BY SPECIAL ARRANGEMENT

A MAGNIFICENT ASSEMBLAGE OF
PAST AND PRESENT STARS OF THE
INTERNATIONAL STAGE

THE ENTERTAINERS

 FOREWORD BY SIR JOHN GIELGUD

WITH A SENSATIONAL CAST OF THOUSANDS

INCLUDING

GROCK ★ GASSMANN ★ BERNHARDT
DUSE ★ GARRICK ★ BOOTH ★ BURTON
GRIMALDI ★ OLIVIER ★ THORNDIKE
BARRYMORE □ KYNASTON □ NOVELLI □ EVANS □ BARRAULT □ MISTINGUETT
POPOV □ ROBEY □ DEBURAU □ ASHCROFT □ HAYES □ GWYNN □ LITTLE TICH
GYPSY ROSE LEE □ BURBAGE □ JOLSON □ CORNELL □ BLONDIN □ GIELGUD
THE LUNTS □ MODJESKA □ BURNS & ALLEN □ ASTAIRE □ IFFLAND □ LAHR
PAXINOU □ IRVING □ BRICE □ KEAN   and 100s of others...

IN WORKS BY

SHAKESPEARE ★ IBSEN ★ MOLIÈRE
MACHIAVELLI ★ STRINDBERG
AESCHYLUS ~ PINERO ~ WILDE ~ GOETHE ~ GENET ~ OSBORNE ~ HECHT
DÜRRENMATT ~ WILLIAMS ~ ZUCKMAYER ~ GIRAUDOUX ~ PIRANDELLO
BRECHT ~ JOHNSON ~ IONESCO ~ CALDERÓN ~ MAETERLINCK ~ CONGREVE
RACINE ~ SYNGE ~ GOGOL ~ DUMAS ~ SCHNITZLER ~ LOPE DE VEGA ~ SHAW
BECKETT ~ COPEAU ~ O'NEILL ~ SARTRE   and many others...

DIRECTED BY

REINHARDT ★ BERGMAN ★ BROOK
KOMISARJEVSKY ○ MEYERHOLD ○ LITTLEWOOD ○ PISCATOR ○ STANISLAVSKY
ZEFFIRELLI ○ STREHLER ○ ZIEGFELD ○ NUNN ○ JESSNER ○ NICHOLS ○ KAZAN

ST. MARTIN'S PRESS

SPECIAL DANCE ARRANGEMENTS ▷ JEROME ROBBINS

First published in the United States of America by
St. Martin's Press, Incorporated, New York, 1980
Library of Congress Catalogue Card Number: 80-52871
ISBN 0-312-25694-4

CONSULTANT EDITORS

Pèpo Angel (France)   Claus Henneberg (Germany)
Michael Aspinall (Italy)   John Lahr (USA)
John Cox (Great Britain)   Trini Lund (Scandinavia)

The Entertainers was conceived, edited and designed by
Harrow House Editions Limited, 7a Langley Street,
London WC2H 9JA, England

General Editor
Clive Unger-Hamilton

Associate Editor
Neil Fairbairn

Art Director
Nicholas Eddison
Art Editor
Clare Judd
Picture Editor
Maggie Colbeck

Production
Kenneth Cowan
Production Editor
Fred Gill
Editorial Assistant
Sue Brown

Contributors Mara Amats, Michael Aspinall, Léonie
Caldecott, Cordelia Chitty, Gordon Davies, Ann Dietrich,
Neil Fairbairn, Stephen Fay, Sarah Harding, Andrew
Hislop, James Keller, John Lahr, John F X Leonard, Ferdie
MacDonald, Brent McGregor, Ethan Mordden, Geoffrey
Smith, Stewart Trotter

Research Christie Brown, Ian Kane, Elspeth Milmore,
Gill Trethowan

Phototypeset in Ehrhardt by Tameside Filmsetting Limited,
Ashton-under-Lyne, England, and in Tiffany and Italian
Old Style by Photo Lettering Services, London, England
Illustrations originated by Reprocolor Llovet S.A.,
Barcelona, Spain
Printed and bound by Graficromo S.A., Córdoba, Spain

CONTENTS

Throughout the book, a system of cross-referencing, by the use of SMALL CAPITAL LETTERS, has been used to indicate where another name in the text has its own entry. Sometimes both Christian name and surname are in capital letters; this is where there is more than one entry with the same surname, e.g. MAX MILLER and ARTHUR MILLER. For quick reference, there is an alphabetical list of the entries on page 306. Unless otherwise indicated in the text, the dates given to the plays are those of first performance.

FOREWORD by Sir John Gielgud

During the sixty years that I have been associated with the world of entertainment, as an actor and director, the revolutionary changes and developments have been almost unbelievable.

The long reign of the actor-manager with his solid, if somewhat egotistic, supremacy, so successful in the late Victorian and Edwardian days up to the First Great War, is gone forever. The music hall is dead. Melodrama, once the staple form of the living theatre, has been usurped by films and television. New styles of production have evolved with the increasing talent of autocratic stage direction. A new school of playwrights has emerged, impatient of old-fashioned techniques and the "well-made" play. Theatre tickets are increasingly expensive, small casts and basic scenery become more and more necessary, except for elaborate musicals. The live theatre is continually on the point of utter extinction, with theatres being torn down, and unemployment rife. Despite this very real threat, the Civic theatre remains an important training ground.

The personal element in live performance remains a unique and irreplaceable occasion for an audience. No mechanical substitute, however superbly recorded, photographed or assembled, can ever supply that particular moment of excitement which is experienced when, in the theatre, a great actor or actress takes the public by the throat.

The acting performances of the last thirty years or so will be available, for the first time in history, for future generations to watch and hear, and no doubt many reputations will inevitably suffer. Our work may be cruelly dissected and possibly ridiculed long after we are dead, and no amount of contemporary approval (on which the previous accounts of acting have always had to depend in the past) will be able to affect the unforeseen opinions of posterity.

The compilers have arranged the biographical detail in such a way that the reader may be enriched in his survey of theatre history. Shakespeare is listed with his contemporaries, Marlowe and Burbage, rather than placed between Seneca and Shaw.

The book touches on the other media, films and television, but is principally concerned with the biographical history of Live Entertainment and the men and women who have so notably contributed to it. Playwrights, impresarios and circus performers are listed as well as more famous personalities, both on the Continent and in America as well as in this country. Irving and Bernhardt might not in their lifetime have been very happy to be billed alongside Barnum and Labiche, but the theatre student of today will surely find the juxtaposition of the names both fascinating and instructive.

This book reflects, with a fascinating wealth of detail, the range of achievement in the Entertainment world. It will remain a magnificent record of a field that is continually changing, with all its ephemeral triumphs and failures, fashions and enthusiasms, clinging to tradition on the one hand while demanding an unceasing infiltration of new talent and originality on the other.

RITE AND RITUAL

For early man, a "play" was a serious matter. A bad production was not simply boring; it represented a threat to survival. In a world where human control was minimal, dramatic ritual provided the only means of mediation between man and the mysterious forces that surrounded him. Imitative action was an attempt to engage these powers, to compel their favour in preserving the conditions that life required.

The plots of primitive drama were basic and unchanging. Invention was not their object, but an exact representation of the vital processes of tribal existence. When the tribe acted out the hunt, they expected the power that had sent animals in the past would understand their request and send them more. In order that there be no mistake the performances had to be carried out in minute detail, repeating the version that had been rewarded before. To please the power and impress him with their sincerity, the community enacted the ritual with passionate fervour and conviction. They translated their emotion into a group dance. They wore grotesque animal masks not just to mimic the quarry they sought but to heighten the occasion, to transport themselves out of their own lives and towards the unknown power. He was sole spectator – and critic. There were no try-outs or rehearsals. Approval was measured by the game the next hunt produced, and a successful "play" would run for the life of the tribe.

Contemporary versions of these prehistoric rituals have existed until the present. American Plains Indians propitiated their rain god by dancing around a sacred tree while a priest poured water over them, repeating the dance till the god responded. If one of the dancers made a mis-step, the rite began again. (In other primitive communities, the offender might have been slain.) Many tribes, like the Coras Indians of Mexico, have made the mask their source of power. War dances combined masks with movement and recitals of past glory.

To early man, no natural process was as awesome as the simple motion of the seasons. Consequently no part of his small dramatic repertoire was more important than the ceremony ensuring that winter would give way to spring. Usually this took the form of a stylized duel, in which the forces of the old year were defeated by the new. Gradually the transition became embodied in a single figure, a priest or king. He would symbolically undergo the process of death and resurrection just as the world died and was renewed in spring. Vestiges of this year-drama are still common, from the "wild men" decked out in horns and animal skins who appear in the villages of northern Europe at midwinter, to the English "Mummers' Play", in which either St George or his adversary is killed in battle, then brought back to life.

One of the most remarkable survivors of the seasonal fertility rite is the ceremony of the Padstow Horse, which takes place in Cornwall, England, on May-day. It shows clearly how the ancient charisma of the mask can still convey the mystery of natural forces. The Padstow mask consists of a black pointed headdress with white markings, a protruding tongue and large ears. Hung from a hoop at the shoulders, a great tent of black, tar-smeared cloth covers the wearer to the ground. Attached in front is a small wooden horse's head; behind hangs a tail. Each year a "May man" leads the horse dancing through the streets, accompanied by traditional music and songs. At intervals the creature sinks down as though dead, then leaps up again. Occasionally he pursues young women and drapes his robes over them. Being caught by the horse is considered a mark of good fortune, particularly for married women. His stylized

Wall-paintings in the tombs of the Pharaohs record the importance of ritual in ancient Egypt. Ceremonies incorporated dancers and musicians (*above*) as part of the community's attempts to praise the gods and invoke their favour

Animals occupied a central place in primitive religions, both as sacrificial offerings and as the incarnation of natural forces. The bull (*right*) and the goat were both associated with Dionysus, the god of yearly regeneration

progress manifests for an audience the hypnotic effect of the ancient rituals. However rudimentary, it is unmistakably drama.

Though transmitting some of the authentic spell, such modern representations are innocent compared to their primitive models. The year-rite was originally enacted with the life-and-death passion that reflected its importance. Deep involvement was still a means of pleasing the god and of achieving union with him. The Abydos Passion Play, performed yearly in Egypt, depicted the three-day procession of the god Osiris and his attendants, who were attacked by the armies of Osiris's treacherous brother Seth. Though "stage battles", the clashes were hard fought, always resulting in a number of deaths. The figure of Osiris himself, symbolically represented, was torn to pieces by Seth on the first day of conflict. His remains were gathered by Isis, the god's faithful wife. On the third day, grief-stricken and weary from battle but victorious at last over Seth's forces, the cortège arrived at Osiris's tomb. There they discovered, rejoicing, that the god had been restored to life. The play's triumphant conclusion augured similar prosperity for the regenerate year.

The Abydos Passion Play was performed for almost four thousand years, until AD 400. According to the historian Herodotus, its highly charged observances influenced the rituals in which the Greeks honoured their year-god Dionysus. His cult had originally inspired the fanatic worship of the Maenads, women who celebrated the god's death and rebirth with frenzied activities that included dismembering a live goat and devouring it. Later rites were less hysterical but still passionate, particularly since Dionysus was both the year-god and god of wine.

In Athens the Dionysian festival comprised a procession with an image of the god preceded by devotees bearing a flowering branch and a huge phallus as signs of his fertility. After them came ecstatic attendants in wine-stained garments and goat skins, and figures in burial robes representing death, which Dionysus' renewing strength would conquer. When the group reached the ceremonial site (a hillside whose slopes could accommodate onlookers) they eulogized the god in songs and dances while a goat was readied for sacrifice. Performed by a chorus with a leader, the *exarchon*, these took the form of dialogues relating the god's sufferings and final triumph.

Some scholars believe that the phases of a Greek tragedy come directly from the stages of Dionysus' tale—his apparent defeat with the arrival of winter, the mourning it inspires followed by the festive recognition of his recovery. Certainly the overall influence is indisputable. The word tragedy comes from "*tragos*" or "goat-song", which immediately confirms the Dionysian link. As the songs and dances of the rite began to be taken less as a literal intercession with the god and more as a commemoration of heroic events, other myths began to be represented. The *exarchon* came actually to take on the function of a character, acting out what he described. The "dromena" ("things done" in honour of the god) became the "drama", a recounting of the relationships between gods and men. Religious observances gave way first to contests between rival choruses, then to incipient works of theatre.

And yet something of the prehistoric ritual endured. Drama would never be cut off from its origins in wonder—the need to represent the significant patterns of life, great and small, in order to understand them. Plots, characters and settings still reflect an audience's concerns even as the theatrical event takes them outside and beyond themselves. The same hopes and fears that inspired the earliest human rituals have remained the stuff that plays are made of, from SOPHOCLES to Neil SIMON.

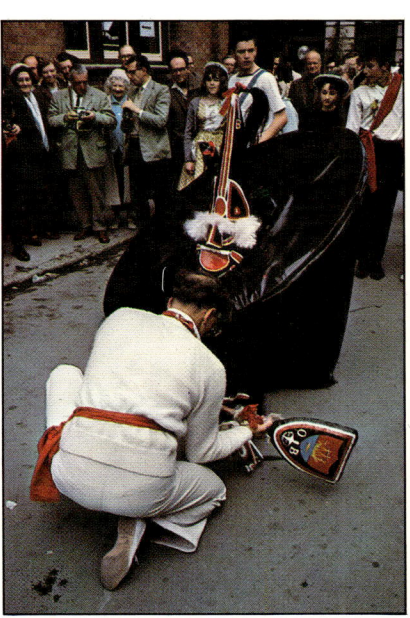

The black and eerie Padstow Horse recreates for modern audiences some of the spell of prehistoric rites. Observances like this one, with its strange, masked central figure, contained the seeds of drama

THE GREEK DRAMA

Greek drama grew out of religious ritual. Tragedy evolved from the worship of Dionysus, god of nature and the vine, in the yearly festivals when winter gave way to spring. He was honoured by dancing and the dithyramb, a hymn performed by a chorus and leader. The choral lyric typically recounted the god's mythic experiences, praised him and celebrated his rejuvenation of the earth. But as the worship of Dionysus came to be taken less literally, the songs evoked other heroic subjects as well. In addition (according to Aristotle) the dithyramb became increasingly dramatic, with the leader acting out the events that his dialogue with the chorus described. Marked by simple plots and spare, formalized action, the early tragedies retained a good deal of their ritual character. The very word "tragedy" in itself recalls the ritual. Derived from *tragos* or "goat song", it refers to the animal associated with Dionysian ceremony as prize and sacrifice.

Comedy seems also to have developed from celebrations of vernal fertility. But the songs and dances that inspired it emphasized ribaldry more than ritual. Aristotle derives "comedy" from "revel-song" and says that the revels included broad jests aimed at passers-by. Another formative element may have been the masquerade, in which people dressed as animals and birds. A choral form of some kind must have influenced the structure of comedy as it had tragedy, but the happier art was also related to Sicilian mime and native Greek burlesque.

A third dramatic type, the satyr play, resembled comedy in mood but tragedy in form. Presented as a concluding piece after a tragic trilogy, it burlesqued tragic action. Mythic heroes confronted absurd circumstances and a company of satyrs – bizarre creatures, half-human, half-animal, in indecent costumes. The plays' rude, vigorous high spirits proved comic relief to the weighty dramas that preceded them.

The city of Athens nurtured all three of these forms. In 534 BC its ruler Pisistratus held a dramatic contest as part of the Dionysian festivals. The first competition was won, fittingly, by THESPIS, who had originated the use of an individual actor separate from the leader of the chorus. Thereafter the contests were a regular part of the City Dionysia in March and April. Three leading poets, chosen by the city, each produced a tragic trilogy and a satyr play. Comedy was not presented competitively until 486 BC, at the Lenaea festival in January, but later both festivals incorporated both forms.

The number of performers in a play gradually changed, according to the demands of individual playwrights. AESCHYLUS reduced the chorus from fifty to twelve and added a second actor. SOPHOCLES later introduced a third.

Despite their classical forms, the character of individual tragedies and comedies also varied in the hands of their creators. Closest to the grandeur of ritual, Aeschylus' works show a divine will shaping the course of events. Sophocles' heroes demonstrate the mysterious coincidence of choice and fate, while EURIPIDES depicts the idiosyncrasies of human character. Comedy as well has its development. The master of Old Comedy, ARISTOPHANES, used a single improbable situation as a starting point for hilarious, satirical and obscene attacks on contemporary folly, often unflinchingly personal. Middle Comedy, beginning at the end of the fourth century, was also satiric but better behaved, concerned more with well-turned plots than individual assaults. New Comedy arose about 336 BC and extended these characteristics. In its stock figures and situations, and its charming treatment of romantic love, it anticipates the modern comedy of manners.

Regardless of period or style, the functional simplicity of the Greek stage illustrates how completely any tragedy or comedy depended on its author's skill. A play succeeded because of its intrinsic interest, not by any novelty in production. The only bit of stage business the Greeks employed was a crane to simulate the ascent and descent of the gods. Scene painting was minimal. Each play was acted against a single decorated

Achilles spears Penthesileia (*far right*). The legends of the Trojan War were told in many epic poems, whose recitation was a source of entertainment (and instruction in communal traditions) long before the playwrights turned to them for dramatic material

Greek actors of the fourth century BC (*below*), both probably "dressed" for comedy. Such performers often adopted a rather lewd and dishevelled appearance. In the vase painting (*right*) from the same period, there is a nice contrast in handsomeness between the balding actor and the tragic mask in his hand

background that established its setting. There was a wooden building on stage, the *skene*, which both provided the actors a place to change and stood for any structure—temple, cave or palace—that would suit the plot. Its three doors also increased the possibilities of comic entrances and exits.

The costumes of the all-male cast were equally simple, consisting of masks of linen, cork or wood that indicated a character's sex and—to a lesser extent—his age and temperament. (Initially realistic, the masks later became imposingly stylized.) For a tragedy, a player wore a long under-robe with a shorter tunic over it, both richly coloured. One of the garments contained sleeves, a distinctive feature probably related to the Dionysian priest's ritual dress. The comic actor wore a kind of short gown, the better to display the red leather phallus that was an outstanding fixture of the Old Comedy. Heavy padding heightened its jocular effect, just as the flowing amplitude of the tragedian's garb invested the player with majesty. Tragic actors, at least, performed in shoes, though not the high "buskins" of popular historical tradition.

The interaction of chorus and protagonists so central to Greek theatre was reflected in the layout of the stage itself. The chorus took up its position in the dancing area (*orchestra*) in the front of the stage. The play's events occurred directly in front of them and on the same level, so that they could indulge in exchanges with the actors as well as comment on the action to the audience.

The role of the chorus as observer and interpreter, and as a kind of representative spectator, points up the essentially public nature of Greek drama. Like its religious antecedents, it involved the whole community. The earliest auditoriums were simply hillsides: only out-of-door, daylight setting could accommodate the crowds of onlookers. Steps were later cut into the hill and a system of fixed seating arranged, but the separate, free-standing theatre only emerged after the greatest Greek plays had been written. Admission was originally free to all, with the best seats reserved for a few officials and foreign guests. Athens instituted a small entrance charge, but subsequently money was set aside to give any citizen the price of a ticket. Such official support—which also extended to playwrights and actors—attests the civic stature of the theatre in Greece, a point of view shared by its dramatists. Though some of the greatest writers of all time, the playwrights regarded their work not so much as self-expression, but as a statement made on behalf of the community. That sense of human significance in Greek drama accounts for its contemporary importance and the esteem of playwrights and playgoers ever since.

Comedy and tragedy were both played at the festivals of Dionysus, who was the Greek god of nature and of wine: that is, the god of those irrational forces in nature which cannot be ignored. Hence the comedies revelled in fantasy, libel, obscenity, blasphemy and bawdry; and the tragedies faced the appalling destructiveness in the human breast.
Left: The wanton god rides a leering goat

Below: The stone carving of a female dramatic mask. All of the parts in Greek drama were in fact played by males

ROMAN ENTERTAINMENT

For the Romans, drama was not a serious affair. Though nominally religious, Roman festivals were an opportunity for magistrates and wealthy citizens to keep the multitude happy with entertainment which was free and acceptable. As early as the first century BC, seventy-six days in the year were devoted to the "Games", in honour of various gods, and fifty-nine of them boasted theatrical presentations. The most important, the "Great Games", lasted for sixteen days in September.

Theatre was a part of life, taken for granted in the Republic. As well as the great comedies of PLAUTUS and TERENCE, many of the old tragedies continued to be performed. During the Empire, the popularity of such performances increased until every town of any size had a theatre, and some (such as Pompeii) an odeon for musical productions. Compared, of course, to contests of strength, the theatre must have seemed tame; consequently amphitheatres and circuses were built to accommodate greater crowds. However, people still flocked to the theatre even if (according to Juvenal) the ordinary Roman found great drama less uplifting than a tight-rope walker.

No early form of tragedy has come to light in Italy, but the seeds of comedy abound. Fescennine verses, jokes by clowns at local harvest festivals, probably combined at an early date with professional music and dance from Etruria to produce *saturae*, not dissimilar in form to music hall entertainment. In southern Italy, a so-called "hilarious tragedy" developed in the areas settled by Greeks. These *phylax* plays, named after the actors, *phylaces* or "gossips", were travesties of mythology or of daily life, and were presented as early as the fourth century BC. Scenes on vases show padded costumes and exaggerated masks, which take away all dignity from god and hero. The Oscan-speaking people of the southern province of Campania developed their own kind of farce called *Atellane*, whose stock characters included a Clown, an Old Gaffer, Fat Cheeks and Hunchback – perhaps a development from *phylax* plays.

Mime appeared on the stage in Rome before the end of the third century BC. It was a solo maskless performance in which women became proficient, the performer being sometimes naked but always indecent. To add to the excitement, the Emperor Domitian had a real crucifixion put into one mime, while Heliogabalus ordered adulterous scenes. Theodora, a mime actress in her youth, later became a powerful Empress. The mime may have survived in the entertainment of the wandering jongleurs of the Middle Ages. Pantomime, a related form of entertainment, catered for slightly more refined tastes. To a musical accompaniment a single actor performed vulgarized material from old tragedy, in dumb show.

Staging in Roman times was one step nearer to the modern theatre than the Greek. The central feature of the auditorium was the raised stage upon which the whole performance took place. In some theatres, a "curtain" made of vellum could be rolled up from a trench in the front of the stage. Behind the stage, the three-doored building grew into a three-storeyed architectural marvel. The orchestra, a semicircle directly in front of the stage, was usually reserved for important guests. The *cavea*, or auditorium, was not a natural hillside, as in classical Greece, but was a building of engineering genius. Like the Greek audience, the Romans were seated by tickets, usually made of bone. As protection from the strong sunlight, a colourful awning was often unfurled over the audience, and in the various intervals scented water was sprinkled about to cool and sweeten the air.

Costume could be Greek or Roman, according to the play staged, and masks were worn to allow doubling of characters and to disguise the fact that (in the great plays at least) men took the parts of women. The authorities responsible for productions would commission a producer, and the successful playwright was encouraged to write boisterous, bawdy scenes, taking care not to make overtly political comments. The lack of originality was staggering. Although Plautus used Greek plots and settings to create patently Roman situations, most dramatists were mere translators of Greek originals. By the time of SENECA (4 BC–AD 65), tragedy was more for recitation than for production.

However much Roman theatre accommodated itself to the taste of the crowd, it could not hold out against the circus and the amphitheatre, which provided real life drama for a people who seem to have preferred excitement to culture. The chariot race in the circus and the beast or gladiatorial contests in the amphitheatre allowed for Rome's most popular sport, gambling; teams of charioteers and gladiators had supporters as ardent as those who today back a horse or a football team. War games reached their most sophisticated in the Flavian Amphitheatre (Colosseum), which could even be flooded to provide the setting for a convincing sea battle.

Public baths, too, became leisure centres to rival any modern facility. By the third century AD they had developed into vast clubs for both sexes, incorporating gymnasia, libraries and gardens; food was provided by itinerant vendors. The baths of Caracalla and Diocletian covered more ground than the Pentagon or the British Houses of Parliament.

In such a sensual and opulent environment it is no wonder that the art of drama declined and fell when the Roman Empire was still a rising power.

The Roman authorities spent lavishly on keeping their unruly subjects entertained. Imposing theatres sprang up throughout the Empire, whose remains are often still visible: this example is near Carthage

This **Roman mosaic floor** (*left*) depicts the nine Greek muses, goddesses of the arts. Left to right, the top row shows Thalia, muse of comedy, Terpsichore (dance) and Clio (history). The centre row has Euterpe (lyric poetry) on the left and Erato (love poetry) on the right; the centre one is unclear. The bottom row is of Urania (astronomy) and two more unidentified

The farcical "mime" plays usually took place on a rough platform raised above the bustle of the market-place. On this vase (*above*) the two ends of a centaur trot on to the stage

Cruelty and danger were the staple fare of spectators at the Roman arena. The mosaic (*left*) captures the terror as a naked slave is forced to try and separate a bear and a bull while another is dragged in to take part in the next event

In Roman drama, as in the Greek, the actors often performed in masks (*above*). Those rehearsing for a "satyr" play in the mosaic (*left*) keep their masks at hand, ready to effect a quick change of character

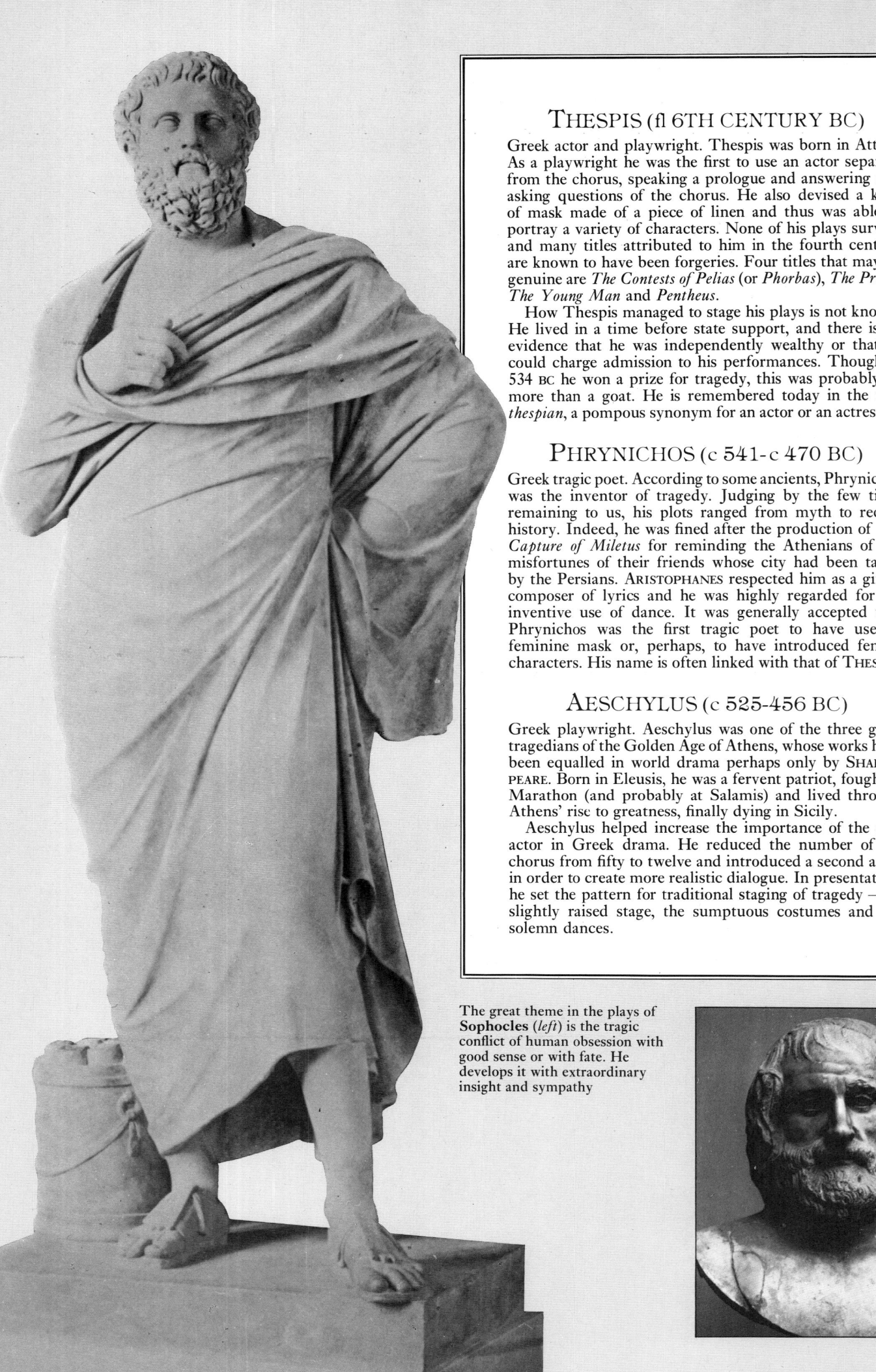

THESPIS (fl 6TH CENTURY BC)

Greek actor and playwright. Thespis was born in Attica. As a playwright he was the first to use an actor separate from the chorus, speaking a prologue and answering and asking questions of the chorus. He also devised a kind of mask made of a piece of linen and thus was able to portray a variety of characters. None of his plays survive and many titles attributed to him in the fourth century are known to have been forgeries. Four titles that may be genuine are *The Contests of Pelias* (or *Phorbas*), *The Priest*, *The Young Man* and *Pentheus*.

How Thespis managed to stage his plays is not known. He lived in a time before state support, and there is no evidence that he was independently wealthy or that he could charge admission to his performances. Though in 534 BC he won a prize for tragedy, this was probably no more than a goat. He is remembered today in the title *thespian*, a pompous synonym for an actor or an actress.

PHRYNICHOS (c 541-c 470 BC)

Greek tragic poet. According to some ancients, Phrynichos was the inventor of tragedy. Judging by the few titles remaining to us, his plots ranged from myth to recent history. Indeed, he was fined after the production of *The Capture of Miletus* for reminding the Athenians of the misfortunes of their friends whose city had been taken by the Persians. ARISTOPHANES respected him as a gifted composer of lyrics and he was highly regarded for his inventive use of dance. It was generally accepted that Phrynichos was the first tragic poet to have used a feminine mask or, perhaps, to have introduced female characters. His name is often linked with that of THESPIS.

AESCHYLUS (c 525-456 BC)

Greek playwright. Aeschylus was one of the three great tragedians of the Golden Age of Athens, whose works have been equalled in world drama perhaps only by SHAKESPEARE. Born in Eleusis, he was a fervent patriot, fought at Marathon (and probably at Salamis) and lived through Athens' rise to greatness, finally dying in Sicily.

Aeschylus helped increase the importance of the solo actor in Greek drama. He reduced the number of the chorus from fifty to twelve and introduced a second actor in order to create more realistic dialogue. In presentation, he set the pattern for traditional staging of tragedy – the slightly raised stage, the sumptuous costumes and the solemn dances.

The great theme in the plays of **Sophocles** (*left*) is the tragic conflict of human obsession with good sense or with fate. He develops it with extraordinary insight and sympathy

In 484 BC Aeschylus won his first victory for tragedy in the City of Athens Dionysia; in all he won thirteen of these prestigious annual competitions. He wrote about ninety plays, of which seven survive: *The Suppliants*, *The Persians*, *The Seven Against Thebes*, *Prometheus Bound*, and his work best known by modern audiences, the *Oresteia*. The latter is the only surviving example of a trilogy from ancient literature; it consists of *Agamemnon*, the *Choephori* and the *Eumenides*.

Plots and characters are epic in conception; the theme throughout is of divine governance in human affairs; man comes to knowledge only through suffering. Ever present in *Agamemnon* is the sin of the house of Atreus, to which the title character belongs. King Agamemnon returns victorious from the Trojan War only to be slain by his wife Clytemnestra who, with her lover Aegisthus, has ruled during his absence. She justifies the act as justice for Agamemnon's sacrifice of their daughter Iphigenia to ensure that the Greek fleet sailed for Troy. To the chorus, she blames all upon the curse on the house, while Aegisthus disclaims any guilt because of the wrong done to his father by Atreus.

The *Choephori* continues the tale of wrong, retribution and personal choice. Orestes, the son of Agamemnon and Clytemnestra, now a grown man, returns home to take vengeance for his father's murder. Clytemnestra and Aegisthus die, but Orestes calls upon himself the wrath of the Furies for the murder of his mother.

The *Eumenides* is set at Delphi, where Orestes has gone, hounded by the Furies. Apollo is on his side, but the Furies, roused by the ghost of Clytemnestra, hound him without mercy. The final scene takes place in a law court in Athens. The Furies prosecute and Apollo defends Orestes. Both sides have irrefutable arguments: the death of his father demanded that the son kill the murderer, but it was forbidden for a son to take the life of his mother. Understandably, the jury of mortal Athenians is unable to come to a verdict; only the goddess Athena's casting vote releases Orestes. Through this divine agency, Aeschylus introduced into tragedy the element of mercy, rare enough in this period.

AGATHARCHOS (fl 5TH CENTURY BC)

Greek painter. Agatharchos of Samos was the first painter to use perspective effectively. He made scenery for AESCHYLUS, but whether he also worked for SOPHOCLES, who is credited with the introduction of scene painting, is not known. His book on scene painting inspired Anaxagoras and Democritus to write on perspective.

SOPHOCLES (c 496-406 BC)

Greek playwright. The great tragedian Sophocles was born near Athens, the son of a prominent local family. Originally he intended to be an actor, but grace and beauty of form did not make up for a weak voice, and he turned his attention to writing. In his ninety years, he wrote at least 123 plays, of which only seven survive: *Ajax*, *Antigone*, *Oedipus the King*, *Electra*, *Women of Trachis*, *Philoctetes* and *Oedipus at Colonus*. He is said to have won twenty victories in dramatic competitions with his plays, the first against AESCHYLUS around 468 BC.

Sophocles took several giant steps towards modern theatrical convention. In the language of his poetry, he left behind the epic style and created a natural flow within the confines of his verse. He also developed and varied the presentation of tragedy, introducing the painted back-drop, an idea which was borrowed by Aeschylus in the *Oresteia*.

But Sophocles' greatest achievement was to abandon the highly stylized tradition of plot revelation and character development. He diminished the importance of the chorus, transforming it into a spectator sympathetic to the actions of individuals. He also introduced a third actor. These solo characters were now free to act out their own tragedies, a technique that has been the essence of drama ever since.

Of his surviving dramas, *Antigone* is often performed, and the confrontation within it of two types of immovability still provides wonderful excitement. Creon, king of Thebes, forbids the burial of his nephew, Polyneices, who has attacked his own state. Antigone contrives to give her brother formal burial, as a sister should. Both are right, both refuse to give way and by the time Creon sees that he must yield, Antigone is dead, his son Haemon, betrothed to her, has hanged himself and Queen Eurydice has killed herself in grief at the loss of her son.

Oedipus the King deals with the tragedy of a man who without his knowledge fulfils a prophecy by killing his father and marrying his mother. This theme is more fatalistic than that of *Antigone*, but, nevertheless, is treated with great sympathy. *Electra*, perhaps Sophocles' most "modern" tragedy, tells of the murder of Clytemnestra by her son Orestes and her daughter Electra in revenge for the murder of their father.

EURIPIDES (c 484-c 406 BC)

Greek playwright. Euripides felt personally for the sufferings and follies of mankind. His understanding of

Euripides (*left*) re-tells the Greek myths as if they involve the actions of ordinary people. In this novel perspective, heroism and weakness are seen to be perilously intertwined; while the gods are viewed sardonically as being either cruel or else the mere reflection of powerful human needs

Clytemnestra stabs her husband in the bath (*right*): a scene which, being violent, takes place off-stage in **Aeschylus'** *Agamemnon*. Vengeance is piled on vengeance until law and persuasion finally bring peace to gods and men

18

ordinary human passions and frailties (rather than the exalted dilemmas of gods or the godlike) has made him the most accessible and popular, in fact the most "modern" of the Greek tragedians.

He was an able student of science and philosophy as well as a successful athlete, but early in his life he fashioned a gloomy view of the times he lived in and of opinions held. Consequently, he retreated to the island of Salamis, where he spent much of his life as a recluse.

Euripides is reputed to have written ninety-two plays, but only seventeen survive. These reveal characters (very often women) torn by the emotions involved in exercising free choice, a privilege rarely extended to the protagonists of Greek drama. *Alcestis* portrays the deep and self-sacrificing love of a wife for an unworthy husband. Another wounded wife is the heroine of *Medea*, a woman of great intelligence and character, who has left her father and murdered her brother for the love of Jason. Alone in a strange land and dependent upon her new husband, Medea becomes a fury bent on a terrible vengeance when Jason deserts her for another woman. All connected with Jason, even her own children, are destroyed by the tormented Medea. *Hippolytus* again deals with the tragedy of a woman. Phaedra, the chaste wife of Theseus, becomes enamoured of her stepson Hippolytus, who repulses her violently. In shame for the love she has professed against her will and for Hippolytus' cruelty, she kills herself, but in revenge leaves behind a letter accusing him of having sexually assulted her. Theseus accepts the truth of Hippolytus' innocence only at the moment of his son's death. The pity of the tragedy is that two virtuous people have died, mainly because of their own virtue: Phaedra because of shame at her one aberration and Hippolytus because, in fact, he did not succumb to her.

There is little place in the tragedies of Euripides for the chorus; consequently it becomes little more than an interlude between acts. The powerful themes he used, though not highly regarded in his own times, have remained popular with playwrights down through the ages.

ARISTOPHANES (c 450-c 385 BC)

Greek playwright. Aristophanes was the greatest exponent of Old Comedy whose work survives. The evidence suggests that writers of Old Comedy were politically conservative and used their work to satirize what they regarded as the excesses of democracy. The theatre for Old Comedy was the same as that for tragedy, but the actors often wore everyday clothes padded to simulate a large belly or a huge behind. The men's costume was usually completed by an outsize leather phallus. The chorus numbered perhaps as many as twenty-four or twenty-eight and took gleeful part in the action.

Eleven plays of Aristophanes have survived: most are enjoyable to a modern audience and many can be regarded as comments on present-day society. *The Wasps* satirizes the jury system at Athens, whereby citizens received a very small fee for doing jury service – a job more like that of judge and jury. *The Birds* takes us to a cloud-cuckoo land between earth and heaven, where birds rule with power to parley with gods, and get their own way. Perhaps the funniest, and certainly the rudest, extant play is *The Lysistrata*. The women of Greece, tired of the long Peloponnesian War, meet and, under the leadership of Lysistrata, decide that they will not give their favours to their husbands or lovers until hostilities cease in the Peloponnese. They take the Acropolis, despite the efforts of old men whom they attack (often in their softest parts). It does not take long for the husbands and lovers to feel the need for peace, but not before the women are also in some distress. A truce is soon agreed upon and with a feast (and all that goes with it) ends one of the best anti-war plays (and one of the most hilarious sexual comedies) ever written. *The Frogs* (like *The Thesmophoriazousae*) depicts EURIPIDES as an amusing bumbling coward. Aristophanes obviously disapproved of the "new wave" in tragedy.

The rest of Aristophanes' work belongs to the type known as Middle Comedy. The chorus is reduced and personal satire plays a small part, if any. Neither *Women in Parliament* nor *The Plutus* has the sting of the earlier plays. Often compared with Rabelais, Aristophanes was not so much opposed to progress as intent on pointing out that progress is a probable myth.

AGATHON (c 447-c 400 BC)

Greek playwright. Apart from the three great tragedians – AESCHYLUS, SOPHOCLES and EURIPIDES – the Athenian Agathon is the only tragic dramatist of any importance. He is known to us through the accounts of ARISTOPHANES, Plato and Aristotle and from a few titles. Only a few lines of his works have survived.

According to Aristophanes, Agathon was a noted dandy who wrote well. Plato set his *Symposium* at the playwright's house and portrayed him with friendly humour. From Aristotle we learn that, following in the footsteps of Euripides, he used his chorus only to provide incidental music between "acts".

Agathon's main claim to fame is that he was the first tragedian to use a plot conceived by himself. The play, called the *Antheus*, was a romantic drama akin apparently to the biblical story of Joseph and Potiphar's wife.

POLUS (fl 4TH CENTURY BC)

Greek actor. Polus is one of the few Greek actors about whom there is any individual information. In the fifth century actors were associated with particular playwrights: Cleander and Mynniscus with AESCHYLUS, Cleidimides and Tlepolemus with SOPHOCLES. In later ages, actors were assigned to playwrights by lot.

Polus, living in a century when actors enjoyed some prominence, is the most interesting; he was probably the first Method actor. He is said to have used an urn containing the ashes of his own son to ensure that he would be sufficiently emotional for the part of Elektra. When Elektra (played by Polus) received the urn said to contain the ashes of her brother Orestes, her grief was genuine.

ALEXIS (c 372-270 BC)

Greek playwright. Alexis, Thurian by birth but Athenian by naturalization, was the uncle of MENANDER and, together with Antiphanes, the most highly regarded writer of Middle Comedy – pleasant, humorous, politically inoffensive situation comedy of urban life, whose plots, while bawdy, move away from myth to family matters, missing children, delayed marriages or even lost treasure.

Only fragments of the 135 titles assigned to him survive. His great contribution to dramatic literature was the introduction of the wily parasite, a most popular part in its varying forms to this day. His modernity is evident in one long fragment, a hilarious scene depicting that most irritating of characters – the gatecrasher.

MENANDER (c 342-292 BC)

Greek playwright. Menander, the chief exponent of the New Comedy at Athens, was introduced to writing by his uncle, ALEXIS, but to love (which formed the basis for most of his plots) by the masterly courtesan Glykera.

His greatest claim to fame is that he and his school developed a dramatic form that is very similar to what is now known as the comedy of manners. Menander's chorus is composed merely of dancers, who mark the end of each of five "acts". The plots are no longer mythical; the characters are of the writer's imagination and develop with the plot. Yet his aim was not primarily comic, it was to portray the quirks of ordinary human beings.

Though Menander is said to have written over one hundred plays, until our time he could be judged only by quotations in other authors (including St Paul, who used his pithy apophthegm: "Evil communications corrupt good manners"). In 1905 a papyrus was discovered which included large sections of four plays and smaller parts of a fifth: the *Heros*, *Samia*, *Epitrepontes* and *Perikeiromene*. In English translations the *Perikeiromene* became *The Rape of the Locks* (1941) and the *Epitrepontes* became *The Arbitration* (1945). In 1957 another play, the *Dyskolos*, was discovered in Egypt. It was first performed in 1959, and was broadcast that same year in England as *The Bad-Tempered Man*.

LIVIUS ANDRONICUS
(c 284-204 BC)

Graeco-Roman playwright and poet. The Father of Roman Theatre, Andronicus was a Greek slave, born at Tarentum in Italy and brought to Rome, where he was freed. Teacher, actor, stage manager, writer of *saturae* (popular variety shows) and of plays, he also translated Homer's *Odyssey* into Latin verse. He wrote and acted in the first Latin comedy and the first Latin tragedy, gaining such popularity that his work ousted the *saturae* from the stage despite the well-known vaudeville mentality of the Roman audience. Once, when his voice failed after too many encores, he introduced a cantor who sang to his gestures while he saved his voice for the spoken word. His inauguration of a guild of actors and writers may be regarded as the prototype Actors' Equity.

NAEVIUS (c 270-c 199 BC)

Roman playwright and epic poet. Gnaeus Naevius, a Campanian by birth, wrote the first Italian national epic, an appropriate accomplishment for the first Italian playwright (LIVIUS ANDRONICUS, his senior by a few years, was a Greek). For the stage he wrote historical plays, two of which are known from fragments to have been about Romulus and the victory won by M. Claudius Marcellus in 222 BC. But his major dramatic contributions were the satiric comedies which went so far as to mock such great contemporary figures as the general Scipio Africanus. He was the first (and last) Roman playwright to be so audacious. Thus he was also the first Roman to write plays in prison—apologies, for he had no wish to be a martyr.

PLAUTUS (c 252-184 BC)

Roman playwright. Titus Maccius Plautus was the greatest comic genius among the ancients after ARISTOPHANES, yet there is very little information about his life. Even his name is in doubt; perhaps Plautus comes from *plotus* (flat-footed). Tradition records that he was of humble origin, born in Umbria, that he made money on the stage, lost it in trade, was forced to work in a flour mill or bakery, and wrote his way back to comfortable means meanwhile. One thing is certain: he created a comedy that was wholly Roman. Not satisfied with mere translations and adaptations of the works of Greek New Comedy, he left only place names and settings as recognizably Greek. Puns, alliteration, topical allusion and jokes (mostly bawdy) all created characters who, though from the stock-in-trade of comedy, were the true, earthy Italians. The action bowls along, interspersed generously with risqué songs, and the whole has the flavour of delightful musical comedy.

Twenty-one of Plautus's 130 plays remain. Two of the best known deal with cases of mistaken identity. In the *Amphitruo* a faithful wife mistakes Zeus for her husband, and in another popular play everyone mistakes the two Menaechmi for each other. The *Amphitruo*, based on a Greek original, might well have a claim as the most imitated play ever written. Jean GIRAUDOUX called his version *Amphitryon 38*, referring to the thirty-seven previous adaptations by such playwrights as ROTROU, MOLIÈRE, DRYDEN, KLEIST and KAISER. The *Menaechmi*, the story of twins separated at an early age, has more than once been adapted, most successfully by SHAKESPEARE in *The Comedy of Errors*. As *The Boys From Syracuse*, a musical comedy by Rodgers and HART, it reappeared in the twentieth century. Another favourite with later writers is the *Miles Gloriosus*, the hilarious adventures of a braggart but cowardly soldier. Numerous clever slaves, too, always one or more steps ahead of their masters, find echoes from the Renaissance to the present day. Plautus has been the inspiration of such seemingly different works as MACHIAVELLI's *La Mandragola* and the musical comedy *A Funny Thing Happened on the Way to the Forum*.

ENNIUS (239-169 BC)

Roman poet and playwright. Quintus Ennius is the acknowledged Father of Roman poetry, but more for his *Annales* (eighteen books of Roman history in Latin verse, adapted to Greek hexameter) than for his plays. Born at Rudiae in Calabria, he learned Greek, Latin and Oscan and was brought by the famous orator Cato to Rome, where he became the friend of such influential Romans as the general Scipio Africanus. His extensive writings for the stage include the *Ambracia*, a description of the Aetolian campaign of 189 BC. About 400 lines remain from at least twenty tragedies written on Greek models. Apparently EURIPIDES was his main inspiration, judging at least from such titles as *Iphigenia*, *Medea*, *Erectheus* and *Hecuba*.

In 169 BC Ennius died of gout – a merry old man, rich in friends but little else.

PACUVIUS (c 220-130 BC)

Roman playwright. Marcus Pacuvius, the nephew of ENNIUS, combined the writing of tragedy with the career of a painter. The first great Roman tragedian, he was only rivalled in his long lifetime by the youthful ACCIUS. Twelve tragedies and one comedy (*praetexta*) remain, the most famous one being his *Armorum Iudicium*, an extract of which was sung at Caesar's funeral and contained the line: "To think that I saved the men who were to murder me." His *Iliona* is associated with a dissolute actor named Fufius. Playing the heroine asleep on the stage, Fufius was supposed to rise when the ghost of "her" son summoned her with: "Mother, I cry to thee." The inebriated Fufius slept on until the helpful Roman public took up the cry, showing that audience participation has a longer history than is generally supposed. Beyond the works listed above, there remain about another 400 fragmentary lines from various lost tragedies by Pacuvius.

STATIUS (c 219-166 BC)

Roman playwright. Caecilius Statius (or Statius Caecilius) was born in Insubrian Gaul, but worked in Rome. Though the ancients regarded him as equal or superior to TERENCE, it is difficult to judge from the titles and frag-

Right: Gambling on the chariot races was highly popular in ancient Rome. Competing teams wore different uniforms of green, gold, purple and (shown in this mosaic) blue

Below: This fresco discovered at Herculaneum shows an actor and his attendants behind the scenes after the performance of a tragedy. Some of the tension lingers as they dedicate a theatrical mask to the gods in thanksgiving for their success. The actor is still absent-mindedly grasping the sceptre of a king. Although the theatre at Roman festivals was largely dominated by comedy, there was also a demand for tragedy for as long as the Republic lasted. The republican virtues of individual dignity and fortitude were celebrated through the performances of the great Greek tragedies in translation and of the lesser imitations by Roman writers such as Ennius, Pacuvius and Accius. Under the Empire, comedy and spectacle gradually took over: this fresco, when inundated by lava in AD 79, was already something of an anachronism

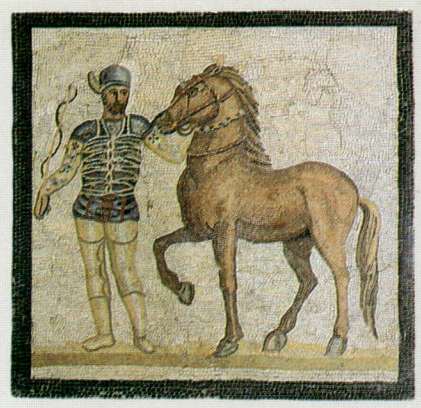

ments that remain, for it is impossible to reconstruct any of his plays. Such lines as there are suggest a Plautine method in the free use of songs and a rollicking sense of fun. Unlike PLAUTUS, however, Statius adhered closely to Greek models, a style that was adopted by his great disciple Terence.

TERENCE (c 190-159 BC)

Roman playwright. In his short career, Publius Terentius Afer became part of the charmed circle of the intellectual Roman élite, his work perfectly expressing the purest native Latin style and idiom. This was an amazing accomplishment because Terence was neither well-born nor a native Italian, but a North African slave, freed after coming to Rome. His adaptations of the Greek New Comedy of MENANDER lacked the bawdy jokes and buffoonery of PLAUTUS. In fact Julius Caesar, who liked their charm, thought they were not very funny at all. But they do contain an abiding interest in the human condition. One of his characters puts Terence's position clearly: "I am a human being, and regard all human affairs as my business". He means ordinary affairs; another remarks "I am Davos, not Oedipus". Nevertheless there is a subtle insight into character, which Terence pursues by showing people reacting differently in similar circumstances. He departed from New Comedy too in his dislike of the monologue, often turning it into dialogue, for he believed that the action should unfold as naturally as possible. For greater dramatic effect he added characters from Greek plays to his *Andria* and *Eunuchus*. He especially loved contrast: Demea, the strict father, and Micio, his easy-going brother in the *Adelphoe*, for instance. Terence also extended the love interest for an audience whose women were much freer than their Greek counterparts.

For his grace and delicacy, Terence was always highly regarded, and by the Middle Ages his works were standard texts. Moreover, in the tenth century, the German nun Hrotsvitha thought him pure enough to imitate in sacred plays of her own. The Renaissance saw an even greater upsurge in his popularity, and his works were translated into many languages. Even in the twentieth century, Thornton WILDER based a novel, *The Woman of Andros*, on the *Andria*.

ACCIUS (c 170-86 BC)

Roman playwright. Lucius Accius was the last writer of tragedy for the Roman stage, and the man who took the florid rhetorical style of his age to its limit without also forgetting that his plays had to be staged. Fewer than 1000 lines of more than forty works survive. These reveal violent, melodramatic plots and majestic characters, who never use one word when more would do. "Get thee from the city" becomes: "*egredere, exi, ecfer te, elimina urbe!*" – four words for "get out"! The most famous quote from Accius (though sometimes attributed to Caligula) is "Oderint dum metuant" ("Let them hate me, as long as they fear me").

AFRANIUS (c 150 BC-?)

Roman playwright. Lucius Afranius was a contemporary of TERENCE, PACUVIUS and ACCIUS. He was most famous for comedy (*togata*), specializing in the lively representation of Italian provincial society. Ancient authorities say that he made much use of MENANDER but often preferred unpleasant themes. *Divorce*, *The Pretender* and *The Exceptus*, three of his forty-four titles which can to some extent be reconstructed, give little evidence of this.

ROSCIUS (c 115-62 BC)

Roman actor. Quintus Roscius Gallus was the most famous actor of his day. A friend of the orator Cicero (who defended him in a legal action) and a favourite of the dictator Sulla, who publicly honoured him, Roscius attained a wealth and status unheard of for one of his profession. He was a master of comedy and a perfectionist who practised his technique with unusual rigour. Though his handsome face was marred by a slight squint, there is no evidence to support the contention that he was the first Roman actor to perform in a mask. He became fabulously wealthy, and in his prime was said to command an annual income equalling half a million pounds sterling.

So great was Roscius's reputation that his name has since become synonymous with great acting. William BETTY, the eighteenth-century boy actor, became known as the "Young Roscius"; Ira ALDRIDGE, the black American actor, was the "African Roscius".

SENECA (c 4 BC-AD 65)

Roman playwright. Lucius Annaeus Seneca the younger was a dramatist, philosopher, satirist and statesman; a tutor to Nero and later his victim. He was born at Corduba (Cordova) in Spain, the son of a famous rhetorician, but spent most of his life in Italy. Despite the apparent hypocrisy of the high moral tone of his writings when set against his self-indulgent life, he has nevertheless had the most profound influence of any ancient writer upon the development of the drama in Europe.

Yet none of his nine tragedies was written to be acted on the stage. A single actor recited all the parts of the most important scenes, or the plays were acted by mimes accompanied by music or dialogue. In fact Seneca seems to have had little theatrical sense: actors become silent, but we are not told when they make an exit; Phaedra kills herself in full view, but her husband ignores the fact until the end of the play; all his characters speak with a rhetorical straining for effect, to the detriment of plot and character.

The titles bear witness to their Greek origin: *Hercules Furens, Troades, Phoenissae, Medea, Phaedra, Oedipus, Thyestes, Agamemnon, Hercules Oetaeus*. Their material, however, is rooted in the Rome of Seneca's day. They are products of rhetorical education and of Seneca's Stoic philosophy, showing the battle between the absolutes of passion and reason. In this (and in the fact that they are written in Latin, and thus were intelligible to the Renaissance writer) lies the reason for their popularity and influence. Moreover, the atmosphere of doom, horror and witchcraft appealed to general taste. His single-line dialogue, his ghosts, witches and corpse-scattered stages all find their repetition in Elizabethen drama. SHAKESPEARE's *Titus Andronicus* is a bloody reminder of Seneca's influence, and *Richard III* an example of Senecan material in the hands of a genius. French classical tragedy as well owes him a great debt; it is interesting to ponder what course European drama might have taken had Greek and not Latin been the *lingua franca* of Renaissance Europe.

ST GENESIUS (?-AD 297)

Roman actor. When performing a parody of Christian rites for the pagan Diocletian, Genesius is said to have declared his own faith after the irreverent "baptism" scene. Immediately the Emperor had him tortured and beheaded. Genesius has since become an enduring symbol of martyrdom, the patron saint of actors and the hero of plays by LOPE DE VEGA, Jean DE ROTROU and numerous others.

THE DARK AGES

Roman decadence killed the legitimate theatre long before barbarian hordes poured out of the north and ushered in the Dark Ages. But even in this decline there was a vital tradition of popular entertainment that was to flourish underground and to re-emerge centuries later and contribute to the rebirth of the theatre. For nearly a thousand years there were no major playwrights, no great actors that history remembers, indeed few written records of theatrical activity of any kind. What traces there are indicate that in the streets of Europe jugglers, clowns, storytellers, acrobats, mimes and minstrels satisfied the universal human need for entertainment and in so doing kept alive vital skills that flourish today. An open space, an attentive audience and skilled performers with a few simple props are all that the theatre needs to survive in even the most hostile environment.

The debased theatrical spectacle that dominated the stage in the late Roman Empire did not survive the barbarian invasions; such decadence offended the unsophisticated but upright conquerors. For a time performances were allowed to continue, but eventually theatres closed and the culture that had seen sex and death actually take place on the stage passed away. Popular entertainers subsequently adapted their art to the taste of the barbarians, who did allow at least some spectacle. Attila the Hun is recorded as having given a banquet in 448 for a delegation from Constantinople. He tried to impress his guests by entertaining them with a recital of heroic deeds, followed by the antics of a Scythian Clown and a Moorish buffoon. Theodoric II, King of the Visigoths in Gaul, was typical in his response to performers who sought to entertain him as he dined. He would permit it provided that nothing was offensive to his guests and that in their acts "virtue should win the heart and the soul as much as singing did the ear".

The Church, which was to keep culture alive through the Dark Ages, had even more reason to object to the sensuality and violence of late Roman theatre. The Roman mimes had satirized the rites of the infant Church, finding baptism particularly amusing. The persecution of Christians had also provided great entertainment, and the lewd spectacles of the mimes aroused the ire of Church fathers, who sermonized against "these wanton words, these ridiculous manners, these foolish tonsures, these ways of walking, these dresses, these voices, that softness of limb, that winking of the eyes, these pipes and flutes, these dramas and arguments—aye, all are full of utter wantonness. Here are to be seen naught but fornication, adultery, courtesan women, men pretending to be women, and soft-limbed boys."

Such comments, common from the fourth century onwards until the Renaissance, not only tell us why the Church objected to the theatre, but more importantly they form the only substantial evidence as to the nature of popular entertainment for an extremely long period. Some nine hundred years later an English cleric wrote very much in the same spirit, describing (as he condemns) three kinds of performers: "Some transform their bodies with gross dance and gesture, now indecently removing their clothes, now donning horrible masks . . . others have no definite profession, but are vagabonds, frequenting the courts of the noble, delighting with scandalous comments concerning those absent . . . There is another class of actor who plays musical instruments for the pleasure of men. Some frequent public drinking places and lascivious gatherings singing lascivious songs and there are others, who are called *jongleurs*, who sing of princes and the lives of saints." Though little is known of the nature of such performers, their role was crucial. They left no dramatic literature, had no great moral impact, yet they kept alive skills that live today and which were to nourish the emergent theatre of the early middle ages.

Though the Church was opposed to the theatre, it unwittingly provided the impetus for a rebirth of drama. In adopting Latin as the language of its liturgy, it assured that the language was studied and widely read. One natural result of this was the preservation of the Latin classics, particularly the playwright Terence, whose high moral tone made him popular with Christian writers. At Gandersheim in Germany a tenth-century Benedictine nun named Hrotsvitha, "German religious and virgin of the Saxon race", wrote plays modelled on Terence. She

feared that some students of Terence "fascinated by the charm and the style, risked being corrupted by the wickedness of the content", and so sought to imitate his manner in order "to glorify the commendable chastity of Christian virgins in the same form of writing which had been used to describe the shameless acts of loose women". (As she added carefully, "avoiding through omission the pernicious voluptuousness of pagan writers".) In her *Abraham* a hermit gallantly rescues his niece from a brothel. Farce creeps into her moral tales in *Dulcitius* where a lecherous young man is given the task of guarding saintly virgins. Hrotsvitha's plays were almost certainly never performed and as such represent more an interesting sideline than a major contribution to the development of drama. She anticipates, however, the spirit of the Renaissance in seeking inspiration in classical texts.

Whatever the role of Latin in the rebirth of the theatre, the liturgy itself was to be crucial. Holy Communion, the central act of faith, is an act of great dramatic significance. The Mass can be seen as a ritual containing theatrical elements. It has participants with clearly assigned roles, including a congregation at once audience and participant, for whom the events represent a central religious mystery. It has a plot of sorts, moving to a miraculous climax. Costumes are worn, incense, music and chant are used to intensify the experience, and the church itself forms a simple "theatre". In the twelfth century, Honorius of Autun wrote on the theatricality of the Mass: "Our tragic author—that is, the celebrant—represents by his actions in the theatre of the church before Christian people the ordeal of Christ and teaches to them the victory of His Redemption." Indeed, the Mass can be seen as a tragedy: a fall from grace, suffering, and the renewal of life.

Resurrection and the defeat of death are archetypal impulses, by no means confined to Christianity. Even today, many rituals survive from the pre-Christian past. In the Dark Ages the Church was in no position to challenge these powerful dramatic traditions; instead it incorporated the most important pagan festivals into its own calendar. Christmas celebrated more than the birth of Christ. It marked the height of winter with all its ambiguity, the longest night past but the severest weather yet to come. Easter was a natural time for celebrating fertility and renewal; it even took its English name from the Anglo-Saxon goddess Eostre.

Thus the ritual battle of George and the dragon or the joyful crowning of a May Queen continued to enrich popular culture. The powerful instincts which these traditions represent were to find their way into the religious theatre of the Middle Ages.

MEDIEVAL THEATRE

Drama in the Middle Ages developed most rapidly within the church, where the theatrical possibilities of the liturgy were to be fully realized. The central mystery of the Christian faith is the Resurrection. It had to be properly celebrated and yet also made memorable to clergy and laity alike. The possibility of a simple dramatization of this event must have occurred to a number of imaginative clerics before anyone actually dared to break with tradition. In the tenth century in the Benedictine monastery at St Gall in Switzerland the leap was made. At first parts were assigned to sections of the choir who engaged in a kind of chanted dialogue during the *introit* of the Easter Mass. One section represented the three Marys, the other the Angel they find when they come upon the empty tomb. He asks them "*Quem quaeritis*" (Whom do you seek?). They reply "Jesus of Nazareth, crucified as He prophesied," at which the Angel announces "He is not here, He is risen as He prophesied. Go announce that He is risen from the tomb." This very simple "play" spread all over Europe; some 400 versions of the *Quem quaeritis* have survived as evidence of its popularity. Eventually it detached itself from the Easter Mass and came to be performed at the morning service, the part of the Angel being taken by individual clerics rather than sections of the choir. Any number of variations were now possible. One version had the three Marys going to buy spices prior to their visit to the tomb. (The spice merchant was a type of pagan quack doctor borrowed from the mumming plays who engaged in comic business with his wife and assistant.) This music drama with impersonation

The flute-player and the young juggler (*left*) are the medieval representatives of very ancient arts. Such figures had been seen in the fairs and markets of Europe ever since pre-Roman times

Among the more bloodthirsty attractions at the medieval fairs was bear-baiting. The exquisite fourteenth-century carving (*below*) in Gloucester Cathedral shows the chained bear, the attacking dog and their mean-faced master with a club. Of the three, the dog was much the most at risk

and rudimentary dialogue was the first halting step towards the great religious dramas of the high middle ages, and the entrance of the profane comic element was crucial. Eventually more complicated plays developed, such as the Passion play from Monte Cassino in Italy, which had some twelve scenes beginning with Judas's betrayal and ending with the Virgin Mary lamenting at the foot of the cross. In this version the hymn of lament is in Italian, indicating the crucial fact that vernacular languages were beginning to creep into church drama.

Naturally Christmas as well as Easter provided great scope for plays. The shepherds seeking Christ provided an equivalent of the *Quem quaeritis* and were quickly followed by the Wise Men; it is part of their story that adds the next element. While searching for the infant Christ, the Magi go to the tyrant King Herod. For the first time a wholly evil character appears. The problem was how to portray this evil in devotional drama. Should a priest take his part? Should evil be portrayed in the church? Comedy was the result. Herod became a buffoon, and a layman played the part. (This was no doubt a relief to the clergy of Padua, for in their version of the play Herod even hit the Bishop with an inflated bladder.)

In Germany, where pagan ritual rather than Church liturgy provided the inspiration for a festival drama, this profane comic tradition was closer to the surface. Carnival plays (*Fastnachtsspiele*) performed in the streets before Lent were secular revels with short humorous scenes from everyday life performed by stock characters. These popular plays later developed into a literary genre in the work of men like Hans SACHS, whose play *The Travelling Scholar* tells the story of how a priest disguises himself as a devil to avoid the wrath of a returning jealous husband. Besides this popular farce tradition there existed more overtly religious plays, but even they, like Dietrich Schernberg's *Play of Frau Jutta*, which deals with a female pope and of pacts with the devil, were considerably different from more devout fare elsewhere in Europe at the time.

In France, parables and the lives of saints and Old Testament prophets formed the subject for liturgical plays. A book of Latin plays from a monastery at Fleury indicates this variety: a *Visit to the Sepulchre*, inspired by the *Quem quaeritis*; a *Herod* and a *Massacre of the Innocents*, performed at Epiphany; Christ's appearance to the disciples on the road to Emmaus; the *Raising of Lazarus*; the *Conversion of St Paul*; and a play about St Nicholas. The story of Daniel also proved popular, forming the subject of two plays, one by students of Beauvais, the other by the wandering scholar-monk Hilarius. He did not make the innovations his name might suggest, but importantly introduced refrains in French into two of his plays. This crucial process continues in *Sponsus* (*The Bridegroom*), an anonymous work of the early twelfth century, which dramatizes the parable of the Wise and Foolish Virgins and is half in Latin and half in French. The final transformation of liturgical drama can be seen in the *Jeu d'Adam* (*The Play of Adam*) which is nearly all in French, was performed outside the church and had little sung dialogue. Out of the already highly dramatic liturgy of the Medieval Church there had developed a drama with dialogue, impersonation and music that incorporated more profane elements and which included everyday spoken language. One step more was required to take the drama finally out of the church into the streets and place it in the hands of the people.

In 1264 Pope Urban IV decreed a new feast, Corpus Christi, which was to commemorate the miracle of transubstantiation. It was to be elevated to the same status as the Virgin Birth and the Resurrection. Rather than celebrate this event at Easter when the calendar of observances was crowded, a new feast was instituted in summer. By the fifteenth century it was an important Church feast all over Europe. The central event of this great ceremony was a procession by both secular and religious leaders through the streets behind the consecrated Host, which was carried in triumph from the church. The procession stopped for worship at various places, arriving at the church or cathedral for a final service. Participants would have included representatives of craft and trade guilds. All over Europe in flourishing trade centres these organizations reflected the prosperity and vitality of a new merchant class. A city like York, which was both an economic and a religious centre, would have had many active guilds. Each guild had a patron saint and each had its own church. They formed part of both the civic and religious structure of the town. At first each guild paraded with banners identifying itself, but as time went on they indicated their devotion and their affluence by elaborate

display. Wagons, called pageants, decorated with rich materials appeared–some with Biblical scenes depicted by costumed tradesmen. In time these figures spoke dialogue written for them: the result was the medieval mystery play.

From these Corpus Christi parades in the north of England developed the great cycles of plays that covered the whole of Biblical history from the Creation to the Last Judgement. Each guild had a play to perform, sometimes appropriate to its trade. For example, the York shipwrights presented the building of the Ark. Each guild organized and financed its own play, looking after elaborate costumes and pageant wagon. The plays were an occasion for great civic as well as religious pride. The wagons moved in procession from station to station through the town, performing at different locations. These great cycles were given in English and contained many comic elements, particularly the mischievous devils and King Herod, a raging villain. Despite their overt religious nature, they were popular plays. Four such cycles survive from medieval England: York, Chester, Wakefield, and the N-town cycle, which was performed at Lincoln among other places. York is the most extensive cycle, with forty-eight plays ranging from the Tanners' production of the Creation and the Fall of Lucifer to the Mercers' (cloth merchants) version of Judgement Day. The York plays are still performed today in a modified version.

Though perhaps the most spectacular way of presenting the great plays, the pageant wagons of northern England were not the only method of staging such epic religious drama. The Cornish *Ordinalia* (a three-part cycle performed on three consecutive days) consisted of the Creation, the Passion and the Resurrection. It was performed in the round, in outdoor theatres that can still be seen today. Earthwork or stone inclines surrounded a central playing space forming an amphitheatre. Stations around the exterior represented various places in the cosmic scheme of things. Hell yawned; Heaven beckoned.

Further evidence for the staging of medieval plays in the round comes from the manuscript of an early fifteenth-century play *The Castle of Perseverance*. It contains a drawing which is a rough stage-plan. In the centre of the arena stands a castle and around the outside of the playing space were located five scaffolds. In the south Flesh; in the west the World; Belial and the other denizens of Hell to the north; in the northeast lay Covetousness and in the east, as per tradition, God in Heaven. The action rages between the Castle and the various symbolic locations, but *The Castle of Perseverance* is crucial to the history of drama for another reason. It is the earliest example of the morality play.

The morality plays were parables using personification to relate religious truth. The heroes were figures like Human Kind of Mankind. Their progress through life was charted and their eventual salvation related as a moral example. In *The Castle of Perseverance* a battle is waged over the soul of Mankind between the forces of Virtue and Vice. There is comic action provided by the various devils and such figures as Backbiter and Lechery, but the play's message is serious. Though allegorical and didactic, the morality play, with its abstract version of the plight of man as he progresses through the world beset by sin, marks the beginning of "psychological drama".

The best known and most sophisticated of the morality plays is *Everyman* (c. 1500). As his name suggests, the title character is representative of humanity. His fair-weather friends, including Fellowship, Kindred, Cousin and Goods, will not accompany him when they realize he has been summoned by Death. Good-Deeds stands by him, however, and advises him to consult Knowledge, with whose help he begins contrition. Everyman next summons Strength, Discretion, and Five-Wits who promise to accompany him, but who gradually desert him until at the graveside even Knowledge departs; Good-Deeds alone can assure Everyman of his salvation.

Religious drama was eventually eroded by the humanistic revolution that began in Italy and swept through Europe during the fifteenth and sixteenth centuries. New ideas engendered by the Renaissance forced the church into an increasingly defensive and repressive attitude. As early as 1548 religious plays were banned in Paris because of degrading innovations. In 1576 the mystery cycle at Wakefield was suppressed. Yet the vital ingredients of the mystery and morality tradition survived to enrich the theatre of a new era. Doctor Faustus or the Fool in *King Lear* could not have drawn breath without their pious ancestry in the sacred drama of the Middle Ages.

The Renaissance brought with it a love of elaborate detail in all of the arts. The forthright plots of the morality and mystery plays were replaced by the delightfully complicated comedies of Machiavelli; the haunting simplicity of the chant gave way to the finely woven counterpoint of Palestrina; and the strong, stylized lines in the paintings of Giotto expanded into the amazing intricacy of Leonardo. The new sensibility is sumptuously expressed in the early sixteenth-century tapestry, "The Departure of the Prodigal Son" (*left*), which can be seen at the Musée de Cluny in Paris

The works of the ancient Roman author Seneca (lovingly transcribed, *right*) were the basis of the first attempts at serious drama in the Renaissance

The carved face of a jester grins cheekily from its place under the seat of a medieval choir stall (*above*)

The action in Memling's painting of the Passion of Christ (*far right*) is influenced by his experience of watching the medieval mystery plays which dealt with the subject

The popular farce of ancient Rome stayed precariously alive in the Dark Ages. The medieval jongleurs (*right*) were its inheritors, playing at fairs and feasts; and (more cruelly) serenading sleeping widows

The Renaissance painting of a procession in Brussels (*below*) shows that the mystery pageants were still being gorgeously mounted. In the middle of the square a wagon bearing the Annunciation is drawn in splendour before another bearing the Nativity (and a perched angel). But the spirit of classicism is also present, in the person of Diana and her nymphs in the near right corner

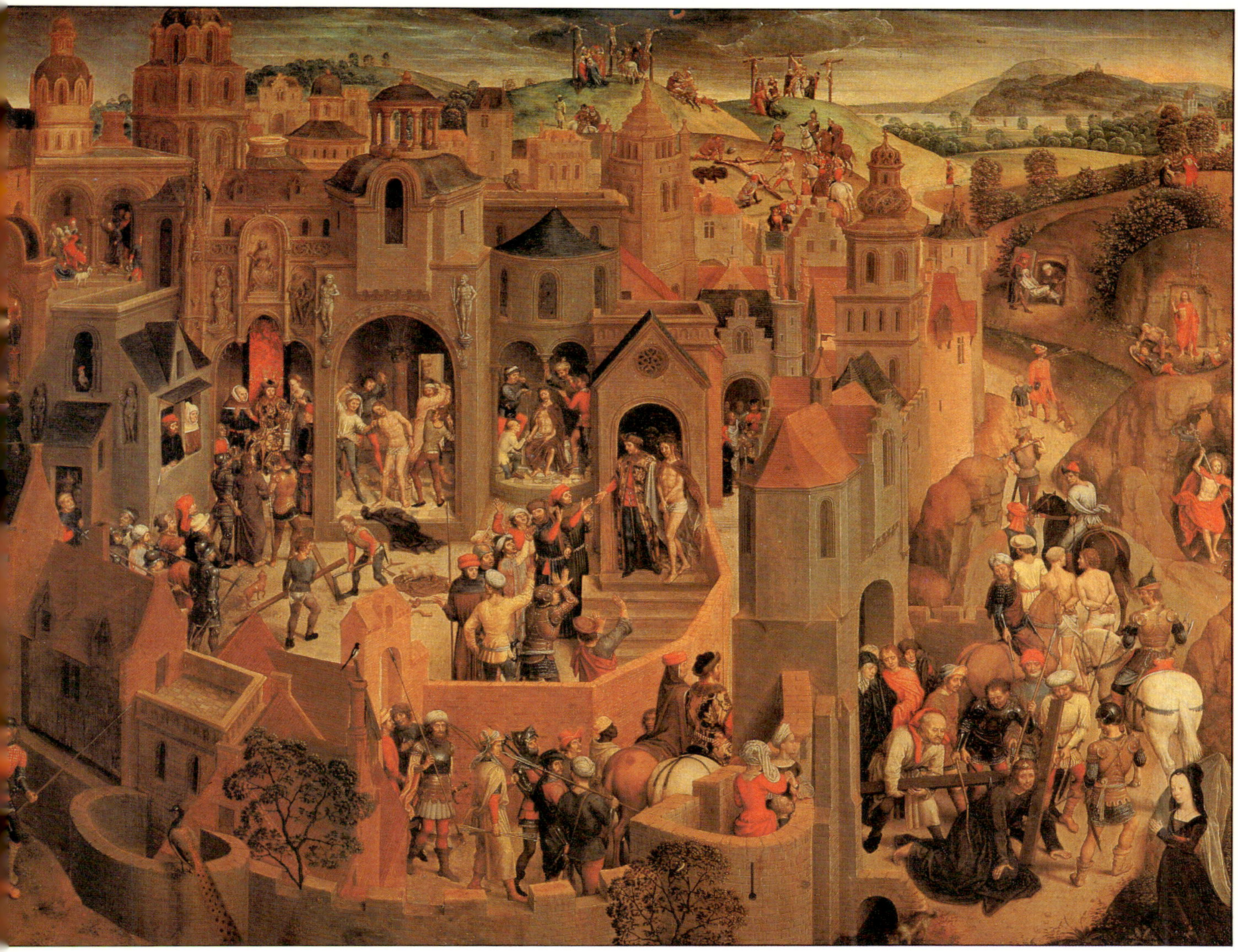

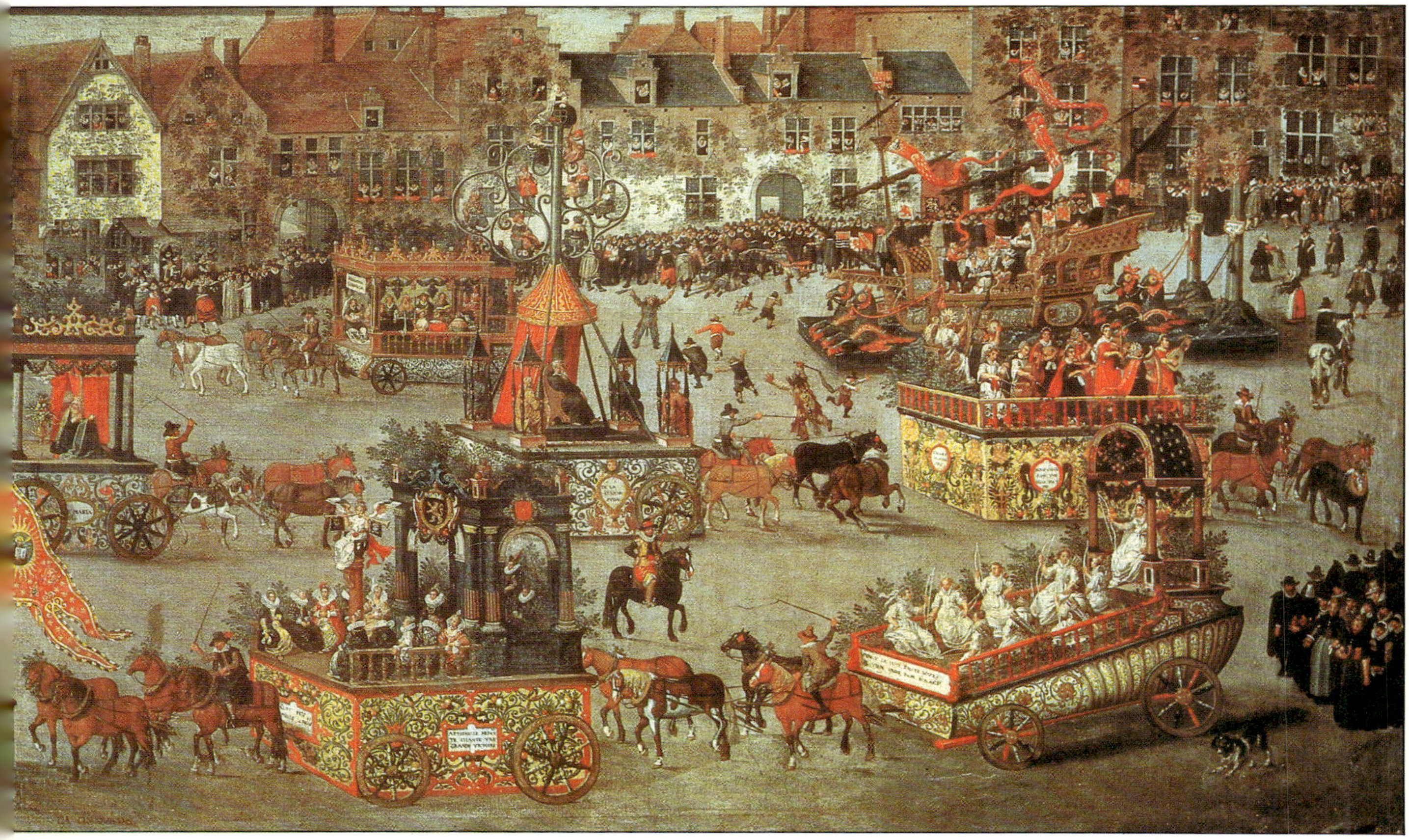

The Renaissance was characterized by a joy in life and knowledge, despite the violence and cruelty beneath the surface of society. History fails to provide a totally adequate explanation for this phenomenon. International commerce encouraged exploration; the Catholic church lost much of its secular power, and the printing press encouraged literacy. Whatever its origins, the Renaissance gave new life to Western theatre

LEONARDO DA VINCI (1452-1519)

Italian artist, architect and inventor. It was a foregone conclusion that when the greatest genius of the Renaissance turned his hand to the theatre he should have been centuries ahead of his time. Leonardo's notebooks contain sketches for scenery, lighting and curtains, but the most significant of his inventions for the theatre is the revolving stage intended for the scenes in Hell in Poliziano's *Orpheus*. It was never used in that performance as casting difficulties held up the production and as a result Europe was not to see such machinery again until four hundred years later, in nineteenth-century Germany.

FERNANDO DE ROJAS (c 1465-1541)

Spanish writer. Rojas is generally accepted as the author of the major part of *La Celestina* (1499), a long novel written in dialogue form. Although not intended for the theatre, this tale of young love and "disorderly lusts" inspired countless theatrical sequels. Spanish playwrights borrowed the plot, scenes, characters and speeches for the next hundred years, during which time it went through over sixty editions.

Rojas was the son of Jewish parents forcibly converted to Christianity, a fact that has led some critics to see *La Celestina* as an allegory of the persecution of the Jews.

Fernando de Rojas's *La Celestina* is the popular title of *La Tragicomedia de Calisto y Melibea*. Celestina herself is a bawd employed by Calisto to seduce the lovely Melibea, and murdered (*left*) for her troubles

GIL VICENTE (c 1465-1536)

Portuguese playwright, poet and musician. Author of entertainments at the Courts of Manuel I and John III of Portugal, Vicente was also a goldsmith and probably Master of the Royal Mint. He produced, composed the music for and acted in his own plays. So great was his fame throughout Europe that Erasmus is said to have learned Portuguese to read Vicente in the original.

His reputation was as a poet and musician, not as a theatrical innovator, since his royal patrons generally commissioned conventional pieces: pastorals in the style of Juan del ENCINA, chivalrous romances and works of devotion. Vicente's farces, however, notably *Farsa de Inês Pereira* (1523), have become classics.

JUAN DEL ENCINA (1469-c 1529)

Spanish playwright, musician and poet. Encina is regarded as the father of the Spanish Renaissance theatre. In the humanistic atmosphere of Italy he broke away from medieval Christian drama and wrote some truly secular plays, the best known of which is the *Egloga de Plácida y Victoriano* (1513). These pastoral entertainments were invariably enlivened by musical interludes and finales (composed by the author) and by the innovative use of comic peasant speech.

Throughout his life Encina was torn between Church and Court. He took minor orders when young, but in 1492 found a position at the Court of the Duke of Alba, where he produced his early works. Ordained in 1519, Encina then forsook worldly fame and went on a pilgrimage to Jerusalem, where he celebrated his first mass.

NICCOLÒ MACHIAVELLI (1469-1527)

Italian political philosopher, statesman and playwright. Machiavelli's name has entered history as a synonym for political astuteness bordering on vulpine cunning, but the Florentine statesman has survived also as a master of prose—on the power of princes, on war and for the stage.

Imprisoned in middle life by the Medici, he spent his latter years in writing, and from this period there comes *La Mandragola* (*c.* 1520), a dark comedy.

The tale of a seduction, written in realistic prose, it perfectly illustrates Machiavellian politics at work in a humbler sphere. The lover, disguised as a doctor, persuades the lady's husband to give his wife a mandrake concoction to cure her sterility, but warns that the first to sleep with her will die. A victim must be found, and the lover himself (now posing as an "innocent" stranger) contrives to be introduced into the lady's chamber. Such unscrupulous cunning reflects the political advice given more seriously in *The Prince*, his most famous work.

In 1520 Machiavelli, once more in favour with the Medici, began a history of the family, and *La Mandragola* was performed before Pope Leo X (himself a Medici). The play has remained popular and has been translated several times into English. It is still performed regularly in Italy, and has even been filmed.

IL BIBBIENA (1470-1520)

Italian playwright. Bibbiena (whose real name was Bernardo Dovizi) was an eminent churchman who is remembered as the author of one of the wittiest and bawdiest comedies of the Renaissance, *La Calandria* (1513). His only play, it was loosely based on PLAUTUS's *Menaechmi*, the same source SHAKESPEARE used for *The Comedy of Errors*. A farcical account of lust, true love, adultery and mistaken identity (between twins of different sexes), the play was widely performed throughout Italy. Bibbiena's ecclesiastical career may have benefited from theatrical acclaim, for he was made a cardinal by the stage-struck Pope Leo X.

LUDOVICO ARIOSTO (1474-1533)

Italian poet and playwright. The five plays of Ariosto are among the first classical comedies of the Renaissance. Their author was a scholarly poet ("tall, thin, bald and stooping" was his own description) who wanted nothing more than to study and write, but who was constrained to pass much of his life in uncongenial occupations. For five years he reluctantly studied law at the University of Ferrara but never pursued a legal career. Instead he became a salaried dependant of the Este family of Ferrara and remained for the rest of his life under its patronage. He was employed at Court, held a military captaincy and received minor orders, varied activities which provided security for his literary work.

In his great poem "Orlando Furioso" he celebrated the Renaissance vision of ideal beauty, but in his plays he adhered to the classical tradition of Latin theatre. The comedies of PLAUTUS with their bawdy intrigues and farcical misunderstandings were obvious influences, but Ariosto updated the old themes, setting four of his five comedies in contemporary Italy. *La Lena* (1528) and *Il Negromante* (1530) are among his best works. An earlier comedy, *I Suppositi* (1509), was successfully translated into English as *Supposes* by George GASCOIGNE in 1566.

LEONARDO·
ᵕVINCI

SEBASTIANO SERLIO (1475-1554)

Italian architect and stage designer. Serlio was in Paris, at the Court of Francis I, when he published his remarkable treatise on theatre architecture, *Le Second Livre de la perspective*, in 1545. It contained designs for a temporary theatre and instructions for stage effects, including coloured lighting, moving heavenly bodies and thunder and lightning. Above all, Serlio designed and described three different perspective stage sets: one each for tragedy, comedy and pastoral scenes. An English translation of 1611 gave the following advice: For comedy "there must not want a brawthell or bawdy house . . . such things are of necessitie to be therein". "Houses for tragedy", on the other hand, "must be made for great personages, for that actions of love, strange adventures, and cruell murthers . . . happen always in the houses of great Lords."

In France this work became an instant success, remaining a vital influence on stage design well into the seventeenth century.

BARTOLOMÉ DE TORRES NAHARRO (c1485-c1524)

Spanish playwright and poet. The early military career of Torres Naharro came to an end when he was shipwrecked and captured by Barbary pirates. Eventually, like many other cultured Spaniards of his time, he made his way to Rome and there took holy orders. He wrote plays which were performed in the households of powerful cardinals, and in 1517 published a volume of his collected works.

Torres Naharro's eight plays were the first classical five-act dramas to be written in Spanish. One of them, the *Comedia Himenea*, published in 1517, anticipates the plays of LOPE DE VEGA with its cloak-and-dagger intrigue and obsession with honour. His most realistic work, the *Comedia Tinellaria* (1516), is a scathing satire on Italian manners and the hypocrisy of the nobility.

DAVID LINDSAY (c1490-1555)

Scottish poet and playwright. Lindsay spent his life at the Scottish court, where he supervised the early education of the infant James V. This royal connection, together with his eminence as a diplomat, may help explain his moral courage as a dramatist. *Ane Pleasant Satyre of the Thrie Estaitis*, staged before the king in 1540, was anything but "pleasant" for some distinguished members of the audience. A long-winded and withering satire which reserves its harshest blows for the clergy, it alternates between severe morality and slapstick comedy. A shortened version has been revived in the twentieth century.

PIETRO ARETINO (1492-1556)

Italian playwright. One of literary history's most Machiavellian heroes began his unscrupulous rise in 1517. Young Aretino had been a bookbinder's apprentice in his native Arezzo and arrived in Rome with no encouraging prospects. Briefly he accepted menial employment, but his wit and ambition found him a wealthy patron in Cardinal Giulio de' Medici, for whom he wrote libellous political broadsheets. Powerful enemies soon outnumbered powerful friends, and in 1526 Aretino was expelled from Rome. He found more fertile ground for his unique blend of blackmail and hypocrisy in Venice, where he prospered until his death. Vowing to "tear apart the names of the great with the fangs of truth", he coerced wealthy patrons to accept his serious literary efforts by threatening to write scurrilous satires about them if they refused. Francis I of France and the Holy Roman Emperor Charles V were eager to keep on friendly terms with Aretino, though other less amiable associates made occasional attempts to kill him.

A notorious libertine, he wrote exuberant (and thoroughly researched) pornography. Amazingly he was also revered as a moralist for his earnest religious tracts (part of an unsuccessful campaign to become a cardinal).

For the stage Aretino wrote one tragedy, *Orazia* (1546), and five brilliant comedies. The latter are marked by their refreshing disregard for classical models and the stock characters that recur in so many Renaissance comedies. Pimps, criminals and courtiers, his constant companions in life, people his stage. It is possible that the protagonist of *Lo Ipocrito* (1545) may have come to life later in MOLIÈRE's *Tartuffe*, while *Il Marescalco* (c.1527) may have served as a model for Ben JONSON's *Epicoene*.

The discovery of perspective gave Renaissance designers the chance to add a new dimension to drama. **Sebastiano Serlio** popularized the art, but was by no means its only master. Baldassare Peruzzi (1481–1537) was another pioneer, contributing the intricate and majestic setting for tragedy (*far left*)

John Heywood (*left*) was a favourite of both Henry VIII and Bloody Mary, but during Elizabeth's reign was forced into religious exile. His wife was a niece of Sir Thomas More.

The German Shrovetide plays, *Fastnachtsspiele* (*right*), were the prelude to a last, riotous pagan carnival before the rigours of Lent. These farcical scenes of domestic life reached a pinnacle of lunacy in the hands of the mastersinger **Hans Sachs**. One typical dimwit tries to hatch a calf from a nest full of cheeses

Aretino died suddenly of apoplexy, though it is tempting to believe the legend that he was carried away "of a great fit of laughing".

HANS SACHS (1494-1576)

German playwright and *meistersinger*. Although Sachs was apprenticed to a shoemaker and is still sentimentally referred to as the cobbler-poet of Nuremberg, it is unlikely that he was able to devote much time to the trade. The leading German dramatist of his day, he wrote more than a hundred plays: moralistic tragedies and comedies with subjects ranging from the Bible to folk tales, but rarely distinguished by any literary or dramatic value. The only original note he struck in these works was his early support for Martin Luther, whose ideas Sachs tried to make generally accessible.

It was with Sachs's 200 *fastnachtsspiele*, pre-Lenten carnival plays, that he made his great theatrical contribution. In works such as *Das heiss Eisen* (1551) he found the ideal balance between earthy farce and his insuppressible urge to moralize.

To the musical world Sachs is the foremost *meistersinger*, a member of the proud society of singers and composers immortalized (along with Sachs himself) by Wagner. Nine years before his death he claimed to have composed over 4,000 songs.

JOHN BALE (1495-1563)

English playwright and bishop. Bale violently rejected the Catholic faith while a student at Cambridge, and thereafter devoted much of his life to attacking it. He was twice exiled when his views clashed with the government's.

He is reputed to have written twenty-two plays, of which only five have survived. Four of these are anti-Catholic diatribes. The fifth, *King John* (1538), is equally polemical, but remains a vital landmark in British drama as the first known history play in the English language.

JOHN HEYWOOD (c 1497-c 1580)

English playwright, poet and musician. Renowned for his mastery of the virginals, Heywood first established himself as a musician at the Court of Henry VIII. Although he was an ardent Catholic and had been involved in a plot against Archbishop Cranmer, he maintained a distinguished place in English cultural life until the Protestant Elizabeth I drove him into exile.

Throughout these years at court he wrote a number of interludes–comic playlets originally intended to amuse guests between the courses of a banquet. *The Four P's* (*c*.1520), in which a pedlar, a palmer, a pothecary and a pardoner compete to see who is the biggest liar, is the best known of these. Heywood's interludes do not reveal any great dramatic flair, but they do represent the first attempts at a purely secular English comedy.

His literary abilities were distilled more perfectly in his grandson, the poet John Donne.

RUZZANTE (c 1502-42)

Italian playwright and actor. Angelo Beolco, known as Ruzzante, was the natural son of a wealthy Paduan doctor. While still a teenager he began writing plays, staging them with his companions at the private theatres or banqueting halls of noble patrons. From the beginning his plays revealed a love and mastery of coarse peasant speech and rough good humour, qualities which have led some scholars to infer that he was one of the "inventors" of the Commedia dell' Arte. It was from one of his most popular low characters, a wily and garrulous peasant called Ruzzante, that he took his stage name.

Neglected for many centuries, several of his plays, including *Anconitana* (1522) and *Moschetta* (1528), have been rediscovered and staged in the twentieth century.

LOPE DE RUEDA (c 1505-65)

Spanish playwright and actor. Trained (like the Portuguese VICENTE) as a goldsmith, Lope de Rueda soon discovered that his greatest talents were theatrical. With touring companies he travelled throughout Spain, gaining special applause for his comic interpretations of pimps, fools and black women. In 1554, as the head of his own company, he performed for King Philip II; his admirers included the young CERVANTES, who considered Rueda "a brilliant actor and a man of sound sense".

Rueda wrote several comedies derived from Italian sources, but the works for which he is remembered today are the *pasos*, short comic plays interpolated for light relief between acts of a more serious work. Of these by far the best known is *Las aceitunas* (1548).

NICHOLAS UDALL (1505-56)

English playwright. As headmaster of Eton College, Udall was renowned for his ready recourse to corporal punishment. Later, as vicar of Braintree (Essex), he was accused of corrupting minors, but after serving a short prison sentence, he recommenced his academic career as headmaster of Westminster School.

The famous comedy for which Udall is now solely remembered is *Ralph Roister Doister*, a rollicking, slapstick farce. It has no great literary merit, owing much to the comedies of PLAUTUS and TERENCE, but achieves historical significance as a herald of Elizabethan comedy.

MARIN DRŽIĆ (c 1508-67)

Croatian playwright. Born in Dubrovnik, Držić took holy orders and worked for a year as cathedral organist, before a ten-year spell in Italy opened his eyes to the vital theatrical life that was emerging there. On his return, he began to write his own highly popular pastorals and comedies, generally for the weddings of well-to-do citizens. Some of these, notably *Dundo Maroje* (1550), are still occasionally performed.

ANDREA PALLADIO (1508-80)

Italian architect. Italy's most renowned architect, Palladio's primary concern was not with the theatre. It was only in the last years of his life that he designed the Teatro Olimpico (see p. 46) in Vicenza, a building he was never to see completed.

The Teatro Olimpico was modelled closely on Roman plans. Palladio's disciple Vincenzo Scamozzi saw the building finished and added a feature of his own: passages at the back of the stage through which perspective street scenes were visible. Despite its elegance and prestige, the Teatro Olimpico was too inflexible to serve as a model for later centuries.

Palladio's influential text, *Quattro libri dell'architettura*, was translated into English by INIGO JONES.

GIOVAN MARIA CECCHI (1518-87)

Italian playwright. Cecchi was a Florentine wool merchant and notary public who found time to become one of Italy's most prolific playwrights. Part of his success lay in the speed at which he worked, a comedy rarely taking him more than ten days to write.

Cecchi's plays include farces and religious dramas as well as comedies, the best known of which is probably *L'Assiuolo* (1550). Many of his works involve a surprising mixture of characters, heralding the development of secular drama in Italy.

JAMES BURBAGE (c 1530-97)

English actor and theatre builder. A carpenter by trade, Burbage became an actor when plays were still performed in inn yards. Aided by his wealthy father-in-law, he built the Theatre, the first permanent playhouse in Britain. A partly covered, circular structure just outside the London city limits, it provided actors with the luxury of backstage changing facilities and wealthier members of the audience with dry seats.

The Theatre was not, as might be supposed, a seat of the highest culture in Elizabethan London. It was often used for displays of sportsmanship as well as for drama. But Burbage never made the "continual great profit" he had expected from his scheme, which was soon to inspire a number of rival buildings. He is none the less revered as the father both of the English theatre, and of one of its great tragic actors, RICHARD BURBAGE.

ÉTIENNE JODELLE (1532-73)

French poet and playwright. In 1552 the twenty-year-old Étienne Jodelle assumed the role of Cleopatra in his own tragedy *Cléopâtre captive*, written that year. Henry II, a member of the audience, was captivated by the production and encouraged the precocious author with 500 crowns. The same evening Jodelle's comedy, *Eugène* (1552), was also produced and the playwright found himself one of the leading literary figures in France. His success did not last. A celebration in his honour organized by fellow poets was condemned as pagan (a goat participated in the festivities). Jodelle returned to poetry and died in neglect.

Jodelle's tragedies, which today seem totally lifeless, were startling novelties in the sixteenth century with their use of classical models and for the introduction of alexandrines (lines of six metrical feet). They inspired the great classic dramas of CORNEILLE and RACINE.

THOMAS NORTON (1532-84)

English playwright. Norton was a law student in London when he and his fellow student Thomas SACKVILLE wrote *Gorboduc* (1562), the first drama in English that can accurately be called a tragedy. Although in form it is based on the Latin tragedies of SENECA, the play exploits English sources for its plot. Gorboduc, King of England, divides his realm between his two sons, Ferrex and Porrex, as disastrous an act of paternal indulgence as that of SHAKESPEARE's King Lear.

GIOVAN BATTISTA DELLA PORTA (1535-1615)

Italian scientist and playwright. Like many educated Italians of the Renaissance, Della Porta, a native of Naples, pursued several branches of learning. Primarily he was a scientist but "science" in his day also included magic and alchemy, practices which compelled the Inquisition to ban his work as wizardry.

He found time to write at least thirty plays, of which fourteen prose comedies survive. These were drawn from a variety of sources, including PLAUTUS and ARIOSTO, and inspired many imitations. *L'Astrologo* (1570) and *I Due fratelli rivali*, first published in 1601, are still admired today. The latter has as its source the same Italian story that SHAKESPEARE used for *Much Ado About Nothing*.

GEORGE GASCOIGNE (c 1535-77)

English playwright and poet. Trained in law, Gascoigne began his career as a member of Parliament. His early literary endeavours were interrupted first by a brief spell in a debtors' prison and, soon after his release, by military service. This found him once again a prisoner, now of the Spanish. In 1574 he returned to England, where for the last three years of his life he wrote poetry and devised Court entertainments.

Gascoigne's theatrical fame rests on two works, *Supposes* (1566) and *Jocasta* (1566). Although both were translations from the Italian, they were important and original, as they appeared in English. The former, taken from Ariosto, was the first English prose comedy, a work that supplied Shakespeare with his subplot for *The Taming of the Shrew. Jocasta*, based on Euripides' *Phoenician Women*, was the earliest English version of a Greek tragedy and, with *Gorboduc* by Norton and Sackville, one of the first tragedies in English.

THOMAS SACKVILLE (1536-1608)

English playwright and politician. Sackville, the first Earl of Dorset, is known to historians as a Lord Treasurer under both Elizabeth I and James I. Long before this political eminence, however, he appeared at Court as a playwright. On New Year's Day 1562, in the presence of the Queen, law students at the Inner Temple performed *Gorboduc*, a work by their fellow students Sackville and Thomas Norton. Written in blank verse, its plot borrowed from Geoffrey of Monmouth, *Gorboduc, or Ferrex and Porrex* is the first known English tragedy.

BATTISTA GUARINI (1538-1612)

Italian poet, statesman and playwright. Before embarking on a diplomatic career, Guarini was a promising poet and teacher in his native Ferrara. He subsequently represented the Este family of Ferrara at the courts of Turin, Venice, Rome and Craców. Even in 1569, at the beginning of these ambassadorial wanderings, he had begun work on the massive pastoral tragicomedy *Il Pastor Fido*, which was only published twenty-one years later. This work, together with its first cousin *Aminta* by Torquato Tasso, reached an enthusiastic international audience in the ensuing century.

Battista Guarini wrote one of the most influential pastoral dramas of all time. *Il Pastor Fido* celebrates the love of Amarilli and Mirtillo, a story beset with bewildering complications

ZAN GANASSA (c 1540-c 1584)

Italian actor. The international reputation of the Commedia dell' Arte was early established by a travelling band of players led by Zan Ganassa. After at least two visits to France (one by special invitation of the king) he took his company to Spain, where, in his own theatre, he enraptured the public, including the young Lope de Vega.

PIERRE DE LARIVEY (c 1540-1619)

French playwright. The brilliant theatre of Molière, which was an unprecedented marvel in the last half of the seventeenth century, had its obscure origins in the nine prose comedies of Larivey, written more than half a century earlier. Larivey was a man of letters in Paris when, according to one story, a performance by the touring Gelosi company in 1577 inspired him to adapt Italian comedy to the French language and culture. His six plays published in 1579 are lively works which are thoroughly French in character. The best of these are *Le Laquais* and *Les Esprits*. Traces of the latter, with its

familiar ingredients of young love, avarice and mistaken identity, reappear later in Molière's *L'Avare* and *L'École des maris*, for example. One departure Larivey made from his Italian models was to reduce the number of female characters in his reworking of the comedies.

Much later, in 1611, Larivey published three more plays, but by then he had taken holy orders and retired to his native city of Troyes, where the writing of almanacs and prophecies replaced the writing of comedy.

JAKOB AYRER (1543-1605)

German playwright. From humble beginnings as an ironmonger's assistant, Ayrer rose to become a state prosecutor as well as one of his country's leading dramatists, in succession to the great Hans Sachs.

Nearly seventy of Ayrer's plays survive: comedies and tragedies of no great literary value, but important for their technical innovations. They reveal his debts to German popular culture (some are written in ballad opera or *singspiel* style) and to the travelling English players who visited Germany in the later sixteenth century. Ayrer's *Comedia von der schönen Sidea* (*c.*1600) may have the same source as Shakespeare's *The Tempest*.

TORQUATO TASSO (1544-95)

Italian poet and playwright. One of the most tragic and romantic figures of the Renaissance, Tasso passed his early manhood in the service of the Este family of Ferrara. In 1575 he completed his great poem "La Gerusalemme Liberata" and immediately set about revising it, a task which so obsessed him that it led to madness. He continued to write sporadically during seven years in an asylum and for eight unsettled years after his release, until his death in Rome.

Tasso was the author of two complete plays, one of which, *Aminta* (1573), a pastoral romance, did much to establish a vogue for the genre. His own sad life has since been the subject of several plays, most notably those of Carlo Goldoni and Goethe.

ROBERT GARNIER (c 1545-90)

French playwright. Garnier began his career as a playwright while a law student in Toulouse. He never forsook the legal profession, serving as a magistrate for most of his working life, but his seven tragedies and one tragicomedy established him in the highest realms of French literature. He "was allowed on all hands", said the scholar Pasquier, "to have eclipsed his predecessors".

His tragedies, including *Porcie* and *Les Juifves* (1583), are classically formal and rhetorical works which rapidly declined in popularity after their initial success. But his works reached England (translated by Thomas Kyd among others), and the form he imposed upon the genre was to influence his great successors Corneille and Racine. *Bradamante*, the first French tragicomedy, with its insistent alexandrine rhythm and its alternating tragedy and humour, is a milestone in French drama.

A fervent royalist who was forced by religious disputes to take sides against his king, Garnier fell into debt and died, it is said, of grief.

RICHARD TARLETON (?-1588)

English actor and clown. According to the most picturesque legend, Tarleton was discovered while tending his father's pigs in Shropshire. A servant of the Earl of Leicester was so delighted by the swineherd's "happy unhappy answers" that he took him to London, where he

Aleotti's Teatro Farnese (*right*) set a style that has continued to the present day. His deep stage, separated from the audience by the now-familiar proscenium arch, permitted the marvellous scenic effects that so fascinated Baroque audiences

Cervantes' *Don Quixote* was an immediate international success. The picture below, from an early English edition, attempts to summarize the action. The original caption reads: "Don Quixote led on by the Folly of an extravagant Love for Dulcinea Del Toboso departs from his house as a Knight Errant in Search of adventures"

became Queen Elizabeth's favourite jester. At Court his power was extraordinary; his political influence occasionally angered the Queen, but more often she was amused, once ordering him to leave her presence because she was laughing so painfully.

By the mid-1570s Tarleton had made the change from the court to the stage. His success was immense. As a member of the Queen's Men he took all principal comic roles, often ad-libbing brilliantly, a practice which Elizabethan clowns constantly indulged in, to the annoyance of both SHAKESPEARE and Christopher MARLOWE. He also wrote an extremely popular comedy, now lost, called *The Seven Deadly Sins*.

Strangely, for an entertainer so generally loved, he never became wealthy. He died while entertaining Emma Ball, a loose woman, at her house in Shoreditch.

GIOVAN BATTISTA ALEOTTI (1546-1636)

Italian architect and stage designer. Aleotti owes his significance as a theatrical architect to just one building. The Teatro Farnese in Parma, built in 1618–19, represented an important development in the art. It was the first theatre to have a permanent proscenium arch separating audience from actors and to make use of painted scenic wings, Aleotti's own invention.

The theatre was seriously damaged in a bombing raid during the Second World War.

MIGUEL DE CERVANTES SAAVEDRA (1547-1616)

Spanish novelist and playwright. The theatrical contributions of Cervantes are dwarfed by his great novel *Don Quixote*. But he was devoted to the theatre and wrote nearly thirty plays.

As a young man in Italy, Cervantes fought in several campaigns, losing the use of his left hand at the battle of Lepanto ("to the greater glory of the right," he remarked). For five years he was held captive in Algiers until finally ransomed, but still his troubles did not end. He endured at least two periods of imprisonment, and humiliating poverty dogged him into middle age.

Eighteen of Cervantes's plays survive. The best of these are the eight short, satirical *entremeses*, or interludes. His one long tragedy *El cerco de Numancia* (*The siege of Numancia*) tells of a gallant Spanish defence against the armies of Rome. It was revived in Madrid in 1937, during the Spanish Civil War, when the city was under siege by the Falangists.

FRANCESCO ANDREINI (1548-1624)

Italian actor. Andreini made a very late debut as an actor. As a twenty-year-old soldier he was captured by the Turks, only escaping from slavery eight years later. Soon after his return to Italy he joined the Gelosi, a Commedia dell' Arte company which he led on a triumphant tour of France. He was a brilliant mimic and skilled writer, whose most famous stage role was the braggart Capitano.

His wife Isabella was the greatest actress of the day, a skilled poetess as well as leading lady of the Gelosi.

Five of their seven children took holy orders. Only the first born, Giovan Battista, won fame as an actor.

PHILIP HENSLOWE (c 1550-1616)

English theatre entrepreneur. Henslowe does not seem to have had a theatrical background; he became neither a player nor a dramatist, but he exercised a great influence on all aspects of Elizabethan theatrical practice.

Soon after marrying the rich widow of his employer, he rented a plot of land on the south bank of the Thames, where once a rose garden had grown. The Rose Theatre grew in its stead and became the first of Henslowe's chain of theatres, which later included the Fortune, Hope and possibly Whitefriars. Aided by his son-in-law, the popular tragedian Edward ALLEYN, he dominated the theatrical scene (excepting the Chamberlain's Men) carefully arranging to have half of England's actors in his debt (and so under his thumb).

Henslowe's business transactions were scrupulously recorded in a diary which is a principal source of information about Elizabethan stage management.

WILLIAM KEMPE (?-1603)

English actor and clown. On the death of Richard TARLETON Kempe became the leading English stage clown. His success was aided immeasurably by the rich new parts that SHAKESPEARE created for him: Dogberry in *Much Ado About Nothing*, Shallow in *Henry IV* and doubtless many others. But his popularity was not merely the result of other men's genius. A brilliant self-publicist, he gained his greatest triumphs by dancing jigs as comic epilogues to plays in which he had just appeared. These jigs, which included words and music, probably suggested to him his most notorious stunt: a long-distance Morris dance from London to Norwich. Nine days of dancing on the road were interspersed with fourteen days of resting his feet. Prosperous and famous, for a while he jigged through Europe, but returned to act and end his days in London. For one so ebullient in life, accounts of his death are obscure. A Southwark church register has a terse entry: "William Kempe, a man."

Will Kempe may not have started a craze for marathon jigging, but he did originate a phrase. *Kemps Nine Daies Wonder* tells of his epic dance from London to Norwich

ROBERT WILSON (c 1550-c 1600)

English actor and playwright. From the sketchy accounts that exist of his life, Wilson was one of the most versatile actor-playwrights of the Elizabethan age. As a member of Leicester's Men and later the Queen's Men he was compared to the great clown Richard TARLETON for his "refined, extemporall witt".

His plays were admired by his contemporaries, but few have survived. *The Three Ladies of London*, about a good-hearted Jew, is probably one of Wilson's works. By one "R.W.", it was published in 1584.

Commedia dell'Arte

On to a ramshackle stage, erected overnight in the corner of a town square or village market place in sixteenth-century Italy, there stepped for the first time two archetypal figures of the comic theatre, Arlecchino (Harlequin) and Pantalone.

They were the creations of the first "professional" theatre, the Commedia dell' Arte. The name itself was given later to itinerant troupes of actors, who by the mid-sixteenth century had combined the arts of the jester and the jongleur with a distinguished tradition of literary farces that claimed ancestry in ancient Greece. Amid the extempore buffoonery of every production, the plot developed strictly according to its written scenario. It was this perfect balance between form and total chaos that distinguished the great troupes and established their reputations abroad as well as in Italy.

As often as not, the stars of the Commedia dell' Arte were the *zanni*, masked comic servants who made fools of themselves and their masters with an infinite vocabulary of practical jokes, horseplay, miming and acrobatics. Each play included two or more *zanni*, several of whom have survived into the twentieth century. Of them all, Harlequin (an Anglicized version of Arlecchino) has survived the best, known by his mask and lozenge-patterned costume. His companions in anarchy included Pulcinella, the hook-nosed and violent ancestor of the English puppet Mr Punch. Pedrolino, a simple peasant boy, was another of the popular *zanni*. Beloved by the French, he metamorphosed into the sentimental and lovelorn Pierrot, whose floppy hat and baggy white suit have become the symbols of wordless devotion. The stock characters of a Commedia dell' Arte company also included at least one pair of lovers, a knavish and braggartly Capitano and the female servant Colombina, later Harlequin's Columbine. (It was in these performances that women had their first opportunities to become actresses, enlisted from the wives accompanying their actor-husbands on the road.) The first recorded entrepreneur of the Commedia dell' Arte was Ruzzante, but the style gained international repute through the work of touring companies such as the Gelosi (see Francesco Andreini, page 37), whose popularity in France greatly influenced Molière and led to the establishment of the Comédie-Italienne. Though its influence faded in the eighteenth century, the Commedia dell' Arte can boast among its surviving descendants Punch and Judy, pantomime and the circus clown.

JOHN LYLY (c 1554-1606)

English playwright. Lyly was by far the most fashionable and imitated playwright of the Elizabethan Court during the 1580s. He arrived in London after studies at Oxford and amazed the aristocratic world with his sophisticated "novel" *Euphues: The Anatomy of Wit* (*c*.1579). Its static plot was enlivened by a complex and elegant style that needed a whole new word to describe it: euphuistic. Lyly continued to write euphuistically in a number of highly successful comedies. Several of these, including *Alexander and Campaspe* (1583–4), *Sapho and Phao* (1583–4) and *Endimion, the Man in the Moon* (1588), were performed by the Children of St Paul's, a company of which Lyly was vice-master in 1590.

Although the grace and wit of his dialogue was an important influence on English drama, the vogue for his plays was brief. Ironically, Lyly's contributions to the stage are today most frequently recalled by SHAKESPEARE's euphuistic parodies in *Love's Labour's Lost*.

HENRY CONDELL (c 1556-1627)

English actor and first editor of SHAKESPEARE's plays. From all accounts Henry Condell deserved his great success in the theatre. A member of the Chamberlain's (later the King's) Men for thirty years, he won the admiration and love of his fellows for his generous nature and devotion to the theatre. In 1619 he was recorded as "of great lyveinge, wealth, and power", and posterity has been as kind to Condell as his own age. As editors of Shakespeare's First Folio collection, Condell and John HEMINGE earned the Victorian tribute inscribed on their memorial in London: "To their disinterested efforts the world owes all that it calls Shakespeare."

JOHN HEMINGE (c 1556-1630)

English actor and first editor of SHAKESPEARE's plays. Heminge was one of the most successful and durable of Elizabethan actors. He joined the Chamberlain's Men probably at their founding in 1594 and acted with them for nearly twenty years. He played in both tragedy and comedy, possibly appearing as the first Falstaff in *Henry IV*. During his long association with the Globe playhouse he became a close friend of Shakespeare, who left him a ring in his will. Heminge's gift to Shakespeare was more substantial. With his colleague Henry CONDELL he edited the First Folio of Shakespeare's plays, a collection that appeared in 1623, giving at a stroke immortality to its author and a world of infinite variety to the stage.

ROBERT GREENE (1558-92)

English playwright. Greene was one of the first authors in England to depend upon writing for a living. A prolific writer of plays and pamphlets, he is remembered today for two dramatic works: *Orlando Furioso* (*c*.1591) and *Friar Bacon and Friar Bungay* (*c*.1591). The former, a bombastic tragedy adapted from ARIOSTO's poem, gave the histrionic Edward ALLEYN a fine chance to shout. The second is a farce which is still remarkably fresh. It is also likely that Greene assisted Thomas KYD with *The Spanish Tragedy* and SHAKESPEARE with *Henry VI* (though in a famous pamphlet he referred to the latter as "an upstart crow").

Greene was fascinated by the seamy side of London life. Throughout his brief adult life he was as celebrated for dissipation as for literature. With his friends Christopher MARLOWE and George PEELE he gave the Elizabethan Age its reckless, godless stamp. He died in

poverty—alone and repentant. "Forget and forgive my wrongs done unto thee," he wrote to his abandoned wife, "and Almighty God have mercie on my soul."

Robert Greene's appetite for pleasure eventually cost him his life. He died penniless, after a surfeit of pickled herrings and Rhenish wine

THOMAS KYD (1558-94)

English playwright. For a dramatist who gave the English public so much of what it wanted—mayhem on the stage—Kyd began his career modestly enough, as a pamphleteer. Early broadsheets, such as *The Truethe of the most wicked and secret Murthering of John Brewen, Goldsmith* must have led directly to such bloodthirsty epics for the stage as *The Spanish Tragedy* (*c*.1588). The latter is a blank verse play of revenge, sometimes short on poetry but extremely generous with blood. Audiences loved it and envious playwrights wrote gory imitations. This one work has established Kyd as a major literary figure.

Most of Kyd's other works are either lost or impossible to identify; one missing play often attributed to him is *Hamlet* (*c*.1588), an inspiration for SHAKESPEARE's later version. He may also have worked on *Titus Andronicus* (*c*.1594), one of Shakespeare's bloodiest plays.

Kyd was a close friend of Christopher MARLOWE; they shared the same lodgings and many of the same habits. Both died wretchedly, though Kyd's end was not, at least, violent. One of the most successful writers of the age, he came to his end in humiliating poverty.

THOMAS LODGE (c 1558-1625)

English author and playwright. The varied life of Thomas Lodge involved him in many adventures and nearly as many literary endeavours. He was a wit, a soldier, a seafarer, an ardent convert to Catholicism, a doctor and a religious exile. He wrote poems, prose romances, religious tracts, medical treatises and plays. Of the latter works, neither *The Wounds of Civill War* (*c*.1594) nor *A Looking Glass for London and England* (*c*.1590), with Robert GREENE, earned him the place in stage history that he won as the author of *Rosalynde* (1590), a popular non-dramatic prose work which inspired SHAKESPEARE's *As You Like It*. *Rosalynde* was written on one of the author's voyages (to the Canary Islands) in 1588: a dangerous year for an Englishman to be at sea.

GEORGE PEELE (c 1558-c 1597)

English playwright. The romantic legend of a brawling and lecherous Elizabethan playwright owes its existence in part to Peele. According to one story he was forced to write for the stage when he spent his bride's dowry shortly after leaving Oxford. In London's theatre world he quickly found acceptance, discovering like-minded companions in Robert GREENE, Thomas KYD and other so-called "university wits".

Peele was a gifted lyric poet and a versatile if undisciplined playwright, whose works include elegant romance in *The Arraignment of Paris* (*c*.1581), history in *Edward I* (*c*.1590) and bombastic tragedy in *The Battle of Alcazar* (*c.* 1588). His best known play is *The Old Wives' Tale* (*c.* 1588–94), a fairy-tale comedy with a complex plot.

Several years after his death there appeared *The Merry Conceited Jests of George Peele*, a book which purported to describe the playwright's dissolute character. Although most of these anecdotes are probably fictitious, there is evidence that Peele's early death was caused by wild living and the resulting venereal disease.

GEORGE CHAPMAN (c 1560-1634)

English poet and playwright. Immortalized by Keats in a famous sonnet ("Much have I travell'd in the realms of gold . . .") Chapman was an outstanding translator of Homer, but he was also a prolific and often brilliant playwright, whose dramatic work has gone largely ignored over three and a half centuries.

In 1596 Chapman's first known play, *The Blind Beggar of Alexandria*, was produced by Philip HENSLOWE at the Rose Theatre. It proved very popular, but later efforts, including *The Old Joiner of Aldgate* and *Eastward Ho!* (1605), fell foul of the law. The latter, a spirited work written with Ben JONSON, contained a slighting reference to James I and resulted in the imprisonment of both authors. Best known of his dramatic works is *Bussy D'Ambois* (1604), in which a strong but flawed hero (a character typical of Chapman's tragedies) comes to inevitable grief. A violent tale of lust and murder, it was probably first performed, like many Jacobean theatrical excesses, by a company of child players.

LOPE DE VEGA CARPIO (1562-1635)

Spanish playwright and poet. Lope de Vega began his literary career at the age of five; impatient to start work but unable to write, he apparently dictated poems to older friends. The author of 1,500 lyric poems and nearly 2,000 plays, Lope wrote a daily average of twenty pages and claimed to have written one hundred of his plays in less than a day each.

He was born in Madrid and educated by the Jesuits. Throughout his life he remained deeply religious but discarded early intentions of becoming a priest. From youth to old age he seems to have been perpetually in love, danger or disgrace, but always in the public eye. He first tasted notoriety when he was found guilty of slandering his mistress's family in verse. Banished from Madrid, he none the less secretly returned to the capital and married into the aristocracy. No sooner had the ceremony taken place than Lope sailed with the Armada of 1588 to England. On his return he experienced a rare period of near-tranquillity, but a second marriage in 1598 again unleashed public hostility. The playwright continued to live with a mistress in Seville while his bride remained in Toledo. In 1614, a year after the death of his second wife, Lope became a priest. Determinedly flouting the vows of chastity, he lived with Marta de Nevares, the woman whom scholars have called his greatest love (perhaps because she was his last). During these final years Lope was stricken with misfortunes. His favourite son was drowned; his beloved daughter Clara was seduced; and Marta went first blind and then insane. Despite these griefs, Lope continued to write, producing his greatest works at an inimitable speed. It is for such energy and resilience that he has been acclaimed "The Phoenix of the Spanish Stage".

Nearly 500 of Lope's plays survive: pastorals, histories, romances, lives of saints, legends, biblical stories and many that defy classification. He wrote in verse of varying metre and generally adhered to a three-act structure, but he was no pedant and freely admitted that his primary concern was to entertain. Perhaps his most original contributions to the theatre were the *comedias de capa y espada*, the cloak and dagger plays which combined love, honour and intrigue in delightful upper-class comedies. Of these *El acero de Madrid* and *El perro del hortelano* are two of the best. Lope never cultivated a taste for pure tragedy, but in at least two of his great plays, *El caballero de Olmedo* and *El castigo sin venganza*, the balance of emotion is decidedly tragic. Of his histories, by far the most popular have been those concerning the Spanish people. *Fuenteovejuna* and *El mejor alcalde el rey* both deal with injustices perpetrated by a corrupt nobility upon the people. In both cases the king ultimately restores order, but Lope's sympathy with the common man has won him a new band of admirers among twentieth-century Marxists.

Lope's plays occasionally betray the superficiality of haste ("What a small streak of lightning for such a loud clap of thunder," said the poet Góngora), but for the vigour and lyrical beauty of his best work as well as for his unnaturally prodigious fecundity, Lope appears today as he did to his contemporary and rival MIGUEL DE CERVANTES – "a monster of nature".

HEINRICH JULIUS DUKE OF BRUNSWICK (1564-1613)

German playwright. A Protestant by birth, Heinrich Julius became a Catholic bishop when he was only fourteen. In 1592, when a company of English actors visited his court at Wolfenbüttel, the Duke found more suitable employment. Stage-struck from the first, he kept a resident company and began to write plays which revealed a typically English delight in clowning and in gore. *Von einem ungeratenen Sohn* (*c.* 1594), a play about Nero, allowed him every excess. Lifeless central characters condemn most of these plays to oblivion, but they were important for introducing prose to German drama.

CHRISTOPHER MARLOWE (1564-93)

English playwright and poet. From his youth to his death Marlowe was at the centre of mystery and intrigue. While a student at Cambridge, he was rumoured to be a Catholic and to have attended a spy school on the Continent. So strong was the talk against him that he was nearly refused his degree. More significantly, he made fine translations of Ovid's "Amores" while still an undergraduate. After leaving university, Marlowe moved to London and in the same year (1587) his first play, *Tamburlaine the Great, Part I*, was produced by the Admiral's Men, with Edward ALLEYN in the title role. The sublime blank verse of the play was a profound influence upon SHAKESPEARE and on a whole later generation of dramatists. *Part II* appeared the following year.

Marlowe's most popular play with his contemporary audiences was probably his next, *The Jew of Malta* (*c.* 1590). The study of an unscrupulous and bloody villain hoist by his own petard, it may have suggested to Shakespeare the character of Shylock. *Edward II* (*c.* 1592) very likely his last play, is a tragic masterpiece, but the work for which Marlowe remains best known is his *Dr Faustus* (*c.* 1590). The legend of the ambitious doctor here found its first great dramatic treatment, confirming the poetic maturity of its author, notably in the anguished passages where Faustus awaits the surrender of his immortal soul to his infernal creditor.

Bad habits Marlowe had acquired at University did not die with public acclamation. He accepted violence on the streets as readily as on the stage and was notorious as an outspoken atheist. Quite probably he also continued to

The title page of a manuscript to one of **Lope de Vega**'s 2000 plays (*left*) betrays the haste with which its author was constrained to write. To critics who complained that his work was careless and inconsistent, Lope replied in an eloquent verse treatise – *The New Art of Making Plays*. In this work he defended his use of popular verse and of gory plots. He was, however, capable of the most exquisite lyrics and renowned for his carefully plotted dramas

One of **George Chapman**'s lesser-known Greek translations was *Battle of the Frogs and the Mice* (*above*). This comic epic tells how the murder of an innocent mouse by a frog sets off a war between the two species. Peace is restored by the intervention of an army of crabs

Christopher Marlowe (*left*) is one of literature's most tragic figures. His plays and poems rivalled those of Shakespeare, yet he died before his thirtieth birthday. One group of modern disciples refuse to believe that two such enormous talents as Marlowe and Shakespeare could have existed simultaneously, and attempt to prove that their hero lived on, assumed another identity and wrote Shakespeare's plays. All indications are, however, that Marlowe died in a tavern brawl, possibly as a result of an argument over the bill

engage in work for the secret service; it may well have been such dark business that led to the final ugly incident at an inn in Deptford. There, one of his companions "stabd this Marlowe into the eye in such sort that, his braynes comming out at the dagger point he shortly after dyed".

A jury decided that Marlowe had struck first. Whatever the truth, he was dead at twenty-nine, and Shakespeare was left without his only serious rival.

WILLIAM SHAKESPEARE (1564-1616)

English playwright. There is frustratingly little personal information available about the greatest English writer. Shakespeare was born in Stratford-upon-Avon, traditionally on 23 April (St George's Day). He attended the local grammar school, free to the sons of city officials, where in the manner of the time he would have studied the Latin dramatists PLAUTUS, TERENCE and SENECA. At eighteen he married Anne Hathaway, eight years his senior and three months pregnant. A daughter, Susanna, was the first-born, followed by the twins Hamnet and Judith.

He soon became restless and by 1592 had moved to London. Before long he was a member of the Chamber-lain's Men (later the King's Men) and remained with them until his retirement from the theatre more than twenty years later. As actor and playwright, Shakespeare rapidly became a successful and important citizen. From his earliest works he revealed uncommon versatility, experimenting with classical farce in *A Comedy of Errors* (1594), courtly satire in *Love's Labour's Lost* (c.1595) and pastoral comedy in *A Midsummer Night's Dream* (c.1595). The first of the history plays also date from this period. The three parts of *Henry VI* (c.1592) and *Richard III* (1593–4) served as apprentice pieces for their greater successors: the two parts of *Henry IV* (1597–1600), and *Henry V* (c.1599). In tragedy, Shakespeare was slower to mature. Between the bloody and conventional *Titus Andronicus* (c.1594) and the sequence of great tragedies beginning with *Hamlet* (c.1601), the only representative of the genre is *Romeo and Juliet* (c.1596).

Such talent provoked an understandably mixed reaction from contemporaries. To the playwright Henry Chettle, Shakespeare was "excellent in the quality he professes", but ROBERT GREENE called him "Shake-scene" and "an upstart crow", angry perhaps that he himself had not received credit for work on *Henry VI*.

"Fresh to all ages": The plays of Shakespeare

To be, or not to be. The most famous line in drama is spoken by drama's most famous character. But Shakespeare's legacy of tragedy extends far beyond *Hamlet. Othello, King Lear* and *Macbeth* form, with *Hamlet*, the most profound body of tragic drama ever written – and all seem to stem from one five-year period (1601-06). In the tragedies is some of the most sublime poetry in the language, expressing penetrating insights into the human predicament. Small wonder that for actor and director alike, these present an enormous challenge. In them is the finest work of the stage's greatest genius.

Such exalted conceptions could not always boast noble ancestors. Shakespeare often drew inspiration from popular sources, including the bloody "revenge tragedies", of which Thomas KYD's *The Spanish Tragedy* is the best known example. Yet he could invest these simple, sometimes crude, plots with an exquisite profanity.

Hamlet is itself a simple story. The young hero returns from university on the death of his father, the King, to find his mother remarried to his uncle Claudius, who now occupies the throne. The ghost of his father appears to tell Hamlet that he was murdered by the new king. Plagued by his inability to exact revenge, Hamlet moves from impotent rage to a tranquil acceptance of life and death in a series of soliloquies that are unsurpassed both as poetry and as portraits of the human soul.

In *King Lear* it is an old man who wilfully destroys his world, and learns too late that he has wrought only death and suffering. *Othello* is the tragedy of a husband driven insane by jealousy to murder his innocent wife; the sadness and remorse of the last two pages of the play are among the most profound and moving in the whole of literature. *Macbeth* chronicles the destruction of a man and his wife by their overweening ambition.

Other tragedies are stories of power (*Julius Caesar* or *Coriolanus* for example) or sometimes of love, like *Romeo and Juliet* or *Antony and Cleopatra*. The infinite beauty and richness of variety that Shakespeare gave to the many faces of tragedy has had an immeasurable effect upon world drama.

Had Shakespeare never written a word other than his comedies, his place in literature would have been assured. As an actor and impresario as well as a dramatist, he understood just how an audience should be entertained. Indeed Samuel JOHNSON, writing in the eighteenth century, thought Shakespeare essentially a comic writer by nature. There are humorous scenes throughout the tragedies; and Falstaff appears at his fun-bellied best in the two parts of *Henry IV*.

There was a flourishing comic tradition in England long before Shakespeare's time. The great medieval mystery cycles were full of boisterous low humour. Travelling players, called interluders, performed knock-about farces in the great houses of Tudor England. The comedies of TERENCE and PLAUTUS were models for later plays in the same spirit.

Shakespeare's genius was to adapt the classical tradition to the England of his audience. One early comedy, *A Comedy of Errors* (1594), uses typical Plautine devices of mistaken identity, intrigue and confusion, combined with the earthy characters who,

It is true that Shakespeare was never very subtle in concealing his sources. Holinshed's *Chronicles* taught him all he needed to know for several of his histories. Christopher MARLOWE may have supplied the ideas for both *Richard II* (*c*.1595) and *The Merchant of Venice* (*c*.1598), and *Hamlet* was an inspired rewriting of another *Hamlet* (perhaps the work of Thomas KYD). Yet as his fame grew, Shakespeare became more sinned against than sinning, his profitable name being put to plays and poems that were evidently not his work.

In 1593, after Marlowe's death, Shakespeare became undisputed master of the stage. His plays were often chosen for performance before Elizabeth I and were later favourites of James I. In 1599 the Chamberlain's Men moved to the south bank of the Thames at Southwark, where among the stews and taverns of the riverside they built the Globe – scene of many of Shakespeare's greatest triumphs.

Throughout twenty years of playwriting, Shakespeare continued to develop. Use of prose in serious as well as comic scenes gave his later works a much wider dramatic range. With these increased skills he wrote, between 1598 and 1600, three of the greatest English comedies: *As You Like It, Much Ado About Nothing* and *Twelfth Night. Hamlet* also dates from this period, while *Othello* (1604), *King Lear* (1606) and *Macbeth* (*c*.1606) consolidated Shakespeare's position as a peerless master of tragedy. It has been argued that the latter three works reflect a period of profound depression; whatever their origin, their inspiration is unquestioned.

Shakespeare never stopped experimenting. His late plays include the magnificent juxtaposition of love and war in *Antony and Cleopatra* (written *c*.1607) and the bitterest of comedy in *The Winter's Tale* (*c*.1611), but the temptations of retirement were becoming increasingly attractive. A part share in the Globe's profits had left him, by middle age, relatively wealthy. Although for years he had not been close to his wife, he had been a generous provider for his Stratford family. In 1611 he retired, dividing his time between houses in London and Stratford. *The Tempest* (1611) is probably the last work which he wrote unassisted. If from that play Prospero can be seen as Shakespeare, the dramatist presents himself as a figure gratefully freed from the contentions of London and the responsibilities of power. He was buried in Holy Trinity Church, Stratford.

except for their Greek names, could be Elizabethan Londoners. Another element – the pastoral – is introduced in *A Midsummer Night's Dream* (*c*.1595) and reappears as late as *The Winter's Tale* (*c*.1611).

It was in the closing years of the sixteenth century that Shakespeare's skills as a comic dramatist fully matured. Though as ready as ever to utilize already extant plots, he became less reliant on stock situations. The eventful progression towards a state of true love became his staple comic fare. The standard happy ending is a reconciliatory marriage (or marriages) that resolves all the preceding mayhem and disorder. Shakespeare's growing mastery of characterization adds new depth to the farcical ruses of mistaken identity and disguise. This is especially true of his subtle studies of sexual identity in *As You Like It* and *Twelfth Night*. Not that the comedy loses all its broadness: there is plenty of the "robust" in such characters as Touchstone (*As You Like It*), Sir Toby Belch (*Much Ado About Nothing*), as well as in the immortal Falstaff.

HISTORIES

"A kingdom for a stage, princes to act, And monarchs to behold the swelling scene!" (*Henry V, Prol.*).

On the bare Elizabethan stage, with little more than a few props, Shakespeare set out to recreate the pageant of English history. In eight plays (*Richard II*, the two parts of *Henry IV*, *Henry V*, the three *Henry VI* plays and *Richard III*) he chronicled one of the most tumultuous periods in the growth of the kingdom. The great prosperity of Elizabethan England had grown out of the political stability brought by Henry VII's victory at Bosworth Field. Shakespeare's purpose in dramatizing the century of turmoil up to the end of The Wars of the Roses was not so much to explore the past, as to use these events to make profound statements about authority, political order and the art of kingship. These were essentially comments on his own time. The defeat of the Armada in 1588, for example, was very recent history and in exploring these national myths, Shakespeare spoke directly to the immediate concerns of his audience – whether at court or in the public playhouse.

So great was the power of these history plays that in 1601 a follower of the treacherous Earl of Essex arranged a performance of *Richard II* on the eve of an uprising, the better to prepare the audience for rebellion and for the death of the monarch. The rebellion was a failure – the play remains a success.

But the history plays are much more than patriotic propaganda. Shakespeare's complex and sophisticated exploration of political philosophy came at a crucial time for the English throne. Queen Elizabeth was nearing death; there was no direct heir, and the political chaos of the century before loomed dark and real.

The plays are peopled with sharply drawn characters, who reveal how often the great events of history are the result of human weakness, and how greatly they affect the lives of common people. *Richard II* and *Richard III* in particular are to be seen as heroic tragedies, as well as histories.

As a record of English history, Shakespeare's plays are far from reliable. It is as a chronicler of the spirit of England, its thought and its feeling, that Shakespeare the historian remains unsurpassed.

44

Romeo and Juliet poise at the balcony in what must be the most familiar love scene in drama; **Henry Irving** and **Ellen Terry** (*left*) conducted their own Victorian love affair far more discreetly. Burnt cork, a turban and **Tommaso Salvini** (*below*) created a commanding *Othello* in the nineteenth century. Titania (**Maggie Smith**, *right*) dotes on the asinine Bottom in *A Midsummer Night's Dream*, until Oberon calls off the game

Macbeth (played by **John Clements**, *above left*) is the most ruthless of Shakespeare's great tragic heroes, but his death is still charged with grandeur and pathos. *King Lear* (*left*, **Werner Krauss**) tests his voice against the elements in a role that leaves actors nearly as exhausted as the passionate king. Such is the prestige of *Hamlet* that many actresses have attempted the title role. **Sarah Bernhardt** (*below*) was one eminent trans-sexual prince; more recently Frances de la Tour enjoyed great success with the part in London

Toby Belch (**Laurence Olivier**, *below*) creates comic havoc in *Twelfth Night*

Richard III (below) has been a favourite role with exhibitionist actors like the unruly **Edmund Kean,** who indulged himself shamelessly in the part. Despite his taste for murder, the hunch-back king excites as much sympathy as loathing. Richard II (foot of page) wins sympathy for his dignified acceptance of his own feebleness. He is played here by **John Gielgud,** with Jill Esmond as his queen

Julius Caesar (above, with **Charles Dullin**) suffers from having too many "heroes": Brutus, forced by conscience to kill his friend; the vengeful Mark Antony and the ill-fated Caesar himself. But in the hands of a great director, the play can make a powerful statement about political ambiguity. Falstaff (below, played by **Friedrich Schröder**) is the most endearing coward in dramatic literature

Rosalind (left) in As You Like It disguises herself as a man to escape her wicked uncle. This "breeches part" was a triumph for **Ada Rehan. Ralph Richardson** (below) as Prospero in The Tempest chides his "dainty Ariel"

EDWARD ALLEYN (1566-1626)

English actor. As the son of an innkeeper, Alleyn was exposed to plays and players from boyhood. Later, when he was a leading actor with the Admiral's Men, he married the step-daughter of the producer Philip HENSLOWE, thus promoting his already successful career.

He was greatest in tragic roles, particularly as the declamatory heroes of Christopher MARLOWE's *Tamburlaine the Great* and *Dr Faustus*. It was during a performance of the latter that a real devil is supposed to have appeared on stage, frightening Alleyn into retirement.

For much of his professional life he was a rival of RICHARD BURBAGE, an actor who had the great fortune of having SHAKESPEARE as his dramatist. Of their qualities, one contemporary source quotes: "Richard Bourbidge and Edward Alleyn, two such actors as no age must ever look to see the like."

RICHARD BURBAGE (1567-1619)

English actor-manager. Burbage first appears in contemporary records not as an actor but fighting outside a theatre in Shoreditch. Later, as the leading actor in England, he created the roles of many of SHAKESPEARE's great tragic heroes, notably Hamlet, Othello and King Lear.

The son of JAMES BURBAGE, he had an ideal upbringing in the new world of the professional theatre. At first, as a member of the Admiral's Men, he was eclipsed by the great Edward ALLEYN, but soon his own quieter and subtler talents gained recognition in the tremendous roles he was privileged to play at their first performances.

In 1599, Burbage and his brother were forced by financial pressures to move south of the river. Accordingly, they dismantled their father's theatre and from its timbers built the Globe in Southwark. They were careful to take Shakespeare with them, and the long association that followed has resulted in England's literary glory and the immortality of Burbage himself.

GUILLÉN DE CASTRO Y BELLVÍS (1569-1631)

Spanish playwright. A friend and successful imitator of LOPE DE VEGA, Bellvís wrote a number of cloak and dagger plays, remarkable for the variety of their sources and monotony of their themes. His theatrical distinction is not based upon these dated studies of the Spanish code of honour but upon *Las mocedades del Cid*, the first play to exploit the story of Spain's legendary hero. This served as an inspiration for PIERRE CORNEILLE's masterpiece, *Le Cid*.

SILVIO FIORILLO (c1570-c1632)

Italian actor. Fiorillo is credited with the creation of two great stock characters of the Commedia dell' Arte. Famous throughout Italy as Capitano Matamoros, the moustache-twirling Spanish braggart, he may also have been the original Pulcinella, the dim-witted servant later to be transformed into Mr Punch. The story goes that Fiorillo put on a monstrous, hooked nose to ridicule an unsympathetic neighbour in Naples, where his company was based.

Two sons toured with him and continued the family tradition, while a relationship with his leading lady may have produced a third, Tiberio FIORILLI, the great Scaramouche, a colleague of MOLIÈRE.

THOMAS DEKKER (c1572-1632)

English playwright. Dekker was an outstanding chronicler of everyday life in London–its streets teeming with tradesmen, pedlars, whores and cutpurses. His reputation rests chiefly on *The Shoemaker's Holiday* (1599), one of the few plays he wrote entirely on his own. This light-hearted comedy is dominated by the genial character of Simon Eyre, who solves everyone's problems and becomes Lord Mayor of London. *The Honest Whore* (1605) and *The Roaring Girl* (c.1611), both written with Thomas MIDDLETON, also contain fine scenes of low life in the city.

Dekker wrote principally for Philip HENSLOWE, collaborating with almost all his famous contemporaries. In *The Poetaster*, Ben JONSON called him "a dresser of plays about the town", but Dekker soon turned the tables on his rival, using the characters of *The Poetaster* in his own play *Satiromastix* (1601). He also published several satirical pamphlets, notably *The Gull's Hornbook* (1609), a tongue-in-cheek guide for would-be gallants, which contains a hilarious account of loutish behaviour of theatre audiences of his day.

It was inevitable that the quarrelsome **Ben Jonson** should one day fall out with Inigo Jones, the designer of the delightful masques he wrote for the Court of King James I

ALEXANDRE HARDY (c 1572-c 1632)

French playwright. One of the most prolific of all dramatists, Hardy is remembered today more for his influence on the French theatre than for any of his nearly 700 plays. He began his theatrical career writing for a touring company of professional actors, turning out plays at a moment's notice for undemanding provincial audiences. Although his works never made him wealthy – many were never even produced – they eventually established him in Paris as France's leading playwright, writing for the great tragedian BELLEROSE.

His plays were mainly tragicomedies, disorganized and often meretricious works that reveal the haste of their creation. More important are the tragedies, including *Marianne* and *La Mort de Daire*, twelve of which survive. Although Hardy's reputation suffered greatly after his death, the abundance and energy of his writings awoke a generation of young playwrights led by PIERRE CORNEILLE and inspired the flowering of French tragedy.

BEN JONSON (1572-1637)

English playwright. Jonson once claimed that he had made less than two hundred pounds out of his plays, yet he was the most successful and respected of all Elizabethan and Jacobean dramatists, his reputation higher even than SHAKESPEARE's. His satirical comedies ridicule the hypocrisy and pretensions of every level of society, from the Court of Queen Elizabeth in *Cynthia's Revels* (1600) to the strumpets and footpads of *Bartholomew Fair* (1614). Jonson was equally renowned for his lyrical court masques, many of them produced in collaboration with the architect and designer INIGO JONES. When in 1616 the king conferred a pension on him, Jonson became (in fact, if not in title) the first Poet Laureate.

His later respectability was in sharp contrast to his rebellious youth. An apprentice bricklayer and then a volunteer soldier in the Netherlands, he only took up writing and acting at the age of twenty-five. Almost immediately he was imprisoned for his co-authorship of *The Isle of Dogs* (1597), a play so subversive it caused all the theatres in London to be closed. A year later he was on trial again for killing a fellow actor in a duel, escaping with his life only by pleading benefit of clergy (his father had been a priest).

Jonson's quarrelsome nature found a more creative outlet in the "War of the Theatres", a battle of words between himself and his rivals John MARSTON and Thomas DEKKER. *The Poetaster* (1601) shows Jonson, in the character of the poet Horace, taking revenge on two rivals who have attempted to defame him.

Jonson's tragedies enjoyed some success, notably *Sejanus* (1603) with Shakespeare and RICHARD BURBAGE in the cast, but he had already found that his genius was for satire as in *Every Man in his Humour* (1598) and *Every Man out of his Humour* (1599). The characters are grotesques, dominated by one ruling passion or "humour", which Jonson mocks mercilessly. One rarely feels any sympathy for his creations; he could not, for instance, have produced a Falstaff. His most memorable character is the protagonist of *Volpone or The Fox* (1606). A cunning, misanthropic miser, Volpone is ostensibly the villain of the piece, but as his misanthropy is fully justified by the petty avarice of those around him, he assumes near tragic grandeur. *The Alchemist* (1610) rivals *Volpone* as his greatest work. Despite its arcane subject matter, *The Alchemist* retains its appeal because of its beautifully constructed plot and its colourful array of swindlers and dupes. Abel Drugger, the simple tobacconist, has been a favourite role with actors from David GARRICK to Alec GUINNESS. Because Jonson's aim was always to castigate folly, some of his comedies seem heavy and pedantic today. His gifts were never so abundant as those of Shakespeare, but he was the first to recognize his friend's superior genius. As ready to applaud greatness as to condemn pettiness, Jonson was a dangerous enemy, a loyal and valuable friend.

INIGO JONES (1573-1652)

English architect and stage designer. While studying in Italy, Jones became acquainted with the flourishing new art of stage design. On his return to England he revolutionized the production of court masques with painted flats for use in perspective scenery, with three-sided painted screens which revolved to effect scene changes in an instant and with the introduction to Britain of the proscenium arch, which today still frames the stage in many theatres. From his first production (Ben JONSON's

In the reign of Charles I the costumes (*left*) and ingenious designs of **Inigo Jones** completely overshadowed the literary content of the masque. Spectacular scenery and dancing rivalled the splendour of Italian court entertainments

In Ben Jonson's *Bartholomew Fair* **Richard Burbage** (*right*) is referred to as the best actor of the age. As the first interpreter of Hamlet, he always heeded the Prince's instruction to the players, "to hold a mirror up to nature"

Masque of Blackness in 1605) Jones dominated royal entertainments, but such success and influence eventually bred a rebellious resentment among his rivals. England's chief architect and stage designer died in disgrace and poverty in 1652.

THOMAS HEYWOOD (c 1574-1641)

English playwright. After studies at Cambridge University (where he failed to take a degree) Heywood worked in London as an actor and playwright. He seems to have applied himself with what John WEBSTER called "right happy and copious industry", for he eventually claimed to have had a hand "or at least a main finger" in over 200 plays. Of these only about twenty-four survive, by far the most famous being *A Woman Killed with Kindness* (1603). This intense drama of adultery in a contemporary marriage was one of the major steps from the Olympian concerns of Elizabethan tragedy to the more pedestrian themes of Jacobean drama. *The English Traveller* (c. 1627) and the two parts of *The Fair Maid of the West*, a tragedy and an adventurous romance respectively, also rise above the mundane. Like Ben JONSON, Heywood wrote for official occasions, collaborating with INIGO JONES on *Love's Mistress* (c. 1636), a masque for the birthday of Charles I.

PIER MARIA CECCHINI (1575-1645)

Italian actor and Commedia dell' Arte author. Cecchini became professionally involved with the Commedia dell' Arte in about 1591 and achieved fame throughout Europe as Fritellino, one of the comic servants or *zanni*. He toured Italy with the Accesi company and later led his own troupe on visits to France. His wife Orsola, generally known by her stage name, Flaminia, was a celebrated actress and beauty.

CYRIL TOURNEUR (c 1575-1626)

English playwright. Tourneur is most celebrated for a work that he possibly never wrote. *The Revenger's Tragedy* (c. 1606), one of the bitterest and bloodiest tales of the Jacobean age, was described by T. S. ELIOT as "an intense and unique and horrible vision of life". Although scholars have recently attributed it to Thomas MIDDLETON, Tourneur's association with the work is traditional and tenacious. His authorship of *The Atheist's Tragedy* (c. 1611), on the other hand, is unquestioned. Unfortunately, nothing in this second play matches the frenzied passion of his (or Middleton's) masterpiece.

As little is known about Tourneur's life as about his writings. After retiring as a dramatist he worked for the Cecil family, and was rumoured to have been involved in secret political work on the Continent. He died of disease while on a naval expedition against Spain.

JOHN MARSTON (1576-1634)

English playwright. Marston trained as a lawyer but turned to the stage in 1600 with his satire *Jack Drum's Entertainment*. This was the first of a number of plays, including *What You Will* (1601), in which he attacked his rival Ben JONSON. Jonson replied with a salvo of his own, ridiculing Marston most effectively in *The Poetaster*. This "War of the Theatres" (which at one point actually came to blows) was amicably resolved when Marston dedicated *The Malcontent* (1604) to his former enemy. Generally considered his best play, this curious mixture of sombre and comic themes has proved more durable than Marston's tragic or extravagantly satiric works. Its tried and tested theme of a people's loyalty to their leader in his absence

was being explored at the same time by SHAKESPEARE in *Measure for Measure*.

Collaboration with Jonson and George CHAPMAN on *Eastward Ho!* (1605) led to jail sentences on a charge of libelling the Scots for all three authors. After a second period of imprisonment in 1608 Marston retired from the stage. Taking holy orders, he became a country parson and rejected his youthful dramatic works.

JAKOB BIDERMANN (1578-1639)

German playwright. Bidermann was a Jesuit professor of rhetoric with a special responsibility for supervising church drama. Although he wrote his plays in Latin and concerned himself solely with religious subjects, he was not above courting the public by alternating farcical with spiritual episodes. Through his innovative use of rapid and dramatic scene changes, he far surpassed his calling of moral instructor. His devils are frequently more entertaining than their angelic antagonists.

Of Bidermann's ten plays, *Cenodoxus* (1602) has been successfully revived in the twentieth century. The protagonist, a learned lawyer whose moral degeneracy is visible to God but not to man, is reminiscent of both Faust and Everyman. In a startling climax, Cenodoxus confounds his grieving friends at his own funeral, rising from his coffin and shouting three times: "I have been justly condemned by God for eternity."

JOHN FLETCHER (1579-1625)

English playwright. Fletcher and his partner Francis BEAUMONT revolutionized theatrical taste with their spectacularly successful series of tragicomedies. Two of the most popular, *Philaster* (1610–11) and *A King and No King* (1611), are romantic dramas set in faraway lands. Despite their concern with honour and kingship they are primarily love stories with contrived happy endings. Public demand for similar escapist romances encouraged unscrupulous publishers to ascribe over fifty plays to Beaumont and Fletcher; in fact they collaborated on only seven or eight.

Fletcher was the son of a Sussex vicar who later became Bishop of London. His first important work, *The Faithful Shepherdess* (1608–9), is full of magnificent pastoral poetry but is hardly dramatic. He needed the more practical Beaumont to restrain his flights of poetic fancy and organize the plot. The most successful combination of their talents is *The Maid's Tragedy* (c. 1611), a bloody tale of love and death at the court of Rhodes.

After Beaumont's retirement in 1613, Fletcher succeeded SHAKESPEARE as chief dramatist to the King's Men and wrote for them until his sudden death from the plague in 1625. He worked briefly with Shakespeare, contributing some scenes to *Henry VIII* (1613), and wrote the major part of *The Two Noble Kinsmen* (c. 1616). Later plays ascribed to Beaumont and Fletcher are usually the work of Fletcher alone or of Fletcher and Philip MASSINGER. These continued to enjoy immense popularity, but suffer in comparison to the works written with Beaumont.

JUAN RUIZ DE ALARCÓN Y MENDOZA (1580-1639)

Spanish playwright. Born in Mexico but a resident of Spain, Ruiz de Alarcón was the continual object of heartless satire on account of his small stature and hunch back. In his play *Las paredes oyen* (1617), he had his imaginary revenge on those that mocked him, including LOPE DE VEGA. In the play, a cripple, like Ruiz the victim of slanderous attacks, wins the girl from his rivals by virtue of superior spiritual qualities. Unlike many of his contemporaries Ruiz led a retiring life, working as a civil servant, and writing primarily for his own satisfaction.

Ruiz left about twenty plays, remarkable for combining entertainment with ethical teaching. His characters (not always realistically drawn) illustrate various vices. Lying was the subject of *La verdad sospechosa*, his best known play, which was later the model for PIERRE CORNEILLE's *Le Menteur* and Carlo GOLDONI's *Il bugiardo*. The influence of Ruiz on these two writers and on MOLIÈRE was immense. His plays mark the beginning of the school of higher, moral comedy that dominated European theatre in the seventeenth century.

THOMAS MIDDLETON (1580-1627)

English playwright. Middleton's plays rival those of SHAKESPEARE for their variety in characters and style. He began his career working for Philip HENSLOWE, and his early comedies, which include collaborations with Thomas DEKKER and John WEBSTER, are highly entertaining pieces: *A Mad World, My Masters* (1604–8) is a brilliant example. The tone of his later plays, however, becomes increasingly sombre. In *A Chaste Maid in Cheapside* (*c*. 1613) laughter has begun to turn sour. Although comedy persists in his revenge tragedies, *Women Beware Women* (1621) and *The Changeling*, written in 1622 with William ROWLEY, the world they portray is a charnel-house of unparalleled horrors. His heroes and heroines are not great figures, but rather victims of cruel jests that "Hell falls a-laughing at".

Throughout a long creative life, Middleton remained a detached observer; comedies and tragedies alike are full of irony. His last great play, *A Game at Chess* (1624), was a fresh departure: a political allegory in which chess pieces represent real figures at the English and Spanish courts. When the Spanish ambassador protested, the play was taken off and author and actors appeared before the Privy Council for upsetting the diplomatic apple-cart.

Renewed interest in Middleton confirms T. S. ELIOT's assessment: "A great observer of human nature, without fear, without sentiment, without prejudice."

JOHN WEBSTER (c 1580-c 1637)

English playwright. Mocked by his contemporaries as a painfully slow writer, Webster nevertheless produced two tragedies that have become classics of the English stage. Nowhere outside the works of SHAKESPEARE is the subject of death presented with such chilling power as in *The White Devil* (*c*. 1610) and *The Duchess of Malfi* (1613–14). Revenge tragedies based on Italian *novelle*, both plays were popular for their spectacular poisonings and stranglings. But plot and the excesses of pseudo-Machiavellian villains were not what mattered to Webster. His greatest scenes are those in which heroes and villains alike confront death and their pasts. Violent passions combine with moments of pathos to produce some of the most memorable dramatic poetry of the Jacobean age.

Webster first appears as a writer in 1602, but of his early work only a few comedies written with Thomas DEKKER survive. Of his two great tragedies, *The Devil's Law Case* (1610–23), a tragicomedy, contains only a glimpse of the earlier Webster, while *The Guise*, a tragedy which the author held in high regard, is lost.

PHILIP MASSINGER (1583-1640)

English playwright. Massinger, the son of a gentleman in the service of the Duke of Pembroke, frequently used the stage to express his political sympathies. In *The Bondman* (1623) he denounced Buckingham, James I's favourite,

while the play for which he wished to be remembered was *The Roman Actor* (*c*. 1626), a plea for artistic freedom set in the reign of the tyrannical emperor Domitian.

When John FLETCHER, with whom he had often collaborated, died in 1625, Massinger took over as writer to the King's Men. Never as popular as Fletcher, Massinger wrote many plays that were later ascribed by publishers to Francis BEAUMONT and Fletcher or simply lost. Legend has it they were used to line a pie-dish (the dimensions of which have never been calculated). *A New Way to Pay Old Debts* (*c*. 1625), Massinger's finest comedy, was forgotten until the late eighteenth century but has since enjoyed unbroken popularity; Edmund KEAN, an early champion of the play, often appeared as Sir Giles Overreach.

philip massinger

Massinger's masterpiece, *A New Way to Pay Old Debts*, satirizes a real-life extortioner of the time, Sir Giles Mompesson. Sir Giles Overreach, as he is called, is finally committed to the madhouse

FRANCIS BEAUMONT (1584-1616)

English playwright. While his collaborator, John FLETCHER, was the greater poet, Beaumont was the more skilled dramatic craftsman. As a judge of what would be effective on the stage he had no equal. Even Ben JONSON took his new plays to Beaumont for approval and correction.

Beaumont's family were Leicestershire landowners. He went to Oxford and then studied law at the Inner Temple in London, where he displayed a talent for satire. The only plays by Beaumont alone are both satirical: *The Woman-Hater* (1606), a Jonsonian comedy, and *The Knight of the Burning Pestle* (1607), a parody of chivalrous romances. (The "Burning Pestle" is a device on the shield of an errant grocer.)

His association with Fletcher, which lasted from 1608 to 1613, produced plays of an entirely different nature. The inspiration for *The Maid's Tragedy* (*c*. 1611) and the great romantic dramas came certainly from Fletcher. The balancing of the action with crowd scenes and comic relief was the work of Beaumont. Without Beaumont's professionalism, Fletcher never again reached the same heights. Beaumont married in 1613 and moved to Kent, where he enjoyed the existence of a country gentleman for the last three years of his life.

TIRSO DE MOLINA (c 1584-1648)

Spanish playwright. Tirso de Molina was the *nom de plume* of Fray Gabriel Téllez, a monk in the order of Our Lady of Mercies and writer of some four hundred plays. Forbidden in 1625 to write any more secular works (on pain of excommunication), he became chronicler of his order and, shortly before his death, Prior of the Monastery of Soria.

Of Tirso's plays, eighty-six survive. Many are religious, based on the Bible and the lives of saints. *El condenado por desconfiado*, the story of a saintly hermit damned for doubting his own salvation, touched on the hotly-debated issue of predestination. A controversial secular piece was *El burlador de Sevilla y convidado de piedra*, the first

CONTINUED ON PAGE 52

The Renaissance stage

Drama spent the first hundred years of the Renaissance in search of a home. During the Middle Ages playgoing had been a spiritual recreation, the very earliest dramas having a church or cathedral as their theatre. Later offerings, such as the cycles of mystery plays, moved outdoors into streets and market places, where religious authorities relied upon faith to draw spectators (and presumably to keep them warm and dry). But with the awakening of interest in secular drama in the early sixteenth century both audiences and actors began to demand more comfortable and secure conditions. Each country found its own solution.

In Italy noble patronage and the study of the Classics evolved gorgeously decorated amphitheatres, with sophisticated scenery and spectacular lighting and machines. The plays performed there were a world apart from the popular (and portable) productions of the Commedia dell' Arte. France was less bound to classic models.

Meanwhile, in Spain and England new-found prosperity and intense theatrical activity had made permanent public theatres an exciting commercial venture. The typical Spanish theatre, the *corral*, was essentially a stage set at the closed end of a three-sided courtyard, the open end forming the entrance. Wealthy patrons sat in the balconies at the sides, while the humbler section of the audience stood in the courtyard below. In effect these *corrales* were very similar to the theatres of Elizabethan London, where the groundlings paid one penny to stand, and the better-off public filled the galleries.

Such diversity in theatrical architecture was short-lived. By the end of the seventeenth century, theatres all over Europe had begun to acquire the familiar characteristics that still exist today.

"According to the ancient custom": The Italian Theatre

The awakening of interest in Greek and Roman plays was naturally accompanied by a desire to re-create ancient theatres. Early dramatic productions were presented on temporary stages erected in the palaces of noble patrons, but with the rediscovery of writings by the Roman architect Vitruvius, Italians determined to establish appropriate theatres for classic drama. One of the most interesting experiments was Andrea Palladio's Teatro Olimpico in Vicenza. Its opening in 1585 was a magnificent social event. An audience of more than 3000 crowded into the semi-elliptical amphitheatre to see a production of SOPHOCLES' *Oedipus Rex*. A dominant feature of this theatre was the permanent Roman *scenae frons*, a back wall and two narrow side walls, richly decorated with statues and reliefs. For the opening production, Vincenzo Scamozzi constructed perspectives of

streets leading to the central archway and the four smaller entrances. At least one was visible from any seat in the audience.

The Teatro Olimpico was the grandest theatre in Europe (a "masterly and admirable work of art", said one spectator), but its neo-classical design did not adapt to changing fashions. In 1580 Bernardo Buontalenti became designer to the theatre in Florence, where his spectacular effects (rolling clouds and gods descending from the heavens) gave audiences a first taste of the Baroque. The need to conceal such backstage activity resulted in the enlargement of the central arch of the *scenae frons* until it contained all the action, scenery and illusion of a production. The proscenium arch, as it is still known, gradually became an effective barrier between audience and actors. In modern times it is often regarded as an impediment to innovative staging, but this child of the Italian Renaissance has remained a tenacious companion of the theatre to the present day.

"This wooden O": the Elizabethan Theatre

The first English theatre was designed not by a classical architect but by an actor. In 1576 JAMES BURBAGE enclosed a traditional travelling stage in a circular building reminiscent of a bull-baiting pit, lined the walls with galleries and called it The Theatre. This simple but novel idea became the inspiration for a number of similar structures: the Curtain, the Rose, the Swan and the famous Globe (built from the timbers of the dismantled Theatre). Round, square or polygonal, all conformed to the same principle: they were enclosed by a high wall and were open to the sky. Performances took place in mid-afternoon, as artificial lighting was impractical and dangerous. Even the few private theatres, roofed buildings converted for dramatic productions, generally relied upon daylight. A contemporary wit advised actors to spend less money on whoring and rather replace the inflammable thatched roofs of their theatres with safer tiles. After the destruction of the first Globe in a fire in 1613, a second Globe was built, and the latter part at least of this advice was taken.

The **Teatro Olimpico** at Vicenza (*left*) was an architectural masterpiece, but it was far too formal for lively productions of contemporary plays. It remained for more versatile stages such as those that sprang up in Elizabethan London to house the great drama of the age. A cutaway model of **a theatre like the Globe** (*below*) reveals its practicality. Productions (*above*) were boisterous events, both on stage and in the auditorium

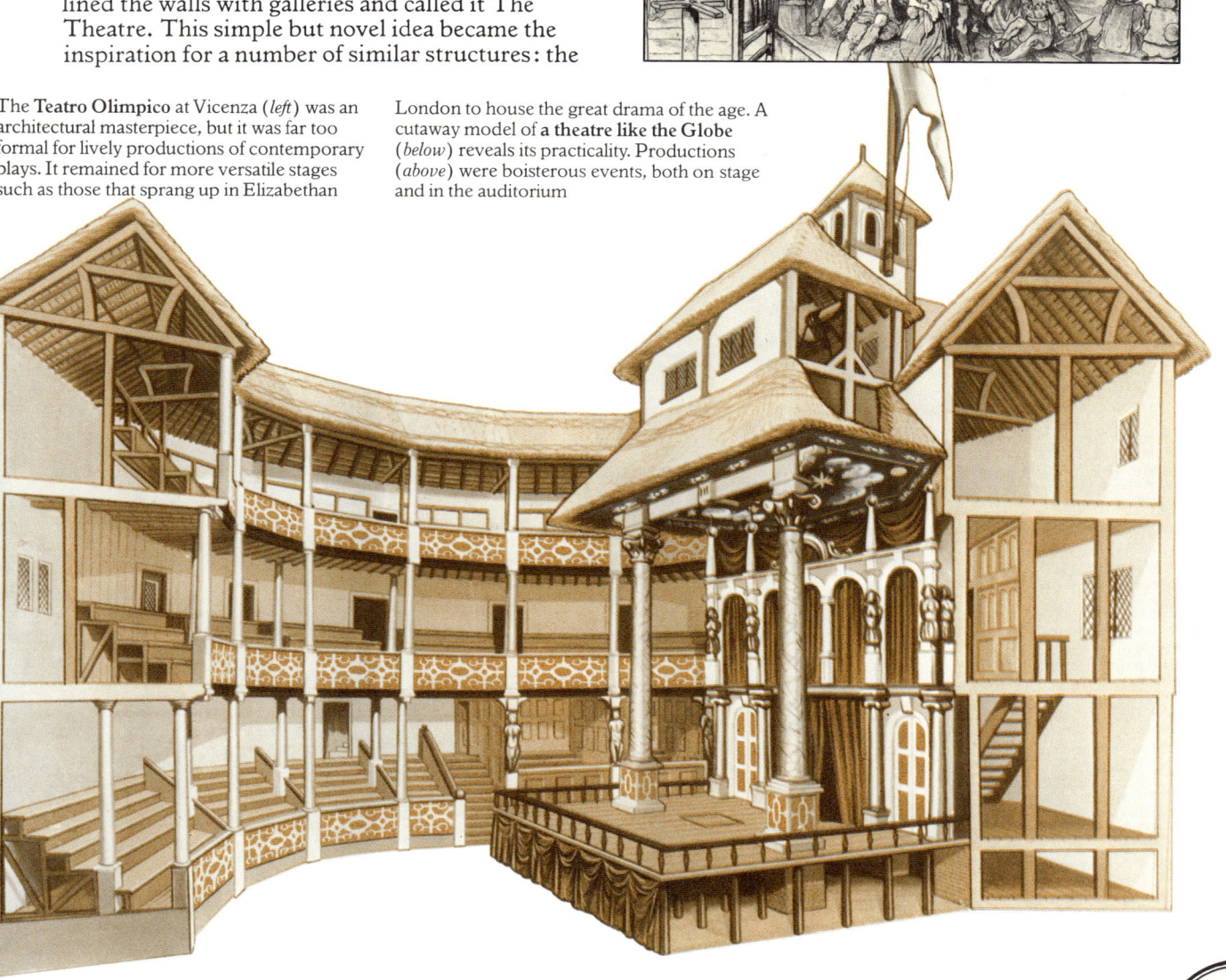

dramatic version of the legend of Don Juan, and the source for plays by MOLIÈRE and Carlo GOLDONI. In Tirso's version Don Juan appears as a courageous rebel against convention, despite his ultimate damnation. Of his comedies the delightful farce *Don Gil de las calzas verdes* has remained particularly popular. The variety of his work and his compassionate insight make Tirso one of the greatest dramatists of Spain's Golden Age. Whether or not he was an illegitimate son of the Duke of Osuna is a literary puzzle that continues to plague scholars.

GERBRAND BREDERO (1585-1618)

Dutch poet and playwright. The common man and woman in seventeenth-century Holland found an amused and compassionate champion in Bredero. The son of a shoemaker, he was a talented painter but lacked the social and educational advantages necessary for success in art. Turning these cultural drawbacks to his own advantage, he wrote romances, comedies and farces, the earthy and comic scenes of which have never been surpassed in Dutch literature. *De Spaansche Brabander* (*c*.1617), a comedy, is a loose-knit and lively portrait of Amsterdam. Of his farces, *De Klucht van de Koe* (1612) is a masterpiece of humour.

ARMAND JEAN DU PLESSIS RICHELIEU (1585-1642)

French statesman and benefactor of the arts. As Louis XIII's prime minister, Cardinal Richelieu was a generous patron of the theatre. After founding the Académie Française, he commissioned the architect Lemercier to build a magnificent theatre in his palace (now the Palais-Royal). Five playwrights, including PIERRE CORNEILLE, were invited to produce new works for it, Richelieu himself suggesting themes and plots. He even had a hand in writing the play chosen to inaugurate the new theatre in 1641. The sets and machinery were spectacular, but the play itself was a failure. Perhaps there was a little professional jealousy in Richelieu's interest in Corneille's masterpiece *Le Cid*. He ordered the Académie Française to prepare a criticism of the work, adding further comments of his own. Corneille tactfully dedicated his next play, *Horace*, to the all-powerful Cardinal.

WILLIAM ROWLEY (c 1585-c 1642)

English actor and playwright. In *The Inner Temple Masque* of 1619 Rowley played the clown Plumporridge,

Elizabethan Londoners frequently went in
fear of the "Roaring Boys", gangs of vicious
louts who thought nothing of blinding or
slitting the tongues of imprudent passers-by.
A fight here between two rival gangs of
apprentices, the Templars and the Alsatians,
shows the other side of Shakespeare's London
in a vivid, but probably realistic, way

so-called because he moved like "one of the great porridge
tubs going to the counter". His tub-like appearance was
also well-suited to the fat bishop in Thomas MIDDLETON's
A Game at Chess.

Rowley is first heard of as a hack writer in 1607 and only
later as an actor. In many of his collaborations he was
responsible merely for revising the text for the purposes of
production. His successful association with Middleton,
which produced *The Changeling* (*c*. 1622) and several other
plays, began in about 1617. Rowley's contribution was
probably small, but he was inspired to try his hand at
unassisted composition. *All's Lost by Lust* (1619), a
tragedy of ravishment and revenge, was his best single-
handed effort. The author himself appeared in it, once
more as the fat clown.

JOHN FORD (1586-c 1639)

English playwright. Ford practised law for several years
before devoting himself to literature. Not until his mid-
thirties did he embark upon the series of theatrical
collaborations that taught him the craft of writing for the
stage. *The Witch of Edmonton* (1621), written with Thomas
DEKKER and William ROWLEY, was the earliest and best

known of these. Seven years later the first of his unaided
works, *The Lover's Melancholy* (1628), was produced by
the King's Men at Blackfriars theatre. Two of his subsequent tragedies, *The Broken Heart* (*c*.1625–33) and *'Tis
Pity She's a Whore* (1629–33), are among the greatest of
Jacobean dramas. The latter, a bloody tale of incest, has
had frequent revivals in the twentieth century. Another
work, the history *Perkin Warbeck* (*c*.1629–34), was called
by T. S. ELIOT "one of the very best historical plays . . . in
the whole of Elizabethan and Jacobean drama".

NATHAN FIELD (1587-c 1620)

English actor and playwright. A rival of RICHARD BURBAGE,
Field became an actor under most improbable circum-
stances. His father, a priest, bitterly opposed all public
entertainment and sent his son safely, as he believed, to
St Paul's School. But at the age of thirteen the boy was
pressed into service as an actor with the Children of the
Chapel Royal and remained in the theatre until his death.
He acted in plays by Francis BEAUMONT and John
FLETCHER and SHAKESPEARE, but his greatest role was as
Bussy d'Ambois in George CHAPMAN's tragedy of that
name.

JOOST VAN DEN VONDEL
(1587-1679)

Dutch playwright and poet. The child of strict Anabaptists, van den Vondel met with strong opposition when he first ventured to write for the stage. He nevertheless persisted in his studies to become a gifted and learned playwright. As well as translating works by SENECA and SOPHOCLES he wrote twenty-four plays. Most of these, including *Gebroeders* (*c.*1640) and *Lucifer*, have Biblical subjects. *Gysbreght van Aemstel* (1637), a work depicting the impermanence of earthly achievements, is still performed in Amsterdam each New Year's day.

FRANCESCO GABRIELLI
(1588-1636)

Italian actor. Francesco Gabrielli's father, Giovanni, was a brilliant impersonator, famous for his solo Commedia dell' Arte performances. Francesco himself had a more modest stage persona. He created the comic servant Scapino and acted with the Confidenti and Accesi companies until his death. It was as a musician that he displayed his father's versatility. Among the many instruments that he played were the guitar, violin, harp, trombone and mandolin. He even became a one-man band in a special play called *Gl' Instrumenti di Scappino.*

BELLEROSE (c 1592-1670)

French actor. Bellerose served his acting apprenticeship in the provinces, but by 1622 was permanently established in Paris as a member of the Comédiens du Roi. As principal actor and later director of this company, he was largely responsible for elevating the role of tragedy in the French theatre, his natural and understated style adding ease and grace to the poetry of PIERRE CORNEILLE. Admirers of his chief rival, the assertive MONTDORY, thought this quiet technique was mere affectation. One critic accused him of speaking his lines while "watching where he would throw his hat for fear of damaging the plumes". In 1643 he retired from the stage in favour of religious fanaticism.

He was married to the actress Nicole Gassot. An enormous, red-haired woman, she was one of France's leading tragediennes.

FRANCOIS LE MÉTEL
DE BOISROBERT (1592-1662)

French poet and playwright. A wit, a womanizer and a priest, the Abbé Boisrobert turned to playwriting at the age of forty. In his youth he had worked as a lawyer in Rouen, but by charming both Cardinal RICHELIEU and the Pope, he became a churchman as well. He was an inveterate gambler, theatregoer and plagiarizer who took his writing as seriously as he took his vows. A founder member of the Académie Française and one of Richelieu's circle of playwrights, he wrote eighteen plays and a parody of PIERRE CORNEILLE's *Le Cid.*

MONTDORY (1594-1651)

French actor. As a young man, Montdory (whose real name was Guillaume des Gilberts) acted in the première of PIERRE CORNEILLE's first play, *Mélite.* In 1630 his company took the work to Paris, where Corneille was recognized as a major playwright and Montdory as one of the greatest tragic actors. As leading actor of the Théâtre du Marais he continued his collaboration with Corneille, most notably as Rodrigue in *Le Cid.* Even bitter critics of the playwright admired the actor. ("The sound of his voice . . .

ennobles the most ordinary and vile sentiments," wrote one.) Unlike his chief rival BELLEROSE, Montdory employed a declamatory style which demanded extreme physical exertion. Perhaps it was this strenuous technique that caused the paralysis of his tongue while he was performing before Cardinal RICHELIEU. The cardinal gave him a generous pension and encouraged him to return to the stage, but Montdory never recovered, dying in neglect after fourteen silent years.

JEAN DESMARETS
DE SAINT-SORLIN (1595-1676)

French poet and playwright. Desmarets was a true Renaissance man, being also an accomplished painter, architect and musician. As a young writer and wit in Paris, he attracted the admiration of Cardinal RICHELIEU, who established him as a founder-member of the Académie Française with the title "first clerk in the department of poetic affairs". The playwright only partly lived up to his lofty title. He wrote seven plays, including *Mirame* (1641), on which he collaborated with the Cardinal. Only *Les Visionnaires*, written in 1637, was a lasting success. A comedy (starring MONTDORY in the original production), it filled the stage with an absurd cast, many of whom were recognizable as caricatures of distinguished Parisians.

Later in life Desmarets regretted his youthful excesses (in which category he included his works for the stage), becoming a devout Catholic and a zealous scourge of the Jansenists who were challenging the Church's orthodoxy.

JAMES SHIRLEY (1596-1666)

English playwright. Soon after becoming an Anglican priest, Shirley converted to Catholicism and was compelled to leave his job as pastor and school teacher in St Albans. He became a prolific and popular playwright, gaining acceptance at court for his lavish masques and even, according to legend, collaborating with Charles I on one comedy. When the theatres closed during the Civil War, Shirley retired to teaching and poetry. With the Restoration in 1660 he was once again England's leading playwright with eight of his plays in the repertory, but he was not long to enjoy his Indian summer. During the fire of London in 1666 he and his wife both perished.

Although he never reached the heights of SHAKESPEARE or Ben JONSON, Shirley was a brilliant craftsman whose tragedies, comedies and masques enjoyed a deserved popularity. *The Traitor* (1631), about Lorenzo de' Medici, and *The Cardinal* (1641) are two of his best tragedies, the last of the noble line that can properly boast direct Elizabethan ancestry. His comedies, on the other hand, reveal the changing tastes in popular entertainment. *The Witty Fair One* (1628), *Hyde Park* (1632) and *The Lady of Pleasure* (1635) show an increasing preoccupation with London life and middle-class manners, a trend that has persisted in the English theatre ever since.

GIAN LORENZO BERNINI (1598-1680)

Italian sculptor, architect, painter and stage designer. Bernini's theatrical activity was only a minor facet of his extraordinary genius, but his work in any medium reflected the flamboyant character of the Baroque. Awestruck foreign visitors described productions with real fire, rivers actually overflowing the stage and sugar plums falling like hail upon the audience's heads.

Bernini's stagecraft was not limited to creating such effects. He also acted in, and produced, plays; it was said he could write a play, design its sets, paint its scenery, invent its machinery and build the theatre.

ANDRÉ MICHEL BARON (c 1600-55)

French actor. Born "Boyron", this leading actor and founder of a dynasty of actors became Baron when Louis XIII mispronounced his name. The son of a merchant, Baron fell in love with the theatre after seeing his first play in Bourges while on business for his father. He was a mainstay of the MONTDORY company at the Théâtre du Marais and later at the Hôtel de Bourgogne, playing "kings in tragedy and peasants in comedy". In 1641 he married Jeanne Ausoult (1625–62), daughter of a well-known theatrical family. She was a success in her own right, performing boys' parts with especial grace and attracting many followers.

Baron's death was fittingly theatrical, the result of a sword wound during a stage fight in CORNEILLE's *Le Cid*. The couple's descendants, most notably their son MICHEL BARON, were to keep the family's name before the public well into the eighteenth century.

PEDRO CALDERÓN DE LA BARCA (1600-81)

Spanish playwright. Calderón is one of the greatest of European dramatists. Though lacking somewhat the lifelike, lyrical vitality of his great countryman LOPE DE VEGA, he surpasses him in depth and richness of structure.

The son of an autocratic government official, Calderón was educated in law and theology by the Jesuits. His youth involved travel, military service and a number of quarrels and duels, in one of which he killed an opponent. His first plays brought him to the attention of the court, and he soon became the leader of Philip IV's select group of dramatic poets. No less successful with the public, he was undisputed master of the Spanish stage after Lope de Vega's death in 1635.

The 1640s marked a crisis for Calderón, inspired in part by the death of his two brothers and reputedly of the mistress who had borne him a son, as well as by the general decline in Spain's national fortunes. In 1651 he became a priest and renounced further writing for the stage. He continued to produce works at the King's command, most notably a series of biannual Corpus Christi plays, but spent the rest of his life in various religious offices, including that of honorary royal chaplain.

Calderón's dual identity as man of the world and man of God is reflected in his dramatic career, in which the two impulses are always present. His early plays, such as *La devoción de la Cruz*, *La cisma de inglaterra* and *La dama duende*, depict the complexity of life and the dangers of monomanic passion. Human responsibility, despite self-ignorance, is most horrifyingly revealed in *El medico de su honra*, in which an innocent wife is sacrificed to the "code of honour". In a violent and uncertain world the qualities of reason, prudence and compassion are obviously vital, but finally even they prove inadequate. As the title of Calderón's most famous play *La vida es sueño* (c. 1635) proclaims, life is a dream, an unfathomable condition of mystery and transcience. Such contentment as is possible depends on an ideal of morality without regard to class, as expressed in *El alcalde de Zalamea* (c. 1638).

Implicitly religious, Calderón's vision is most clearly evident in his *autos sacramentales*, the one-act allegories written for the feast of Corpus Christi. Typical of them is *El gran teatro del mundo*, in which human life is presented as a play written and directed by God. The later works in the series, such as *El pastor fido*, are among Calderón's most moving. These are meditations on the fall of man and his redemption, in a style characteristically combining formal beauty and profound humanity, offering ultimate happiness outside the world's illusions.

Calderón (*above*). The poet Shelley was moved to translate some of his plays. Another later champion was Edward Fitzgerald, "author" or "translator" of *Omar Khayyám*

Bernini's near-magical ability to handle marble is nowhere better seen than in *Apollo & Daphne*. In front of the viewer, the nymph Daphne seems to change into an oak-tree (*below*)

JODELET (c 1600-60)

French actor. An outrageous and incorrigible improviser with a nasal voice and a naturally comic face, Jodelet (born Julien Bedeau) was perhaps the greatest comedian of his time, spanning in his career the old rowdy tradition of the Commedia dell' Arte and the new comedy of manners. He performed both for MONTDORY at the Théâtre du Marais and for the rival company at the Hôtel de Bourgogne, making such a success with his broad, earthy humour that a series of plays was written specifically for him, incorporating his name in their titles. Most prophetic of these was *Jodelet, ou le maître-valet* by Paul SCARRON, in which he played the type of cunning, comic servant who was to remain a staple theatrical figure from MOLIÈRE to BEAUMARCHAIS. It was as the valet in Molière's *Les Précieuses ridicules*, a part based completely on the persona he had originated, that Jodelet made one of his last appearances.

TRISTAN L'HERMITE (c 1601-55)

French poet and playwright. If Tristan's highly romanticized autobiography can be believed, he killed a cook while a young page at court. Mistaking the poor man for a ghost, he ran him through with his sword. There followed equally fanciful exploits in England and Norway, but his crime was eventually pardoned and he returned to France to serve the Duke of Orléans.

Tristan was a remarkably original (if somewhat precious) lyric poet, whose finest tragedy, *Mariane*, was produced in 1636, the same year as CORNEILLE's *Le Cid*. These two plays were seen to "counterbalance" each other, Corneille's characters speaking "the jargon of gallantry", Tristan's "the language of the heart".

Personal tragedy overtook Tristan when he lost his wife and child. Until then he had been a carefree adventurer and gambler. He consoled himself by employing the young Philippe QUINAULT and encouraging the boy's talent as a playwright.

FRANÇOIS HÉDELIN ABBÉ D'AUBIGNAC (1604-76)

French critic and playwright. Aubignac's principal contribution to French drama was his treatise *Le Pratique du théâtre* (1657). This important work asserts the validity of the Aristotelean unities of time, place and action as the proper basis for an effective play. In all his theoretical writings Aubignac inveighed against what he considered ignoble and outlandish dramatic practices and the disrepute they brought on both the art and the profession. His zeal for reform ranged from the well-made play to the well-made theatre, sparing no offender, while in church his sermons were known for their histrionic qualities. His own plays (first among them *Zénobie*, 1647) were intended to serve as models, but met with indifferent success, not least because of the enemies, including CORNEILLE, that his criticism had earned him.

JEAN MAIRET (1604-86)

French playwright. Mairet's first plays, *Chryséide et Arimand* (1625) and *Sylvie* (1626), established him as a popular dramatist. These were conventional pastoral tragicomedies, but *Silvanire* (1630) marked the first attempt to apply the doctrine of the unities to the genre. In his preface to this play Mairet explained his theories, and later fully realized them in 1634 with the production of *Sophonisbe*, the first true tragedy in the French classical style. Noble in sentiment and wholly consistent in structure, it broke with the past and influenced such dramatists as PIERRE CORNEILLE.

Long a favourite of the nobility, Mairet abandoned the stage for the diplomatic service in 1640.

PIERRE CORNEILLE (1606-84)

French playwright. The production of Pierre Corneille's *Le Cid* in 1637 lifted French tragedy from a morass of classical scholarship and emphatically established a great new age of drama. From a play by Guillén de CASTRO Y BELLVÍS, Corneille extracted a love story as immortal as Romeo and Juliet. Paris flocked to see the lovers, Rodrigue and Chimène, torn between passion and family honour (Rodrigue kills Chimène's father in a duel to avenge an insult to his own father). The success of this unashamedly romantic drama provoked jealous hostility from lesser writers, who accused Corneille of immorality, vulgarity, plagiarism and disregard of the classical unities of time, place and action. On the orders of Cardinal RICHELIEU, the Académie Française investigated the case, upholding the criticisms, but adding that the play was nevertheless first-rate entertainment.

Corneille was no newcomer to the stage at the time of this dispute; *Le Cid* was his ninth play. The first, *Mélite* (c. 1629), a comedy written while he was still a young lawyer in his native Rouen, so impressed MONTDORY's visiting company that they took the piece straight to Paris. There the playwright became one of Richelieu's coterie of "Five Authors", but relations between the two were never amicable, and worsened with the furore over *Le Cid*.

Horace and *Cinna*, both performed in 1640, mark the beginning of Corneille's great series of historical tragedies, set mainly in ancient Rome. Unlike RACINE, Corneille preferred history to myth, and politics were always central to his dramas. With the emergence of France as a great power, his themes were particularly relevant to the age. Auguste in *Cinna* is his portrait of a noble, generous ruler and stoic hero. This ideal, much admired by Napoleon (if not by Richelieu and Louis XIV), was further developed in *La Mort de Pompée* (1642–43) and *Nicomède* (1651).

Corneille's heroes are superhuman, called upon to make extreme sacrifices, yet capable of great tenderness and humanity. For many his finest work is *Polyeucte* (1641), a "Christian tragedy", in which the hero characteristically chooses martyrdom despite the passionate pleas of his wife. As if to seek relief from this high seriousness, Corneille turned once more to the Spanish theatre, this time with completely different results. *Le Menteur* (c. 1643), adapted from Juan Ruiz de ALARCÓN, was a comedy of manners. "It is only a translation," wrote VOLTAIRE, "but it was this translation that gave us MOLIÈRE."

By 1650 he was "le Grand Corneille" (partly to distinguish him from his younger brother, Thomas), and his reputation seemed assured. But political unrest and the complete failure of *Pertharite* (1651) sent him back to Rouen, where he retired to translate "The Imitation of Christ" by Thomas à Kempis. Friends urged him to take up writing for the theatre again, which he did in 1659, but he was now in direct competition with Racine. His earlier masterpieces were frequently revived by the actor FLORIDOR, but his new plays knew limited success. After 1674 he wrote no more for the stage.

For most of his life Corneille held a government post in Rouen and led a quiet existence, although stanzas

Playwright **Pierre Corneille** (*right*)
founded a great era of drama
in seventeenth-century France

addressed to the beautiful actress Marquise DU PARC have led to speculation concerning this provincial respectability. He was a perfectionist in his writing, spending hours polishing a single line. Strangely his heroes are hot-blooded men of action, a fact which contributed to the unpopularity of his work in the cooler, intellectual climate of the late seventeenth century. The Romantics, on the other hand, loved his plays for the violence of their passions, the impossibility of their dilemmas, the colour of the language and the resonance of the verse.

WILLIAM DAVENANT (1606-68)

English playwright and theatre manager. Davenant never refuted the story that he was SHAKESPEARE's illegitimate son; the legend added to his status as the most eminent surviving link with the golden days of Elizabethan and Jacobean theatre. His first play, *Albovine* (*c.*1629), was his most successful tragedy, and *The Wits* (1634) his finest comedy. The Court admired his masques, and on Ben JONSON's death Charles I made him Poet Laureate.

Turning soldier in the Civil War, Davenant was knighted for his services to the Royalist cause and joined Charles II's exiled Court in Paris. Oliver Cromwell's forces finally caught up with him as he was sailing to America to become Governor of Maryland. Imprisoned for more than a year in the Tower of London, he returned to the theatre on his release, evading the ban on theatrical entertainment in force since 1642 by billing *The Siege of Rhodes* (1656) as "music and instruction". It is sometimes considered the first English opera.

At the Restoration only two theatrical companies were given a licence, Thomas KILLIGREW's King's Players and Davenant's Duke's Men. As manager of this company (which included Thomas BETTERTON), Davenant could

hardly fail. Meanwhile he devoted himself to the improbable task of rewriting Shakespeare (sometimes with John DRYDEN) and to the building of a theatre in Dorset Garden. He died as his company was about to move to these quarters.

TIBERIO FIORILLI (1608-94)

Italian actor. Tiberio Fiorilli was universally known as Scaramouche, the Commedia dell' Arte character he made his own. He first chose the part because he was hungry and the play included a scene in which Scaramouche ate some hard-boiled eggs. Fiorilli always dressed in black, carried a guitar and played without a mask. Without uttering a word, he could keep an audience laughing for fifteen minutes or more.

He took London and Paris by storm and was considered by MOLIÈRE to be the greatest actor of the age. Even when Fiorilli was in his eighties, his agility as a dancer and acrobat continued to astound. His reputation was marred only by his notorious meanness.

FLORIDOR (1608-71)

French actor. It is a mystery why the young nobleman Josias de Soulas should have forsaken a promising career as a musketeer to go on the stage. Changing his name to Floridor, he formed a company that toured the provinces, visited London and finally went to Paris in 1637. There, at the Théâtre du Marais, began his lifelong association with PIERRE CORNEILLE, Floridor playing the leading roles in *Horace*, *Cinna* and *Polyeucte*.

By 1650 he had taken over from BELLEROSE at the Hôtel de Bourgogne as Orator and First Lover (he had to pay for the privilege, but received Bellerose's old cos-

In 1650 Paris was treated to the first of many *pièces à machines*, Pierre Corneille's *Andromède* (*left*), designed by the "great wizard" **Giacomo Torelli**. In machine plays the aerobatics of the cloud-borne deities totally eclipsed the routine classical drama taking place at ground level

Paul Scarron's *Roman Comique* recounts the hazardous life of a travelling theatre company. Here (*right*) the players receive a typically warm welcome in Le Mans, the town where Scarron had ill-advisedly begun his career as a cleric before discovering his talent for writing farce

tumes into the bargain). Subsequently Corneille transferred his allegiance to his friend's new company.

Nobody ever had a harsh word to say about Floridor. His acting was apparently calm, assured and naturalistic. He alone was spared in MOLIÈRE's parodies of contemporary actors.

Many of his later roles were in plays by RACINE. After playing Titus in *Bérénice*, Floridor fell seriously ill and was urged by his confessor to quit the stage.

JOHN MILTON (1608–74)

English poet. While John Milton, old and blind, sought to "justify the ways of God to Man" in *Paradise Lost*, London was enjoying the earthly delights of the Restoration. Just such revels had been the subject of Milton's youthful masque, *Comus*, performed at Ludlow Castle in 1634. Comus, son of Bacchus and Circe, tries unsuccessfully to seduce a young virgin. The contrast, poetic rather than dramatic, between the sensuality of Comus and the lady's stern virtue makes it the finest masque in the English language. It has often been revived in this century: the music is by Henry Lawes.

GIACOMO TORELLI (1608–78)

Italian stage designer and theatre architect. Known as the Great Wizard on account of his spectacular sets and lightning scene changes, Torelli first came to public notice at the Teatro Novissimo in Venice. Using trolleys connected to a central winch, he could move five sets of wings on or off the stage at once.

In 1645 Torelli was invited to Paris, where he started a vogue for spectacular plays like CORNEILLE's *Andromède*. He also redesigned MOLIÈRE's theatre, the Petit Bourbon,

but the machinery and sets he built for it were burned by a jealous rival. Before Torelli, designers had always been primarily painters or architects; he was the first full-time professional.

JEAN DE ROTROU (1609–50)

French playwright. VOLTAIRE called Rotrou "The true founder of French theatre" for instilling decorum and nobility into dramatic literature. Certainly, next to his close friend CORNEILLE, he was the best playwright of his day and one of the most prolific, producing thirty plays by 1634. Much of this labour was simply due to economic necessity, Rotrou having no other income – and a fondness for gambling. His financial position was eased when he was given a pension and appointed a *lieutenant civil* for his native town of Dreux, but as late as 1647 he was forced to sell his great tragedy *Venceslas* to pay a gambling debt. *Saint Genest* (1646), another major work, tells the tragic history of the Roman actor-martyr GENESIUS. A popular comedy, *Les Sosies* (1636), and a Spanish-style tragicomedy, *Laure persécutée* (1637), reveal his mastery of other dramatic forms.

For his integrity and charm Rotrou was universally admired. His virtues were ultimately displayed when he insisted on returning to Dreux at the outbreak of an epidemic. There, like one of his own selfless and committed heroes, he discharged his office until he himself fell victim to the plague and died.

PAUL SCARRON (1610–60)

French playwright, novelist and poet. Until 1640 Paul Scarron was Abbé Scarron, secretary to the bishop of Le Mans. His ecclesiastical career had been for the most

CONTINUED ON PAGE 62

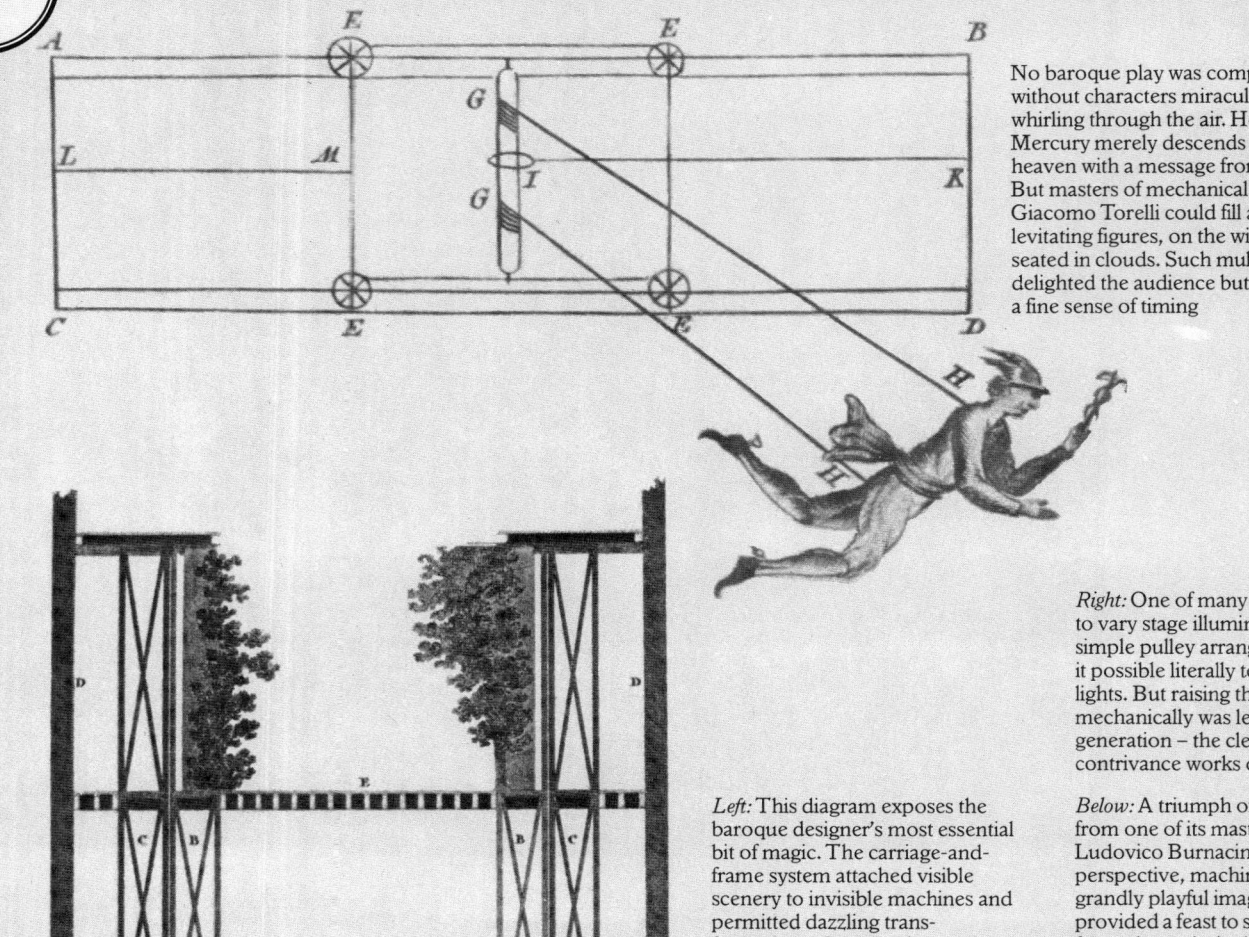

No baroque play was complete without characters miraculously whirling through the air. Here Mercury merely descends from heaven with a message from the gods. But masters of mechanical illusion like Giacomo Torelli could fill a stage with levitating figures, on the wing or seated in clouds. Such multiple feats delighted the audience but demanded a fine sense of timing

Right: One of many early attempts to vary stage illumination, this simple pulley arrangement made it possible literally to lower the lights. But raising them mechanically was left to a later generation – the clever contrivance works only one way

Left: This diagram exposes the baroque designer's most essential bit of magic. The carriage-and-frame system attached visible scenery to invisible machines and permitted dazzling transformations. Cunning fostered illusion: the audience saw foliage or a splendid courtyard but not the stagehand and pulley that changed one into the other

Below: A triumph of stagecraft from one of its masters, Ludovico Burnacini. Combining perspective, machinery and a grandly playful imagination, he provided a feast to suit everyone's fancy. A precisely detailed city blazes on the horizon, an oarsman battles stormy seas all taking place in the mouth of a fire-breathing monster

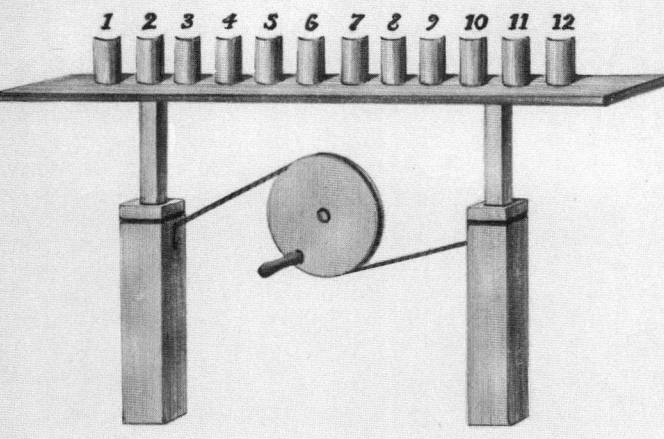

Above: For the audience, this chariot swept through the air without visible means of support

Below: A ship rocks over billowing seas in heavy weather. A wooden model simulates the vessel; its bobbing motion is achieved by offstage wires. The churning waves are four sections of painted cloth turned on spits; extra waves appear behind the craft. All these techniques resemble (with modifications) many that are still in use today

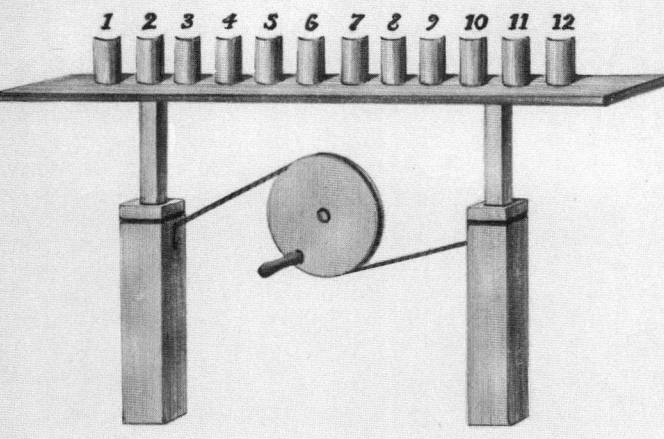

"Ingenious magick": Baroque machinery

Baroque theatre aimed above all to astound. The stage was never confined by walls and floor. It was a place of infinite expansion and endless surprise. The designer's art could create the illusion of any location; his machines could transform it in an instant. The key to this freedom was the carriage-and-frame method of shifting scenery invented by Giacomo TORELLI. Painted panels (wings) on either side of the stage were attached to frames slotted in the stage floor. Below the stage these rested on carriages running on tracks. By means of a windlass and counterweights, one man could move the whole apparatus and so alter the scene above him as quickly as new panels were inserted in the frames. In seconds a great hall became a forest, fire turned to water or Heaven to Hell. And with the wings themselves painted in perspective, the stage appeared to possess infinite depth.

Within this protean setting occurred the amazing effects that made Baroque drama seem truly magical. Men in flight, rivers with ships and spouting fish, pillars and chariots of fire became devices so standard that in 1638 Niccoló Sabbatini published a manual showing anyone how to achieve them. The descent of a man in a cloud, for instance, required a vertical beam behind the backdrop to which a sliding triangular frame was attached. The "cloud" was a basket or platform concealed by painted canvas and connected to the frame, which was then operated backstage by a pulley. But by the time Sabbatini's book came out, all its contrivances had been rendered obsolete by the busy ingenuity of competing designers. Torelli, aptly named the Great Wizard, could join two figures in mid-flight. One of his prologues, set in a harbour, featured Justice coming down in a cloud from heaven and Neptune arriving in a shell-chariot drawn by sea-horses. (Innocence was obliged to enter on foot.) A classic feat of 1701 presented a globe hanging in mid-air, which first advanced, then opened to reveal gold, precious stones, coloured metals and "a great number of musicians . . . without the spectator being able to discern the Pulleys and Machines that directed the whole".

Playwrights as noted as CORNEILLE took advantage of mechanized wonder; the plot of his *Andromède* (1650) depended on such effects. But one of the triumphs of seventeenth-century stagecraft was the wedding in 1628 of Ranuccio II and Margherita of Tuscany, at the Farnese theatre in Parma. At the climax, Neptune arose from a sea simulated by slowly turning spiral columns laid lengthwise. All at once illusion became reality. From tanks below the stage water filled the auditorium, and through side doors "marine monsters and floating islands" appeared, leaving the audience dumbfounded. Before such magic, as a Baroque theatregoer observed, "a Spectator stands in need of his Reflection, to put him in Mind that all is purely the Effect of the Machinery".

The pious cant of **Molière**'s *Tartuffe* fails to effect his planned seduction

part forced on him by an unsympathetic stepmother, but had not seriously diminished his appetite for pleasure. A crucial event in Scarron's life was an attack of rheumatism severe enough to leave him a permanent invalid. Far from inducing sober reflection, this misfortune freed his literary talents, paradoxically creating an outlet for his wit and high spirits.

His gifts for farce and satire revealed themselves at once in two plays written for the great comedian JODELET (*Jodelet ou le maître-valet*, 1643; *Jodelet duelliste*, 1645) and in *Don Japhet d'Arménie* (1647). These are vigorous burlesques, deriding artificiality and aristocratic pretension. His later work turned more to tragicomedy, and was also an influence on MOLIÈRE.

Scarron's success as author and wit made him the centre of a brilliant salon, frequented by aristocrats and intellectuals. The most unexpected of his glittering prizes was his marriage (probably unconsummated) in 1652 to a penniless orphan, Françoise d'Aubigné, who became Mme de Maintenon and wife of Louis XIV.

NIKOLAUS AVANCINI (1611-86)

Austrian playwright. Avancini entered the Society of Jesus in 1627, and his art is the full expression of Jesuit philosophy. Of noble birth, from Brez in South Tyrol, he came to Vienna in 1640 as Professor of Rhetoric, a title which implied close involvement with drama.

Jesuit drama aimed to overwhelm its audience with colossal representations of the forces of nature, of spiritual and temporal history. The most extravagant effects were employed to make the stage an image of the power of God, His Emperor and Church. For forty years Avancini provided such exercises in apotheosis as *Pietas Victrix* (1659) for the Court of Leopold I.

THOMAS KILLIGREW (1612-83)

English manager, playwright and courtier. Killigrew's enthusiasm for the theatre revealed itself early. When extras were called for at London's Red Bull Playhouse ("Who will go and be a devil, and he shall see the play for nothing?"), a very young Tom would always volunteer.

All his life, Killigrew was a man of the Court. Royal page to Charles I as a boy, then groom of the bedchamber and master of the revels to Charles II, he had a natural part in the easy licentiousness of the Restoration. But his wit was often aimed more at exposing the king's weaknesses than encouraging them. Killigrew's reputation as a "merry droll" spared him royal disfavour, but on one occasion his raillery earned him a box on the ear from a less tolerant lord.

His plays, though slight, reveal a predictable skill at repartee and (despite his description of himself as "an illiterate courtier") an awareness of theatrical developments in other countries. Typical of both is *The Parson's Wedding* (c. 1640), a lusty adaptation from CALDERÓN.

Killigrew's place in theatrical history was assured when, in 1660, he was granted (along with William DAVENANT) one of two royal patents to open a theatre. Later in that year, Killigrew's King's Players performed the first licensed dramatic production of the Restoration. He went on to establish the Drury Lane Theatre and The Nursery, a school for actors.

Wenceslaus Hollar's vision of   The gloomy Silesian sage
Thomas Killigrew (*above*)   **Andreas Gryphius** (*below*)

ANDREAS GRYPHIUS (1616-64)

German poet and playwright. Gryphius's austere and complex character grew from the troubled events of his youth. His father died in 1621; his mother in 1628. He went to live with his brother in Glogau, but saw the city almost completely destroyed by fire in 1631. And throughout these years his native Silesia, a centre of literature and learning, was torn by religious strife in the horrors of the Thirty Years War.

Gryphius's early intellectual gifts ripened at the University of Leyden and in travel throughout Europe. He returned to Silesia in 1647, refusing offers of university posts elsewhere, and remained there as a government official until his death.

The literary fruit of his experiences and abilities is dark and didactic. Gryphius's constant theme is the vanity of earthly values, the necessity of stoic virtue and Christian faith. His tragedies, among them *Ermordete Majestät, oder Carolus Stuardus*, celebrate the patient suffering of noble heroes, while such comedies as *Horribiliscribrifax* anatomize human folly. In both genres he commands a language passionate, highly wrought and inventive.

HAUTEROCHE (c 1617-1707)

French actor and playwright. During a long career at the Hôtel de Bourgogne, Hauteroche played major supporting roles in all RACINE's tragedies as well as many leading comic parts. His ponderous style of acting was parodied by MOLIÈRE in *L'Impromptu de Versailles*, but when Hauteroche himself turned to writing he adopted Molière as his model. *Crispin médecin* (1670) exploited the vogue begun by Molière for attacking doctors, while *Crispin musicien* (1674) satirized the new mania for opera.

MADELEINE BÉJART (1618-72)

French actress. Whether or not Madeleine Béjart and MOLIÈRE were ever lovers, their careers were indissolubly linked. As early as 1643, when Molière was only twenty-one, they founded the Illustre-Théâtre in Paris, and, after its failure, toured the provinces together for thirteen years. The company owed much to Madeleine's practical business sense. She was not only leading lady; at various times she was administrator, accountant and wardrobe-mistress, all the while bringing up Armande, her young sister (or daughter, said her enemies), whom Molière later married.

When the company found fame in Paris in 1658, Madeleine gave up playing tragic heroines and in Molière's comedies usually took the part of the witty servant-girl, her greatest creation being the cheeky, down-to-earth Dorine in *Tartuffe*. Throughout the scandals that surrounded Molière she remained loyal. Fittingly the two died within a year of each other.

AGUSTÍN MORETO Y CABAÑA (1618-69)

Spanish playwright. Moreto's career typified the comfortable existence a writer could lead within the Catholic Church. The son of a rich Italian merchant, he attended university, served in the army and in 1642 took minor orders, obtaining a sinecure which left him free to live in Madrid. There he was befriended by CALDERÓN and produced over seventy plays.

Although no great poet, Moreto had an eye for a good plot, borrowing freely from other dramatists. From LOPE DE VEGA he took the story of his brilliant comedy *El desdén con el desdén* (1654), in which a lady spurns all suitors until she is similarly spurned. He was also famed for character studies such as *El lindo Don Diego*, a portrait of a society dandy who spends his day at the dressing-table. His finest religious drama is *San Franco de Sena*, in which a young gambler loses his eyes as the result of a short-sighted wager.

SAVINIEN DE CYRANO DE BERGERAC (1619-55)

French poet, philosopher and playwright. The fictional Cyrano of Edmond ROSTAND's play, with his enormous nose and insatiable appetite for duels, gives a very distorted impression of an extraordinary man. Extravagant action and extravagant language were the two passions of this courageous soldier and radical free-thinker. Wounded in the throat at the siege of Arras in 1640, he left the army and threw himself into the political and intellectual life of Paris.

Cyrano's baroque excesses of language were most successfully employed in fantastic, satirical tales. In his two plays, flights of linguistic fancy tend to obscure the action. His comedy *Le Pédant joué* contains too much parody of verbose scholars, but elements of the plot and lines of dialogue were later used very effectively by MOLIÈRE in *Les Fourberies de Scapin*.

La Mort d'Agrippine (1653) was a Roman political drama in the style of CORNEILLE. Some fine verse, in which a conspirator justifies his immorality and defies religion, brought Cyrano into conflict with the authorities. They shed no tears when, shortly afterwards, a piece of timber fell on his head. The wound proved fatal.

CATHERINE DE BRIE (c 1620-1706)

French actress. When Catherine du Rozet joined MOLIÈRE's troupe in 1650, she was an immediate success. A year later her new husband, Edmé de Brie, was accepted into the company and allowed to play extremely small parts, but he never seems to have come between Catherine and the playwright.

She was probably Molière's lover and later, when his marriage failed, he turned to her again for consolation (there were apparently no hard feelings between her and Molière's wife, ARMANDE BÉJART). After the playwright's death she followed the company (now under Armande's direction) from the Palais-Royal to the theatre in rue Guénégaud and in 1680 was one of the founder members of the Comédie-Française.

Catherine's greatest success came in the role of Agnès in *L'École des femmes*. When she finally stepped down to let a younger actress take the part of the innocent teen-ager, the public demanded her return, and she continued to play Agnès until her retirement at the age of sixty-five. Catherine's nature was simple and affectionate, although many found her stupid. Her figure too provoked mixed reactions: some found her exquisitely slim and graceful; others described her as a skeleton. Her comic acting, on the other hand, must have been unique and brilliant to a degree; reports from those who saw her perform are unanimous in their acclaim.

MOLIÈRE (1622-73)

French playwright and actor. Before Molière, comedy in France was considered an unimportant genre. He and his company raised it to a rank equal to that of tragedy and founded a theatrical tradition that has lasted to this day. The price he paid for his success was high; personal happiness and health were sacrificed to his one great love, the theatre.

In 1642 the young Jean-Baptiste Poquelin met the actors Madeleine and Joseph BÉJART and grew dissatisfied with his law studies. The following year he founded a theatre company with the Béjarts, changed his name to Molière, and devoted his life to the stage. The Illustre-Théâtre soon incurred large debts, and in 1645 Molière was briefly imprisoned. Leaving Paris, he toured the south of France in Charles Dufresne's company, eventually taking over the troupe, which was reinforced by the talents of René and Marquise DU PARC and Catherine DE BRIE.

Molière's ambition was always to be a great tragic actor, but provincial audiences demanded comedy, and he obliged with *L'Étourdi* and *Le Dépit amoureux*, his earliest surviving works.

Commanded to play before Louis XIV in 1658, Molière presented CORNEILLE's *Nicomède*. The reception was tepid, and in an attempt to save the day, he played one of his own farces, which enchanted the Court. Under the patronage of the king's brother, the troupe was allowed to use the Petit-Bourbon theatre. At first they had to play alternate nights with the comedians of Tiberio FIORILLI, an actor on whose natural style Molière is said to have based his own, but in a later home, the Palais-Royal, the tables were turned and the Italians paid Molière rent for the use of the stage.

Public acclaim came with *Les Précieuses ridicules* (1659), a farcical satire on the pretentious language and mannerisms of young Parisiennes. The stock figure of the cuckold in *Sganarelle* (1660) was equally farcical, and enemies began to sneer at these lightweight offerings and demand something more substantial. The first production at the Palais-Royal was *Dom Garcie de Navarre* (1661). Molière considered it his finest work, and its failure hurt him deeply. It was his first and last attempt at pure tragedy, but his great comedies were all to contain that seed of tragedy, which gives pathos and humanity to otherwise ridiculous characters.

In *L'École des femmes* (1662), his first five-act comedy in verse, the old bachelor Arnolphe brings up his ward, Agnès, in complete seclusion, hoping to make her his dutiful, submissive wife. He finds himself instead an accomplice to her elopement with the young and handsome Horace. The revolutionary style of this piece provoked a war of pamphlets and parodies between Molière and the actors of the Hôtel de Bourgogne, aided by MONTFLEURY. Molière was forced to justify his ideas of comedy in *La Critique de L'École des femmes*, which appeared in 1663.

In 1662 Molière had married ARMANDE BÉJART, twenty years his junior, so the subject of *L'École des femmes* was close to his heart. It was not clear whether Armande was Madeleine Béjart's sister or her daughter, and the scurrilous actor Montfleury *père* suggested that she was Molière's own daughter by Madeleine. Fortunately Molière could rely on the support of the king, who stood godfather to his first son.

Louis XIV's patronage subsequently placed Molière in an embarrassing situation. The first version of *Le Tartuffe* (1664) was performed at Court, but banned from public performance through the influence of the pious but powerful Jansenist sect, who saw themselves parodied in the arch-hypocrite. *Dom Juan* (1665) also met with opposition from the Church, for although the cynical libertine of the title is dragged down to Hell, there is powerful logic in his denunciations of others' hypocrisy.

In Molière's masterpiece, *Le Misanthrope* (1666), there is a strong autobiographical strain. Alceste despises the insincerity of mankind, yet is in love with the young coquette Célimène. Molière played Alceste and Armande Célimène at a time when their marriage had failed and they were living apart. The play was not well received, neither was *L'Avare* (1668). *Le Médecin malgré lui* (1666) was a brilliant one-act farce, but not until *Le Tartuffe* was finally produced in public in 1669 was Molière's reputation fully restored. With the success of *Le Bourgeois gentilhomme* (1670) at Court and *Les Femmes savantes*

(1672) in town, fortune seemed to smile on him at last. But royal patronage was unrelated to public applause, and in 1672, for complex political reasons, the king withdrew his support. Ailing and disconsolate, Molière continued to act. On the fourth night of *Le Malade imaginaire* (1673) he suffered a convulsion, which, professional to the last, he disguised as a grimace. He finished the play, but died that night.

Armande, a torment to him throughout their married life, lived on to champion his works and consolidate his unique reputation.

THOMAS CORNEILLE (1625-1709)

French playwright and scholar. It was a mixed blessing to be the younger brother of the illustrious PIERRE CORNEILLE. The worthy, if inferior creations of Thomas do not bear comparison to the elder Corneille's works, but during his lifetime they were highly successful. He produced forty plays, including the romantic tragedy *Timocrate* (1656), which ran for six months, a record unequalled in the century. His relations with his brother were surprisingly cordial, the two marrying sisters and living together or side by side until Pierre's death. Thomas later took his brother's seat in the Académie Française and quietly abandoned playwriting for the more reflective occupation of scholarship.

GEORGE VILLIERS DUKE OF BUCKINGHAM (1628-87)

English courtier, statesman and playwright. Buckingham was a notorious debauchee in an age when only the most spectacular licence attracted attention. Raised with the royal children after the murder of his father, he fought and intrigued for Charles II throughout the Civil War. His own estates were confiscated by Parliament, but Buckingham reclaimed them by marrying the daughter of the general to whom they were assigned. This lady was later supplanted by a mistress, the Countess of Shrewsbury, whose husband Buckingham had mortally wounded in a duel.

A man of parts (some of which he used more than others), Buckingham wrote *The Rehearsal* (1671), a witty satire on the kind of heroic drama most associated with DRYDEN. The latter's reply, in verse, is underneath the picture opposite. This device of a play about a play was later adapted by SHERIDAN in *The Critic*.

CHARLES HART (?-1683)

English actor. Hart, with Thomas BETTERTON, was one of the leading actors of the Restoration stage. Though less resourceful than his rival, he was acknowledged to possess a "finer presence". He excelled in the roles of Hotspur and Othello–appropriately, since he was the great-nephew of William SHAKESPEARE.

A romantic figure both in life and art, Hart was a Royalist cavalry officer in the Civil War and later the drama coach and reputed first lover of Nell GWYNN.

JOHN DRYDEN (1631-1700)

English poet, playwright and critic. Before emerging as a major satirical and narrative poet in his late forties, Dryden dominated Restoration drama. He developed the rhymed heroic play then in vogue, expanding the themes of love, honour and fate sometimes to the point of comic absurdity. The two massive parts of *The Conquest of Granada* (1670, 1671) and *Aureng-Zebe* (1675) are exuberant exercises in violence and bombast, but they

This scene from the painter Hogarth's "Marriage à la Mode" (*above*) adds a moral comment to **Dryden**'s zestfully immoral play

George Villiers (*right*), who "in the course of one revolving moon; Was chemist, fiddler, statesman, and buffoon"

include lucid, unsettled arguments which betray an author more subtle than such a dramatic form would permit. The extravagant emotion of these plays was mocked by the Duke of BUCKINGHAM in *The Rehearsal*, a burlesque which featured the barely disguised Dryden directing an especially ludicrous tragedy.

But Dryden's heroic plays are not so slight as Buckingham imagined. They burst at the seams with an outpouring of ideas and images. Dryden finally found a quieter and more suitable means of expression in blank verse. *All for Love* (1677), a thoughtful version of the story of Antony and Cleopatra, and the disturbing, near tragic *Don Sebastian* (1689) are among his best plays.

Apart from *Marriage à la Mode* (*c*.1672), his bleak comedies lack the polish of those of his young friend William CONGREVE. But there is coarse energy and a powerful satirical insight in *Secret Love* (1667), *The Kind Keeper* (1678) and *The Spanish Fryar* (1680). Dryden also developed his comic genius by writing verse prologues and epilogues for plays. These poems, recited before and after performances by a popular member of the company (Nell GWYNN is said to have entranced Charles II with the epilogue to *Tyrannic Love*), entertained the audience with bantering commentary on topical affairs. He wrote 102 such pieces altogether.

As a writer of more substantial verse, Dryden was indebted to the theatre. The supple and lively satires of his maturity, including "MacFlecknoe" (1678), "Absalom and Achitophel" (1681) and "The Hind and the Panther" (1687), are a perfect fusion of the conversational style learned in the prologues and the uninhibited imagery and argument practised in the early drama.

His public outspokenness was dangerous. In one famous incident he was beaten by hired thugs near his home in Covent Garden (the Earl of ROCHESTER was popularly held responsible for this crime). An enthusiastic though critical supporter of the Stuart monarchy and a convert to Catholicism, he lost the laureateship conferred on him in 1668 when the Protestant William of Orange assumed the throne after the Revolution twenty years later. To supplement his modest private income, Dryden returned briefly to writing plays, but he found that he could earn a substantial living by poetry when he published his retelling of Virgil's "Aeneid" (1697). A portly old man, he frequently sat in Will's Coffee House and talked with the young writers who came to pay homage.

MARQUISE DU PARC (1633-68)

French actress. In 1653 Marquise-Thérèse de Gorla, a dancer, married René du Parc (*c*. 1630–64), known as Gros-René, the chubby comedian of MOLIÈRE's company. Thus began her remarkable career both as actress (especially in tragic roles) and as turner of famous heads. At various times Marquise was pursued by Molière, Pierre and Thomas CORNEILLE, the poet La Fontaine and RACINE, but throughout her married life she remained faithful to her husband. On his death in 1667, she joined the Hôtel de Bourgogne company both as the title player of Racine's *Andromaque*, and as the author's mistress. When she died suddenly he was accused of poisoning her, but a clumsy abortion was the more likely cause.

GEORGE ETHEREGE (c 1634-c 1691)

English playwright and courtier. With the performance in 1664 of *The Comical Revenge, or Love in a Tub*, George Etherege emerged as the first major Restoration dramatist. It seems clear from the play that the author must have spent some of his youth in France, since his work reveals the influence of MOLIÈRE. The sexual intrigue, the brilliant and cynical dialogue and the elegant portrayal of fashionable London society were standard features of Restoration comedy for years to come. This style was

You, the audience I

"The lewdest persons in the land, apt for pilfery, perjury, forgery, or any roguery, the very scum, rascality and baggage of the people, thieves, cutpurses, shifters, coseners; briefly an unclean generation and spawn of vipers." According to the biased contemporary testimony of an English Puritan, these were the early playgoers.

There was some truth in the condemnation. The theatre was cheap entertainment and attracted an audience seeking good sport, not moral instruction. The raucous atmosphere of the pit (the area in front of the stage) was especially offensive to the pure-minded. In France, Spain and Italy it was an all-male province. In England women could enter but none of the better sort did, fearing "privy contacts". The "groundlings" stood packed together, jostling and joking, diverted as much by what they did as by what they saw. Including expert cutpurses and (in England) prostitutes, they produced a confusion of jabbering, quarrelling, eating and drinking. The theatre seemed no place for a respectable work of art, and resembled a medieval fair more than a haven of culture. Even the most serious performances could include tumbling, vaulting, juggling and fireworks, and were never complete without a clown.

Housing such goings-on, the theatre was bound to have a reputation for "tumults and outrages". The authorities kept a nervous eye on the uproar. Once, in London in 1602, they attempted an ultimate solution, arresting all frequenters of playhouses, bowling alleys and

perfected by Etherege himself in *She Would if She Could* (1668) and above all in *The Man of Mode* (1676), with its archetypal foolish dandy, Sir Fopling Flutter.

In addition to scattered verse and witty letters, these three plays comprise Etherege's entire literary output. "Gentle George" was too involved in living the Restoration to give it much expression in literature. Indeed *The Man of Mode* would never have been written if the Earl of ROCHESTER, a libertine companion, had not chided him into it. "Easy Etherege" invariably indulged his "noble laziness of mind", married a rich wife, had a daughter by Rochester's mistress and carried out several diplomatic appointments, dying in Paris in an obscurity reminiscent of his origins. But his theatrical contributions survived to shape the works of WYCHERLEY, CONGREVE, SHERIDAN and WILDE.

THOMAS BETTERTON (c 1635-1710)

English actor and manager. In theatrical history there is no more gratifying marriage of professional skill, individual worth and mutual devotion than Betterton and his wife Mary (?–1712). As an actor, "infallible Tom"

was pre-eminent. Possessing none of the natural graces of his only possible rival, CHARLES HART, he made up for a squat frame and rather gravelly voice with a genius for characterization. COLLEY CIBBER praises his "temper'd spirit" and notes that every line he spoke satisfied judgement, ear and imagination. As Hamlet he was extraordinary, basing his interpretation on that of Joseph Taylor, whom SHAKESPEARE had reputedly coached in the part. He was still successful in the role at seventy, and in the Ghost Scene created such an atmosphere of terror that the actor playing the ghost said he was more frightened of Betterton than Betterton was of him. As a man he was modest, cheerful, honest and generous, particularly to young actors. These qualities made him an ideal manager, and he assumed leadership of the Duke's Company after DAVENANT's death, first sharing it with Davenant's son, then, from 1695, on his own.

His wife, known as Mrs Sanderson, was her husband's equal in professional and personal reputation. She, likewise, was a distinguished interpreter of Shakespeare. On Thomas's death, after forty-eight years of marriage, she temporarily lost her senses. Two years later she was buried beside her husband in Westminster Abbey.

brothels. The scheme came to nothing when it turned out that among the detainees were "Gentlemen and servingmen; lawyers, clerks, countrymen with law causes, the Queen's men, knights, and as it was credibly reported one Earl". This should have come as no surprise; gentry and nobility shared in the theatrical feast, occupying the boxes and galleries around the pit. As much as the carefree groundlings, the better classes made the spectators part of the show. Occasionally they also contributed to disorder by a haughty reluctance to even pay for their entertainment.

Depending on the mood of a London crowd, it was said, you might begin with MARLOWE and wind up with *The Merry Milkmaid*. In Paris and Madrid unpopular productions attracted whistles and jangling keys; in London, howls and applecores. Yet audiences there were exceptionally receptive. An enactment of Bacchus courting Adriadne utterly captivated a London house: "... the company presently was set on fire, they that were married posted home to their wives; they that were single vowed very solemnly to be wedded." Such pure involvement was as characteristic as boisterousness, for early audiences possessed the great virtue of unselfconscious delight. However rough and unpredictable their manners, playgoers loved lively and well-spirited action, and could applaud SHAKESPEARE as enthusiastically as the jigs of Will KEMPE. The illustration here shows a much better-behaved crowd than was usual, being the private theatre of Cardinal Richelieu at a performance before King Louis XIII in 1641.

Le grand siècle

The great age of French drama was conceived as much in the fashionable salons of Paris as at the Académie Française. At these elegant gatherings enlightened ladies and men of letters cultivated wit, finesse, *galanterie* and linguistic purity. They could dispute all afternoon about acceptable replacements for the word "because", and delighted in discovering eloquent euphemisms for the simplest terms. Thus a humble fan became a "zephyr"; a fireplace "the empire of Vulcan"; and a broom "the instrument of hygiene". MOLIÈRE mocked their sillier excesses in such plays as *Les Précieuses ridicules*; but at their best the salons manifested a care for precision which has been a hallmark of French culture ever since.

In this milieu dramatic theorists were naturally fastidious, and placed great emphasis on the "three unities" of time, place and action. Basing their ideas on a rather narrow reading of Aristotle, they decreed that a serious play should be restricted to one day and one place, and should have one unbroken story line. In fact, Aristotle, sensible pragmatist, had said nothing so dogmatic; all the major Greek writers would have failed this test miserably. Hence it was inevitable that men of the calibre of CORNEILLE and RACINE should find themselves in constant conflict with the pundits. But their very revolt combined with the disciplining effect of the "rules" to produce a drama of powerful clarity and intensity. Thus the voracious passion of Racine's Phèdre is all the more horrifying for being contained within the formal conventions of alexandrine verse; and the impossibility of the plight of Andromaque (or Alceste, or Polyeucte), is rendered even more appalling by the ruthless and clinical economy with which it is portrayed.

> Ce n'est plus une ardeur dans mes
> veines cachée :
> C'est Vénus tout entière à sa
> proie attachée.
> This is no longer passion lurking
> in my veins :
> It is Venus herself, fixed upon
> her prey. (*Phèdre*, Act 1, scene 3).

The power of these tragedies resides mainly in the poetry. Traditionally, they are presented with a minimum of movement, gesture and scenery; the delivery of the verse is supreme. Corneille's hyper-moral heroes and Racine's murderously exalted heroines exist in a spirit world wholly removed from the gaudy abandon of the English tradition. Truth is more important than colour; the world is pared down to its essentials. Thus Racine's vocabulary comprises a mere 2000 words, against SHAKESPEARE's 24,000. Physical action is also

PHÈDRE

There is an overwhelming pity in Racine's presentation of the fatal love and jealousy of Phèdre (*left*) in his greatest play. He retired after writing it, weary of the intrigue and emotional turmoil which was such a part of the theatrical life of Paris

Molière is the great master at portraying the follies of social pretension. M Jourdain in *Le Bourgeois gentilhomme* (*right*) goes to immense lengths to pass himself off as an aristocrat. He accepts his daughter's suitor only when the latter disguises himself as the son of the Grand Turk

Although indubitably the founder of French classical tragedy, Pierre Corneille reveals a much more Romantic impulse than his austere younger contemporary, Racine. *Le Cid* (*far right*) is at once a tale of military courage and a complex drama of young lovers in danger

banned: Phèdre is not seen to take poison before we witness her death; Le Cid's glorious victory is won offstage; and Hippolyte's violent end is only described (since he is killed by a sea monster this is understandable).

For these reasons Corneille and Racine do not "travel" well. When deprived of their poetic force, their plays seem static. The same is unfortunately true of Molière's great comedies, notably *Le Misanthrope* and *Tartuffe*. But there was a lighter side to the *grand siècle*: the generous patronage of kings and cardinals enabled Corneille and others to experiment with elaborate Machine Plays involving monsters, gods descending from heaven, sinners departing to hell, seascapes and a plethora of scenic novelties inspired by Giacomo Torelli and the Italian players visiting Paris. Spectacular ballets and pageants were also greatly favoured, and Molière indulged himself outrageously in mixed-media shows such as *Le Bourgeois gentilhomme*, a satire with musical interludes.

As theatre seats were expensive, there were no groundlings to demand the cruder entertainment found in English drama. But performing conditions were far from ideal. The great success of *Le Cid* established the dubious precedent of allowing the audience to overflow on to the stage, and it often became difficult to distinguish the performers from the even more splendidly attired spectators.

Unruliness was common (and murder not unknown) notably among members of the Court, who felt their station excepted them from many proprieties, including payment. Nor did the acting companies always live up to ideals of their writers; commercial rivalry encompassed bribery, chicanery and even arson. The church only added to this confusion. Though the great Cardinals Mazarin and Richelieu were influential sponsors of the drama, the lesser priesthood presented a united front against it. Since the actors' stock-in-trade was simulation, they were agents of the devil and were denied the sacrament; even Molière, once a protégé of the demi-god Louis XIV, was refused the last rites and a decent burial. As the great comic writer himself remarked, in his *Critique de L'École des Femmes*:

> C'est une étrange entreprise que celle de faire de rire les honnêtes gens.

> It's an odd way to make a living, making honest people laugh.

The Sun-King, who had contributed so vitally to the rise of classical drama, also accelerated its decline. Under the sway of his mistress, Mme de Maintenon, Louis finally decided that the theatre was indeed profane, and the founding of the Comédie Française in 1680 came too late to save French drama from a period of relative sterility.

PHILIPPE QUINAULT (1635-88)

French playwright and librettist. The son of a baker, Quinault was taken into service by the playwright TRISTAN L'HERMITE, who generously gained acceptance for the boy's first plays by presenting them as his own. In the period from the decline of CORNEILLE to the rise of RACINE, Quinault's sentimental tragedies won him extravagant praise and rapid social advancement. The mawkish tragedy *Astrate, roi de Tyr* (1664) was immensely popular. A comedy, *La Mère coquette* (1665) had more fibre to it, but it was only when Quinault started working with the composer Lully that he found his true vocation as an opera librettist.

LUDOVICO BURNACINI (1636-1707)

Italian stage and costume designer. Ludovico's brilliant career under Leopold I in Vienna has eclipsed the work of his father Giovanni (?-1655). But the elder Burnacini was also celebrated as a theatre architect and stage designer, building the Court theatre in Vienna and equipping it with the new wing-settings which made possible rapid and complex scene changes. Perhaps Giovanni's greatest triumph was the temporary structure erected at Regensburg in 1653, ingenious enough in construction and machinery to be dismantled and shipped by barge to Vienna. Ludovico worked with his father on such projects, mastering the art of grandiose display in scenery and costume, which he later applied in every medium, from water festivals and horseback ballets to opera and religious pageants. It was natural that he would be attracted by the spectacular religious plays of Nikolaus AVANCINI. His work on the latter's *Pietas Victrix* was appropriately stupendous.

JEAN BÉRAIN (c 1637-1711)

French theatrical designer. Bérain shaped and dominated High Baroque design in Europe for thirty years. He supervised entertainments at the court of Louis XIV and was scenic designer to the Paris Opéra, applying himself to all aspects of design, from furniture to firework displays. Perhaps Bérain's genius was greatest as a costume designer. His unique creations were a combination of contemporary fashion and his own exotic fantasy.

GIUSEPPE DOMENICO BIANCOLELLI (c 1637-88)

Italian actor. Under his stage name of Dominique, Biancolelli revolutionized the Commedia dell' Arte role of Harlequin, transforming him from the traditional slapstick buffoon to a witty, comic character. Biancolelli himself was a cultured and intelligent actor who was working in Vienna when Cardinal Mazarin invited him to join the Italian troupe in Paris. Although a speech defect forced him to deliver his lines with a distinctive throaty voice, he was a great actor with enough influence at Court to persuade Louis XIV to allow the actors of this ostensibly foreign company to speak in French (previously, Italian companies had been obliged to use their native language). Eventually, Biancolelli himself found it expedient to adopt French nationality.

In 1663 Biancolelli married Orsola Cortesi (c.1632-1718), later the leading lady of the Comédie-Italienne (as the Italian company became known). Several of their eight children joined the troupe. Francesca, known as Isabella, played amorous parts; Caterina, who was immortalized by the painter Watteau, became famous as Colombina. She and a brother, Pietro, were members of the Comédie-Italienne when the troupe was finally banned for satirical indiscretions in 1697.

EDMÉ BOURSAULT (1638-1701)

French playwright. At the age of thirteen Boursault was an illiterate nonentity, newly arrived in Paris; ten years later he was an aggressive, self-educated young playwright and a rival of MOLIÈRE. A journalist for much of his life, he satirized his own profession in his best play, *La Comédie sans titre* (1683). Two later plays based on Aesop have a satirical intent, but are tiresomely moralistic.

GUILLAUME BRÉCOURT (1638-85)

French actor and playwright. Brécourt acted with MOLIÈRE's company for only two years before his quarrelsome nature forced him to leave. He had more success at the Hôtel de Bourgogne, where he took leading roles in works of RACINE, including Britannicus in the first performance of that play. In 1680, however, he lost his temper and killed a coachman. As luck (or at least legend) would have it, he saved the king's life during a boar hunt and was allowed to return from exile in Holland. Back in Paris, Brécourt joined the Comédie-Française, but his remaining years were few and were spent partly in debtors' prison (whence he continued to act, being accompanied to rehearsals and performances by his gaoler). *La Feint mort de Jodelet* (c. 1659) is one of his earliest and best plays. *L'Ombre de Molière* (1674) is a generous tribute to his former mentor.

CHARLES VARLET LA GRANGE (1639-92)

French actor and manager. La Grange's combination of spirit, practicality and loyalty made him an especially useful member of MOLIÈRE's troupe. As an actor he possessed "rare intelligence and taste", good looks and an impressive bearing, which enabled him to play the role of a young lover successfully throughout his career. At the same time a sound business sense prompted him to keep exact records of works performed, receipts and general affairs, for which scholars have been grateful. These traits stood him in good stead when he assumed leadership of the company on its founder's death. In devotion to his master's memory he produced the first collected edition of Molière's works in 1682. In a generous and elegant introduction, La Grange was among the earliest to acknowledge the playwright's genius.

ANTOINE-JACOB DE MONTFLEURY (1639-85)

French playwright. A lawyer and state official, Montfleury first wrote for the stage out of family loyalty, becoming resident writer to the Hôtel de Bourgogne, where his father Zacharie was one of the leading actors. *L'Impromptu de l'Hôtel de Condé* (1664) was a riposte to MOLIÈRE's *L'Impromptu de Versailles*, in which his father's company had been parodied. In this play the young Montfleury merely satirized Molière's mannerisms as an actor. His father took the feud more seriously. Deeply hurt at the fun made of his enormous girth and the thunderous emphasis he gave to his lines, Zacharie accused Molière of marrying his own daughter. Few people paid much attention to this accusation, and Montfleury *père* died a few years later as a result of his exertions in the role of Oreste in *Andromaque*. Montfleury *fils* continued to write for the theatre, producing comedies very similar in style to those of his family's mortal enemy.

Ludovico Burnacini's design (*above*) for *The Golden Apple* shows how successfully Baroque stagecraft could simulate natural settings. But productions also took place out-of-doors. Below and to the left are three garden theatres, favoured settings for operatic productions.

The Archbishop of Salzburg created this theatrical grotto (*above*) by enlarging a natural cave. Two years later it saw the first production of opera in Northern Europe

An outdoor theatre always reflected the fancy of its patron. This eighteenth-century example (*right*) was built to resemble a Romantic ruin. Rough stones and straggling weeds were deliberate, calculated parts of the whimsical whole

Open-air drama epitomized the grandeur of the baroque, with nature itself providing a background for spectacle. The "hedge theatre" was standard in courts and in country houses. Set in a formal garden, its stage was a grassy rectangle bordered by wings of pruned trees receding into perspective; an amphitheatre accommodated noble spectators. Though silent now, the theatre in the park at Herrenhausen, Hanover (*above*) retains its former stateliness

JEAN RACINE (1639-99)

French playwright and poet. Orphaned when only four years old, Jean Racine was raised by the Jansenists of Port-Royal, a radical Catholic community convinced of man's corrupt nature and dependence on God. There he received an excellent if eccentric education. When the Port-Royal schools were suppressed by the state, he worked on his own, reputedly reading Greek in the woods. From this austere and lonely boyhood arose a master of tragic drama.

In 1658 he went to Paris to study philosophy, but the glittering literary life and the flattering patronage of the poet La Fontaine attracted him instead. In 1660 an ode for Louis XIV's marriage earned him critical praise and a sum from the royal treasury. Racine's family, disturbed at these activities, sent him to study theology with an uncle at Uzès in 1661, but he soon returned to Paris, where, encouraged by MOLIÈRE, he embarked as a dramatist with the tragedy *La Thébaïde* (1664). His next tragedy for Molière, *Alexandre* (1665), brought both success and scandal when, during rehearsals, he took the play secretly to the rival Hôtel de Bourgogne company, who hurried it on to their stage during Molière's run. Racine may have been dissatisfied with Molière's production, but the deed made him appear ambitious, devious and ungrateful. That view seemed confirmed when he enticed Molière's leading actress (and his own mistress), Mlle DU PARC, to the Hôtel de Bourgogne for his tragedy *Andromaque* (1667). Her sudden, somewhat mysterious death further clouded his reputation. He had also severed his relations with his former friends at Port-Royal in an open letter violently denouncing their opposition to the theatre.

But while his character was pilloried, his plays were acclaimed. *Andromaque*'s great success established its author as PIERRE CORNEILLE's main rival. The hostility between the two playwrights was apparent in the old man's glowering attendance at Racine's *Britannicus* (1669), and increased in 1670 when, perhaps not coincidentally, they both wrote on the same subject. (The public favoured the younger man's *Bérénice*.) Both honours and controversy surrounded Racine's next masterpieces, *Bajazet* (1672), *Mithridate* (1673) and *Iphigénie* (1674). Suddenly, after *Phèdre* (1677), he stopped writing for the theatre. This decision at the height of his fame predictably provoked a buzz of malicious speculation: the popularity of another version of the Phaedra story caused him to retire, suggested his critics, or the infidelity of his mistress, or repercussions from his satiric attacks on the Court. But Racine was not necessarily driven from the stage. Louis XIV had offered him the full-time post of historiographer, he and Port-Royal had been reconciled and he had married a pious woman of some fortune. Whether the playwright had undergone the religious conversion he claimed or was simply weary of turmoil, his last tragedies, *Esther* (1689) and *Athalie* (1691), both based on biblical subjects, were written only at the request of the king's wife for private performance. He devoted his final years to raising seven children and writing a history of Port-Royal.

Racine's plays describe the inexorable destructiveness of passion, particularly the passion of love. Their overwhelming effect is due to his acute psychological insight and to his unparalleled simplicity of language and structure. Perhaps the greatest poet among French dramatists, Racine charted the emotional predicament of his characters and its inevitable course; feelings, fate and the movement of the play all seem equally irresistible. He differs from Corneille in this utter concentration and above all in his conception of the power of human will. For Corneille man is capable of heroic resistance to temptation; for Racine he is totally powerless against the demonic force of love.

Of all the plays, perhaps *Phèdre* best epitomizes Racine's obsessive vision of life. Phèdre, wife of Thésée, is the victim of a consuming and illicit desire for her stepson, Hippolyte. ("Venus in all her might is on her prey," says the heroine, confessing herself enslaved to hopeless passion.) Torn by guilt, she attempts to conceal her obsession, but the fatal sequence of misjudgements and malignities it engenders destroys both her and the young man. Innocent and corrupt, aware of sin and beyond assistance, she represents, as a Jansenist said, "one who has not been granted grace". It was just such a hope that grace would be granted him that seems to have compelled Racine, after a lifetime of passion, to forfeit his art.

CHARLES SEDLEY (c 1639-1701)

English courtier, poet and playwright. Sedley was a noted Restoration figure, an intimate of Charles II, famed for debauchery, wit and occasional playwriting. In a notorious escapade in 1663 he appeared naked and drunk on a tavern balcony, and delivered a blasphemous oration, for which he was stoned, fined and gaoled. Marriage to a virtuous wife, however, ultimately converted him to respectability, and he became a distinguished and conscientious member of Parliament.

Chief among his plays are *The Mulberry Garden* (1668) and *Bellamira* (1687), occasionally witty comedies written in an uneasy combination of prose and verse.

APHRA BEHN (1640-89)

English playwright, novelist and poet. Aphra Behn's position as England's first professional authoress has overshadowed her genuine abilities as a dramatist. She was brought up in Guiana, where her father was lieutenant-governor. In England she married a wealthy Dutch merchant, but by 1666 was reduced to a state of penniless widowhood. After this she worked for a time as a government spy in the Low Countries, though her only reward seems to have been a period of imprisonment for debt. After her release, Aphra Behn turned to writing to support herself and in the eighteen years from 1671 produced fifteen plays, as well as novels and poetry.

Her most successful dramatic work was *The Rover* (1677), a comedy which was frequently revived during the following century. Much of Aphra Behn's work has been criticized for its coarseness, but it is important to see this as the reflection of a quite extraordinarily coarse age. It would be fairer to view her as a fiercely independent spirit and writer of real talent and warmth, the first woman playwright to live by her own lights and make her way in a man's profession.

Aphra Behn's *The Rover* spares no details of how hot-blooded Cavaliers spent their exile in Europe

EDWARD KYNASTON (c 1640-1706)

English actor. Before actresses were fully accepted on the Restoration stage, Ned Kynaston, the last great boy-heroine, set a formidable example of how to play female roles. At a performance of Ben JONSON's *Epicoene* Pepys found him "clearly the prettiest woman in the whole house", and COLLEY CIBBER described him as "so beautiful a youth that the ladies of quality prided themselves in taking him with them in their coaches to Hyde Park in his theatrical habit". Ladies did not drive Kynaston from the stage. Although some critics complained of his "disagreeable tones in speaking, something like whining", he successfully assumed male roles, SHAKESPEARE's Henry IV being one of his triumphs. "To the last of him his handsomeness was very little abated," wrote Cibber, "even at past sixty his teeth were sound."

JOHANNES VELTEN (1640-c 1693)

German actor-manager. The "father of the German theatre", Velten led an academic life in Wittenberg and Leipzig until 1665. In that year he joined the theatre company of Karl Paulsen, assuming the role of Paulsen's son-in-law in about 1672. From 1678 until his death he led his own troupe, the Kursächsische Komödianten, which played throughout Germany with a repertory of eighty-seven plays.

Velten's reputation was greatly exaggerated by misinformed admirers in the eighteenth century, but it is clear that he was one of the first German managers to use actresses instead of boys in female roles. He also enhanced the meagre German repertoire with fourteen plays by MOLIÈRE as well as with several English adaptations. His version of *Hamlet*, performed in 1686, was entitled *Fratricide Avenged*.

WILLIAM WYCHERLEY (1640-1716)

English playwright. Wycherley was born to wealthy parents in the west of England. Unable to resist the fleshly delights of London after the restoration of King Charles II, he quit his law studies and became a fashionable wit, a friend of the Duke of BUCKINGHAM and a favourite of the king. Four plays which were first performed between 1671 and 1676 distinguished him as a remarkable and serious talent in an age of dilettantes. But a poorly concealed secret marriage in 1680 annoyed his noble patrons into withdrawing their support; the playwright was left a social exile, whose shrewish wife let him out of the house only to go to the tavern next door. When her death a year later released him from the bondage of matrimony he was thrown into debtors' prison "where he continued", says a contemporary, "seven Years in a close Imprisonment, almost forgot by his old Friends". Although restored to royal favour on his release, he wrote no more plays in his bitter old age. At seventy-six, determined to deprive a nephew of his inheritance, he married a young bride. Eleven days later he died.

Two early comedies, *Love in a Wood* (1671) and *The Gentleman Dancing Master* (1672), are dwarfed by the reputations of the two later works. Today *The Country Wife* (1675) is regarded as one of the finest comedies in the language, although its coarse plot and obsessively salacious dialogue have troubled audiences and directors well into this century. Horner, the lecherous protagonist who publicly feigns impotence in order to make sexual conquests, was too vicious a hero for later tastes, yet too beguiling to ignore. In 1766 David GARRICK was forced to tame the original with his own gentle adaptation, *The Country Girl*. *The Plain Dealer* (1676) was Wycherley's greatest success in his own day. Inspired by MOLIÈRE's *Le Misanthrope*, it tells the story of Manly, whose rage against the hypocrisy of his age reveals a moral passion that is rarely evident in Restoration drama. "Manly" Wycherley, as he became known, still reigns as England's lewdest moralist.

Explicit references to sex kept
William Wycherley's work from
the stage for two hundred years

ARMANDE BÉJART (c 1642-1700)

French actress. To the friends of MOLIÈRE, Armande was the younger sister of the noted actress MADELEINE BÉJART; to his enemies (including the actor MONTFLEURY), she was Madeleine's daughter—perhaps even by Molière. Molière had good reason for promoting the former case, for in 1662 he married the young Armande. Within a year of marriage she had taken to the stage, and for the next decade created the roles of her husband's most celebrated heroines, including Elmire in *Le Tartuffe*, Élise in *L'Avare* and Célimène in *Le Misanthrope*, her greatest success. Whatever honour she brought to the plays of Molière, she brought none to Molière himself, whose devotion to his capricious wife was answered only with strife and infidelity. "If you know what I suffer you would pity me," the playwright said to the poet Chapelle.

After her husband's death, Armande married happily and assumed leadership of the Théâtre du Marais troupe, repeating her successes in the plays of Molière.

CHARLES CHEVILLET CHAMPMESLÉ (1642-1701)

French actor and playwright. Today Champmeslé is remembered more as a complacent cuckold than a man of the theatre, but he was an able actor in both comic and tragic roles and the writer of several successful comedies, including *Le Florentin* (1685). With his erring wife, the renowned MARIE DESMARES CHAMPMESLÉ, he acted for the Théâtre du Marais, the Hôtel de Bourgogne and later the Comédie-Française, always keeping on the best of terms with RACINE and other of his wife's lovers. Warned of his death in a dream, Champmeslé paid for a Mass to be said for himself and died the same day.

MARIE DESMARES CHAMPMESLÉ (1642-98)

French actress. "RACINE writes plays for La Champmeslé, not for posterity," wrote Mme de Sévigné, who was

Nell Gwynn (*left*, in a romantic study by Charles Landseer) was an actress for only five years, retiring at the age of twenty. Previously she had sold oranges at the Drury Lane Theatre. Charles II, a connoisseur of more tangible sweetmeats, plucked her from the stage

Charles-Rivière Dufresny (*right*) noted that the critics condemned comic playwrights either for copying or for not copying Molière. But his own carelessly witty plays delighted the Paris audiences

John Wilmot, second Earl of Rochester (*far right*, a portrait attributed to Jacob Huysmans). The obscenity of much of his verse continues to obstruct appreciation of his fine qualities as a satirist and poet. His tender love lyrics are often marred by excessive coarseness

familiar with all the essential Parisian gossip. The Lady she referred to was indeed a continual subject of speculation–mistress of the great playwright and for thirty years the unchallenged queen of French tragedy.

She was born Marie Desmares in Rouen, where she fell in love both with the stage and with the young actor CHARLES CHAMPMESLÉ. After a few seasons with provincial companies, the couple moved to Paris, where, in 1670, the unknown Marie appeared as a last-minute understudy in Racine's *Andromaque* at the Hôtel de Bourgogne and became a star overnight. Racine, terrified before the performance that the newcomer would ruin his masterpiece, fell on his knees with relief and admiration at its conclusion and promptly fell in love with his heroine. For the next seven years he was her coach and lover, creating for her the title roles of *Bérénice*, *Iphigénie* and *Phèdre*. Although she had her critics (including Racine's son Louis), everyone agreed that her voice was an exquisitely modulated instrument, capable of wringing tears from the driest eye in the house.

Marie was no more faithful to Racine than to her husband (the poet Boileau attributed six lovers to her), but she remained loyal to the stage, appearing with the Comédie-Française from its formation in 1680 until the last year of her life.

THOMAS SHADWELL (c 1642-92)

English playwright and poet. One of the unworthiest Poets Laureate of all time, Shadwell will live for ever in the annals of incompetence thanks to John DRYDEN's satirical poem "MacFlecknoe".

Shadwell's comedies, the best of which is *Bury Fair* (1689), were hastily constructed but popular for their crude satire of contemporary fashions. Although he borrowed freely from MOLIÈRE, Shadwell preferred to proclaim himself a disciple of Ben JONSON. It was Dryden's criticism of Jonson, in fact, that triggered off their interminable battle of words. Poor, fat, beer-swilling Shadwell was doomed to lose the unequal contest. Writing in ironic praise of the various sons of "Dullness", Dryden felled him at one blow:

"The rest to some faint meaning make pretence,
But Shadwell never deviates into sense."

CHRISTIAN WEISE (1642-1708)

German playwright. At a time when German drama was in a sorry state, one small outpost of intense theatrical activity was the Grammar School at Zittau, where Weise was headmaster. Sixty of the plays he wrote for the school's annual three-day festival survive. The actors were senior students, who, on the first day, presented a biblical work, on the second an historical one and on the third a "free" work, usually a comedy. One of Weise's innovations was his use of the traditional comic figure Pickelhering to make extempore comments. His serious works had a schoolmasterish tendency to preach.

JOHANN OSWALD HARMS (1643-1708)

German painter and stage designer. Harms benefited from extensive travel, particularly in Italy, where he absorbed the baroque spirit of painting and stagecraft. But in Vienna in 1673 he came to know the work of the great Italian designer Ludovico BURNACINI. Subsequently Harms interpreted the Italian example according to German motifs, establishing a native style in stage design. In 1677 he was named "Court and chief theatre painter" of Dresden; one of his first works there was for the high-sounding *Musical Opera and Ballet concerning the actions of the Seven Planets* (1678).

JOHN WILMOT
EARL OF ROCHESTER (1647-80)

English courtier, poet and playwright. In an age of the utmost licence, Rochester (against stiff competition) may well have been the greatest libertine of the Restoration. He arrived at Court at the age of seventeen, handsome, brilliant and a graduate of Oxford. Early escapades, such as the abduction of a carefully protected young heiress, spread his notoriety throughout the land. Later ones, such as the responsibility for thrashing John DRYDEN within an inch of his life, should probably not be laid at his door; indeed in later life Rochester forswore profanity and discovered his faith.

He was a writer of cynical and erotic poetry, which is sometimes of surpassing beauty. Of the two plays which have been ascribed to him, *Valentinian* was adapted from BEAUMONT and FLETCHER, while *Sodom*, so startlingly frank in its elegant pornography, still remains on the classified list at The British Library in London three hundred years later.

MME BEAUVAL (c 1648-1720)

French actress. A foundling raised by a washerwoman, then trained in two provincial theatre companies, Jeanne Olivier de Bourguignon married a fellow-player, Beauval, in about 1665. His amiable deference and her marked tendency to domineer produced a satisfactory marriage and anything from ten to twenty-eight children, coupled with a joint career on stage with the companies of MOLI-ÈRE, the Hôtel de Bourgogne and finally the new Comédie-Française. Mme Beauval was celebrated both for tragedy and comedy, and Molière incorporated her idiosyncratic and barely controllable giggle into the character of Nicole in *Le Bourgeois gentilhomme*. He also praised her hus-

band's "instinctive comprehension" of comic parts. Typically, when after an imagined slight Mme Beauval suddenly informed the Comédie-Française of her retirement, she informed her husband of his retirement too.

CHARLES-RIVIÈRE DUFRESNY
(c 1648-1724)

French playwright. Dufresny's striking resemblance to his ancestor Henri IV made him a great favourite of Louis XIV, who did his utmost to find suitable employment for this indolent and extravagant young man. He displayed a genius for landscape gardening, but soon tired of it, whereupon the king granted him a licence to manufacture ice, a privilege the playwright sold to pay off his debts.

Dufresny's first theatrical works were written for the resident Italian troupe in Paris, often in collaboration with Jean-François REGNARD. When the two quarrelled and split up, Dufresny continued to write successful prose comedies. Witty, realistic dialogue made up for the slack construction of his best works, *L'Esprit de contra-diction* (1700) and *Le Double veuvage* (1702). Any money he made was gambled away, but he usually managed to borrow from wealthy patrons. When unable to pay a laundry bill, he married his washerwoman, a lady of exceptionally repulsive appearance.

NELL GWYNN (1650-87)

English actress and orange-seller. Nell Gwynn is remembered today for the beauty and high spirits that attracted Charles II. A failure in tragedy, her success at comedy was due to quickness in body and wit, an instinct for daring and a peculiarly infectious laugh. Her origins had encouraged such devil-may-care qualities. Born in Hereford – or perhaps in an alley off Drury Lane (she herself said she was brought up in a brothel) – she was coached for the stage by her lover CHARLES HART. Nell made her debut in 1665, but retired five years later in the role of King Charles's mistress, after bewitching him in the Epilogue to DRYDEN's *Tyrannic Love*. She remained his favourite till he died, with his famous final directive: "Let not poor Nelly starve."

THOMAS OTWAY (1652-85)

English playwright. After a misguided attempt at acting on leaving Oxford, Thomas Otway won fame as a playwright with his tragedy *Alcibiades* (1675). This production unfortunately brought to his notice the actress Mrs BARRY, for whom, it is generally believed, he cherished a lifelong and tragically unrequited passion. His second play, *Don Carlos* (1676), was a great success and revealed in its preface Otway's social standing as a favourite of the Earl of ROCHESTER. But that favour proved capricious and, weary of love and of patrons, the playwright enlisted for military service in Flanders in 1678. In the years following his return he produced some of the finest work of the age, particularly in the verse tragedy *Venice Preserved* (1682). Its genuine, passionate torment, owing something to the example of RACINE, makes the heroic drama of many of his contemporaries seem like mechanical bombast.

Otway's abilities went almost unrewarded. (A man who once rebuked a noble for mistreating an orange-seller was not the type to inspire lordly condescension.) He died in an alehouse in the meanest poverty. The tale that he choked to death on the first crust of bread he had eaten for days may be apocryphal, but conveys a characteristic spirit: *se non e vero, e ben trovato*.

MICHEL BARON (1653-1729)

French actor and playwright. The orphan son of André Baron was performing with a juvenile theatrical troupe when he was discovered by MOLIÈRE. The playwright was quick to take advantage of the young actor's natural flair, his obsession with the stage and his dramatic gifts, and groomed him for stardom.

Baron's disillusionment with the low esteem in which the acting profession was held may have been responsible for his premature retirement. He had enjoyed consummate success with Molière's troupe, the Hôtel de Bourgogne and the Comédie-Française, but from 1691, for nearly thirty years, France's greatest actor lived quietly as a gentleman, writing occasional plays and acting in private performances. Then in 1720 he just as suddenly returned to the stage, playing the same heroic parts to the same rapturous acclaim.

Baron's legacy to the art he practised was exactly as he would have wished: a more natural and expressive style of acting and an elevation of the actor's social status.

NATHANIEL LEE (c 1653-92)

English playwright. Lee came to London from Oxford, keen to act. His ambition was supported chiefly by a splendid voice, but was doomed by ungovernable stage-fright. He turned to writing, and produced bombastic and extremely popular tragedies such as *The Rival Queens* (1677), gory theatrical showpieces only occasionally elevated by moments of real feeling. Lee's main characteristic was "unbounded fancy" to the extent of morbidity. He became an alcoholic, was confined to Bedlam from 1684 to 1683 and died after a drunken fall one night in the snow.

ANGELO COSTANTINI (c 1654-1729)

Italian actor. Born into a family of actors, Costantini first came to public notice in Parma and Venice as a Harlequin. (His brother, Antonio, and son, Gabriele, were both later to achieve fame in the role.) Called to Paris, he found DOMENICO BIANCOLELLI unwilling to admit a second Harlequin at the Théâtre Italien, so he devised a new (unmasked) character called Mezzetino.

In 1697 Louis XIV closed the theatre, angry at the caricaturing of his mistress, Mme de Maintenon, by the Italians (an incident for which the Costantini family were widely held responsible). Angelo left on an unfortunate tour of Eastern Europe, where the Elector of Saxony effectively ended his stage career with twenty years' imprisonment for flirting with a royal favourite.

JEAN-FRANÇOIS REGNARD (1655-1709)

French playwright. Regnard was a charming, rich dilettante who, with little apparent effort, assumed the mantle of MOLIÈRE as France's leading comic writer. But long before achieving this theatrical status, he had established a glamorous reputation with picturesque accounts of his own youthful adventures. Pursuit of a married lady led to his capture by pirates, who sold him as a slave to a Turk. By the time of his ransom Regnard had become chief cook for his master. After his release he continued to travel widely, even visiting the far north of Lapland.

Regnard's works, full of intrigue and joyful immorality, are closer to Italian comedy than to Molière. As his mastery of verse improved, so did his plays; *Le Légataire universel* (1708) was his crowning achievement. With *Les Folies amoureuses* (1704) it remained in the repertory of the Comédie-Française for 200 years, in part, no doubt, because of the rascally servant character who foreshadows the plays of BEAUMARCHAIS.

JEAN-GALBERT DE CAMPISTRON (1656-1723)

French playwright. More than a hundred years after his death, Campistron was immortalized in a line of verse by Victor HUGO, but hardly in the way he would have liked. "*Sur le Racine mort le Campistron pullule!*" effectively describes him as a maggot crawling over the body of the dead RACINE, a libellous judgement if only because Campistron wrote during his master's lifetime. Productions of *Alcibiade* and *Andronic* in 1685 were extremely well received, as was *Tiridate* (1691), a shameless imitation of *Phèdre*, in which the hero is consumed by incestuous passion for his sister.

FERDINANDO GALLI-BIBIENA (1657-1743)

Italian stage designer. Throughout the eighteenth century the Bibiena dynasty designed entertainments and theatres for almost every royal house in Europe. Bibiena was the birthplace of Giovanni Maria Galli, a minor artist, whose two orphaned sons, Ferdinando and Francesco, were brought up by their father's colleagues, the former specializing in painting, the latter in architecture.

Ferdinando was for twenty-eight years chief painter to the Duke of Parma. Later he worked in Barcelona and then for the Emperor Charles VI in Vienna. When encroaching blindness threatened his career, his third son, GIUSEPPE BIBIENA, succeeded him. Ferdinando's ideas on "angle perspective" were not original, but he was the first to exploit them systematically. The centre of the

Much desir'd in England: The first actresses

In the vast public theatres of Elizabethan England, nobody minded that women's parts were played by boys. In the more intimate court theatres of the reign of Charles I, however, audiences began to realize that something was missing, for many of them had travelled in Europe and seen French and Italian actresses. It remains a mystery why women did not appear on English stages sooner than they did. The Restoration of Charles II quickly made up for lost time. During his long exile in Paris, Charles had developed a taste for playgoing and actresses and was determined to continue to enjoy these pleasures on his return to London. The King's charter to the theatre managers Thomas KILLIGREW and William DAVENANT contained much pious humbug, stating that in old plays "the women's parts therein have been acted by men in the habit of women, at which some have taken offence". Women were therefore permitted to give "harmless delight" and "useful and instructive representations of human life".

The role of first English actress is usually granted to Margaret Hughes, who played Desdemona in 1660 and later became mistress of the King's cousin, Prince Rupert. Such was the usual destiny of an attractive actress, for the theatre was little more than a noisy bawdy-house. (For a fee, the beaux could go round to the ladies' dressing-rooms.) Small wonder that, in order to protect his leading ladies, William Davenant arranged for Mrs Saunderson, Mrs Davenport, Mrs Davies and Mrs Long to lodge in his own house. Mrs Saunderson, the least attractive, won most renown for her acting, marrying Thomas BETTERTON and excelling in SHAKESPEARE opposite her husband. Like Lady Davenant before her, she took young actresses into her house and trained them. Among these were Elizabeth BARRY and Anne BRACEGIRDLE: the first great female stars of the London stage.

In an age when the words "actress" and "whore" were almost synonymous, those that married, married actors. The others, whose salaries were half those of their male counterparts, could only hope to find rich protectors, who would settle money on them. The classic case, of course, was Nell GWYNN, pictured below.

Towards the end of the century, English actresses began to win respect for their professional talents, as their French counterparts already had. Mrs Barry and Mrs Bracegirdle became powerful voices in theatre politics, and the system of benefit performances augmented the salaries, at least of the successful. Of course actresses still had lovers and protectors, but they could now dictate the terms (Mrs Barry's were notoriously steep). Their unorthodox morality even came to be accepted in polite society.

stage shows the corner of a building, and there are two vanishing-points, one on either side, set low to create an illusion of soaring height.

Francesco's greatest contribution was to improve the audience's view of the stage. The raked seating of his theatres in Rome, Vienna, Verona and Nancy has been copied right down to this century. Antonio, Ferdinando's fourth son, studied under his uncle and designed the Teatro Comunale of Bologna, while two other sons worked mainly in Prague and Mannheim. The Bibiena theatre, a Baroque wonderland of decoration and illusion, was a central image of culture in the eighteenth century.

ELIZABETH BARRY (1658-1713)

English actress. When the management of the Dorset Garden Theatre despaired of making an actress of the young Elizabeth Barry and discharged her after a year, the Earl of ROCHESTER protested that a girl could hardly be expected to portray a passion she had never felt. By coaching her first in passion and then in acting, he produced the greatest leading lady of the age. "In the art of exciting pity," wrote COLLEY CIBBER, "she had a power beyond all actresses I have yet seen." At her best playing opposite Thomas BETTERTON in OTWAY's tragedies, she was unmatched as Monimia in *The Orphan* and Belvidera in *Venice Preserved*.

Otway's passionate feelings for Mrs Barry were never returned, but the loves of many others were during her long and scandal-ridden career. In the theatre she usually behaved with dignity, although in one notorious incident she found an opportunity during a production of NATHANIEL LEE's *The Rival Queens* to stab and wound a rival actress on stage.

THOMAS SOUTHERNE (1660-1746)

English playwright. Born in Ireland, Southerne adapted easily to London literary life. He was befriended by John DRYDEN and while still very young won reputation and wealth from his ephemeral, sensational plays. *The Loyal Brother* (1682), a piece of Tory propaganda, was followed by three comedies heavy with sex and corruption. Although discerning enough to hail his protégé William CONGREVE as the new Dryden, he himself forsook comedy for melodrama based on the popular novels of Aphra BEHN. *The Fatal Marriage* (1694) and *Oroonoko* (1695) were resounding successes and survived well into the eighteenth century.

FLORENT CARTON DANCOURT (1661-1725)

French playwright and actor. When Dancourt fell in love with the actress Marie-Thérèse Lenoir de Thorillière (1663-1725), daughter of one of MOLIÈRE's troupe, he immediately abandoned his law studies for the stage. Dancourt, a fine comic actor, but ponderous in tragedy, and his wife, described as "good, when she could be bothered", joined the Comédie-Française while still young and grew to be hardy and beloved perennials in their more than thirty years of service with the company.

Dancourt's comedies give a vivid, satirical portrait of a society obsessed with money and social status. *Le Chevalier à la mode* (1687) clearly established his superiority as a playwright (if not as an actor) over his brother-in-law, MICHEL BARON. It was followed by *La Maison de campagne* (1688), which was translated into English by John VANBRUGH, but many of his fifty plays treated subjects of only ephemeral interest. He retired in 1718, to write psalms and supervise the building of his tomb.

EVARISTO GHERARDI (1663-1700)

Italian actor. Gherardi's father, Giovanni, came to Paris as Flautino, so-called for his ability to imitate musical instruments with his voice. After an unusually complete education in philosophy, languages and presumably music, Evaristo took over as Harlequin at the Théâtre Italien in Paris. His brief career ended after a fall on the stage of a private theatre.

JOHN VANBRUGH (1664-1726)

English architect and playwright. Vanbrugh's Flemish extraction proved no obstacle to his becoming an archetypal English gentleman: bluff, courageous, witty and above all supremely confident of his own abilities. He could sit down and design a country house, write a comedy or dash off a translation, all with equal facility. Even a spell in the Bastille failed to curb his happy creativity. While a young officer, he visited Calais and was inexplicably arrested as a spy. Imprisoned for eighteen months, he is said to have passed the time working on his comedy *The Provok'd Wife* (1697).

The unrealized potential of the characters in COLLEY CIBBER's *Love's Last Shift* prompted Vanbrugh to write a sequel, *The Relapse, or Virtue in Danger* (1696). Two plots are uneasily welded together, but in Lord Foppington and Sir Tunbelly Clumsey he revealed his unrivalled talent for caricature. *The Provok'd Wife* has a better-contrived plot than *The Relapse*, and the cowardly, drunken Sir John Brute, who drives his wife to the point of adultery, is a magnificent creation. Vanbrugh's style was rough and colloquial in contrast to the careful elegance of William CONGREVE. (To Cibber his dialogue "seem'd to be no more than his common conversation committed to paper".) But his absurd characters and mastery of comic situations place him among the greatest of Restoration dramatists.

Attacks on the immorality of his plays combined with the demands of his new career as an architect put an end to any original writing for the stage, but he continued translating from the French. *The Confederacy* (1705), based on Florent DANCOURT's *Les Bourgeoises à la mode*, was an immense success once it had left Vanbrugh's own Queen's Theatre. The appalling acoustics in this huge building made it the one failure in his career. His greatest designs, notably Castle Howard and Blenheim Palace, were controversial but won acceptance through the overwhelming impression created by their sheer size.

Sir John finally returned to the stage two years after his death. *A Journey to London*, completed by Cibber as *The Provok'd Husband* (1728), showed that Vanbrugh had lost none of his old vigour.

CATERINA BIANCOLELLI (c 1665-1716)

Italian actress. The daughter of one of the great Commedia dell' Arte actors, DOMENICO BIANCOLELLI, Caterina was as celebrated a Columbina as her grandmother had been before her. In fact Columbina became her stage name, though her vivacity and intelligence, grace and charming voice fitted her for any part. A Parisian favourite from her debut with the Théâtre-Italien in 1683, she retired when it closed in 1697, declining to join the Théâtre-Français.

SUSANNAH CENTLIVRE (c 1667-1723)

English playwright and actress. Although she never won great fame as an actress, Susannah Centlivre was a popular provincial player with a singular talent for interpreting men's roles. Curiously, it was while appearing as Alexander the Great at Windsor that she fascinated her third and last husband, Joseph Centlivre. He was chef to the royal family and their marriage permitted the poet Alexander Pope to mock Susannah as "the cook's wife in Buckingham Court". As a playwright she was worthy of more consideration and enjoyed considerable success. Originally writing to support herself after the death of her second husband in a duel, she produced nineteen plays, almost all comedies. Sometimes criticized for coarseness, their overall effect is witty, lively and attractive. The best of them, such as *The Wonder: A Woman Keeps a Secret* (1714) and *A Bold Stroke for a Wife* (1718), were performed throughout the eighteenth century. David GARRICK chose the former for his farewell appearance in 1776.

ALAIN-RENÉ LE SAGE (1668-1747)

French novelist and playwright. Le Sage's considerable literary industry was forced on him when an uncle squandered his inheritance. From the time of his marriage in 1694 he supported his family exclusively by writing, achieving fame, but never great wealth, with novels such as *Gil Blas* and numerous works for the stage. His early plays were Spanish adaptations, the one-act comedy *Crispin, rival de son maître* (1707) being his first original piece and an indisputable success. The Comédie-Française rejected his next comedy *Les Étrennes*, but Le Sage reworked and expanded it into *Turcaret* (1709), the most remarkable piece of satire since MOLIÈRE. Before the première, he refused a large bribe to withdraw it, and the play's scathing depiction of greed and callous opportunism, particularly in the world of finance, caused a sensation. Le Sage later ceased writing for the Comédie-Française, objecting partly to the grand style of acting and partly to their tampering with an author's text. He spent the rest of his dramatic career producing over a hundred sketches for the Théâtre de la Foire, the unofficial troupes that performed at fairs and festivals.

Although he had devoted much of his life to the theatre, Le Sage was bitterly disappointed when two of his three sons insisted on becoming actors. Under the stage-name of Montménil, René-André Le Sage won especial renown for his performance in his father's *Turcaret* with the Comédie-Française.

WILLIAM CONGREVE (1670-1729)

English playwright. "A spoilt child of life and art", Congreve dismissed his own remarkable talent as cavalierly as he would a tiresome mistress, thereby depriving the English stage of its greatest comic playwright since the great Ben JONSON.

Born near Leeds into an old Staffordshire family, he was raised and educated in Ireland, where his father was an army officer. In England he made a pretence of studying law, but soon began frequenting literary circles. When he showed his new friend John DRYDEN a comedy he had written some years earlier to amuse himself while ill, the great poet pronounced it the most brilliant first play he had ever seen. With Dryden's help *The Old Bachelor* was produced in 1693, assuring overnight fame for its author. Later that year Congreve presented *The Double-Dealer*, a better though less successful play than its predecessor. A third comedy, *Love for Love* (1695), was as clear a triumph as the first work, and his only tragedy, *The Mourning Bride* (1697) (though neglected today), brought him renewed acclaim. But in 1700, *The Way of the World*, now regarded as his masterpiece, was received with little more than indifference, and Congreve vowed

Le Sage (*above*) was the first important French writer to live by his pen

Elizabeth Barry (*above*) was taken into the country by the notorious Earl of Rochester to learn her craft

As well as writing plays **Vanbrugh** (*below*) designed some of the largest buildings in England

A reign of pleasure

When Charles Stuart returned to England in 1660 to become Charles II, he found a country that had lain for more than ten years under a strict Puritan rule. Immediately the new king reversed the dour order of the preceding decade. He restored the Anglican faith as the official religion, reinstated the old noble families as social and political leaders, and encouraged all the amusements in which healthy young men like himself delighted: riding, fencing and hunting; women, gambling and wine; music, dance and, of course, the theatre. A vast number of his serious-minded subjects were horrified by such goings-on in the capital, but Charles himself was unrepentant. "God will never damn a man for allowing him a little pleasure," said the Merry Monarch.

Charles and his Court took pleasure very seriously indeed; they worked hard to appear frivolous and reckless. "To be easy oneself and to make everybody else so," was Charles's own definition of a gentleman, but in practice this philosophy meant that a man was "easy" towards money, easy towards women and easy towards death. The young lords and ladies of Restoration England were a cynical crowd. They had seen religions come and go, alliances betrayed and dead men carted like rubbish through the streets of London. It is no wonder that their drama should have been so insistent upon wit and sexual pleasure – so determinedly amoral.

With few exceptions, playwrights of the Restoration did not consider themselves professional writers. A reputation as a serious dramatist might have ruined a young rake's advancement in this casual society. Most men of talent would have looked for their model to the gifted and depraved Sir George ETHEREGE, whose three plays appeared over a period of twelve years. The last and best of these comedies, *The Man of Mode*, was a looking-

Martin Powell directs a performance of *A Tale of A Tub*. He stands in front of the stage of his puppet theatre, in the Covent Garden district of London, wielding a wand which he used to help explain the action. Powell appears also to have toured widely and successfully on the Continent with his spectacular and original troupe of marionettes and their operators

Joseph Addison (*left*) looks on while his friend Martin Folkes examines a seal in Button's Coffee House, Covent Garden. Coffee houses were popular meeting-places for intellectuals in the seventeenth century; Pope, Dryden and Steele all frequented Button's, whose owner had worked for Addison

Colley Cibber (*below*) takes a pinch of snuff. He was a notoriously rude and vain man who nevertheless knew how to make a play successful. His version of Shakespeare's *Richard III* remained the definitive performing edition for over a hundred years

glass for courtly society. Dorimant, its elegant and womanizing hero, was generally presumed to have been modelled on the EARL OF ROCHESTER. Sir Fopling Flutter, the ridiculous man of mode of the title, was a spiteful portrait of Beau Hewit, an affected contemporary. "Easy Etherege", as he was known, broke his neck in a drunken fall down a flight of stairs.

Sir Charles SEDLEY was another profligate playwright, whose lyric poetry is still justly praised. Characteristically, his companion Rochester admired the seductive quality of his verse:

Sedley has that prevailing gentle art,
That can, with a resistless charm impart
The loosest wishes to the chastest heart.

Other great "playwrights" of the Restoration never wrote a play at all. Charles Sackville, the Earl of Dorset, was an attractive and talented man who led a charmed life. "I know not how it is," said the admiring Rochester, "but my Lord Dorset can do

anything, and yet is never to blame." "Anything" included the murder of an innocent tanner whom he had mistakenly believed to be a thief, and a notoriously high-spirited brawl in a Covent Garden tavern. Yet Sackville was one of the most respected arbiters of literary taste, advising William WYCHERLEY on *The Plain Dealer* and the DUKE OF BUCKINGHAM on *The Rehearsal*. He just didn't have time to write plays himself. "He was so lazy," wrote a contemporary, "that though the King seemed to court him to be a favourite, he would not give himself the trouble that belonged to that post".

The unreigned self-indulgence of the Restoration lasted scarcely more than two decades. Rakes and wits died young or turned respectable. In the theatres sentimentality supplanted cynicism. Writing in 1702, the playwright John Dennis bemoaned the demise of the idle and educated audiences of the Restoration. "For that was an age of Pleasure," he concluded, "and not of Business."

never again to write for the stage.

His reaction may have been due to honest anger compounded by uncertain health, but throughout his short career Congreve had never regarded himself as a mere literary professional. Playwriting was a gentlemanly accomplishment, one facet of the life of a wit in Restoration society. It may well have been that the public rejection of his last and best play was a pretext for a retirement he desired in any case. Certainly, outside of two librettos and a small share in an adaptation from MOLIÈRE, he exerted himself no further for the theatre. In all respects he led the life of a gentleman, cultivating a wide range of literary and aristocratic friends, who cherished his company, and enjoying very close (though indeterminate) relationships with the actress Mrs BRACEGIRDLE and the Duchess of Marlborough. Despite later blindness and ill health, he cultivated such acquaintances until his death after a carriage accident.

The wit and invention of Congreve's dialogue increases with each play, but his works reveal a corresponding advance in feeling and moral refinement. The marvellous scene from *The Way of the World* in which Mirabell and Millamant discuss their forthcoming marriage is unsurpassed as repartee; it also enshrines a view of marital relations at once civilized and tender.

But the easy grace of the Restoration did not encourage profundity, and Congreve, its greatest playwright, casually renounced his literary pastime.

MARTIN POWELL (fl 1709-14)

English puppeteer. The hunchbacked Powell first made his reputation in the fashionable resort of Bath. He then played five consecutive seasons in his own London theatre before returning to the obscurity of the fairgrounds. Competing for the first time against flesh and blood rivals of the Drury Lane Theatre and the opera, Mr Punch and his fellow puppets acquitted themselves with honour. They were large marionettes, perhaps as tall as three feet high, for on one famous occasion Mr Punch did battle with a live pig. This was in a parody of Italian opera, one of the most popular features of their

extensive and original repertoire.

Powell was assisted by his "servants" and at least two actresses, who received benefit performances just like leading ladies of the stage. His London theatre boasted magnificent perspective scenery, spectacular machines, footlights and even an orchestra.

COLLEY CIBBER (1671-1757)

English playwright, actor and manager. Cibber bore the most withering censure that his censorious age could provide. True to prediction, all his merits (along with his numerous vices) have survived.

The young Cibber turned to playwriting when pressure from his growing family impelled him to supplement his modest income as an actor. *Love's Last Shift* (1696) established him as a brilliant comic playwright and gave the stage another absurd Restoration fop (played by Cibber himself) in the person of Sir Novelty Fashion. Further successful comedies such as *The Careless Husband* (1704) combined wit with sentiment, cannily exploiting his audiences' fashionable readiness to weep. Quick to respond to popular taste, he rewrote *Richard III* (1700) to everyone's (except possibly SHAKESPEARE's) satisfaction. In 1710 he became one of the managers of the Drury Lane Theatre, while continuing to act and write. His surprising and controversial appointment as Poet Laureate in 1730 crowned his career and further infuriated his enemies.

Today Cibber is remembered for his gossipy and informative autobiography – and for his extreme unpopularity with men of genius. His facility, success, supreme self-confidence and unfailing opportunism attracted the withering scorn of Alexander Pope, Henry FIELDING and Samuel JOHNSON, among others. Cibber was unabashed; he loved the theatre and rendered it good service. His best role was himself, and he played it with spirit and conviction.

JOSEPH ADDISON (1672-1719)

English essayist, poet and playwright. Son of a churchman, classical scholar, man of letters and statesman, Addison

George Farquhar's *The Constant Couple* (*above*) contained the popular "breeches part" of Sir Harry Wildair. It was a favourite role of actresses

The blood-and-thunder plays of **Crébillon** (*below*) were immensely popular throughout the eighteenth century, though they made very little money for the dramatist

was too much the moralist ever to be a good playwright. His Roman tragedy *Cato*, however, had a famous opening night and an extended run in 1713, principally because of its relevance to contemporary politics. Both Whigs and Tories identified with the hero in his commitment to liberty and justice against Caesar's growing power. An equally sententious comedy, *The Drummer*, failed in 1715.

RICHARD STEELE (1672-1729)

English essayist, playwright and manager. After an Oxford education, Steele became a Guards officer sufficiently dashing to fight a duel (and father an illegitimate child). His subsequent repentance coloured all his literary work, including hundreds of moral essays and four comedies. *The Funeral* (1701) was a lively success, but *The Lying Lover* (1703) and *The Tender Husband* (1705) were marred by obvious moralizing. Thereafter Steele was connected with the stage as governor of the Drury Lane Theatre and editor of a theatrical paper. His last play was *The Conscious Lovers* (1722), a tearful comedy that perfectly judged the sentimental spirit of the times.

MARC-ANTOINE LEGRAND (1673-1728)

French actor and playwright. Legrand's thick body and grotesque face were natural assets to his comic skill, but they thwarted his persistent ambition to succeed in tragedy. He was more successful as a teacher (instructing Adrienne LECOUVREUR in acting, tradition has it) and as a playwright, specializing in comedy and drama directly drawn from contemporary events. His most notable coup was *Cartouche* (1721), based on the career of a famous bandit. Legrand began writing the play when its subject was arrested, used the convict as technical advisor, and tidily closed a profitable run the night before the poor man's execution.

ANNE BRACEGIRDLE (c 1674-1748)

English actress. For much of her childhood, Anne Bracegirdle was cared for by the actors Thomas and Mary BETTERTON. She is reputed to have appeared on stage from the age of six, making her debut as a page carrying Mrs BARRY's train. Later these two actresses were to reign jointly as leading ladies of Betterton's company, but as Mrs Bracegirdle never attempted any of the roles Mrs Barry had created, direct comparisons were avoided. Fortunately William CONGREVE's comedies contained fine parts for both actresses, Mrs Bracegirdle being the original Millamant in *The Way of the World* and Angelica in *Love for Love*.

Mrs Bracegirdle's virtuous conduct was as well publicized as her rivals' affairs, but this merely added extra spice to her considerable attractions. Congreve's devotion to her (he is said to have secretly married her) was rivalled by that of the playwright Nicholas ROWE, who, according to COLLEY CIBBER, seemed to make "his private court to her in fictitious characters". As soon as she felt her charms were waning, she retired and after 1707 returned to the stage only to support Betterton in his benefit performances.

PROSPER JOLYOT DE CRÉBILLON (1674-1762)

French playwright. The name of Crébillon epitomizes the degenerate state of French tragedy, fifty years after its golden age. The principal ingredients of his works were parricide, infanticide and incest. After his first play,

Idoménée (1705), the poet Boileau described him as "RACINE drunk", though less discerning critics soberly judged him to be every bit Racine's equal. His most successful farrago of blood, lust and disguise was *Rhadamiste et Zénobie* (1711), in which a father and two sons are all in love with the same woman.

A pitiful wreck of a man in his old age, Crébillon nevertheless remained VOLTAIRE's only serious rival as a writer of tragedy, and as such was shamefully exploited by enemies of the great philosopher.

NICHOLAS ROWE (1674-1718)

English playwright. To eighteenth-century audiences, even to the usually perceptive Samuel JOHNSON, Rowe's tragedies were among the finest in the English language. He qualified as a barrister, but the success of *The Ambitious Stepmother* (1700) and the charms of the actress Anne BRACEGIRDLE persuaded him to continue to write for the stage. By far the most popular of his plays was *The Fair Penitent* (1703), an adaptation of *The Fatal Dowry* by MASSINGER and FIELD. The role of "Gay Lothario" was a fine vehicle for Thomas BETTERTON and later David GARRICK, while Elizabeth BARRY, Anne OLDFIELD and Sarah SIDDONS all shone as Calista.

Rowe's edition of SHAKESPEARE's plays was a piece of sound scholarship, but his own attempts to write "in imitation of Shakespeare's style" *The Tragedy of Jane Shore* (1714) and *The Tragedy of Lady Jane Grey* (1715) had little in common with the master's works. He did at least introduce a moral, patriotic tone that had long been lacking on the English stage, for which he was duly rewarded, becoming Poet Laureate in 1715.

SCIPIONE MAFFEI (1675-1755)

Italian man of letters and playwright. A "Renaissance man" two centuries behind the times, Maffei wrote prolifically on history, philosophy, politics, science and theology and was also a pioneer in archaeological fieldwork. When he found time for drama, he demanded an end to imitations of French tragedy and a return to the purer Italian models of the sixteenth century. His own theatrical output was necessarily small: two rather lifeless comedies and *Merope* (1713), a remarkably successful tragedy, which was admired throughout Europe. Both VOLTAIRE and Vittorio ALFIERI were impressed enough to write their own versions of the play.

JOSEPH ANTON STRANITZKY (1676-1726)

Austrian actor. Stranitzky founded a tradition of popular Viennese theatre that was to last for over a century. Hanswurst, the clown he created and frequently represented on stage, was a character of mixed parentage, his costume deriving partly from local peasant dress, partly from the Commedia dell' Arte. In the many scenarios written by Stranitzky himself, Hanswurst's role is not fixed. In farces, he is usually the central character, while in sentimental love stories he is a servant who makes down-to-earth and ribald comments on the action.

GEORGE FARQUHAR (1678-1707)

Irish-born playwright. Alcohol and perennial poverty cut tragically short the life of one of England's most promising playwrights. Farquhar was early attracted to the theatre, but after a brief spell on the Dublin stage found he had little talent for acting, and went to London to try his hand at writing comedies. *Love and a Bottle* (1699) was not well received, but his second effort, *The Constant Couple or a Trip to the Jubilee* (1699), was an immense success. Sir Harry Wildair from that play became a classic stage character and made a name for the actor Robert Wilks, who became Farquhar's closest friend.

Three relative failures and an unfortunate marriage damaged Farquhar's health and finances, but did not dampen his spirits. *The Recruiting Officer* (1706) at last brought some earthy, country realism to a stage too-long populated by fashionable city fops. In an age which delighted in women masquerading as men, Anne OLDFIELD's appearance in breeches as Sylvia guaranteed the play's success, but Farquhar's circumstances refused to improve. Wilks had to give him twenty guineas to keep him alive while he wrote his last and greatest play, *The Beaux' Stratagem* (1707). The author did not live to enjoy the fruits of its success, and with his death the era of Restoration Comedy came to an end.

PIER FRANCESCO BIANCOLELLI (1680-1734)

Italian actor. The youngest son of DOMENICO BIANCOLELLI, Pier Francesco was known as Dominique Fils. On the threshold of his career, the Théâtre Italien in Paris was closed and he was forced to tour Italy and the provinces of France, making his name as Harlequin and Pierrot. These were unhappy years; his son died and later his wife went mad.

When the Italian company was re-formed in Paris in 1716, Biancolelli was naturally a leading member, taking the part of the valet, Trivellino, who appears in several of MARIVAUX's comedies, and writing many successful parodies of productions at the rival Comédie-Française. During his lifetime the Italian theatre in Paris evolved from clowning to the most sophisticated French comedy.

PHILIPPE NÉRICAULT DESTOUCHES (1680-1754)

French playwright. The early comedies of Destouches, especially *L'Irrésolu* (1713) and *Le Triple Mariage* (1716), display such a sure sense of theatre that critics were convinced he must have been an actor. His career took a new turn when he was included in a diplomatic mission to England about 1717, spending six years there before returning to Paris and to writing. His adventures in England, which included a clandestine marriage, he used in the plot of *Le Philosophe Marié* (1727).

His best known play, *Le Glorieux* (1732), is a study of an arrogant, impoverished count obliged to marry a rich bourgeoise to save his estates. Like much of his later work, it is strangely cold, not funny enough to produce laughter nor pathetic enough to produce tears.

BARTON BOOTH (1681-1733)

English actor. To his wealthy family's distress, Booth left Trinity College, Cambridge, to join a company of strolling players. So great was his ability that before he was twenty he was at the prestigious Lincoln's Inn Fields Theatre, where he rapidly became second only to the great Thomas BETTERTON, whose Hamlet he put into the shade with his memorable and haunting Ghost.

He seized his chance after Betterton's death, and his success in the title role of Joseph ADDISON's *Cato* brought considerable financial rewards from grateful Tory politicians (who saw themselves portrayed as the hero). After obtaining a one-third share in the management of the Drury Lane Theatre, Booth grew lazy, but could still rally to create a fine Othello.

ANNE OLDFIELD (1683-1730)

English actress. According to legend, Anne Oldfield was discovered by the playwright George FARQUHAR, who overheard her reading in the back room of the tavern where she worked. At Farquhar's insistence, Christopher Rich grudgingly took her on at the Drury Lane Theatre, but for some time she failed to fulfil her promise. Then the astute COLLEY CIBBER gave her the part of Lady Betty Modish in his own play, *The Careless Husband*, and her reputation was finally secured. Appropriately she was at her best in roles by Farquhar: Sylvia in *The Recruiting Officer* and Mrs Sullen in *The Beaux' Stratagem*.

Anne Oldfield always preferred playing comedy to tragedy, but on the retirement of Mrs BARRY and Mrs BRACEGIRDLE, all their great tragic roles were hers for the taking. Praised for her clear delivery, her sense of dress and above all for the beauty and expressiveness of her eyes, she enjoyed triumph upon triumph right up to her death. Despite two long-standing public liaisons (and two illegitimate children), she was deemed respectable enough to be buried in Westminster Abbey.

LUDVIG HOLBERG (1684-1754)

Norwegian-born Danish historian, playwright, poet and essayist. The "Father of Danish literature" spent the first twenty-two years of his life in his native Norway. A man of unusual physical and intellectual energy, Holberg devoted his early manhood to epic wanderings around Europe. Having hardly any money, he travelled hundreds of miles on foot, nearly killing himself through hunger and exhaustion. The aim of this odyssey was to become familiar with all the current movements in European thought. He spent two years in Oxford teaching languages and the flute for a living and reading voraciously in the Bodleian Library. But it was France that influenced him the most, both in philosophy and the theatre, where his chief mentor was MOLIÈRE.

The year 1722 saw the opening of the first Danish-language theatre in Copenhagen, where Holberg was already an eminent professor. On the strength of this and his enormously successful mock-heroic poem "Peder Paars" he was made director. By 1727, when the theatre closed, he had written nearly thirty comedies. These were mostly satires of human folly; *Erasmus Montanus* (1723) mocked the pedantic academic; *Den politiske Kandestøber* (1722), the political know-all. The delightful *Jeppe paa Bjerget* (1722) is a portrait of the ignorant Danish peasant, downtrodden and drunk, but redeemed by his humour and common sense.

Holberg's plays are but a small fraction of his complete works, which include a history of Denmark, a satirical novel in the manner of Swift and countless philosophical essays, including a surprisingly modern discussion of the role of women in society. His extraordinary versatility and single-minded devotion to European culture was to prove the cornerstone of modern Danish literature.

JOHN GAY (1685-1732)

English playwright and poet. On the strength of just one play, the unassuming Gay became the most talked-about writer of the day. The furore provoked by *The Beggar's Opera* (1728) amazed his more illustrious contemporaries, the poets Pope and Swift, who had always regarded Gay as a likeable nonentity, a social and literary hanger-on.

Gay's early pastoral poetry was feeble, derivative stuff. Only when he turned to satire did he discover where his true talent lay. His first play to be performed, *The What D'ye Call It* (1715), is a lively farce, containing one of his best known ballads, "Twas when the seas were roaring", but its reception gave no indication of the success he was later to achieve. The original idea for *The Beggar's Opera* was tossed idly to Gay by Swift, who suggested that "A Newgate pastoral might make an odd pretty sort of thing." The satirizing of leading politicians as thieves, highwaymen and pimps drew a far wider audience than the London theatre had ever known; ballads from this musical play were on everybody's lips and Gay's fortune was made. A sequel, *Polly*, though banned from the London stage, was another instant best-seller.

Gay's services were now in universal demand. He completed the librettos of two operas but died at the height of his fame. No English playwright has ever been so honoured at his death as was Gay in his magnificent funeral in Westminster Abbey.

PIERRE CARLET DE CHAMBLAIN DE MARIVAUX (1688-1763)

French playwright, novelist and journalist. Throughout his youth and early manhood Marivaux seemed destined for a dazzling literary career. But life in the fashionable salons of Paris was so beguiling that the well-to-do young dilettante might never have begun work in earnest had he not lost all his money in a speculative Mississippi venture. In 1720, obliged at last to make his living as a professional writer, he started his own newspaper, *Le Spectateur français*, modelled on Joseph ADDISON's *Spectator*. He also became a brilliant and highly individual playwright.

Marivaux attempted various forms of comedy, but always returned to his favourite theme, the concealment and declaration of love, as in his two classic pieces, *Le Jeu de l'Amour et du Hasard* (1730) and *Les Fausses Confidences* (1737). The comedy lies in the nuances of the dialogue, as the lovers attempt to discover each other's true feelings. This verbal skirmishing became known as "marivaudage". A perceptive observer of feminine wiles, Marivaux was an accomplice, not a critic, of these society games.

These seemingly lightweight offerings seldom appealed to the audience of the Théâtre-Français, where one of Adrienne LECOUVREUR's rare failures was in the 1727 production of *La Surprise de l'amour*. VOLTAIRE accused Marivaux of "weighing flies' eggs on spider's web scales". It was not until the mid-nineteenth century that the accuracy of his psychological insights was fully appreciated. Thus Marivaux wrote mostly for the Théâtre Italien, which possessed in Silvia (Gianetta Benozzi) an actress equal to the subtlety of his plays. In recent years Madeleine RENAUD has skilfully evoked the original spirit of his delightful heroines.

ALEXIS PIRON (1689-1773)

French poet and playwright. Piron's first comedy, *Arlequin Deucalion* (1722), was designed to get round a law that forbade the use of dialogue at the Théâtre de la Foire (the Comédie-Française and the Comédie-Italienne shared a monopoly on dramatic productions). This "play" contained one speaking role, a great deal of mime and a talking parrot. A more serious comedy, *Les Fils ingrats* (1728), was a forerunner of the sentimental *comédies larmoyantes* of Pierre de LA CHAUSSÉE, but most of Piron's energies were devoted to annoying people with mischievous, witty epigrams. His best known play, *La Métromanie* (1738), satirizes his own mania for writing occasional verse. It also contains several hits at his lifelong enemy, VOLTAIRE.

In 1753 Piron was elected to the Académie Française but was immediately expelled, the king having recalled a notoriously obscene Priapic ode penned by the reckless Piron in his youth.

Ludvig Holberg (*below*) was the Danish Goethe. Historian, novelist and poet, he also single-handedly (and almost as an afterthought) founded a tradition of drama in the Danish language

The sensitive wit in the plays of **Pierre Marivaux** (*below*) has always charmed French audiences. Like his successor, Musset, he develops deep insight in the lightest of plots

Anne Oldfield (*above*), beautiful in figure and voice, reigned on the English stage at the beginning of the eighteenth century. Voltaire was delighted to discover that her clear delivery enabled him to understand a play in English

John Gay's *The Beggar's Opera* (*below*) was produced by John Rich, "making Gay rich and Rich gay". This raffish work in words and song was a great hit again in recent times when Brecht updated the satire in *The Threepenny Opera*

PIERRE-CLAUDE NIVELLE DE LA CHAUSSÉE (1692-1754)

French playwright. La Chaussée was over forty when he took up writing for the stage. All he had written before *La Fausse Antipathie* (1733) were some scabrous tales for the amusement of other idle, rich, young men like himself. The contrast between these tales and his sentimental, tear-jerking *comédies larmoyantes* provoked a great deal of comment, to which La Chaussée replied that he merely gave people what they wanted. His own behaviour, especially towards women, was also in marked contrast to the morality of his plays. *Le Préjugé à la mode* (1735), one of his most popular plays, was a glorification of the figure of the tender, loving wife. All his works enjoyed enormous success and established the handkerchief as an essential piece of playgoing paraphernalia.

ADRIENNE LECOUVREUR (1692-1730)

French actress. Throughout her brief career, Adrienne Lecouvreur was the unchallenged favourite of Parisian audiences. Competition was not strong; she was said to be the only actress at the Comédie-Française "capable of weeping or complaining without terrifying us, as the others do by their bawling". She had spent ten years in the provinces before her debut there in 1717 in Prosper de CRÉBILLON's *Electre*. Her triumph caused great jealousy back-stage, for the established actresses could not compete with her beauty and natural style of playing. Her voice was weak, but she made up for this with great control and clarity. Excelling in all the major tragic roles of RACINE and CORNEILLE, she was especially moving as Pauline in the latter's *Polyeucte*. Her weakness in comedy was usually overlooked by indulgent admirers.

Her lover (at least the most important one) was Maurice de Saxe, later to become Europe's greatest general, and she moved freely among the aristocracy. Yet so strong was the enmity of the church for the stage that she was buried at night in unconsecrated ground. The great atheist VOLTAIRE, who had been her close friend, was justifiably enraged, pointing out that in England that same year Anne OLDFIELD, an actress of no greater stature, had been buried in Westminster Abbey.

Adrienne Lecouvreur appeared in the leading roles of plays by her friend Voltaire at the Comédie-Française

JOHN RICH (c 1692-1761)

English actor-manager. Once, a nobleman whom John Rich had rebuked for crossing the stage during a performance drew his sword and, still rankling, returned later with hooligans determined to burn down the theatre. Apart from the isolated incident such as this, John was as popular as his father Christopher (a notoriously mean manager) had been unpopular, and suffered only the normal vexations of a manager's life. His achievements included the première of John GAY's *The Beggar's Opera*

(which was said to have made "Gay rich, and Rich gay") and, in 1732, the founding of a new theatre in Covent Garden, London.

Rich's most enduring contribution was the introduction of pantomime to England, which he presented every Christmas from 1717 to 1760 with himself as Harlequin.

DUFRESNE (1693-1767)

French actor. Dufresne delighted both himself and his audiences with his acting. He favoured the natural style of MICHEL BARON instead of stilted declamation, and recalled Baron in his splendid voice and presence, perhaps even surpassing him in good looks. Some critics thought he shared Baron's interpretative genius as well, but most found him "more dazzling than deep" and preferred him in lighter roles. Warranted or not, he was definitely Baron's equal in self-love. Though never realizing (or admitting) it, he provided the pattern for the vain and arrogant hero of DESTOUCHES's satire *Le Glorieux*, a part he played with real insight, to universal approval.

GEORGE LILLO (1693-1739)

English playwright. Lillo spent his early years as a jeweller in his father's shop, an experience of the tradesman's world that inspired his one famous play. *The London Merchant* caused a sensation in 1731 because it defied the classical requirement that tragedy present great actions and noble figures in elevated verse. Instead Lillo depicted the downfall of an apprentice seduced by a prostitute into murdering his uncle "in artless strains, a tale of private woe". The audience at its première had brought along copies of the old ballad on which the play was based, prepared to mock, but were moved to tears by its homely realism and moral sentiment. The work was a favourite throughout the eighteenth century, especially for holiday performances as a warning to apprentices. This new conception of domestic tragedy in prose influenced such continental playwrights as Denis DIDEROT, Gotthold LESSING and ultimately even IBSEN.

JAMES QUIN (1693-1766)

English actor. Quin was the last great exponent of grand and formal tragic acting before this style was swept aside by the free, intuitive technique of David GARRICK. In comic roles, however (above all as Falstaff), he performed much more naturally, revealing a warm and intelligent personality. He was popular both on stage and in society, despite an occasional outspokenness that led to two fatal duels. Their differences did not keep him and Garrick from eventually becoming friends, and on Quin's death Garrick wrote the epitaph.

VOLTAIRE (1694-1778)

French philosopher, novelist, historian, poet and playwright. Throughout his restless life Voltaire was involved with the theatre not only as author of more than fifty plays but as amateur actor and producer. His first work, *Oedipe* (1718), brought him fame and a return to favour, after one of his chronic scrapes with authority had deposited him in the Bastille. Another offence exiled him for two years to England, where he discovered the plays of SHAKESPEARE. Fascinated by the energy and variety of plot and character in England's greatest playwright, Voltaire tried to graft these characteristics to the French classical tradition. His first effort, *Brutus* (1730), was a failure, as was *Eriphyle* (1732), in which a *Hamlet*-style ghost only made the audience laugh. *Zaïre* (1732), however, was a great success, its combination of Moorish hero and Christian heroine inspired both by *Othello* and RACINE's *Bajazet*. Voltaire's purpose in adapting Shakespeare and in using exotic settings and sumptuous decor was to bolster the waning fortunes of pure French tragedy. But he soon realized that his innovations were only hastening its demise by indulging the popular taste for sensational effects. He reacted ultimately by repudiating Shakespeare as a "drunken savage" though an undoubted genius, and wrote his last plays only in strict classical form.

Voltaire's dramatic interest utilized only a fraction of the feverish energy that created *Candide*, thundering pronouncements, intellectual feuds, love affairs and a precarious domestic existence. Typically, his last residence incorporated property on both sides of the Franco–Swiss border to ensure a refuge from whichever government pursued him, and it was from here, in 1778, that Voltaire returned to Paris to oversee his last play, *Irène*. He received a tumultuous welcome at the opening night. But the excitement proved too much, and the theatre, fittingly, provided the last public occasion of his life.

François Marie Arouet (better known as **Voltaire**) derived his pen-name from an anagram of his surname and the initial letters LI– standing for *Arouet le jeune*

GIUSEPPE GALLI-BIBIENA
(1696-1757)

Italian theatre architect and stage designer. Giuseppe was perhaps the most illustrious member of the extraordinary family who were masters of Baroque stage design all over Europe. His father, FERDINANDO GALLI-BIBIENA, founded the dynasty, and Giuseppe succeeded him as Theatre Architect at the Court of Vienna in 1727. He had already served the Emperor Charles VI in Prague, creating the Castle Garden Theatre in 1723 and mounting magnificent open-air opera productions. Later, assisted by his son Carlo (1725–87), Giuseppe designed and built the Margrave's Opera House in Bayreuth (1744–48), beautifully integrating stage and auditorium in a masterpiece which still stands today. The use of transparent scenery was his own innovation, but above all Giuseppe carried on the family wizardry at painted perspective scenery, employing a diagonal instead of central viewpoint, which opened space dramatically through fabulously ornate columns and arches.

CAROLINE NEUBER (1697-1760)

German actress-manager. Caroline Neuber's elopement at twenty to escape an autocratic father gave early notice of her strong, independent character. She and her husband Johann spent ten years with provincial theatre companies before establishing their own troupe in Leipzig, with "die Neuberin", as she was known, determined to raise the crude contemporary standards of acting and repertoire. Johann Christoph GOTTSCHED, an outspoken partisan of French Classicism, shared her convictions, and in 1727 the Neuber company began to produce Gottsched's translations of RACINE and CORNEILLE, as well as original works that adhered to the exacting new standards. For some time the project had considerable impact, highlighted by the ritual burning in 1737 of Hanswurst, the stock figure of German rustic comedy. Caroline's dedication, acting prowess and skill as manager and teacher made her an ideal colleague, but gradually she grew as tired of Gottsched's inflexibility as she had of her father's. Finally, the playwright insisted his tragedy *Der sterbende Cato* be presented in Roman costume. "Die Neuberin"

Caroline Neuber was a most serious and high-minded actress, for many years a colleague of the intellectual playwright Gottsched

derided him by decking her actors in pink tights, then responded to his public rage with a prologue depicting him as a bat-winged and benighted pedant.

This episode ended a fruitful collaboration, but the Neubers were finding themselves in other difficulties as well. Tours to Hamburg and Russia had gone badly, partly due to Caroline's habit of lecturing the audience, and the troupe lost its favoured position in Leipzig. The long decline in their fortunes was speeded by the Seven Years War, during which Caroline and her husband died in impoverished retirement.

PIETRO METASTASIO (1698-1782)

Italian poet, librettist and playwright. An extremely precocious boy, Metastasio was taken up and trained by the Abbé Gravina of Rome's Arcadian Academy, who bequeathed him a large part of his estate. His graceful talent for poetry, singing and improvisation recommended him to salons and academies alike, and his popularity increased with the success of his opera libretto *Didone abbandonata* (1724) and an heroic play, *Catone in Utica* (1727). The former featured Marianna Bulgarelli, a noted singer and the first of three women, all named Marianna, who gave him aid and comfort. For fifty years he also enjoyed imperial favour at the Court of Vienna, producing there the long series of librettos for which he is best known, chief among them *La Clemenza di Tito* (1734) (later to find its most famous setting to music—albeit in an altered form—by Mozart). Metastasio's lyricism, as effortless as his life, rather excluded passion, but was ideal for the wedding of words and music.

JOHANN CHRISTOPH GOTTSCHED (1700-66)

German critic and playwright. According to GOETHE Gottsched was "tall, broad and awesome", physical characteristics that surprisingly had an early influence on his literary career. The would-be man of letters fled his native Prussia in 1724 to avoid recruitment into a special regiment of huge, oversized grenadiers and found Leipzig, his new home, an ideal centre for his ambitions. There as professor, journalist and leader of a learned society, he carried on a vigorous campaign to reform German literature. He loathed the theatre's anarchic blend of bombast and buffoonery (particularly the popular clown Hanswurst) and demanded a dignified new drama modelled on French Classicism. With his wife and disciples he began to create a dramatic repertoire of translations, adaptations and original works, which were performed by Caroline NEUBER's theatre company. Gottsched's influence was at its height in the 1730s, but his authoritarian views never went unchallenged. His own turgid but popular tragedy *Der sterbende Cato* (1732) was attacked as being borrowed from French and English sources. Gottsched and the equally strong-minded Neuber quarrelled over this production, among other things, and ended their alliance in 1741. Thereafter he was a spent force, however imposing, but his convictions had helped mould public taste and cleared the way for greater dramatists such as Gotthold Ephraim LESSING.

CHARLES MACKLIN (c 1700-97)

Irish actor. Macklin's restless energy led him from theatre to theatre for the best part of a century. A clown, a Harlequin and a keen boxer in his youth, in his later years he opened a tavern and ran a drama school.

Macklin made his name in 1741 when, at his suggestion, *The Merchant of Venice* was put on in its original form. Bastardized versions had made Shylock a cheap comic character; Macklin restored dignity and terror to the part. As a rule, the pre-eminence of David GARRICK and SPRANGER BARRY kept Macklin in supporting Shakespearean roles, but he once gave a memorable Macbeth at Covent Garden. Another incidence of his playing second fiddle to Garrick was his affair with the tempestuous actress Peg WOFFINGTON, who was for many years the mistress of Garrick.

Love à la Mode (1759) and *The Man of the World* (1781), two comedies written by Macklin himself, were extremely popular and provided the author with the opportunity to play Scotsmen less heroic than Macbeth: Sir Archy McSarcasm and Sir Pertinax McSycophant.

FRANÇOIS BOUCHER (1703-70)

French painter and designer. As a painter, Boucher is best known for his charming pictures of aristocrats at play in Arcadian landscapes. This atmosphere was in vogue on the stage as well, which made him the ideal master to provide sets, scenery and costumes for its pastoral swains and coquettes. He worked ingeniously for both the Paris Opéra and Opéra-Comique and, off-stage, illustrated the 1734 edition of MOLIÈRE's plays.

THEOPHILUS CIBBER (1703-58)

English actor. One of COLLEY CIBBER's "dozen or so" children, Theophilus was a byword for irresponsibility. Not lacking talent, which his father painstakingly encouraged, he was applauded as Pistol in *Henry IV* and as the first George Barnwell in George LILLO's *The London Merchant*. But his imprudence kept him in debt and trouble, forcing him to give benefit performances "for myself and my creditors" and ultimately to take money from his wife's lover while the three lived together. This scandal led to court action, a duel with James QUIN, the end of the marriage and a blight on his career. After years of hack-work he drowned in a storm while sailing to Dublin—"a fair player and sad rogue".

JOHANN FRIEDRICH SCHÖNEMANN (1704-82)

German actor. Schönemann had the good fortune to be a member of Caroline NEUBER's company in Leipzig at the time of her historic feud with the pedantic theorist Johann GOTTSCHED. In 1740, when Neuber went off to Russia in a huff, Schönemann took over what was left of the troupe and set off on the first of many financially successful tours of northern Germany.

A fine actor in his youth, especially as the comic valet in plays by MOLIÈRE, Schönemann neglected his duties in later years. He was so busy pursuing young actresses and buying horses that the direction of his forsaken company passed to the actor Konrad EKHOF.

HENRY FIELDING (1707-54)

English novelist and playwright. Fielding's brief but eventful career as a writer for the London stage had one momentous consequence: the advent of censorship in the theatre. It was largely the outspokenness of Fielding's satire that provoked Prime Minister Robert Walpole into passing the notorious Stage Licensing Act of 1737, empowering the Lord Chamberlain to prevent the production of any play. Not until 1968 was this act repealed.

Before arousing official disapproval, Fielding experimented with many genres besides satire: comedies in the style of CONGREVE, translations of MOLIÈRE, parodies and farces. *The Tragedy of Tragedies, or The Life and Death of Tom Thumb the Great* (1731), a lively burlesque of contemporary dramatists, remained in the repertory long after his political satires were forgotten.

Walpole had first been angered by the portrayal of corrupt election practices in *Don Quixote in England* (1734). In 1736 Fielding formed his own company at the Little Theatre in the Haymarket and abandoned all restraint. The highly successful *Pasquin* and *The Historical Register for the Year 1736* attacked the clergy, the Royal Family and Walpole himself.

As a magistrate and novelist, later in life Fielding

continued to campaign energetically for social reform. His first novel, *Joseph Andrews*, was intended merely as a burlesque, but while he never lost his contempt for the hypocrisy, meanness and corruption he saw in society, he found scope in the novel for a joyful celebration of humanity, an impulse which culminated in his masterpiece, *Tom Jones*.

BERNARDINO GALLIARI (1707-94)

Italian painter and stage designer. Bernardino was the acknowledged head of the Galliari dynasty, but his talents lay in figure-painting and landscapes; he was "quite incapable of doing a pedestal or a niche". This side of the business was therefore left to his brother, Fabrizio (1709–90). With other members of this closely knit family, they worked predominantly in Milan and Turin, but received frequent summonses to the courts of Austria and Germany.

CARLO GOLDONI (1707-93)

Italian playwright. Despite unrelenting opposition from the theatrical establishment, Goldoni realized his lifelong ambition, putting an end to the improvised buffoonery of the Commedia dell' Arte and creating a new style of higher, literary comedy. His works contain no great comic types like those of MOLIÈRE; instead he drew a carefully observed picture of the preoccupations and manners of Venetian society.

His early years, as recounted in his delightful memoirs, were the classic childhood of a prodigious playwright. By the age of eleven he had completed his first play and at fourteen ran off briefly with a troupe of strolling players. After obtaining a degree in law, he continued his involvement with the stage, writing scenarios for the actors he encountered in his travels. Only when he married did he settle down to practise law, first in Venice and then further south in Pisa.

In 1748 Goldoni became resident playwright for the Teatro Sant' Angelo in Venice, where he made up for lost time by turning out sixteen plays in one year. Early pieces like *La Vedova scaltra* (1748) retain the characters of the Commedia dell' Arte, but they are no longer masked. The comedy arises from character rather than from ridiculous situations, and the settings of the plays are realistic, the coffee shop in *La Bottega del caffè* (1750) and the inn in *La Locandiera* (1753). The heroine of the latter piece, Mirandolina, the hostess of the inn, is typical of Goldoni's spirited female characters. Proud and resourceful, she humbles her two presumptuous old suitors by marrying her faithful assistant.

Venetian audiences clamoured for more gentle mockery of their shortcomings, and in fourteen years Goldoni wrote over 200 plays, many of the finest being in local dialect. In *Le Baruffe chiozzotte* (1762), the quarrels of a small fishing village are settled by a young lawyer, thought to be Goldoni's self-portrait.

Goldoni's innovations do not seem so revolutionary today. His implied criticism of society was softened by the charm and vitality of his plays, yet hostility from rival playwrights made him the centre of bitter controversy. In 1762 he accepted Louis XV's invitation to become director of the Comédie-Italienne in Paris. *Il Ventaglio* (1763) is the only major work of this period, for he now wrote mainly in French.

Goldoni never returned to his beloved Venice. In later years he led a sad existence, pensioned off by the king, half-blind and in poor health. With the Revolution of 1789 his pension was stopped. It was about to be restored to him when he died in poverty.

Henry Fielding, creator of *Tom Jones* and *Tom Thumb*

Playwright **Carlo Goldoni**, Italian realist

J. C. Gottsched (*above*), pioneer German classicist

Macklin (*below*), one of theatre's toughest characters

Diderot (*above*). His writing on theatre was much greater than his writing for it

Below: an unusually benign **Dr Johnson** (*right*) with his friends Boswell and Goldsmith at the Mitre tavern

CHARLES COLLÉ (1709-83)

French playwright, librettist and *chansonnier*. Collé's memoirs give a vivid account of the theatrical activity in great private houses, where most of his songs and satirical farces were first performed. These were often too obscene or too critical of authority to receive public performance. *La Vérité dans le vin* (1747), an outspoken attack on the clergy, circulated widely, but was banned by the Archbishop of Paris. Royal displeasure decreed a similar fate for *La Partie de chasse de Henri IV* (1774), the charming tale of a simple miller who gives his king a lesson in political morality.

SAMUEL JOHNSON (1709-84)

English critic, essayist and lexicographer. Johnson's contribution to English theatre (leaving aside his invaluable criticism and his edition of SHAKESPEARE) was one single, unmemorable offering.

After leaving Oxford, Johnson set up a school near Lichfield. When it failed, he went to London with one of his pupils, the young David GARRICK, bringing with him a tragedy, *Irene*. "The labour of introducing it on the stage" proved to be "in a very high degree vexatious and disgusting", but it was finally produced in 1749 by Garrick, who had become manager of the Drury Lane Theatre. Little more than a succession of moral debates, it was allowed to run for nine nights, earning the author three hundred pounds. Notwithstanding this mildest of successes, aspiring playwrights remained eager for his literary approval.

CARLO ANTONIO BERTINAZZI (1710-83)

Italian actor. When Bertinazzi joined the Comédie-Italienne in 1741 the 200-year-old tradition of the Commedia dell' Arte in Paris was drawing to a close. By that year these so-called "Italian" productions were performed entirely in French, and Bertinazzi, whose grasp of the language was tenuous, was obliged to make his debut in *Arlecchino muto per forza* (*Harlequin forced to hold his tongue*). Never completely happy with the spoken word, he had no equal as a mime, receiving the highest praise from both Carlo GOLDONI and David GARRICK. When the Comédie-Italienne was disbanded in 1780, so great was Bertinazzi's popularity that he alone was allowed to stay on in the new French company.

CHARLES-SIMON FAVART (1710-92)

French playwright and librettist. Favart's talent for the theatre enabled him to give up his career as a pastry-cook to write tart comedies, stuffed with popular tunes. The fame he achieved with *La Chercheuse d'esprit* (1741) led Favart and his wife, the actress Marie Duranceray, to be engaged by the Maréchal de Saxe to entertain the troops in Flanders, but the tyrannical Marshal (who had previously revealed a penchant for actresses in Adrienne LECOUVREUR) had other plans for Mme Favart, and the couple were forcibly separated. Reunited after the Marshal's death, they worked together happily and fruitfully for twenty years. Favart became director of the Opéra-Comique, where his light musical entertainments *La Fille mal gardée* (1758) and *Les Trois Sultanes* (1761) established his wife as the rage of Paris.

KITTY CLIVE (1711-85)

English actress. A great comedienne, throughout her career Kitty Clive longed to play serious roles. The results were unfortunate. Playing Portia to Charles MACKLIN's historic Shylock, she incongruously parodied a prominent London lawyer. Events like this led to interminable rows with David GARRICK, to whom she wrote long, abusive, semi-literate letters. Somehow the two remained the best of friends.

Kitty Clive first made her name as a pert and sprightly singer in *Love in a Riddle*, a ballad opera by COLLEY CIBBER, and kept up her singing in immensely popular parodies of Italian opera. She retired in 1769, by then "full-blown and florid", to live in "Clive's-Den", which became a favourite resort of leading men of letters. Samuel JOHNSON admired her particularly: "What Clive did best, she did better than Garrick. She was a better romp than any I ever saw in nature."

KONRAD ERNST ACKERMANN (1712-71)

German actor-manager. A skilled painter and an efficient surgeon, Ackermann could also ride and fence as well as any gentleman. On leaving the army, however, he joined Friedrich SCHÖNEMANN's company and sealed his destiny by falling in love with Sophie Schröder, the leading lady.

Unlike his colleague Konrad EKHOF, Ackermann was no theorist; he played the roles that he enjoyed. These ranged from Barnwell in George LILLO's *The London Merchant* to Rodrigue in CORNEILLE's *Le Cid*. The company he founded in 1751 still depended largely on the French classics and the comedies of Ludvig HOLBERG, for Ackermann's importance was not as an innovator. His aim was simply to maintain high standards of acting.

The company's great opportunity came in 1767, when, with the playwright Gotthold Ephraim LESSING, they were invited to form the first national theatre in Hamburg. Ackermann was an excellent Sergeant Werner in Lessing's *Minna von Barnhelm*, but by that time the old actor-manager had become fat and easy-going, as happy just to sit and smoke his pipe.

CHARLOTTE CIBBER (1713-60)

English actress. The youngest and most eccentric of COLLEY CIBBER's children, Charlotte spent most of her life, on stage and off, dressed as a man. A disastrous marriage to a dissolute violinist obliged her to earn a living to support their child. This she did in a bewildering variety of jobs. Two interesting but unsuccessful roles in her sporadic acting career were Macheath in a revival of John GAY's *The Beggar's Opera* and Fopling Fribble, a satirical portrait of her father in a farce by Henry FIELDING. Between stage appearances she worked as an oil-dealer, a puppeteer, a sausage-seller and as valet to a nobleman. Charlotte apparently used her masculine disguise to court young ladies, yet throughout her bizarre, tragic existence, she retained a childlike innocence.

DENIS DIDEROT (1713-84)

French encyclopedist, philosopher, man of letters and playwright. Although only a part-time playwright, Diderot had as strong opinions about the stage as about sex or religion. He urged his fellow-dramatists to abandon the passions of classical tragedy and deal instead with the moral dilemmas of everyday bourgeois life: "Le drame bourgeois," as it was called. This theory had enormous influence, especially on the plays and critical writings of Gotthold LESSING. Diderot's own domestic tragedies, *Le Père de famille* (1761) and *Le Fils naturel* (1771), however, were poor advertisements for his theories. *Le Fils naturel* had to wait fourteen years for its first (unsuccessful) performance, and both plays were as sentimental and platitudinous as the *comédies larmoyantes* of Pierre de LA CHAUSSÉE.

Oddly, Diderot's philosophical works contain more lively and realistic dialogue than his work intended for the stage. A casual comedy of his old age, *Est-il bon? est-il méchant?* (1781), is far superior to his earlier plays, not being marred by an overwhelming desire to moralize.

MARIE-FRANÇOISE DUMESNIL (1713-1803)

French actress. Neither a great beauty nor even a commanding presence on the stage, Mlle Dumesnil, when roused, could play with a force and fire that none of her rival tragediennes could approach. The audience standing in the pit of the Comédie-Française would draw back several yards in terror at the sound of her impassioned imprecations. Her blazing eyes, exaggerated gestures and strangled sobs were much appreciated by VOLTAIRE, who gave her all his best tragic roles, her greatest triumph being in his *Mérope*. For other parts she had to compete with the great Mlle CLAIRON, and rivalry between the two was intense. Clairon accused Dumesnil of being permanently drunk. She certainly did have some recourse to the wine bottle, losing interest in the proceedings when not inspired by emotion or alcohol.

After her retirement in 1776, Mlle Dumesnil led a simple life, doing her own cooking and mending. Bed-

ridden in her old age, she lay among the chickens that scratched for food in her bedclothes.

MARIE-ANNE DANGEVILLE (1714-96)

French actress. The daughter of an actress and a dancer at the Opéra, Mlle Dangeville (known as Mme Antoine) was already well known on the stage when she made her official debut at the Comédie-Française at the age of sixteen. As a soubrette, especially in comedies by MARIVAUX, she had no rival. Untouched by scandal and admired by all, she retained her vivacity and girlish looks for over thirty years. One miscast role in a tragedy by VOLTAIRE, however, dissuaded her from trying to extend her theatrical range.

LEWIS HALLAM (1714-56)

Anglo-American actor-manager. Puritan opposition to the theatre in eighteenth-century America was strong (*Othello* had to be billed as "a moral dialogue in five acts"), so it was a hazardous venture when, in 1752, Hallam sailed to the colonies with his entire family and a sizeable company of actors. In Williamsburg and Philadelphia they played in makeshift halls, but in New York they took over and rebuilt an existing theatre, presenting the whole classical repertoire of the London stage, from the plays of SHAKESPEARE to George LILLO's *The London Merchant*, and plays by VANBRUGH.

After Hallam's death, his wife married another actor-manager, David Douglass. Their two companies united to form the American Company, in which Hallam's son, LEWIS HALLAM the younger, became the leading man.

PEG WOFFINGTON (c 1714-60)

Irish-born actress. Although a happy balance of beauty and humility, Peg Woffington first captivated the Dublin public in the role of a dashing young man. As Sir Harry Wildair in George FARQUHAR's *The Constant Couple* she repeated her success in London, where her tall, slim figure delighted every man in town. With typical gener-osity, she accommodated as many as she could, living for a time in a *ménage à trois* with the actors David GARRICK and Charles MACKLIN. Rival actresses, understandably less welcoming, found that Peg could be as spirited off stage as on. The spiteful Mrs Bellamy, who declared open war, suffered a stabbing for her pains.

Woffington's generosity to her poor family (her father had been a bricklayer) was matched by her loyalty to the public. In a long succession of triumphs, particularly as the young heroines in SHAKESPEARE and CONGREVE, she only once missed a performance. Her one unattractive feature was her voice. Her harsh barks and occasional squeaks were a gift to arch-mimic Tate Wilkinson, who parodied Woffington on stage, just as Samuel Foote had guyed her lover, Garrick. By a strange twist of fate it was into Wilkinson's arms that she collapsed while playing Rosalind in *As You Like It* in 1757. Semi-paralysed, she never returned to the stage.

DAVID GARRICK (1717-79)

English actor, manager, playwright and poet. Garrick's appearance as Richard III on 19 October 1741 transformed the English stage. James QUIN summed up the older generation's amazement: "If the young fellow is right, I and the rest of the players have been all wrong." Their grandly stilted style of heroic acting was swept aside by a realism "alive in every muscle and in every feature".

Of French and Irish ancestry, Garrick was raised in Lichfield, where as a schoolboy he organized amateur theatricals. Intending a career in law, he walked to London in 1737 with his former teacher Samuel JOHNSON. According to Johnson they arrived with fourpence between them, but shortly afterwards a legacy permitted Garrick to take up his uncle's trade of vintner. Business brought him into contact with the theatre and rekindled his interest in the stage. In April 1740 his comedy *Lethe, or Esop in the Shades* was produced at the Drury Lane Theatre. His debut as actor followed in March 1741, as an anonymous substitute for an indisposed Harlequin at Goodman's Fields Theatre. Apprehensive about his family's reaction to his new career, he performed under

David Garrick (*far left*) had small but expressive features and a resonant voice, with which he dominated the eighteenth-century English stage. Ironically, the cultured founders of London's exclusive Garrick Club in 1831 at first barred actors as unworthy of membership

Modern taste has restored the fantastic plays of **Carlo Gozzi** to favour with children and adults, as in this production (*left*) of *Il Re cervo* (The King Stag)

Garrick's lover for many years was the incomparable **Peg Woffington** (*right*). So revered was "The Woffington" that she was privileged to become the only female admitted to London's sought-after Beefsteak Club

an assumed name until his legendary appearance as Richard III made further secrecy futile. All London knew that "Garrick, a wine merchant" was sensational, and the crowds at the unlicensed, out-of-the-way theatre soon included "a dozen dukes a night". He was immediately engaged by Drury Lane for an unprecedented salary and in the summer of 1742 played opposite his mistress Peg Woffington in Dublin to such acclaim that a coincident outbreak of illness was dubbed "Garrick fever".

Except for separate years in Dublin and at Covent Garden Theatre, Garrick spent his whole professional life at Drury Lane, of which he became co-manager in 1747. On stage he made his effect not by imposing a style but by exploring a role's individuality. He was a master of all types of role, the clownish Abel Drugger in Jonson's *The Alchemist* being as important in his repertoire as Hamlet. Despite his painstaking preparation, Garrick believed that a characterization only revealed its complete nature in the mysterious alchemy of performance. The "electrical fire" he generated on stage was his unique gift, the power that enabled him, as Lear, to move not just the people in the stalls but the theatre staff as well to tears.

As a manager his contribution to theatrical history was no less important. It included devoted, if unfortunately altered, productions of Shakespeare, the introduction of concealed stage lighting and naturalistic backdrops, and the long-overdue removal of spectators from the stage.

Garrick retired in 1776 after a poignant series of fare-well performances repeating his greatest roles. For three years thereafter he entertained both in town and country with unfailing theatricality. "He could not sit down to have his hair dressed without terrifying the barber with every shade of expression." When he died and was buried in Westminster Abbey, his old friend Johnson maintained that his passing had "eclipsed the gaiety of nations".

SPRANGER BARRY (1719-77)

Irish actor. "Handsome as a god", Barry held his own in an era dominated by David Garrick. In a famous contest of 1750 the two played Romeo at different theatres. A female observer noted that if she had been Juliet in the balcony scene, Garrick's passion would have convinced her he would come up to her, "but had Barry been my lover, so seductive was he that I should certainly have jumped down to him". Barry was also a matchless Othello, but his "gay and splendid" private life was marred first by a disastrous investment in a Dublin theatre and at last by a wasting and terminal illness.

His final years were brightened by a late second marriage to the tragic actress Anne Dancer. His devotion to her was so total that he would only act if she appeared as his leading lady.

KONRAD EKHOF (1720-78)

German actor-manager. Originally a post office clerk known for "trustworthiness and beautiful handwriting", Ekhof made his debut in Leipzig with the Schönemann company in 1740. There he created a realistic style previously unseen in Germany, where serious acting was still synonymous with the static classicism of Caroline Neuber. In 1753 he founded an academy for the reading and discussion of plays, but the venture failed because of his chronic obsession with detail. This same minute care fostered his superb dramatic technique, allowing him to understand and interpret a vast range of roles, from comic German peasants to the tragic Oedipus. Ekhof was less successful as a manager, but did valuable work at the new National Theatre in Hamburg and in the closing years of his life at the small Court Theatre in Gotha. A simple, homely man, Ekhof was unconcernedly aware that some contemporaries thought him an "odd duck"; his more general and appropriate title was "the German Garrick".

CARLO GOZZI (1720-1806)

Italian playwright and poet. Gozzi came from a Berga-masque family of witty, aristocratic ne'er-do-wells. He was a passionate conservative, particularly keen to maintain the farcical improvisations of the Commedia dell' Arte against the realistic plays of Carlo Goldoni. To challenge them for public favour and show the old genre's adaptability, Gozzi concocted *L'Amore delle tre melarance*

(*The Love of Three Oranges*) (1761), a fantastic piece based on a fairy-tale, combining the Commedia figures, exotic settings, magic and spectacle. The play had a great if short-lived vogue, and Gozzi turned out nine more on the same fabulous lines, including *Turandot* (1762) and *L'Augellin belverde* (1765). They were all written for the popular troupe of Antonio Sacchi. Gozzi's efforts to preserve the tradition came to an end when the company disbanded in 1769.

MLLE CLAIRON (1723-1803)

French actress. Mlle Clairon "made the utmost use of her capacities in art as in love". The illegitimate daughter of a seamstress, she returned from her first visit to the theatre mimicking the actors and repeating scores of lines from memory. Trained at the Comédie-Italienne and in the provinces, in 1743 she joined the Comédie-Française, where she astonished everyone with her triumph as Phèdre, a role that Mlle DUMESNIL had made her own. Although ten years later she abruptly altered her acting technique from traditional grandiloquence to a more natural delivery, Clairon remained beloved by the public (and by the many rich and noble admirers whose passion was rarely unrequited). Perpetually strong-minded, she campaigned for historical accuracy in costuming, and once went to prison rather than accept a dismissed colleague's reinstatement.

Mlle Clairon left the Comédie-Française in 1766, spending the years of retirement with her friend VOLTAIRE, and later with her lover, the Margrave of Ansbach. She died in poverty, but even in old age could act scenes from *Phèdre* with "majesty and fire".

KARL THEOPHILUS DÖBBELIN (1727-93)

German actor-manager. Döbbelin's success was due more to bluster than to merit. He was an actor totally without subtlety, a manager most skilled at ballyhoo. But he did have an enthusiasm for the stage, played leading roles with Caroline NEUBER and Konrad ACKERMANN, and with his own Berlin-based company helped increase the dramatic repertoire and support the creation of a national theatre. LESSING regarded Döbbelin as a lunatic, but was indebted to him for the first productions of several of his plays, including the verse drama *Nathan der Weise* with Döbbelin in the title role.

JEAN-BAPTISTE NICOLET (1728-96)

French actor-manager and acrobat. The son of a puppeteer, Nicolet established himself in 1760 on the Boulevard du Temple with a troupe of thirty actors, fifty dancers, twenty musicians and trained animals (such as the talented monkey, Turco). To the displeasure of the official theatres, this motley company insisted on including light plays in its repertoire, but Parisians were delighted, and in 1772 Louis XV gave it recognition as the "Spectacle des Grands Danseurs du Roi". After the Revolution the troupe became in name what it had been in fact, the "Théâtre de la Gaîté".

LEKAIN (1729-78)

French actor. VOLTAIRE noticed Henri-Louis Caïn in an amateur production and praised his gifts, but advised him against an acting career. When the stage-struck apprentice would not be dissuaded, Voltaire built him a theatre in his own home, trained him for six months and arranged a debut with the Comédie-Française in the title-role of his tragedy *Brutus*. The event, in 1750, had a mixed reception, with the young enraptured, the ladies only aware of Lekain's bull-like ugliness, and his fellow-actors resentful of his talent. His probation with the company dragged on for eighteen months, until Louis XV declared, "He has made me cry, I who scarcely ever shed tears. I accept him!" This intense communication was Lekain's great skill, earning him the title of "the French GARRICK". His devotion to his craft overcame his physical disadvantages just as it impelled him to seek professional reforms and frequently to overexert himself. At the height of his fame he died of a chill caught after a performance of Voltaire's *Adélaïde du Guesclin*. He was buried the same day the philosopher returned to Paris from exile.

GOTTHOLD EPHRAIM LESSING (1729-81)

German playwright and critic. The first great German dramatist, Lessing urged fellow writers to abandon the French classics and turn to English models, especially in the use of blank verse or prose rather than the inevitable alexandrine. His own early works, however, were comedies in the style of MOLIÈRE. The best of these, *Der junge Gelehrte* (1748), was performed by Caroline NEUBER's company while Lessing was still a student at the University of Leipzig. It is only with *Miss Sara Sampson* (1755) that he made his first great break with tradition. A domestic tragedy written in prose was now possible thanks to the success of George LILLO's *The London Merchant* and the theories of *drame bourgeois* evolved by DIDEROT in France.

Lessing's critical essays (on art, poetry and philosophy as well as theatre) made him many enemies, including VOLTAIRE, the favoured philosopher of Frederick the Great. This prevented him from gaining the coveted post of Royal Librarian in Berlin. Obliged to seek employment at the courts of minor German principalities, he often had difficulty in getting his works performed.

His fortunes changed when, in 1767, he was appointed resident dramatist and critic to the newly formed National Theatre in Hamburg and his great comedy *Minna von Barnhelm* at last reached the stage. Konrad EKHOF played Major von Tellheim, a dishonourably discharged officer, innocent of any offence, whose exaggerated Prussian sense of honour nevertheless prevents him from marrying his fiancée. Realistic and topical, yet still funny today, it is one of the few eighteenth-century comedies to have survived in the German repertoire.

Lessing's most influential work, *Emilia Galotti* (1772), hardly complies with the author's ideal of tragedy that deals with everyday moral problems. The play is set at an Italian court, where the heroine is abducted by a debauched prince. She persuades her uncomprehending father to stab her to death, not because she fears a fate worse than death, but because she is horrified to discover her own latent sensuality. The play had many imitators, but Lessing himself abandoned the theatre to write on philosophical and moral problems. His only other theatrical work was *Nathan der Weise* (1779), a poetic drama that makes a powerful plea for religious tolerance.

Lessing's appeals to reason and compassion were forgotten briefly by the writers of the *Sturm und Drang* movement in their exaltation of genius and individual liberty. Yet later, both GOETHE and SCHILLER acknowledged him as the founder of German theatre.

FEODOR GRIGORYEVICH VOLKOV (1729-63)

Russian actor. The fame of Volkov's amateur performances in the town of Yaroslavl was such that in 1752 the Russian royal family summoned his company to Court. After a free education had smoothed their rough provincial manners, Volkov, Ivan DMITREVSKY and others formed the first permanent Russian theatre company in 1756, with Volkov as its leading actor.

Despite the generous patronage of Tsar Peter III, the young actors took part in the revolt that led to his over-throw and the accession of Catherine the Great.

OLIVER GOLDSMITH (1730-74)

Irish-born playwright, poet and novelist. "No man was more foolish when he had not a pen in his hand, or more wise when he had." Contemporary accounts bear out Samuel JOHNSON's summing-up of Goldsmith, an awk-ward ugly man, whose jokes always fell flat and whose finances were in perpetual chaos.

Goldsmith left Trinity College, Dublin, to study medicine in Edinburgh. Any knowledge he may have acquired was clearly forgotten in the two years he spent wandering across Europe, begging for money by playing the flute. When he set up as a doctor in London, he attracted hardly a patient and, on applying to be a mere hospital orderly, was considered unqualified for the job.

Undertaking any literary work available, Goldsmith led a hand-to-mouth existence. The manuscript of his great novel *The Vicar of Wakefield* was hastily sold for sixty pounds to pay off his landlady. His first play, *The Good-Natured Man* (1768), was refused by GARRICK but produced by George COLMAN the elder at Covent Garden.

The crowning achievement of Goldsmith's career, *She Stoops to Conquer* (1773), remains one of the finest and most frequently revived of English comedies. In answer to objections that the misunderstanding around which the plot revolves was completely incredible, the author claimed that he himself had once mistaken a private house for an inn. Such a blunder would have been typical of this unfortunate man, who, when asked on his death-bed if his mind was at ease, replied, "No, it is not."

PIERRE-AUGUSTIN CARON DE BEAUMARCHAIS (1732-99)

French playwright, polemicist, spy and arms dealer. By the age of thirty, Pierre-Augustin Caron was an international financier and a favourite of the King of France. The son of a watchmaker, he had effected this heady rise through the social ranks by inventing a revolutionary watch mech-anism and by teaching harp and guitar to the four daughters of Louis XV. The title "de Beaumarchais" came from one of the properties of his first wife, a conveniently rich widow, who died ten months after the marriage.

Beaumarchais' capacity for intrigue more than matched that of his great creation, Figaro. In 1764 he travelled to Spain, ostensibly to avenge his sister, jilted by a certain Clavijo (the story became the subject of GOETHE's *Clavijo*), but at the same time he was engaged in numerous business deals and in furnishing the future King of Spain with a mistress.

Literary success did not come so easily. *Eugénie* (1767) and *Les deux amis, ou Le Négociant de Lyon* (1770) were ponderous *drames bourgeois* in the style of DIDEROT.

When Beaumarchais was left a fortune by his protector and mentor in the world of finance, the disappointed heir contested the will. From that day on the playwright spent much of his life in the courts (with not infrequent visits to prison). He vented his anger against a corrupt establish-ment in his *Mémoires contre Goëzman*. Their overnight success saw him hailed as a champion of liberty. Despite this new role, he returned to royal service as a secret agent and blackmailer. He also proposed that Louis XVI should

sell arms to Americans in the War of Independence and, at his own expense, fitted out a fleet for the purpose.

After many revisions *Le Barbier de Séville* finally reached the stage in 1775, and the scheming servant Figaro became a folk-hero. The pace of this dazzling comedy of intrigue leaves audiences no time to draw breath, for the engineering of the plot is worthy of Beaumarchais the master watchmaker. The battles over copyright that followed its success were nothing to the disputes provoked by his second comic masterpiece, *Le Mariage de Figaro* (1784), inferior in construction to the earlier work, but not in its satire. As the king considered it seditious, *Figaro* had to pass through the hands of six censors, one of whom Beaumarchais unwisely referred to as "a flea". For this insolence he was thrown into prison, but was freed through the influence of the king's brother (who later played Figaro in a Court production that co-starred Queen Marie-Antoinette as Suzanne).

Le Mariage de Figaro has been seen by some to herald the French Revolution, but most of Beaumarchais' satire was inspired by personal grievance, and Figaro's spirit of freedom is one of selfish hedonism rather than a socialistic ideal. When the Revolution did come, the ageing Beaumarchais could no longer turn history to his advan-tage. An unsuccessful three-year expedition to buy sixty thousand rifles left many in doubt as to which side he was on. His last theatrical venture was also a failure. A much-changed Figaro was hissed when he appeared in *L'Autre Tartuffe, ou La Mère coupable* (1792), an ill-advised return to the moralizing drama of his youth.

Such aberrations are easily forgotten; Beaumarchais is honoured today for his exuberant love of life, which gave birth to the peerless Figaro and inspired the immortal operas of Mozart and Rossini.

The escapades and adventures of
Beaumarchais' life are as sensational
as anything he wrote

GEORGE COLMAN (1732-94)

English playwright. Colman's two most popular comedies, *The Jealous Wife* (1761) and *The Clandestine Marriage* (1766), were both written in collaboration with David GARRICK. When the great actor refused to play the part intended for him in the latter play, Colman set up as a rival manager. At the Covent Garden Theatre and then the Haymarket Theatre, he continued to write, translate, adapt and edit plays.

Unfortunately, protracted legal actions (he lost a nine-year case to the litigious Charles MACKLIN) took their toll on his sanity, and he spent the last four years of his life locked up in an institution.

His son, George Colman the younger (1762–1836), took

You, the audience II

In the early eighteenth century the theatre was still a place to flirt, fight, show off and occasionally to watch plays. Playgoing was fashionable, playhouses comfortable, and the price of tickets beyond the reach of the very poor. In London the pit was now furnished with benches. These were occupied not by the rowdy groundlings of the sixteenth century but by "Men of Quality, particularly the younger Sort", and "Ladies of Reputation and Vertue". Though "the younger Sort" dallied with the orange-sellers, and elegant masked prostitutes sat among the ladies, the mood was a good deal more refined than Elizabethans would have appreciated.

Despite this new civility, critics still said sourly that people "came not to see Plays, but act their own". Samuel Pepys, a true devotee, acknowledged that he loved to look at the fine women in glittering gowns almost as much as at the work being staged. King Charles II and his rival mistresses were attractions in themselves. Country gentlemen, lords, ladies and well-to-do citizens confirmed the theatre as a temple of modish society.

Audiences were by no means staid. They had whims and prejudices which they were not slow to express. The pit, for all its quality, on occasion compelled a complete change of programme by the sheer volume of protest. Hapless performers were bombarded with dried peas; a French dancer, at a time of strained cross-channel relations, was knocked down by an apple. The stage itself was as ever the particular haunt of lounging fops, and their frequent unconcern for the performance increasingly piqued both actors and those of the audience with any interest in the play. During one performance of *Macbeth*, a nobleman sauntered across the proscenium to talk to a crony. The manager, John RICH, rebuked him, slaps were exchanged and swords drawn; the offended beau returned later with a mob to vandalize the theatre.

The new status of the pit banished persons of no quality to the upper gallery, far from the stage, but they could still exhibit an Elizabethan restlessness. For a time Covent Garden admitted footmen without payment to swell attendance, but these "savage spectators" soon provoked an "intolerable disturbance". The new pit rebelled against the old rowdiness and forced their servants' eviction. But the footmen responded with riots that only the army was able to quell.

Other countries faced similar conditions. Noble families owned the theatres of Venice, and their young relations took full advantage of their privileged status. They brought masked courtesans into their private boxes, causing "confusion" and "surprizing Accidents". They spat into the pit, which on the Continent was still a standing area, and tossed down "snuffs and ends of candles".

Paris had seen an improvement in behaviour during the seventeenth century, but armed noblemen and soldiers still tried to enter without paying. Contemptuous *petits-maîtres* bought the privilege of stage seating, sometimes positioning themselves directly in front of the audience. Perhaps as protest or practical joke, a rich citizen once bought all the stage tickets for a performance in advance and passed them out exclusively to hunch-backs. In the boxes ladies chatted, drank tea and played with their dogs, sometimes taking up places for eight with their voluminous skirts. The pit remained all-male, proud of its reputation for passionate display and true connoisseurship.

over from his father as manager of the Haymarket. Though a playwright of talent, he was a weak and dissolute man. He delivered his best comedy, *John Bull; or, the Englishman's Fireside* (1803), to the theatre act by act as he needed the money.

IVAN AFANASYEVICH DMITREVSKY (1733-1821)

Russian actor and director. On the death of Feodor VOLKOV in 1763, Dmitrevsky took over as leading actor in the Russian National Theatre. He rose to become director, and travelled frequently to the West to study the contrasting styles of David GARRICK and LEKAIN. His own playing was cold and classical in heroic Russian drama, but he was a magnificent interpreter of MOLIÈRE.

In 1812, aged seventy-nine and long since retired, he was fired by patriotism to take the stage once more in a rousing piece of anti-Napoleonic propaganda.

CHRISTOPH MARTIN WIELAND (1733-1813)

German poet, novelist and playwright. After a period of youthful frivolity, Wieland ended his days as a scholarly classicist and honoured companion of GOETHE at the Court of Weimar. His one major play, *Lady Johanna Gray* (1758), was completed as a result of a chance encounter with Konrad ACKERMANN and Sophie Schröder, who played the title role. For a time Wieland's prose versions of SHAKESPEARE were the best in the German Language, but they were rendered obsolete by the inspired verse translations of August SCHLEGEL. His story "Lulu, or The Magic Flute" was the source for SCHIKANEDER's libretto to Mozart's opera.

ISAAC BICKERSTAFFE (c1735-c1812)

Irish-born playwright and librettist. The success of his comic opera *Love in a Village* (1762) made Bickerstaffe England's most popular living playwright. But fame turned overnight to notoriety when rumour branded him a sodomite. In fear of his life (sodomy carried the death penalty) he made a hasty escape to France, where he spent forty years of friendless and penniless exile. David GARRICK received a plea for help from the "poor wretch", but failed to answer it.

Bickerstaffe used a wide variety of sources, from CERVANTES to the novels of Samuel Richardson. His charming lyrics (for which the young Charles DIBDIN wrote much of the music) were the chief reason for the success of his insubstantial works, which were continually revived long after his self-imposed exile.

THOMAS GODFREY (1736-63)

American playwright and poet. Godfrey was a reluctant apprentice to a watchmaker when the Provost of the College of Philadelphia recognized his literary talent, released him from his contract and encouraged him to write. The young poet met other artists and absorbed colonial culture, particularly the plays given by the American Company. This experience of live drama so impressed him that after military service and a move to North Carolina he wrote a verse tragedy. Submitted to the American Company in 1759 but not produced until 1767, a year after its author's death from fever, *The Prince of Parthia* was the first American play ever to be professionally performed. Its influences, including SHAKESPEARE and LILLO, clearly stem from productions given in Philadelphia by HALLAM.

ANTOINE FRANCONI (1738-1836)

Italian circus manager and animal trainer. Franconi was a penniless Venetian aristocrat, whom poverty drove to become an animal trainer. Assisted by a violent temper, he tamed lions, fought bulls and at length took up the equestrian displays popularized by Philip ASTLEY. After meeting Astley in Paris in 1783, Franconi opened his own amphitheatre in Lyons. He returned to Paris in 1791 (narrowly escaping the guillotine), and from 1793 presented grand historical equestrian dramas. These shows, along with the clever antics of canaries, stags, elephants and clowns, proved very popular in France and numbered among their enthusiasts Napoleon himself.

Succeeded by his sons and apprentices, Franconi established a circus dynasty that spread around the world.

LEWIS HALLAM JR (c1740-1808)

Anglo-American actor-manager. Hallam was one of the early stars of the American stage, appearing with the American Company under the management of his stepfather David Douglass. He played Romeo opposite his mother and later performed in the first production of the first all-American play, Thomas GODFREY's *The Prince of Parthia*. After the Revolution Hallam became co-manager of the troupe. He was instrumental in overcoming wartime anti-theatre laws, initially by presenting scenes from plays as "moral lectures".

PHILIPPE DE LOUTHERBOURG (1740-1812)

French stage designer and painter. Loutherbourg abandoned religious studies for the gaudy illusions of the theatre. After working in Paris and Italy, he lived most of his life in England and became David GARRICK's scenic director at the Drury Lane Theatre, creating marvellously new and innovatively realistic backdrops. He used silk filters with stage lights to produce varied colours and subtle effects of motion, and replaced the traditional Baroque wings with painted set pieces to make staging more flexible. Some of his most grandiose accomplishments came in pantomimes such as *The Wonders of Derbyshire or Harlequin in the Peaks*. Essentially travelogues, their real subject was Loutherbourg's remarkable scenery, combining "geographical accuracy with romantic picturesqueness". Loutherbourg eventually left to create his own scenic extravaganza *Eidophusikon*.

PHILIP ASTLEY (1742-1814)

English circus pioneer and equestrian artiste. More in love with horses than with cabinet-making, "the creator of the modern circus" ran away from home at seventeen to join the cavalry. He distinguished himself as a trainer and trick-rider as well as a hero in battle, and on leaving the service was presented with his general's own white charger. Back in England, Astley set about publicly exhibiting his prowess. In 1768 he appeared in an improvised ring near the Thames, riding "with one foot on the saddle and one on his head". A few years later a grander show incorporated clowns, acrobats and singers in "Astley's Amphitheatre", a ring built to accommodate the thousands who flocked to see these spectacles. A believer in both aggressive advertising and expansion, he opened amphitheatres throughout Britain, making himself so well known that Samuel JOHNSON said Astley could attract a crowd by standing on a horse and preaching a sermon. Short of that, his displays ultimately included "pantomime, magic, tragedy and comedy" both on and off horseback, as well as solo feats by the "Little Military Learned Horse" Billy, who could dance, count, fire a rocket and make tea.

In 1783 Astley built an amphitheatre in Paris, but its operation was complicated by revolution and war between France and England. The old cavalryman escaped from one scrape only by commandeering a coach at pistol-point. The most important result of his time in France was his meeting with Antoine FRANCONI, who further popularized Astley's concept of the circus throughout Europe and the New World.

CAGLIOSTRO (1743-95)

Italian conjuror and occult poseur. Cagliostro was one of the last conjurors to claim genuine magic powers. Born Giuseppe Balsamo in Sicily, he entered a life of petty crime until he discovered how willing people were to believe in magic. After tricking a goldsmith out of a large sum of money with promises that he would use his magic spells to find treasure, Balsamo was forced to leave Palermo. Calling himself the Comte de Cagliostro and posing as a magician and doctor, he travelled with his bride across Europe in a carriage drawn by four horses.

In 1780 they arrived in Strasbourg, where the naive inhabitants were amazed by this mysterious aristocrat who claimed to have the power to restore youth. Needless to say, the couple's stay was short but lucrative. They came to Paris in 1785 and Parisians were soon flocking to the magician's soirées. The seance room was draped in rich materials, and in the corners burned candles placed in magical formations. Under Cagliostro's power, a young girl would go into a trance before a glass ball and predict the future.

Unfortunately these thrilling performances came to an end when the magician was thrown into the Bastille, implicated in the notorious "Affair of the Diamond Necklace". Later released, he went to Rome in 1789, but was arrested again and died in prison.

HANNAH COWLEY (1743-1809)

English playwright. Provoked by the dullness of a contemporary play, Mrs Cowley wrote her first work, *The Runaway*, in two weeks. GARRICK produced this sentimental comedy to great applause in 1776. Thirteen other plays followed, the most successful being *The Belle's Stratagem* (1780), performed by Lewis HALLAM, JR in America in 1794 and revived throughout the nineteenth century. Indifferent to the public reception of her pieces, Mrs Cowley never attended her opening nights and stopped writing in 1794 as abruptly as she had begun.

The old Commedia dell' Arte traditions lingered on well into the eighteenth century. This engraving of **Harlequin** in mourning, from *Le Viellard amoureux*, shows the popular mime and actor Carlo Bertinazzi (see page 91) in the part. David Garrick particularly admired his expressive back

Early circus

Like the drama, the circus had its beginnings in religious ritual. Both the ancient Egyptians and Greeks honoured their gods with splendid processions of exotic animals. Pageants included chariots drawn by antelopes, elephants and ostriches, and cages of peacocks, leopards and lions. Greek trainers anticipated modern circus acts by teaching horses to dance and bears to wrestle.

Later Roman festivals were more grandiose, held in gigantic arenas like the Circus Maximus. Chariot races and gladiatorial combat were the main attractions, but animal acts also appeared. Equestrian artists thundered around the ring standing on two horses, in the style that came to be known as "Roman Riding", lions and an elephant walked a tight-rope. Acrobats, jugglers and rope dancers were featured as well, but the most unique and brutal spectacle was the wholesale slaughter of animals. Lions and tigers fought each other or attacked elephants or giraffes. Soldiers massacred hundreds of exotic creatures. At the dedication of the Colosseum in AD 80, 5000 beasts were killed in a festival lasting one hundred days.

Such colourful but savage entertainment disappeared with the Roman Empire itself. For over a thousand years the spirit of the circus survived feebly in the various itinerant performers who juggled, somersaulted, or exhibited their animals wherever they could. But the modern circus only emerged in 1768, when an ex-cavalryman named Philip ASTLEY opened a "riding School" in a London field to

show off his equestrian skills. He soon had a permanent amphitheatre and a show that included such circus fixtures as acrobats, tumblers, rope-walkers and clowns. It was clear that this was no mere equestrian display. When Astley appeared in Paris the police authorized him to present only those parts of the programme that took place on horseback, since variety acts would infringe a monopoly owned by another theatre. But the canny dragoon mounted an entire stage on the backs of horses and the show went on as before.

Astley's success inspired other impresarios. Antoine FRANCONI opened his own amphitheatre and founded a circus dynasty. The illustration above depicts the range of entertainment the Franconis provided. The circus came to America with John Bill RICKETTS who had been a star rider with Astley's competitor and former clown, Charles Hughes. Ricketts' admirers included George Washington, and his example gave rise to numerous small travelling circuses. Brightly painted wagons and canvas tents became familiar and welcome sights in nineteenth-century America.

Such one-ring touring shows remained the international pattern until 1870, when the American W. C. Coup conceived the idea of simultaneous acts in more than one ring. The old rather intimate circus would soon give way to extravaganzas that even the Romans might have approved. Coup and his partner enlisted the aid of the arch-showman P. T. BARNUM, and "The Greatest Show on Earth" was born.

FRANÇOISE-ROSE VESTRIS
(1743-1804)

French actress. Mme Vestris owed her 1768 debut with the Comédie-Française to her noble admirer the Duc de Duras. After high-powered private instruction from the actors LEKAIN, Mlle DUMESNIL and Mlle CLAIRON, she made a triumphant public appearance in VOLTAIRE's *Tancrède*. But her instant popularity was not enduring. Critics gradually found her acting style limited and superficial, dependent on a fine figure more than intelligence, and "fire in the eyes" more than "blood in the veins". She also aroused disfavour for jealous intrigues against her rival, Mlle Sainval. She continued to have some reputation as a tragic heroine, however, and Voltaire praised her performance in his *Irène*.

FRIEDRICH LUDWIG SCHRÖDER
(1744-1816)

German actor-manager. Stepson of the actor-manager Konrad ACKERMANN, Schröder profited from his father's experience but suffered from his unpredictable temper. The latter was strikingly illustrated when the company departed from Königsberg in 1756 and young Friedrich was mysteriously left behind. He lived in a vacant theatre and supported himself by renting it out and doing odd jobs, before finally locating his family in Switzerland.

Originally more interested in acrobatics than in drama, Schröder began seriously to learn his trade when the great actor Konrad EKHOF joined the troupe in Hamburg in 1764. Though treating the older man so rudely that he eventually left, Schröder carefully studied the revolutionary realism of his performances, applying his observations first to his own acting and, from 1771, as artistic director of the company.

Over the next ten years Schröder transformed German drama. He introduced the most modern playwrights, including GOETHE and LESSING, and presented their work in the radically new terms it required. Gone were French costumes and declamation. The new style was natural and passionate, its intensity the result of Schröder's concern for a unified performance. His productions of SHAKESPEARE, the first on the German stage, were as great a revelation. *Hamlet* began the series in 1776, and Schröder himself was an outstanding King Lear in 1778. His epoch-making tenure as manager ended in 1781, from a salary dispute, and public innuendo that his overbearing manner had driven an actress (his own half-sister) to suicide.

Schröder returned to Hamburg in 1786, never achieving the same artistic heights but becoming wealthy and revered. Once, reflecting on his career, he had remarked that an actor's life was second in unpleasantness only to a theatre manager's. In 1798 he quit them both for retirement in the country.

CHARLES DIBDIN (1745-1814)

English playwright, actor and song-writer. Dibdin's quarrelsome nature may have compelled him to create the one-man shows in which, as director, writer and performer, he had no one to contend with but himself. He was also a popular composer of ballad operas, tuneful and often irreverent descendants of GAY's *The Beggar's Opera*. Of these, *The Waterman* (1774) was his most successful. But it is for his exquisite sea songs that Dibdin is now remembered. "Tom Bowling"—a song he composed when his seafaring brother was tragically drowned at Cape Town in 1780—and "The Lass that Loved a Sailor" are sentimental masterpieces, as moving today as they were two centuries ago.

DENIS FONVIZIN (1745-92)

Russian playwright and pamphleteer. As a government employee in St Petersburg, Fonvizin was deeply concerned with the reaction and repression he witnessed in Russia. His progressive opinions found a voice in dramatic satires, two of which, with their national flavour and lively, popular language have become classics of the Russian theatre.

The Brigadier is a tale of confused love affairs, brought to life by a stinging satire of the minor Russian nobility's bungling mimicry of French manners. *The Minor* (1782), considered his best play, satirizes the stupidity, brutality and greed of the provincial gentry.

Although he was an active member of the Reform Party and a writer of many polemical essays, Fonvizin was tolerated at first by the repressive regime of Catherine the Great. Later, relationships became strained, and in 1783 he was forced to retire from public life.

THOMAS HOLCROFT (1745-1809)

English playwright and actor. During a wandering youth Holcroft worked as a stable-boy, shoemaker, tutor and strolling player. From 1770 he was a theatre prompter in Dublin and in 1777 came to the Drury Lane Theatre as an actor. The next year his short play *The Crisis* was produced there, followed in 1781 by the full-length sentimental comedy *Duplicity*. After seeing BEAUMARCHAIS' *Le Mariage de Figaro* in Paris in 1783, Holcroft translated it from memory (a suspiciously prodigious feat since he had received no formal education) and introduced it to London as *The Follies of a Day* in 1784. But his most lasting contributions to the stage were melodramas such as *A Tale of Mystery* (1802), the first of their kind in English.

LAURENT MOURGUET (1745-1844)

French puppeteer. Undaunted by a depression in the silk trade, Mourguet, a weaver of Lyons, started a marionette theatre in the city's Public Gardens. He created Guignol, the drunken and jocular caricature of a Lyonnais silk-weaver. With his inseparable companion Gnafron, his bossy wife Madelon and their precocious son Guillaume, Guignol delighted his audiences, and Mourguet moved to a permanent theatre, where Guignol became France's favourite puppet.

DUGAZON (1746-1809)

French actor. Dugazon, whose real name was Jean-Baptiste-Henry Gourgaud, was a leading comic actor with the Comédie-Française. He could contort his face into the most grotesque grimaces, and was at his best in the farcical comedies of Marc-Antoine LEGRAND and Paul SCARRON. He also wrote some moderately successful plays himself.

He was unhappily married to Louise-Rosalie Lefèvre, the star of the Théâtre Italienne. Mme Dugazon excelled in the sentimental domestic drama of the time, causing those who saw her to sob and even to faint.

JOHN HENDERSON (1747-85)

English actor. Although he had no personal advantages whatever, Henderson worked diligently for success on stage, modelling his style on that of his friend David GARRICK. After five years of playing in the provinces he made his London debut as Shylock and, despite a poor voice and unimpressive physique, was an immediate success. An able Hamlet and a magnificent Falstaff,

Henderson died in his prime (from overwork it is said), but won the posthumous gratification of being buried beside Garrick in Westminster Abbey.

JOHN O'KEEFFE (1747-1833)

Irish playwright. "O'Keeffe might well be called our English MOLIÈRE," wrote William Hazlitt of the man whose farces, comedies and comic operas delighted English and American audiences at the end of the eighteenth century. Only one of these has been regularly revived, but the unfailing success of *Wild Oats* (1791) suggests that others have been unfairly neglected.

A promising actor and painter in his youth, O'Keeffe went blind when still in his twenties, and was forced to earn his living entirely as a writer.

DOMINIQUE SÉRAPHIN (1747-1800)

French puppeteer. Séraphin first opened his renowned shadow theatre in the Lannion Gardens at Versailles in 1776. There he charmed the aristocracy with his *Ombres Chinoises*, using articulated silhouette puppets. (Initially these were constructed out of stout card and thin cord; it is generally conjectured, however, that later in his career he made at least some use of hand puppets.) His great success prompted him to move to Paris, where he soon won wide acclaim with the *Spectacle des Enfants de France* in the new galleries of the Palais Royal, and gave daily performances to audiences of all ages. Apparently these productions were particularly popular among the clergy, being the only ones to which they could go in their cassocks. Of his large repertoire the best known is *Le Pont Cassé* (1784), in which a traveller and a workman carry on an angry argument from either side of a river. Séraphin's descendants continued to run the theatre for seventy years after its creator's death.

HEINRICH LEOPOLD WAGNER (1747-79)

German playwright. Wagner was not always popular with his fellow *Sturm und Drang* writers, especially with GOETHE, who accused him of plagiarizing his *Faust* material in *Die Kindermörderin* (1776). A socially conscious middle-class tragedy, it is the tale of a butcher's daughter who kills her illegitimate child. Wagner also published anonymously a satire against the critics of Goethe's *Werther*. This well-intentioned defence embarrassed the great man considerably, because people thought him responsible for Wagner's mediocre doggerel.

VITTORIO ALFIERI (1749-1803)

Italian playwright, poet and writer. Born into a noble family in Piedmont, Alfieri found the repressive atmosphere of eighteenth-century Italy intolerable. In his early twenties he travelled restlessly, frequently falling in love and continually railing against the tyranny he perceived throughout Europe. He longed to see Italians rise up in a new spirit of unity, but it was not until 1775, when he wrote *Cleopatra*, his first play, that he found a means of expressing these feelings.

In 1777 he met and fell in love with the wife of the Count of Albany, pretender to the English throne; their relationship was to last until Alfieri's death. In the next nine years Alfieri wrote another eighteen tragedies, all with historical or biblical subjects. They preserve the strict classical form of French tragedy, but in their content herald the Romantic age. Among the best are *Oreste*, *Virginia*, *Filippo* and, most notably, *Mirra* and *Saul*. Saul is a superhuman and tragic figure, racked by the inner conflict of the opposing forces of tyranny and freedom. This struggle is at the heart of all the tragedies.

In his last years Alfieri completed *Vita*, his memoirs, and made himself Knight of his own Order of Homer.

JOHN EDWIN (1749-90)

English actor. Edwin was a popular comic actor who preferred to play himself than to adopt the identity of the character he was playing. Said a contemporary: "He was irresistibly comic, but he was always Edwin." This method of playing frequently led to departures from the text. Once, when a character Edwin was portraying was accused by another, Cranky, of being ugly, he turned to the audience and said, "I submit to the decision of the enlightened British public which is the ugliest . . . I, Cranky or that gentleman in the front row."

Edwin was at least able to assume fictitious roles long enough to earn a distinguished reputation in the plays of John O'KEEFFE. His son, another John Edwin, was likewise an actor.

JOHANN WOLFGANG VON GOETHE (1749-1832)

German poet, playwright, novelist and scientist. "All my works are fragments of a great confession," wrote Goethe. A year before his death several fragments, on which he had worked for over fifty years, were united to form his masterpiece, the dramatic poem *Faust* (1831). He had been fascinated by the legend ever since watching a puppet-play of Dr Faust as a child. Unlike MARLOWE's *Doctor Faustus*, Goethe's hero is not damned, but borne up to Heaven by angels and granted salvation for his tireless attempts to understand the whole universe. Throughout his life Goethe sought the same understanding, not by means of abstract thought (he had "no organ" for philosophy) but through poetry and science.

Goethe studied to be a lawyer and even practised briefly in his native Frankfurt, but the law was no place for a young poet who wanted to embrace the whole natural world. He was at first torn between his admiration for Greek classicism and his enthusiasm for SHAKESPEARE. The latter "gothic" inspiration held the upper hand long enough for him to provide the *Sturm und Drang* movement with its greatest and longest work, *Götz von Berlichingen* (1773). Even in a later revision, it ran over six hours. *Clavigo* (1774), the tragedy of a poet who deserts his lady for his art, was the best of his other youthful plays, but the most sensational product of this period was the novel *Die Leiden des jungen Werthers* (*Young Werther*), a love story which made Goethe a household name and created a vogue for yellow waistcoats and suicide among the sensitive youth of Europe. Until he was in his seventies, a series of love affairs continued to feed Goethe's poetic imagination with tragic separations and sufferings.

Invited to Weimar by the young Duke Karl August, Goethe made this tiny city his home – and consequently the literary capital of Europe. As well as court poet, he was, at various times, superintendent of roads and of finances, a soldier and eventually a Minister of State. A long, platonic affair with a married lady of the Court inspired his two great classical plays, *Iphigenie auf Tauris* (1787) and *Torquato Tasso* (1790). Both were rewritten from earlier prose versions during Goethe's two-year stay in Italy, where he had revelled in the sensuality of classical sculpture and of the girl he lived with in Rome (significantly he refers to her as "Faustina"). He also completed *Egmont*, but this play, with its fusion of liberty and love, belongs to his earlier, Romantic period.

Goethe dictating to his secretary in the study of his little house at Weimar, now in East Germany. The delightful building may still be seen, and is virtually unaltered

On his return to Weimar, Goethe lived with Christiane Vulpius, a girl of humble birth, who bore him five children. Domesticity dulled his muse and he devoted more time to science. His theories of colour and of plant evolution have since been discredited, although they were the result of painstaking research. He also made a contribution to anatomical knowledge, discovering a small bone between the upper and the lower jaw.

During his long tenure as director of the Ducal theatre, Goethe befriended the playwright SCHILLER, ten years his junior and now also a resident of Weimar. An early riser and a lover of fresh air, Goethe was at first physically repelled by the unhealthy Schiller, who rose at noon and reeked of tobacco, but as each recognized the other's genius, they worked together on a journal, corresponded daily, competed as writers of ballads and produced each other's works in the theatre. "You have given me a second youth and made me a poet again," wrote Goethe to the younger man, who finally prompted him to resume work on *Faust*.

After Schiller's death, Goethe's interest in the theatre waned and he returned to other abandoned projects: his vast novel about the education of man, *Wilhelm Meister*, and the autobiographical *Dichtung und Wahrheit*, in which Goethe the man and Goethe the artist appear inseparable. His art was more than his life's work; it was his life. No man has ever embodied European culture so fully as Goethe, and few have so magnificently enriched it.

FRIEDRICH MÜLLER (1749-1825)

German playwright. Müller, who prided himself on his painting and liked to sign his works "Maler [painter] Müller", spent the latter half of his life in Rome, earning his living as a tourist guide. Like many minor members of the *Sturm und Drang* movement, he aped the great GOETHE, producing a version of the Faust legend, *Fausts Leben dramatisiert* (1778), and *Golo und Genoveva* (1811), a knightly epic in the style of Goethe's lengthy *Götz von Berlichingen*.

GIUSEPPE PINETTI (1750-1800)

Italian conjuror. When a professor in Rome, Pinetti was so encouraged by the students' praise of his scientific experiments that he decided to take up magic. He became famous all over Europe for his conjuring. Audiences were amazed by this small, elegantly dressed man, with his gold and silver apparatus and his astonishing illusions. In one of them, the "Philosophical Bouquet", he poured liquid over a tree, and it was instantly covered in oranges.

In 1783 Pinetti went to Paris. He drew large audiences, but things became rather difficult with the publication of *The Conjuror Unmasked*. Although it did not actually name Pinetti, this work denounced him as a fraud and explained his tricks. It was Pinetti's turn to disappear. He left for London and took a theatre in the Haymarket for a season, where he introduced the trick of "second-sight"—a new act that held the public spellbound. Blindfolded, Madame Pinetti would describe objects belonging to the audience, an illusion that was achieved by the use of a complex code of words. Pinetti travelled all over Europe, finally going to Russia, where he died of a fever.

EMANUEL SCHIKANEDER (1751-1812)

Austrian director, actor, librettist and playwright. Brought up in poverty, Schikaneder joined a travelling theatre company in 1773 and quickly proved his talent as an actor and writer. By 1778 he had his own company, and during a long stay in Salzburg he and Mozart became close friends. In 1784, encouraged by the praises of the Austrian Emperor Joseph II, Schikaneder took his company to Vienna, where, after a few unsettled years, he became the manager of Vienna's Theater auf der Wieden.

Schikaneder had no high artistic ideals except the box-office. He knew what the Viennese public wanted: a mixture of music, magic and farce that suited his loud and lively acting and his love of lavish sets and elaborate stage effects. In 1791 he suggested the idea of *Die Zauberflöte* (*The Magic Flute*), an opera involving all these popular elements, to Mozart. As well as writing the libretto, Schikaneder played Papageno, creating the part especially for his own comic talents.

By the end of the century Schikaneder's fortunes began to change. His extravagance had put the theatre deeply into debt, and the Viennese had lost interest in his plays. He continued to direct, moving to the Theater an der Wien in 1801, but without his audience's enthusiasm his work deteriorated.

The difficult political situation and his waning success combined to reduce him to poverty. In 1812, on his way to work at a new theatre, Schikaneder went suddenly mad. He never really recovered, and died a few months later in Vienna during another "nervous attack".

In his youth, **Schikaneder** earned his living as an itinerant violinist in Bavaria before he joined up with a theatre company in Augsburg in his early twenties

RICHARD BRINSLEY SHERIDAN (1751-1816)

English playwright, manager and politician. Sheridan was born in Dublin, the son of Thomas Sheridan, an actor, and Frances Sheridan, a novelist and playwright. He went to England, and entered Harrow as a law student.

In 1773, after an interrupted elopement and two duels, he won the lovely Elizabeth Linley. Although she was an accomplished singer and money was a continual problem, Sheridan never allowed his wife to perform professionally. Instead he turned his talents to writing, and in less than four years had written the plays which were to stamp him as one of England's greatest and most famous playwrights. With his very first work, *The Rivals* (1775), he captured a comic spirit, neither lascivious nor sentimental, that had been sorely lacking from the eighteenth-century stage. *The Rivals* has remained in the repertoire, and Mrs Malaprop, its comic ogress, has a place in the English dictionary she so shamefully malappropriated. This was followed by *St Patrick's Day or The Scheming Lieutenant* (1775) and *The Duenna* (1775). *The School for Scandal* (1777), for many his greatest play, is an exquisitely plotted comedy of manners which has remained even more familiar than *The Rivals*. In 1776 Sheridan bought David GARRICK's share in the Drury Lane Theatre and two years later became the sole owner. He was only 27 years old.

Sheridan's main ambition was to be accepted in London society. Often referred to as "the player's son" he abhorred the stigma of being "theatrical". He turned to politics and the Whig Party in particular, becoming a member of Parliament in 1780. The time and effort he put into this career was unfortunately at the expense of Drury Lane. An eloquent speaker in the House, he became equal in political status to Charles James Fox, William Pitt and Edmund Burke.

Two years after Elizabeth's death Sheridan married the very young Esther Jane Ogle, daughter of the Dean of Winchester. Their marriage was fraught with difficulties, but Esther stood by him gallantly to the end. Sheridan lived constantly beyond his means, with the bailiffs never very far away.

In 1799 he adapted and presented *Pizarro* at Drury Lane (from *Die Spanier in Peru* by August KOTZEBUE). A long-winded melodrama, it was his first attempt at writing since *The Critic*, a farce, in 1779.

Disaster struck in 1809 when the Drury Lane Theatre burned down. It was tens of thousands of pounds in debt, and Sheridan sat at the Piazza Coffee House watching the flames and getting very drunk. "Cannot a man take a glass of wine by his own fireside," he said with painful irony.

After the fire Sheridan went steadily downhill, from drink and lack of money, dying in dire poverty in 1816. London honoured him for his theatrical past and buried him in Poet's Corner, Westminster Abbey, next to Garrick as posterity demanded and not with the politicians as he himself would have preferred. It was the last ironic comment on the picaresque adventure which was Sheridan's life.

FRIEDRICH KLINGER (1752-1831)

German playwright. An orphan raised in poverty, Klinger established himself as a literary figure with the help of GOETHE, who had paid in part for his law studies. He was a member of the group *Sturm und Drang* ("Storm and Stress"), which centred around Goethe and opposed rationalism in favour of the emotions. This influential movement was named after a retitled play by Klinger himself (although the original title, *Der Wirrwarr*, meaning "Confusion", was just as appropriate). Like other plays of his youth, including *Otto* (1775) and *Die Zwillinge* (1776), this unperformable work was full of improbable situations and extravagant language.

In 1776 Goethe, fearing that *Sturm und Drang* was becoming excessive (and might harm his career), dissociated himself from the movement. Rebuffed by his former patron, Klinger fought in the War of Bavarian Succession, where the real storm and stress of battle tempered his theatrical effusions. He then embarked on a more successful and practical career in Russia, writing philosophical novels and plays which better reflected his measured life-style.

SARAH SIDDONS (1755-1831)

English actress. For thirty years Sarah Siddons ruled the British stage. Painted by Joshua Reynolds and Thomas Gainsborough, admired by King George III and Samuel JOHNSON, she was more esteemed even than her brother, the great tragedian JOHN PHILIP KEMBLE.

Not that the early career of Sarah Kemble suggested such glories. Although her theatrical family put her on the stage when very young, they removed her from it when, aged fifteen, she fell in love with an actor. Three years later Sarah married another actor and returned to the theatre as Mrs Siddons. A disastrous London debut under David GARRICK in 1775 confined her to working in the provinces, but in 1782 she triumphed as Isabella in Thomas SOUTHERNE's *The Fatal Marriage* at the Drury Lane Theatre. Thereafter her career as a tragic actress in parts such as Zara in CONGREVE's *The Mourning Bride* and, notably, Lady Macbeth, prospered brilliantly.

A strikingly beautiful and dignified woman, Sarah Siddons excelled in mime, and her flexible voice was said to have "the melancholy yet shattering tone of the nightingale". Her rhythmic delivery annoyed some. Garrick wondered how her speech acquired its "ti-tum-ti", and another critic referred to its "hobble-ti-trot". So accustomed was Mrs Siddons to reciting blank verse that she often made the most ordinary remarks in perfect iambic pentameter.

George III, when mad, mused long on her supposed elopement with the artist Thomas Lawrence, but Sarah, who was a public prude (and considered the role of Rosalind in *As You Like It* a bit risqué), had allowed the painter to capture her only on canvas. Unfortunately, she was unable to prevent him breaking the hearts of two of her daughters.

WOJCIECH BOGUSLAWSKI (1757-1829)

Polish actor, director and playwright. Boguslawski was a major dramatic figure of his time; he wrote more than eighty plays, translated *Hamlet* and successfully presented works of MOLIÈRE and LESSING. As director of the Polish National Theatre and a distinguished actor, he did much to expand the repertoire and improve the standard of acting in his native land.

JOHN PHILIP KEMBLE (1757-1823)

English actor. Although critics judged him harshly towards the end of his career, Kemble and his sister, the great Sarah SIDDONS, ruled the stage for many years, assisted by numerous relations.

At a Catholic seminary in France the young Kemble impressed his fellow students with his prodigious memory. Choosing to exercise this gift in the theatre rather than the cloisters, he worked hard on his art during seven years in the English provinces before making his London debut as Hamlet in 1783. The ease with which he wore the robes of kings and princes was his greatest asset, and he shone in noble, tragic roles, playing almost every leading Shakespearean part. In comedy he was handicapped by a lack of humour, but won praise for his intelligent reading of the texts.

After managing the Drury Lane Theatre for fifteen years, Kemble purchased a sixth share of the Covent Garden Theatre for £23,000. Almost ruined when the theatre burned down in 1809, he was forced to charge more for seats in the new building, and for several weeks his Macbeth was interrupted by cries of "Old prices, old prices". He gave his last performance there in 1817 as Coriolanus, the part of the stern Roman having always been that best suited to his cold and haughty style. By this time, however, enthusiasm for Edmund KEAN's more emotional playing had caused Kemble's declamatory style to be condemned as "a petrification of sentiment, that heaves no sigh and sheds no tear; an icicle upon the bust of tragedy".

FRANÇOIS ANDRIEUX (1759-1833)

French playwright. At times a lawyer, judge, political figure, professor and, from 1829, Perpetual Secretary of the Académie Française, Andrieux found time to write several successful comedies, notably *Les Étourdis* (1787). A determined defender of the Classical tradition, he read Honoré de BALZAC's play *Cromwell* and told the author that he should pursue any career except that of a writer.

AUGUST IFFLAND (1759-1814)

German actor, playwright and manager. At a time when the German theatre was convulsed by change, Iffland was its great establishment figure, reassuring his conservative audiences with glamour, skill and cheap sentiment.

Although he was excellent as the violent Franz Moor in SCHILLER's *Die Räuber*, Iffland the actor was better suited to comedy, developing brilliant characterizations by careful observation of dress and gesture. He was appointed Director of the Berlin National Theatre in 1796, where he remained for the rest of his life. There his productions, many for his own plays, made lavish use of costume and scenery. Iffland the author was skilled but unadventurous, a moralizer who preferred the public to weep rather than think. Of his sixty-five plays, only *Die Jäger* (1785) survived well into the next century. Nearly as devoted to wine and women as to the theatre, he was not accounted a good citizen by his contemporaries. But his great abilities, his gift of popularization and his discerning encouragement and help that he gave to young actors (including LUDWIG DEVRIENT) have assured Iffland of a major place in German theatre history.

Sheridan. His courtship of the lovely Elizabeth Linley involved much wrangling with her father (the composer Thomas Linley), two duels with a rival suitor and a romantic elopement to France

FRIEDRICH SCHILLER (1759-1805)

German playwright and poet. The early careers of the two giants of German literature had nothing in common. While GOETHE enjoyed privilege, Schiller suffered the injustices of feudal despotism. His father was in the service of the tyrannical Duke of Württemberg, who had absolute control of the young man's destiny. Sent to the Military Academy at the age of thirteen, despite all protestations that he wanted to become a priest, Schiller was forced to study first law and then medicine, and eventually to become a low-ranking medical officer in the Duke's army. There all he learned was the heavy-handed administering of drugs, a method of treatment he later prescribed for himself during long illnesses.

All Schiller's feelings of anger and rebellion were poured into his first play, *Die Räuber* (1782). Franz Moor, a grotesque archetype of evil, cheats his brother Karl out of his father's love, his inheritance and his fiancée. Karl, in a confused desire for justice, becomes the leader of a band of robbers, but cannot prevent his men from committing atrocities in his name.

After travelling to Mannheim to see August IFFLAND as the original Karl Moor, Schiller was placed under arrest and forbidden to write any more for the stage. Although loth to leave his family, he fled back to Mannheim under a false name, but there found his former friends in the theatre unwilling to help a deserter from a Duke's army.

A period of extreme poverty brought on the illness that afflicted Schiller for the rest of his life (he suffered from repeated bouts of pneumonia, combined with severe digestive troubles). On top of this, *Fiesko* (1782) was a failure, but eventually, with *Kabale und Liebe* (1783), a domestic tragedy in the style of LESSING, he began to gain

"To die of singing": German Romanticism

The golden ages of theatre in Spain, England and France coincided with eras of political power and material prosperity. For two centuries the princedoms of Germany had hardly known sufficient years of consecutive peace even to erect a theatre, let alone find time to write for it. Finally, in the relative stability of the eighteenth century, rival courts began to compete, not by hiring mercenary soldiers, but by patronizing the arts. In the theatre, however, there existed little tradition to build on; the Austrian court was obsessed with Italian opera, while in the north the only players were fairground tumblers. The first major companies, those of Caroline NEUBER, Konrad ACKERMANN and Konrad EKHOF relied heavily on French classics. Leipzig, where the word of the scholarly Francophile Johannes GOTTSCHED was law, resembled a miniature Paris.

These tentative beginnings kindled a theatrical Renaissance that was to encourage some of the greatest poets, playwrights and actors the West has ever seen. The first playwright to rebel against the imitation of the French was Gotthold LESSING, who saw that contemporary English works, notably George LILLO's *The London Merchant*, provided far more suitable models. A true rationalist, he believed in presenting the problems of the day in a realistic bourgeois setting, using prose rather than ponderous alexandrines.

No sooner had Lessing indicated one possible direction for the development of German theatre, than the *Sturm und Drang* (storm and stress) movement set off in another. The inspiration of the young GOETHE and the circle he gathered round him in Frankfurt was SHAKESPEARE. The use of blank verse and freedom from all classical restraints in form and language made for powerful poetry but unperformable plays. Realistic, middle-class dramas still remained popular (especially when they included seduction and abandonment), but more energy was devoted to epic struggles between good and evil. Everyone identified with *Faust*.

This cult of genius and rage, a premature flowering of the Romantic spirit, found its greatest playwright in FRIEDRICH SCHILLER. When *Die Räuber* was put on in Mannheim in 1781, a member of the audience likened the theatre to a madhouse; "Complete strangers fell sobbing into one another's arms, and fainting women tottered towards the exits. The effect was of universal release, as when a new creation bursts forth from out of the mists of Chaos."

Goethe was by this time in Weimar, the city state that became the European centre of classical Greek ideals. When Schiller followed him there, he too realized the importance of form in his later masterpieces, from *Wallenstein* to *Wilhelm Tell*. Goethe's and Schiller's productions at the ducal theatre, however, were (by all accounts) extremely amateur. Even on the professional stage, the only actor-manager who really met the challenge of new theatrical styles was the great Friedrich SCHRÖDER. In his later years at Weimar, Goethe tried to evolve a ritualistic, pseudo-Greek style of playing. This was in reaction to the highly emotional acting then fashionable, typified by the manic excesses of LUDVIG DEVRIENT.

The most popular dramatist of the age was not one of the literary giants, Goethe, Schiller or Heinrich von KLEIST (whose understated style was too subtle for contemporary taste), but the man of the world and reactionary politician, August von KOTZEBUE. With the skill of a professional playwright, he knew just how to keep audiences on the edge of their seats with crude melodrama. The Romantics turned likewise to sensationalism. Fate, a powerful element in the great tragedies of Schiller became the sole ingredient in the plague of *Schicksalsdrama* (fate drama) unleashed by Zacharias Werner. The theatre was still a novelty and simple emotion appealed. Germany needed a further period of reflection to assess the legacy of its golden age.

a wider reputation. Invited to Leipzig by unknown admirers, he worked on his vast, poetic tragedy *Don Carlos* (1787). Over 6000 lines in length, it is more objective than his earlier works and even gives tyranny, in the person of King Philip II of Spain, a chance to justify itself.

Although historical accuracy was not a strong point of *Don Carlos*, Schiller, on Goethe's recommendation, obtained the post of Professor of History at the University of Jena, where work on a history of the Thirty Years War inspired his great Wallenstein trilogy, *Wallensteins Lager*, *Die Piccolomini* and *Wallensteins Tod*, completed in 1799. This epic tragedy, which is dominated by an idea of "fate", similar to that of classical drama, was performed at Weimar, where Schiller was now collaborating with Goethe on productions in the Ducal Theatre. In contrast to the "Olympian" Goethe, who was aloof and formal with his actors, Schiller proved a more practical director,

with a ready sympathy for his actors.

As he knew his end was approaching, Schiller wrote tirelessly for the theatre. *Maria Stuart* (1800), his best-loved play, is a hymn to the triumphant inner freedom attained by the heroine when she renounces her ambitions in a corrupt, political world. *Die Jungfrau von Orleans* (1801), a highly symbolic version of the story of Joan of Arc, and *Die Braut von Messina* (1803), a Greek tragedy complete with chorus and set in Norman Sicily, were followed by the more down-to-earth *Wilhelm Tell* (1804).

More limited in range than Goethe (his plays all treat similar themes), Schiller was nevertheless far more aware of world events and also of developments in philosophy. Immanuel Kant examined the question of whether there was such a thing as absolute good. It is Schiller's fascination with the political implications of this problem that has made his plays so relevant to succeeding generations.

Friedrich Schiller (*above*) was at times able to relax, but most of his life was a frenzy of poetic activity and a desperate struggle to survive. In his youth he fought to make a living as a writer, and just as he achieved critical recognition he began his long battle against illness. "In the end", he wrote to Goethe, "I shall perhaps have salvaged what was worth preserving." *Traveller Overlooking a Sea of Fog* by Caspar David Friedrich (*left*) sets the age to perfection

JOHN BANNISTER (1760-1836)

English actor. Bannister inherited the irrepressible good humour of his father, "honest Charles Bannister", whom he followed onto the stage of the Drury Lane Theatre. His inauspicious beginnings in tragedy were soon forgotten with his comic triumph as Don Ferolo Whiskerandos in SHERIDAN's *The Critic*. "The first low comedian on the stage", he made many roles his personal property, including Tony Lumpkin in GOLDSMITH's immortal comedy *She Stoops to Conquer*.

LOUISE-FRANÇOISE CONTAT (1760-1813)

French actress. A massive beauty "cut from a block of purest marble", Mlle Contat made her name as Suzanne in BEAUMARCHAIS' *Le Mariage de Figaro*. Her spirited portrayal of romantic heroines at the Comédie-Française (she was especially admired in MARIVAUX) was mirrored by an extremely active love life off stage. This produced a growing family of illegitimate children, to whom she was an excellent mother.

During the French Revolution, Mlle Contat was imprisoned for her royalist sympathies. She was saved from the scaffold by a young actor, who, although a revolutionary himself, destroyed her dossier so that she never appeared before Robespierre's dreaded Committee of Public Safety.

JOHN BILL RICKETTS (1760-99)

English-born "Equestrian Hero". Trained as a trick-rider at Philip ASTLEY's Circus in London, Ricketts chose an unpropitious time for an Englishman to emigrate to the rebellious United States. Yet, despite continuing hostilities between England and America, he became well known around Philadelphia and even went riding with George Washington. His act included dancing and juggling on horseback and jumping from one mount to another through a hoop. His *pièce de résistance* was a "leap over a ribband extended twelve feet high" from a kneeling position in the saddle.

Assisted by Signor Spinacuta and The Polander Dwarf, Ricketts developed his show into a regular circus with acrobats and rope-dancing. An amphitheatre was built for him in New York, but almost immediately it burnt to the ground. After this disaster Ricketts set sail for England, but he and his whole company perished when their ship was lost in a storm.

AUGUST VON KOTZEBUE (1761-1819)

German playwright. Serious writers and critics held Kotzebue in utter contempt; German patriots thought he was a Russian spy; yet public demand made him the most popular playwright in all Europe. Even GOETHE, who loathed him, was obliged as director of the Duke's theatre in Weimar to put on no fewer than eighty-eight of his plays.

As a young diplomat, Kotzebue found favour at the Court of St Petersburg and rose to become Governor of Estonia. His involvement in Russian politics later earned him a life sentence in Siberia, but he was freed after only four months through his influence with the Tsar. An implacable opponent of Napoleon and of the German democratic movement, he scorned any form of idealism, just as he affected cynical indifference to any elevated literary activity.

The international success of plays like *Menschenhass und Reue* (1789) created a taste for melodrama that was to last throughout the nineteenth century. With mystery, sensational recognition scenes and crude emotionalism, Kotzebue achieved startling theatrical effects. He claimed he could write any kind of play on any subject. In fact he produced over two hundred, attempting every genre from romantic tragedy in *Die Spanier in Peru*, which contrasts the noble Incas with their brutal Spanish conquerors, to satirical comedy in *Die deutschen Kleinstädter* (1803), the portrait of a small provincial town that apes the cultural life of the big cities.

Kotzebue was stabbed to death by a young student, an event which the Austrian statesman Metternich used as an excuse for repressive control of all political movements in Germany. The assassin, Karl Ludwig Sand, was executed and became a martyr to the cause of democracy. Goethe saw the death of his literary enemy as "a necessary consequence of the moral order of the world".

LOUIS-CHARLES CAIGNIEZ (1762-1842)

French playwright. A wealthy lawyer and local dignitary in Arras in the north of France, Caigniez was ruined by the Revolution. Desperate for money, he went to Paris, where he took up writing for the popular theatre. His first success was a comedy, *Le Dîner des bossus* (1799), but it was with *La Forêt enchantée* (1800) that he found his true metier as a writer of melodrama. For thirty years he rivalled Guilbert de PIXÉRÉCOURT for the title of "the RACINE of the boulevards". One of his plays, *La Pie voleuse*, provided the libretto for Rossini's opera, *La gazza ladra* (*The Thieving Magpie*).

FRANÇOIS-JOSEPH TALMA (1763-1826)

French actor. Talma began acting in elegant theatricals in London, where his father's dental patients included the Prince of Wales. The family's sympathies, however, were decidedly anti-royalist. After his debut with the Comédie-Française in 1787, Talma caused a sensation in Marie-Joseph CHÉNIER's republican drama *Charles IX* in 1789. His radical fervour in the title role galvanized the audience, disturbed his colleagues and ultimately closed the theatre.

Talma's passion for reform also involved theatrical practice. As an actor he favoured "dignity and natural truth" instead of artificial gestures, and continued the campaign for authentic costuming begun by Mlle CLAIRON and LEKAIN. Both his politics and his art appealed to Napoleon, who asked him to perform at great gatherings of state. Offstage, Talma tended to "simplicity and indecision"; his personal life was a confusion of wives, mistresses and children.

MARIE-JOSEPH CHÉNIER (1764-1811)

French playwright and poet. Chénier rode to fame on the crest of the French Revolution. His tragedy *Charles IX* (1789) defied royal censorship, expounding democratic principles to the receptive public. He was a member of the Convention that sent King Louis XVI to the guillotine, but his fortunes declined with the rise of Napoleon. His once-successful play *Timoléon* (1794) was burnt by government order, the actress Mme VESTRIS managing to save just one copy.

WILLIAM DUNLAP (1766-1839)

American playwright, manager and man of letters. America's first professional dramatist, Dunlap became infatuated with the theatre while studying painting in

London. His comedy *The Father, or American Shandyism* (1789) began his long association with the American Company, of which he became manager in 1798, succeeding LEWIS HALLAM, JR. Dunlap wrote and administered assiduously but, plagued by illness and backstage rivalries, went bankrupt in 1805. From 1806 to 1811 he served the company as assistant stage-manager, then supported himself mainly by writing. His publications included a valuable *History of the American Theatre* (1832), but only one of his fifty plays appeared in print.

AUGUST WILHELM VON SCHLEGEL (1767-1845)

German man of letters. Schlegel made SHAKESPEARE seem almost as much a German as an English playwright. The translations he published between 1797 and 1810 with Ludwig and Dorothea TIECK conveyed Shakespeare's power with unprecedented fidelity. Through them, Shakespearean passion and dramatic form became paramount influences on the German stage. Schlegel also translated CALDERÓN as well as DANTE and CERVANTES. Only slightly less important, his lectures *Über die dramatische Kunst und Literatur* (1809–11) were the first attempt to formulate a worldwide historical theory of drama. His gifts were not creative, and his own classical play *Ion* (1803) failed despite the support of GOETHE.

Schlegel's translations of Shakespeare are still commonly performed in Germany today.

August von Schlegel came from a distinguished literary family. His uncle Johann was a playwright and critic; his brother Friedrich, a philosopher and Sanskrit scholar

ZACHARIAS WERNER (1768-1823)

German playwright. Debauched and mentally unstable as a youth, Werner ended his days a Catholic priest. He is chiefly remembered as the inventor of the *Schicksalstragödie* (fate tragedy). Because his mother and best friend had both died on the twenty-fourth of February, he chose this date as the title of his doom-laden tragedy, *Der vierundzwanzigste Februar* (1810), in which an unfortunate family contrive to exterminate themselves, always choosing the same fatal date (and even the same knife) for their bloody deeds. The play was produced by GOETHE (on the twenty-fourth of February). Its success made accursed families and menacing coincidences a staple ingredient of German theatre for the next thirty years.

TORRINI (c 1770-c 1820)

French conjuror. As a young medical student, Torrini had fled France after the execution of his father in the Revolution. He continued his studies in Naples, but was fascinated by magic, in particular by the tricks of Giuseppe PINETTI, whose illusions he shamelessly plagiarized. Great rivalry sprang up between the two; there are numerous anecdotes of both magicians interrupting and ruining each other's performance.

Torrini's brilliant career took him all over Europe, even to Constantinople, and earned him the favour of high society. It was terminated tragically when his son was killed on stage by the accidental substitution of live ammunition for blank during an illusion. Torrini went mad and died soon after.

GUILBERT DE PIXÉRÉCOURT (1773-1844)

French playwright. The haughty Comédie-Française scorned Pixérécourt, but for thirty-five years he thrilled the public with his melodramas. Performed at the unpretentious boulevard theatres, their standard formula never failed and varied only slightly. In fifty-nine plays purity defeated villainy at the last gasp, after evil machinations and hair's-breadth escapes.

For Pixérécourt such tension and violence were facts of life. He fled France at the outbreak of revolution and fought briefly with a royalist army before returning secretly to Paris. Only a friend's intervention saved him from Republican justice. Already the author of sixteen unperformed plays, he eked out a living for his family painting fans until his first theatrical success in 1797. He produced his best-known melodrama, *Coelina, ou l'Enfant du mystère* in 1800. Quickly translated into other languages, this classic story tells of an innocent maiden defamed and exiled by the lies of a rejected suitor. The scoundrel is finally exposed and captured with the timely aid of some passing archers.

Pixérécourt lost his fortune in a theatre fire and died after a long illness. His trite but vital plays influenced the Romantic drama of HUGO and DUMAS. In France, with some justification, he is known as the father of melodrama.

LUDWIG TIECK (1773-1853)

German playwright and manager. Tieck's best plays are his satiric fantasies based on fairy-tales. In *Der gestiefelte Kater* (1797) a talking cat makes his master's fortune while the stage character of the author ridicules melodramatic conventions. Tieck also wrote lengthy verse dramas such as *Leben und Tod der heiligen Genoveva* (1799), but he is best known for his completion of SCHLEGEL's translations of SHAKESPEARE. Although his daughter Dorothea did much of the actual writing, Tieck supervised the project and used the new versions in a celebrated series of dramatic readings in Dresden. His own reputation as a writer gradually waned, and from 1825 to his death he worked as a theatre director in Dresden and Berlin.

ROBERT ELLISTON (1774-1831)

English actor-manager. Elliston regularly found himself "in great difficulties by his own fault", but few actors have enjoyed such acclaim from their contemporaries. Leigh Hunt thought him second only to GARRICK in tragedy and "the best lover on the stage". Lord Byron could imagine "nothing better than Elliston in gentleman's comedy". Offstage he was the perfect Regency gentleman, with a flashing smile and a manner at once graceful and hearty. An enthusiastic manager, known as The Napoleon of Drury Lane, he was often extravagant, but remained "the joyousest of spirits".

MATTHEW LEWIS (1775-1818)

English novelist and playwright. Lewis acquired a reputation for Gothick horror with his novel *The Monk* (1796), from which he gained the nickname "Monk"

Mr Punch (*below*) was born as Pulcinella, the hook-nosed and mischievous servant of the Commedia dell' Arte. By the early nineteenth century he had taken his familiar English name and become the villainous hand puppet who murders his family. This engraving depicts a Neapolitan performance

A tyrant behind the scenes at the Comédie-Française, **Mlle Mars** (*above*) was a delightful comic in the plays of Molière

The agile clown **Grimaldi** (*right*) became so crippled in his old age that each evening the landlord of his tavern had to carry him home

Lewis. His spine-chilling expertise with murders, ghosts and graveyards transferred superbly to the theatre. *The Castle Spectre* (1797) was the first in a series of stage works that included an equestrian melodrama, *Timour the Tartar* (1811). Lewis's plays abounded with evocative music, atmospheric scenery and stunning effects. They also required actors athletic enough for perilous leaping escapes. The audience meanwhile revelled in "fits of hysteria and fainting".

Lewis's own demise was aptly macabre. He died of yellow fever on a voyage from Jamaica and was buried at sea. The coffin slipped its weights and, instead of sinking, carried its lifeless cargo off into the unknown.

HEINRICH VON KLEIST (1777-1811)

German playwright. Kleist is now considered to be one of the greatest of German dramatists, but his demonic genius flourished and died unrecognized by his contemporaries. Only two of his plays were performed in his lifetime, and Kleist himself never saw his work on the stage.

After serving in the army, and a short spell as a farmer in Switzerland, Kleist turned to writing. His first play *Die Familie Schroffenstein*, completed in 1803, was followed by *Robert Guiskard*, but in a fit of despair he burnt the manuscript of this second play and joined Napoleon's army to invade England and "expire in the beautiful death of battle". Thwarted in his aim, he was later arrested by the French as a spy.

In 1811, Kleist shot himself after first shooting an incurably sick woman who had begged him to kill her. The author of eight brilliant novellas and one of the greatest masterpieces of German comedy, *Der Zerbrochene Krug* (1808), he died impoverished.

JOSEPH GRIMALDI (1778-1837)

English clown. Grimaldi was the most beloved theatrical performer of his day. Comic, acrobat, dancer, mime, singer and swordsman, he excelled in melodrama as well as in farce and pantomime. In an age which lacked great dramatists, his tumblings and songs were major contributions to the stage. Equally at ease as Mother Goose or "the Bold Dragoon", he delighted audiences at the Covent Garden Theatre for seventeen years. But it was as a pantomime clown that Grimaldi was at his most inventive. Joey, as the character became known, ousted the Commedia dell' Arte figure of Harlequin from pre-eminence in his harlequinade. Before long, Joey the clown was as popular in the circus ring as on the stage; as familiar in America as at Covent Garden.

Grimaldi's early childhood was dominated by his severe and eccentric father, who worked as a ballet master, and once feigned death to discover how his family would react to his demise. Joe feigned sorrow. By the time his father really did die, Grimaldi, aged nine, was already a veteran of the stage and indulging in his own eccentricities, such as collecting flies.

Grimaldi's private life lacked the mirth of his public appearances. His brother mysteriously vanished; his son, who had some early success on the stage, drank himself to death; and Grimaldi himself was forced from the stage by a crippling affliction. The clown who had begun his career under the stage motto "Hence, Loathed Melancholy" spent his last fourteen years in sad retirement.

MLLE MARS (1779-1847)

French actress. The greatest comic actress of her age, Mlle Mars radiated sweet innocence on stage, but behind the scenes ruled the Comédie-Française with despotic authority. Younger actresses walked in terror of her, for she would demand that anyone who crossed her be dismissed.

The illegitimate daughter of a member of the company, she joined as a skinny sixteen-year-old ingénue, a perfect Agnès in MOLIÈRE's *L'École des femmes*. Her subsequent triumphs were the result of dedicated study; she waited many years, for example, before attempting the great coquette, Célimène, in Molière's *Le Misanthrope*. Her intelligent playing brought out every nuance in the comedies of Molière and Pierre de MARIVAUX, but the vital exuberance of the Romantic theatre proved to be beyond her range. Not wishing to be passed by as fashions changed, Mlle Mars accepted leading roles in plays by Victor HUGO and ALEXANDRE DUMAS *père*, but drove the authors mad with persistent requests that they tone down the poetic excesses of their language.

LUDVIG DEVRIENT (1784-1832)

German actor. Devrient was a temperamental man and a heavy drinker, whose emotional style, ill-suited to the dignified classical tradition, restricted him to character parts or wild heroes such as King Lear. In 1814 he went to work with August IFFLAND in Berlin, where he gave fine performances as Falstaff and Shylock. Devrient took over the company in 1819 and, in spite of drinking and related amnesia, continued to act until weeks before his death.

LOUIS ANGELY (1787-1835)

German playwright, actor and director. Angely's farces were enormously popular among the Berlin bourgeoisie in the 1820s and 1830s. He worked at the Königsstädter Theater from 1822 onwards, and wrote more than a hundred plays. These were mostly borrowed from French vaudeville farces, but Angely cleverly adapted them to everyday life in Berlin. Among the most popular were *Sieben Mädchen in Uniform* (1826) and *Das Fest der Handwerker* (1828).

MLLE GEORGE (1787-1867)

French actress. Mlle George's early success was due as much to her statuesque beauty and eminent lovers as to her interpretations of RACINE. Her conquests included heads of state from Talleyrand to the Tsar of Russia, but a much-vaunted affair with Napoleon probably lasted no more than one night.

Mlle George's invasion of Russia took place four years before Napoleon's. In the middle of a season with the Comédie-Française in 1808 she eloped with a ballet dancer to St Petersburg. Forced to return by the war, she was reinstated in the Comédie-Française at the insistence of the Emperor. After Waterloo, her Bonapartism and violent temper made her so unpopular in the company that she was dismissed.

On a tour of Belgium she met Charles Harel, who, as leading impresario of Romantic drama, was to mastermind her second career. Mlle George's fiery passion was ideal for the forceful heroines of Victor HUGO's *Lucrèce Borgia* and *Marie Tudor*. As she grew older, she appears to have made a speciality out of what were then contemporary roles. In addition to the two Hugo plays above, she was also extremely popular in two plays by DUMAS *père*: *La Tour de Nesle*, and *Christine* (1829). Harel, her lover for many years, eventually went bankrupt, but Mlle George did not give up. Over fifty and overweight, she attempted several comebacks, but Parisian audiences now had eyes only for the beautiful RACHEL. Eventually retirement was forced upon her, and she died forgotten.

Ferdin. Raimund

Edmund Kean (*left*) rejected the company of high society that stardom made available to him. He preferred drinking with his tosspot friends in rowdy taverns

Raimund (*right*). His magical plays are often redolent with melancholy. His own life was likewise afflicted with the anguish of his unbalanced mind

EDMUND KEAN (c 1787-1833)

English actor. Kean's delight in creating legends about his life has confused fact and fiction, but he undoubtedly experienced an unsettled boyhood and a turbulent youth. He appears to have first gone on stage at the age of three, as Cupid in a Drury Lane ballet. When eight years old, according to one attractive tale, he walked to Portsmouth and went as a cabin-boy to Madeira. Hating the discipline, he managed to convince both the captain and a doctor that he was deaf. He was sent home, keeping up the deception for several months and, on reaching port, danced a hornpipe on the quay before running off into the crowd.

As a young man Kean wandered the provinces, using his talents in any way he could, even as a circus acrobat. He worked with many companies, and although poor and unrecognized, remained convinced of his own abilities. In 1814 he was finally offered a contract at the Drury Lane Theatre. Neither actors nor audience expected much from the newcomer, but his Shylock enthralled them and success came literally overnight. An idol of the stage, he went on to play Richard III, Hamlet and Iago, always at his most effective in moments of emotion or villainy. "To see him act", said Coleridge, "is like reading Shakespeare by flashes of lightning." As Sir Giles Overreach, the grasping hero of Philip MASSINGER's *A New Way to Pay Old Debts*, he had many of his audience in a state of shock.

In 1820 Kean went to America. Greeted with enthusiasm in New York, he stormed out of a theatre in Boston, angered by the small audience. While he was in New York, he put up a monument to the actor George Cooke, and had his body removed from the Strangers' burial ground and reinterred. It is said that he retained a toe-bone for himself, a souvenir that he treasured until his wife threw it out of the window.

Back in England, Kean continued to rule the stage, but in 1825 his infatuation with one Mrs Cox led her husband to bring an action against the actor, and substantial damages were awarded. His pride suffered more than his pocket. Audiences turned against him, and although he did eventually regain their favour, his acting was no longer what it had been. He drank heavily, and by the age of

forty-six was an old man. Kean collapsed on stage during a performance of *Othello* and died six weeks later.

THEODORE HOOK (1788-1841)

English journalist and playwright. At sixteen Theodore was already writing the words to comic operas by his father, the composer James Hook. While still a teenager he began to write plays on his own; *Tekeli* (1807) was one of the most popular melodramas of the time.

A remorseless wit and practical joker, Hook delighted London in 1809 with the Berners Street Hoax. When crossed by a Mrs Tottenham, he sent 4000 letters inviting attendance at her address. On the appointed day, half London converged upon the street: coal wagons, chimney sweeps, bakers, undertakers, lawyers, philosophers and even the Lord Mayor. Hook was forced to leave England until the hue and cry had died down.

In 1813 he went as accountant-general to Mauritius; by 1817 £12,000 had disappeared. He went to prison for two years, describing his ignominious return from the tropics as due to "a slight disorder in the chest". For the last twenty years of his life, writing continued to furnish his living; wit, his place in society.

MIKHAIL SHCHEPKIN (1788-1863)

Russian actor. Born a serf and apprenticed in obscure provincial theatres, Shchepkin won his freedom and became a star of the Imperial Theatre of Moscow when he was in his early thirties. He was a great exponent of "Narodnichestvo populism"—the movement away from classical, foreign influences towards an art born from the soul and soil of the Russian people. His natural approach to acting became the dominant style, and was to have a profound effect on the work of STANISLAVSKY.

FERDINAND RAIMUND (1790-1836)

Austrian playwright and actor. Raimund fell in love with the theatre while selling sweets for a living in the aisles. He longed to play tragic roles, but his poor diction and

unimposing build made this impossible. His talent for comedy, however, was quickly recognized.

As a playwright, Raimund was a master of popular comedy, a mixture of farce, magic and song, written in Viennese dialect. His first play, *Der Barometermacher auf der Zauberinsel*, was performed in 1823. Although he continued to write in this tradition, Raimund was a solemn man, who did not consider his work purely as lighthearted entertainment. There are evident moral undertones in *Der Alpenkönig und der Menschenfeind* (1828) and in his most ambitious play, *Der Verschwender* (1834). Good triumphs over evil, and virtue is rewarded; Raimund extended the possibilities of folk comedy.

But he himself was not to experience the happy ending of his plays. Bitten by a dog, he shot himself, believing that he had rabies.

WILLIAM BETTY (1791-1874)

English actor. When William Betty, a boy of twelve, made his London debut in 1804, the audience became so wild with excitement that the military had to be called out. For the rest of the season there was talk of little else. The "Young Roscius" was hailed as a genius, and the Prime Minister, the younger Pitt, adjourned the House of Commons in order to see him as Hamlet. Master Betty played most of the great Shakespearean roles, but his success was short-lived; he was jeered as Richard III, and eventually left London for the provinces.

Well past his prime in 1812, he attempted to return to the stage, but was a complete failure.

FRANZ GRILLPARZER (1791-1872)

Austrian poet and playwright. Grillparzer came from a tormented family. His mother and brother both committed suicide. His father, a lawyer and a semi-recluse, strongly disapproved of his son's poetry, yet the boy would discover him late at night reading tales of knights and spirits.

Grillparzer expressed many of his own sufferings in plays, whose deeply felt psychological understanding is far ahead of its time. In *Sappho* (1818), *Das goldene Vliess* (1821) and *Hero und Leander* (1831) powerful feelings and intense emotional conflicts are sensitively portrayed in verse. Although his plays were much admired, Grillparzer always felt a certain shame at the exposure of things so intimate and personal on the stage. When his comedy *Weh dem, der lügt* (1838) was censored, he ceased to write for the public. Subsequent plays are bitter and critical self-portraits. *Libussa*, which he considered his best, was also written during this period.

In 1827 Grillparzer participated in a melancholy scene. He wrote Beethoven's funeral oration, and was a torch-bearer at the ceremony.

EUGÈNE SCRIBE (1791-1861)

French playwright. Scribe was one of the new breed of professional authors that emerged in the nineteenth century to make large fortunes from their writing. He wrote over 400 pieces, some in collaboration, including vaudevilles, comedies and librettos for comic operas.

He began his career at the café frequented by Parisian vaudeville writers. Drinking champagne, seven or eight authors would invent a farce and send it off to the theatre. Soon Scribe was writing successful vaudevilles on his own; then, not content with these one-act farces, he began to write longer and more complex comedies. Among these were *Bertrand et Raton* (1833) and *Le Verre d'eau* (1840). Bourgeois audiences loved his plays. They were topical, the characters and situations were familiar, and their sanity and solid morality were a comfort in a France upset by the Revolution of 1830. Scribe's plays may have lacked depth, but they were masterpieces of plot, carefully constructed down to the finest detail. Perhaps the best example of this facile perfection (or the "well-made play" as the style became known) is *Bataille de dames* (1851). *Adrienne Lecouvreur*, written with Ernest Legouvé, is his only tragedy.

"That greatest nongenius of drama", Scribe has often been condemned as trite and worthless, but his achievements as a craftsman cannot be denied, nor his influence on later realistic drama forgotten.

Introverted and intolerant, **Macready** (*right*) became a great tragedian through sheer application. He quarrelled with all his stage partners, such as Samuel Phelps, Helen Faucit and Charlotte Cushman; and was particularly put out when people noticed that he and Cushman looked uncannily alike. His rivalry with Edwin Forrest ended in a fatal riot

Andrew Ducrow (*above*) showed great style in circus displays which combined horsemanship with mime

Deburau (*below*) gave a subtle dignity to the character of the hopeful and ever-disappointed Pierrot

ANDREW DUCROW (1793-1842)

English equestrian and circus owner. At seven Ducrow was already appearing in Philip ASTLEY's equestrian displays. His father, a circus strongman called the Flemish Hercules, encouraged the boy's career with regular floggings. As an adult, Ducrow overwhelmed audiences by his style as much as by his horsemanship. They adored his "Living Statuary" in which, standing on horseback, he imitated heroes of the past, striking a motionless pose above his thundering steed. Dramatic sketches were also great favourites, especially *The Courier of St Petersburg*, in which he entered on two horses, straddled a third and controlled several others on reins. Sometimes the animals themselves starred, demonstrating their courage and intelligence. Ducrow employed clowns and other two-legged acts, but to the end his motto remained "cut the dialects and get to the 'osses".

WILLIAM CHARLES MACREADY (1793-1873)

English actor and manager. Macready had no desire to enter the theatre, but the debts incurred by his father, a theatre manager, forced him to leave school at sixteen to come to his aid. He made his London debut at the Covent Garden Theatre in 1816, playing Orestes in Ambrose Philips's *The Distrest Mother*. But it was his performance as Richard III in 1819, thought by many to equal Edmund KEAN's, that brought him recognition as a great tragic actor. Macbeth, Lear, Hamlet and Henry IV were to be some of his finest roles. In the 1820s he visited America and France, where his performances were well received. Macready studied his parts carefully: "I cannot act Macbeth without being Macbeth," he explained. He lacked the fire of Kean or GARRICK, but his acting was sensitive and superbly controlled.

Macready was intolerant of poor management and second-rate performances. He was also bad-tempered and a snob. In 1837, after years of disputes, he became manager of Covent Garden and was finally able to work to his own high standards. One of the first men to conceive of a production as a whole, not as fragmented parts, Macready insisted on full crowd rehearsals and commissioned magnificent sets and backcloths. He remained at Covent Garden for two years, and later managed the Drury Lane Theatre; but his artistic principles lost him money, for he proudly ignored the box-office as unworthy of his attention.

Macready's quarrel with the American actor Edwin FORREST caused his last tour of America to end in disaster. About twenty people lost their lives in the riots at the Astor Place Opera House, where Macready was acting.

He gave his last performance in 1851 as Macbeth, a part he had played nearly 150 times.

ALEXANDER GRIBOYEDOV (1795-1829)

Russian playwright. Griboyedov's verse play *Woe From Wit* is still the masterpiece of Russian comedy, occupying a unique place in the national culture. By the end of the nineteenth century, according to one scholar, sixty-one phrases from this single work had become everyday Russian expressions.

Chatsky, the play's hero, returns from three years in Europe with liberal ideas and the misfortune of being both enlightened and clever. In Moscow he encounters nothing but monotony, vulgarity and self-indulgence: "What novelty can Moscow show me? Today a ball, tomorrow two or three." All the action takes place within twenty-four hours in the house of a rich and servile civil servant. In such a world it is no wonder that the sane Chatsky is ultimately considered to be the madman.

"In *Woe From Wit*," complained the poet PUSHKIN, "the question arises, 'Who is being witty?' and the answer is Griboyedov." Yet to have packed so much bite and sarcasm into four elegant conversational acts is the wit of a genius.

Griboyedov wrote several earlier comedies, but his energies were diverted by a diplomatic career that ultimately cost him his life. He was murdered in Tehran, while serving as Minister Plenipotentiary.

TYRONE POWER (1795-1841)

Irish-American actor. The sudden death of the Irish actor Charles Connor gave Power the opportunity to prove himself the leading comic Irishman on the English stage. In roles such as Sir Lucius O'Trigger in *The Rivals*, as well as in his own comedies (*O'Flannigan and the Fairies*, for instance), he brilliantly parodied his countrymen. Returning from one of his trips to America, Power was drowned in a shipwreck in the Atlantic.

His grandson, Tyrone Edmond Power (1869–1931), acted almost entirely in America. He was with Augustin DALY's company in New York from 1890 to 1898, playing with such leading actresses as Mrs FISKE and Julia Marlowe. His son, Tyrone Power Jr. (1914–58), also began his career in the theatre, but it was as a cinema heart-throb that he was to reach international stardom.

JEAN-BAPTISTE GASPARD DEBURAU (1796-1846)

French mime. The lonely, tortured, white-faced clown, forced to smile against his will, is today part of the repertoire of any mime. This was the romantic creation of Jean-Baptiste Deburau, whose life became legend in the film *Les Enfants du Paradis*.

But Deburau was not limited to melancholy interpretations. Although he always appeared in the black skull-cap and long, white, large-buttoned gown of Pierrot, his range was considerable. He could be "joyful, sad, sick, healthy, aggressive, defensive, a musician, a poet, a simpleton", but he was "always poor, just like the common people". It was this that made him the star attraction of the rumbustious *Boulevard du Crime*, the centre of popular entertainment in Paris.

Deburau's father had toured Europe with a troupe of acrobats before setting up at the Théâtre des Funambules. Deburau himself turned down frequent invitations to leave his father's theatre for more prestigious companies, preferring to stick with the poor plots, stale jokes and repetitive tumbling routines that had made his name. Knowing his limitations, he never attempted a speaking role, but his reputation did not suffer.

After leaving the flower-girl he had lived with for many years, Deburau became a suspicious, neurotic man. He died as a result of a fall on stage, and his huge funeral was said to have been attended by every beggar, thief, whore and seamstress in Paris.

BOCAGE (1797-1863)

French actor. With his handsome and expressive face, alluring voice and keen intelligence, Pierre-Martinien Tousez, known as Bocage, was one of the leading interpreters of Romantic drama. His fine acting contributed to the early success of plays by DUMAS *père*, George Sand and Victor HUGO, his greatest triumph being Buridano in Dumas *père*'s *La Tour de Nesle*. Although his popularity

did not diminish, he was beset by illness and financial difficulties in later years, and died in poverty.

MME VESTRIS (1797-1856)

English actress-manager and singer. Besides appearing as Mozart's Cherubino, Lucia Elizabetta Vestris was an enthusiastic specialist in such virile roles as Macheath and Don Juan. Her performances in breeches offered to her numerous followers an opportunity to admire her ample charms ("What a breast – what an eye! What a foot, leg and thigh!" ran one contemporary ditty). Her historic importance lies in the tasteful and realistic staging and costumes her work inspired. Scorning the casual daubing which had hitherto characterized English stage decor, she made such innovations as using real door-knobs in her sets. She also imposed her own critical standards upon such works as *Romeo and Juliet* and *A Midsummer Night's Dream* (typically choosing in the latter to play Oberon, the King of the Fairies). Sometimes her fastidiousness went too far. She allegedly donned kid gloves and silk to play a milkmaid, and in another play had a pair of slippers sewn on to her feet every night (for better shape) to be discarded after each performance.

At sixteen Lucy had married the Parisian dancer Auguste-Armand Vestris, an outrageous rake who soon abandoned her. She then embarked on a strenuous and lucrative career of illicit adventure, contriving at one time to be kept simultaneously by two admirers. A later marriage to her stage partner Charles Mathews seems to have reformed her. Together they became a respected force in London theatre management, notably at the Lyceum, but eventually their fortunes ebbed and Charles was imprisoned for debt as Lucy lay dying.

ALFRED DE VIGNY (1797-1863)

French poet, dramatist and novelist. Vigny shocked traditionalists of the French theatre with his adaptations of SHAKESPEARE, such as *Shylock* and *Othello*. The violence of language and the dynamic English manner of acting adopted by the French cast in this latter play came as a revelation to audiences who had never before heard spoken on the stage such a vulgar word as "handkerchief" in classical theatre, and certainly were not accustomed to such natural expression of emotion.

La Maréchale d'Ancre (1831), an original play, met with only partial success, but *Chatterton* (1835), based on the life and suicide of the young English poet, had a triumphant reception. Vigny's mistress of many years, Marie DORVAL, distinguished herself in the part of Kitty Bell. Their tempestuous relationship ended in the same year, and Vigny wrote nothing more for the stage.

PAULINE-VIRGINIE DÉJAZET (1798-1875)

French actress. Déjazet was one of the most popular actresses of her day, excelling in vaudeville and musical comedy. She was renowned for playing male roles (including VOLTAIRE and Napoleon) and for witty, malicious women characters who came to be called "Déjazets" after her. The Palais-Royal was the scene of some of her major successes, but in 1859 she started her own theatre, the Théâtre Déjazet. It had originally been Les Folies-Nouvelles, and with her son as manager, she worked happily there for many years.

When ALEXANDRE DUMAS *fils* asked her to star in *La Dame aux camélias* Déjazet refused, saying that the work would be a success, but only if there was a revolution and she did not act in the play. History proved her right.

MARIE-THOMAS DORVAL (1798-1849)

French actress. Dorval was the archetypal French Romantic actress, as passionate in person as she was on the stage. The poet Théophile Gautier said she was "nature itself, all womanhood united in one woman". Mistress of Alfred DE VIGNY, she startled audiences with her dramatic fall down a staircase in his play *Chatterton* (1835).

Finding the Comédie-Française too restricting, Dorval preferred to appear in popular theatres where she could "rumple up her dress to her knees without any consideration for the standards of the Conservatoire".

HONORÉ DE BALZAC (1799-1850)

French novelist and playwright. Balzac's plays were mainly adaptations, often in collaboration, of his own novels and short stories. From *Le Père Goriot* he extracted *Vautrin* (1840), a play that was banned because the actor Frédérick LEMAÎTRE appeared in a wig that made him look like King Louis-Philippe. For Balzac, the theatre suffered from the need to have actors translate an author's ideas to the audience: "Better to deal with God himself than his saints," he said. Balzac himself was dealing with God when he had his greatest theatrical success, the posthumous *Mercadet*, performed as *Le Faiseur* (1851).

ALEXANDER PUSHKIN (1799-1837)

Russian poet, novelist and playwright. Throughout his short life Pushkin was regarded by tsarist authorities as a dangerous revolutionary. In fact, he was a true revolutionary only in his writing. He overthrew the stale power of French classicism, replacing it with Russian myths and history; and from the Russian language he created a supple and powerful voice that came as a revelation to his contemporaries. He was a master of poetic forms, from exquisite erotic lyrics to the great narratives for which he is best known: "Russlan and Ludmila", "The Gypsies" and his masterpiece "Eugene Onegin". For the stage he wrote four "little tragedies", character studies in verse, and one great tragedy, the historical drama *Boris Godunov*. This work reveals Pushkin's debt to SHAKESPEARE. No longer bound to inflexible French alexandrines, he wrote in a mixture of prose and verse, capturing a wealth of emotion and characterization that had previously been denied to Russian dramatists. In the fall of Tsar Boris he also chose a radical new theme. So convincingly did he describe the corruption of power and a people's rebellion, that Russian censors forbade the production of *Boris Godunov* until 1870.

Pushkin spent much of his life in domestic exile. Although he was a minor official with the foreign office, his early sympathies with the Decembrist rebellion of 1825 and his subsequent liberal opinions made him a marked man. But revolutionary politics were far from Pushkin's mind; he wanted simply to be allowed to write in peace. In February 1837, stung by insults to his wife, he challenged a guard's officer to a duel. Some are convinced that Pushkin was forced into this impulsive act. If so, the plot succeeded; the supposed enemy of the state (and the greatest poet Russia has ever known) died of a stomach wound in St Petersburg.

JAMES HENRY HACKETT (1800-71)

American actor. Hackett was one of the first American character actors. In various guises throughout the USA and England he played the stage Yankee, a bluff comical figure with a heart of gold. He often adapted existing plays to create a vehicle for the part.

A master of dialect, Hackett was equally popular as the epitome of the Westerner, Nimrod Wildfire, but he did not restrict himself to patriotic caricatures. In 1833 he won critical admiration in London for his Falstaff.

FRÉDÉRICK LEMAÎTRE (1800-76)

French actor. Lemaître became famous overnight when, without consulting either authors or cast, he parodied the role of Robert Macaire in the dull melodrama *L'Auberge des Adrets*. Encouraged by his success, he developed the part into the play *Robert Macaire* (1834). Critics saw Macaire as a symbol of the greed of contemporary society; Gustave FLAUBERT considered him the greatest dramatic figure since Don Juan. The censors banned the play.

Lemaître was one of the greatest romantic actors of

Pushkin (*above*) ushered in a great age of Russian literature. His major play *Boris Godunov* is strangely neglected in the West

Balzac (*right*) was a large, convivial and generous-spirited man who poured immense energy into his novels and very little into his plays. But many of the ninety or so novels and stories in his panoramic masterpiece, *La Comédie humaine*, have been dramatised by others

Dumas *père* turned many of his own Romantic novels into plays. *Right*: the pathetically abandoned figure of "The Man in the Iron Mask" in the third of his D'Artagnan stories, *Le Vicomte de Bragelonne*

Van Amburgh (*far right*) trained his beasts harshly with an iron bar, but relied thereafter on an extraordinary empathy. He was once discovered perched in a gum tree with an opossum, patiently trying to teach it to read. When finally and fatally mauled by a lion, he still managed to throttle it with his hand down its throat

his day. Although he was successful as Hamlet and Othello, he was at his best in the modern roles, which allowed him to unleash his passionate temperament upon a sobbing or terrified audience. With Marie Dorval he had a number of successes in melodrama, and Alexandre Dumas *père* wrote especially for him the title role of *Kean*, a dramatic biography of the fiery English actor.

Lemaître's last great romantic role was in Lamartine's *Toussaint L'Ouverture* (1850), after which changing tastes exiled him to lesser parts in small theatres.

ISAAC VAN AMBURGH (1801-65)

American animal tamer. Van Amburgh's power over jungle cats was attributed variously to his protruding eyes or his Indian blood. From his earliest years he had charmed skittish horses, foxes and even wild mice until a chance encounter with a circus presented him with bigger game. He was soon the Lion King, touring with his own menagerie, drawing crowds by coating his arm with blood and thrusting it into a lion's mouth, or putting a lamb and small child between a beast's paws. Van Amburgh's magic failed at last, when a lion mauled him fatally during a violent storm.

EDUARD DEVRIENT (1801-77)

German actor, singer, director and theatre historian. Eduard and his two brothers Karl (1797–1872) and Emil Devrient (1803–72) carried on the great Devrient tradition in a more sober, professional manner than their temperamental uncle, Ludwig. A fine baritone, Eduard helped give German opera its own particular style of singing, before the tragic loss of his voice obliged him to concentrate on straight drama. A tireless organizer, he acted and directed in Berlin and Dresden before becoming Director of the Hoftheater in Karlsruhe. His *Geschichte der Deutschen Schauspielkunst* was the first full history of the German stage.

The eldest brother, Karl, was famed for playing the great roles of Wallenstein, Faust and Lear. But perhaps the greatest actor of the three was Emil, who adopted a classical, measured style of delivering verse and worked for most of his career at the Dresden Court theatre.

CHRISTIAN DIETRICH GRABBE (1801-36)

German playwright and essayist. As a young man Grabbe abandoned legal studies and moved to Berlin to become a writer, but after boring Ludwig Tieck and quarrelling with the great poet Heinrich Heine, he returned disconsolately to work in his provincial hometown as a military lawyer. Dismissed for negligence, he found a benefactor who published his work, but finally Grabbe fell out with him as well.

Grabbe's work is as colourful and chaotic as the legends surrounding his life. *Don Juan und Faust* (1829), an attempted integration of Mozart and Goethe, is probably unstageable, but the equally experimental *Napoleon oder Die hundert Tage* (published in 1831) successfully foreshadows expressionist techniques, while the cynical comedy, *Scherz, Satire, Ironie und tiefere Bedeutung* (published in 1827) has even today lost little of its sting.

JOHANN NEPOMUK NESTROY (1801-62)

Austrian playwright and actor. "I believe the worst of every man, including myself, and I have rarely let myself down," runs one of the typical aphorisms that punctuate Nestroy's satirical comedies. But in his life he showed no sign of the bitter sarcasm that pervades his plays, even when his wife deserted him.

During a brief career as an operatic bass, Nestroy was notorious for improvising and introducing comic business, talents he exploited to the full when he took up acting. A lean, angular figure, he delighted in playing grotesques, and wrote himself many parts to suit his style. *Der böse Geist Lumpazivagabundus* (1833), which retained the fairy-tale setting of the plays of Ferdinand Raimund, was his most popular work. Later, more realistic farces included *Zu ebener Erde und erste Stock* (1835) and *Einen Jux will er sich machen* (1842).

ALEXANDRE DUMAS (1802-70)

French novelist and playwright. The world's first great purveyor of romantic adventure, Dumas *père* thrived on

the memory of his father, a West Indian half-caste who became a general in Napoleon's army. Despite gestures of Republican fervour, he diverted most of his energy to amorous intrigues and to his many swashbuckling, historical novels and dramas. These were written with little regard for style or originality, often being plundered from the works of lesser contemporaries.

For a time Dumas was the leading playwright of the Romantic movement, his standing higher even than Victor HUGO's. *Henri III et sa Cour* (1829) was performed at the Comédie-Française before the epoch-making production of Hugo's *Hernani*. *Antony* (1831) was also produced there, but Dumas later rewrote it as a (not disinterested) favour to the lovely actress Marie DORVAL. From then on he helped to make the Théâtre de la Porte-Sainte-Martin the citadel of Romantic drama. His greatest success was *La Tour de Nesle* (1832), a macabre melodrama that contained very few lines by its supposed author. An interesting failure was *Kean* (1836), based loosely on the life of the great English actor. (It has come to life this century in a version by Jean-Paul SARTRE.)

Dumas' later plays were usually adaptations of his own novels, including the world-famous *Les Trois Mousquetaires* and *Le Comte de Monte-Cristo*. In 1847 he founded his own theatre, but it failed and Dumas faced bankruptcy. His extravagance with regard to women, clothes and jewellery was legendary. ALEXANDRE DUMAS *fils*, by then a highly successful writer himself, kept the "dear simple-minded, great man" in comfort. They had not always got on so well. *Fils* had previously objected bitterly to his *père's* cast-off mistresses and shoes.

VICTOR HUGO (1802-85)

French poet, novelist and playwright. Although Hugo's writing and philosophy dominated French Romantic literature of the nineteenth century, his early poems respected a classical restraint in form and language. But when he turned to the theatre, he joined in the fashionable enthusiasm for SHAKESPEARE. His first play, *Cromwell* (published in 1827), was not performed, but its preface became the bible of Romantic drama. Its thesis is that tragedy and comedy should exist side by side; the playwright should "mix the grotesque with the sublime". The censors did not agree, for his next offering, *Marion de Lorme*, was immediately banned.

In 1830 Hugo finally had a play, *Hernani*, accepted by the Comédie-Française; not since CORNEILLE's *Le Cid* had French theatre known such controversy. The fantastic plot gave little offence, but Hugo's disdain for the classical unities, and the unprecedented freedom of the verse and language were little short of revolutionary. On the first night two rival groups set out, one to hiss, the other to cheer. The piece was inaudible, but the cheers won the day. The following year saw his quasi-apotheosis, with the publication of his best known novel, *Notre Dame de Paris* (*The Hunchback of Notre Dame*).

Hugo's best plays are those in verse. The finest of these is *Ruy Blas* (1838), the only one to combine tragedy and comedy successfully and the only one regularly performed today. His prose pieces, like *Lucrèce Borgia* (1833), are little better than melodrama. It was during a rehearsal of the latter that Hugo met Juliette Drouet, a young actress of limited talent. Embittered by his wife's brief liaison with the critic Sainte-Beuve, Hugo sought consolation with Juliette. The passion soon went out of the affair and he was reconciled with his wife, but he long continued to practise a form of bigamy.

The failure of *Les Burgraves* (1843) put an end to Hugo's ambitions in the theatre. By now he was deeply involved in politics. He had been a Royalist, but in 1848 became a supporter of Louis-Napoleon. His politics moved rapidly to the left, until he tried to incite the common people of Paris to revolt. In 1851 he escaped to Belgium and moved to the Channel Islands.

Hugo's return to Paris during the Franco–Prussian War brought further political disappointments, but under the Republic he became Senator for life. His magnificent funeral was a worthy tribute to his genius, and he was buried among France's national heroes in the Panthéon.

EMIL DEVRIENT (1803-72)

German actor and singer. Like his brother EDUARD DEVRIENT, Emil worked as a salesman before taking to the stage, where he played *Liebhaber* (lover) roles in most of the German classics and won acclaim as an operatic bass. Devrient's greatest fame coincides with his thirty-seven-year stay at the Dresden Court theatre, where he excelled in such idealistic Goethean roles as Tasso and Egmont. On tour in London, he was a superb advocate of many hitherto unseen German masterpieces, besides playing a Hamlet which even Englishmen were compelled to acknowledge as authoritative.

GUSTAVO MODENA (1803-61)

Italian actor. An ardent patriot as well as a theatrical innovator, the young Modena would insert inflammatory political speeches into his scripts. After the suppression of the uprisings against Austria and the Pope in 1831, in which he was an active combatant, he spent many years in exile, aiding the Republican cause of his friend Giuseppe Mazzini. Once, facing starvation in London, he took to reciting Dante in the intervals between concert-pieces. This proved so popular that his audiences subscribed to help pay off his debts.

A political amnesty allowed Modena to return to Milan, where he formed his own company. His belief in psychological realism, and insistence that plays should have contemporary relevance, greatly influenced the young generation of Italian actors. Both Tommaso SALVINI and Ernesto ROSSI studied under him.

SAMUEL PHELPS (1804-78)

English actor-manager. In 1843 Phelps took over the historic Sadler's Wells Theatre in the northern outskirts of London and turned it into a centre for the production of classical English drama. All but four of SHAKESPEARE's plays were among the works performed there during the next eighteen years. Some of these Phelps rescued from oblivion; *Antony and Cleopatra*, for example, was produced for the first time in a hundred years.

Phelps trained a generation of younger performers, and appeared on stage regularly himself. One of his most popular roles was Bottom in *A Midsummer Night's Dream*, confirming reports that he was better at pathos and comedy than at passion. He was, however, in a position to take on tragic roles when he liked, acting them in an old-fashioned declamatory style. A crusty, difficult man, Phelps nevertheless knew how to relax: he is said to have been familiar with most of the trout streams in the country.

JEAN EUGÈNE ROBERT-HOUDIN (1805-71)

French conjuror. The apparatus of today's conjurors is still based largely on the inventions of the phenomenal Robert-Houdin, whose genius for intricate mechanics was fostered in his family's clock-making business in Blois. He made his reputation by constructing clockwork automata, robot-like figures that could answer questions and make profile drawings. These were the rage of the Paris International Exhibition of 1844. The following year he ventured on to the public stage in his Théâtre des Soirées-Fantastiques. Eschewing the traditional decor of the magician, he appeared in a simple black suit, with the minimum of paraphernalia. A born entertainer, he produced a perfect blend of fun and breathtaking illusions, the highlight of the show being the "Suspension by Ether" of his young son. He went on to exploit the potential of electricity and magnetism, creating ever more spectacular effects in his many tours of Europe.

No jealous guardian of his trade-secrets, Robert-Houdin delighted in debunking any fraudulent claims to supernatural powers. At the request of the French government (and at the risk of his life) he exposed as charlatans the sword-swallowing, fire-eating monks who were trying to foment revolt in the colony of Algeria.

EDWIN FORREST (1806-72)

American actor. Forrest was the first great American tragic actor. Massive in presence and voice, he was not at his best in quiet roles (one critic described him as "a vast animal, bewildered by a grain of genius"), but no one could doubt his ability to electrify audiences with his energy and passion.

Born in Philadelphia, he was inspired by acting with Edmund KEAN while still in his teens. When he first appeared in New York as Othello he was only twenty, but his uninhibited style expressed the virility and confidence of a young country, and he soon became the idol of working-class audiences throughout the USA. The figure of the manly rebel in American theatre and film may be traced in part to roles specially written for Forrest: the Indian chief in *Metamora* and the slave, Spartacus, in *The Gladiator*.

Actors playing rough scenes with him learned first-hand what a powerful actor Forrest was. It is said that once, after an argument, six villains whose part it was to attack him did so in earnest. The uncomprehending audience applauded Forrest's "acting" as he threw them all off stage.

In fact he was a brooding, often selfish man who made enemies easily. Rivalry with the English tragedian MACREADY erupted into the Astor Place Riots of 1849, when troops killed some twenty-two among thousands of his fans protesting at the presence of the Englishman. In the same year he tried to divorce his wife on a suspicion of adultery. After she filed a counter-suit and won, he appealed unsuccessfully five times in the next eighteen years. As a bitter old man, complimented on his playing of Lear (his Shakespearean roles had indeed grown more subtle over the years), Forrest replied that he "played" others, but "I *am* Lear!"

IRA ALDRIDGE (1807-67)

American-born actor. The first great Negro actor – nicknamed "the African ROSCIUS" – Aldridge was born in New York, not in Senegal as he liked people to think. As a boy he learned that a black actor had no future in the USA when the African Theatre, where he first performed, was closed by hostile whites. At the age of seventeen he emigrated and never returned home.

This brave step turned out to be a lucky one, for Aldridge was welcomed in Britain, where the abolition of slavery had recently become a popular cause. At first he played slaves aspiring to freedom, such as the tragic hero of *Oroonoko* (by Thomas SOUTHERNE from the novel by Aphra BEHN) and the humorous Mungo in Isaac

The first American actor to win international acclaim, **Edwin Forrest** (*above*) amazed London with the fury of his King Lear

Robert-Houdin (*below*) used his impressive scientific talents to create fantastic illusions. Here he lifts a child by one hair of its head

BICKERSTAFFE's *The Padlock*. Naturally, he also played Othello, but his resonant voice and original interpretations soon commanded the great white roles as well.

After a successful appearance in London in 1825 Aldridge slowly perfected his style for nearly twenty-five years in the provinces. When he appeared briefly in London in 1833 the audiences greeted him warmly, but the critics – unlike their provincial colleagues – were racist and hostile. A third visit in 1848 finally won their unreserved acclaim.

Soon after his London success, Aldridge set out on the first of five triumphant European tours. He travelled to the farthest Russian provinces and played Lear (for the first time) in St Petersburg. In this role, his greatest interpretation, he made up a pale and ancient face but left his hands black. A British subject, Aldridge died on tour at Lodz in Poland, by then one of the best-known and best-loved actors in the world.

THOMAS DARTMOUTH RICE
(1808-60)

American actor. The first blackface white comedian (or "Ethiopian delineator" as they were called) "Jim Crow" Rice was famous for a single song and dance he claimed to have learned from watching a crippled Negro stableman:
    Weel about and turn about and do jis so;
    Eb'ry time I weel about I jump Jim Crow.
Rice bought the man's clothes, added his own topical verses, and made the act into the craze of the next decade, even taking it to England in 1836.

With its combination of English melody and African movement – shuffle and hop of the feet and strong play with the arms and shoulders – it gave white men a reassuring vision of their simple, uninhibited slaves. Rice danced it unchanged well into the fifties. At the Bowery Theatre in New York he performed it between the acts of *Richard III*, giving sometimes twenty encores.

NIKOLAI VASILYEVITCH GOGOL
(1809-52)

Russian novelist and playwright. The hero of Russian liberals for his realistic satire of bureaucracy and his indictment of serfdom, Gogol ultimately confounded his admirers with totally contradictory, reactionary opinions. His masterpieces are works that can be taken on many levels, from tropical satire to allegories of the human soul.

Gogol was born into the Cossack gentry of the Ukraine. The religious mysticism of his mother, who was to be the only woman in his life, does much to explain his apparent *volte-face* at the end of his career. As a young man he tried acting, poetry, the civil service and teaching, all with little success. He even tried to run away to America, but got no farther than Germany.

A collection of Ukrainian folk-tales established his literary reputation, which reached its height with a performance of *The Government Inspector* before the Tsar in 1836. One of the finest comedies of mistaken identity in any language, it contains a wonderful gallery of petty provincial dignitaries who mistake a penniless dissolute for the official of the title.

Confused by the varying reactions to the play, which many condemned as seditious, Gogol moved to Rome, where he lived for twelve years, working mainly on his epic comic novel *Dead Souls*. A pleasant comedy of bourgeois manners, *The Marriage* (1842) was untypical of work he produced in exile, which became increasingly symbolic and concerned with spiritual, rather than social, reform. At the same time mental and physical illness were causing an irrevocable breakdown. After a pilgrimage to the Holy Land in 1848, Gogol gradually lost all hold on reality and finally the very will to live.

FANNY KEMBLE (1809-93)

English actress. Frances Anne Kemble became a star as Juliet in her first appearance at the Covent Garden Theatre in 1829. Her playing of both tragic and comic heroines over the next three years reversed the fortunes of the manager, her nearly bankrupt father, Charles Kemble. She was equally successful in New York when she acted there with her father in 1832. Small and dark-haired, she had a natural talent for the subtle gestures which express passion with decorum.

Although born into a distinguished theatrical family – Sarah SIDDONS was her aunt – Fanny had never aspired to be an actress, and in 1834 she married and retired to a plantation in Georgia. The marriage failed, and from 1848 to 1868 she gave popular readings of whole SHAKESPEARE plays in Britain and the USA. Her two books of memoirs reveal a lively and intelligent woman, and contain shrewd assessment of the theatre in her time.

PHINEAS TAYLOR BARNUM (1810-91)

American showman. The patron saint of promoters, Barnum believed that the sole purpose of what he called "the show business" was providing entertainment. Marvels and marvellous deceptions were its chief attractions, and as "Prince of Humbugs" he proudly supplied them.

His first coup as a showman came in 1835, after years of clerking in general stores, organizing lotteries and running a newspaper. He purchased Joice Heth, an ancient blind black woman with four-inch fingernails who claimed to be 161 years old and the former nurse of George Washington. Lured by Barnum's sensational advertising campaign, crowds flocked to hear her reminisce about "dear little George". Barnum increased the take by planting a letter in a Boston newspaper declaring that Joice was a rubber dummy and her owner a ventriloquist. When she died that year and an autopsy showed she was no older than eighty, Barnum professed injured innocence.

After several lean years, he bought Scudder's American Museum in New York, a lacklustre collection of historical and scientific "curiosities". From 1842 he transformed it with giants, dwarfs, animals, albinos, an Indian village, variety acts, a 3000 seat playhouse and the Feejee Mermaid, a hairy embalmed creature purportedly half-human, half-fish. Always it was his avowed monomania for publicity that made the enterprise "the town wonder and talk".

That same year he made one of his greatest discoveries, the midget Tom THUMB. After successfully exhibiting him, Barnum took the "bright-eyed little fellow" across the Atlantic. In London he artfully presented him to the nobility first, by invitation only. When Queen Victoria commanded a private audience, Tom's ensuing public renown was guaranteed. Back home, Barnum paid tribute to European culture first by building a fantastic pseudo-Oriental mansion in imitation of George IV's pavilion at Brighton. Then in 1849 he engaged the Swedish soprano Jenny Lind for a mammoth concert tour, at an astronomical fee. Hitherto unknown in provincial America, the "Swedish Nightingale" became a legendary success because Barnum touted her "charity, simplicity and goodness" as much as her voice.

Barnum had his setbacks, including bankruptcy and public outrage at the frauds to which his genial autobiography confessed. When the American Museum burned down for the second time in 1868 he thought of retiring. But in 1870 circus men W. C. Coup and Dan Costello offered him a share in their vast new show, and

Barnum leapt at the chance. Such innovations as three rings of simultaneous entertainment were Coup's idea, but Barnum was the great attraction. In 1873 he bought out his partners, and in 1881 merged with James A. BAILEY to form the original Greatest Show on Earth. In 1882 he engineered one last sensation, buying the renowned elephant Jumbo from the London Zoo. Only too late did an irate English public discover the sale. An emotional campaign to save the great beast for the nation simply provided Barnum with free publicity, and he recouped Jumbo's cost within a week of his arrival in America.

But by the time of Barnum's last English tour in 1889, all was forgiven. There, like everywhere else, the old showman basked in the warm public recognition that, of all his creations, he was the most remarkable. At his death two years later an obituary rightly prophesied, "His name is a proverb already, and a proverb it will continue."

ALFRED DE MUSSET (1810-57)

French playwright and poet. Musset was the quintessential Romantic: his life a chaos of disordered passions, his writings obsessed with love. Yet his plays have a delicate wit and a structural cohesion which are found in the work of no other Romantic dramatist.

The turning point in his life was a disastrous visit to Italy in 1833–34 with the novelist George Sand. When she fell ill in Genoa he turned for a while to other women; when he fell ill in Venice she went off with the doctor. Heartbroken, Musset returned to his native Paris and considered the affair in plays and in a series of beautiful lyric poems, "Les Nuits" (1835–37). The direct personal emotion in the poems makes a break with the exotic and public Romanticism of his early mentor, Victor HUGO. But the plays go further, avoiding Romantic self-absorption altogether.

Although they are now classics of the stage, Musset's plays were written for reading only, after the disastrous première of an early work made him wary of public performances. In *Lorenzaccio* (1834) this freedom from stage conventions is fortunate; the play is a succession of short, swift scenes which never cloy. It remains the one popular historical drama of French Romanticism.

But most of Musset's plays are not historical. *Les Caprices de Marianne* (1833), *On ne badine pas avec l'amour* (1843), *Il ne faut jurer de rien* (1836), *Un Caprice* (1837) and *Il faut qu'une porte soit ouverte ou fermée* (1848) are vague about time and place. Set in a slightly unreal and unpredictable world, they combine pure feeling with a refreshing sense of irony. Surrounding a pair of young lovers with a small cast of comical characters, each of these plays focuses subtly on the sad and funny complications of the heart.

CHANG AND ENG (1811-74)

The Siamese twins. Chang and Eng, forced into partnership by a thick ligament joining the base of their chests, were in fact Chinese. They were discovered at the age of nineteen by a Scottish merchant, who exhibited them in Europe and America as the "Siamese Double Boys". The exploitation of such an oddity was meat and drink to Phineas T. BARNUM, who bought their contract, thus beginning a most unfortunate relationship. Barnum in fact disliked the twins, hardly mentioning them in his autobiography, and they could not stand Barnum. Worse still, they now found they could not stand each other. Eng was a quiet, even-tempered chess-player, Chang a quarrelsome drinker with a taste for women. And for all the money they had made, no surgeon would dare attempt to separate them.

Chang and Eng bought a plantation in North Carolina, where, at the age of forty-two, they married two sisters. Each wife had her own mansion, the twins spending three days with one and three with the other, an arrangement that produced twenty-one children. The loss of their slaves in the Civil War forced them to tour again to restore their finances. They eventually retired to the plantation once more, where they died within a few troubled hours of each other.

GEORG BÜCHNER (1813-37)

German playwright. Büchner's death of typhoid in his twenty-fourth year deprived Europe of a doctor, a revolutionary thinker and a dramatist of genius. His three plays remained unperformed until the present century.

He qualified as a doctor, like his father, and entered into revolutionary politics as an emotional reaction to the exploitation he saw in the still largely feudal German states. His manifesto *Der Hessische Landbote* urged an immediate peasants' revolt. Forced to flee to Zurich, where he taught zoology and comparative anatomy, Büchner continued to reflect on political problems, his works becoming profoundly pessimistic.

Much of the dialogue of his first play, *Dantons Tod* was drawn from contemporary records of the French Revolution. The sympathetic, pleasure-loving Danton, who sent so many to their death, embodies the contradictions of the individual revolutionary. As he faces his own death, he reflects on the helplessness of man faced by historical forces beyond his control. The alternation of tragic and comic scenes in swift succession shows Büchner's debt to SHAKESPEARE. His one comedy, *Leonce und Lena*, owes more to Alfred DE MUSSET.

It was *Woyzeck* that revealed the full extent of Büchner's originality. Little more than a fragment, it is the story of a simple soldier driven by jealousy to murder his wife. The brief, impressionistic scenes and the horrific images swirling through the poor soldier's confused brain create an atmosphere of tension more in the manner of the cinema than the theatre. At the end of the nineteenth century these startling new techniques were finally recognized. Büchner was hailed by Gerhart HAUPTMANN as a forerunner of naturalism, but it was the unprecedented style of *Woyzeck* rather than its naturalistic storyline that was to influence the development of modern drama.

"Jim Crow" Rice first performed his blackface act in frontier towns along the Ohio River. Very soon he was being feted in New York; and his solo turn expanded into the Minstrel Show

FRIEDRICH HEBBEL (1813-63)

German playwright and poet. Unable even to begin his studies until he was twenty-two, Hebbel, the son of a builder, suffered from a degree of poverty few other young writers can have experienced. Restless and dissatisfied, he travelled around Europe until he at last found peace of mind in Vienna with the actress Christine Enghaus (1817–1910), whom he later married. She was a fine interpreter of Hebbel's majestic heroines, especially in the title role of his first play *Judith* (1840).

Passionate love is a recurring theme in Hebbel's tragedies, where exceptional individuals are forced to bow before the demands of society or history. *Herodes und Mariamne* (1849), his finest such work, seems a classical verse play dealing with the superhuman emotions of legendary figures, yet its psychology of sexual relations is remarkably modern. He almost always used biblical or mythical sources (Greek myth in *Gyges und sein Ring*; German in his ambitious version of *Die Nibelungen*, 1861), but his one play in a contemporary setting, *Maria Magdalena* (1848), is no less powerful. Like all Hebbel's works it ends with the message of hope, that the sacrifice of the individual will create a better, more understanding and compassionate society.

FRANZ VON DINGELSTEDT (1814-81)

German director and writer. Forgetting his youthful gestures of revolutionary idealism, Dingelstedt accepted a job at the Stuttgart Court Theatre. Officially he was the dramaturge, but it was not so much for his plays that he was to become renowned as for his new approach to direction: his insistence on overall effect as against virtuoso solo performances, and his dynamic use of crowds to create a powerful sense of history. From Stuttgart he went to Munich, then Weimar, where (assisted by the composer Franz Liszt) he staged a vast cycle, comprising almost all the SHAKESPEARE histories and the whole of SCHILLER's *Wallenstein* trilogy.

In 1867 Dingelstedt moved to Vienna to take over the Court Opera. For the last ten years of his life he ran the prestigious Burgtheater, his productions giving great impetus to the rise in status of the director.

EUGÈNE LABICHE (1815-88)

French playwright. Compared in his day to MOLIÈRE, Labiche brought the arts of vaudeville and farce to hilarious perfection. He wrote more than 170 works for the stage, often as senior partner in a collaboration. A number of his farces, such as *Le Chapeau de paille d'Italie* (1851) and *La Cagnotte* (1864), are still popular. The former simply tells of the persistently absurd problems which beset a pleasant young man whose horse eats a hat, but it moves with delightful logic and wit.

Labiche excelled at showing how stock characters cope with abnormal situations in a hilariously predictable way. The gentle satire shows a delicate insight into human reactions: *Le Voyage de M Perrichon* (1860), for example, describes a man who is grateful to one he is able to help, but not at all to one who is helpful to him.

CHARLOTTE CUSHMAN (1816-76)

American actress. Charlotte Cushman, the greatest American actress of the nineteenth century, once remarked, "My earliest recollections are of dolls' heads ruthlessly cracked open to see what they were thinking about." Not surprisingly, she was best at playing determined women, such as Lady Macbeth, Nancy in *Oliver Twist* and the gypsy, Meg Merrilies, in *Guy Mannering*. Her tall, somewhat unfeminine figure also suited her to male roles, notably Romeo to the Juliet of her sister Susan (1822–59). She made a virtuoso piece out of the part of Queen Katharine in SHAKESPEARE's *Henry VIII*, but in other productions of the same play she became an equally convincing Cardinal Wolsey. Her greatest asset was a husky voice, which enabled her to express the most powerful emotions without the ranting histrionics that afflicted so many of her colleagues.

The fact that Cushman's closest attachments were to other women seems to have been accepted by Victorian society. By the acting profession, her ambition and capacity for work were received with awe. After failing miserably as an opera singer, and spending seven years learning to act on the principal stages of New York and Philadelphia, she suddenly controlled her talents in a season of acting with William Charles MACREADY. The English tragedian was patronising but impressed, and at his urging she went to London, where her greatness was immediately recognized. Billed with her overbearing fellow countryman Edwin FORREST on her arrival in 1845, she demolished him with her passionate performance. Later in the tour she outshone Macready himself: as Lady Macbeth she "literally dragged him off the stage" after Duncan's murder.

Cushman's return to the USA was a triumph. She retired several times at the peak of her career, but always came back, and towards the end kept acting through six out of seven years of cancer. A few months before her final performance, a vast crowd in New York escorted her with blazing torches from the theatre to her hotel, where among the fireworks above the cheering throng appeared the sparkling effigy of a local politician. Asking who it was, the great lady was told, "That is Shakespeare, Miss Cushman."

ALEXANDER SUKHOVO-KOBYLIN (1817-1903)

Russian playwright. Cultured, aristocratic and wealthy, Sukhovo-Kobylin was accused in 1850 of murdering his French mistress. The subsequent years of arrest, trials, sentences, reversals of verdict, appeals and counter-appeals were to form the basis of his plays.

Krechinsky's Wedding (1855), the first of his famous trilogy, is a comedy of manners; the second, *The Law Case*, is a bitter indictment of red tape and hypocrisy in which the individual is called "nothing" and The State is "the forces"; part three, *Tarelkin's Death*, deals with surreal interrogations and grotesqueries with the accuracy of bitter experience.

It was MEYERHOLD's 1922 production of *Tarelkin's Death* which became a "text-book of constructivism". Circus devices, contrivances and tricks were used to stage ideas. A hero would be tossed into the air by a spring in his chair, or a policeman explode like a jack-in-the-box, compelling actors to calculate their stage-business with the precision of acrobats.

ALEXEI KONSTANTINOVICH COUNT TOLSTOY (1817-75)

Russian poet, playwright and diplomat. Although he was born into the most privileged class of tsarist society and was a close friend of Alexander II, Tolstoy maintained an artistic independence which often led him into conflict with the authorities. He is best remembered in theatrical annals for *Tsar Fyodor Ivanovich*, which was given an opulently realistic production by STANISLAVSKY in 1898 at the opening of the Moscow Art Theatre. This was the second trilogy of historical verse plays dealing with Ivan The Terrible (the others are *The Death of Ivan The Terrible* and *Tsar Boris*). Tolstoy had problems getting the trilogy past the censors because it dealt scathingly with royalty and the seamy side of the clergy. The plays were finally performed uncut only after the Bolsheviks seized power, and then with great artistic, popular and political acclaim.

BOGUMIL DAWISON (1818-72)

Polish actor. The son of poor Warsaw Jews, Dawison worked as a clerk before making his debut in 1837. Twelve years later he had sufficiently refined his thick (and unpopular) Polish accent to find employment at the Vienna Burgtheater. Pale, skinny and dishevelled, he won fame for excitability that bordered on the grotesque, especially in such roles as King Lear and Othello. At the Dresden Theatre he quickly became a rival to EMIL DEVRIENT, whose exalted style formed an interesting contrast to Dawison's more earthy realism, but in 1864 ill-feeling between them forced Dawison to leave. There followed a series of triumphant tours, until cerebral illness cut short his career.

IVAN TURGENEV (1818-83)

Russian novelist and playwright. Ivan Sergeyevich was born in a forty-roomed manor just south-west of Moscow, to a tyrannical mother who ruled her children with a knout as mercilessly as she did her serfs. His retreats into the seclusion of the gardens and countryside of Spasskoe were to be the only peace of his battered childhood. Later, this idealized landscape, where nightingales sang in dark cypresses and the only flower to scent the air was the rose, became the trademark of his classically controlled, yet lyric style. At nineteen he published his first poems; at twenty-five, he experimented with the theatre in the manner of Prosper Mérimée. *The Imprudence* was romantic and pseudo-Spanish, but his next comedy, *Penniless*, deals more realistically with flighty, impoverished noblemen of high ideals and no will. *The Parasite*, written for Mikhail SHCHEPKIN in 1847 (but censored until 1861) was influenced by GOGOL, as was *The Bachelor. Lunch With The Marshal of Nobility* was to be the beginning of genuine originality, pointing the way to his greatest play, *A Month in the Country*. Written in 1850, *A Month in the Country* was so mutilated by the censors that it only appeared in 1872. Since then it has established itself as a perennial favourite both in Russia and in the West. Turgenev's preoccupation with the psychological development of his characters in the play was to influence profoundly the drama of CHEKHOV.

Most of Turgenev's life was spent abroad. For years he lived in the family entourage of the singer Pauline Garcia Viardot, with whom he had fallen in love in 1843 (he travelled with her on her European tours, and his daughter by a seamstress was brought up with the Viardot children). After the death of his sadistic mother, he became a wealthy man, but he was always short of funds because of his unbusinesslike character. His long affair with Mme Viardot may never have been consummated, though it lasted for more than forty years.

Turgenev was the first Russian writer to gain recognition in Europe. Oxford gave him an honorary degree; FLAUBERT, ZOLA, Daudet and The GONCOURT Brothers wined and dined him in Paris. Yet, cut off from Russia, old before his time, he became hypochondriac, and the turbulence he so aptly chronicled in his novels *Fathers and Sons, Sportsman's Sketches, A House of Gentlefolk, Smoke* and *On the Eve* finally overwhelmed him.

LOLA MONTEZ (c 1820-61)

Irish courtesan, dancer and moralist. Lola appeared as a "Spanish" dancer in cities from London to Dresden. She was expelled from Warsaw after publically denouncing the ruling despot (an amorous dwarf); she whipped a policeman in Berlin and a journalist in Melbourne; she became Franz Liszt's mistress, gossiped with the Tsar and persuaded at least one lover to die for her in a duel. As mistress of the ageing King Ludwig I of Bavaria, she helped to topple the Jesuits from power. Thereafter she lived on her notoriety, appearing as herself in numerous Broadway shows, writing and lecturing on Beauty, Nobility and Morality. Though married to at least two men (possibly simultaneously) the entertaining Lola died in impecunious and penitent solitude.

ÉMILE AUGIER (1820-89)

French playwright. In an age of tearful sentimentality Augier was an anti-Romantic; his plays defend the bourgeois ideals of marriage and honesty. He first tried out these themes in classical verse-comedies, but after seeing the success of ALEXANDRE DUMAS *fils' La Dame aux camélias* he turned to realistic prose.

Some of his best plays, including *Le Gendre de Monsieur Poirier* (1854) (written with Jules Sandeau) and *Le Mariage d'Olympe* (1855), explore the effect of conflicting values within marriage. The latter is a reply to Dumas, giving a sardonic account of the marriage of a prostitute who does not have a heart of gold. Needless to say, Paris preferred Dumas's more sentimental version.

Later plays consider money and the professions. *Le Fils de Giboyer* (1862) caused an uproar with its anti-clericism. In fact, Augier's didactic streak is meant to provoke, but it rarely spoils the play. His attacks on middle-class avarice and ambition were tempered by a touching faith in what was best in bourgeois society. The results of this balance were believable characters and honest plots. Late in life he showed a delightfully irresponsible impulse in the farce *Le Prix Martin* (1875), written in collaboration with Eugène LABICHE.

DION BOUCICAULT (1820-90)

Irish playwright and actor. Boucicault was one of the most successful and glamorous men of nineteenth-century theatre. An actor, playwright, innovator, lobbyist and romancer, he wrote 150 plays, or else adapted them, for in his own words "plays are not written, they are rewritten". The best known were *The Octoroon* (1859), which daringly considered inter-racial marriage, and the Irish melodramas *The Colleen Bawn* (1860) and *The Shaughraun* (1875), but his first play, *London Assurance* (1841), written when he was twenty-one, has a recent reputation as something more: a bridge between the comedy of SHERIDAN and WILDE.

Boucicault's own life was a melodrama in itself. He was born in Dublin, the illegitimate son of the author of *Dr Lardner's Cabinet Cyclopedia*. His mother, a Mrs Boursiquot, christened him Dionysius, but when he wrote *London Assurance* he was Lee Moreton, and when he married for the first time in Paris he was known as Viscount Boucicault. Finally he settled for Dion as "a suitable patronymic to suggest the subtle, magical qualities of a necromancer". He married three times (the last time bigamously) and died in New York, where he had taught in an acting school in Madison Square Garden.

Boucicault's work, and his stage Irishmen, quickly became unfashionable after his death; but if the critics stopped admiring it, J. M. SYNGE and Sean O'CASEY did not, because it influenced them both. It was also thoroughly professional. Boucicault rehearsed carefully, which was uncommon then; he introduced fireproof scenery and the box set.

He was also keen to please (and happy to plagiarize). Borrowing a French play called *Les Pauvres de Paris*, he changed its title to *The Poor of London*, or *New York* or *Liverpool*, depending on where it was playing. Despite his freedom with other men's work, he successfully lobbied the US Congress to establish author's copyright. Since *The Colleen Bawn* was the most popular Irish play of the century, his motivation was clear.

LOUISA LANE DREW (1820-97)

American actress-manager. A distinguished comedienne and for many years (1861-92) the formidable manager of the Arch Street Theatre in Philadelphia, Mrs Drew survived to become a grand matriarch of the stage. She was the mother of two fine actors, JOHN DREW JR (1853-1927) and Georgiana (1856-93) and the grandmother of Lionel, ETHEL and JOHN BARRYMORE. Her third husband, John Drew, whom she married in 1850, was famous for his comic Irish roles.

Louisa's own theatrical forbears went back to the Elizabethans. She was already a seasoned trouper when (as Louisa Lane) she emigrated to the USA from London at the age of seven with her actress mother. In America she became famous in the SHERIDAN roles of Mrs Malaprop and Lady Teazle, making a reputation for herself backstage by arriving at the first reading of a play with her lines already memorized. As a producer Mrs Drew was familiar with the theatre from top to bottom; it is said she was as good a carpenter as any who worked for her.

FYODOR DOSTOYEVSKY (1821-81)

Russian novelist. "I am a realist in the highest sense of the word; that is to say, I depict all the depths of the human soul," wrote Dostoyevsky in his diary. No stranger to the depths himself, this epileptic, convict and compulsive gambler wrote some of the greatest novels in the world. The plays adapted from *The Brothers Karamazov*, *The Idiot*, *The Possessed*, *The House of the Dead* and *Crime and Punishment* were to be inspirations for NEMIROVICH-DANCHENKO's productions at the Moscow Art Theatre. Dostoyevsky's analyses of the beauty, intensity and evil of the human heart still inspire vivid dramatization.

GUSTAVE FLAUBERT (1821-80)

French novelist and playwright. Flaubert's interest in the theatre far exceeded his talent for it, though his novels and short stories have often been dramatized. He wrote a number of plays which were not produced, but when his great friend the poet and playwright Louis-Hyacinthe Bouilhet died, Flaubert completely rewrote Bouilhet's play *Le Sexe Faible* and persuaded Carvalho, director of the Paris Vaudeville Theatre, to produce it. Carvalho changed his mind during rehearsals and produced instead Flaubert's harsh satire on political parties, *Le Candidat* (1874). Whistles, insults, chaffing and raillery caused Flaubert to withdraw the play after four nights. In 1914 Carl STERNHEIM produced his German adaptation of the play with more success.

RACHEL (1821-58)

French actress. Rachel brought the seventeenth-century masterpieces of French tragedy back to life. Born Elisabeth Félix, the child of Jewish pedlars, she spent her early years singing for coins in the streets and cafés of Lyons and Paris. Her family was too poor to afford a good education, but in Paris she began to attend Saint Aulaire's school of drama, where she studied passionately to master the classics of the French stage. She finally won a place at the Conservatoire and began at the Comédie-Française, where one director remarked that she had a good voice and a gift for tragedy but not the figure for it, and another that she might have the figure for comedy but not the voice. Impatient to be on the stage, she left at fifteen and, taking the name Rachel, made her debut in melodrama at one of the smaller Paris theatres, the Gymnase.

The influential critic Jules Janin noticed her; few others did. It was Joseph Samson who took her into the Comédie-Française in 1838. She made her debut at the end of the season as Camille in CORNEILLE's *Horace* before an audience of hardly twenty. Playing a number of parts during the summer, she remained unnoticed until Janin returned from a trip to Italy and turned all eyes upon her. Here was the actress who would revive RACINE and Corneille! Here at last was a return to classical simplicity, after the overblown excess of the Romantics. Suddenly all Paris was flocking to see the young actress who, small, narrow-shouldered and hardly pretty, spoke her verses so simply and naturally. Her sudden outbursts of passionate love, anger or jealousy seemed quite impossible from such a meagre frame.

Rachel became an emblem in the battle between classicism and Romanticism, which at that time in France was also a conflict between tradition and the threat (or promise) of revolution. She was renowned for her numerous and distinguished lovers, including Walewski, son of Napoleon and Maria Walewska.

In 1843 Rachel performed what may have been her greatest stage role – Phèdre. Roxane in *Bajazet* and Hermione in *Andromaque* were other triumphs in plays of Racine. Later she attempted Romantic drama, but Eugène SCRIBE's *Adrienne Lecouvreur* was her only success. She repeated her triumphs all over Europe and in Russia. Eventually her love life and cupidity became obsessive. She began to lose favour with the arrival in Paris of Adelaide RISTORI, who stole many of her admirers. That year Rachel left to act in America; she returned exhausted and ill, to die soon after of consumption.

EDMOND AND JULES DE GONCOURT (1822-96 AND 1830-70)

French men of letters and playwrights. The famous *Journal* of the inseparable *frères* Goncourt, kept daily over many years, is one of the great social documents of the nineteenth century. The highly strung and morbidly sensitive brothers were more fascinated with the details of life than with events, and accordingly their jointly written art histories, novels and plays are all documentary in approach – in a sense, extensions of the *Journal*. Such verisimilitude repelled the first audience of their one interesting play, *Henriette Maréchal* (1865), which anticipates ZOLA in its naturalism. To the Goncourts' dismay (they were interested in observing evil, not reforming it) it also provoked an anti-government riot.

ADELAIDE RISTORI (1822-1906)

Italian actress. Adelaide Ristori, one of Italy's most celebrated actresses, was born into the theatre. She first appeared on stage in a basket, aged three months; she was soon playing small parts and, at fourteen, her first lead. She joined the Compagnia Reale Sarda, one of the best in Italy, and by nineteen was the leading actress. Over the next ten years her finest roles included the leads in Eugène SCRIBE's *Adrienne Lecouvreur* and SHAKE-SPEARE's *Romeo and Juliet*.

In 1846 the noble Marchese Capranica del Grillo fell madly in love with her. Secret meetings and much plighting of earnest troths followed, until his disapproving family consented to their marriage. As befitted her new position, in 1851 Ristori left the stage. Not surprisingly, she returned a year later, stipulating that she would play "morally acceptable" parts. In Paris in 1855 she triumphed in Vittorio ALFIERI's *Mirra*. Three years later the Austrians threw her out of Venice for arousing nationalist sympathies among the Italian population with *Giuditta*, written for her by Giacometti.

Ristori was tall, imposing and dignified; her acting powerful and passionate, suiting to perfection such parts as Lady Macbeth and SCHILLER's Maria Stuart.

So great was her fame that on her eightieth birthday the king paid his respects in person.

THÉODORE DE BANVILLE (1823-91)

French poet, playwright and critic. De Banville favoured verse drama, a discipline which presented no apparent difficulty: "I write in verse with the same ease that I write to my tailor." Though now remembered for his poems, his plays were very popular in their time, among them the verse comedies *Le Feuilleton d'Aristophane* (1852) and *Les Fourberies de Nérine*, a variation of MOLIÈRE's *Les Fourberies de Scapin*, written in 1864. The prose comedy *Gringoire* (published in 1866) has survived the best: for in it, the leading role provides irresistible opportunities for virtuoso display, which were exploited with great success by both Constant-Benoît COQUELIN and ZACCONI. De Banville was a respected critic and man of letters.

ALEXANDER OSTROVSKY (1823-86)

Russian playwright. Ostrovsky abandoned his law studies in Moscow because of their cost, and found work as a court clerk instead. For the aspiring young playwright this was an ideal occupation; the daily litigations of smug merchants, petty despots, attractive wastrels and ladies with beautiful souls became his inspiration. *Bankrupt*, his first play, was considered subversive, and Ostrovsky lost his job. But he gained a vast supportive audience for the rest of his life. Of the eighty plays he wrote, many are still the mainstay of repertory companies throughout Russia. Their aphorisms accurately observed customs, national songs, and that nineteenth-century Russia still "smelling of barns and grocery-shops", and are as popular as ever.

He deals best with the nouveau-riche and conservative middle-class – their domestic tyrannies, their intellectual pettiness, their egotism and greed – all desperately assuming gentility. *A Profitable Job* (1857) is about government clerks with nagging wives; *Wild Money* (1859), about gold-diggers. In *Without Dowry* (1863) he describes aristocrats with pretensions where their hearts should be. In his masterpiece *The Storm*, Katerina, the heroine, hovers between purity of the soul and the harshness of reality. Set in a provincial town, the play is a crucible for any aspiring actress. Entire reputations have risen and fallen over the expression of Katerina's woes.

Ostrovsky's "realistic objectivity" required a new school of acting. The Maly Theatre, which specialized in the production of his plays, became known as "Ostrovsky's House". Senior actors and actresses there were expected to play almost any part.

During the early Soviet Period, the critic Lunacharsky's admonition, "Back to Ostrovsky", was a slogan of The People's Commissariat for Enlightenment. Ironically, Ostrovsky had become a symbol for twentieth-century conservatism.

DAN RICE (1823-1900)

American clown, strongman and circus owner. Rice first tasted show business success as part-owner of a talking pig. When the garrulous porker died, Rice the strongman was born. But brawn alone bored him. Performing at P. T. BARNUM's American Museum he purposely dropped the huge barrel of water he was "struggling" to lift, revealing that it was really almost empty. Such roguishness led him to his real vocation as a clown, though it also made him a difficult employee. He became famous for his mock-Shakespearean orations, invincible repartee and comic equestrian feats. He was equally well known for hard drinking, brawling and a habit of walking out on contracts. Still for years he remained the First Clown of America. Once in Washington D.C. both House and Senate suspended their deliberations to attend one of his performances. It was an appropriate gesture, for Rice regularly appeared in the guise of Uncle Sam, with red, white and blue suit, top hat and whiskers. Unfortunately, he turned out to be a less durable figure than his model, declining finally into bitter alcoholic obscurity.

The wisecracking Mr Bones and Mr Tambo, and the sentimental medley of blacked-up singers and dancers of the touring Minstrel Show, were a familiar sight in America and England from about 1840

BLONDIN (1824-97)

French tight-rope walker. With one performance Blondin turned ropewalking from a clever skill into a death-defying act. He arrived in America in 1859 as a star member of the illustrious Ravel troupe. Bored with their traditional feats, he announced that he would traverse a rope stretched across Niagara Falls. Before 25,000 breathless spectators he strolled the 1100 feet in eight minutes, pausing *en route* to do a back somersault. Then he carried a heavy camera and tripod half-way across, stopped to take pictures and returned walking backwards. He made a second complete crossing with a chair, on which he first sat, then stood. His audience's nerves suffered even more in months to come as Blondin added a frightening number of variations, repeating his jaunt in turn blindfolded and wrapped in a sack, pushing a wheelbarrow, with a piggy-back passenger, in heavy chains and finally on stilts. ("Sit quiet," said Blondin to his nervous passenger, "or I shall have to put you down.") The same derring-do subsequently amazed European sceptics. High above awful chasms Blondin danced, played a fiddle or cooked omelettes on a portable stove. He retired at last to a peaceful old age, still toasted as "the Hero of Niagara".

124

Ibsen (*right*) left Norway at the age of thirty-six with as much relief as he had felt on escaping from provincial Skien at fifteen. His art needed detachment and the slow distillation of memory. Most of his great plays about the constrictions of small-town life were written while he lived in Rome, Dresden, Munich and the Tyrol. In the space of twenty-seven years he visited his native country only twice

Alexandre Dumas *fils* (*below*) anticipated Ibsen in the writing of realistic drama. Although lacking the latter's poetic power and psychological insight, he was one of the first playwrights who dared to question middle-class morality

The law required the half-clad ladies of Miss Warton's "Poses Plastiques" troupe to keep perfectly still on stage, making them ideal subjects for the earliest photographs. For this picture (*above*) taken in 1856, the exposure time was something like fifteen minutes

The romantic ardour of **Ernesto Rossi**'s performance in such roles as Amleto (*below*) conveyed something of the true Shakespearean spirit to foreign audiences who could not understand his Italian

ALEXANDRE DUMAS (1824-95)

French playwright and novelist. Dumas *fils* wrote *La Dame aux camélias* (sometimes called *Camille*) as a novel in 1848, but it was the stage version, written for money in eight days and performed in 1852, which caught the public's imagination. Inspired by the author's own attachment to one Marie Duplessis, it tells of a courtesan who, reformed by the pure love of her suitor, is eventually persuaded to leave him for his own good. They are reunited only when the strain has broken her health, and she dies in his arms.

Beneath the sentimental plot (which has considerable power, as Verdi realized when he used it for his opera *La Traviata*) Dumas posed social questions which were taboo in the theatre at the time. Today the play may seem as romantic as any escapist entertainment written by ALEXANDRE DUMAS *père*, but to the contemporary playgoer it was realistic. *Le Demi-monde* (1855) strengthened his reputation for dealing with sordidly real subjects. It describes the world of moral twilight where women who have fallen down the social scale mingle with those who are climbing it. *Le Fils naturel* (1858) and *Les Idées de Mme Aubray* (1867) deal with illegitimacy. Illegitimate himself, Dumas *fils* had an uneasy rivalry with his more ebullient father, complaining wryly, "I'm tired of having to have your discarded mistresses and shoes."

In his later plays he moralized too much. But his best work, like that of his contemporary AUGIER, is well plotted and defends liberal bourgeois values with a clear insight into human nature. Unlike Augier, he does not concentrate on character (the courtesan Marguérite is an exception) but uses dialogue brilliantly to evoke the society of the age he lived in.

HIRAM W DAVIS (1825-1905)

American circus freak. Hiram and his brother Barney (1827–1912) were billed as "Plutano and Waino, The Original Wild Men of Borneo". According to Phineas BARNUM's typically inventive publicity, they were captured in the East Indies after a pitched battle with a ship's company seeking water. In reality they were mentally subnormal, physically stunted and inoffensive; but they were abnormally strong and could easily lift men of twice their weight. Sensation-seekers were unfailingly impressed by their hairiness and propensity for gibbering. On their Ohio tombstone is written: LITTLE MEN.

LOUIS-ARSÈNE DELAUNAY (1826-1903)

French actor. Delaunay's talents were first spotted by Théophile Gautier, the critic whose opinion could make or break reputations on the Paris stage. Duly becoming *jeune premier* at the Comédie-Française, Delaunay excelled above all in the works of Alfred DE MUSSET: as Perdican in *On ne badine pas avec l'amour* and as Coelio in *Les Caprices de Marianne*.

After playing the same roles for nearly forty years, Delaunay began to feel his eternal youth was wearing thin, though his popularity never waned. When he was finally allowed to retire, the takings at his benefit performance broke all existing records.

GEORG, DUKE OF SAXE-MEININGEN (1826-1914)

German director and designer. Succeeding to the small dukedom of Saxe-Meiningen in 1866, the "Theatre Duke" not only ruled his country liberally but devoted himself to the radical reform of the Court theatre. Staging, scenery, costume and lighting gradually changed completely. Georg absorbed a bewildering diversity of influences: Japanese art, for example, showed him the charm of asymmetry on stage. Twice a widower, his third wife (actress Ellen Franz) extended Georg's visual reforms to the dramaturgical and literary levels. Struck by the Shakespearean productions of Charles Kean, as well as by Wagner's synthesis of the arts, the Duke worked out every production in lengthy rehearsals. Removing the inflexible scenic wings he frequently used a multi-level stage, especially for the crowd scenes at which he was expert ("During a battle all run about," is one appropriate instruction). The general public first saw the Meininger Troupe in SHAKESPEARE's *Julius Caesar* in 1874. Over the next twenty years, Meiningen's company visited nine countries, performing before such directors as STANISLAVSKY and ANTOINE, who brought his reforms into the mainstream of twentieth-century theatre.

ERNESTO ROSSI (1827-96)

Italian actor. The first time the inhabitants of such distant parts of the world as Romania and South America saw SHAKESPEARE's works on stage they were (as likely as not) performed in Italian by Rossi's indefatigable, global touring company. International fame came to Rossi as early as 1855, when he and Adelaide RISTORI captivated Paris as Paolo and Francesca in Silvio Pellico's *Francesca da Rimini*. It was in France too that his Romantic style of playing Shakespeare was most admired. He emphasized the remorse of Macbeth, the sexual passion of Othello and the madness of King Lear, while his Hamlet was remarkable for the tenderness with which he treated Ophelia. Only in England did the critics refuse to add to the eulogies heaped upon him in every city from St Petersburg to San Francisco.

'LORD' GEORGE SANGER (1827-1911)

English circus proprietor. Sixth child of a strolling showman (who had seen Nelson fall at Trafalgar), "Little Georgie" drummed up trade for his father's peep-show and toured up and down England at a time when smallpox and riots were rife throughout the land. To an act of tight-rope-walking canaries he added conjuring and *poses plastiques*; he became known as "His Lordship" and founded a circus dynasty by marrying one of the first so-called Lion Queens. Soon, an oyster smoking a clay pipe provided enough money to buy Astley's Amphitheatre and open the Sanger Circus. By 1871 he was staging spectacular pantomimes such as *Lady Godiva*.

There is no doubt of Sanger's genius for showmanship. When sued by Buffalo Bill for plagiarism, Sanger said, "If he's the Honourable William CODY, then I'm Lord George Sanger from this out." Queen Victoria, it seems, was amused; at any rate she made no objection. In retirement, the inventor of the three-ring circus wrote *Seventy Years a Showman*, and was killed by one of his own manservants running amok with an axe.

HENRIK IBSEN (1828-1906)

Norwegian dramatist and poet. Ibsen was born in the small town of Skien to a merchant who, like SHAKESPEARE's father, was ruined in his son's youth, forcing Henrik to become a chemist's assistant for six years in the tiny seaport of Grimstad. Before leaving for Bergen, Ibsen wrote two historical plays and fathered an illegitimate son. During six years as stage manager at the Bergen National

Theatre he finished four more plays, though still apprentice pieces in subject and style. In 1858, now Director of a Christiania theatre, he married the steadfast Suzannah, who bore their only child, Sigurd. With small success he wrote *The Vikings at Helgeland* and, after five fruitless years of poverty and despair, completed *Love's Comedy*, a modern verse satire. It was rejected by his own theatre, which went bankrupt. Living off moneylenders, Ibsen finally achieved stage success with *The Pretenders*, a tragedy. A government grant then gave him the opportunity to go abroad.

Leaving Norway in 1864, Ibsen settled in Europe for twenty-seven years. In Rome he wrote his verse play *Brand*, whose idealistic hero (reminiscent of Ibsen himself) cries: "All or nothing." Bitterly aware of the stage's technical limitations he wrote this and his next play for the reading public. Back home, though not acted for nineteen years, it was a big success, making its author famous throughout Scandinavia. Next he took a Norwegian folk hero the very opposite of Brand and wrote his vigorous tragicomedy *Peer Gynt*. Peer has no deep awareness of his own nature. He thinks of himself as a human onion, all layers and no centre. His epitaph is "Here lies No-one." After the success of this play as a book, Ibsen moved to Dresden, attended the opening of the Suez Canal, wrote his first modern prose comedy, *The League of Youth*, and in 1871 published a book of his shorter poems, his farewell to verse.

From then on, although poetry flowed beneath the well-plotted surface, Ibsen wrote in prose. Small-town society and unhappy domestic circles confine his characters from without; fruitless idealism and the stifling memory of the past obsess their inner lives. Female characters frequently express his anger with society. In the first of his twelve great modern dramas he saw women like Lorna Hessel as representing *Pillars of Society* (1877). *A Doll's House* (1879), its successor, gave the stage one of its great heroines. In the play's final act Nora, no longer a doll-wife, literally slams the door on her old life. *A Doll's House* caused a sensation at its first production, making Ibsen internationally famous. In the twentieth century, as the sound of slamming doors grew deafening, Nora became the patron saint of feminism. *Ghosts*, written in 1881, was even more startling, syphilis and incest becoming symbols for the grim power of the past. Unable to see beyond these forbidden subjects, managers and critics violently rejected the play. It was only while Ibsen was writing a bitter commentary on his relation to society in *An Enemy of the People* (1882) that *Ghosts* received its world première in Chicago.

Ibsen bewildered the public with his later plays, resorting increasingly to symbolism in order to express his obsession with social and spiritual freedom. *The Wild Duck* (1884) is a pathetic study of self-deception and myopic idealism. Like so many of Ibsen's plays it ends with a bang – this the gunshot that tragically kills little Hedvig Ekdal. *Rosmersholm* (1886) and *The Lady from the Sea* (1888) continue to dramatize the conflict between the demands of total freedom and conventional restraint. *Hedda Gabler* (1890), arguably Ibsen's best play, presents a woman who is driven to suicide when her Dionysian passions clash with a conventional and uncomprehending society. "But people don't do such things," says a bewildered character as yet another gunshot has died away.

In 1891 Ibsen returned home permanently to write his nemesis for a megalomaniac, *John Gabriel Borkman* (1896), and three portraits of the artist as an old man passing judgement on himself. These are *Little Eyolf* (1894), *The Master Builder* (1892) and finally *When We Dead Awaken* (1899). The latter reflects back on its author's life, though rather more severely than SHAKE-SPEARE had in *The Tempest*. It was Ibsen's last play, what he called "a dramatic epilogue". Paralysed by a stroke, he wrote no more.

LEO TOLSTOY (1828-1910)

Russian novelist and playwright. So great is Tolstoy's fame as a novelist that his works for the stage are often overlooked. Yet they are central to his philosophy and include among them several classics of the Russian theatre.

Tolstoy's major plays all date from the years following his spiritual conversion. In middle age he put on a peasant's shirt and boots and became, in the traditional Russian mould, a *Bogoiskatel* – a Seeker after God. Although he never entirely gave up the privileges of his aristocratic birth, his work thereafter was an attempt to fuse the peasant's simple life with an equal simplicity of spirit. In *The Power of Darkness* (written in 1886), murder, greed and incest define the moral emptiness of the peasants' existence. So inflammatory was its tone that this drama was banned from production in Russia for eleven years. An equal pessimism underlies the comic intrigues of *The Fruits of Enlightenment* (1891), while *The Living Corpse* savagely attacks the inhuman "justice" of the legal system. *The Light That Shines in Darkness* tells the story of a nobleman who attempts to give up his wealth in order to achieve spiritual purity. Though this autobiographical work occupied him for many years, Tolstoy never lived to complete the final act. He died of pneumonia in a provincial railway station.

After writing *War and Peace* and *Anna Karenina*, **Tolstoy** decided to renounce sex and possessions. His play *The Light that Shines in Darkness* poignantly reviews the effect of this on his family

JOSEPH JEFFERSON (1829-1905)

American actor. Joseph Jefferson was the third and greatest actor of that name. His grandfather had led a distinguished career in New York and Philadelphia; his cheerful, less-talented father toured with his family on the theatrical circuits of the South and Midwest. Young Joseph was already on stage at the age of four, doing a blackface routine with THOMAS "Jim Crow" RICE. When his father died, the thirteen-year-old boy took over the family troupe, barnstorming even into Mexico. He joined Laura Keene's New York company in 1856 and had great success in *Our American Cousin* (1858). Then in 1865 he achieved international fame with his witty, sensitive portrayal of Rip Van Winkle, a role that may have been based on memories of his father. Jefferson continually refined his interpretation of Rip over the forty years he performed in the play, eventually achieving a total identification with the character. When he retired in 1904, after seventy-one years on the stage, the play disappeared completely from the repertoire. He was also a great success in Richard Brinsley SHERIDAN's *The Rivals*, a play that has proved more durable.

THOMAS WILLIAM ROBERTSON (1829-71)

English playwright. Failed actor, failed journalist and for many years a failed writer of melodramas, Tom Robertson managed to persuade the popular Edward Sothern to act in his indifferent play *David Garrick* in 1864. Encouraged by a taste of success, he surprised London a year later with his unusually realistic approach in a much better work, *Society* (1865). In the remaining years before his early death, comedy-dramas such as *Ours* (1866), *Caste* (1867 – his best) and *School* (1869) founded a new tradition of realism in the British theatre.

His plots may have been contrived, his characters simple, but for the first time in England real people did ordinary things on stage such as drinking from tea-cups and making roly-poly pudding. Their conversations were believable, unlike those of contemporary melodrama and burlesque. Robertson also portrayed the effect of society on behaviour, as AUGIER and DUMAS *fils* had begun to do in France.

He and the BANCROFTS (his theatre-managers and, with John Hare, his principal actors) deliberately broke with the custom whereby a play was directed by an actor as a vehicle for himself. Robertson produced his own plays. W. S. GILBERT considered that Robertson "invented stage-management". Under his direction the actors on stage became an ensemble, working subtly with each other without drawing attention to themselves. Less appreciative critics than Gilbert have attributed to Robertson another theatrical innovation: "The cup-and-saucer drama"; but his works are unreasonably neglected.

TOMMASO SALVINI (1829-1915)

Italian actor. After Edmund KEAN, Salvini was considered to be the greatest Othello of his century. His handsome figure and musical voice – he had sung in opera – mesmerized audiences all over the world. In 1875 London was spellbound by Salvini; the critic Clement Scott wrote "He was a torrent, a tornado, a mountain." His Othello was convinced by Iago only at the last possible moment, when passion overwhelmed him. STANISLAVSKY himself studied Salvini's acting closely, another witness to the uncommon realism of his performance.

TOM BELLING (c 1830-?)

American circus performer. In the 1860s Belling, a circus vagabond, was working as an acrobat for the Renz circus in Berlin when the owner suspended him for incompetence. On a bet, he crept down to ringside wearing a wig and riding coat, both turned back to front. There he ran straight into Herr Renz. In a panic, he stumbled into the ring, tripping and falling as he tried to escape. The audience howled at the new act, calling out "auguste, auguste" (a Berlin dialect word meaning "stupid") in appreciation of Belling's stupid antics. At that moment the "Auguste" clowning style of fumbling slapstick was born, to be perfected by such modern artists as COCO.

ROBERT HELLER (c 1830-78)

English conjuror. Heller's first attempt at conjuring was not a great success. His admiration for ROBERT-HOUDIN resulted in blatant imitation; he dropped his real name of William Henry Palmer, appeared on stage in a black wig, and even spoke with a French accent. After performing in England and America, he abandoned magic and instead taught the piano.

Marriage to a wealthy heiress gave Heller the chance to return to magic. In Heller's Hall on Broadway, he relied upon his enormous wit and charm, delighting audiences with shows that combined music and magic, and his famous "gift" of second sight. In this trick, members of the audience wrote what they chose on a piece of paper. The conjuror would then say what was on the paper while it was still in their hands. His secret lay in the pasteboards upon which they leaned to write, for inside was another slip of paper which bore the imprint of their message. Heller also used electricity in many tricks. He died at the height of his career, stipulating in his will that all his apparatus be destroyed.

MATILDA HERON (1830-77)

Irish-born American actress. A wild, passionate performer, Matilda Heron on stage resembled "a high-pressure first-class Western steamboat, with all her fires up". This was *The New York Herald*'s impression of her as Camille, the role she made her personal preserve all over the States. While on holiday in Paris, Matilda saw DUMAS' *La Dame aux camélias* and herself made "a crude but faithful translation, in which bad English takes the place of good French". As no better version existed and Heron's playing was inimitable, the piece (together with Medea, her one other starring role) made her a fortune, which she gaily spent and gave away.

JULES LÉOTARD (1830-70)

French trapeze artist. Léotard was the original "daring young man on the flying trapeze". Other acrobats had performed on a fixed, suspended bar but no one had ever set it swinging freely, much less leapt from one bar to another in mid-air. Assisted by his father, who pushed the second trapeze to him at the crucial moment, Léotard astonished Parisians in 1859 with his effortless gliding, for all the world "like a tropical bird jumping from branch to branch". Death from smallpox cut short his fabulous European career. He left to later daring young men (and women) both the challenge of his invention and the simple but revealing costume that still bears his name.

JOSEPHINE BOISDECHINES (1831-?)

Swiss-born circus freak. Known as Madame Clofullia, Boisdechines was the original Bearded Lady; she was covered from head to toe in dark hair. After touring in Europe she was engaged by Phineas BARNUM, along with her equally hairy offspring, *Little Albert or the Infant Esau*.

Her debut with Barnum's "Great American Museum" was followed by a summons for deception; but medical testimony cleared her (of being a man) – it would appear that the charges had been secretly laid by Barnum himself in a characteristic bid for free publicity. At the peak of her career Boisdechines was earning a fabulous sum of money for herself and her employer. Her husband was known – not inappropriately – as Fortune Clofullia Jr.

VICTORIEN SARDOU (1831-1908)

French playwright. Sardou claimed to have learned his craft by reading the first acts of plays by SCRIBE, then writing the last acts himself. Whatever his method, with AUGIER and DUMAS *fils* he dominated the French stage in the latter half of the nineteenth century. His success was not immediate, but he found an early champion in the actress Virginie DÉJAZET and later in Sarah BERNHARDT, who were not put off by his rule that a playwright should always torture the heroine.

Sardou was the chief craftsman of bourgeois drama;

mechanical devices and formulae prevail. *Pattes de mouche* (1860), a comedy, is typical of his well-made, contrived plays. He claimed to be a champion of realism, and the public was apparently convinced. But BERNARD SHAW dismissed Sardou's work as "Sardoodledom", and, crossly condemned "Diplomacy Dora and Theodora and La Toscadora and other machine dolls from the same firm. . . ." So unremarkable were the plots that critics sometimes resorted to reviewing the costumes, as in *Théodora*, his greatest success with Bernhardt. Sardou's melodrama *La Tosca* was immortalized by Puccini in 1900, but only his witty laundress, the title role of *Madame Sans-Gêne*, is regularly revived.

BJØRNSTJERNE BJØRNSON (1832-1910)

Norwegian playwright, poet and novelist. Even though his reputation has diminished in the twentieth century, Bjørnson was a writer of stature, whose fame in his lifetime equalled that of his friend and rival IBSEN. Whereas Ibsen observes the human heart, Bjørnson observes Norway. As an editor and orator he played an important part in securing Norwegian independence from Sweden, and his plays and stories have a strong local feeling in keeping with their writer's nationalism.

The best of a series of early plays on historical, national themes is *Sigurd Slembe* (1862), the tragic trilogy of a character resembling a more noble Macbeth. At this time he also wrote his great poetic saga, "Arnljot Gelline" (1870). But in *The Newly-Married Couple* (1865) he began to examine his own society through realistic prose drama – a shift in form which the less precocious Ibsen was to emulate some years later. *The Editor* (1874), *A Bankruptcy* (1874) and *Leonarda* (1879) followed, all lively pieces in the style of AUGIER.

Bjørnson is eloquent above all in four late plays: *En Hanske* (1883) – which takes a hard look at the double standard of sexual morality – *Over Aevne I* (1883), *Over Aevne II* (1895) and *Paul Lange og Tora Parsberg* (1898). In these plays he explores human needs and motives kindly but without sentimentality. The last is based on an episode in his own life, when Bjørnson had to denounce a friend and political colleague, who then committed suicide. He was awarded the Nobel Prize for literature in 1903. Bjørn, his son, was a well-known actor.

EDWIN BOOTH (1833-93)

American actor. Booth provided a refinement and sensitivity that had long been lacking from the American stage. His forte was spirited intensity, not ferocity. He was the opposite in every respect of his thundering predecessor Edwin FORREST (after whom he was named). The actress Charlotte CUSHMAN urged him in vain to remember that Macbeth was "the grandfather of all the Bowery villains" who crowded the New York theatres. But whatever his shortcomings as a warrior-king, he was a splendid student-prince – on either side of the Atlantic one of the best Hamlets of the nineteenth century.

Booth's melancholy was real. The unbalanced mind of his actor-father, Junius Brutus Booth, and of his brother JOHN WILKES BOOTH was a source of grief to him (the two brothers played with a third, also called Junius Brutus, in a memorable *Julius Caesar* not long before John assassinated President Lincoln). Perhaps as a consequence he appeared not to set too high a price on his life. Once, when a man fired three shots at him on stage, he stepped to the footlights and identified the attacker. His life was dogged by violence: in Scotland he was stabbed in the arm by an over-excited Laertes in *Hamlet*.

As a young man Booth acted in California and the still wild West, and at twenty-one toured the Pacific islands and the raw British colonies of Australia. A tour of Britain itself in 1861 was unsuccessful, but his return there in 1880–82 was a triumph, when he and HENRY IRVING acted together, alternating the parts of Othello and Iago on different evenings. With the great Ellen TERRY in the role of Desdemona, the play is reputed to have worked much better on those evenings when it was Booth's turn to play Iago, the part of Othello suiting Irving much better. Booth had "made and lost three fortunes on SHAKESPEARE" in theatre management. Bankrupted in 1873 by his biggest venture, Booth's Theatre in New York, he easily recouped his losses with more successful tours of the United States. His sensitive and thoughtful interpretations, particularly of classical roles, continued to delight both Europe and America.

HENRY JAMES BYRON (1834-84)

English playwright and actor-manager. Abandoning both medicine and law, Byron wrote burlesques, farces, comedies and extravaganzas. They served as a perfect vehicle for Marie Wilton, and Byron went into brief partnership with her and her future husband Squire BANCROFT, taking over a tramp-infested London theatre known as the Dusthole and transforming it into the fashionable Prince of Wales's. To modern ears the leaden alliterations and obvious punning of such works as his extravaganza *La Sonnambula, or The Supper, The Sleeper and the Merry Swiss Boy* (1865) have lost something of their original charm. But the generous Charles Dickens was impressed by the pithiness of *The Maid and the Magpie* (1858), remarking: "It begins at eight, and it's over by a quarter past nine."

ADAH ISAACS MENKEN (1835-68)

American equestrian actress. The dying tradition of equestrian drama was given a new lease of life by Menken's unusual talents, or more specifically by the shapeliness of her legs. *Mazeppa*, an equine dramatization of a poem by Lord Byron, had been a mainstay of Astley's Amphitheatre in London but never with a lady in the hero's roles. In America Menken met with only moderate success, but in England the spectacle of her scantily-clad body lashed to a horse's back packed the theatre for six months. The horse clambered as slowly as possible up mountain crags, prolonging the patrons' enjoyment of its rider's famous legs in their flesh-coloured tights.

Menken's origins were Creole, but the public, misled by her married name, thought her the epitome of Hebrew beauty. In fact she had adopted the faith of her second husband and retained his name throughout many subsequent marriages. She appeared in circuses and also in pedestrian drama, aspiring to be a great classical actress, but usually relying on revealing costumes for success. In pursuit of literary recognition, she energetically seduced famous writers. The ageing rake, ALEXANDRE DUMAS *père*, was a willing accomplice, but the sexually confused poet Algernon Charles Swinburne was a distinctly embarrassed and unsatisfactory lover (all he did was bite, she complained). She then arranged for the mass publication and distribution of photographs of herself and these two celebrated conquests. London and Paris in particular were as thrilled as they were shocked by her extravagant and bold behaviour.

An edition of Menken's poems, boasting a dubious foreword by Charles Dickens, was a disastrous failure but, as she wrote in a letter to a friend shortly before her death, she had certainly lived life to the full.

WILLIAM SCHWENK GILBERT
(1836-1911)

English librettist, playwright and producer. In 1861 a legacy enabled Gilbert to forsake the Civil Service for legal studies, but by the time he was called to the bar he was already writing humorous verses for *Fun* magazine, and on taking up playwriting he won instant and lucrative success. In 1870 he met the young composer Arthur Sullivan, and under the management of Richard D'Oyly Carte their operatic burlesques and satires became a national institution. In the comedy *Engaged* (1877) and in such operettas as *HMS Pinafore* (1878), *Iolanthe* (1882), *The Mikado* (1885) and *The Gondoliers* (1889) Gilbert's sophisticated wit imparts a uniquely sly sense of anarchy which has helped it outlive the passing of the Victorian era. Gilbert vigorously opposed Sullivan's Wagnerian aspirations, fearing that the sheer tonnage of such "serious" music would smother his elegant librettos. But he too lived to regret his comic vocation, complaining: "I have been scribbling twaddle for thirty-five years to suit the public taste."

Gilbert was a physically courageous man, though as a motorist his lack of self-regard made him something of a hazard to others. He died in his seventies while rescuing a girl from drowning.

LYDIA THOMPSON (1836-1908)

English actress, dancer and manager. In 1868 *Lydia Thompson and her English Blondes* arrived in New York with a unique brand of entertainment. Nominally classical burlesque, in which her lovely girls played male parts in musical dramas, it was really a blithe celebration of feminine charms. The ladies were gorgeous in tights, tunics and short skirts, and freely interrupted the "plot", whether set in ancient Greece or Sherwood Forest, with outbursts of gay song and leggy dance. One reviewer pronounced the spectacle "a bewilderment of limbs, belladonna and greasepaint". But it attracted a wide audience, by no means exclusively male, and pointed the way to modern burlesque.

HENRY BECQUE (1837-99)

French playwright. Though he has since been recognized as one of the first exponents of naturalist drama, Becque was unappreciated by his contemporaries. His early comedy *L'Enfant prodigue* (1868) and the socialist drama *Michel Pauper* (1870) had a certain success, but the total failure of *L'Enlèvement* (1870) drove him to abandon writing and become a stockbroker. (This brought near bankruptcy, prevented only by the intervention of his brother.)

On his return to the stage, he shocked and pleased the public in turn with *La Navette* (1878) and *Les Honnêtes femmes* (1880), before his first important play *Les Corbeaux* was produced in 1882. In this ugly slice of life, a bereaved wife and her daughters are beset by unscrupulous men after their inheritance. Some sympathized with Becque's attempt to show life as it was, but most condemned a play that depicted middle-class hypocrisy and corruption so frankly and brutally, with no hint of a moral. *La Parisienne* (1885), about a calculating, coquettish wife who coolly plays games with the emotions of husband and lovers, was likewise poorly received. It has been translated as *Woman of Paris*.

A stubborn and unbusiness-like man, Becque spent his last years in poverty, forgotten and starving, until friends came to the rescue. His ultimate importance as a dramatist has been left for later generations to discover.

Adah Isaacs Menken (*above*) rides bare-legged to notoriety

Edwin Booth (*below*) brought decorum to the American stage

JOHN AUGUSTIN DALY (1838-99)

American manager and playwright. Daly's acting company (which included JOHN DREW and Ada REHAN) set the highest standards in their productions at his theatres in London and New York. But he is as often remembered for his melodrama *Under the Gaslight* (1867), which featured the "nick-of-time" rescue of a victim tied to a railroad track. When Dion BOUCICAULT copied the idea, Daly sued and secured the American rights.

HENRY IRVING (1838-1905)

English actor-manager. Irving dominated the English stage during the second half of the Victorian era. The son of a humble salesman, he fell in love with the theatre on seeing Samuel PHELPS play Hamlet, but his puritanical mother considered drama a work of the devil, and Henry was put to work as a clerk. On receiving an unexpected bequest, he bought himself some theatrical props and costumes (including three swords) and went to act in the north. After ten unhappy years he arrived in London, and in 1871 became a sensation overnight for his performance in Leopold Lewis's *The Bells*, a melodrama he was to repeat more than 800 times. In 1878 Irving took over the management of the Lyceum where, with Ellen TERRY, he reigned for a quarter of a century.

Mrs Irving, who had no time for her husband's calling, enquired after the first night of *The Bells*, "Are you going on making a fool of yourself like this all your life?" Irving replied by leaving her instantly. A romance with Ellen Terry consoled him until well into the 1890s.

In 1895 Irving became the first-ever actor-knight, but soon thereafter his good fortune began to ebb. Most of the Lyceum props were destroyed by fire in 1898 and, touring to make good the loss, he was laid low by pneumonia. The sale of his books and prints helped him to regain solvency, but a further blow came when the Lyceum, faced with expensive alterations, had to close. In 1902 he and Ellen Terry finally parted and Irving, still in poor health, continued to tour. Three years later he was playing Tennyson's *Becket* in a provincial playhouse. His last words as the martyr on stage were: "Into Thy hands, O Lord." He died within the hour.

Irving's knighthood – and the fact that Queen Victoria confessed to being "pleased" – was a remarkable achievement in that prudish society which had so often regarded the stage as the province of satanists and whoremasters. His thoughtful and faithful interpretations of SHAKESPEARE did much to extricate the theatre from the banality into which it had sunk. His *Hamlet* was by all accounts a masterpiece. Discarding the traditional tragic plumes, Irving wore the now-famous black tunic, adorned only by a simple gold chain.

He had many detractors. In his deportment and diction he cultivated a melodramatic eccentricity often at odds with his role; and his voice was apparently unequal to such parts as King Lear and Othello. Nor had he any literary discrimination, preferring the opportunities offered by ephemeral melodramas, and rejecting IBSEN and SHAW. The latter became his most vocal critic, but recognized that Irving's sheer magnetism set him in a class apart, remarking ruefully: "We feel that we could watch him sitting down for ever."

Though as celebrated as any English actor has ever been, the "Knight from Nowhere" died in poverty.

TOM THUMB (1838-83)

American midget. Less then two feet tall at the age of five, Charles S. Stratton was discovered by P. T. BARNUM, America's greatest showman, and duly Barnumized into "General Tom Thumb, a dwarf eleven years of age, just arrived from England". So great was his success that the deception was soon dropped, and Barnum and the little General set sail to conquer Europe. Skilful publicizing of such incidents as the General's singing of "Yankee Doodle" to Queen Victoria, and impersonating Napoleon for the Duke of Wellington made Barnum a fortune during their three-year tour.

Barnum denied that the General's marriage to another of his dwarfs, Lavinia Warren, was just a publicity stunt. He was genuinely fond of his creation and made him rich enough to cultivate a taste for high living, racehorses and big cigars. The General grew to a height of three feet four inches, but his weight increased disproportionately and he died of an apoplectic stroke.

JOHN WILKES BOOTH (1839-65)

American actor and assassin. John was possibly as talented as his father, JUNIUS BRUTUS BOOTH, and his brother, Edwin, but he lacked the latter's discipline on stage and inherited the former's unbalanced mind.

Particularly dashing as Romeo, he made a successful tour of the South in 1860–61 at the beginning of the Civil War. But his most spectacular performance was his leap to the stage from the President's box after assassinating Abraham Lincoln at Ford's Theatre in Washington D.C., on 14 April, 1865. His confused idea had been to strike a final blow for the defeated South.

Although he escaped on a horse waiting at the back of the theatre, Booth had broken a leg on landing, and this injury impeded him. After twelve days he was trapped in a burning barn and shot – though whether by a soldier or by his own hand has never been determined.

JOHN NEVIL MASKELYNE (1839-1917)

English conjuror. Maskelyne first attracted attention by exposing the fraudulent activities of the American Davenport Brothers, spirit mediums who held English audiences transfixed at the time. Long fascinated by conjuring tricks, he used his mechanical skill, learnt as a watchmaker's apprentice, to construct a box from which he could escape while closely bound by ropes. With this box he was able to imitate the Davenports' performances, proving that no occult powers were needed.

Maskelyne went on to perform for many years at the Egyptian Hall in Piccadilly. He was one of the most inventive conjurors of his time. Amongst his most impressive tricks was "Cleopatra's Needle". This involved a hidden lifting device that enabled him to carry a large obelisk as though it were very light. He would then place it upon a table, whereupon, to the audience's astonishment, two or three people would emerge. Maskelyne's mechanical figures, or automata, baffled everyone. "Psycho", an oriental figure, played whist and performed card tricks, yet it was impossible to see how he was controlled. In fact he was operated by means of compressed air.

Many famous magicians worked with Maskelyne at the Egyptian Hall and later at England's "home of mystery", St Georges Hall, which his descendants ran until 1933.

HELENA MODJESKA (1840-1909)

Polish actress. Modjeska was loved and admired in America and England with the same fervour as in her native land. In 1861 she appeared in an amateur production for charity and it was immediately clear that she would be an actress of extraordinary talent. From 1869 she was the

The last-minute rescue (as in **John Augustin Daly**'s *Under the Gaslight*, *left*) was a common ingredient of that most popular nineteenth-century dramatic form, the melodrama. The spectacle of innocence in danger was deeply fascinating to audiences of all classes, and great actors from Siddons to Irving played melodrama alongside the classics. Though domestic trauma (*Fifteen Years of a Drunkard's Life* etc) was ever a popular theme, the most abiding subject was murder. *Maria Marten; or, The Murder in the Red Barn* and *Sweeney Todd, the Demon Barber of Fleet Street* still curdle the blood today. Encouraged by the way such gruesome goings-on could pack the theatre, producers spared no expense to provide spectacular effects: train wrecks and even earthquakes could take place on stage

Queen Victoria's coachbuilder made a special carriage for **Tom Thumb** to ride in state (*left*). He was the most famous but not the shortest midget in circus history. Lucia Zarate (1863–89) was a mere twenty inches tall and weighed under five pounds at the age of seventeen

Henry Irving (*right*, in a caricature by Max Beerbohm) had a fondness for the melodramatic pose. His Richard III, nasal and grotesque, seems to have been based on accounts of the great Edmund Kean's portrayal. The interpretation was similarly transmitted to Laurence Olivier, and thence to the permanence of film

John Wilkes Booth (*below*) leaps on to the stage after assassinating President Lincoln at the theatre

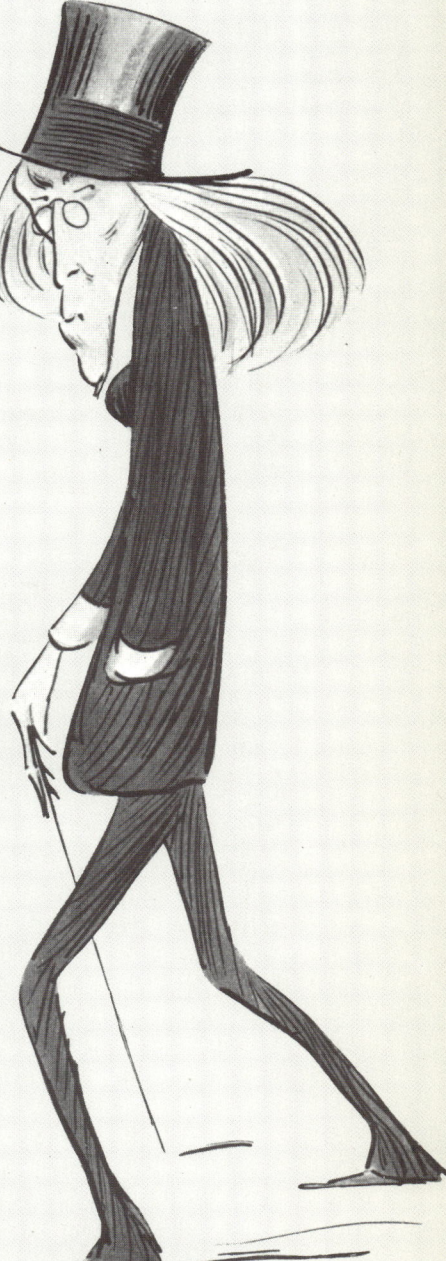

Carl Hagenbeck's Singhalese Caravan (*left*). This contemporary woodcut is a fine advertisement for the advantages of the kind treatment of animals. In 1907 the great animal-gentler founded the Stellingen Zoo near Hamburg

In 1912 London audiences were privileged to see Holland's finest actor, **Louis Bouwmeester**, in a piece called *La Grippe* (*right*). He did not give his celebrated Shylock in England until he was nearly eighty, but was then warmly applauded in the part in London and Stratford

All vehicles, from Hamlet to the most trivial light comedy, came alike to the peerless **Sarah Bernhardt** (*far right*), seen here as Frou-Frou in an 1879 cartoon from *Vanity Fair* magazine

shining light of the Warsaw stage, until in 1876 she and her husband left for California to start a farming colony.

The project failed, and within a year (having mastered English) Modjeska was acting again. She had to fight for an audition, but her debut in Eugène SCRIBE and Legouve's *Adrienne Lecouvreur* in San Francisco was a smash hit. In the next twenty-eight years she toured America twenty-six times and the British Isles three times, as well as revisiting Poland. Her finest roles were SHAKESPEARE's Juliet and Ophelia, SCHILLER's Maria Stuart, and Nora in IBSEN's *A Doll's House*.

Majestic and beautiful in tragedy, Modjeska was passionate yet never lacking in refinement. The American stage was greatly enriched by her energy and devotion to the theatre.

SQUIRE BANCROFT (1841-1926)

English actor-manager. Bancroft and his wife effected a quiet revolution in Victorian theatrical taste. In 1865 Marie Wilton (1839–1921), anxious to leave burlesque and to act in plays of her own choosing, joined forces with young Squire Bancroft, leased a London theatre known as the "Dusthole" and refurbished it as the Prince of Wales's. A whole new public was drawn by the unusually comfortable seats and by the muted, realistic comedies of the Bancroft's prize discovery, T. W. ROBERTSON. There was a riot when the couple (who married in 1867) bought the rival Haymarket theatre and squeezed out the rougher patrons by abolishing the pit and putting the good seats in front of the stage (where they remain today).

The Bancrofts retired to well-earned prosperity while still in their forties. But Squire (later knighted on behalf of them both) occasionally returned to acting, notably in a hazardous duel on a dim stage with HENRY IRVING. Both actors were too short-sighted to know that they barely missed maiming each other.

CONSTANT-BENOÎT COQUELIN (1841-1909)

French actor. Now principally remembered as the creator of Cyrano de Bergerac in ROSTAND's play (which ran from

1897 until 1899), Coquelin is often called *aîné* to distinguish him from his brother Ernest and son Jean, also actors. Though he worked sporadically with the Comédie-Française he preferred to pursue his career independent of any particular theatre or company. He also wrote three important books on acting including *L'Art et le comédien* (1880). Charming and stylish, he was at home in bold, open comedy, especially that of MOLIÈRE. Daudet wrote of him: "M Coquelin is a man who can make you hear Beethoven when he is playing 'Au Clair de la Lune'."

LOUIS BOUWMEESTER (1842-1925)

Dutch actor-manager. Bouwmeester was the most important Dutch tragedian of his day. Encouraged by his actor-father, he made a stage debut at six and, after thirteen itinerant years, found his first permanent engagement at the Salon des Variétés in Amsterdam. Here he gradually achieved recognition (though mostly in mediocre plays) and was soon touring with his own company. He joined the Netherlands Theatre in 1879 and founded the Haarlem Theatre in 1903. Bouwmeester travelled widely, excelling as Tartuffe and Macbeth, and especially as a comic and humane Shylock, a role he continued to play well into his eighties.

ALEXANDER HERRMANN (c 1843-96)

French-born conjuror. As a child Herrmann repeatedly ran away from home to join his brother, Carl Herrmann (1816–87), a well-known conjuror. The two toured together until 1869 when Alexander went back to Europe alone. In London he was an instant success, and gave one thousand performances at MASKELYNE's Egyptian Hall.

"Herrmann the Great" finally settled in the United States and went in for grand illusions, one of which was "Cremation", during which his wife was burned alive and ghosts danced over her casket. His acts became more and more sensational. When he devised a trick in which he had to catch, on a plate, bullets fired at him from five guns simultaneously his insurers became sufficiently alarmed to withdraw his life policy.

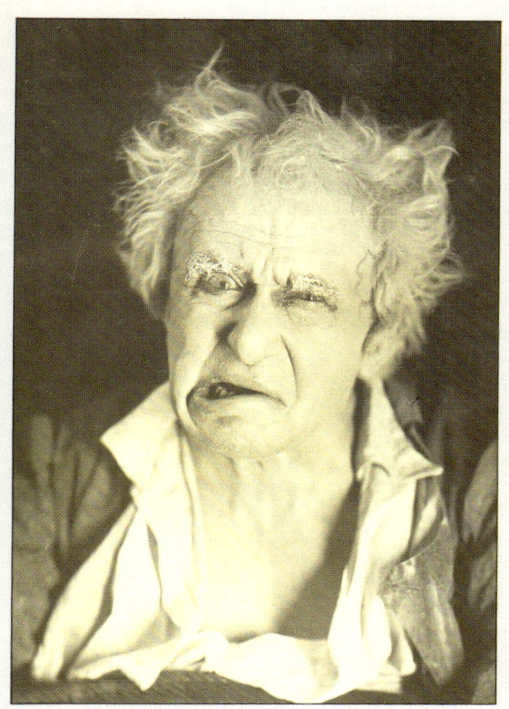

You may search this page in vain for further information on the French conjuror **Bautier de Kolta** (*below*). The great illusionist's biography has been cunningly concealed on page 134

Although on stage Herrmann made use of his naturally satanic appearance, he was a genial man. He had an irrepressible desire to amuse and could not stop playing tricks. At dinner his wine glass would disappear as he lifted it to his lips; in the street a taxi fare would appear out of thin air; Herrmann even took cigars out of President Grant's whiskers. He became enormously rich and travelled America in a luxurious private railway carriage that had once belonged to Lillie LANGTRY.

SARAH BERNHARDT (1844-1923)

French actress. At the age of fourteen, Sarah Bernhardt hoped to become a nun. Instead she was sent to the Paris Conservatoire to train for the stage, and four years later made her debut at the Comédie-Française in RACINE's *Iphigénie*. In 1863, after only a year with the company, she stormed off, establishing a pattern of impetuosity which was to last throughout her career: "Quand même" was her constant motto.

Bernhardt quickly won a following at the *Théâtre de l'Odéon*, where she served a crucial apprenticeship with a young, dynamic company in a Bohemian milieu. In 1869 her success in Coppée's *Le Passant* marked a Romantic revival, culminating with the 1872 production of HUGO's *Ruy Blas*, in which Bernhardt's "golden" voice and inspired verse-speaking won her critical acclaim. Lured back to the more traditional Comédie (a move which one critic described as bringing "the wolf into the fold") she created in 1874 a Phèdre to rival RACHEL's, a realistic study of guilt-ridden love. Offstage she painted and sculpted, and in 1878 ascended in a hot-air balloon.

Her reception during the Comédie's 1879 London season was little short of ecstatic, as was her impact on the USA (which she toured in order to pay off 100,000 francs legal compensation to the Comédie for having walked out on them once more). Henry James sneered "She is too American not to succeed in America," and he was right. The tour, fuelled by inspired publicity stunts, established her as an international superstar. Subsequently she toured most of Europe, Russia and Australia, entering into a short-lived marriage in 1882 with a Greek actor named Damala. Her best-known role was Marguérite in *La Dame auc camélias* by DUMAS *fils*, and she was closely connected with the popular plays of SARDOU, in which she demonstrated her singular talent for infusing melodrama with a sense of classical nobility. She also made a minor speciality of men's parts in such plays as MUSSET's *Lorenzaccio*, ROSTAND's *L'Aiglon* and a renowned production of *Hamlet*, which took place in her own *Théâtre Sarah Bernhardt*. Even after an old wound forced her to have her right leg amputated in 1914, the "divine Sarah" continued to act. The woman Edmond DE GONCOURT called "the most remarkable phenomenon of the nineteenth century" died while making a film at the age of seventy-nine.

ELI BOWEN (1844-?)

American circus freak. Bowen's feet were joined directly to his hips. In the days before cinema and television banalized the extraordinary, it was predictable that he should be snapped up by a circus. He was not, however, content to be a passive sideshow curiosity, and worked hard to become a tumbler, eventually becoming renowned as the "Legless Aerial Gymnast, the Perch Pole Marvel".

Bowen's partner, Charles Tripp, was billed as "The Armless Wonder". He could feed and shave himself, write, smoke and paint, besides having a pretty wife and three children (as the publicity salaciously noted).

As a double-act the two were irresistible, and the comedy of their mutual repartee seems to have done much to dignify the misfortune which they and their employers exploited. A contemporary photograph shows the pair posing with gentlemanly insouciance on a tandem. It is serenely absurd.

CARL HAGENBECK (1844-1913)

German animal trainer and circus owner. Before Hagenbeck, wild animal acts depended on terror and brute strength. With iron bars and whips, tamers bullied their charges into simple manoeuvres. But Hagenbeck preached "sympathy with the animal". Introduced around 1880, his "gentling" method created affection and trust over a long, patient course of training. The dramatic results appeared in his own circus, but above all spread to animals and trainers he sent all over the world. Animal acts became much more inventive. Based on kindness, they also became safer because, as a Hagenbeck trainer said; "Lions know who to kill and who not to kill."

BAUTIER DE KOLTA (1845-1903)

French-born counjuror. De Kolta was the inventor of many famous tricks and illusions. He had little of the elegance so important to the performances of other conjurors, and habitually appeared in a large, baggy dress-suit that bulged with hidden secrets. His tricks, however, were faultlessly executed. De Kolta, whose real name was Joseph Bautier, often worked with John Nevil MASKELYNE at London's Egyptian Hall. It was here that in 1886 he first demonstrated "Black Art". On a stage hung with black cloth and lit only at the front, people and objects could be made to disappear by being quickly draped in black velvet. In his famous trick, "the Flying Bird Cage", the conjuror took in his hands a small cage containing a live bird; then, with a swift movement, both cage and bird disappeared. The cage was in fact collapsible and was drawn up inside his sleeve, often killing the bird. The Society for the Prevention of Cruelty to Animals complained about this trick, but, when asked to give a demonstration, de Kolta was wise enough on this occasion to see that the bird remained unharmed.

EDWARD HARRIGAN (1845-1911)

American playwright and actor-manager. The duo of Harrigan and Hart delighted New York from 1872 to 1884 with their good-humoured parodies of the Irish, German and black Americans who formed the bulk of the audience. Tony Hart (1857–91), fifteen when the partnership began, was a charming singer, comedian and female impersonator. Ned Harrigan had as many talents. An accomplished actor and writer, he made a financial success of three theatres, and formed and trained his own acting company.

Songs tended to turn into sketches (eighty in all) and many of these in turn became full-length plays. One particularly popular sketch, *The Mulligan Guard* expanded into a whole series of Mulligan plays (*The Mulligan Guard Ball*, *The Mulligan Guard Chowder*, etc), with Harrigan indulging in political shenanigans as the Irish proprietor of a corner store, and with Hart as his wife.

After the team broke up (the rivalry of their wives was said to be the cause) Harrigan continued his career successfully as a straight comic actor, but never captured on his own the energy and originality of his partnership with Hart.

"BUFFALO BILL" CODY (1846-1917)

American frontiersman and showman. Buffalo Bill had been a Pony Express rider, Civil War scout and bison-killer extraordinary when journalists from back east decided to make him a legend. A flood of dime novels inflated his exploits. Bill's reaction was "Gosh! What they say!", but he lent his name to them, sometimes as author. From 1880 he even appeared in inane myth-making plays like *Scouts of the Prairies*. However, publicity from such dubious ventures gave him the chance to present some real frontier skills in the great Wild West Show he founded in 1883. Its famous, frantic "Indian attacks" may have

been simulated, but the incredible feats of shooting and riding, the colour and non-stop excitement were as genuine as the performers' own hard-drinking conviviality. Supported by a host of cowboys, Indians and animals, its stars included the dead-eyed Annie OAKLEY, the great chief Sitting Bull and Buffalo Bill himself. The very image of the western hero, with flowing hair, flashing eyes and buckskin suit, he opened the four-hour show with a dramatic solo ride, as well as leading a cavalry rescue and a buffalo hunt. The extravaganza was an international sensation. In London, as enthralled as any commoner, Queen Victoria attended three times to shiver at the "quite fearful Indians who came so close". After thirty years of thrills the show came to an end in 1914, succeeded by several hopeless attempts at imitation.

AUGUST LINDBERG (1846-1916)

Swedish actor and director. Many established theatres in Scandinavia refused to touch IBSEN's more controversial works, so it was left to Lindberg's travelling company to stage the first production of several pieces, including the notorious *Ghosts*. The naturalistic acting required for the part of Oswald and other leading roles was markedly different from the energetic style, full of sweeping gesture, previously employed by Lindberg in SHAKESPEARE. For a long time his great versatility was acknowledged everywhere except in Stockholm, a city that had treated him harshly ever since he had worked there as a waiter at the age of fifteen; he was over fifty when the capital finally accepted him. In his later years there he gave celebrated one-man versions of *The Tempest*, *Faust*, *Oedipus Rex* and of course *Peer Gynt*.

What he had done for Ibsen, his son Per Lindberg (1890–1944) tried to do for German expressionist drama. He studied under Max REINHARDT in Berlin and was also a great admirer of Erwin PISCATOR. As a director he was subject to too many influences to develop a distinctive style of his own, but in the cinema was Sweden's most original talent before the era of Ingmar BERGMAN.

ANNA SWAN (1846-88)

American giantess. Born in Nova Scotia, Swan inevitably became one of the exhibits in the "Great American Museum", Phineas BARNUM's freak show. She was seven feet five and a half inches tall, and greatly obliged her patron by marrying a giant, Captain Martin Bates, and having a baby weighing twenty-four pounds.

Swan was twice caught in fires at the "museum". On the second occasion her weight (one-fifth of a ton) proved too much for the damaged staircase, and she was trapped. All would have been lost had not her colleagues thought of knocking a hole in the wall of the building and winching her to safety with a derrick. Her best friend, the Living Skeleton, witnessed the rescue but was too frail to be of much assistance.

Swan was reputedly a fine actress. There are reports of her appearing in New York as Lady Macbeth; contemporary reviews have not, however, survived.

JAMES BAILEY (1847-1906)

American circus entertainer. Small, shrewd and tireless, Bailey developed a talent for publicity and became, while still in his early thirties, the principal rival of P. T.

The picture on the left offers a vintage view of one of entertainment's classic spectacles. The public originally associated the vast multi-ringed circus, teeming with excitement, with P. T. BARNUM. A show that was "by design overwhelming" was typical of him, though the unprecedentedly large display that bore his name from 1871 was actually conceived by his partner, W. C. Coup. Aficionados complained that continuous activity in two or three rings made it impossible to concentrate on a particular act.

But the "greatest show" was less interested in discrimination than in dazzlement. All its performers were top-notch, its animals unique, its programmes marvellous. The circus was a kaleidoscope, its colours and images constantly shifting to form one long, dizzying experience.

Barnum and James A. BAILEY, a circus genius, joined forces in 1880. It was Bailey who added the third ring and took the show triumphantly to England. It soon included acts not traditionally seen in the big top, eye-filling pageants on varied themes like the tribute to "modern modes of locomotion" featured in this poster. Bailey became sole owner after Barnum's death in 1891 and subsequently took the show on a grand five-year tour of Europe.

But during his absence the RINGLING Brothers had emerged as heirs to circus eminence. When Bailey died they added his "greatest show" to their own and the "Ringling Brothers and Barnum and Bailey" became the colossus it still is today.

The astonishing skills of **Buffalo Bill**'s Wild West Show took a breath of the frontier as far east as England

Ellen Terry (*above*) as Lady Macbeth, in a painting by John Singer Sargent

Aristide Bruant (*below*) created a vogue for audience insult

BARNUM. After the first elephant born in captivity was advertised by Bailey's circus, Barnum himself suggested a merger. And so in 1880, "The Greatest Show on Earth" was born. When Barnum died, Bailey succeeded him as America's Circus King.

In 1897 Bailey set out on a five-year tour of Europe, sometimes competing with the ghosts of circuses past in Roman amphitheatres. Returning home triumphant, he found a new rival waiting for him; Wisconsin's RINGLING brothers had begun to dominate the American scene. Bailey sold them the smaller of his two circuses, and on his death three years later the Ringlings took over "The Greatest Show on Earth". A mild-mannered man (when irritated he would merely chew a rubber band), Bailey claimed to live by the motto: "Give the people the best – spare no expense and they'll reward you."

CHARLOTTE CRABTREE (1847-1924)

American singer, dancer and actress. Lotta Crabtree was the darling of the California gold fields. Coached by the voluptuous Lola MONTEZ and supported by an indomitable mother, from the age of eight she toured the rough camps, charming the miners with gay laughter, sentimental songs and agile dances. She had a similar effect in San Francisco beginning in 1859, and her mother took her east in 1864. Lotta's breakthrough there came in 1867 as star of the irresistibly maudlin *Little Nell and the Marchioness*. She continued to play such roles until her retirement in 1891, retaining all her girlish vivacity and winsome appeal.

GUISEPPE GIACOSA (1847-1906)

Italian playwright. When the Italian public demanded realism on stage, Giacosa had no difficulty in turning from historical melodrama to naturalistic, bourgeois pieces in the style of IBSEN. While *Una partita a scacchi* (1871), the medieval romance that first brought him success, has remained popular, however, imitations of Ibsen (*I tristi amori*, 1888) and *Diritti dell' anima* (1894)) have not borne revival so well.

At the height of his fame Giacosa wrote *La Signora di Challant* (1891) for Sarah BERNHARDT, travelling with her to New York to see it open, while Eleonora DUSE played the part in Turin. In the end he guaranteed the immortality of his words, not in his plays but as a collaborator in the librettos of three great Puccini operas, *La Bohème*, *Tosca* and *Madam Butterfly*.

ELLEN TERRY (1847-1928)

English actress. Probably no other English actress has ever been so popular. Ellen Terry had a clear voice and a large-boned, pre-Raphaelite beauty; her special talent was to invest each character with her own swift, lively grace. She was utterly natural, on stage and off, in an age which was often pompous. This suited some roles more than others. Her greatest were those of Beatrice and Portia, characters very like herself; but there was little evil in her Lady Macbeth, and she refused to play in the sombre new dramas of IBSEN.

Terry's lack of ambition dismayed her great fan, BERNARD SHAW, with whom she had a famous correspondence (she put off actually meeting him, from an unfounded fear that he would be disenchanted). During her great acting partnership with HENRY IRVING from 1878 to 1902 at the Lyceum theatre, she submitted to his total direction – and Irving, who was probably also her lover, arranged everything to suit himself. Terry never played Rosalind, the perfect role for her, because there was no corresponding part for Irving, but she never showed resentment.

This was a temperamental generosity, rather than female subjection, for there was a fiercely independent side to her. She retired from the theatre at twenty-one to live for six years with an architect in the country, in defiance of Victorian morality. When poverty broke up the relationship (the love of her life, despite three brief marriages) it was to support two illegitimate children that she resumed acting. Proud of being a professional woman, Ellen Terry supported women's suffrage. And she was one of the few people brave enough to praise Oscar WILDE after his conviction for homosexuality.

AUGUST STRINDBERG (1849-1912)

Swedish writer and dramatist. Strindberg was the son of a bankrupt merchant and his former maidservant, origins that nourished a lifetime of emotional instability. After leaving university, he wrote plays, preoccupied (like IBSEN) with history and folklore. But even by the age of twenty-three, in *Master Olof*, he had rejected both traditional dramatic conventions and a seemly reverence towards Swedish history.

A schoolmaster, librarian, journalist, novelist and writer of scientific and political treatises in his youth, Strindberg left Sweden in 1883 to live in Europe, where he wrote ceaselessly. Indeed his sixty-two plays are only a portion of his total literary output (which are collected in a standard edition of fifty-five volumes).

His first popular theatrical success was *Lucky Peter's Journey* (1882), a fairy-tale fantasy which introduces a theme central to the plays of his last years: that of the quest. A production of *The Father* in 1887 established him as one of the most powerful dramatists in Europe. This naturalist drama, together with *Miss Julie* and *Creditors* (both 1888), expose Strindberg's obsession with the war between the sexes. Marriage is a battlefield and women are predators and vampires. To combat what he saw as imminent world domination by women, he passionately embraced Nietzsche's theory of the Superman. (Not long after, he divorced his first wife; neither of his subsequent wives stayed with him.) This sexual obsession culminated theatrically with *The Dance of Death* (1900), a bitter work that has proved a macabre magnet for some of the greatest actors and directors of the twentieth century.

Writing no more plays for six years, Strindberg dabbled in the occult and alchemy, trying to make gold. Finally he suffered a mental breakdown, and after a year in a sanatorium, returned to writing; his experiences later appeared in *Inferno*, an extraordinary prose account of his near-madness.

From then on his plays attempted to find ways of expressing psychological and spiritual realities, verging on the mystical. In this search, Strindberg evolved techniques that would be widely imitated by expressionist dramatists. He wanted a stage where "Time and space do not exist; on a slight groundwork of reality, imagination spins and weaves new patterns made up of memories, experiences, unfettered fancies, absurdities and improvisations." In the spirit of this, he wrote *The Road to Damascus*, *A Dream Play* (1901), *The Ghost Sonata* (1907) and his last play, *The Great Highway* (1909), all generated by an obsessive questing journey for some meaning in a world which is more Hell than Heaven.

Strindberg devoted the last three years of his life to writing pamphlets on politics, sociology and philosophy. His immensely varied plays had to wait until after the First World War for a new generation of theatre artists to explore and to give them life on the stage. His drama has had a profound influence on both European and American

dramatists. Perhaps his most fruitful disciple is stage director and film-maker INGMAR BERGMAN: it has been said that every Swede has a Strindberg phase – it lasts from the cradle to the grave.

ALEXANDER GIRARDI (1850-1918)

Austrian actor and singer. Vienna's best-loved actor for over forty years, Girardi first captured the public's imagination with his singing of a Strauss waltz. His death (he was playing Weyring, the violinist in Arthur SCHNITZLER's *Liebelei* at the time) marked the end of that city's great era of carefree entertainment. It was in the plays of Austria's master of fantasy, Ferdinand RAIMUND, that his natural comic gifts found their greatest expression, particularly as Fortunatus Wurzel in *Der Bauer als Millionär*. Fittingly, the flat-topped peasant hat he wore in this and many other famous roles became known as a "Girardihut".

ARISTIDE BRUANT (1851-1925)

French chansonnier, poet and cabaret-owner. As Toulouse-Lautrec's famous poster suggests, Bruant cultivated the figure of the aloof, artistic dandy, dressing in a black velvet suit, wide-brimmed hat, high boots and scarf. This pose, developed as a defence against the hostility he had experienced as a timid fifteen-year-old provincial in Paris with not a penny to his name, became part of his entertainment as well. Le Mirliton, his cabaret which succeeded SALIS's Le Chat noir, set a fashion for abusing its well-to-do customers; his songs, which he delivered in a solemn, bass voice, complained continually that the audience was too stupid to understand. The local people of Montmartre loved him for championing the poor and oppressed in their own *argot*, and even put him up as their Parliamentary candidate.

DANIEL FROHMAN (1851-1940)

American manager. Like his brother CHARLES FROHMAN, Daniel acquired a passion for the stage from the actors who frequented his father's Broadway cigar store. He became business manager of the Madison Square Theatre in 1880 and hired David BELASCO as director in 1882. But his greatest years were to come at the Lyceum Theatre from 1887–1902. There Frohman trained his company in the smoothly realistic acting and well-knit ensemble that contemporary drama required, enjoying particular success with works by PINERO and HENRY ARTHUR JONES.

HENRY ARTHUR JONES (1851-1929)

English playwright. The prolific and forthright Jones reawakened English drama from a century of make-believe, but his plays have not lasted well. Persuaded that drama must show every aspect of modern life, particularly social problems, he helped break new ground for serious playwrights but, while deft and often comic, his own plays remained bogged down in melodrama. Others such as GEORGE BERNARD SHAW were to write the masterpieces to which he himself was unable to rise. (Shaw was a personal friend until the irascible Jones quarrelled violently with him.)

Victorian audiences were unprepared for his more advanced subjects. In *Michael and His Lost Angel* (1896) a clergyman is involved in adultery; Mrs Patrick CAMPBELL gave up her part in the seventh week of rehearsal because one particularly "offensive" scene took place in church, and the play itself ran for only ten performances. Jones's most successful works were *The Liars* (1897) and *Mrs*

Cabaret I: Paris

Artists and criminals have always had much in common. Paris's first true cabaret – Le Chat noir – was an open acknowledgement of this long association. In 1881 Rodolphe SALIS moved his apartments from the fashionable Latin Quarter to the disreputable Montmartre district of Paris, and held regular meetings of artists, poets and songwriters who consciously identified with the surrounding *canaille*. Once a week he would invite the public, and so cabaret was born amid the intimate fumes of wine, pastis and tobacco. The performers, who wrote their own material, were dedicated to the destruction of bourgeois values; and the audience were often savagely attacked from the stage.

Salis closed Le Chat noir in 1897, but Le Mirliton sprang up on its original site. This was started by Aristide BRUANT, who continued Le Chat's policy of audience insult. His songs, filled with rage at the establishment and at social inequality, exemplified his belief in social change. By the turn of the century, the cabaret had become a meeting-place for avant-garde artists such as Picasso and APOLLINAIRE. But its latent violence soon erupted, and the Montmartre cabaret disintegrated as rogues and roughnecks took its anti-social ethos all too literally. After the horrors of the First World War the angry iconoclasm of the Dadaists gave it a new lease of life; but jazz was sweeping through Paris, and soon the particularly Parisian flavour of the cabaret, with its celebration of the local *argot*, was all but dead.

Cabaret audiences were peopled with artists, who would meet to formulate new ideas – and to concoct hoaxes to expose the vacuity of popular taste. One of them, Roland Dorgelès, invented the school of Excessivism and "discovered" Boriali, its

leading exponent. Boriali was in fact a donkey called Lolo, who painted with a brush tied to his tail. His masterpiece "Et le soleil se couche sur l'Adriatique" was exhibited at the Salon des Independants, and received serious reviews. The authorities were outraged

Dane's Defence (1900), but, as the critic William Archer said, his plays lacked "that subtle quality – distinction".

ERMETE NOVELLI (1851-1919)

Italian actor-manager. Novelli's long, bony nose and body did not immediately endear him to the public, but his expansive character, expressive face and gift for characterization and mimicry soon did. In 1883, after working with Luigi BELLOTTI-BON, he formed his own company. His great triumphs were always in tragedy; *Hamlet* (with an impressively realistic ghost scene), *Othello* and plays by IBSEN became the stock-in-trade of his repertoire. Some disapproved of his naturalistic acting – Adelaide RISTORI accused him of speaking like a village grocer. His greatest parts mixed comedy and tragedy: Shylock, for example, and the lead in Jean Aicard's *Le Père Lebonnard*. Novelli's attempt (in 1900) to found a permanent theatre in Rome was a tragic failure.

WHIMSICAL WALKER (1851-1934)

English clown. "Whimmy" was as famous a clown as GRIMALDI and GROCK. He ran away from home at nine, and made his first circus appearance as a tumbler at ten. His special comic trademarks were a "red-hot" poker for jabbing other clowns in the pants, and a wonderful array of animal assistants. Chief among the latter was Tom the donkey, who sang before Queen Victoria. Whimmy made the last appearance of his seventy-year, worldwide career before the great-great-granddaughter of Queen Victoria. His final turn coincided with Princess Elizabeth's first visit to a circus. Tom was no longer available for an aria, but England's future queen delighted in the antics of the old man and his red-hot poker.

LADY GREGORY (1852-1932)

Irish playwright. Augusta Gregory was an immensely capable Anglo-Irishwoman who not only helped to found and then direct the Abbey Theatre, but wrote extensively for it. She was drawn to the theatre by twin loves: for W. B. YEATS and for the trot and rhythm of the dialect speech of the peasantry in Galway, where she was born. Her work lacks imaginative power and contains the unconscious snobbery of her class (she was married to an English colonial civil servant, becoming a Lady when he was knighted). She wrote more than thirty plays, the best of which – *Spreading the News* (1904), *The Rising of the Moon* (1907) and *The Workhouse Ward* (1908) – were sprightly, bitter comedies of Irish life; they were also the most popular plays in the repertoire during the first twenty-five years of the Abbey's history.

WEEDON GROSSMITH (1852-1919)

English actor, novelist and playwright. Grossmith is best known for *Diary of a Nobody*, the brilliantly funny novel about Victorian middle-class life, which he wrote with his brother George, a performer in GILBERT and Sullivan's Savoy operas. Weedon was himself an extremely popular comic actor. GEORGE BERNARD SHAW had a high opinion of him and wrote of his performance in Arthur Law's *The Ladies' Idol* in 1895, "The audience . . . laughs whenever he opens his mouth. He accordingly opens his mouth very often, and shuts it again, with hilarious results." Shaw's complaint was that his comic talents were wasted. Nevertheless he had a great success in his own play, *The Night of the Party* (1901). A man of many talents, Grossmith was also a good painter and a crack shot. Two nephews, George and Lawrence, were also actors.

ALBERT RINGLING (1852-1916)

American circus owner. Dazzled by the DAN RICE circus one day in 1870, Al Ringling and his four brothers decided on the spot to create a show of their own. Their first effort consisted of a home-made panorama with an admission fee of ten pins. In 1882 they became the Ringling Brothers' Classic and Comic Concert Company, performing music and skits in small-town opera houses. By 1885 they had a patchwork tent, three horses, a dancing bear and a blind hyena (optimistically billed as *Hideous Hyena Striata Gigantium*), to which they soon added two elephants and a whole variety of acts.

By 1890 their "great moral show", offering "neatness, clean performances and fast movement", was performing all over the mid-West. Within twenty years they had absorbed the fabulous Barnum and Bailey circus itself, to become literally "The Greatest Show on Earth". For years the Ringling extravaganza, with its special one-hundred-car railroad train and tent that could hold ten thousand, was synonymous with the thrills of the circus. Even today, with the big top replaced by modern stadiums, the show still generates the excitement that inspired the "five ringling" circus one hundred years before.

RODOLPHE SALIS (1852-97)

French cabaret impresario. Salis founded Le Chat Noir, the first and most famous Parisian cabaret. Taking an old house in the seedy suburb of Montmartre in 1881, he invited friends along to talk and to perform their work. Soon Paris was beating a path to his door, and Salis opened to the public, offering drink to anyone "who earned his thirst artistically". In songs, poems and sketches, artists such as Aristide BRUANT and Alphonse ALLAIS struck out at the hypocrisy and corruption of the Establishment; needless to say, its more prominent members were soon risking insult to attend performances.

Needing more room, in 1885 Salis removed the contents of Le Chat Noir (in midnight procession) to rue Victor-Massé, also in Montmartre. Here the most popular feature became the Théâtre d'Ombres, in which shadows of cut out shapes were projected on to a screen as a play or an illustration to sharp and amusing satirical comment by Salis. Today, Montmartre cafés still offer tourists emasculated imitations of such wit and invention.

JOHN DREW (1853-1927)

American actor. Despite the example of his famous mother, the son of LOUISA LANE DREW showed no early inclination to act. And when he finally made his debut he showed no signs of nerves, much to her vexation. Such effortlessness became the younger Drew's stock in trade, sometimes obscuring the care with which it was achieved.

He frequently appeared with the Augustin DALY company (winning particular renown in SHAKESPEARE) and in 1892 became a member of CHARLES FROHMAN's troupe, where he starred in sophisticated modern comedy. To the end of his life, he worked hard to cultivate the impression recorded by an early critic: "John Drew doesn't act, he just behaves."

JOHNSTON FORBES-ROBERTSON (1853-1937)

English actor-manager. Forbes-Robertson, the greatest Hamlet of his day, did not much like acting. He wanted to paint, yet went on the stage at twenty at the suggestion of others. Popular for his good looks, fine voice and elegant natural style, he worked with Samuel PHELPS, Squire and

Lady BANCROFT, Henry IRVING and John Hare. In 1881 he played Romeo to Helena MODJESKA's Juliet. Nearing forty before venturing into management, he never settled down to one theatre, but toured extensively with his own companies.

Forbes-Robertson first played Hamlet at forty-four. He spoke the lines with such beauty that it was to make him more money than any other part. Mrs Patrick CAMPBELL played Ophelia. He was long in love with this notoriously cruel actress, but eventually, while on tour in GEORGE BERNARD SHAW's *The Devil's Disciple*, transferred his affection to the young American GERTRUDE ELLIOTT, his new leading lady. They were soon engaged, and Shaw wrote to Ellen TERRY, "I foresaw it, and wanted a clause in the contract against it. However, he might do worse. She . . . will mend his extensively broken heart." They were, in fact, very happy.

Forbes-Robertson's other famous performances were in *Caesar and Cleopatra*, written for him by Shaw, and Jerome K. Jerome's *The Passing of the Third Floor Back*. In 1916 he appeared on stage for the last time and then gratefully retired. Later he wrote, "I stripped myself of Hamlet's garb with no sort of regret, but rather with a great sense of relief."

LILLIE LANGTRY (1853-1929)

English actress. The daughter of the Dean of Jersey, Lillie married a rich diplomat, who unwisely brought her to London. There she became an almost legendary society beauty and shocked her patrician friends by taking to the stage. She made a name for herself as Rosalind in *As You Like It* and Kate in *She Stoops to Conquer*, but her fame was based as much upon her social grace as upon ability. Lillie commanded a galaxy of distinguished admirers: an American enthusiast built a luxury railway-carriage for her; Oscar WILDE wrote a poem to her while camping all night on her doorstep; and Millais painted her holding a flower (after which she became known as the "Jersey Lily"). She became a mistress of the Prince of Wales, who set her up in a house in Bournemouth and eventually bequeathed her to his nephew, Prince Louis Battenberg. Lillie became fabulously rich, owning a yacht, a Californian ranch and a racing-stable.

HERBERT BEERBOHM TREE (1853-1917)

English actor-manager. Six feet tall with flaming red hair, Beerbohm Tree had a personality to match his appearance. After ten successful years as an actor, he turned to management in 1887 in order to choose his own roles. He chose well, and was soon able to take over the Haymarket Theatre. Tree excelled in character parts; while playing Lord Illingworth in Oscar WILDE's *A Woman of No Importance* he continued to live the part off-stage. Wilde remarked: "Herbert becomes *de plus en plus Oscarisé*; it is a wonderful case of Nature imitating Art." *Trilby*, an adaptation of George du Maurier's novel, with Tree as Svengali, was an immense success. Profits helped to build Her Majesty's Theatre (*His* Majesty's after the death of Queen Victoria), where Tree moved in 1897.

Here his productions became more and more spectacular. Ignoring criticism that the plays were drowned in extravagance, he had live rabbits in *A Midsummer Night's Dream*, a rocking boat splashed with waves in *The Tempest*, and, in *Richard II*, a real horse. The public loved it, but Tree tired quickly of novelty and would refer to a play as "an obstinate success". He was not a great Shakespearean actor, but he knew how to make the plays commercially successful. He ran SHAKESPEARE festivals from 1905 to 1916 and founded The Royal Academy of Dramatic Art in 1904.

Tree's wife, Maud Holt (or Lady Tree, 1863–1937, for he was knighted in 1909), was a fine comic actress. The Trees were often joined on stage by their daughter Viola.

ALPHONSE ALLAIS (1854-1905)

French comic writer and monologuist. Allais's humour was usually described as "Anglo-Saxon" because his monologues, impelled by their own absurd and often macabre logic, were delivered with deadpan solemnity. Immensely popular at Rodolphe SALIS's Le Chat Noir and other Montmartre cabarets, he also wrote vaudeville pieces and contributed regular columns to weekly magazines. His jokes were not always as improbable as they seemed. A pharmacist by training, he once discoursed at length on stage about how to kill microbes by heating them up and then cooling them down, thus accidentally describing the pasteurization of milk.

FRANÇOIS DE CUREL (1854-1928)

French playwright. When Curel's first play, *L'Envers d'une Sainte*, was put on by ANTOINE's Théâtre Libre in 1892, it was praised by the critics but booed by uncomprehending audiences. So conscious was he of his failure to reach the average theatregoer with his intellectual analyses of the moral issues of the times, that he rewrote continually in an attempt to clarify his intentions. In the first version of *La Fille sauvage* (1902), the last act is a Wagnerian sing-song in Bayreuth; in the final version it takes place among a tribe of cannibals. *Le Repas du lion* (1897), an intelligent piece on the problems of capitalism and labour, underwent six major revisions.

Curel's greatest success came late in life with *L'Âme en folie* (1920). The title refers to the state of being in love, a more appreciable theme than those of his earlier works.

OSCAR WILDE (1854-1900)

Irish playwright, poet and man of letters. Oscar Fingal O'Flahertie Wills Wilde was the son of a Dublin eye surgeon. Though he remained unmistakably Irish throughout his life, he spent only twenty years in his native land; the rest he lived in England "where he laughed", as one Irish critic remarked, "at England and English ways to such good purpose that the English themselves laughed with him." Until, that is, he was convicted of "committing acts of gross indecency with other male persons" in 1895 and confined in Reading gaol for two years. This event is itself the plot for many plays and films, and gave the English the last, cruel laugh on Wilde who, when released, fled into exile and died wretched and penniless in Paris three years later.

The young Oscar was a brilliant classical scholar at Oxford, whence he arrived in London with "immeasurable ambitions". Like the Prime Minister of the day, Benjamin Disraeli, Wilde understood that "to enter high society, a man must either have blood, a million or a genius". He managed quite easily on his genius, though he first caught the public's attention with his studied flamboyance. In knee breeches or a green carnation he was a notorious figure on the American lecture circuit.

Before his fatal affair with the young and neurotic Lord Alfred Douglas, Wilde married and had two children. He was a successful poet, writer and journalist, but it was not until he was thirty-eight that his first London stage success, *Lady Windermere's Fan* (1892), was produced. The sentimental morality of this comedy was leavened by such brilliant (if now familiar) lines as "I can resist everything except temptation." His notoriety was further increased by the banning of his second play *Salomé*, but the next year *A Woman of No Importance* appeared. The sentiment was, this time, neatly punctured by Wilde, who declared that its moral was "Good women cause more trouble than they are worth."

It was followed, in 1895, by the first performances of *An Ideal Husband* ("To love oneself is the beginning of a life-long romance") and *The Importance of Being Earnest* ("None of us are perfect. I myself am peculiarly susceptible to draughts") within two months of each other. Wilde's reputation was not only made, but justified, for the second of these – his last play – is perhaps the most perfect comedy in the English language: a comedy quite without a meaning or moral. It was followed by tragedy; within weeks he was arrested, within months he was bankrupt, and when he finally received his sentence of two years' hard labour, the prostitutes danced in the streets.

WILLIAM GILLETTE (1855-1937)

American actor and playwright. The success of a 1974 revival of *Sherlock Holmes* (1899) proved that a Gillette play could still hold an audience. Holmes was a character typical of Gillette, who wrote nearly all his works as star vehicles for himself. He favoured an understated realism, a reserved but steely strength that could burst into decisive action. His Civil War dramas *Held By The Enemy* (1886) and *Secret Service* (1895) also featured this exemplary sang-froid. But "no living man would pick up a cigar and proceed to chew it coolly, the instant after he has been shot in the arm . . ." remarked a cynical critic of the latter play.

ARTHUR WING PINERO (1855-1934)

English playwright and actor. In the years before the First World War, Pinero was a force in English drama to rival GEORGE BERNARD SHAW. He worked as an actor under IRVING, who encouraged him to take up playwriting. Thereupon Pinero produced a number of successful farces, notably *The Magistrate* (1885) and *Dandy Dick* (1886). He is better known today for his more serious works, including *The Second Mrs Tanqueray* (1897) and *Trelawney of the Wells* (1898). The former, which earned its author fame as the English IBSEN, once seemed courageously modern in its portrayal of a "fallen woman", but Shaw, who distrusted all things "Pinerotic" found it merely torrid, while many other Victorian critics bemoaned Pinero's literary dialogue and his tendency towards genteel expressions and comfortable attitudes. None-the-less, the play provided a splendid vehicle for Mrs Patrick CAMPBELL, and subsequent interpretations have won it recognition as a compulsive and searching character study.

OTTO BRAHM (1856-1912)

German director, critic and historian. Die Freie Bühne, a theatre company founded in Berlin in 1889 to pursue the same naturalist aims as ANTOINE's Théâtre Libre in Paris, was the joint creation of nine men, but Brahm immediately emerged to become its inspiration and leading director. Previously he had been a radical theatre critic (frequently at odds with the newspapers he worked for) and in 1887 had published a notable essay on IBSEN, and in particular on *Ghosts*. Accordingly, this was Die Freie Bühne's first production (a Sunday matinée in a theatre kindly loaned for the occasion). It was soon followed by the two most influential works of the new German naturalist school, HAUPTMANN's *Vor Sonnenaufgang* and *Die Familie Selicke* by Arno HOLZ and Johannes Schlaf.

After finding a stable home for his company at the Deutsches Theater, Brahm was responsible for bringing a young actor called Max REINHARDT from Salzburg to Berlin. Ironically it was to be Reinhardt's impressionist style of theatre that finally killed off the precise naturalism that Brahm had laboured so hard to establish.

RÉJANE (1856-1920)

French actress. While the intelligentsia worshipped Sarah BERNHARDT, the less pretentious Parisians reserved their adoration for Réjane, the unrivalled queen of vaudeville and light comedy. She had something of Bernhardt's eccentricity, driving around in a carriage drawn by two mules (a present from the King of Portugal), but her greatest qualities were her vivacity and spontaneity. "Compared to her," wrote her son, "all other women seemed to be suffering from some illness."

Réjane made her debut at the Vaudeville Theatre in

The beautiful and spirited Emilie Charlotte le Breton (otherwise known as **Lillie Langtry**) shone as Cleopatra (*below*)

1875, but her talent and beauty did not come to full flower until the 1890s, when a second-rate, sentimental piece called *L'Amoureuse* made her and Lucien Guitry the idols of Paris. Most of her material was equally trivial, with the notable exception of SARDOU's *Madame Sans-Gêne*, in which she created the title role, later playing it in London and New York.

In middle age Réjane turned successfully to serious drama, even playing Nora in IBSEN's *A Doll's House*. She died, like Bernhardt, while making a film.

GEORGE BERNARD SHAW
(1856-1950)

Irish playwright. When George Bernard Shaw died at the age of ninety-four the lights were dimmed on Broadway, *The Times* devoted its first leader to his life and the Indian Cabinet adjourned. All were entirely suitable obsequies. Shaw, the stubborn Irishman, was by then an English institution. A prolific and beloved playwright and critic, he had also become an influential socialist philosopher, one of the most effective propagandists against the Empire.

Shaw did not start writing plays until he was thirty-six, having lived penuriously as an unpublished novelist in the sixteen years since he had exiled himself from his native Dublin. "I am not enamoured of poverty, of obscurity and the ostracism of contempt . . . these were all that Dublin offered the enormity of my unconscious ambition," he wrote later.

But he could never really divorce himself from his Irish birth; it was his delight to be witty and ungenerous at the expense of his adopted country, where he was, none-the-less, revered. One of his many biographers, the Irish writer St John ERVINE, says, "Had he written as vehemently against the policies of the [Irish Free State] in a time of comparative peace as he wrote against the policy of the English at a time of war, he would soon have found himself serving an indeterminate sentence in Kilmainham Prison [in Dublin]." Not that Shaw ought to be remembered for the quality of his political judgement: among the men he praised were Stalin and Mussolini.

But it is this outrageousness which is a characteristic of his finest plays. Shaw may have started writing them late (late enough to be deeply influenced by the realism of Henrik IBSEN) but his output was prodigious, not only because he lived to a great age, but because he could write remarkably quickly in the shorthand he had learned as a boy. He wrote about fifty plays, and each was accompanied by a preface which was rarely brief.

Many of the plays are entirely forgettable, but he wrote more good ones than any dramatist in English during the nineteenth and twentieth centuries. The best are not necessarily the best known. The appealing plot of *Pygmalion* (1913), uncluttered with philosophical dialogue, has made it one of his most popular plays and an ideal vehicle for the musical *My Fair Lady*. Plays like *Major Barbara* (1905) and *St Joan* (1923), though successful on stage, became more famous when they were made into films, and both have produced excellent performances by three generations of actresses – Sybil THORNDIKE, Wendy HILLER, Siobhan McKENNA and Judi Dench, for example. Actors and actresses revel in the strength of personality of Shaw's leading men and women: the title role of *Candida* (1895), Jack Tanner in *Man and Superman* (1905), Caesar and Cleopatra (from the play of that name) and King Magnus in *The Apple Cart* (1929). In all, a dozen or more plays by Shaw appear regularly in the English-speaking theatrical repertoire. (His idiosyncratic style has never translated especially well into other languages.)

Many critics believe Shaw's best play to be *Heartbreak House*, written shortly after the end of the First World War, in which he describes (accurately, history would suggest) the end of the leisurely, cultured society of pre-War Britain. Captain Shotover, the play's "hero" states: "The captain's in his bunk drinking bottled ditchwater; and the crew is gambling in the forecastle. She will strike and sink and split. Do you think the laws of God will be suspended in favour of England because you were born in it?"

Despite his elderly preference for dictators, Shaw's plays show a passion for the destruction of idols, a contempt for conventional wisdom ("He who can, does. He who can't, teaches"), a love of strong women, and an inability to stop arguing with God. A man of considerable conceit, Shaw would have had no trouble explaining this: "All great truths begin as blasphemies," he wrote.

He died a lonely man, having outlived his wife, Charlotte, whom he had married at the age of forty-one, choosing then to settle down after a decade of philandering. (His second play, *The Philanderer*, is an autobiographical work.) This did not prevent him, however, from verbal seductions, the most famous of which was the actress Mrs Patrick CAMPBELL. Shaw died immensely wealthy. Since 1950 royalties have made the estate even richer, which is gratifying for the three major beneficiaries: The British Museum, the National Gallery of Ireland and London's Royal Academy of Dramatic Art.

In his old age, **Shaw** was frustrated and distressed at his own inability to die

MAX DEVRIENT (1857-1929)

German actor and director. The son of Karl Devrient, Max rapidly established himself in Vienna in the official role of "Young Lover and Character Actor", though the hierarchy demanded that to begin with he play only "second" (i.e. unrequited) lovers. He later made a name for himself as an actor of unusual power in both tragedy and comedy. Old and white-haired, he had a dignified presence on stage, but he is best remembered for such evil roles as Mephistopheles, Richard III, and Gessler in SCHILLER's *Wilhelm Tell*.

LE PETOMANE (1857-1945)

French petomane. Swimming in the sea as a youth, Joseph Pujol found that he could imbibe water through his anus. He soon discovered that he could also inhale air and entertained his friends by exhaling it with a variety of amusing noises. Giving up his trade as a baker, he set off to tour the provinces with a ripping show. In 1892, he approached Monsieur Zidler at the Moulin Rouge, called for a bowl of water to ensure a fresh performance and gave his audition, imitating the farts of young girls, brides on their wedding night (and the morning after), playing tunes on a pipe and finally blowing out a candle.

Le Petomane was taken on immediately (admittedly he performed in the garden) and, with the slogan "the only one who pays no authors royalties", became the hottest act in Paris. Pujol retired in 1914, but lived to a ripe old age.

HERMANN SUDERMANN (1857-1928)

German playwright and novelist. Sudermann's world-wide reputation was based on *Heimat* (1893), or more precisely on the role of Magda, the misunderstood daughter who leaves home and becomes a singer. After both Sarah BERNHARDT and Eleonora DUSE had played the part, it became an essential test for young actresses who aspired to similar greatness. Although theatrically very effective, *Heimat* (*Magda* in the English translation) suffers from the same weaknesses as *Die Ehre* (1889), the piece that made Sudermann one of the leaders of the naturalist movement in Germany. The contrast between the characters is too black and white, and facile solutions beg the questions the plays have posed. *Sodoms Ende* (1890) was a far stronger dose of naturalism, but it proved too much for Berlin (the Sodom in question).

Sudermann maintained his much-publicized rivalry with Gerhart HAUPTMANN by experimenting with many new dramatic styles. The most successful of his later plays were those set in his homeland of East Prussia, notably *Das Glück im Winkel* (1895) and *Johannisfeuer* (1900); but even these bear little comparison with the more profound theatre of Hauptmann. It is hard now to believe that for over twenty years both playwrights were invariably mentioned in the same breath.

ERMETE ZACCONI (1857-1948)

Italian actor. Zacconi's naturalistic acting was a shock to many who considered it an insult to great drama. But he introduced Italians to much that was new and exciting in the theatre. He played with numerous small groups before joining Giovanni Emanuel's company in 1884, where he established himself as one of Italy's foremost actors.

In 1894 Zacconi formed his own company, which became known for outstanding performances of contemporary drama. He himself played Oswald in the Italian première of *Ghosts*. *Kollege Crampton* and *Fuhrmann Henschell* by Gerhart HAUPTMANN, Alfred DE MUSSET's *Lorenzaccio* and SHAKESPEARE's *Othello* were other distinguished productions. In later years Zacconi had great successes in Alfredo Testoni's *Il Cardinale Lambertini*; he also enjoyed a concurrent career as an early film actor.

GEORGE ALEXANDER (1858-1918)

English actor-manager. Oscar WILDE maintained that, on stage, Alexander did not act, he behaved. But in Wilde's comedies he behaved extremely well. As Lord Windermere in *Lady Windermere's Fan* and John Worthing in *The Importance of Being Earnest* he was able to be himself, the perfect English gentleman. When he attempted a character part, the results were unfortunate. BERNARD SHAW's comment on Alexander's playing of a doddering old man was blunt: "The sole merit of the performance is that it deceives nobody."

Alexander's finest performance was as the Prince (and his double) in *The Prisoner of Zenda*. His great contribution to the English stage (for which he was knighted) was his management for more than a quarter of a century of the fashionable St James's Theatre. One great opportunity that he missed was putting on the plays of Shaw. The part of Higgins in *Pygmalion* was written with Alexander in mind, while Mrs Patrick CAMPBELL was to play Eliza. "Go on for another play with Mrs Campbell I will not," declared Alexander. "I'd rather die."

ANDRÉ ANTOINE (1858-1943)

French actor and director. Antoine was a clerk with the Paris Gas Company until he founded the Théâtre Libre in 1887. Here he became a champion of naturalism and an ally of Emile ZOLA, one of whose plays he dressed with his mother's own furniture carried across Paris by hand-cart. Encouraged by the critics, Antoine turned professional and presented almost two hundred plays, including works by IBSEN, STRINDBERG, BECQUE and HAUPTMANN. He insisted that actors be conversational rather than rhetorical, and urged them to behave as if unaware of the presence of an audience. Touring Europe, he established the importance of his naturalistic production methods and of the new playwrights he introduced. As director of his own Théâtre Antoine and, until 1914, of the Odéon, he became the unquestioned master of naturalism in Europe. Although his theories were quickly superseded, the director who used real meat to dress the set of a butcher's shop can still claim to be one of the inspirations of the modern theatre.

GEORGES COURTELINE (1858-1929)

French playwright. Courteline's experiences of the army and civil bureaucracy inspired some of the funniest French plays of the nineteenth century. His research for these pieces, however, was not always wholehearted. He once held a job in a Government department for two years, during which he was never seen in the office, paying a fellow-employee half his pay to do the work. He was originally a successful short-story writer and did not at first consider his farces important. He wrote them for friends to perform in a Montmartre club, until André ANTOINE recognized their quality and began to produce them at his Théâtre Libre.

Courteline's numerous comedies were traditional in style, but the observation was acute and the wit biting. *Lidoire* (1891), the first to be produced, and *Les Gaîtés de l'escadron* (1895) satirize army life. *L'Article 330* takes the Law as its target. Others deal with the weaknesses and peculiarities or ordinary people – he liked to think of himself as something of a moralist. In *Bourbouroche* (1893), his masterpiece, a rich old bachelor chooses not to know that his mistress is deceiving him, despite discovering a young man in her apartment. Courteline's plays were long successful at the Comédie-Française. He wrote little after 1900, partly because of ill-health, and because the act of writing was always a laborious process for him.

ELEONORA DUSE (1858-1924)

Italian actress. A spiritual, almost mystical quality made Duse the greatest tragic actress of her time. She was born to the hard life of a travelling player, but at first showed

CONTINUED ON PAGE 146

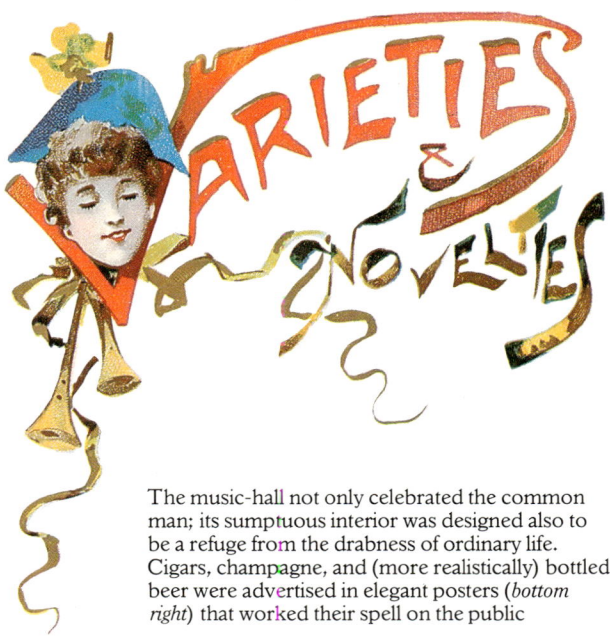

The music-hall not only celebrated the common man; its sumptuous interior was designed also to be a refuge from the drabness of ordinary life. Cigars, champagne, and (more realistically) bottled beer were advertised in elegant posters (*bottom right*) that worked their spell on the public

The comic Scotsman **Will Fyffe**

The sheet music for the songs of music-hall stars was marketed as fiercely as the top ten records are today. The examples (*centre right*) of songs by **Dan Leno** and **Marie Lloyd** show that a similar care was lavished on attractive covers. The warm and subtle suggestiveness of Marie Lloyd made her the most popular star of all. T. S. Eliot considered that she uniquely expressed "the soul of the people" who were her audience

George Robey (*below*) and Dan Leno were two of the earliest stand-up comics, mixing monologue with song

Music Hall

Music hall grew from the British love of drinking and singing. In the notorious supper rooms that sprang up in the 1830s, young men-about-town could get a meal after a visit to the theatre (women were rigorously excluded) and listen to songs of breathtaking obscenity. The proceedings were ruled over by a Chairman, who, gavel in hand, would introduce a mixture of amateur and professional performers – and occasionally perform himself if an artiste failed to show up. Some of these managers became wildly ambitious, and set up vast variety saloons where over a thousand people could be fed and entertained. But still women were kept out, or at best allowed to watch the all-male entertainment from behind grilles at the back of the gallery.

By the 1840s the saloons had got quite out of hand and were illegally performing plays, operas and ballets in addition to the regular comic turns. The Lord Chamberlain clamped down with the 1843 Theatre Act, which forced the saloons either to become legitimate theatres – and not sell drink in the auditorium – or to confine themselves to musical numbers and get their customers as drunk as they liked.

Charles Morton, a brilliant manager, seized on the change in the law to create a new entertainment: music hall. He would continue to sell drink, but would admit women and put on reputable acts. Night after night his Canterbury Hall, built in 1852 on the site of a skittle alley next to a pub, attracted "respectable mechanics and small tradesmen with their wives, daughters and sweethearts", who listened to the latest musical offerings of Offenbach and even excerpts from the newly composed *Faust* of Gounod.

From here the craze for music hall spread to the middle and lower classes, and by the 1860s so many new halls had been built that it became necessary to employ agents to conduct the affairs of the artists. A

singer could appear in as many as four different theatres in a single night; the dash by brougham across London entailed split-second timing. Unfortunately the physical exertion was not the only demand on the strength of the artist. Theatre etiquette insisted that a star performer bought drinks for everyone else on the bill – and accepted more in return. In such a way, many an artist drank his polite way to an early grave.

Inevitably managers became even more ambitious, and towards the end of the nineteenth century an attempt was made to get the upper classes into the halls as well. The luxurious London Pavilion was opened in 1878 – far removed from the rough and tumble of the original Supper Rooms – and bar counters were gradually excluded from the auditoriums. Electric numbers on the proscenium arch (indicating the identity of the performers) made the job of the genial Chairman redundant. By the time of the first Royal Command Performance in 1912, when George V visited the Palace Theatre with Queen Mary, smoking was forbidden in the auditorium by royal request, and Marie LLOYD, the darling of the public, was not asked to appear as her act was thought too vulgar.

From then on the halls went into a rapid decline. Oswald Stoll had opened his genteel Coliseum in London and insisted on vetting each act before it appeared. Tea rooms on every level of the theatre replaced the usual bars, and an attempt was made to educate the public with Russian ballet and French tragedy. Ragtime swept across London, making the favourite songs of the halls seem rather *passé*: and the new style of revue from Paris emphasized the disconnected nature of the traditional variety bill.

It was the cinema and radio that finally killed off music hall. Formerly, an artist could survive on the same act for years; one appearance on radio and his act was blown for good. And when the talkies appeared they provided far more novelty than any number of illusionists and speciality acts.

The deadpan **Little Tich** (*right*)

Wilton's (*above*) which closed in 1887, is today awaiting restoration as the oldest surviving music-hall building in London.

little enthusiasm for acting (at the age of four she had to be urged on stage with a slap). At fourteen, playing Juliet in the ancient Roman arena at Verona, she suddenly became intoxicated by her art. "Every word, before leaving my lips, seemed to have passed through the warmth of my own blood," she explained.

Her style had so little of the extravagance of melodrama that many advised her to give up. Finally, in 1878, Giovanni Emanuel chose her to be the ingénue in his new company. Her first triumph was in the title role of Emile ZOLA's *Thérèse Raquin*. Joining Cesare Rossi's company as leading actress, she became bored with the melodramatic repertoire and might have given up acting had she not seen Sarah BERNHARDT in 1881. Determined that she too would inspire people to love great art, Duse brought DUMAS *fils'* *La Frincesse de Bagdad* alive with the spontaneity of her acting and was hailed a genius. She formed her first company in 1886. An affair with the poet Arrigo Boito also inspired her career. She admired him passionately, and strove to absorb from him all the culture that she had been denied in childhood. He translated SHAKESPEARE's *Antony and Cleopatra* for her, a play in which she excelled.

Duse was a small woman of grave beauty, but she had extraordinary powers of expression. When CHEKHOV saw her in Russia in 1890 he wrote "I speak no Italian . . . but I felt I understood every word." She toured extensively in Europe and the Americas, where, despite a worsening chest complaint, all were amazed by the intense sincerity and simplicity of her acting.

Still she longed for greater roles and, on falling in love with the poet Gabriele D'ANNUNZIO in 1894, felt she had found the man to write them. They vowed to restore poetry to Italian drama, but the treacherous D'Annunzio gave *La Città Morta* to Bernhardt, dashing off the inferior *Sogno di un mattino di primavera* for his lover. In 1897 Parisians gave Duse a wildly enthusiastic reception in this and Dumas *fils'* *La Dame au camélias*. She continued to dedicate herself to D'Annunzio's work, but when, in 1904, she became ill while preparing *La Figlia di Iorio*, he refused to postpone the play and found a replacement. This was the last straw for Duse, who had already seen their affair described in his novel *Il Fuoco*. Turning to other plays, notably those of IBSEN, she now gave some of her finest performances as Hedda Gabler, Nora in *A Doll's House* and, above all, Ellida in *The Lady from the Sea*.

In 1909, without warning, Duse gave up acting. She withdrew to meditate and read and, on the outbreak of war, devoted herself to visiting the wounded. In 1921 she returned to the stage, and died on tour in the United States three years later. In age, as in youth, she was an idealist, ceaselessly striving for greater truth and perfection in her art.

JOSEPH KAINZ (1858-1910)

Austrian actor. There exist no records of Kainz's most interesting performances as a young man, for these were given in the small hours of the morning before an audience of one, King Ludwig II of Bavaria, whose admiration for Kainz was as total and eccentric as his admiration for Wagner. Berlin audiences soon endorsed the mad monarch's opinion of the young actor when he moved to the newly founded Deutsches Theater. After ten years as the capital's leading actor (appearing chiefly in SHAKESPEARE and German classics like KLEIST's *Prinz Friedrich von Homburg*) he broke a contract because he was not getting the roles he felt he deserved. As a result he was effectively blacklisted by all the major theatres. This prompted him to undertake the first of his successful tours of America.

Kainz returned to Berlin for a while, creating the part of Heinrich the bell-founder in HAUPTMANN's *Die versunkene Glocke*, but eventually he found his way back to Vienna, where his career had started twenty-five years before. There at the Burgtheater he gave new depth to the heroes of Franz GRILLPARZER. Although Kainz's approach to his work was cerebral, he established an emotional involvement with his role that none of his contemporaries could match.

VLADIMIR NEMIROVICH-DANCHENKO (1858-1943)

Russian director and manager. Nemirovich-Danchenko began his career as theatre critic, drama teacher and playwright. His play on a double suicide, *The Worth of Life*, won the GRIBOYEDOV Prize – the highest accolade of the theatrical year. Among his pupils were some of the brightest lights of the next generation: the actress Olga KNIPPER and the producer MEYERHOLD. As a teacher, he argued for "inner-technique", and was opposed to "surface-memorization". He felt that a play had to become a living and breathing reality, its characters real people, long before a single line was learned.

When it looked as if his reforms for the Maly Theatre in Moscow were going to be rejected, Nemirovich-Danchenko wrote to STANISLAVSKY and arranged a meeting. For eighteen hours in the Slaviansky Bazaar restaurant these two visionaries plotted to overthrow the theatrical establishment. When the Moscow Art Theatre opened in 1898 the founders (now co-directors) were to revolutionize the attitudes, production techniques, staging and philosophy of the entire theatrical world.

DAVID BELASCO (1859-1931)

American director, manager, playwright and actor. Known as "the Bishop of Broadway" for his pseudo-priestly dress and dictatorial manner, Belasco served his stage apprenticeship in California. Barnstorming in frontier mining towns taught him to produce well-made, crowd-pulling plays remarkable for their spectacular effects and unusual attention to realistic detail. His legendary version of the Passion Play, for instance, featured a real flock of sheep. In 1882 he became stage manager at New York's Madison Square Theatre, and in 1887 at the Lyceum, expanding his reputation for action and naturalism. For one play he bought and transferred to the stage the complete contents of a shabby furnished room, down to the peeling wallpaper. By the 1890s he was a major Broadway force, and by 1902 had his own Belasco Theatre. As playwright (usually in collaboration) he turned out hits like *The Girl I Left Behind Me* (1893), but he is best remembered (thanks to Puccini's grandly sentimental operas) for *Madam Butterfly* (1900) and *The Girl of the Golden West* (1905). Belasco's influence also extended to promoting such stars as Fanny BRICE and Katharine CORNELL. In the twentieth century, a new generation largely disdained his unabashed realism and theatricality, but in 1923 STANISLAVSKY paid tribute to Belasco's achievements by making him an honorary member of the Moscow Art Theatre.

JAMES MATTHEW BARRIE (1860-1937)

Scottish playwright and novelist. When J. M. Barrie was six his brother died. This loss had a devastating effect both on him and on his mother, who consoled herself by smothering her remaining son with maternal passion. James never outgrew her, spending the rest of his life in a hopeless search for the boyhood he had missed. "Courage", he said, "is the thing. All goes if courage goes."

These problems are the inspiration of the novels which made Barrie's name in the 1890s. Equally, in his most famous play, *Peter Pan* (1904), he takes childish refuge in the magic dispensed by the invisible spirit Tinkerbell; but the popularity of this inspired fairytale resides also in the character of Captain Hook, an unforgettable incarnation of the hostility which Barrie perceived in the real world.

The earlier comedy, *The Admirable Crichton* (1902), expresses Barrie's disillusionment in terms of humorous cynicism: a lord and his butler are marooned and exchange roles, but on returning to "civilization" effortlessly revert to their original status. Similarly, the main characters of *Dear Brutus* (1917), finding themselves in an enchanted forest, are offered a magical opportunity to relive and repair their lives. They too merely succeed in repeating their original mistakes. *Quality Street* (1902) and *What Every Woman Knows* (1908) are two more typical comedies that remain in the repertory.

For all his cynicism Barrie never grew up. His marriage was an attempt to replace his "little mother", and probably remained unconsummated. But a subsequent relationship with a real young mother and her sons was more satisfying and led to the composition of *Peter Pan*.

Critics such as G. B. SHAW vilified Barrie's work as vapid and "Pinerotic". Others maintain that he transformed a human weakness into an artistic strength, agreeing with George Rowell's view that "while PINERO exploits the sentimental, Barrie explores it".

BESSIE BELLWOOD (1860-96)

English music hall artiste. Women were only just emerging as stars of music hall when Bessie Bellwood gave up skinning rabbits for her father to emulate the great Marie LLOYD. She never acquired the sophistication of her rival, remaining true to her Irish-Cockney origins. Her legendary exploits include thrashing an uncooperative cabman, biting a nobleman's ear and sticking a pin in a footman to see if he was real. Her equally aggressive stage act was accompanied by a constant battle of words between herself and the gallery, in which she invariably wiped the floor with her hecklers. Appropriately, "Wotcher Ria", the song that became her signature tune, described a typical music hall slanging match (in this case between the gallery and a working girl, who has paid a shilling to sit downstairs with the toffs).

ANTON CHEKHOV (1860-1904)

Russian short-story writer and dramatist. Chekhov's childhood in the tiny seaport of Taganrog was, in his own words, "mutilated" by his despotic grocer father who avoided debtors' prison by taking his family to Moscow. Anton was left behind. Later, as a Moscow medical student, he supported his family by writing pieces for a comic weekly, and after qualifying as a doctor still found time to write several collections of stories. In all he wrote over seven hundred short stories, becoming one of the greatest masters of the form the world has known. "Medicine is my lawful wife and literature is my mistress," was how he explained his double life. He also dashed off several curtain-raiser farces, including *The Proposal, The Bear* and *The Wedding*. In spite of his own low opinion of these playlets they have remained successful and highly entertaining. His full-length plays, however, were not so gratefully received. Both *Ivanov* (1887) and *The Wood Demon* (1889) had disastrous first productions. Chekhov decided that he was not a playwright.

For a time he fell under the sway of TOLSTOY's humanitarian ideas, but finally, reacting against his repressive upbringing, he achieved a sceptical independence of judgement. In a letter he perhaps came closest to formulating his own philosophy: "My holy of holies is the human body, health, intelligence, talent, inspiration, love and absolute freedom–freedom from violence and falsehood, no matter how the last two manifest themselves." Politically he was inclined to champion individual initiative and personal effort. In 1890 he suddenly left his practice, travelling six thousand miles for a three-month visit to the penal colony on Sakhalin island. He returned with material for a book which was not published until five years later.

In 1892 Chekhov acquired a country estate, where he settled with his parents, sister and younger brothers. Although he was a keen gardener and fisherman, country air did not improve his health. After many restless travels he suffered a severe lung haemorrhage as a result of advanced consumption. But even in hospital he continued to work, writing one of his finest stories, *The Peasants*.

In 1896 the first production of *The Seagull* in St Petersburg was a fiasco. But in spite of a vow never again to write for the stage, two years later he revised *The Wood Demon* as *Uncle Vanya* and the new play was produced successfully in the provinces. In that same year (1898) the newly formed Moscow Art Theatre performed *The Seagull* with great success. So bagan Chekhov's fruitful association with this theatre. Chekhov married actress Olga KNIPPER in 1901, but his deteriorating health separated them for much of the time; he lived mostly in Yalta while she stayed in Moscow acting in his last two plays: *Three Sisters* (1901) and *The Cherry Orchard* (1904, which, curiously, he saw as a farce).

Each of Chekhov's four great plays is set in rural Russia and describes the boredom and monotony that beset the idle landowning class. All reveal the vast gap that separates expectation and actuality. Here is a world of trivial everyday actions that casually reveal profound human truths. Audiences feel both inpatience with the characters' inability to act and a discomfort at finding their own impotence so unflatteringly portrayed.

Chekhov died in a German health resort in 1904. His body was transported back to Moscow in a boxcar marked "oysters"–an ironic touch he might well have put into one of his own short stories.

CHARLES FROHMAN (1860-1915)

American manager. For thirty years a leading impresario, Charles Frohman did all his business exclusively by verbal contract. His Empire Stock Company (founded in 1892) included stars like JOHN DREW and Maude Adams. He arranged outstanding productions of plays by BELASCO, PINERO and MAUGHAM, and had a particular sympathy for works of J. M. BARRIE. It was Frohman who presented Maude Adams's classic performance as Peter Pan in 1904. His reputation for personal honesty and professional acumen was transatlantic; he eventually controlled several theatres in London and New York. It was in 1915, travelling between one continent and the other, that he was among those lost with the *Lusitania*.

DAN LENO (1860-1904)

English comedian. During his short life Leno became the most popular man on the English music hall stage: "The GARRICK of the Halls." Born George Galvin, a child of song and dance artistes, he spent a large part of his early years in a dressing-table drawer, and at four went on the stage as "Little George, the Infant Wonder, Contortionist and Posturer". By nine he was earning his own living, dancing and singing with his brother in provincial music halls and pubs. He was often out of work and hungry, but in 1883 won a clog-dancing championship. This helped to get him his first important engagement, at Forester's Music Hall in London in 1885. The next year he had great success in the pantomime *Jack and the Beanstalk*, and his future was assured.

Leno was the star of pantomime at Drury Lane from 1883 to 1903, usually playing the dame. A master of the grotesque, he was renowned for his caricatures: the shop-walker, the station master or the gossiping old Mrs Kelly. Among his best acts was a delightfully ambiguous song about lodgers and landladies' daughters: "Young Men Taken In and Done For."

Leno even had a comic journal named after him and, after a Royal Command performance before Edward VII in 1901, he became known as "King's Jester".

ANNIE OAKLEY (1860-1926)

American sharpshooter. At the age of eight Phoebe Ann Moses frightened the life out of her mother by killing a squirrel with one shot through the window of their cabin in Ohio. When she was fifteen, a Cincinnati hotel-keeper, learning of her prowess with a gun, arranged a competition between her and Frank Butler, a renowned exhibition shot. To his surprise, she beat him; a year later they married, and soon they were touring as "Butler and Oakley" (the stage name Annie assumed for her act). In 1885, after a spell with the Sells Circus, they joined Buffalo Bill's Wild West Show. "Little missy", as CODY called her, was often the opening act, and the sight of "this frail girl among the rough plainsmen" was guaranteed to draw the crowds. She could shoot a cigarette out of her husband's mouth backwards (with the aid of a mirror) or hit forty-nine out of fifty clay pigeons in a row. Her fame travelled before her as she toured with the Wild West Show, but the woman Sitting Bull called "Little Sure-Shot" never lost the shy simplicity of her youth. She was careful with money, and had the same skill with an embroidery needle as with a gun. "What a pity there are not more women in the world like that little one," remarked the Prince of Wales on meeting her. She and Butler, who gave up his career to manage hers, were inseparable. They died within twenty days of each other.

ADA REHAN (1860-1916)

Irish-born American actress. Rehan's real name was Crehan, but it was once felicitously misprinted on a playbill, and the modification stuck. She was, according to her colleagues, a paragon of dedicated professionalism. The principal object of this devotion was Augustin DALY's theatre company, where she formed an unforgettable partnership in Shakespearean comedy with JOHN DREW. In 1891 she laid the cornerstone of Daly's London theatre, and, two years later for the inaugural production, she repeated her greatest role, Katharina in *The Taming of the Shrew*. Described as ample and opulent in the manner of a Gainsborough portrait, she also made an ideal Lady Teazle in SHERIDAN's *The School for Scandal*.

RABINDRANATH TAGORE (1861-1941)

Indian writer, scholar and mystic. Tagore was the son of a celebrated maharishi. Much of his work seems obscure to the Western imagination, notably a series of symbolic dramas concerning a mysterious king: *The King of the Dark Chamber* (1910), *Red Oleanders* (1924) and others. But Tagore's aim of blending Western and Oriental sensibilities found particular success in such lyrical plays as *Chitra* (1892), a re-enactment of a Sanskrit epic embodying dance, song and mime.

Tagore devoted himself to revitalizing ancient folk traditions, particularly at the Visva-Bharati University, which he himself founded. He won a Nobel Prize and a Knighthood, but relinquished the latter honour as a protest against British colonial policies.

ADOLPHE APPIA (1862-1928)

Swiss stage designer. Appia dreamed of the theatre as a magical escape from the sombre Calvinism of his childhood home. At nineteen he eagerly attended a performance of Gounod's *Faust* in Geneva, but was bitterly disappointed with its uninspired visual design. While studying music in Leipzig and Dresden, he immersed himself in ideas for reforming the use of light and space on stage. His early writings on Wagner and *La musique et la mise-en-scène* (1899) call for artistic unity in the theatre, expressive lighting (which technical innovations soon made possible), three-dimensional, sculptured sets and clean, stylized lines. Flat sets with pseudo-realistic detail made a ludicrous contrast with rounded human figures moving in front of them, he insisted, and as for curtains they were "ridiculous and barbarous". Sadly he had few chances to put his theories into practice, and when opportunities occurred, they were often marred by incomprehension on the part of those carrying out his designs (he was a shy, stammering man, who imposed his will with difficulty) and of the critics who viewed them. A short-lived experiment in Paris in 1903 only plunged him back to his mountain retreat near Geneva.

In the choreographer Emile Dalcroze (1865–1950), whose eurythmics influenced modern dance from Isadora Duncan to Diaghilev and onwards, Appia found a kindred spirit, collaborating with him on the seminal production of Gluck's *Orpheus* at Hellerau in 1912. The two men shared a classically inspired desire to create the "perfect fusion of all media of expression". But although the director COPEAU and the designer CRAIG did much to disseminate his ideas, Appia was in his sixties before he designed *Tristan und Isolde* at La Scala and *Das Rheingold* and *Die Walküre* in Basle. Wagner acolytes were shocked at the simplicity to which he had reduced the set and costumes, and critical cries of "too monotonous" filled the newspapers. By then, however, the ideals of Appia had found powerful exponents in both the sung and spoken theatre. He has since been generally recognized as the father of modern theatre design.

GEORGES FEYDEAU (1862-1921)

French comic playwright. Son of the stockbroker and novelist Ernest-Aimé Feydeau, Georges was the master of modern French farce. He wrote prolifically for more than thirty years in the tradition of MOLIÈRE, BEAUMARCHAIS, SARDOU and LABICHE, scoring his first big success with *Tailleur pour dames* at the Théâtre de la Renaissance in 1886. Pushing the comedy of breathless adultery and bedroom doors to a new satirical pitch, Feydeau's dialogue had a wittiness and his plots an ingenious complexity calculated to leave an audience thoroughly entertained. Among his best known comedies are *La Dame de chez Maxim* (1899), *La Puce à l'oreille* (1907), *Occupe-toi d'Amélie* (1908) and the later one-act farces *On purge bébé*, *Mais n'te promène donc pas toute nue!* and *Hortense a dit: J'm'en fous!*, the titles of which are an indication of their popular appeal. In 1892, two of his plays ran for over 1000 performances in the Palais-Royal and the Théâtre des Nouveautés. His critically disdained "ephemeral comedies" retained their popularity long after their author's death, becoming a regular part of the repertory of the Comédie-Française (to the horror of some) and of the

RENAUD-BARRAULT company. Madeleine Renaud, along with the original Mme Cassive, is one of the best actresses to have portrayed the beautiful and sharp-tongued women around whom many of Feudeau's bedroom intrigues revolve. The 1950s saw a revival of interest, including Noel COWARD's adaptation of *Occupe-toi d'Amélie* as *Look after Lulu*. *Un Fil à la patte*, originally produced in 1894, made the Comédie-Française one of the most popular Paris theatres of the late fifties.

GERHART HAUPTMANN (1862-1946)

German playwright, novelist and poet. Hauptmann is always considered Germany's great naturalist writer, yet fewer than half his more than forty plays fit easily into this category. For him the suffering of the poor was just one face of man's tragic existence, and his "naturalism" in depicting it was no aesthetic doctrine, just honesty.

Hysterical opposition to the representation of squalor on stage gave Hauptmann's first play, *Vor Sonnenaufgang* (1889), as stormy a first night as Berlin had ever witnessed. At one point in the play, when a midwife is summoned, a doctor in the audience brought out a pair of forceps to throw on stage. There were strong objections, too, to the use of Silesian dialect. Hauptmann's masterpiece, *Die Weber* (*The Weavers*, 1893), contains even more dialect. It is remarkable as the first great tragedy, not of an individual, but of a whole social mass. A group of linen-weavers are driven by starvation to attack the factory-owner's house, only to be shot down by the militia. As the author himself put it, human misery is the real heroine of the play.

Hauptmann's prolific output in these early years ranged from vigorous comedy in *Der Biberpelz* (1892) to bleak introspection in *Einsame Menschen* (1891). The play, how-ever, that indicated the direction Hauptmann's later work would follow, was *Hanneles Himmelfahrt* (1893). It begins in typically grim naturalistic fashion, with a fourteen-year-old girl lying at the point of death after having tried to drown herself to escape from her brutal, drunken stepfather. The "action" of the play, however, is the child's delirious vision of Heaven, a mystical longing for some higher existence. This vein Hauptmann pursued in the sad fairy-tale pieces *Die versunkene Glocke* (1896) and *Und Pippa tanzt* (1906).

After the First World War, Hauptmann's early pieces were regularly revived, for since his winning the Nobel Prize in 1912 they had become classics. But his new works, which expressed increasing horror at the course history was taking and urged the need for spiritual renewal, were greeted largely with incomprehension. More isolated than ever during the Second World War, he worked on his vast Greek tetralogy, *Iphigenie in Delphi, Iphigenie in Aulis, Agamemnons Tod* and *Elektra*. This apocalyptic vision of an accursed world plunging into chaos and barbarism remained unperformed until 1962, when Erwin PISCATOR directed it to honour the centenary of Hauptmann's birth.

MAURICE MAETERLINCK (1862-1949)

Belgian poet, playwright and philosopher. Maeterlinck was Belgium's greatest symbolist poet; likewise his *Pelléas et Mélisande* is the outstanding drama of symbolism. It is strange, however, that the dialogue of this particular play shows (as the English drama critic Harold Hobson has remarked) that "the proper way to write poetic drama is to use unpoetic speech".

The play is infused by an unsettling eroticism and set in a gloomy Nordic castle; the action controlled by a perverse and mysterious fate. It is a superb example of the power of static drama to evoke suspense, horror, melancholy and sensuality. In the earlier *La Princesse Maleine* (published

in 1889) the Edgar Allan Poe-inspired atmosphere is, however, simply too lurid to be convincing on stage. Conversely, Maeterlinck's later works are lacking in power, though the popular *L'Oiseau bleu* (*The Blue Bird*, 1908), a childlike fantasy partly inspired by *Peter Pan*, was given a celebrated première by Konstantin STANI-SLAVSKY in Moscow. Thereafter Maeterlinck was increas-ingly accused of sentimentality and although he won the Nobel Prize in 1911, his reputation waned. His supposed immorality—and his alleged anti-Catholicism—deferred the award of any honour by his own country until in 1932 he was made a Count. He retired to his home near Nice, and died there, practically forgotten.

ARTHUR SCHNITZLER (1862-1931)

Austrian playwright and novelist. As a doctor practising in Vienna at the time Freud was expounding his theories of psychology, Schnitzler was keen to discern repeated patterns in human behaviour, particularly in sexual relationships. The most extreme example of this in his dramatic works is *Reigen* (1900), now better known in Max Ophüls's film version, *La Ronde*. It has ten charac-ters; a man has an affair with a woman, who then has an affair with another man and so on until the last meets the first and the chain has gone full circle. Despite superficial differences, the fundamental experience of each affair is the same. There is a similar purposelessness to the seven seductions of the hero of Schnitzler's first play, *Anatol* (1893), while in the later *Liebelei*, an idle aristocrat's trifling with the affections of a poor working-class girl ends in tragedy.

Of more interest than these ironic pictures of decadent Viennese society is *Der grüne Kakadu* (1898), a mysterious one-act play, set at the time of the French revolution, in which what seems like comic play-acting turns suddenly into grim and very real murder.

SHOLEM ANSKI (1863-1920)

Russian playwright. Anski was the pseudonym of Solomon Rappoport, whose Yiddish play *The Dybbuk* (1920) was a startling success in war-torn and starving Moscow. Based on a Jewish legend of the power of the dead to take pos-session of the living, it is the story of a poor student who dies when he seeks the devil's aid to gain his loved one. Love and justice eventually prevail, and the couple's souls are united in death.

VAKHTANGOV's 1922 production of *The Dybbuk* was the glory of the Moscow Habima company, founded in 1917 to devote itself to Hebrew culture. It left Russia in the 1930s to settle down permanently in Israel, taking Anski's masterpiece with it.

HERMANN BAHR (1863-1934)

Austrian critic, playwright, novelist and essayist. For forty years the vociferous champion of every new move-ment in the German theatre, Bahr began as an admirer and imitator of IBSEN. He assisted Otto BRAHM and Arno HOLZ in the establishment of the Freie Bühne in Berlin, but rejected naturalism almost immediately. After lending enthusiastic support to the causes of Impressionism and Expressionism, he ended his days a devout Catholic.

As well as writing and lecturing on the theatre, litera-ture, music and art, Bahr found time to write a new comedy almost every year, the best of these being *Das Konzert* (1909). His practical experience in the theatre included working as a director for Max REINHARDT in Berlin and the influential position of dramaturge at the Vienna Burgtheater from 1918.

GABRIELE D'ANNUNZIO (1863-1938)

Italian poet, playwright and novelist. D'Annunzio led an outrageous, epic life, revelling in the twin images of poet and superhero. As early as 1883 he created a scandal by eloping with the aristocratic Duchessina di Gallese, and marriage did not prevent numerous liaisons. His affair with Eleonora DUSE, whom he met in 1894, was one of the great love stories of the decade (he even wrote a novel about it, to the annoyance of the actress). By then his passionate poetry and novels were well known, but it was for Duse that D'Annunzio began to write verse drama. The plays' immense popularity owed less to their merit than to her talent and his notorious reputation. Duse appeared in *Sogno di un mattino di primavera* in Paris in 1897, Sarah BERNHARDT in *La Città morta* in 1898. That year D'Annunzio moved to a large villa near Florence, where he led a life of luxury and wild extravagance far beyond his means.

D'Annunzio's plays revolve around the self-inspired "superman" figure, the artist-hero-genius. Violently sensual, they celebrate man's primitive instincts. In *La Gioconda* (1899), Lucio, a sculptor, loves his wife but is obsessed by La Gioconda, his model, his passion and the inspiration of his genius. His wife is maimed saving his masterpiece from destruction, and Lucio leaves to follow La Gioconda. *Francesca da Rimini* (1901) is loosely based on the fifth canto of Dante's *Inferno. La Figlia di Iorio* (1904), the play that has lasted best, was inspired by the memory of drunken peasants seen chasing a woman in a village of his native Abruzzi. It is a powerful play in its poetry and its evocation of primitive superstition. (Duse did not appear in the première as their affair had ended.)

By 1911 D'Annunzio had run up huge debts, and left for France to escape them. There he wrote plays in French, including *Le Martyre de Saint Sébastien* (1911), with music by Debussy. The war finally gave him the chance to be a hero. He rushed back to urge Italy to join the conflict and, volunteering at the age of fifty-two, served with mad courage in army, navy and airforce (scattering his own pamphlets from his flying-machine over Vienna).

Furious that Italy was not given the port of Fiume in the 1919 peace treaty, he took the town with his own battalion and held it for several months. Such posturing xenophobia greatly impressed Mussolini, who adopted the black shirts worn by D'Annunzio's men and created him Prince of Montenevoso in 1924.

VLADIMIR DUROV (c1863-1934)

Russian clown and animal trainer. Circus-goers in tsarist Russia chuckled at Durov's jibes at authority while they marvelled at his power over animals. The ingenious clown exploited his pets' most characteristic natural movements, with food as a constant enticement. A scratching hen could be taught to play the zither; the crane's stiff hop could be refined into a kind of dance. He trained his star pig Chushka to "shoot" a clown with a pistol, then roll his body out of the ring with her snout. Her devotion to Durov's tidbits even permitted him to harness her to a balloon. Another of his great attractions was a model ship manned entirely by rats, who demonstrated all the seaman's skills, including lowering a lifeboat. Durov's principles and achievements are still visible today in the Animal House he founded in Moscow in 1902.

ARNO HOLZ (1863-1929)

German playwright, poet and theorist. With his principles of naturalist drama, which he scrupulously followed in *Die Familie Selicke* (1890), Holz "set the idiom of the German theatre of the next fifteen years". Hermann BAHR, the outspoken Austrian critic, did not intend this assessment of his former friend's influence as a compliment. Holz's pinpointing of every gesture, cough and breath refined the art of writing to an almost photographic detail, though it limited the actor's scope for interpretation.

Once his association with Johannes Schlaf (co-author of *Die Familie Selicke*) had ended, Holz too became sceptical of his own dogma. Of his later plays the most significant was *Sozialaristokraten* (1896), a satire on cultural elitism of which Holz himself had not been entirely innocent. But essentially it is for the former play that he will be remembered. Its grim and hopeless depiction of life had a profound effect on the later writing of HAUPTMANN.

The colourful, swashbuckling exploits of **Gabriele D'Annunzio** (*far left*, in conversation with Mussolini) gave the Fascist movement a great boost in the years after the First World War

Noel Coward was so taken with the acting style of **Marie Tempest** (*left*) that he created the part of Judith Bliss in *Hay Fever* especially for her

The company of the Moscow Art Theatre (right). Its two founders were **Nemirovich-Danchenko** (wearing a pale jacket and hat on the extreme left of the middle row) and **Stanislavsky** (facing the camera in a pale hat, centre front). Also pictured is the playwright **Gorky** (wearing a pale shirt and dark hat, second from the left in the third row from the front)

KONSTANTIN STANISLAVSKY
(1863-1938)

Russian actor, director and producer. Stanislavsky was born Alexeyev, the son of a rich merchant. A keen amateur actor in his youth, after schooling and European travel he gradually developed into an outstanding performer, taking his stage name from a retired Polish actor. He then set out to find an acting style more truthful than the histrionics that had prevailed throughout the nineteenth century. He helped to establish a permanent company of amateur actors and, in 1898, he and NEMIROVICH-DANCHENKO founded the Moscow Art Theatre.

CHEKHOV's *The Seagull* made the Art Theatre's name; it even adopted a seagull as its emblem. All of Chekhov's subsequent plays were premièred there, but this did not stop the playwright from complaining about what he thought were distracting and unnecessary production details—in particular, sound effects. Stanislavsky loved to relate how Chekhov had threatened to write a play with dialogue like, "How wonderfully quiet it is here, not a bird to be heard, not a dog barking . . . no clock ticking, no bells ringing, and not a single cricket chirping."

Stanislavsky's acting method—which he never ceased to protest was not The Method—involved great attention to ensemble playing and the subordination of acting to the playwright's purpose. He called for actors to use their emotional memories to give truth and immediacy to their characterization. He stressed that an actor cannot portray a state of mind, only an action, and that a character's life begins offstage and continues offstage after the actor exits. While staging GORKY's *The Lower Depths* in 1902, Stanislavsky made his actors study vagrants close at hand—so successfully that spectators in the first rows feared being infested with vermin.

But believing that there was a reality within fantasy he pushed beyond naturalism. Above all he felt that the actor must not just depict surface matters but express the spiritual. Hence his productions of plays such as MAETERLINCK's *The Blue Bird*. He also encouraged other innovators such as MEYERHOLD and Gordon CRAIG, but in his striving for new forms of expression Stanislavsky was mostly disappointed. In his last years, determined "to put down on paper what a young actor ought to know", he wrote *Building A Character and Creating A Role*, still two indispensable textbooks for students.

In spite of Bolshevik attacks on the Art Theatre, Stanislavsky survived both Soviet philistinism and his weak heart to die peacefully in his bed, unlike so many fellow artists of his nationality and generation.

JULES RENARD (1864-1910)

French novelist and playwright. Renard's unhappy childhood, caught between the mutual antipathy of his Catholic mother and his Freemason father, is reflected in his novel *Poil de Carotte* (1894) and other works. Contemptuous of symbolist writers such as Mallarmé, he adopted a dry, often savagely incisive style. He later adapted *Poil de carotte* and another novel, *L'Écornifleur*, a bitter attack on social hypocrisy, for the stage. His plays, like SHAW's, broke away from the melodrama and romanticism of the period. Devoured by fear and hatred of his mother, portrayed in *La Bigote* in 1909, Renard was a pessimist. But such fulfilling relationships as he had with his wife gave plays like *Le Plaisir de rompre* (1897) and *Le Pain de ménage* (1898) a tender sincerity.

MARIE TEMPEST (1864-1942)

English actress. Marie Tempest's beginnings were shrouded in colourful legend. She claimed to have been presented as a young girl to the Prime Minister, Gladstone, who went to great lengths to dissuade her from becoming an actress. Heedless of his dull advice, she studied singing and was soon the object of delirious adulation on both sides of the Atlantic as a soprano in operetta and musical comedy. It was not until the turn of the century that she took up straight acting, making the transition as Becky Sharp in an adaptation of Thackeray's *Vanity Fair* and Kitty in *The Marriage of Kitty* (a piece written for her by her second husband, Cosmo Charles Gordon-Lennox).

In later years Marie Tempest was much loved in the plays of Noel COWARD and other drawing-room comedies. For her definitive interpretation of well-spoken, well-dressed, well-preserved middle-aged women, in addition to possessing a most exquisite curtsey, she was created a Dame of the British Empire.

VESTA TILLEY (1864-1952)

English music hall artiste. At the age of five, "The Great Little Tilley" was already appearing on the music hall stage in male attire. Within weeks of arriving in London in 1873 she created a reputation singing "The Pet of Rotten Row" and "Near the Workhouse Door". Although very pretty and feminine, she always wore military or civilian male dress on stage. "Girls", she cried out in a typical song, "if you'd like to love a soldier, you can all love me!" During her long career, Vesta Tilley introduced an enormous number of still-familiar songs, including "After the Ball" and "Burlington Bertie".

FRANK WEDEKIND (1864-1918)

German playwright and actor. Wedekind was at times an advertising executive, secretary to a circus and a cabaret singer, while his activities as a satirical journalist earned him a spell in prison. His masterpiece, *Frühlings Erwachen*, written in 1891 but not performed until 1906, describes the sexual awakening of three adolescents. Their repressive society drives one to suicide and another to an abortion which kills her; the third is persuaded to choose life only on the intervention of a masked figure – presumably the author himself. The play is both a documentary of social oppression and a celebration of sex as a profound and beautiful spiritual force which can – if misunderstood – turn to evil. Wedekind's sympathy for youth sufficiently transcends the morbidity of his material to make the work a classic precursor of Expressionism.

His message is less clearly articulated in *Erdgeist* (written in 1895), *Die Büchse der Pandora* (1904) and *Der Marquis von Keith* (1901). The heroine of the first two, Lulu, is a femme fatale who has already been corrupted; indeed in all of Wedekind's later work his stage teems with gangsters, prostitutes and perverts, an unforgettable symbol of the self-conscious decadence of his time.

MRS PATRICK CAMPBELL (1865-1940)

English actress. Mrs Campbell was one of the great characters of the stage, legendary for both her humour and her tantrums. Much to the family's horror, when her young husband left her with two small children she decided to use her histrionic talents to earn a living. Her first London engagement was in melodrama. In the première of *The Trumpet Call* in 1891 she won the public's admiration for keeping her cool when an article of clothing dropped about her ankles.

In 1893, still relatively unknown, Mrs Campbell was given the part of Paula in *The Second Mrs Tanqueray*, Arthur Wing PINERO's daring new play about a woman with a "past". She swept London off its feet at the first performance (or more literally on to its feet, for the audience crowded across the stage at the end of the evening). She remained for some years "in her 'Tanqueradiance'" – as GEORGE BERNARD SHAW wrote to Ellen TERRY. Her finest parts included Ophelia and Juliet, Rita in IBSEN's *Little Eyolf* and the title role in Hermann SUDERMANN's *Magda*. An intense if platonic relationship led Shaw to write *Pygmalion* (1914) for her. Mrs Campbell was a great if inconsistent actress; her eyes were dark and mysterious, her wit notoriously sharp and her behaviour wildly temperamental. She acted into the 1930s, also working for a short time in Hollywood.

MINNIE MADDERN FISKE (1865-1932)

American actress and director. After years of juvenile roles, Minnie Maddern made her adult debut in 1882 in a part originally intended for her idol, Lotta CRABTREE. Her girlish charm was so devastating that it provoked a fist-fight between two future theatrical giants, CHARLES FROHMAN and David BELASCO. But sentimental comedies did not satisfy her. In 1890, already a star, she married the editor of the *New York Dramatic Mirror* and abruptly retired. She returned to the stage three years later as Mrs Fiske, an exponent of a restrained naturalistic style of acting and a devotee of modern playwrights like Henrik IBSEN. Her come-back had been in *Hester Crewe*, an earnest new work by Harrison Grey Fiske, her husband. For the rest of her career she excelled in such grave works as Ibsen's *Hedda Gabler* as well as comedy. At least one admiring critic was confident that she could triumph "in a dramatization of the telephone book".

WILLIAM CLYDE FITCH (1865-1909)

American playwright. As a young man in New York, Fitch set himself up as a dandy, writing children's stories and receiving friends in a blue velvet coat. His first success as a playwright was *Beau Brummell* (1890), and by 1901 he had found the perfect ingredients for commercial success, with four plays running at the same time in New York. One of these, *Captain Jinks of the Horse Marines*, was a star vehicle for ETHEL BARRYMORE. He also wrote successes for Lillie LANGTRY and Helena MODJESKA. His first-hand knowledge of drawing-room society was turned into witty but over-sentimental plays again and again. Fitch was generously described as the CONGREVE of his period.

AGNES SORMA (1865-1927)

Austrian actress. No German-speaking actress had appeared in Paris for nearly thirty years (the French did not easily forget their ignominious defeat in the Franco-Prussian War) when Sorma made a triumphant visit there in 1899. She was soon acclaimed all over the Continent as one of the most sensitive interpreters of IBSEN, particularly as Nora in *A Doll's House*.

Sorma's first successes had come playing SHAKESPEARE's young heroines opposite the great Joseph KAINZ, but as she matured, she went on to create many of the leading roles of Gerhart HAUPTMANN, who particularly admired her beauty and natural grace.

WILLIAM BUTLER YEATS (1865-1939)

Irish poet and playwright. W. B. Yeats was Ireland's greatest poet and tragedian, but only his poetry has achieved lasting popularity. His theatrical reputation lingers because he was a founder, and for thirty-five years the managing director, of Dublin's Abbey Theatre.

Yeats was born in Dublin, the son of John Butler Yeats, a famous portrait painter. Although brought up in Sligo, in the west of Ireland, his middle-class Protestantism somewhat alienated him from the Irish peasantry whose stories and music were such an inspiration. By the time he was living in London in the 1890s, already a reputable poet, he had become a nationalist of an unusual variety: Yeats scorned politics, wishing only to create a heroic and romantic conception of Ireland.

In Ireland at that time poetry was a spoken rather than a literary tradition, so Yeats decided that the best medium to arouse "the primitive emotions of the music of sound" was a theatre. He collected some actors, a patron and a building, and founded the Abbey. It opened in 1904 with the first performance of his verse drama *On Baile's Strand*.

The most popular of his plays is *Cathleen ni Houlihan* (1902), which is the one most easily construed as a political parable. Cathleen is Ireland in the guise of an old woman, who, when asked what she hopes for, replies: "The hope of getting my beautiful fields back again; the hope of putting strangers out of my house." Though the emotions are fairly primitive, the play is more comprehensible than others which rely on poetry for their impact. These, like *The Land of Heart's Desire* (1894) and *The King's Threshold* (1904) were a staple of the early repertoire of the Abbey, but the plays were (one critic noted) "written to his own requirements, and he had no followers".

As political nationalism flowered, so W. B. Yeats' own passion declined.

"Romantic Ireland's dead and gone,
    It's with O'Leary in the grave,"
he wrote in "September 1913". In the stylized Nō drama of Japan he found an alternative, timeless appeal. But although he stopped writing plays for the general public, he clung tenaciously to the managing directorship of the Abbey until his death in 1939.

LÉON BAKST (1866-1924)

Russian designer and painter. With his extraordinary stage designs Léon Bakst, or Lev Samoylovich Bakst Rosenberg, opened up a new world to those who saw Serge Diaghilev's Ballets Russes. In the early years of this century he designed productions of tragedies by SOPHOCLES at the Imperial theatres, and ancient Greek art remained a strong influence in his work. In 1909, when he was thrown out of St Petersburg for being Jewish, he joined Diaghilev and accompanied the Ballets Russes to Paris. Europe was amazed. Bakst's most successful designs included those for Rimsky-Korsakov's *Schéhérezade* (1910) and Debussy's *L'Après-midi d'un faune* (1912). His exhilarating use of colour, his genius for making every detail of costume and scenery combine in the creation of a stunning overall visual effect, and the strong and unfamiliar oriental influence in his work revealed new possibilities and had immense influence not only in the theatre but in painting, fashion and even interior design.

JACINTO BENAVENTE (1866-1954)

Spanish playwright, poet and journalist. Benavente released the Spanish theatre from the stranglehold of melodrama, making it once more a potent social force. His early plays are stinging satires on the corrupt and self-satisfied Madrid aristocracy. *El nido ajeno* (1894) proved too strong, but *Gente conocida* (1896) made him famous. He used masks and Commedia dell' Arte techniques in his greatest play, *Los intereses creados* (1907). Leandro (Good), deeply in debt, asks the help of Crispin (Evil), who neatly and dishonestly solves the problem, justifying his own right to exist. Other important plays are *La noche del sabado* (1903) and *La malquerida* (1913). Benavente was a prolific playwright, completing 172 plays, though his later works rarely achieve the same force and pungency.

HARRY CHAMPION (1866-1942)

English music hall comedian. Champion was a stalwart survivor from the early days of the East End halls. After starting his career (like LITTLE TICH and so many other stars) as a black-faced comedian, he devised a style of patter and singing based entirely on speed. He had no objection, he said, to singing six songs in two minutes and

A children's book written by **Frank Wedekind** (*above*) affords some relief from the violent, suppressed sexuality that pervades his plays

The sheet music cover of one of the hits rattled off by **Harry Champion** (*below*), the Cockney speed-specialist of Music Hall

154

getting paid for it. Wearing an absurd billy-cock hat and waving his arms in manic frenzy, he sang such classics as "Boiled Beef and Carrots", "'Enery the Eighth" and, far and away the best of his songs, "Any Old Iron". The miracle was that he never fluffed a single word, reaching the end of each number in breathless triumph.

LOTTIE COLLINS (1866-1910)

English music hall singer and dancer. Originally a Gaiety chorus girl, Lottie Collins played the halls as a skipping-rope dancer. Back at the Gaiety, in 1891 she caused a sensation with a song she had acquired in America and had rewritten for an English audience. Clad in the most enormous hat and a long red dress, she timidly reached the chorus of her song, and exploded with "Ta-ra-ra Boom-de-ay". She waved her handkerchief and broke into a wild dance, her long blonde hair streaming. "The hat bobbed, the short skirts whirled and she showed a positive foam of petticoats." A star was born and the song became a classic.

ROMAIN ROLLAND (1866-1944)

French writer, musicologist and playwright. Rolland was an idealist whose works celebrate international brotherhood and the humanitarian philosophies of TOLSTOY and Gandhi. Music, which he saw as a spiritual bond between men, formed the subject of many of his books, including his massive novel *Jean-Christophe* and a six-volume life of Beethoven. As a dramatist, Rolland sought to write for the common man, as he explained in *Le Théâtre du peuple* in 1903. *Les Loups* (1898), the first of his *Tragédies de la révolution*, was inspired by the Dreyfus case. In his second play cycle, *Tragédies de la foi*, as in his essay *Au-dessus de la mêlée*, he expounded his pacifist ideals. This and his socialist mysticism were not popular in a war-torn Europe, but he was awarded the Nobel Prize in 1916.

RAMÓN MARÍA DEL VALLE-INCLÁN (1866-1936)

Spanish novelist and playwright. Valle-Inclán came from a proud family of poor aristocrats. He successfully avoided taking a law degree, partly by wandering about his native Galicia collecting legends and stories. Attracted by the mysterious letter x, he was lured to Mexico to work as a journalist. But by 1895 he was in Madrid, where his sharp tongue cost him his left arm after an attack from a critic whom he provoked.

Typical of Valle-Inclán's early plays is *Farsa Infantil de la cabeza del dragón* (1909), a sophisticated and satirical piece for children. He also wrote verse plays about his favourite theme: the Carlist Wars. Other works, including some for puppets, show him terse and realistic, especially when looking at poverty and vice, as in *El Embrujado* (1913) and *Divinas palabras* (1920). *Luces de Bohemia* is a particularly scathing attack on corrupt Madrid society, one of several such plays which the author called *esperpentos*.

ALBERT BASSERMANN (1867-1952)

German actor. Overcoming a weak, nasal voice, Bassermann became the most celebrated actor on the Berlin stage. He emerged from the relative obscurity of the Meiningen Court Theatre to play in TOLSTOY's *The Power of Darkness* at the Deutsches Theater for Otto BRAHM. Brahm's regular diet of IBSEN and HAUPTMANN sustained him for a while, but in 1909, when he joined Max REINHARDT, his versatility was fully realized. As Mephistopheles, Lear and Shylock he struck terror into the hearts of all who saw him. He later struck up a close understanding with Leopold JESSNER, playing Gessler in Jessner's historic production of SCHILLER's *Wilhelm Tell*.

Under Nazism, Bassermann made his way, via Switzerland, to the USA, where he had some success in films. Returning to Europe aged almost eighty, he attempted to feature himself and his wife in IBSEN's *Ghosts*, but finally had to admit that he was past his prime.

JOHANNE DYBWAD (1867-1950)

Norwegian actress. Johanne Dybwad began her career on the Berlin stage in 1887. Two years later she played Hilde Wangel in the world première of IBSEN's *The Lady From the Sea*. A second Hilde–the same character developed in depth in *The Master Builder*–remained one of her outstanding interpretations.

For forty years Dybwad was the leading actress of the Norwegian National Theatre. She played a total of 192 roles and gained an international reputation from tours that included successful appearances in Paris and Berlin. Only her vain insistence on playing youthful roles when an old lady tarnished her reputation. In one especially notorious production she tottered nimbly about the stage as a sixty-seven year-old Ariel in *The Tempest*.

JOHN GALSWORTHY (1867-1933)

English novelist and playwright. The novelist D. H. Lawrence dismissed Galsworthy as one of "the rule and measure mathematical folk". Indeed, his precise legal education combined with the lessons he learned from GEORGE BERNARD SHAW to create carefully observed and structured plays. The immensely popular novels of *The Forsyte Saga* and plays such as *The Silver Box* (1906) and *Strife* (1909) struck just the right balance between craft and conscience for a public who had at last grown accustomed to hearing important issues aired in fiction and drama. *Justice* (1910) was an enormous success. Its description of the ordeals suffered in trial and prison by a weak-minded thief so impressed the Home Secretary, Churchill, that he was moved to initiate penal reforms.

Galsworthy was awarded the Order of Merit in 1929 and the Nobel Prize for Literature in 1932. Later plays such as *Escape* (1926) dated quickly, but recent revivals of his best work suggest that these social dramas are as much the creation of an artist as of a reformer.

YVETTE GUILBERT (1867-1944)

French *diseuse*. Among the early admirers of Yvette Guilbert were ZOLA, Daudet, the GONCOURTS, Monet and Toulouse-Lautrec, who drew her when she sang at the Cabaret Divan Japonais in the early 1890s. Later she became the star of famous revue theatres, including the Ambassadeurs and the Folies-Bergère in Paris, and the Old Empire and the Coliseum in London, where her visits were always popular. She successfully toured most of Europe, as well as the USA and North Africa. Tall and thin, she relied more on her dramatic interpretation of songs than on her beauty. Her long black gloves, originally resorted to in poverty, became a characteristic mark of distinction. Later in her career she acted in Murnau's film *Faust* (1926) and played Mrs Peachum in BRECHT's *Die Dreigroschenoper* in 1937.

LUIGI PIRANDELLO (1867-1936)

Italian playwright, novelist and poet. One of the great masters of modern drama, Pirandello believed that reality is unfathomable, that every human being is "the juxta-position of infinite blurred selves". His plays strip away illusion only to reveal further illusion beneath. They depict life as a "ceaseless, everlasting masquerade in which we are the involuntary actors".

He learned instability and uncertainty at first hand. Life in his native Sicily was harsh and violent, outwardly controlled by the Catholic Church and a rigid social code. His wealthy, overbearing father defied the Mafia with his fists. His mother, like Pirandello himself, was quiet and sensitive. He began writing poetry as a teenager and, after attending university in Germany, settled in Rome to pursue a literary career. In 1894 his father arranged a marriage for him with the daughter of another prosperous Sicilian. Quite content, the couple were supported in their early years by the family business. But a financial disaster left them penniless and induced a mental breakdown in Pirandello's wife. He had to teach for a living, while caring

Luigi Pirandello, Italy's greatest playwright, combined a unique tragic vision of life with a warm love of the stage and understanding of the actor

for his increasingly paranoid and abusive spouse. In 1918, when her threats and recriminations drove their daughter to attempt suicide, he finally agreed to have her committed.

Throughout this domestic agony, Pirandello continued to write. He only turned to the theatre in 1912, but in 1916 alone wrote nine plays, chief among them the utterly characteristic *Così è' (se vi pare) – Right You Are (If You Think You Are)*. Composed in six days, the work concerns an attempt to determine the truth of a woman's identity. At the end of a searching inquiry the woman reveals that she is, in fact, just "whoever you think I am".

Pirandello's "humour" is inseparable from pity. Life in a world of hopeless complexity requires compassion and tolerance. Role-playing is necessary to make sense of the chaotic present. *Sei personaggi in cerca d'autore* (1921), which won Pirandello an international reputation, exam-ines the idea of roles in the theatre itself. A rehearsal is interrupted by the appearance of six masked "characters" from an unfinished play. They exist in their roles alone, which they proceed to act out. The theatre company try to imitate them, but the characters object to their distortions and falsifications. Finally their play ends in tragedy, and the characters depart grief-stricken, while the actors uneasily assert that the drama is only make-believe. *Ciascuno a suo modo* (1924) and *Questa sera si recita a soggetto* (1930) are also plays within a play, showing that art, however "false" it seems, is more "real" than life. Pirandello's manipulations of "actors", "characters" and "spectators" weave his audience into the paradox.

His masterpiece may be *Enrico IV* (1922), which makes sanity and madness appear as difficult to separate as illusion and reality. For twenty years the play's hero, supposedly insane, has impersonated a German emperor. Suddenly he reveals that for most of that time he has consciously assumed the pose, and has only embraced "the reality of a true madness" to escape "the terrifying world of wretchedness". Without warning, however, he kills his former mistress's lover and resumes his mad persona – if indeed he had ever abandoned it.

In his last years, Pirandello himself was an ironic, enigmatic figure, travelling constantly, indifferent to possessions. Awarded the Nobel Prize in 1934, he answered journalists' questions while typing out the word "buffoonery". Dying, he left instructions for the simplest possible funeral and a list of those who might attend, headed "Pirandello".

EUGENE SANDOW (1867-c 1924)

German-born strong-man. One legend has it that Sandow studied anatomy in Brussels, where he met the improbably named Professor Louis Attila, who induced him to give up medicine and go into show business. They went on tour together, and Sandow first came to the attention of the public (and the police) when he demolished a number of Try-Your-Strength machines.

While trying his strength and his luck in New York he met the cunning Flo ZIEGFELD, who had yet to get started as an impresario. The American entrepreneur soon had the beefy giant out of his leotard and into a skimpy pair of briefs, inviting society matrons to feel Sandow's muscle after the show, in return for a contribution to a deserving charity. In this way the fledgling promoter first demon-strated his instinctive flair for acceptable erotic chic (a talent which he later famously exploited with his volup-tuous Ziegfeld Girls).

Sandow was clearly very strong, lifting pianos (with their pianists) and rooms full of people. He also wrestled with a lion; though there was some dispute as to the physical well-being of the beast at the time. He died trying to lift a broken-down car out of a ditch.

JOSEPH WEBER (1867-1942)

American comedian. Joe Weber was born in the Bowery section of New York, one of a Polish Jewish butcher's seventeen children. In the same neighbourhood, also from Poland, lived a tailor whose son Lewis later took the name of Fields. Weber and Fields met at school, from which it was said they were expelled for practising hand-stands and clog dances. Poverty forced them to start performing as a team in 1876 as a black-faced acrobatic song and dance act. The two boys dressed in oversized clothes, Weber heavily padded and Fields in built-up shoes. By 1883, after a long apprenticeship in ten-cent theatres, they were receiving forty dollars a week.

Weber and Fields travelled all over America with cir-cuses, road shows and finally with their own company – playing for laughs the immigrants' broken English, which had been the language of their youth. After some time in burlesque, they opened a theatre (the Weber and Fields'), where their ethnic parodies of popular plays met with great success. In their hands *Cyrano de Bergerac* became *Cyranose de Bricabrac*. Because of new fire laws, their theatre closed in 1904 and "Weberfields" parted company. With the decline of burlesque, they independ-ently concentrated on musicals, vaudeville and films.

Lew Fields' son Joseph became a playwright; Dorothy, his daughter, was one of Broadway's and Hollywood's most successful lyricists.

PAUL CLAUDEL (1868-1955)

French poet and playwright. Plagued by the conflict in his youth between fervent Catholicism and an adulterous

CONTINUED ON PAGE 158

American Vaudeville

Vaudeville was born in frontier America. Long before the Civil War, honky-tonks and gambling dens were offering free entertainment to lure thirsty cowboys and their womenfolk inside. The first performers banded together in minstrel shows, but singing formed only a small part of their repertoire. Unusual dances were *de rigueur*: the bayonet-dance, the egg-dance, the spade-dance, the hootchy-kootchy and the soft-shoe shuffle.

Some acts showed a desperate ingenuity. One man danced while playing the harp; another "played" the xylophone with his feet; an underwater trombonist also caused quite a stir. The mystifying effect of crude gas lighting lent extra credibility to the ghost shows, to the musician who made his navel sing and to the man who played a cat-piano (by pulling their tails). In this atmosphere such performers as HOUDINI were bound to succeed. Melodramas were also much favoured.

An astonishing variety of comedians – from Gallagher & SHEAN to W. C. FIELDS – grew up in vaudeville. A typical early act consisted of two blackface comics reacting to a whiteface

Among the more intrepid acts thrown up by Vaudeville must have been Miss Billie May, who needed jodhpurs to cope with The Famous Boxing Cats. The performance itself, however, was morally unquestionable. The famous puss Carol (seated, *top centre*) was rumoured never to have lost a single fight

At its greatest, Vaudeville was the playground of some of the finest talent in America: Bert Lahr, Gallagher & Shean, W. C. Fields and a whole host of others. Naturally, there was another side to the coin. A thousand shows were born and died again for any great production that lingers in the memory today. The illustration sports the (barely) inimitable Bothwell Brome and company in the revue *Broadway Bits* (*right*)

"Interlocutor" (stooge), whose naiveté was established by an English accent. Indeed during the heyday of immigration, racial comedy – Jewish, Irish, Italian, German, Negro – was the mainstay of such acts as WEBER and FIELDS.

The robust charms of Eva TANGUAY, Lillian Russell and Elsie Janis were much in demand. In the early days actresses doubled as bar-girls and strumpets, and obscenity flourished in cheerful sketches concerning haymaking and other dalliance. But under the influence of the "Father of Vaudeville", Tony Pastor, such frolics were exiled to the limbo of burlesques and girlie-shows. Pastor cleaned up vaudeville, but others cleaned up the profits, notably the United Booking Office, which eventually controlled 400 theatres. These manipulators legitimized variety, turned it into showbiz, attracted such celebrated visitors as BERNHARDT, LANGTRY, LAUDER and GUILBERT, and paved the way for the up-market revues of ZIEGFELD and Shubert. Finally films were introduced into vaudeville shows as a side-attraction; and five years after the first talkie, *The Jazz Singer* (based on a vaudeville act), they had triumphantly unseated their live competition.

love affair, Claudel dwelled constantly in his drama on the theme of human love sacrificed or lost for the sake of divine grace.

His writing had an exotic, sweeping independence. In both poetry and plays, he tended to express himself through the free verse of his idiosyncratic *verset claudelien*. His early plays are highly symbolic, only anchored to reality by their celebration of earthly beauty, inspired in *La jeune fille violaine* by nostalgia for his native Tardenois. *Partage de midi* (published in 1904) marks the start of his mature period by attaching a realistic domestic situation to his spiritual view of man. *L'Annonce faite à Marie* (1912, a later version of *La Jeune fille violaine*) attracted praise for its passionate portrayal of medieval faith. *Le Soulier de satin*, an epic drama more in the Elizabethan than the French tradition, and produced by Jean-Louis BARRAULT in 1943, established Claudel as a playwright who, if not to everyone's taste, frankly and forcefully expressed religious vision in the modern theatre.

MAXINE ELLIOTT (1868-1940)

American actress. ETHEL BARRYMORE once described Maxine Elliott as "the Venus de Milo with arms". In spite of such classic beauty, her Shakespearean roles with the Augustin DALY company were coolly received in New York and London. She fared much better in the modern plays of Clyde FITCH, such as *Her Own Way* (1903). Offstage, glamour surrounded her on both sides of the Atlantic. One admirer, the millionaire banker J. P. Morgan, reputedly financed the building of the Maxine Elliott Theatre in 1908, and her friends in London included King Edward VII.

MAXIM GORKY (1868-1936)

Russian novelist, poet and playwright. At the age of eight, Alexei Peshkov was turned out of doors by his grandfather and made to earn his own living. Subsequently he spent his youth on the road as a choir boy, gardener, dishwasher, baker and nomadic labourer. At nineteen, he shot himself, but survived and took the name Maxim Gorky, or "Maxim the Bitter".

In 1898 a book called *Sketches and Stories* made him a household name. He met CHEKHOV, who urged him to use fewer adjectives, introduced him to TOLSTOY and pestered him to write for the stage. His first play, *The Smug Citizens* (1901), was censored, and failed at the Moscow Art Theatre, but in the next year *The Lower Depths* scored a triumph. STANISLAVSKY's production of this down-and-out drama was so realistic that spectators in the front row were afraid of catching lice. Although Gorky fell out with the Moscow Art Theatre, he continued to write plays, including *Enemies*, *Summer Folk* and *The Children of the Sun*, many of which were banned in Russia until after the Revolution.

From 1906 until 1913, Gorky lived in Capri and wrote only prose. After the Revolution he devoted himself to saving Russian culture and aiding writers and intellectuals. Lenin never refused Gorky's requests. In 1921, he went abroad again for his health and did not return to Russia until his sixtieth birthday celebrations in 1928 when he was awarded the Order of Lenin, Although he was acclaimed as the father of Socialist realism, Gorky never joined the Communist Party and during his last years became increasingly uneasy about the Soviet régime. Before his death—a suspected poisoning—he wrote the last of his fourteen plays: two works in a proposed cycle on the fall of the tsarist regime, and leading up through the next decades to the 1930s. The two completed works have not received the attention in the West that they deserve.

EDMOND ROSTAND (1868-1918)

French poet and dramatist. Rostand imbued his plays with the colourful ebullience of his Marseilles background, which came as a relief for Parisian audiences weary of demanding naturalistic drama. *Les Romanesques* (1894), a witty variation of the Romeo and Juliet theme, was followed the next year by *La Princesse lointaine*, in which Rostand gave full rein to the escapist yearning for the romance and glamour of an earlier age. The sentimentality which marred such works as the biblical *La Samaritaine* (1897) was dispelled by humour and by the brilliant performance of CONSTANT COQUELIN in *Cyrano de Bergerac* (1897). The nobleman with the nose like a peninsula is a wonderful comic creation and the play has gained lasting popularity in spite of an often superficial verse dialogue. Once again the heavy-handed pathos of *L'Aiglon* was redeemed by Sarah BERNHARDT's performance as Napoleon's unfortunate heir, and its 1900 production in her theatre was a resounding popular success. *Chantecler* (1910) and the unfinished *La Dernière nuit de Don Juan* show Rostand turning towards allegory and moral symbolism, at the expense of theatrical effect.

AL SHEAN (1868-1949)

American comedian. Al Shean was already a well-known comedian when he first teamed up with Ed Gallagher in 1912 for *The Rose Maid*. From then on, although he continued to appear in musicals and revues, his name was indissolubly linked with his partner's. Even after a bitter quarrel separated them for six years after 1914, they reunited and immediately took up where they had left off. The *Ziegfeld Follies* of 1922 crowned their partnership, and introduced "Mr Gallagher and Mr Shean", the nonsense song which made its title characters household words. Their success had one even further-reaching effect: Al Shean's alluring habit of flinging handfuls of nickels to boys in the streets convinced his nephews, the MARX Brothers, that show business was a glamorous career.

LITTLE TICH (1868-1928)

English music hall comedian. British music hall was not a readily exportable commodity, yet Tich's mixture of mime, juggling, acrobatics, song and dance made him internationally famous. In Paris he was revered as a genius, his reputation higher there than at home. Critics all agreed that his success did not depend on his size (he was four feet six inches tall). "He would have been just as funny had he grown to the height of seven feet."

Born Harry Relph, the sixteenth son of an innkeeper, not only was Tich very little, he also had six digits on each hand. He went into show business with a strong sense of grievance, reflected in stage characters, both male and female, who were often aggressive and sometimes possessed by a kind of "fury".

Tich started his career as a black-faced comedian, touring small provincial halls and public houses. One of the routines picked up in these "spittoons" became the best known feature of his act: his "Big Boot Dance". The wooden-soled boots thumped on the floor as Tich performed a frenzied dance. They were also props for his clowning and acrobatics, their enormous length enabling him to lean forward, legs straight, at gravity-defying angles. Tich himself hated his boots and eventually dropped them from his act. He despised such easy applause, but was proud of his forty years of unbroken success and remained aloof, cultivating in private life an almost aristocratic disdain, and enjoying the friendship of such figures as Toulouse Lautrec.

FIRMIN GÉMIER (1869-1933)

French actor and producer. Gémier was a contemporary and disciple of STANISLAVSKY, whose techniques he both used and taught. He himself was a flamboyant actor, famed for powerful performances as Ubu Roi in JARRY's play and Petruchio in *The Taming of the Shrew*. After working with his teacher ANTOINE at the Théâtre de l'Oeuvre, he became manager of the Théâtre de la Renaissance in 1901. He later succeeded Antoine in his own Théâtre Antoine, and from 1921 to 1930 was director of the Odéon.

Gémier wanted to bring theatre to the people. In between popular productions in Paris, he toured with his Théâtre National Ambulant, trying to establish dramatic centres all over France. In 1920 he founded the Théâtre National Populaire. His influence reached through his pupil DULLIN to the great generation of actor-producers, including VILAR and BARRAULT.

ANDRÉ GIDE (1869-1951)

French novelist, critic and playwright. Gide's fiction, as well as his social and literary criticism, is founded on a self-searching morality which has influenced several generations. The recurrent motif of his life was reaction—first against his puritanical upbringing, then against the moral stultification fostered by society in general. In his plays, Gide broke away from the "unintelligent subordination to realism" he saw in the theatre, and advocated a return to the ideals of classical tragedy. Archetypal mythic or historical figures abound, as in *Le Roi Candaule* (1901), and the later, dryer *Oedipe* and *Thésée*. This dramatic style did not at first find a wide audience. *Saül*, a long and complex drama touching on themes familiar from the rest of his fiction (the nature of power and homosexuality) had to wait twenty-five years from its inception at the turn of the century for a post-war audience sympathetic to Gide's cult of liberation and moral individualism. *Le Retour de l'enfant prodigue* had the same youthful appeal (and nearly as long to wait for a production). A fruitful partnership with the RENAUD-BARRAULT company in the 1940s led to Gide's highly successful translations of SHAKESPEARE, notably *Hamlet*, produced by the company in 1946. His adaptation for them of Kafka's *The Trial* in 1947 also had an impact; the same year he won the Nobel Prize for literature. The Comédie-Française production of the satirical *Les Caves du Vatican* in 1950 affirmed his commitment to the theatre as a channel through which his intellect unceasingly balanced answers with questions.

AURÉLIEN-FRANÇOIS-MARIE LUGNÉ-POE (1869-1940)

French actor and director. The young Aurélien Lugné added the surname of Edgar Allan Poe to his own, because he felt himself a kindred spirit of the author of *Tales of Mystery and the Imagination*. His early productions were certainly mysterious, and made considerable demands on the audience's imagination; the lighting was extremely murky, and Lugné-Poe himself wore the same, often quite inappropriate black frock-coat in almost every piece. The Théâtre de l'Oeuvre, the company he founded in 1893 was to be the home of "symbolist" drama, but, as such, its only notable achievement was the production of MAETERLINCK's *Pelléas et Mélisande*. Although Lugné-Poe encouraged new French writers, almost all his successes came with foreign works (he produced everything from IBSEN and STRINDBERG to plays translated from Chinese and Sanskrit). Of the French works, the most significant (and most misunderstood) was Alfred Jarry's *Ubu Roi*.

Lugné-Poe was universally admired as an actor of great sensitivity, but his innovations as a director did not always receive the acknowledgement they deserved. The Théâtre de l'Oeuvre closed in 1899 to reopen in new permanent premises in 1919. In the intervening years, Lugné-Poe surprised everyone by becoming an impresario, managing the European tours of Eleonora DUSE in the works of Ibsen. This seemed an act of disloyalty towards his wife, Suzanne Després, who, as Nora in *A Doll's House*, was deemed at least the equal of the great Italian tragedienne.

WILLIAM VAUGHN MOODY (1869-1910)

American poet and playwright. Moody's father was a steamboat pilot; he himself became an academic and intellectual. Originally a poet, he turned to drama to express the conflicting human elements he discovered in his own life. *The Great Divide* (1909), his most popular play, concerns the marriage of a refined New England woman to a coarse but vital Westerner. Earlier he had written unperformed verse dramas, including *The Masque of Judgement* (1900), which depicted a similar tension between man's sensual and spiritual natures and his resulting rebellion against God. Among the first American attempts to reach a wide audience with serious philosophical themes, his plays anticipated the work of O'NEILL.

GEORGE ROBEY (1869-1954)

English music-hall comedian. In spite of his stage image of sophisticated vulgarity, Robey took great trouble to publicize his middle-class life-style. He encouraged the lie that he had been educated at Cambridge and freely discussed his love of classical music and *objets d'art* (he was, in fact, an accomplished painter). On stage, however, "The Prime Minister of Mirth" was a master of music hall technique. Behind his trademark of heavy black eyebrows he created a gallery of characters. He would tell his audience that he had not come there to be laughed at, and when they persisted, he would cry out, "Desist!" (at which they laughed all the harder). He was also a great pantomime dame. During the First World War, he performed in revues, introducing the song "If you were the only girl in the world". Then came straight comic roles. In films he played Sancho Panza opposite Chaliapin as Don Quixote, and the dying Falstaff in OLIVIER's *Henry V*. Robey wrote two volumes of autobiography, which reveal an outstandingly perceptive observer of his times and of the profession in which he excelled. Not long before he died, he was honoured with a knighthood.

STANISLAW WYSPIANSKI (1869-1907)

Polish playwright, designer and poet. Wyspianski's plays and designs combined new ideas of "total theatre" and an architectural conception of the stage with traditional Polish music, costumes and architecture. Some plays, such as *Akropolis*, written in 1903-4, and *The Return of Ulysses* (1907) have biblical or ancient Greek settings. Others deal with social and political problems, dramatizing important moments in Poland's history. His greatest play, *The Wedding* (1901), is among these. As it ends guests follow a scarecrow in a wild dance, ignoring the call to join Poland's struggle. In 1901 he was the first to produce Adam MICKIEWICZ's masterpiece *Forefathers' Eve*. Wyspianski's popular plays had a lasting influence on Polish drama.

Once again **Florenz Ziegfeld** unveils the latest models of American beauty in his annual *Follies*. The styling and bodywork of his creations was impeccable; many he tested himself to see how they handled. As a dictator of fashion and creator of stars in the twenties, he enjoyed more power than the movie moguls

Olga Knipper, who was to become the grand old lady of the Russian stage, joined the Moscow Art Theatre at its inception in 1898. She played Irina (*below right*) in one of Stanislavsky's first productions, *Feodor Ivanovich*

Patriotic Scotsmen have never forgiven **Harry Lauder** (*below*) for the damage he did to their image abroad. The English loved his mixture of kilted comedy and sentimental songs, and in 1919 they awarded him a knighthood for his contribution to the war effort

RAGGEDY RAG

Words by GENE BUCK

Music by DAVE STAMPER

F. ZIEGFELD JR's
15th ANNUAL PRODUCTION

ZIEGFELD
FOLLIES
OF
1921

STAGED UNDER THE
DIRECTION OF
EDWARD ROYCE

Two Lovely Lying Eyes

What a World This Would Be!

Sally, Won't You Come Back?

I Can't Resist Them
    (When They're Beautiful)

The Princess of My Dreams

The Legend of the Golden Tree

In Khorassan

Everytime I Hear a Band Play

Roses In the Garden

Raggedy Rag

You Must Come Over

HARMS
INCORPORATED
NEW YORK

FLORENZ ZIEGFELD (1869-1932)

American impresario. Flo Ziegfeld's first chorus line made its debut in a tent in Chicago, "The Dancing Ducks of Denmark" did indeed cavort—and even chortle—in a most unusual way; they were a great attraction until an animal-welfare official detected a number of gas burners under the metal stage. Even more short-lived was Ziegfeld's "Invisible Brazilian Fish", a hoax which the public saw through in no time.

His first real chance arrived in the person of Eugene SANDOW, a strong-man whom Ziegfeld refashioned into a well-exposed and highly profitable Adonis. Ziegfeld next wooed and won the beautiful French starlet Anna Held, promoting her even more extravagantly: she gave interviews reclining in négligés or bathing in milk. The press lapped it all up, and Held was a celebrity before she had even been seen on stage.

By 1906 the public demanded stronger fare. Ziegfeld's answer was *The Parisian Model*, a show greeted by scandalized allegations of immorality, many planted in the newspapers by Ziegeld himself to ensure a good box-office. This new style, based on the *Folies-Bergère*, developed into the renowned *Ziegfeld Follies*, which ran from 1906 to 1943. Early revues were overtly erotic, but thereafter they emphasized elegance, and moments of nudity were brief, meeting the American demand for implied rather than revealed sensuality. Ziegfeld had a genuine pride in his unspoken equation between wealth, elegance and sex. His aim was to "Glorify the American Girl", and to this end he treated his theatres like colleges of femininity, demanding that his charges should be equally lady-like offstage as on, and insisting that the conspicuous glamour which audiences flocked to worship should be authentic: his stars wore real silk, while for a stage "banquet" gourmet food was provided, along with gold utensils and sumptuous napiery.

In 1912 Ziegfeld was divorced by Anna—surprisingly, since he had never legally married her; but Lillian Lorraine, who had been understudying her dramatic and domestic roles, filled her place. The prize of real marriage fell to Ziegfeld's next star and concubine, Billie Burke.

In all Ziegfeld promoted an astonishing range of celebrities, including MARILYN MILLER, Fanny BRICE, Will ROGERS, Eddie CANTOR and W. C. FIELDS. He was a tyrannical producer, and such employees as George Gershwin, Richard Rodgers and LORENZ HART – though prepared to turn in a score at a moment's notice—resented his arrogance. Ziegfeld also drove himself to the edge of insanity, as his manic appetite for women suggests. The Depression finished him. Unwilling to accept the financial restrictions of that era, and refusing to admit the increasing irrelevance of his extravagant productions, he spent wildly and died leaving Billie a million dollars in debt.

IRMA GRAMATICA (1870-1962)

Italian actress. Daughter of a prompter and a costume maker, Irma was already on stage at the age of three. She worked with Eleonora DUSE, whose qualities of simplicity and purity she shared, and in 1896 became Ermete ZACCONI's leading actress, excelling in plays by SHAKESPEARE and Gerhart HAUPTMANN. From 1900 she ran her own companies, reaching her peak in such plays as *Dal tuo al mio* by Giovanni Verga. In later years she often worked with her sister. The less beautiful Emma (1875–1965) battled her way on to the stage against all advice, finally forming her own company in 1909. She gave some of her best performances in the plays of IBSEN, and (like Sarah BERNHARDT) enjoyed assuming male roles, including a memorable Hamlet. She also worked extensively in the cinema and on television, and in later life was very popular in the United States.

OLGA KNIPPER (1870-1959)

Russian actress. Olga Knipper studied drama with NEMIROVICH-DANCHENKO at the Moscow Philharmonic Society, where the other star pupil was MEYERHOLD. She became known for her interpretations of CHEKHOV's subtle heroines, applying the rigorous Method of STANISLAVSKY. Until 1917 she was one of the reigning queens of the Moscow Art Theatre.

Chekhov, entranced, wrote to Olga: "I do love you, I love your letters, I love the way you act and the way you walk. The only thing I don't love is the way you spend ages at the washbasin," and married her. After his death in 1904 she rededicated herself to the theatre.

HARRY LAUDER (1870-1950)

Scottish music hall singer and comedian. Lauder (born Hugh MacLennan) first made a hit in England, where he ran out of material one night in his Irish act in Birkenhead and had to fill in with his native songs. Wearing a kilt and wielding a crooked stick, he developed a potent Scottish mixture of sentiment and dour comedy, and took London by storm. Several world tours made him the best known living Scotsman. His songs included "I love a lassie", "Roamin' in the Gloamin'", and—the words often lost amid squeals and grunts—"Stop yer ticklin', Jock".

MARIE LLOYD (1870-1922)

English variety artist. "Our Marie" to millions of Londoners, Lloyd epitomized music hall gusto and Cockney wit. Critics accused her of lewdness, but her songs were never coarse. Their good-humoured suggestiveness depended on her delivery. As one of her titles proclaimed, "Ev'ry Little Movement has a Meaning All Its Own".

She made her debut at fifteen at the music hall where her father worked as a waiter. A year later she was a star, delighting audiences with her big blue eyes, golden hair and buxom charm. Early in her career she was the naughty ingénue, all ribbons and lace, later on the winking *grande dame* with fabulously frilly gowns, pink tights, diamond garter and cane. Her lifelong professional eminence was marred only by her exclusion from the first Royal Variety Performance in 1912, on vague grounds of impropriety. The sexual innuendo (and parodying of drunkenness on stage, as in "I'm One of the Ruins that Cromwell knocked Abaht") worked well in the East End, but not "up West". But personally she suffered from three unhappy marriages and a compulsive generosity that was too often unreturned. Her universal appeal was demonstrated both by the huge crowds at her funeral and by Sarah BERNHARDT's assertion that Marie Lloyd was the only woman of genius on the English stage.

NELLIE WALLACE (1870-1948)

English comedienne. Nellie was not a pretty girl, but she made a comic virtue of her appearance. After many years of acting in straight plays she became a star as a music hall soloist, singing in her typical staccato manner such songs as "I Lost Georgie in Trafalgar Square". Her costume was equally diverting. "Those bonnets of hers and the wretched little tippet of moth-eaten fur" are what made her unforgettable for one admirer. She was also at home in revue and was a particularly villainous witch in *The Sleeping Beauty*, one of the many pantomimes in which she could indulge her talent for caricature.

LEONID ANDREYEV (1871-1919)

Russian playwright. Andreyev's plays were acclaimed and performed for almost as short a span as his own life. His nightmare images and celestial landscapes appealed to all the great directors of his day. STANISLAVSKY interpreted *The Somebody in Grey* as a personification of fatalism brooding on death. In 1909 NEMIROVICH-DANCHENKO discovered metaphysical truths battling against the spirit of darkness in *Anathema*, and MEYERHOLD produced *The Life of Man* in 1907. The symbolism of *King Hunger* terrified thousands of theatregoers, and everyone brooded over the Duke of Lorenzo's duel with his double in *The Black Masks*. The plays were so Romantic, so full of awesome images, that LEO TOLSTOY felt compelled to respond: "Andreyev wants to frighten me but I am not scared," he said.

SERAFÍN AND JOAQUÍN ÁLVAREZ QUINTERO
(1871-1938 AND 1873-1944)

Spanish playwrights. The Álvarez Quintero brothers wrote cheerful, witty, often sentimental dramas full of the character and colour of their native Spain. Success came remarkably early in Seville in 1888 with *Esorima y amor*. Moving to Madrid, they wrote nearly 200 more plays in a partnership that lasted a lifetime.

In *El amor que pasa* (1904) girls living isolated lives in the country dream of perfect lovers who never arrive. Problems arise in *Doña Clarines* (1909) with a girl who insists on telling the truth. In the more serious but equally popular *Malvaloca*, a respectable man finally defies society by marrying the girl he loves in spite of her having a "past". Harley GRANVILLE-BARKER who, with his wife, translated eight of the plays, remarked, "This is not profound drama, but it is alive."

JOHN MILLINGTON SYNGE
(1871-1909)

Irish playwright. Synge wrote the finest single play in the history of the Irish theatre. Yet when *The Playboy of the Western World* was first produced at the Abbey Theatre in 1907 it caused a riot. Sections of the audience believed it was an unpatriotic satire on Irish peasant life. Synge was not interested in their nationalism, but it is true that his comedy was merciless. The hero, a young man called Christy Mahon, arrives in a village claiming to have killed his father, and is much admired for this bold deed. The villagers' respect makes him genuinely bold; he wins races and disarms women. When his father appears, very alive and vengeful, Christy is stripped of his illusions and flees. But to Pegeen Mike, the heroine, he is still the greatest living playboy in the Western World.

It was one of only six plays written in eight years before Synge's early death, and it sprang, as did *Riders to the Sea* (1904)—perhaps the best one-act play in English—from his taking the advice of W. B. YEATS. As a young man Synge lived in Paris, but Yeats told him, "You will never create anything by reading RACINE . . . go to the Arran Islands." In the West of Ireland Synge learned the poetic realism of Gaelic English, and, unlike most of his contemporaries, he distilled it into an intensely dramatic form.

CHARLES BLAKE COCHRAN
(1872-1951)

English impresario. C. B. Cochran (known as "Cockie") was a promoter on the grand scale. Willing to take risks because he loved the glitter of the theatre even more than he loved money, he staged spectacular revues and musicals, and the plays of J. M. BARRIE and Noel COWARD.

He was fascinated by the cavernous London showplaces of Olympia, Earl's Court and Wembley. There he arranged wrestling, roller-skating, a Midget City of 100 dwarves, and a vast rodeo, which was advertised by riders rampaging through the West End lassoing people at random. Cochran also livened up a SHAKESPEARE festival with a zoo and a circus (few bothered with the drama).

In 1911 the Cochran pageant-play, *The Miracle* (directed by Max REINHARDT), employed a cast of 1500 and gave a start to a generation of actors who in later years would disconcertingly ask him if he remembered them.

EDWARD GORDON CRAIG
(1872-1966)

English designer, director and actor. Craig produced fewer than ten plays in his long life, but he radically influenced modern theatre. The illegitimate son of Ellen TERRY, he first went on stage when he was six years old. By the age of sixteen he was a member of HENRY IRVING's company, with whom he continued to act until 1898 when his visions and ambitions were no longer compatible with a performer's life.

Craig believed that theatre should be an overwhelming emotional experience "like some ancient religious ceremony", composed equally of acting, words, line, colour and rhythm. The director should have absolute control over all dramatic elements. Beginning in 1900, his productions of opera, and of plays by IBSEN and SHAKESPEARE, spurned realism to concentrate on atmosphere, and employed unprecedented lighting effects and abstract sets. Too innovative and eccentric for English managers, Craig left for Europe in 1904. The rest of his life was a whirl of mainly theoretical activity. He wrote a number of books (chief among them the widely translated *On the Art of the Theatre*), edited his own magazine, *The Mask*, from 1908 to 1929 and exhibited stage designs. But he produced only five more plays. These included Ibsen's *Rosmersholm* for Eleonora DUSE and a famous *Hamlet* with STANISLAVSKY. "Poor as a fish" in his last years, he was still exuberantly devoted to "the dear Theatre" and honoured by such modern masters as Jean-Louis BARRAULT.

WILLIAM FAY (1872-1947)

Irish actor. Together with his brother Frank (1870–1931), William Fay founded the acting company which performed the plays of W. B. YEATS, Lady GREGORY and J. M. SYNGE, making the Abbey Theatre in Dublin famous and influential within five years of its foundation in 1904. William was the producer and chief comic actor; Frank coached Yeats in playwriting, the company in speaking, and took the leading tragic roles. Both clashed with the Abbey's directors, led by Yeats, and the brothers left the theatre in 1908. Their Irish nationalism was more cultural than political, and their preoccupation with artistic standards antagonized some members of the Abbey's audience.

HARRY TATE (1872-1940)

English comedian. Tate's famous "Motoring" sketch was among the most successful of all music hall acts. Born Ronald Macdonald Hutchinson, he took his stage name from an old employer (Henry Tate & Sons, sugar refiners) and began his career as a mimic. "Motoring" made him a star. As a pompous car owner trying to mend his broken machine, he was infuriated by the inane comments of his son. His stiff, bristling moustache twitched and twirled to express every possible emotion. This sketch and others such as "Billiards" and "Fishing" remained popular for years. With the decline of music hall, Tate deftly switched to revue. He died from injuries received in one of London's first air raids.

GERALD DU MAURIER (1873-1934)

English actor-manager. Du Maurier made his name in the first productions of J. M. BARRIE's *The Admirable Crichton* and *Peter Pan* (in which he played both Mr Darling and Captain Hook) and then went on to more debonair roles. He had a thin voice and a gaunt face, but his nonchalant stage-presence charmed theatregoers who saw him in 1906 as the gentleman thief in *Raffles*.

ALFRED JARRY (1873-1907)

French writer and playwright. At the age of fifteen, Jarry lampooned one of his teachers at the lycée in Rennes with a scurrilous puppet play. In 1896, it was performed as *Ubu Roi* at the Théâtre de l'Oeuvre, with Firmin GÉMIER as the monstrous Ubu, the archetype of power-hungry, bourgeois Philistinism. With its aggressively offensive first word, "Merdre" (which could be loosely translated into English as "shirt"), and its Punch and Judy ferocity, the play caused a sensation and was condemned by the critics and a large section of the public. "There are times", commented the more sympathetic poet Catulle Mendès, "when, the pavements cracking, the sewers like volcanoes explode and ejaculate."

The "perfect anarchy" of which Jarry dreamed may have contributed to his inability to match the violent achievement of *Ubu Roi* in his later Ubu plays or other works. Although the posthumous publication of his *Gestes et opinions du docteur Faustroll, pataphysicien* confirmed his cult status among the surrealist movement, Jarry did not live to benefit from it. Lack of revenue from his writing brought penurious obscurity, and he died at the age of thirty-four from tuberculosis aggravated by drink and malnutrition. Meanwhile his legend grew; absurdists like IONESCO later formed a *Collège de Pataphysique*, which celebrated the "science of imaginary solutions" expounded in *Faustroll*. For example, Newton's apple may as well demonstrate the ability of an apple to pull the planet towards it as vice versa.

Jarry's masterpiece, *Ubu Roi*, is still regularly performed, evidence of the savage vitality of its anarchic "hero", Ubu, the king. The English comedian Spike Milligan has reworked the play for a London audience.

MISTINGUETT (1873-1956)

French music hall singer, actress and dancer. The great Rodin once declared that if ever he had to sculpt the muse of music hall she would have the legs of Mistinguett. Towards the end of her career, however, audiences were lucky to catch even a fleeting glimpse of those priceless limbs, so surrounded was she by ballyhoo and extravagant ostrich plumes.

Mistinguett was well into her thirties when her sketches and dance routines at the Moulin Rouge and Folies-Bergère first made her a Parisian institution. One of her partners at that time was Maurice CHEVALIER. An energetic, comic dance number ended with the two of them rolled up inside a carpet. Legend has it that their passion was first kindled while they waited for the stagehands to disentangle them. The affair did not run smoothly, but on occasions Mistinguett showed remarkable devotion. When Chevalier was captured during the First World War, his lover did not rest until she had secured his release, once

being arrested at the Swiss border as a suspected spy.

Mistinguett had a sure sense of popular comedy, making several forays into straight acting, notably in the title role of SARDOU's *Madame Sans-Gêne*. But for the last twenty years of her long career she was principally a revue-artist. With songs like "Mon Homme" and "J'en ai marre", she would make her entrance at the Casino de Paris, gliding down a gilded staircase in costumes worth almost as much as the legs they nearly concealed.

Jeanne Bourgeois, or **Mistinguett**, the fiery "La Miss" of French music-hall

MAX REINHARDT (1873-1943)

Austrian director. The youngest child of a large orthodox Jewish family, Reinhardt was a bank clerk before he took up acting. At the Deutsches Theater in Berlin he worked under the great naturalist director Otto BRAHM, but soon grew tired of "sticking on a beard . . . and eating noodles and sauerkraut on stage every night", and left to organize a number of experimental groups, including a cabaret. After winning acclaim for a glowing production of *A Midsummer Night's Dream*, in 1905 he took over control (partly by buying it outright) of the Deutsches Theater. His work here offered a refreshing contrast to the ponderous realism of the naturalists, and his adventurous imagination and lightness of touch brought a new dimension to many ostensibly grim plays, notably IBSEN's *Ghosts* and Frank WEDEKIND's *Frühlings Erwachen*. A master of architectural sets, inventive lighting and music, and meticulously disciplined crowd scenes, he discovered new colours in SHAKESPEARE, while his vast and genial productions of SOPHOCLES' *Oedipus Rex* and AESCHYLUS' *Oresteia* did much to re-establish the Greek classics. But the monumentality of Reinhardt's concept of drama appeared most unforgettably in his awe-inspiring productions—in five cities—of Vollmöller's *The Miracle*.

Reinhardt was undogmatic—even shy—and his reputation as the father of "director's theatre" derives largely from the respect he afforded his actors: he established the precedent that "total theatre" can be achieved better by inspiration than by domination.

In 1920 he helped to found the Salzburger Festspiele, the original modern cultural festival, and here championed works by Hugo von HOFMANNSTHAL. By now, however, the expressionist movement (of which Reinhardt had been an early advocate) had become hostile to "illusionary" theatre, and from 1920 he lived mainly in Austria. Increasingly isolated, he handed over the Deutsches Theater to the Nazis in 1933 (accompanied by a courageous letter to Goebbels) and from then on worked more spasmodically—and largely abroad. In 1938 he abandoned his home and his fortune to live out his old age in American exile.

LILIAN BAYLIS (1874-1937)

English manager. The eccentric Lilian Baylis created the Old Vic out of the Royal Victoria Coffee and Music Hall in working-class London, and worked there from 1898 to 1937. Her purpose in staging opera (in English) and drama (especially SHAKESPEARE – hers was the first theatre ever to put on all of his plays) was to enlighten the local residents and keep them out of the public houses. A very small audience grew over the years until she realized her ambition of taking over Sadler's Wells Theatre to house the opera (and to introduce ballet).

Religious and stubbornly practical, she prayed, "Oh God, send me some good actors and cheap!" An early arrival was the young Sybil THORNDIKE, who was told by a friend, "There's a strange woman running a theatre in Waterloo Road, . . . you will find her exciting, Syb, because you are as mad as she is." Edith EVANS, John GIELGUD, RALPH RICHARDSON and generations of great actors also cut their teeth at the Old Vic, and they all returned, attracted by Miss Baylis's single-mindedness. Dumpy and motherly, coercive and gauche, she wore the robes of an honorary M.A. from Oxford with dignity on opening and closing nights – Queen Mary was then the only other woman to have been so honoured.

MAY GERTRUDE ELLIOTT (1874-1950)

American actress. Early in her career, Gertrude was taken firmly in hand by her illustrious older sister MAXINE ELLIOTT, and became a star in the 1899 London production of Clyde FITCH's *The Cowboy and the Lady*. Her effervescent performance as the ingénue stole the show from her sister and attracted the attention of no less a figure than Johnston FORBES-ROBERTSON. He subsequently made her a member of his company, then married her. They acted together until his retirement in 1913, after which she toured widely and successfully on her own.

HUGO VON HOFMANNSTHAL (1874-1929)

Austrian playwright and poet. Hofmannsthal's early works for the stage are so heavy with symbolism and exquisite poetry that they appeared somewhat static in performance. His subsequent awakening to what he called *Existenz* made him reject this subjectivity in favour of a more dramatic technique and an appreciation of the real world. This phase coincided with his friendship with two very practical men: Max REINHARDT, who produced many of his plays from *Elektra* (1903) onwards, and the composer Richard Strauss, who collaborated with him on such operas as *Der Rosenkavalier* (1911) and *Ariadne auf Naxos* (1912). Among Hofmannsthal's stage master-pieces are *Jedermann* (1911), a version of the *Everyman* play; *Der Schwierige* (1921), a high comedy; and *Der Turm* (1925), a drama based on CALDERÓN.

WILLIAM SOMERSET MAUGHAM (1874-1965)

English novelist, short-story writer and playwright. V. S. Pritchett has likened Maugham to a very dry Martini, and dry wit is the hallmark of his plays. Maugham, now most famous for his short stories and novels, had no admiration for drama, considering it "one of the lesser arts, like woodcarving or dancing", but he hoped to make money from it. He first had a play produced in 1901-2; by 1908 he had four running simultaneously in the West End: *Lady Frederick*, his first success, *Mrs Dot*, *Jack Straw* and *The Explorer*. His elegant well-made comedies avoided sentimentality and became the height of fashion both in London and New York.

A number are masterpieces of their kind, particularly *The Circle* (1921), on the dilemmas of impulsive action, and *The Constant Wife* (1926). Some later plays such as *East of Suez* (1922) and *The Sacred Flame* (1928) are more serious. When *Sheppey* (1933), about an altruistic barber who wants to give away his lottery prize-winnings, was not appreciated, Maugham abandoned playwriting. He spent his later years in a villa on the French Riviera, where he boarded up all the seaward windows and gaily entertained his friends.

VSEVOLOD MEYERHOLD (1874-c 1940)

Russian director. Meyerhold was baptised into the Orthodox Church with the Old-Russian name of Vsevolod at the age of twenty-two. Before that he was plain Karl Theodore Kazimir, a Lutheran of German-Jewish background. He studied drama with NEMIROVICH-DANCHENKO and acted with The Moscow Art Theatre, then combined acting and directing with his own group. His symbolist, anti-realist ideas merged with the radical political ones of socialism into a totally new approach to the theatre. STANISLAVSKY was impressed enough to appoint him director of The Studio, and so began a rivalry that was to last all their lives. Meyerhold thought that words were merely "a design on the fabric of movement". To him actors were patterns; they moved and spoke with precise artificiality. This philosophy was so totally opposed to Stanislavsky's psychological realism that the theatre was closed, and Meyerhold moved on. At The Komisarjevskaya Theatre his actors became bas-relief against flat canvases instead of settings. The owner, actress Vera KOMISAR-JEVSKAYA, protested that he gave her no part worthy of her, and fired him.

In 1908, Meyerhold was appointed one of the director-producers of the Imperial Theatres, in Petrograd. There, and in his own independent productions, he continued to refine techniques culled from Japanese Kabuki, Spanish and Chinese theatre, and the Commedia Dell' Arte. He fought for Constructivism, masks, revolving stages, magic and mysticism. He felt anyone with normal reflexes could become an actor, and coined the term "biomechanics" to explain how.

His genius was all-pervasive and revolutionary, and when the revolution (of which he had at first been an ardent supporter) started devouring its own children, he was one of its chief victims. At the First All-Union Congress of directors in 1939, he condemned the theatre of social-realism as "gloomily well-regulated averagely arithmetical, stupefying, and murderous in its lack of talent . . . where once there were the best theatres of the world".

Some say he was arrested and tortured to death. Others contend he was released after years of imprisonment and committed suicide (earlier his wife, the actress Zinaida Raikh, had been found with her eyes gouged out and covered in stab wounds – an act attributed to robbers). The world lost probably its greatest theatrical innovator.

BERTRAM MILLS (1874-1938)

English circus manager. Mills knew nothing about show business when he set out to create the most ambitious circus seen in Britain. A prosperous carriage-builder, passionate about horses, in 1920 he booked the American RINGLING Brothers for a Christmas season. When they cancelled he had six months to find his own circus.

Travelling the world to find acts, he prepared a dazzling show and arranged an extravagant opening-night dinner for the press. The circus was a wild success, and the dinners became an annual event, the list of distinguished guests once reaching 1493. Both in London and on the road Mills's show remained an institution, with its fabulous grand parades, exotic costumes, beautiful animals and world-class artistes (including the WALLENDAS and COCO).

BERT WILLIAMS (1874-1922)

American comedian. Photographs of Bert Williams show a proud, sensitive black man. But his fame depended on his assuming the shuffling, slow-witted stereotype of the stage Negro. His first success came as half of a comic duo. He and his partner George Walker danced, sang and clowned as "The Two Real Coons" and scored their greatest triumphs in a number of all-black musicals, including the popular *In Dahomey* (1903). After Walker retired because of illness, Williams became a solo star, one of the main attractions of the *Ziegfeld Follies*. But acclaim for his perceptive comic monologues did not diminish the racial prejudice that poisoned his life off-stage. His constant awareness of that cruel paradox led to the heavy drinking and overwork that finally killed him. His co-star W. C. FIELDS supplied an epitaph: "Bert Williams is the funniest man I ever saw and the saddest man I ever knew."

HARRY HOUDINI (1876-1928)

American escape artist and conjuror. With a mixture of courage, strength, showmanship and deft trickery, Houdini made a reputation for being able to free himself from any physical restraint. After emigrating as a child to the USA from Budapest, he named himself after the great French conjuror ROBERT-HOUDIN (his real name was Ehrich Weiss) and began his career in obscure shows and circuses. Then on a visit to London in 1900 he persuaded the police to handcuff him to a pillar at Scotland Yard. Handcuffs were child's play to an expert locksmith like Houdini (he simply tapped them in a certain way), but the stunt won him international fame.

Houdini had to plan ever more elaborate escapes in order to keep his public. He was manacled and enclosed in boxes, safes, milk cans, mail bags and paper bags, which were then covered by a screen. He was put in coffins and buried (or immersed in water – where he once remained for an hour and a half). He hung head-down, strait-jacketed, roped and manacled, six storeys above a crowd of thousands. He conjured an eagle on to his shoulder and made an elephant disappear.

His secret lay in preparing hidden catches and panels in his containers, and in using hidden keys, often with the help of an accomplice. Those who checked his equipment never detected the trickery. While being examined naked before being locked in a gaol, he hooked the key on to the inspecting doctor's clothes and retrieved it afterwards with a slap on the back.

Once, diving roped and manacled from a high bridge in Melbourne, Australia, he dislodged a corpse from the river bottom. As it rose, the aghast spectators thought it was Houdini; Houdini himself, on surfacing beside it, was so shaken that he had to be rescued. But the very real dangers in his act (even with all his tricks he had to be quick and skilful) did not generally alarm him: it was the audience's nerves that were at risk.

Finally, Houdini was fatally slow. Punched in the stomach by a young man who was testing the magician's legendary strength, he failed to brace himself and died of peritonitis.

Harry Houdini (*above*), about to be lowered into the sea, chained and manacled inside a casket. The equipment used for this, his most spectacular and dangerous feat, was always painstakingly checked, in case an irresponsible practical joker had tampered with it

The great black American comedian, **Bert Williams**, at the height of his popularity in the Ziegfeld Follies of 1910. The indignities suffered by Williams in order that sophisticated New Yorkers might laugh at the antics of a simple "coon" proved too much for his sensitive genius

166

HENRI GHÉON (1875-1944)

French playwright, poet and novelist. While serving in the First World War, Ghéon (born Vangeon) rediscovered the faith he had discarded as a young man. As a result, in 1915 he returned to Catholicism, which remained an inspiration for his drama. *L'Eau-de-vie* had already been produced in 1914 by Jacques COPEAU in his experiments at the Théâtre du Vieux-Colombier; now Ghéon went on to write over ninety plays. Simple but effective poetic dramas, often similar in form to medieval mystery plays, they included *La Parade du pont au diable* (1925) and *Le Noël sur la place* (1935). Some he wrote for Copeau, among them one of his best, *Le Pauvre sous l'escalier* (1921). Ghéon's plays are still very popular in religious groups and schools.

EDGAR WALLACE (1875-1932)

English novelist, journalist and playwright. Edgar Wallace was the author of some 150 detective novels and fourteen plays. The titles of the latter convey their flavour: *The Terror* (1927), *The Squeaker* (1928), *On the Spot* (1930), *The Case of the Frightened Lady* (1931). His works were usually composed into dictaphones or taken down by high-speed typists, but their style was lucid and unpretentious and appealed to chambermaids and tycoons alike.

Wallace's portrayal of the seamier side of life was undoubtedly authentic. Born in East London and brought up by a fish porter, he discovered SHAKESPEARE while a boy and at the same time learned the ways of criminals and police from his environment. He became a soldier, and later one of London's top journalists, with a passion for horse racing. It was only then that Wallace began writing thrillers.

HARLEY GRANVILLE-BARKER (1877-1946)

English actor, producer, manager, playwright and critic. As a young actor, Granville-Barker was renowned for his athletic lightness and grace. He had begun to act at fourteen; by his twenties he was playing the lead in the premières of a string of SHAW plays. Later, as director of the Court Theatre, he remained an enthusiastic champion of modern playwrights, including Shaw, IBSEN, GALSWORTHY and HAUPTMANN.

There were also sensational productions of SHAKESPEARE, notably *The Winter's Tale* and *Twelfth Night* in 1912, and *A Midsummer Night's Dream* in 1914. The sets in these productions were semi-abstract, and brightly coloured and lit; the action had an elegant fluency and the speech was quick and clear.

Of his own works, the best plays combine sensuality with a cool, rational dialogue. *The Voysey Inheritance* (1905), *Waste* (1907) and *The Madras House* (1910) take a very modern view of sex; *Waste* was banned for mixing politics and abortion. Granville-Barker retired early to a life of scholarship. The literary critic and the man of the theatre are beautifully combined in his influential *Prefaces to Shakespeare*.

MAX PALLENBERG (1877-1934)

Austrian actor. Pallenberg's comic genius was widely recognized, but he had to wait until he was over fifty to find a part in which the character's fantasy really matched his own. This was the title role in Erwin PISCATOR's historic adaptation of *The Good Soldier Schweik* (1928). At last he could alternate freely between grim realism and extempore buffoonery, without abusing the script or disconcerting the rest of the cast.

In 1914, after many hard years as a comedian in small-town Austria, Pallenberg was brought by Max REINHARDT to the Deutsches Theater in Berlin. He enjoyed success in plays as diverse as Georg KAISER's *Von Morgens bis Mitternachts* and Ferenc MOLNÁR's *Liliom*, but the kind of theatre he was born to play in did not yet exist. When he was killed in an air crash, many lamented the fact that he had never played in the masterpieces of BRECHT.

LIONEL BARRYMORE (1878-1954)

American actor. Lionel never shared his sister ETHEL BARRYMORE's exalted view of their profession. "Anyone can be an actor," he said. "And if you need five dollars you can be an author." His debut at fifteen with his grandmother Mrs John DREW was a casual disaster, and he spent the next few years mostly playing basketball, boxing and painting. A fit of dedication brought him success and critical acclaim in 1902 in *The Mummy and the Humming Bird*, but two years later he went to Paris to paint full time. Only necessity forced him back to the stage in 1909. He and his brother John had a hit in George du Maurier's *Peter Ibbetson*, and his work in *The Copperhead* and *The Jest* was widely applauded. But his *Macbeth* was panned, and following several other short-run plays, Barrymore left for Hollywood in 1925, where the money was better and the work less taxing.

GEORGE M. COHAN (1878-1942)

American playwright, composer, actor and producer. One critic denounced Cohan's typical hero as a "vulgar, cheap, blatant, ill-mannered . . . smart Alec". But his shows reflected precisely the aggressive optimism of pre-First World War America, as well as his own cocky personality. He came to prominence with the family vaudeville act, *The Four Cohans*. His first hit as playwright-composer and star was the musical *Little Johnny Jones* (1904), in which such songs as "I'm a Yankee Doodle Dandy" and "Give My Regards to Broadway" expressed a new kind of urban patriotism. Shows like *George Washington Jr* (1906) celebrated America not just in such strutting anthems as "You're a Grand Old Flag" but in their fast-moving, high-powered colloquial style.

Cohan turned out a long series of hit plays, musicals and individual songs like the First World War classic "Over There". But he fared less well in the cynical 1920s. Though busy as a producer and successful as an actor (particularly in Eugene O'NEILL's 1933 *Ah, Wilderness!*) his great years remain the early ones recalled in his film biography *Yankee Doodle Dandy* starring James CAGNEY.

LORD DUNSANY (1878-1957)

Irish playwright Edward John Moreton Drax Plunkett, eighteenth Baron, was a member of the Anglo-Irish aristocracy, though his education at Eton and Sandhurst made him more Anglo than Irish. After returning from the Boer War, he turned to big-game hunting, cricket and playwriting. Dunsany's first play, *The Glittering Gate*, was produced at the Abbey Theatre in 1909, the first of five to be performed there. But the themes were fatalistic and pessimistic, and the audience for his work was always larger in London and New York than in Dublin.

LEOPOLD JESSNER (1878-1945)

German director. Jessner's intense, intellectual concentration on the text of a play was a reaction both to unimaginative traditionalism and to the Romantic impressionism of Max REINHARDT. In 1919 he became director of the Berlin Staatstheater, where his first production was SCHILLER's *Wilhelm Tell*. This play had previously been solemnly recited before a backdrop of picturesque Alpine scenery. Jessner re-emphasized the radicalism of the play, and reduced the set to a flight of central steps, which were to become the trademark of his productions. He later introduced BRECHT into the theatre's repertoire and gave Erwin PISCATOR the opportunity to put on his revolutionary adaptation of Schiller's *Die Räuber*. Neither his choice of material nor his own work, which included an antimilitaristic *Hamlet*, endeared him to the authorities, and he was forced to resign from the Staatstheater. With the rise of Nazism, Jessner joined the German theatrical migration to Hollywood.

GEORG KAISER (1878-1945)

German playwright. Towards the end of the First World War, the general feeling that people were becoming cogs in an industrial and military machine helped Kaiser's expressionist plays to reach a surprisingly wide audience. *Die Bürger von Calais*, written several years previously, and *Von Morgens bis Mitternachts* were both first performed in 1917. There followed three connected plays, *Die Koralle* (1917), *Gas I* and *Gas II* (1918 and 1920), about a millionaire's son who tries to liberate his father's employees from their work in a gas factory.

Although theatrically very effective, Kaiser's plays are extremely abstract, dealing with ideas rather than characters. One favourite expressionist idea was that of the "New Man", capable of transcending an outworn morality. Kaiser put this idea into practice himself by selling his wife's house and pawning her belongings. His attempt to justify this action in court did not enhance his reputation, and he received six months for theft.

FERENC MOLNÁR (1878-1952)

Hungarian playwright and novelist. Molnár's blend of delicate fantasy and sceptical irony had enormous appeal in the twenties and thirties, but the charm of his forty-odd plays has since waned. His reputation in Budapest, where he led a carefree and Bohemian café life, was nothing compared to his fame abroad. *As Ördög* (*The Devil*), 1907, was produced simultaneously at two New York theatres, and *Liliom* (1909) enjoyed even greater international success, especially when sweetened and condensed as the musical *Carousel*.

As well as such fantasies of Heaven and Hell, Molnár wrote cynical pieces like *A testör* (1911), in which an actor dresses up as a guardsman to seduce his own wife (it proves a futile exercise, as she claims she recognized him all the time). *Játék a kastélyban* (1926) also tampers wittily with reality in the manner of PIRANDELLO.

BILL "BOJANGLES" ROBINSON (1878-1949)

American tap-dancer. Robinson worked as a waiter until he was lucky enough to spill oyster soup over the agent Marty Forkins. The little dance that he did to pacify Forkins got him a contract and he was soon appearing in night-clubs and vaudeville, where his skill, energy and exuberance so amazed and excited audiences that he always had to be last on the bill; no one could follow his act. Robinson appeared in a number of all-Negro shows, beginning with *Black Birds of 1928*, where "his feet were as quick as a snare drummer's hands". A highly inventive dancer, his most famous act was the Stair Tap, performed up and down a flight of steps. Bojangles consumed large

quantities of ice-cream, and always danced in his winter underwear.

CARL STERNHEIM (1878-1942)

German playwright, novelist and critic. The son of a wealthy banker, Sternheim often lived in conspicuous luxury. From his privileged position he satirized the selfish hypocrisy of the new Prussian middle class in a series of plays known collectively as *Aus dem bürgerlichen Heldenleben*. *Die Hose* (1911) caused the greatest stir, as it concerned the agonized self-doubt of an heroic civil servant whose wife loses her knickers in public. The hero, Maske, reappeared in *Der Snob* (1913) and became a household name for the archetypal self-important petty bourgeois. But Sternheim's best play was *Bürger Schippel* (1912), a more serious condemnation of the German class system.

EVA TANGUAY (1878-1947)

French-Canadian vaudeville artiste. The "Sambo Girl", the "Cyclonic Comedienne", and the "Electrified Hoyden", Eva Tanguay thrust herself from obscurity to stardom with an act that was unashamedly and boisterously sexual. "I am not beautiful, I can't sing, I do not know how to dance," she admitted, but strength of personality and sparsity of clothing overcame such handicaps. "It's all been done before but not the way I do it", she sang, and her behaviour confirmed this was no idle boast. She once threw a stagehand downstairs and grandly paid the

Bill "Bojangles" Robinson danced his way to Hollywood, (and taught his famous Stair Tap to Shirley Temple)

Grock (*above*) exemplifies the dual nature of the clown. Behind him is the smiling mask that the public sees, while in front of it the clown stands weeping. Overcome with emotion, his own image belies his state of mind

Early circus proprietors quickly realized that the menagerie (*below*) was an unfailing attraction. Wild animals even took to the stage, albeit reluctantly, for such savage spectacles as *The Brute Tamers of Pompeii*

fine with a thousand dollar bill. Middle age and the financial collapse of 1929 brought her career to a reluctant and unhappy end. She lost all her fortune, and died virtually blinded by cararacts.

ETHEL BARRYMORE (1879-1959)

American actress. Ethel Barrymore began her distinguished career in the family barn, playing the consumptive courtesan in *Camille* with her brothers John and Lionel. She became a public star in 1901 as Mme Trentoni in *Captain Jinks of the Horse Marines*. Versatility was as much her trademark as her willowy beauty, graceful bearing and melodious voice. She played frothy comedies, SHAKESPEARE and IBSEN with equal success, but her favourite role was the schoolmistress in EMLYN WILLIAMS's *The Corn is Green*, which ran on Broadway for four years. A substantial film career had begun for Ethel Barrymore as early as 1914. Her looks and bearing fitted her admirably for countless movie appearances.

JACQUES COPEAU (1879-1949)

French actor and director. Copeau's vision of a "pure" theatre relying upon gesture and mime, simple sets and atmospheric lighting was an important reaction against late nineteenth-century realism. In 1913 he founded the Théâtre du Vieux-Colombier, where his company achieved the highest of standards in their performance of works ranging from SHAKESPEARE to Paul CLAUDEL. In 1924 he moved his school of young actors to Burgundy, where they worked in the fields with local peasants and became known as Les Copiaux. The company was later taken over by Michel Saint-Denis.

Copeau believed that one man, if of sufficient faith and will, could construct a theatre of absolute purity that would appeal to all mankind. He failed in this high ambition as he did in his attempt to "make anew the French theatre", but his work has continued to exert a significant influence in England and America, as well as in France.

BARRY JACKSON (1879-1961)

English theatre manager and director. Sir Barry Jackson was not only prepared to invest large amounts of his own money in various projects, he also showed an artistic enterprise and flexibility in the management of the two theatrical institutions which he founded: the Birmingham Repertory Theatre, built in 1913, and the Malvern Festival, held for the first time in 1929. Never afraid to be unconventional, he dressed Hamlet in plus-fours, and mounted a production of BERNARD SHAW's *Back to Methuselah* which took four days to perform. From 1945–48 he directed the Shakespeare Memorial Theatre.

ALLA NAZIMOVA (1879-1945)

Russian actress. A principal performer of the St Petersburg Theatre, Nazimova toured both Europe and America with her actor-husband. She made her home in New York after an English-speaking debut there in IBSEN's *Hedda Gabler*. Between stints of success in Hollywood films, she remained an interpreter, in the grand traditional manner, of the plays of CHEKHOV, TURGENEV and O'NEILL, but she is probably best remembered for her sensuous film portrayal of Salome (1923).

WILL ROGERS (1879-1935)

American wit and vaudeville comedian. Only in America could a man combine a rope-throwing cowboy act with political comment, but Rogers's unschooled wit made him a popular, homespun American philosopher. "His appeal went straight to the heart of the nation," wrote Franklin D. Roosevelt. Rogers himself characteristically dismissed his role as court jester. "I don't make jokes; I just watch the government and report the facts," he quipped when he first introduced a political tone into his act in 1915. By 1922 he had his own newspaper column to comment on contemporary affairs and was making regular appearances in the *Ziegfeld Follies*. He also aired his views on the world in a number of books and films, though not to everyone's taste: "The bosom friend of senators and congressmen was about as daring as an early Shirley Temple movie," commented James Thurber.

RICHARD TESCHNER (1879-1948)

Czech puppeteer. Blessed with diverse artistic talents, Teschner turned to puppetry for an aesthetic unity which he found lacking in his painting, mosaics and stage design. He dispensed with the human voice in his work, deciding that it was out of scale with puppets (though he did admit it was necessary for the German Punch, Kaspar), and concentrated on the effects produced by different lighting techniques.

Teschner is best known for his use and development of Javanese rod-puppets, which were controlled from below the stage. The work of his puppet theatre in Vienna was a major influence on puppetry in the West.

GUILLAUME APOLLINAIRE (1880-1918)

French poet and playwright. A poet of the French avant-garde and an advocate of the application of cubism to literature, Apollinaire completed only one play, but its staging was a notable event in the history of the theatre. *Les Mamelles de Tirésias* (1917) opens with Thérèse, bedecked with saucepans and brooms, railing against the drudgery of being a housewife. Suddenly, a large beard is placed on her chin, she casts off the balloons which had served as her substantial "mamelles" and declares herself to be a man. Tirésias, as he is now known, fathers 40,049 children in eight days and only avoids being arrested by a sterile policeman because of the intervention of a fortune-teller, who turns out to be a repentant Thérèse, his former self. The curtain fell on the first night to an uproar of boos and applause. The word Apollinaire coined to describe his drama was "surrealist".

An illegitimate son of a Polish emigrée, Apollinaire was acquainted with the surreal in life as well as in art. He was once charged and imprisoned in error for stealing the Mona Lisa. He died from wounds received for his adopted country in the First World War.

ALEKSANDR BLOK (1880-1921)

Russian poet and playwright. The great symbolist, whose poetry agonized over the spiritual destiny of his land, was put in charge of repertoire in the theatre section of The Commissariat of Enlightenment in 1918. Despite the devastations and shortages of the Civil War, he published a series of the world's dramatic classics and helped create theatre for young people. With GORKY and Lunacharsky he sponsored the Great Dramatic Theatre in Petrograd and became chairman of its board of directors.

MEYERHOLD staged Blok's poetic dramas *The Little Showbox* and *The Stranger* in 1915. But most of his other plays, *The King in the Marketplace* and *The Song of Destiny* for example, were considered "flowers too delicate not to wilt in the footlights".

LUIGI CHIARELLI (1880-1947)

Italian playwright. Chiarelli's first and greatest stage success, *La Maschera e il volto* (1916), launched a new dramatic style. Dubbed *teatro grottesco* by its author, the play exposed the absurd effects of social codes of behaviour. Its hero cannot pardon his wife's infidelity because of his belief in a husband's right to vengeance. He sends her away secretly, claiming to have killed her. Tried and acquitted (largely due to the testimony of her lover), he finds himself threatened with imprisonment when his chastened spouse reappears. Ultimately the reunited couple are forced to flee.

Chiarelli's "grotesquery" was a great influence on PIRANDELLO's examination of human feeling and social disguise. Other plays, *Fuochi d'artificio*, for example, had less of an impact.

TILLA DURIEUX (1880-1971)

Austrian-born actress. Durieux was spotted by Max REINHARDT, who brought her to Berlin in 1903. Her first great triumphs came playing opposite Alexander MOISSI, notably as Jocasta to his Oedipus in Hugo von HOFMANNSTAHL's *Oedipus Rex*. Throughout her long career she was deeply committed politically. During the First World War she even went to Switzerland on a secret, abortive peace mission. In the twenties she was associated with revolutionary projects, both on stage and off, appearing frequently in the anti-bourgeois plays of Frank WEDEKIND.

After fleeing Nazism in 1933, she settled in Zagreb, where at the age of sixty she was an active partisan in the Second World War.

WILLIAM CLAUDE FIELDS (1880-1946)

American vaudeville comedian. Fields's life was indistinguishable from his work: an act of comedy, juggling and hard liquor. At the age of eleven he ran away from home and became a petty criminal of exceptional talent. In later life he confined his stealing to other performers' material, while guarding his own routines with a zeal only equalled by his protection of his vast wealth. Obsessed with the fear that he might once again become destitute, he kept his money under a variety of assumed names.

Until he was in his forties, Fields was renowned for being one of the best jugglers in the world. From 1915 to 1921 he performed in the *Ziegfeld Follies*. His tramp juggling act was comic, but it was not until the play *Poppy* (1923) that he made his long-desired move to acting. Soon he developed into one of the greatest comic figures in show business, with his distinctive nasal drawl and masterly timing. An announcer in a sketch addresses Fields: "I have no sympathy for a man who is intoxicated all the time." "A man who's intoxicated all the time does not need sympathy," is the measured retort. Fields did not believe in dining on an empty stomach.

Behind the cynicism of Fields there was a man of great sensitivity. A proverbial despiser of dogs and children, he once arranged for a dog that had been apprehended for drunkenness to be adopted by friends and, as he left his home for the last time to enter the sanatorium, he placed a large red rose in the now empty lily pond where the son of Anthony Quinn had drowned.

GROCK (1880-1959)

Swiss clown. Little Adrian Wettach made his first professional appearance at the family inn, playing his fiddle

In **O'Casey**'s tragedy of civil war, *Juno and the Paycock* (*left*) the men's heroic fantasies are punctured by female realism. Juno Boyle tells her maimed son, "Ah, you lost your best principle, me boy, when you lost your arm. Them's the only sort o' principles that's any good to a workin' man"

"I spent the afternoon musing on Life. If you come to think of it, what a queer thing Life is! So unlike anything else." **P. G. Wodehouse** (*right*) muses here in his own drawing room as if awaiting his manservant Jeeves, who "moves from point to point with as little uproar as a jellyfish"

Liquor and women were lifelong weaknesses of **John Barrymore** (*far right*). His first experience of the former came at the age of five when finishing off the glasses after a dinner party. He was sexually initiated, he claimed, at fourteen

and performing acrobatics. He joined in a clown act with one of his father's friends at the age of twelve, and in 1903 became Grock.

Musical skill masquerading as incompetence was Grock's matchless speciality. Beginning in 1911, his wordless and hilarious struggles to extract results from several instruments made him internationally famous. He appeared in theatres as well as circus rings, but he was everywhere a clown, shuffling out in painted face, voluminous coat and oversize shoes, dragging a huge instrument case from which he would produce a miniature violin. Where finance was concerned, Grock was far from the fumbler he seemed on stage. In 1954 "the emperor of clowns" (as J. B. PRIESTLEY had called him) retired serenely to an imperial mansion beside a Swiss lake.

ALEXANDER MOISSI (1880-1935)

Austrian-born actor. Moissi worked in Vienna and Prague before moving to Berlin to become the leading man in Max REINHARDT's great pre-war company. He excelled in the plays of IBSEN and SHAW, but the legendary beauty of his voice was more effective in highly emotional roles like Oedipus in Hugo von HOFMANSTAHL's *Oedipus Rex*. After the First World War he found another ideal vehicle in TOLSTOY's *The Living Corpse*, which he performed everywhere from Moscow to New York, acting it in three different languages: German, Italian (his mother tongue) and even in English.

SEAN O'CASEY (1880-1964)

Irish playwright. It was remarkable that O'Casey ever became a playwright. He was born a Protestant in a Dublin slum, the last of thirteen children of whom only five survived. He could not afford the price of a ticket to the Abbey Theatre, but he read widely, being especially fond of SHAKESPEARE and the Irish melodramatist Dion BOUCICAULT. Despite their widely different backgrounds, he shared one particular quality with an earlier literary Dubliner, Jonathan Swift: "A savage indignation which gnawed his heart."

O'Casey was vigorously anti-clerical, pro-socialist and pro-nationalist; during the dramatic general strike in Dublin in 1913, he was one of the chief assistants to its leader, James Larkin. In the following year he was briefly secretary to the more populist of the nationalist militias, the Irish Citizen Army, though he soon quarrelled with them and left. This was the backcloth to three great plays, written with a flourish between his forty-third and forty-sixth birthdays. Each reflected the chaos which the Easter Rising of 1916 and the Civil War had inflicted on the ordinary people of Dublin. "The whole worl's in a terrible state o' chassis," moaned Joxer Daly in the second of these plays, *Juno and the Paycock* (1924). It was only after he received twenty-five pounds from the Abbey for *Juno* that O'Casey finally stopped working as a labourer. The play had an equally profound effect on the Theatre itself: it saved the Abbey from bankruptcy – artistic as well as financial.

These three plays, *The Shadow of a Gunman* (1923) then *Juno* and *The Plough and the Stars* (1926), were all conceived as tragedies, but their humour is so irrepressible that they are better described as tragicomedies. *The Plough and the Stars* dealt ironically with religion, patriotism and sex, three subjects about which many Dubliners were singularly lacking a sense of humour. There was a riot at its première in the Abbey. "You have disgraced yourselves again," fumed YEATS at the audience, though he rejected the next work, *The Silver Tassie* (1929), an anti-war morality play. In return, O'Casey rejected the Abbey, Dublin and Ireland. Unfortunately, once removed from his roots he never wrote so well again.

STANLEY HOUGHTON (1881-1913)

English playwright. Houghton was the best known member of the Manchester School, a group of dramatists who attempted with the use of everyday language to create a realistic social drama. Unlike some of the other members of the group, however, he could amuse his audience as well as instruct them with his views of society. He could shock them too. In his most successful play, *Hindle Wakes* (1912), the pregnant Fanny Hawthorn refuses an offer of marriage from her lover, a factory owner's son. "You were an amusement – a lark," is the answer of the emancipated Fanny to the proposal.

FREDERICK LONSDALE (1881-1954)

English playwright. Lonsdale's early works were librettos for musicals such as the phenomenally popular *The Maid of the Mountains* (1917). It was not until he was in his forties that he wrote the stylish comedies for which he is

best remembered: *The Last of Mrs Cheyney* (1925), *Spring Cleaning* (1923) and *On Approval* (1926). Though a private soldier and an able seaman before turning to writing, he set his plays in aristocratic circles, which allowed him to indulge freely his passion for epigrams. Shortly before his death, he received a knighthood.

GREGORIO MARTÍNEZ SIERRA (1881-1947)

Spanish playwright, novelist, poet and manager. In 1899 Martínez Sierra married the poet Maria de la O Lejárraga and gained both a wife and a lifelong collaborator. She assisted him in producing over fifty original plays and as many translations, including works by IBSEN, SHAW and SHAKESPEARE. Influenced initially by MAETERLINCK, his style is restrained and tender, illuminating domestic events and quiet virtue. His masterpiece, *Canción de cuna* (1911), based on his wife's convent upbringing, portrays the maternal longings of a group of nuns.

An innovative manager, from 1917 to 1925 Martinez Sierra introduced foreign repertoire and modern techniques to the Teatro Eslava. He also presented the plays of daring new Spanish writers, including the first work of Federico GARCÍA LORCA.

PABLO PICASSO (1881-1973)

Spanish painter, sculptor, stage designer and playwright. Picasso's stage work reflected his ceaseless artistic development. His jaunty cubist screen for Jean COCTEAU's ballet *Parade* (1917) received more acclaim than the production itself. His designs for Stravinsky's ballet *Pulcinella* employed the harlequin figures of his "rose period" paintings, and his settings for Cocteau's play *Antigone* mirrored his neoclassical interest. Surprisingly, Picasso found time to write two plays of his own. *Les Quatres petites filles*, written in 1952, was never performed, but Albert CAMUS directed a reading of the earlier *Le Désir attrapé par la queue* in 1944. This Dada frolic featured an all-star literary cast, including Jean-Paul SARTRE.

PELHAM GRENVILLE WODEHOUSE (1881-1975)

English novelist and playwright. P. G. Wodehouse was one of the most accomplished and prolific comic novelists in the English language. A master of prose and the complicated plot, he created the immortal Jeeves, manservant and mainstay of Bertie Wooster.

He collaborated in many comedies and musicals for the stage, including *A Damsel in Distress* (1928) with Ian Hay and *Who's Who* (1934) with Guy BOLTON. He also adapted a number of foreign plays, notably those of the Hungarian playwright Ferenc MOLNÁR. Sean O'CASEY once described him as "English literature's performing flea". Wodehouse, who was impressed by the "sterling artistry" of the flea, took it as a compliment.

STEFAN ZWEIG (1881-1942)

Austrian novelist, poet and playwright. Significantly, Zweig called his autobiography *Die Welt von Gestern* (*Yesterday's World*), for he saw his ideal of a humane Europe, civilized by a common culture, crumble in two world wars. An ardent Francophile, he translated the works of his friend Jules ROMAINS, and one of his highly successful biographies was of another French playwright, Romain ROLLAND. Equally interested in English theatre, he made a brilliant adaptation of Ben JONSON's *Volpone*.

The First World War inspired Zweig's one great original play, *Jeremias* (1917), a passionate condemnation of the barbarism of war. But the Second World War destroyed Zweig's dreams for ever. Forced to flee Austria, he and his young second wife travelled to Brazil, where together they committed suicide.

JOHN BARRYMORE (1882-1942)

American actor. Son of the actor Maurice Barrymore, John inherited his father's pride in wilful eccentricity as well as his ability. When the boy was dismissed from one of a series of schools and protested he hadn't done anything, his father shouted "Why in God's name not? Aren't you a Barrymore?" As if to escape subsequent admonition, John spent the rest of his life being "a Barrymore" – a brilliant actor and a vain, alcoholic womanizer.

More interested in art than in acting as a teenager, he made a lacklustre debut in 1903, but his natural gifts soon established him as a leading man in romantic comedy. The extent of those gifts truly emerged in 1916, when Barrymore starred in John GALSWORTHY's grim drama *Justice*. His performance as a cockney bank clerk

You, the audience III

Not at all typical of a 1900 music hall crowd, this rather glum group has assembled for the last show ever to be presented at the "Canterbury", one of variety's most famous venues. The old house had fallen victim to competition, but all over England other music halls were flourishing, providing hearty comedy, song and dance to primarily working-class audiences. Their prosperity – and the increasing "family" nature of their programmes – was due largely to the upper-class orientation of the legitimate theatre. Well-to-do audiences wore evening dress and generally behaved with irreproachable decorum. Smooth, highly polished dramas described the gentle crises of upper-class society – the cad, the social climber, the "woman with a past". Meanwhile, the other classes and their families fled to the music halls.

Glittering respectability had obvious limitations. The "well-made play" for the well-heeled patron strangled all other kinds. What a critic called "organized monotony" was supported by syndicates of promoters who controlled theatres and theatrical fare. One of them, the American producer CHARLES FROHMAN, pictured the public as "tired children at the end of a day. They want a Cinderella story." It was only with the advent of the free theatre movement, started in France in 1887 by André ANTOINE, that more challenging works began to reach the stage. Everywhere, independent productions of Henrik IBSEN, GEORGE BERNARD SHAW and Anton CHEKHOV gradually provided an alternative for more serious playgoers. But by that time too, the music hall audience was turning to the novel pleasures of the cinema, and more and more houses were going the way of the Canterbury.

gaoled and hounded to suicide was a revelation. In 1920 a masterly version of *Richard III* reaffirmed his new status. He prepared the part for months, studying the text minutely and taking lessons in voice production. He worked even more exhaustively on *Hamlet* in 1922. "One of the most memorable in the history of American theatre," said a critic of the opening night. He repeated this triumph in London in 1925, but the anticipated great career did not materialize. Barrymore returned to Hollywood and years of bad movies, bad publicity and a great deal of drinking. In 1939 he toured in a feeble comedy, deliberately trading on his debauched image. Audiences came to see him "belching, ad-libbing and, hopefully, being drunk on stage". For the first great modern Hamlet, the rest might better have been silence.

JOHN DRINKWATER (1882-1937)

English playwright, actor and director. Drinkwater found a surprising ally in his early attempts to promote poetic drama when chocolate manufacturer George Cadbury commissioned his "masques" as sustenance for the minds of factory workers. With Barry JACKSON, Drinkwater was also a founding spirit of the Birmingham Repertory Theatre, where he both acted and directed.

Verse plays such as *Cophetua* (1911) and *X = O* (1917) established his critical reputation, but it was in prose, with *Abraham Lincoln* (1918), that Drinkwater achieved popular success in London and New York. Subsequent historical plays were less well received; it was not until 1927, with his comedy *Bird in Hand*, that he had another substantial theatrical hit.

JEAN GIRAUDOUX (1882-1944)

French novelist and playwright. Giraudoux was one of the most distinguished of modern authors. In his hands, French drama became once again the province of literature and not just a craftsmanlike product to divert the audiences of the Boulevard theatres. He defined French theatre in terms of the sovereignty of speech, and made much use of elaborately wrought language and great formal debates, contrasting them suddenly with a meticulous focus on trifling detail. Dialogue is the essence of his theatre, but he also revived the use of the monologue to give greater range to his characters' speech.

Giraudoux was a career diplomat whose professional interests often impinged upon his art. The need for a better understanding between France and Germany was the theme of his play *Siegfried* (1928), a dramatization of his novel *Siegfried et le Limousin*. *Siegfried* tells the story of a French soldier who loses his memory on the battlefield and is re-educated as a German by a German nurse. The absurdity of all war is the theme of *La Guerre de Troie n'aura pas lieu* (1935), which was adapted by Christopher FRY as *Tiger at the Gates* (1955). He frequently explored the relationship between opposing forces in his drama, whether it was gods and man as in *Amphitryon 38* (1929), paganism and the Old Testament in *Judith* (1931) or man and woman in *Sodome et Gomorrhe* (1943).

Giraudoux was horrified by the frenzy of the conflict at the Harvard-Yale football game when he spent a year at Harvard University. He experienced the horrors of a greater conflict when he was wounded in the First World War. This experience made him a vehement supporter of peace between France and Germany. The Nazi invasion of France shattered his hopes and also placed him in an awkward position: as minister of propaganda in the Vichy government, he felt obliged to ban the production of his own plays. He finished his famous play *La Folle de Chaillot* (*The Mad Woman of Chaillot*) in 1943 and wrote on the manuscript the prediction: "This play was first performed on October 19th, 1945." In fact, it was performed on 19 December, but Giraudoux had been dead for over a year.

THEODORE KOMISARJEVSKY (1882-1954)

Russian director and designer. Komisarjevsky, one of the most inspiring theatre personalities of his time, began his career in St Petersburg at the theatre directed by his sister Vera (1864–1910). She was a leading actress, adored by her audiences and by the symbolist playwrights to whose work she was so suited. After her death Komisarjevsky started his own theatre, where he put on imaginative and deeply considered productions often of symbolist plays. There his futuristic opera design for productions such as Offenbach's *The Tales of Hoffmann* were exciting innovations.

In 1919 Komisarjevsky left for England, where, with the actor John GIELGUD, he revitalized CHEKHOV's gloomy reputation. His experiments with SHAKESPEARE (such as the aluminium scenery for his 1933 *Macbeth*) were not at first appreciated; but in 1936 his *King Lear* won over both audiences and critics. He settled in America in 1939.

HENRI-RENÉ LENORMAND (1882-1951)

French playwright. In dark and moving plays, Lenormand dramatized the struggle between man's conscious and subconscious feelings, showing him to be a victim of his own subliminal, destructive desires. To effect such a dramatization of the mind, he used a series of tableaux, lighting up first one part of the stage and then another, and ignoring a normal sequence of scenes. The first successful play was *Le Temps est un songe*, produced in 1919 by Georges PITOËFF, who directed a number of Lenormand's works. International recognition came with *Les Ratés* (1920), a study of the destruction wrought by uncontrollable jealousy. In a number of plays such as *Le Simoun* (1920) it is an oppressive, tropical climate that becomes the destructive force, releasing suppressed and violent emotions.

ALAN ALEXANDER MILNE (1882-1956)

English playwright, novelist and children's writer. Most of A. A. Milne's thirty plays exhibit the same kind of gentle humour as his children's classic, *Winnie-the-Pooh*. He came to the theatre by way of a mathematics degree at Cambridge and several years of arduous ill-paid work as a freelance journalist. It was only during army service in the First World War that he found the time to begin writing plays. *Wurzel-Flummery* (1917) was the first of a regular series that included *Mr Pim Passes By* (1919) and a dramatization of Kenneth Grahame's *The Wind in the Willows* (1929), which has remained a staple Christmas entertainment under the title *Toad of Toad Hall*.

SYBIL THORNDIKE (1882-1976)

English actress. "I only want to be lots of different people. Isn't that what acting's for?" In over fifty years on stage Sybil Thorndike had ample opportunity to fulfil her simple wish. She established herself as a versatile and dedicated performer.

Sybil showed an early penchant for drama when she and her brother used to act out High Mass, using cough syrup for Communion. She made her stage debut in 1904 and toured the United States, playing 112 Shakespearean roles, both male and female. In 1908 she married Lewis Casson, forming a domestic and theatrical partnership that would last for sixty years. Four years at the Old Vic, again playing female and male parts (due to a wartime shortage of men) increased her abilities. In 1920 a season of matinées, alternating EURIPIDES' *The Trojan Women* and *Medea*, and SHAW's *Candida*, won her great critical acclaim. Then she achieved similar popular success with two years of gruesome thrillers, presented in repertory by the Grand Guignol Company. Her subsequent triumphs included the lead in *St Joan* (which Shaw had written with her in mind), Lady Macbeth, and the school-mistress in EMLYN WILLIAMS's *The Corn is Green*.

Dame Sybil's lifelong concern for people revealed itself in her campaign to establish Actors' Equity, her frequent village tours and the support she constantly gave to young performers. Though crippled with arthritis in her old age she remained active virtually until her death, ignoring her rueful self-assessment: "I do everything too much."

Grand Guignol originated in Paris, but its morbid obsession with violence and the supernatural appealed to English audiences as well. This gory picture decorated the poster advertising a season of Grand Guignol plays at the Little Theatre in London. Sybil Thorndike starred there in the 1920 productions of *The Tragedy of Mr Punch* and *The Unseen*

ALEXEI NIKOLAYEVICH TOLSTOY (1882-1945)

Russian novelist and dramatist. The former count and returned emigré who understood and profoundly loved Russia, was recognized as a leading Soviet writer only in the 1930s. Patriotic interpretations of pseudo-history obsessed the period, and Alexei Nikolayevich rode the crest of that wave as an apologist. The play *Peter The Great* (from his epic novel) went through three separate political boot-lickings before it was acceptable to The Party. A rehabilitation of Ivan The Terrible was accomplished in two plays: *The Difficult Years* and *The Eagle and His Mate*, in which "the mate", Tsar Ivan's adored wife, is poisoned by the boyars in a parallel to the alleged Trotskyist poisoning of Alliluyeva, the wife of Stalin.

KARL VALENTIN (1882-1948)

German cabaret artist. Valentin performed in Munich beer halls and theatres, often dressed as a cyclist and wheeling a battered old tricycle. A tall, gangling, tragicomic figure, he had the air of a man continually at odds with the world. Although his use of the Bavarian dialect gave him a popular regional appeal, his comedy was far more universal. With his absurd sense of humour, he was constantly challenging accepted ideas and conventions. Bertolt BRECHT worked with Valentin in the 1920s, a collaboration that influenced several of his early plays.

HJALMAR BERGMAN (1883-1931)

Swedish playwright, poet and novelist. The same demon that gave Bergman his furious creative energy and inspired him to experiment continually with new literary forms, also drove him to lead a restless, nomadic life.

His early plays, much influenced by MAETERLINCK, did not reach a wide audience. The most original were *Dödens Arlekin* (1917) and *Herr Sleeman kommer* (1917), bizarre, symbolic tragedies in which man is prey to sinister and irrational forces. Then a complete change of style produced two immensely popular comedies, *Swedenhielms* (1925) and *Patrasket* (1928). The former, which revolves around the winning of a Nobel prize, is a rare example of a Swedish author mocking the national characteristics of his countrymen. Bergman died alone, in a Berlin hotel room.

ST JOHN ERVINE (1883-1971)

Irish playwright. Ervine, a Fabian Socialist like George Bernard SHAW, had an Ulsterman's contempt for nationalist drama. His plays, however, were often first performed in Dublin at the Abbey Theatre, of which he became manager in 1915, announcing that no acceptable plays were being written in Ireland, except by himself. His finest play, *John Ferguson*, was produced in 1915.

Ervine's preoccupation (already present in *Mixed Marriage*, his first play produced there in 1911) was the destructive power of religious bigotry. "Onderneath the Cathlik an the Prodesan there's the plain working man," says one of his characters. It was not a popular theme in Dublin, and the plays were not revived.

LUCIE HÖFLICH (1883-1956)

German actress. Between the ages of twenty and fifty, Lucie Höflich acted almost entirely for the Deutsches Theater in Berlin. There she restored character and vigour to classical roles which had too long been played with simpering sentimentality, the great, tragic role of Gretchen in GOETHE's *Faust* being a prime example. She developed into a fine character actress and became a mainstay of the realistic dramas of Gerhart HAUPTMANN and IBSEN. For a time she was married to the great screen actor Emil Jannings.

RAIMU (1883-1946)

French actor. Raimu was the stage-name of Jules-Auguste-César Muraire, the son of an upholsterer from Toulon. At first a music-hall singer, he was discovered by Lucien Guitry and became a celebrated comic actor after appearing in Marcel PAGNOL's *Marius* (1929). Although he became a notable success playing MOLIÈRE at the Comédie-Française, he was so sensitive about his proverbial meanness that he always refused to play in Molière's *L'Avare* (*The Miser*). As late as 1944, he made what many critics and audiences regard as the peak of his theatrical achievement. This was again Molière, and again the Comédie-Française, as the preposterous Monsieur Jourdain in *Le Bourgeois gentilhomme*.

POUL REUMERT (1883-1968)

Danish actor. Reumert was the greatest Danish actor of this century. His powerful naturalistic style and ability to portray complex states of mind and subtleties of character gave new life to many great roles. Among his most famous were Peer Gynt in IBSEN's play, MOLIÈRE's Tartuffe and Captain Edgar in STRINDBERG's *The Dance of Death*. BRECHT greatly admired his acting and offered him plays, but Reumert's disagreement with the playwright's theories on drama prevented any collaboration. In a career that lasted well into his eighties, Reumert played nearly 400 different roles.

EUGENE VAKHTANGOV (1883-1922)

Russian director and actor. E. B. Vakhtangov believed that theatre should both purify and elate the audience. As a director at the Moscow Art Theatre he tried to achieve a balance between uninspiring realist theatre and the glittering artificiality of the avant-garde.

In 1918 Vakhtangov discovered that he had cancer. Nevertheless, his greatest work was done in the last four years of his life. Among his powerful and disturbing productions were STRINDBERG's *Eric XIV* and a Yiddish performance of *The Dybbuk* by Sholem ANSKI. His final production was Carlo Gozzi's *Turandot*. By now in great pain, Vakhtangov went to rehearsals enveloped in a fur coat, his head wrapped in a wet towel. Despite his own suffering and the general gloom of Moscow, the production was a triumph of gaiety and exuberance. Its creator died three months later.

HARRY WHANSLAW (1883-1965)

English puppeteer. Whanslaw's enthusiasm for what he called "The Toy that Never Grows Old" breathed new life into English puppetry. His childlike delight in model theatres went into his textbook *Everybody's Theatre* and inspired the creation of a number of puppet workshops, first among them his own London Marionette Theatre. An artist and book illustrator by training, Whanslaw designed his sets, created his actors (both marionette and glove puppets) and directed the productions. These varied entertainments included scenes from the Bible, SHAKESPEARE and burlesque.

GUY BOLTON (1884...)

Anglo-American librettist and playwright. Bolton practised architecture before turning in 1913 to writing for the stage. Particularly prolific in musical comedy he frequently wrote in collaboration with other authors. With Fred Thompson and the Gershwins he wrote *Lady, Be Good!* (1924), while one of thirteen shows he co-authored with P. G. WODEHOUSE was Cole PORTER's *Anything Goes* (1934). A longtime associate of Jerome Kern, Bolton wrote the script for *Till the Clouds Roll By*, a sentimental film biography of the composer.

JANE COWL (1884-1950)

American actress and playwright. An actress of great versatility, Jane Cowl made her debut in 1903 under the direction of David BELASCO. She became well known in such amiable and popular comedies as *Lilac Time* (which she co-authored) and *Smilin' Through*. But her greatest triumphs came as a Shakespearean actress, beginning with Juliet in 1923. Her later career included contemporary plays by Robert SHERWOOD, Noel COWARD and GEORGE BERNARD SHAW.

RUTH DRAPER (1884-1956)

American solo actress. In 1914 England's Queen Mary "heard a little American lady recite too delightfully". Though pleased at such praise, Ruth Draper considered herself a character actress rather than reciter. Her repertoire of sixty solo dramatic sketches required her to assume or suggest over three hundred personalities in

Sybil Thorndike and Arthur Wontner starring in *Village Wooing* by George Bernard Shaw

Ruth Draper (*above*) plays an English artist in her own sketch *In a Church in Italy*

"The Nigger Minstrel of Eastbourne" (*below*) was a seaside black-face comic

settings from London society to the New England aristocracy, and in moods from hilarity to pathos. As an admirer observed, "She seemed to have lived countless lives and remembered them all."

The shy, delicate daughter of wealthy parents, Ruth Draper would spend whole afternoons acting out solitary plays based on the idiosyncrasies of visiting tradesmen. Her skills were soon recognized. Assisted by her parents' wide range of acquaintances, she appeared (at first privately) in Europe and America, often before heads of state and royalty. She did not make an official theatre debut until 1920 in London, but it established her for the general public as a unique performer.

Working on a bare stage with a minimum of props, Ruth Draper achieved her effects by a mastery of voice, gesture and movement. She composed all her own sketches. Typical of them is *In a Church in Italy*, which depicts English and German tourists, a local girl in love and an anguished peasant woman seeking relief in prayer. She maintained that her gift was to "see the world always through the eyes of a child". But a London critic said of her performance, "At the bottom of it all lies her sympathy. She can jest because she understands."

ALEKSANDRA EXTER (1884-1949)

Russian stage designer. A talented painter, Exter brought to the theatre her technical experiments with colour, cubist philosophy and the radical French and German aestheticism of the "Knave of Diamonds", an intellectual club she helped to found in 1910.

Theatre sets, she felt, should intensify or cool emotion, not merely illustrate locale. Colour should be made to sing and move; she spoke of "the music of painting" and "the rhythm of form". A major influence on many designers, Exter created what she called "dynamic costume" – make-up applied directly to the body to emphasize musculature or to mask the face. Her costumes themselves became moving, painted sculptures made up of varying weaves and textures. The basic geometric shapes of cubism were also to affect her sets for TAIROV, whose principal collaborator she became at The Kamerny Theatre in Moscow in 1916.

After the Revolution Exter settled in France, where her many designs, though exhibited in maquette form, were seldom realized.

LION FEUCHTWANGER (1884-1958)

German playwright and novelist. Internationally, Feuchtwanger is best known for his novel *Jud Süss*. His own life-story also reflects the unsettled fortunes of the Jews of the Diaspora. After studying for a literary doctorate at Munich and Berlin, he lived with his wife in Provence, Calabria and Sicily, earning little from his writing. The outbreak of war found him in Tunis, where he was briefly interned as an alien. His wife contrived to smuggle him back to Germany, and after serving in the army he returned to Munich, where his plays were invariably disrupted by the Left or banned by the authorities. He tried anew in Berlin, but became a natural target for the burgeoning Nazi party. In 1933 news reached party ears of criticisms made of Hitler by Feuchtwanger in the United States. On his return to Europe he found his villa vandalized, his pets killed and his car and a manuscript missing. There followed the inevitable period as a refugee in Switzerland, France and finally America.

A collaborator with Bertolt BRECHT, Feuchtwanger is remembered for his concern with decent human values and social issues. This is evident not only in his expressionist and realist plays but also in his realizations of ancient dramas such as AESCHYLUS' *The Persians* and the Indian legend *Vasantasena*. Later playwrights such as DÜRRENMATT and ARTHUR MILLER found inspiration in the work of Feuchtwanger.

WALTER HUSTON (1884-1950)

Canadian-born American actor. In 1905 Walter Huston was fired from a touring company for forgetting most of his only line in a new play. After working for a power company in the American West, he went into vaudeville in 1909, doing song-and-dance numbers with his wife. At last, in 1924, he returned to legitimate acting with a powerful performance in Eugene O'NEILL's *Desire under the Elms*. "An incurable old ham", as he called himself, Huston excelled in character roles both on stage and in films, although he continued to exercise his talent for tragedy, notably in a 1936 production of *Othello*. He made one of his last appearances in a play directed by his son, the film director John Huston.

WERNER KRAUSS (1884-1959)

German actor. Krauss was one of the foremost European actors of the century. The mark of his greatness lay, as is so often the case, in his skill at expressing meaning through gesture and movement. He is internationally famous for his frightening performance in the silent film *Das Kabinett des Dr Caligari* (1919), but his stage interpretations of Macbeth, Julius Caesar and King Lear were unrivalled in Germany. He also gave distinguished service to the expressionist theatre in such productions as Max REINHARDT's *The Miracle*.

During the Second World War, Krauss acted the title role in the distorted Nazi version of Lion FEUCHTWANGER's *Jud Süss* with such loathsome efficiency that he was later prosecuted by an Allied tribunal. The judges were unimpressed by his defence that he was interested only in the dramatic possibilities of the role, although they did congratulate him on his court-room histrionics.

He finally reasserted himself as an actor, however, and in his seventies played Lear once again in a performance of overwhelming power and sadness.

BARRY LUPINO (1884-1962)

English pantomimist. The Lupino dynasty of actors, dancers, acrobats and clowns was founded by Giorgio Luppino, an Italian political exile and puppeteer, who had come to England in the early seventeenth century. In true family tradition, Barry Lupino first appeared on the stage at the age of two months. Touring the world and writing over fifty pantomimes himself, he became the king of pantomime dames.

Barry's brother, Stanley (1894–1942), who was principally a comic revue actor, wrote an account of the clan's recent history, from their father George (1853–1932) (who could perform 210 pirouettes on a handkerchief) and uncle Arthur (1864–1908) (who was Nana the dog in James BARRIE's *Peter Pan*) to the Hollywood career of Stanley's daughter, Ida (1918 . . .). In the twenties and thirties, it was Lupino Lane (1892–1959), a nephew of Barry and Stanley, who brought further glory to the family name in musical comedies, invariably playing the "shy, rather worried little man". In one such role he helped to launch London's pre-war dance-craze, the Lambeth Walk.

GEORGES PITOËFF (1884-1939)

Russian actor and director. Pitoëff came to Paris in 1922 intending to "renew" the theatre. Although he regretfully concluded that the public would first have to be renewed, he did at least surprise his audiences by using perfumes on stage and distributing flowers.

Pitoëff was responsible for producing many plays by foreign playwrights, including SHAW and PIRANDELLO. As an actor he was a brilliant Hamlet, but he could never rid himself of his strong accent. Once asked "Who is concerned about the French language?" he replied "Me, I massacre it." His wife Ludmilla (1895–1951) was a distinguished actress who mastered French sufficiently to triumph in such roles as Shaw's Joan of Arc.

GASTON BATY (1885-1952)

French director, designer and playwright. Baty believed in a "total theatre". "Painting, sculpture, the dance, prose, verse, song, music, these are the seven chords stretched side by side on the lyre of drama," he said. Opposed to the dominance of language in theatre, he made a famous attack on *Sire Le Mot* (His Majesty, the Word). The repertoire of his company, La Chimère, ranged from RACINE and SHAKESPEARE to BRECHT, but Baty played down the role of the actor in his productions; in fact he devoted the last years of his life to working with puppets.

FERNAND CROMMELYNCK (1885-1970)

Belgian playwright. An actor in his youth, Crommelynck was able to devote himself entirely to writing when his "lyric-farce" *Le Cocu magnifique* brought him international fame in the 1920s. This play, his only work to be popular in English, is the grotesque and tragic study of a man determined to prove his loving wife unfaithful. Other plays, all written in French and dating from between the wars, show equally obsessive tendencies. *Tripes d'or* (1925) concerns a paranoid miser who powders his gold, eats it and dies of constipation.

CHARLES DULLIN (1885-1949)

French actor and director. Dullin's conviction that drama should be "a complete spectacle" led him to draw on a wide variety of sources while director of Le Théâtre de l'Atelier (1922–41). Music hall, the Commedia dell' Arte, mime, dance and even the drama of Japan found their way into experimental performances of both contemporary drama and the classics. One of the most famous of his later productions was the masked wartime première of SARTRE's *Les Mouches*.

A gifted actor himself, Dullin was better known for his remarkable pupils. Among them was a trio of the century's greatest mimes: Étienne DECROUX, Jean-Louis BARRAULT and MARCEL MARCEAU.

JÜRGEN FEHLING (1885-1968)

German director. Fehling was among the great Berlin directors in the 1930s. He concentrated initially on satire and comedy, which he directed with deftness and sensitivity. Later his productions became more violent and unsettling, performed on stark sets and steeply raked stages. He was particularly revered for his treatment of SHAKESPEARE (his 1937 *Richard III* was a dark and chilling production), Heinrich von KLEIST and Ernst Barlach.

WILL FYFFE (1885-1947)

Scottish music hall comedian. The man who, on so many Saturday nights, sang "I belong to Glasgow" came in fact from Dundee, where his stage-struck father ran a tiny theatrical company. His apprenticeship in straight drama stood him in good stead in music hall, for his comic songs were only incidental interludes between his celebrated character sketches. When Fyffe impersonated the Ship's Engineer, so brilliant was his acting that audiences claimed they could smell the engine-room. Other favourite pieces included a Poacher-turned-Gamekeeper so realistic that a man once stopped the show by crying out "That's me!"

SACHA GUITRY (1885-1957)

French playwright and actor. Sacha was the son of Lucien Guitry (1860–1925), one of the most popular actors of his day. Lucien had appeared in DUMAS *fils' La Dame aux camélias* (1878) at the Gymnase, but it was after Sarah BERNHARDT asked him to join her company in 1893 that he achieved his greatest successes.

Sacha's career as an actor got off to an unfortunate start. When the young man appeared without his wig and twenty minutes late for a performance, the father and son quarrelled and did not speak to each other for thirteen years. Sacha's career suffered further when he was sacked after falling over the set of another play.

As a playwright Sacha was more successful. *Nono* (1905) was an early success in a dramatic career that included 130 plays, varying from sentimental comedies to dramatic biographies, revues and operettas. In spite of the family estrangement, Sacha's early works were written with his father in mind and, after a reconciliation, Lucien appeared in a number of his son's plays, notably *Pasteur* (1919). Sacha himself acted with great success in many of his works, indulging his brilliant abilities at improvisation.

All of Sacha Guitry's five wives were actresses. The most famous of these was Yvonne Printemps, who played the composer in her husband's *Mozart* (1925).

RING LARDNER (1885-1933)

American short-story writer, journalist and playwright. Ring Lardner always knew his stories had two kinds of reader. One group revelled in their "top layer of wild nonsense" – ingenious plots, laughable characters and hilarious use of everyday speech. The other relished Lardner's cynicism – his deep contempt for everything he described. Both would have enjoyed his Broadway hit *June Moon* (1929), which he concocted together with the irrepressible George S. KAUFMAN. Witty and cleverly constructed, it satirized the dullness and pettiness of Tin Pan Alley.

Mainly for his own amusement, Lardner also wrote several dramatic sketches featuring bizarre word-play and surrealist association. Their titles are indicative: *Clemo Uti* (The Water Lilies), *The Tridget of Griva*, *I Gaspiri* (The Upholsterers) and *Cora, or Fun at a Spa*. Their sardonic absurdity shows another side of this ex-baseball writer whom a critic called "the greatest and sincerest pessimist America has produced".

FRANÇOIS MAURIAC (1885-1970)

French novelist and playwright. In 1937, despairing of his achievements as a novelist, Mauriac declared "I want to write plays" and went to a performance of *Don Giovanni*: "There is no more wonderful stimulant than Mozart for a man who wants to launch into dramatic art," he explained. His first play, *Asmodée* (1937), was produced at the Comédie-Française and directed by Jacques COPEAU, but Mauriac complained, "It is just a novel of mine put into dialogue." His next play, *Les Mal-Aimés* (1945), drew large audiences, although its stuffy, bourgeois setting annoyed contemporary critics. *Le*

The bizarre plays of **Witkiewicz** kept audiences away in their millions

Al Jolson's Negro impersonations (*above*) made it easier for white audiences to revel in the extravagant pleading of songs such as "Swanee" and "Sonny Boy"

The great expressionist painter **Kokoschka** (*below*) wrote several nerve-jarring plays in his youth. The work of his old age included gorgeous theatre sets

Passage du Malin (1947) and *Le Feu sur la terre* (1950), both studies of the physical or spiritual possessiveness of love, were not successful and Mauriac returned to novel-writing (which he thought he had abandoned forever) and to political journalism for such papers as *Le Figaro*. He was awarded the Nobel prize for Literature in 1952.

JULES ROMAINS (1885-1972)

French novelist, playwright and poet. Walking one evening in Paris, Romains suddenly became aware that the street had a collective being and conscience. This was the inspiration of *Unanimisme*, the philosophy that became a concept vital to his writing. In Romains' plays *L'Armée dans la ville* (1911) and *Cromedeyre-le-vieil* (1920) groups such as a town or an army of occupation assume a personality of their own. *Unanimisme* is important even in the brilliant comedies for which Romains is most famous. These include farces featuring M Le Trouhadec, a professor of geography, and *Knock, ou le Triomphe de la médecine* (1923), in which a fanatical and fraudulent doctor works a whole town into a frenzy of hypochondria.

ALEKSANDR TAIROV (1885-1950)

Russian director. Tairov was a great and influential craftsman of the stage. He founded the Kamerny Theatre in 1914, and there experimented with his own theories of drama. His actors had also to be jugglers, dancers and acrobats. Tairov no longer used flat, picture-like sets; instead there were three-dimensional, architectural designs within which the actors moved on different levels, using rhythmic body movement as well as words. The first important production of this kind was Innokenty Annesky's *Famira Kifared* (1917). The set was an elaborately lit three-dimensional cubist design with cone-cypresses and cube-rocks. Remarkably, Tairov managed to avoid becoming involved in politics and maintained his theatre's independence for some time. In the 1930s, however, he was made answerable to an official committee. He continued to work at the Kamerny until it closed, one year before his death.

STANISLAW IGNACY WITKIEWICZ (1885-1939)

Polish playwright, painter, philosopher and novelist. Witkiewicz called his profoundly pessimistic philosophy "Catastrophism". The Russian Revolution (during which he fought on both sides) first alerted him to the precariousness of European civilization, and the Second World War was just the catastrophe he had foretold. Shortly after the Russian invasion of Poland he committed suicide.

As a young man his ambitions had centred chiefly on painting; he had once accompanied his anthropologist cousin on an expedition to India and Ceylon, as official artist and photographer. But while his art remained expressionist in style and found an appreciative audience, his surreal plays were thirty years ahead of their time. The convoluted form of works like *The Water Hen* (1922) suggest the world of Samuel BECKETT. Other plays, like *The Metaphysics of the Two-headed Calf* (1928) and *The Shoemakers* (1934) bear little resemblance to any works of his contemporaries, although all his thirty-odd pieces can be said to foreshadow IONESCO's Theatre of the Absurd.

Witkiewicz's insistence on form rather than plot, the liberties he took with language, and his constant references to scientific theories, won him an ever-growing reputation as a lunatic. Taking this to heart, he enthusiastically dedicated *The Madman and the Nun* (1925) to all the lunatics in the world.

JOHN MURRAY ANDERSON (1886-1954)

American director and producer. In 1919 Anderson inaugurated *The Greenwich Village Follies*. He owed the "Follies" title to ZIEGFELD, but the show's success came from his own extraordinary good taste. Where most revues relied on spectacular gaudiness, Anderson used simplicity, subtlety and imagination. His colour effects were unprecedented – "even burlap became exotic when he sprayed it with paint". To his revues, Anderson contributed song lyrics and sketches. He left the *Follies* in 1924 to stage musicals, circuses and even aquacades. These later productions were as witty and tasteful as his first, especially two *Almanac* revues, the second of which closed his career in 1953.

AL JOLSON (1886-1950)

American singer and actor. Jolson's overwhelming voice, manic energy and shameless sentiment made him a legendary black-face entertainer. Son of a rabbi, he came to America from Russia at the age of seven and was immediately attracted to the popular culture of the New World, running away from home to sing in saloons or to follow the circus. After an anonymous stage debut in a crowd scene in 1899, he played in vaudeville and with minstrel troupes. A star's illness provided his big chance in 1909, and his first solo "mammy song" was an instant hit. For fourteen years beginning in 1911 he sparked the musicals produced by the Shubert brothers at New York's Winter Garden Theatre. His stage character was the black-face "Gus", but, whatever the plot, Jolson was always Jolson. On one occasion he bounded out on stage in mid-act and exclaimed, "I'll tell you how the story comes out: the fellow gets the girl. Now shall we go on with it or do you want to hear me sing?"

After 1925, radio and movies largely replaced Jolson's stage work. His eyeball rolling, tear-jerking, show-stopping charisma made him a natural choice to star in *The Jazz Singer*, the first talking picture.

OSKAR KOKOSCHKA (1886-1980)

Austrian painter and playwright. One of the purest exponents of the ideals of expressionism in painting, the young Kokoschka extended his theories to the theatre in *Mörder, Hoffnung der Frauen* (set to music by Paul Hindemith), a terrifying picture of the violence of men to women. The subsequent scandal cost him his job as a teacher in Vienna, but he found consolation and fresh artistic inspiration in Alma Mahler, the voracious widow of the composer Gustav Mahler. When their three-year affair began to echo the screams and shouts of his own drama, Kokoschka escaped to serve in the army.

Kokoschka's horror at the destructiveness of the war, during which he was seriously wounded, inspired his most fruitful period of dramatic writing, but after *Orpheus und Eurydike* and *Der brennende Dornbusch* (1919) his interest in the theatre waned. In his old age, when finally recognized as one of the masters of colour and movement in modern painting, Kokoschka designed spectacular sets for the Vienna Opera House and Burgtheater.

ETTORE PETROLINI (1886-1936)

Italian actor and playwright. Petrolini was one of the most influential and inspiring men in the Italian theatre between the wars. From 1903 he worked for several years in third-rate theatres and "cafe-concerts". In the noise and smoke of those cafes, fighting for the attention of hostile audiences, his aggressive style and colourful repertoire took shape. A successful tour of Uruguay in 1907 encouraged Italians to pay him more attention, and from then on his fame grew. Comedies were written for him and he also wrote his own, among them *Nerone* (1918), *Gastone* (1924) and *Chicchignola* (1931).

For Petrolini, nothing was sacred. His audiences adored yet hated him, for he tore away at the foundations of their world. One minute he was a shambling, mincing idiot, the next, his nutcracker face became more sinister as he launched into bitter jokes and vicious satire. But Petrolini also delighted Italians with his gift for pure nonsense. The idiocy of such sketches as *I Salamini*, about a string of sausages, was irresistible. In his fascination with the absurd, Petrolini set new and vital trends; he was a generation ahead of his time. Such was his fame throughout Europe that he was even allowed to play his own version of MOLIÈRE's *Le Médecin malgré lui* at the Comédie-Française.

BEN TRAVERS (1886...)

English playwright. To Londoners in the 1920s the word "farce" meant the Aldwych Theatre and Ben Travers. It was Travers who every year for nine years provided the Aldwych Company with a ludicrous but beautifully constructed piece of sustained panic. He admitted that the formula for farce was simple: "Act two – the sympathetic and guileless hero is landed into the thick of some grievous dilemma or adversity. Act one – he gets into it. Act three – he gets out of it." His first three Aldwych farces were his most successful: *A Cuckoo in the Nest* (1925), *Rookery Nook* (1926) and *Thark* (1927). (*Rookery Nook* has since been revived by almost every provincial repertory and amateur company in Britain.) The series ended with *A Bit of a Test* (1933), a courageous but ill-fated attempt to combine the author's passion for cricket with his talent for comic situations.

Travers's own favourite of his farces was a later work, *Banana Ridge* (1938). The author himself appeared in it, heavily disguised as a Malay servant and speaking genuine Malay. More recently, at the age of ninety and after years of apparent retirement, he proved that his formula still held good with *The Bed Before Yesterday* (1976).

ED WYNN (1886-1966)

American comedian. Wynn, "the perfect fool", burst upon New York at the age of sixteen in a comedy act with Jack Lewis. Introduced at a single-performance benefit show, it ran for two years. He remained to become one of vaudeville's most familiar and popular stars, chatting, interrupting himself, lisping and giggling, always wearing an old hat, baggy, ill-matched clothes and a big pair of shoes that accumulated $3,000 worth of repairs over thirty-seven years.

He finally reached Broadway in *The Ziegfeld Follies of 1914*. In the 1915 *Follies* he shared an act with W. C. FIELDS, who became so angry at Wynn stealing the laughs that he stunned him with a billiard cue. Wynn wrote three Broadway shows: *Ed Wynn's Carnival* (1920), *The Perfect Fool* (1921) and *The Grab Bag* (1924), then went on to enjoy a successful Hollywood career. He also co-authored *Simple Simon* with Guy BOLTON and, as the owner of many shows in which he starred, was President of the Ed Wynn Production Company.

GEORGE ABBOTT (1887...)

American playwright, director, producer and actor. George Abbott came to New York as an actor in 1913, but his real interest lay in what he called "the practical matter of how to make a show". He became known in the 1920s as writer, director and "doctor" of other people's plays. Such shows as *Boy Meets Girl* (1935) and *Pal Joey* (1940) were, in Abbott's hands, among the outstanding productions of their generation. Particular triumphs in the 1930s were *Twentieth Century* (1932), which he directed and co-produced, and *Three Men on a Horse* (1935), which he directed and co-authored. In 1937 he turned a failed comedy, *Room Service*, into one of the season's great successes. He collaborated on a string of long-running musicals in the forties and fifties, most notably *Where's Charley?* (1948), *The Pajama Game* (1954) and *Damn Yankees* (1955). Three of the biggest hits of 1962 were George Abbott productions, earning him citation for "most effective individual contribution to the theatre".

LYNN FONTANNE (1887...)

English-born American actress. Lynn Fontanne's marriage to Alfred LUNT in 1922 enchanted theatregoers and founded a celebrated acting partnership. The bride had made her debut in 1905 with Ellen TERRY, then came to New York with Laurette Taylor. Her regal beauty and commanding presence captivated audiences and critics – as well as her future husband, who fell down a short flight of stairs when they were introduced. In 1921 the title part in George S. KAUFMAN and Marc CONNELLY's *Dulcy* established her as a star, but she made all her subsequent performances as half of "Lunt-Fontanne". The team became famous for subtle, stylish playing, particularly in the comedies of GEORGE BERNARD SHAW, Noel COWARD and Robert E. SHERWOOD. Though a critic once accused her of "listening lovingly to the sound of her own voice", for forty years Lynn Fontanne epitomized a refinement rare on the modern stage.

GERTIE GITANA (1887-1957)

English music-hall singer. Billed as the "Dainty Comedienne" in 1900, Gertie Gitana became the pure and wholesome idol of the music halls, delivering tender songs with convincing sincerity. A typical speciality, "Never Mind", assured her listeners that "there's sunshine after rain and gladness follows pain". She retired in 1938, but in 1947 made a comeback as part of the *Thanks for the Memory* package of former music-hall headliners, appearing with them in the 1948 Royal Variety Performance. Even today a trace of her winsome sentimentality survives in "Nellie Dean", a Gitana favourite which still elicits the tribute of a drunkard's tear.

REINHARD GOERING (1887-1936)

German playwright. Although he spent much of the First World War in a sanatorium with tuberculosis, Goering wrote *Seeschlacht* (1918), a highly topical nautical drama set in the gun-turret of a cruiser at the Battle of Jutland. As the sailors discuss mutiny and duty, they realize they are merely the insignificant agents of some monstrous fate. In *Die Südpolexpedition des Kapitäns Scott* (1930) he found an even more extreme situation to symbolize mankind's struggle against adverse destiny, a struggle that Goering himself eventually gave up by taking his own life.

LOUIS JOUVET (1887-1951)

French actor and producer. Jouvet was a central figure in the French theatre between the wars. He produced and acted in the plays of modern writers such as Jules ROMAINS (notably his *Knock* of 1923), Jean COCTEAU and especially Jean GIRAUDOUX, but was equally well known for his productions of MOLIÈRE. Disliking the design of modern theatres, he often worked on Elizabethan or medieval-style stages.

Although Jouvet began his career by bringing theatre to the masses, he spent most of his life in films, and delighting smart Parisian audiences with his companies at the Comédie des Champs-Elysées and the Théâtre de l'Athénée. A disciple of the great teachers COPEAU and STANISLAVSKY, he turned to a type of acting nearer the theatre of the absurd for his last production, an adaptation of GRAHAM GREENE's novel *The Power and the Glory*. He undertook to appear in the play as "expiation" for having directed Jean-Paul SARTRE's *Le Diable et le bon Dieu*. Sartre had promised him that the character Goetz would turn to Good in the second act. Jouvet had only reluctantly accepted that play after assurances from the Church that there was an after-life. He died while rehearsing his part in Greene's drama – the priest.

GEORGE KELLY (1887-1974)

American playwright, director and actor. Kelly acquired his skill at composing well-made plays in his years as a vaudeville actor. His first hit, *The Show-off* (1924), was based on a comic sketch he had written for himself. The next year, *Craig's Wife* won him a Pulitzer Prize for its penetrating analysis of a destructive woman. Thereafter Kelly indulged his interest in human (generally female) behaviour, but *Daisy Mayme* (1926), *Behold the Bridegroom* (1927) and *Maggie the Magnificent* (1929) were received with more respect than enthusiasm. *Philip Goes Forth* (1931), an ironic portrait of corruption by success, fared no better. Kelly proclaimed himself "enormously uninterested" in the theatre until 1936, when he attempted a comeback with *Reflected Glory*. But critics again complained of a lack of warmth (except when Tallulah BANKHEAD was on stage). Ten years later he tried again with *The Deep Mrs Sykes* (1945) and *The Fatal Weakness* (1946), but public reaction was the same. Kelly retired to Hollywood, where the family name was given new lustre by the film stardom and the marriage of his niece, Grace.

PIER MARIA ROSSO DI SAN SECONDO (1887-1956)

Italian playwright. A native of Sicily, Rosso spent much of his life in northern Europe, where he wrote many of his works, including a major study of Luigi PIRANDELLO. His popular success rests largely upon the 1918 play *Marionette, che passione!* in which three characters who meet in a restaurant are seen to be the powerless and despairing toys of fate. In other plays, including *La bella addormentata* (1919) and *Il ratto di Proserpina* (1954), he ironically invested modern life with a mythic quality and continued to explore the theme of human impotence. Rosso's plays have been infrequently staged in England and the United States.

LEON SCHILLER (1887-1954)

Polish director. Born in Cracow, Schiller moved to Paris in his early twenties. There he met the English designer Gordon CRAIG, whose revolutionary new concept of "total" theatre came as a revelation to him. Schiller's subsequent originality as a director arises equally, however, from the fact that he did not immediately enter the world of serious theatre but spent a rather odd interlude first as a cabaret singer and journalist in Warsaw, then as a music student in Vienna.

On his return to Poland he quickly made a mark as a

theatre director. His production of liturgical and romantic Polish dramas created an enormous impression, but his progressive views led to a spell of imprisonment and later to a brief internment in Auschwitz.

Schiller's return to the "forgotten tradition of nativity and mystery plays" (as one compatriot remarks) tended to free his productions from the tyrannical dominance of "literature". For him, as for Bertolt BRECHT and others, the theatre and its audience were more important than the playwright and his text.

MAXWELL ANDERSON (1888-1959)

American playwright. In styles ranging from sub-SHAKESPEARE to situation comedy, Anderson challenged American audiences with a succession of tragedies, comedies, fantasies and histories – more than thirty in as many years of writing for the stage. Some were hits, but a number of them left the public puzzled and disappointed. There was the feeling that here was a man too versatile and prolific for his own good.

Anderson was unknown as a playwright until 1923, when the production of his verse drama *White Desert* won him critical acclaim. The following year, in collaboration with a journalist colleague, he found the perfect formula for Broadway success with *What Price Glory?* A play about the First World War, neatly combining sex, violence, romance and realism, it told the story of two American marines and a whore in wartime France. Critics and audiences found it strong, compelling stuff.

Anderson never wrote another play quite like it. He was an ambitious and individualistic playwright whose most valuable contribution to the American theatre was his largely fruitless attempt to establish verse as a popular modern dramatic medium. *Elizabeth the Queen* (1930) and *Mary of Scotland* (1933), both poetic histories, had modern counterparts in *Gods of Lightning* (1928), a poetic treatment of the sordid Sacco-Vanzetti political executions, and *Winterset* (1935), its masterly sequel. With *Both Your Houses* (1933), a political satire, he won the Pulitzer Prize, and wearing still another hat he wrote the musical comedy *Knickerbocker Holiday* (1938) to music by the exiled German composer Kurt Weill.

It was on film that Anderson reached his biggest audience. *Key Largo* and *Anne of the Thousand Days* are familiar to millions who have never heard of the author.

IRVING BERLIN (1888...)

American composer and lyricist. When he was only eight years old, Israel Baline teamed up with a singing beggar called Blind Sol in the streets of New York's Bowery. By his twenty-first birthday he was a full-time song writer and two years later a national celebrity as the writer of "Alexander's Ragtime Band". The result was that America's most famous popular composer had no

Irving Berlin sang with these rather dubious beauties in the wartime hit, *This Is the Army* (1942): he was also its author

The beautiful **Gladys Cooper** (*above*) at twenty-one: she was later made a Dame of the British Empire. Soigné Frenchman **Maurice Chevalier** (*right*) in a precocious pose

Poet and intellectual sage, **T. S. Eliot** (*below*) makes some suggestions at a rehearsal in 1951 of his play about the martyrdom of Thomas Becket, *Murder in the Cathedral*

time for schooling and could neither read nor write music.

The movies claimed him early and rewarded him richly ("Cheek to Cheek" alone earned him $250,000), but he continued to write music and lyrics for Broadway shows until the early 1960s. Throughout this long career he has shown an uncanny ability to assess the mood of the public with songs such as "Oh, How I Hate to Get Up in the Morning" from *Yip, Yip Yaphank* (1918), "Easter Parade" from *As Thousands Cheer* (1933) and "Fools Fall in Love" from *Louisiana Purchase* (1940). Two of his musicals, *Annie Get Your Gun* (1946) and *Call Me Madam* (1950), were long-running Broadway hits.

No one seems to begrudge Berlin his success. "Irving Berlin has no *place* in American music; he *is* American music," wrote Jerome Kern. The man who can only play the black notes on a piano may have earned the title George Gershwin gave him: "The American Franz Schubert."

JAMES BRIDIE (1888-1951)

Scottish playwright. To his medical colleagues, Bridie was Dr Osborne Henry Mavor, consultant at a Glasgow hospital. Not until 1928 (and then under the name of Mary Henderson) did he see his first play produced. The success of *The Sunlight Sonata* was the beginning of a fertile career as a dramatist. Such plays as *The Anatomist* (1930), *Tobias and the Angel* (1930), *A Sleeping Clergyman* (1933) and *Daphne Laureola* (1949), have been compared to the work of SHAW, an admirer and fellow moralist. Witty and inventive, many of these plays show a distinctive religious preoccupation. The Devil frequently makes an appearance.

MAURICE CHEVALIER (1888-1972)

French singer and actor. Urbane, mischievous and straw-hatted, his lower lip protruding (as if perpetually poised for an "*ooh-là-là*") Chevalier was everyone's vision of the debonair Parisian. Seductive when young and suggestive when old, but never remotely dangerous or dirty, he charmed audiences all his life with a beguiling repertoire of song, dance, mimicry and anecdote.

From the age of twelve Chevalier was singing in Paris cafés and by 1910 had reached the Folies-Bergère, partnering (both on stage and off) the cabaret star MISTINGUETT. Wounded and imprisoned during the First World War he returned to entertainment with *Hullo, America* in London, although it was not until ten years later in 1929 that he actually said hello to America at ZIEGFELD's theatre in New York. In the years that followed, his international reputation was established in a series of Hollywood films, including several saccharine partnerships with Jeanette MacDonald. His French following diminished somewhat with the Second World War because of his continued performances under the German occupation, but by then his international fame as the archetypal Frenchman was irreversibly established. "Paris has two monuments," said playwright Jean COCTEAU, "the Eiffel Tower and Maurice Chevalier."

BOBBY CLARK (1888-1960)

American comedian. Clark made his first New York appearance as a clown in the Ringling Brothers Circus. His long and successful partnership with Paul McCullough began in 1905. In 1912 they took their comedy act into vaudeville, followed in 1917 by five years on the burlesque circuit. Throughout these years they retained a vulgar, slap-stick humour, Clark's painted-on spectacles adding to the absurdity of the routine.

Clark and McCullough appeared in the first of many successful musical comedies, *The Ramblers*, in 1926. Ten years later McCullough committed suicide. Deeply upset, Clark was unsure of continuing alone, but his appearance in the 1936 *Ziegfeld Follies* erased all doubts. He remained one of the pillars of Broadway comedy.

GLADYS COOPER (1888-1971)

English actress. From her earliest appearances on the Edwardian stage to her elegant portrayal of old Mrs Higgins in the 1964 film of *My Fair Lady*, Gladys Cooper was an actress distinguished for combining intelligence and ability with radiant beauty. She began her stage career as a chorus girl, and achieved general recognition in SHAW's *Man and Superman* in 1911. Although she continued to win praise for comedy, few critics thought her capable of a convincing dramatic performance until 1922, when she astonished London with her moving portrayal of Paula in a revival of Arthur Wing PINERO's *The Second Mrs Tanqueray*.

After a 1934 New York debut, Gladys Cooper reached a whole new audience in films such as *The Song of Bernadette*, while maintaining close ties with the living theatre, most notably in Enid Bagnold's *The Chalk Garden*. Only ill health forced her to retire from the stage.

CLEMENCE DANE (c 1888-1965)

English novelist and playwright. Winifred Ashton took her pen-name from the London church of St Clement Dane's. She had already been a teacher, portrait painter, actress and novelist when *A Bill of Divorcement* (1921) displayed her gifts as a playwright. She produced over thirty plays, with historical subjects a special interest. *Will Shakespeare* (1921) dramatized the playwright's life, *Wild December* (1932) the Brontës, and *Till Time Shall End* (1958), Queen Elizabeth I.

THOMAS STEARNS ELIOT (1888-1965)

American-born poet, critic and playwright. Against all odds, Eliot's career as a popular playwright was a success; not a whimper, but a resounding bang (to use his own imagery). The man who had immortalized despair in his poems proved himself a first-rate entertainer.

Born in St Louis and educated at Harvard, Eliot went to Europe for further studies and from the outbreak of the First World War lived mostly in England. His early writings were poetry and criticism. Only in 1935, seven years after his adoption of English nationality and the Anglican faith, did he publish his first complete play. An austere verse treatment of Thomas à Becket's death, *Murder in the Cathedral* was a surprising success, but Eliot did not continue in this style. *The Family Reunion* (1939) and *The Cocktail Party* (1949) were set in contemporary middle-class England and, although written in verse, had none of the deliberate poetical aura of his first play. *The Cocktail Party*, produced shortly after Eliot had received the 1948 Nobel prize, was by far his most successful stage work, running for a year on Broadway.

Audiences were flattered in finding themselves able to understand and even enjoy the work of a great and "difficult" poet. The familiar clutter of modern life (psychiatrists, neuroses, loveless affairs, alcohol and mundane jokes) combined with ostensibly undemanding verse to convince the public that philosophy was fun.

Behind the smiling mask, Eliot was as sober as ever, his commitment to self-knowledge and spiritual fulfilment as genuine in his box-office hits as in his profoundest poetry. As if a serious message were not enough, the formal Eliot based his plays on classical models, finding impeccable pedigrees for several of them among the drama of ancient Greece. Two later verse plays, *The Confidential Clerk* (1953) and *The Elder Statesman* (1958), did not achieve the same popularity, but by then their author had made his point and retired.

EDITH EVANS (1888-1976)

English actress. "Her face was like a city in illumination," said the critic James Agate after having seen Edith Evans perform. The remarkable vitality and inner beauty to which he referred continued to illuminate the English stage for more than sixty years.

Edith Evans was well into her twenties before she left her job as a milliner for a career on the stage. Despite early critical praise and the support of Ellen TERRY, she failed to win popular success until 1924, when she appeared as Millamant in CONGREVE's *The Way of the World*. ("The finest comedy performance I have ever seen on the stage," wrote novelist Arnold Bennett.) Her role as one of England's greatest actresses was thereafter never questioned.

Throughout her career Edith Evans excelled in comic and Shakespearean roles, especially as the Nurse in *Romeo and Juliet* (although the languorous beauty of Cleopatra escaped her). As Mrs Malaprop in SHERIDAN's *The Rivals* and Lady Fidget in WYCHERLEY's *The Country Wife* she was unchallenged, while in plays by her contemporaries SHAW and Christopher FRY she proved herself equal to the challenge of twentieth-century drama. But her most popular characterization will remain WILDE's Lady Bracknell, a role she immortalized with her aghast exclamation: "A handbag?"

CURT GOETZ (1888-1960)

German dramatist and actor. It is not without justification that Goetz is known as the German Noel COWARD. Not only did he write roles for himself with a meticulous comic nuance, but he acted them to perfection. He made his name first as an actor before the First World War and then as the author and star of two cycles of grotesque comedies: *Nachtbeleuchtung* and *Menagerie* (1920).

He was especially distinguished in the plays of GEORGE BERNARD SHAW and became a celebrated film actor, playing in Pabst's renowned *Die Büchse der Pandora* (1928).

FRANTIŠEK LANGER (1888-1965)

Czech playwright and novelist. For much of his life Langer combined the careers of army doctor and playwright. After active service during the First World War he became one of Czechoslovakia's leading literary figures, alternating social satires such as *The Camel Through the Needle's Eye* and *Grand Hotel Nevada* (1927) with realistic tragedies, including *The Outskirts* (1925). In England during the Second World War, he was chief medical officer of the Czech army in exile. In 1947, having returned to his homeland, he was honoured by the title of "National Artist".

EUGENE O'NEILL (1888-1953)

American playwright. O'Neill was born into the theatre. As a boy he accompanied his actor-father James on endless national tours of a production of *The Count of Monte Cristo* (O'Neill Senior played Edmond Dantès more than 6000 times, crippling his status as one of the great American tragedians). This nomadic childhood led to several unsettled years, including one at Princeton University, from where he was suspended in 1907 for what he accurately described as "hell-raising". There followed a secret and short-lived marriage, work as a merchant seaman, profitless gold prospecting in Honduras, stints as an actor and stage manager with his father, and frequent spells of drunkenness and unemployment. Ill health compelled him to slow down in 1912, and he emerged after six months in a sanatorium cured of tuberculosis and inspired to become a playwright.

Several of his early works were one-act plays, realistic episodes from his seafaring days, including *In the Zone* (1917) and *The Moon of the Caribees* (1918). These modest productions rapidly established his reputation among critics. By 1920, with *Beyond the Horizon* playing to packed houses on Broadway and having earned his first Pulitzer Prize, he was already regarded as America's leading dramatist.

Edith Evans, equally at home in tragedy and comedy, was one of the great ladies of the modern English stage

Eugene O'Neill. His slow, massive plays explore human failure with compassion and integrity

Oskar Schlemmer saw costume and stage design as an extension of avant-garde painting and sculpture

O'Neill was never swayed by adulation. Although he continued to write commercially successful plays, he was moved solely by a compulsion to express his tragic visions, most persistently that of man's ideals suffocated in a world dominated by appearances and materialism. Impatient with "the banality of surfaces" in realistic drama, he experimented with unconventional techniques; asides to the audience in *Strange Interlude* (1928); masks in *Lazarus Laughed* (1928); classical models in *Desire under the Elms* (1924) and *Mourning Becomes Electra* (1931), or even two actors playing one role in *Days Without End* (1934).

From 1934 to 1946, depressed and in ill health, he published nothing. Even the Nobel prize in 1936 failed to flatter him back to public life. But he had been far from idle, as he revealed after the war with *The Iceman Cometh* (1946), recalling his days among the drunken and down-and-out, and *A Moon for the Misbegotten* (1954), a tragic picture of his alcoholic brother. Stricken by a debilitating disease that left him, though mentally sound, unable to write, he died with an undiminished reputation as America's greatest playwright.

Three years after O'Neill's death, the autobiographical *Long Day's Journey into Night*, for many his greatest play, provided a stark and dramatic obituary.

OSKAR SCHLEMMER (1888-1943)

German painter, director, set designer and dancer. Schlemmer's early training as a dancer was a continual inspiration to his work as a director and designer. His art shows a fascination with the human figure; for him ballet was moving sculpture. In his *Triadische Ballett* (1921), three figures dressed in strange, brightly coloured costumes made from bits of wire, fabric, rubber and metal, moved about the stage forming a series of geometric patterns. The emphasis was on movement rather than dancing in the traditional manner.

Schlemmer also applied his bold, geometric art to the theatre, designing sets for both plays and operas. These included *Mörder, Hoffnung der Frauen* (1921), by the expressionist playwright Oskar KOKOSCHKA, Christian GRABBE's realist drama, *Don Juan und Faust* (1925), and Arnold Schoenberg's opera *Die glückliche Hand* (1930).

FRIEDRICH WOLF (1888-1953)

German playwright. Wolf was a key figure in East German theatre. As a young man he was influenced by the expressionist school, but in the 1920s, when he became a Marxist, political commitment began to inspire his work. Living in Nazi Germany, Wolf was inevitably made to suffer for his beliefs; he emigrated to Russia in 1933, returning to East Berlin after the War.

An exponent of social realism, Wolf was often too politically insistent to be a great dramatist, but several of his plays profit from the passion of his beliefs. *Cyankali* (1929), one of his most successful works, attacks the German government's anti-abortion policy. In *Professor Mamlock* (1934) a Jewish surgeon commits suicide when life in Nazi Germany becomes intolerable. A comedy, *Burgermeister Anna* (1950), examines the society of newly created East Germany.

JEAN COCTEAU (1889-1963)

French poet, novelist, playwright, stage designer and actor. "To enclose the collected works of Cocteau one would need a warehouse, and how even then could one catalogue such a bewildering assortment of poems, plays in verse, plays in prose, mythologies, natural histories, travels, drawings, tins of films, phonograph records, etc?" wrote W. H. AUDEN. Cocteau, the *enfant terrible* of the avant-garde, applied his talents not only to all the traditional arts and literary genres, but also to cinema and ballet. He collaborated with some of the greatest artistic figures of the century, the painter Pablo PICASSO and the composer Erik Satie for the ballet *Parade* (1917), for instance. He wrote the libretto for Igor Stravinsky's *Oedipus Rex*, and the composer acknowledged that he was "a theatrical and cinematographic inventor of the highest order. His best caricatures are as good as any but Picasso's." Yet it is Cocteau himself, the supreme narcissist, a priest of art (as he saw himself), who is as memorable as any one of his many works.

After the First World War, Cocteau dismissed his early "waking books" and "began to dream" and experiment with his poetry. "A great literary masterpiece is but a dictionary in disorder," he declared. Experiment was an

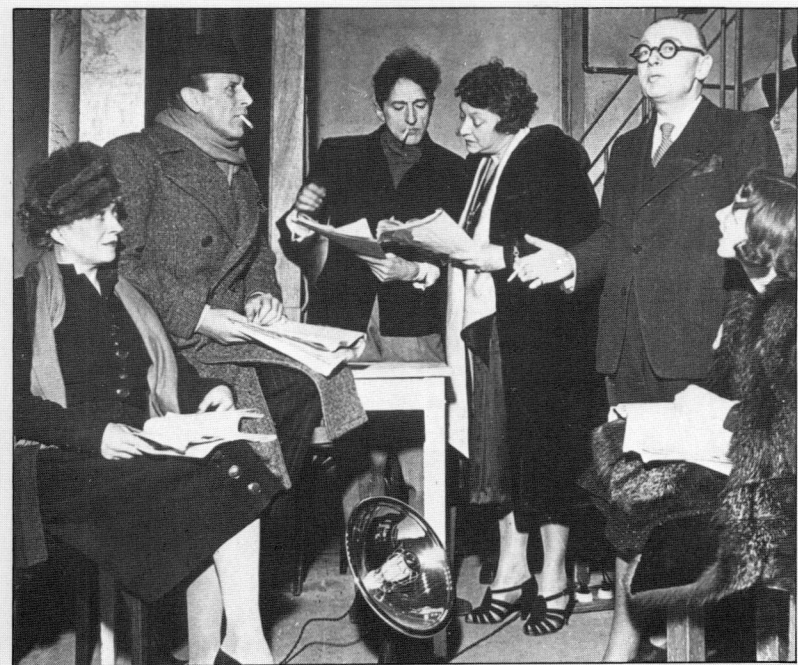

Jean Cocteau (seen tousle-haired at a 1930 rehearsal *left*) was a many-faceted genius. An example of his stage and costume design is pictured *above*

essential part of his thirty-odd stage works (including ballets). He tried nearly every dramatic form: a Greek play – *Antigone* (1922), "pantomime-farce" – *Le Boeuf sur le toit* (1920), tragic monologue – *La Voix humaine* (1930), melodramas, romantic dramas and contemporary psychological thrillers. His masterpieces are generally regarded to be *Orphée* (1926), which uses the legend of Orpheus to explore poetic inspiration, death and time, and *La Machine infernale* (1934), which discusses the nature of free will in a world in which gods construct infernal machines to ensnare human beings.

Cocteau once described himself as a poet of the night. His obsession with death, the alienation he felt as a homosexual and his addiction to opium were a part of the darker side of his artistic brilliance. Above his tomb is the inscription *Je reste avec vous*, a characteristically confident assumption that has so far proved prophetic.

GEORGE S KAUFMAN (1889-1961)

American playwright and director. A brilliant Broadway technician, George Kaufman professed "no philosophy except that the theatre is entertainment, and good entertainment pays". As a teenager, he submitted comic sketches to newspapers and by 1912 had his own column. Drama criticism for *The New York Times* and *Tribune* was his entrée to the theatre. He formed the first of a lifetime of writing partnerships with Marc CONNELLY, and in *Dulcy* (1921) they produced a hit for the actress Lynn FONTANNE. Their collaboration (but not their friendship) ceased in 1924 with *Beggar on Horseback*. In 1925 Kaufman wrote *The Cocoanuts* on his own, but it took titanic – and usually unsuccessful – efforts to keep the MARX Brothers from rearranging it every night as they pleased. The play's famous "Viaduct/Why a duck" sequence is typical of its creator's fast-paced punning wit.

The next fifteen years were the Kaufman era on Broadway. His astonishing series of hits included *The Royal Family* (1927) and *Dinner at Eight* (1932) written with Edna Ferber, and the musicals *Strike up the Band* (1930) and *Of Thee I Sing* (1931) with Morrie Ryskind. With MOSS HART he produced one of his few serious plays, *Merrily We Roll Along* (1934), as well as the hit comedies *You Can't Take It With You* (1936) and *The Man Who Came to Dinner* (1939). His charmed touch as writer and director served him well into the 1950s.

As amusing as the characters he created, Kaufman enjoyed a late-blooming career as a television personality.

GABRIEL MARCEL (1889-1973)

French philosopher, playwright and critic. Converted to Catholicism in 1929, the philosopher Marcel is often referred to as a Christian existentialist. His plays discuss philosophical and spiritual questions. Often they are set among a family at a moment of crisis, when the characters are forced to face themselves and their inability to understand life. *Un homme de Dieu*, published in 1925, deals with the painful re-examination of a wife's long-forgiven infidelity. Among his other plays are *L'Iconoclaste*, published in 1923, *La Chapelle ardente*, published in 1931, and *Le Dard* (1937).

Marcel was occasionally to be observed asleep at the performance of his own plays.

VIVIAN VAN DAMM (1889-1960)

English showman. VD, as he was known, bought London's Windmill Theatre in 1932 and began presenting "non-stop flesh and blood" vaudeville nine hours a day. A rare judge of public taste, he introduced "classical tableaux" composed of groups of nude lovelies. The Lord Chamberlain approved the spectacle as long as the lights were low and the ladies remained motionless. To VD it was, of course, pure culture. Supported by a large and attentive male audience, Van Damm maintained that the Windmill "never strayed from the path of sheer artistry"; at the end of the Second World War, his proud boast "we never closed", was taken up and transformed by the London public: "We never clothed."

ANTON BRAGAGLIA (1890-1960)

Italian director. Shortly after the First World War Bragaglia's Teatro degli Independenti in Rome was the centre for avant-garde theatre in Italy. In a tiny underground room amid the ruins of an ancient Roman bath, a company of non-professionals acted, mimed and danced before a crowd of Bohemians and intellectuals. Although the theatre closed in 1931, Bragaglia continued to promote experimental and foreign works in translation. Two of his greatest successes while director of the Teatro delle Arti in Rome were Thornton WILDER's *Our Town* and Eugene O'NEILL's *Mourning Becomes Electra*.

KAREL ČAPEK (1890-1938)

Czech novelist, playwright and journalist. In *R.U.R.* (1920), his most famous play, Čapek imagined a race of mechanical men rising up against their human masters. He called the automatons "robots", and both the name and its uneasy associations have endured. Čapek wrote the play with his brother Josef (1887–1945), known equally for his cubist paintings. Their next collaboration, *The Insect Play*, in which all the characters are insects, was a Kafkaesque fantasy on the dangers of regimentation. These works were well received, but the third production, *Adam the Creator* (1927), was a comparative failure.

In the decade that followed Čapek suspended his dramatic activity and concentrated on fiction, journalism and increasingly on politics. The success of the new Republic of Czechoslovakia had always been one of his guiding passions, and he worked tirelessly in support of its democratic ideals. His efforts were spurred by the growing power of Nazi Germany, a menace that eventually forced his return to the stage as a means of raising the alarm. *Power and Glory* (1937), again using elements of fantasy, was a denunciation of public apathy *The Mother* (1938) justified the deaths of young men who died fighting oppression. But in the same year *The Mother* was performed, the Munich agreement spelled doom for Czechoslovakia. Čapek died soon after, and three months later the robots of the Third Reich marched into Prague.

MARC CONNELLY (1890...)

American playwright, director, producer and actor. Connelly first made his reputation collaborating with George S. KAUFMAN on a number of successful comedies. Their partnership had begun in 1921 with *Dulcy*, and ended profitably and amicably with two shows in 1924: *Be Yourself* and *Beggar on Horseback*.

Then in 1928 he bought the dramatic rights to *Ol' Man Adam an' his Chillun*, a version of the Old Testament as interpreted by a black Southern preacher. His famous adaptation, *The Green Pastures*, presented with an all-black cast in 1930, played to packed houses and won the author a Pulitzer Prize.

Connelly's later plays were less successful, but he remained variously active in the theatre. He was a notable teacher of his craft, encouraging younger playwrights to aim higher than the "sure-fire" Broadway hit.

KÄTHE DORSCH (1890-1957)

German actress. Käthe Dorsch was one of the most versatile actresses of the twentieth century. She appealed equally to critics and to the least critical of popular audiences, bringing to all her roles, from *The Merry Widow* to LESSING's *Emilia Galotti*, an admirable combination of involvement and technique. After a number of successful years in operetta, Käthe Dorsch adapted her talents to non-musical drama. In Berlin and Vienna she continued to exercise her extraordinary range in works by IBSEN, SHAW and FEYDEAU.

GÖSTA EKMAN (1890-1938)

Swedish actor and director. The unconventional and sometimes crudely eccentric performances of Ekman infuriated Swedish critics. But throughout his career he could silence even his loudest detractors with an illuminating interpretation: MOLIÈRE's Tartuffe, for example, played as an English snob. He was especially skilled at comic roles, including Joseph Surface in SHERIDAN's *The School for Scandal*, and was extremely successful in a 1931 production of Lehár's operetta, *The Merry Widow*.

In 1931 Ekman became director of the Våsa Teater in Stockholm. Although his reputation as a film actor continued to grow, his greatest performance may have been on his own stage in the title role of *The Hangman*, Pär LAGERKVIST's moving anti-Nazi parable.

HALLIE FLANAGAN (1890-1969)

American manager. Renowned as a teacher of drama, Mrs Flanagan was appointed head of the Federal Theatre Project in 1935. This government-sponsored scheme aimed first to provide jobs during the Depression and second (in the words of a presidential aide) to promote "free, adult, uncensored theatre". It came close to this ideal during its short life, with centres throughout the USA presenting a spectrum of plays from EURIPIDES to the most controversial contemporary works. But controversy finally killed the project. A Congressional committee suspected "un-American activities" and summoned Mrs Flanagan to inquire, among other things, if Christopher MARLOWE were a Communist. Despite her determination, Congress denied further funding in 1939.

WALTER HASENCLEVER (1890-1940)

German playwright and poet. In the decade after the First World War Hasenclever was one of the most influential of European playwrights. *Der Sohn* (1914), which celebrates a son's rebellion against his tyrannical father, was correctly interpreted by the radical youth of Germany as a condemnation of political suppression. Other highly stylized and symbolic plays included *Antigone* (1917), an updated version of SOPHOCLES; and *Die Menschen* (1918), in which a corpse returns to life only to be executed as his own murderer.

Surprisingly, Hasenclever's strident, expressionist works gave way in the 1920s and 1930s to social comedies which only occasionally, as in *Napoleon greift ein* (1930), revealed the political preoccupations of his youth. A committed pacifist, Hasenclever was to commit suicide in France on the eve of the Nazi invasion.

ALAN PATRICK HERBERT (1890-1971)

English novelist, playwright, humorist and politician. A. P. Herbert was well known for his novels, humorous articles and satirical poems, but derived the most pleasure from writing musical comedy. His shows included *Riverside Nights* (1926), *La Vie Parisienne* (1929), *Derby Day* (1932) and *Big Ben* (1946). Well produced and with star casts, they were a great success on the London stage.

A man of wide interests, Herbert was also Independent member of Parliament for Oxford University from 1935 to 1950. He was a confirmed campaigner, raising his voice on endless issues from the Divorce and Obscenity Laws to jargon and spelling, and only hampered by his inability to resist flippancy at even the most serious moments. "People must not do things for fun", he said in *Uncommon Law*. "There is no reference to fun in any Act of Parliament." First published in 1935, this book (as *Misleading Cases*) was a popular television series.

HEINZ HILPERT (1890-1967)

German director and actor. Hilpert was a schoolmaster at the outbreak of the First World War. Although he began his theatrical career immediately after the Armistice, he never entirely abandoned the structured and reasoned methods of the schoolroom. As director of the Deutsches Theater in Berlin, as well as at theatres in Vienna and Göttingen, Hilpert created realistic and often humorous productions of plays by BRUCKNER, SHAKESPEARE, CHEKHOV and ZUCKMAYER.

STANLEY HOLLOWAY (1890...)

English actor. Holloway was born in East London. Throughout a career that included musicals, films and SHAKESPEARE, he always returned to the cockney humour and the unmistakable haccent of 'is burfplice.

After a theatrical apprenticeship as an entertainer at English seaside resorts, Holloway became an established star in London with a popular variety show called *The Co-Optimists*. Despite his experience in films and musicals, he was apprehensive when Laurence OLIVIER asked him to play the First Gravedigger in his 1947 film of Hamlet. Upon discovering that he could play Shakespeare as a Cockney, and having repeated this success at the Old Vic in 1951, he later played Bottom in *A Midsummer Night's Dream* at the Edinburgh Festival. Since 1956 Holloway has been inextricably associated with the role of Alf Doolittle, the philosophical dustman in *My Fair Lady*. His Shakespearean days are over. "I've no desire to finish my career by playing King Lear," he wrote in his delightful autobiography.

GROUCHO MARX (1890-1977)

American comedian. The Marx Brothers nurtured their genius for chaos over long undisciplined years in vaudeville. Encouraged by their mother, Groucho and his brothers Chico (1891–1961), Harpo (1893–1964) and Gummo (1894–1977) toured as *The Four Nightingales*. Reaction to the boys' singing was overwhelmingly indifferent. Their frustration exploded one epic night in Texas in a spontaneous orgy of manic high spirits and general mayhem. The spectators were taken aback but delighted, and the Marx Brothers' image was made. From then on their act was virtually spontaneous throughout. Groucho recalled, "We always played to ourselves, never the audience." Alive to the moment, they might sing, or even make book on a passing cockroach.

Their berserk improvisations brought the Marx Brothers to Broadway in 1924, with Zeppo (1901–79) replacing Gummo in the hit revue *I'll Say She Is*. The *Cocoanuts* (1925) was another triumph, though George S. KAUFMAN was appalled at the way its four stars systematically dismembered his dialogue. Audiences came to that show and its sequel *Animal Crackers* (1928), expecting each performance to be unique. Theatre managers might complain, "You go talk to those crazy men, I can't do anything with them", but a legend was in the making. Hollywood came next, and the rest is anarchic history.

KURT TUCHOLSKY (1890-1935)

German satirist. Tucholsky waged a personal battle against oppression in Germany between the wars. He published books and articles under numerous pseudonyms, and wrote extremely popular and bittersweet satirical songs and poems for that stronghold of dissent, the cabaret. But as the power of the Nazis grew, Tucholsky came to doubt the value of such passive protest. In 1933 his books were publicly burnt and he left Germany. Two years later he poisoned himself.

FRANZ WERFEL (1890-1945)

Austrian novelist, playwright and poet. In the horrors of war and the persecution of his fellow Jews, Werfel discovered a philosophy that was both despairing and compassionate. "There is an essential tragedy in the world . . . from which the understanding soul suffers most," he wrote with unabashed self-pity.

Even before service in the First World War, Werfel expressed his bitter anti-militarism in *Die Troerinnen* (1916), in which the Trojan Wars assume an unexpected relevance to twentieth-century Europe. A subsequent trilogy, *Spiegelmensch* (1921), shows the hero confronted with his vicious *alter ego*. Werfel also dealt effectively with religious and historical subjects, but it was with *Bocksgesang* (*The Goat Song*, 1922) that he had his greatest success outside Germany. The story of a monster born of normal human parents, who inspires a violent peasant revolt, *The Goat Song* has an immense theatrical impact that is missing from much of the rest of Werfel's drama.

Best known as a novelist, Werfel enjoyed especial fame while a Californian exile for a film version of his novel *The Song of Bernadette*.

GEORGE WHITE (1890-1968)

American producer and dancer. For years, *George White's Scandals* vied in splendour with the *Ziegfeld Follies*. White had grown up dancing for pennies in cheap New York clubs, but in 1912, after an appearance in Paris, he returned home smitten with the French *revue à grand spectacle*. His own great spectaculars began in 1919, opulent productions with lavish costumes and designs, gorgeous chorus girls, star singers and dancers. George Gershwin wrote much of the music. White produced a conventional musical in 1927, but every alternate year until 1930 saw a new *Scandals*, each more brilliant and expensive than its predecessor. Other successes of these salad days were two outstanding comedies: *Runnin' Wild* (1923) and *Manhattan Mary* (1927).

The series faltered in the depression, and in 1939 it stopped completely. White transferred his revues to films and nightclubs with limited success. An extravagant and profligate man, he filed for bankruptcy several times and was once imprisoned for causing a fatal automobile accident. A revival of the old *Scandals* in 1963 displayed only a nostalgic hint of the former, glorious days.

MEMO BENASSI (1891...)

Italian actor. When the great Eleanora DUSE emerged from retirement in 1921, she chose Benassi to be her lead-ing man. Three years later he returned from a tour of the United States with the body of his benefactress, but by then his reputation as one of Italy's best young actors was well established.

Benassi was a powerful and often eccentric performer (in one production he recited Hamlet's famous soliloquy while playing solitary chess). Among his major roles were Oswald in IBSEN's *Ghosts* and Shylock in SHAKESPEARE's *The Merchant of Venice*.

FANNY BRICE (1891-1951)

American singer and comedienne. Fanny Brice's poor and polyglot background shaped her comic art. Born on New York's lower east side, she absorbed the district's welter of cultures, characters and human incident. Sympathy with the poor prompted her to steal beer for them from her father's saloon. But poverty also appealed to her sense of drama. She concocted such tales of her family's destitution as had her friends in tears.

Renowned as a neighbourhood singer, she made a public debut at thirteen, winning first prize at a Brooklyn amateur night. Her professional career was slower getting started. George M. COHAN fired her from his chorus line for her inability to dance. At fifteen Fanny Brice toured in a show called *A Royal Slave*, playing the part of an alligator. But she soon made a name singing in burlesque, and in 1910 her rendition of a Yiddish dialect number catapulted her into the *Ziegfeld Follies*. Year after year she was one of the revue's biggest stars. Known for comic songs and caricatures, she surprised her fans in 1921 with a poignant version of the torch song "My Man".

Her desire for wider dramatic opportunities led her first to have her nose straightened and then to do a straight play, *Fanny*, in 1926. But she was still at her best in revue, performing old and new songs, changing moods in an instant and satirizing the pretensions of "high art".

During the 1930s Fanny Brice gave more and more time to radio, and in the last decade of her life her infant character, the irrepressible "Baby Snooks", made her famous to millions who had never seen her on stage. Posthumously, in the 1960s, Fanny Brice became familiar to a generation who had neither seen nor heard her through *Funny Girl*, the hit musical based on her life and starring Barbra Streisand.

FERDINAND BRUCKNER (1891-1958)

Austrian playwright. It was many years before Ferdinand Bruckner was discovered to be a pseudonym for the poet and director Theodor Tagger. Bruckner first appeared as the writer of *Krankheit der Jugend* (1926), a play that showed the youth of Germany as self-indulgent and suicidal. He revealed a brilliant sense of stagecraft with *Die Verbrecher* (1928), in which the action unfolds in seven rooms, all of which are visible simultaneously to the audience. *Elisabeth von England* was a skilful combination of romance and politics.

Bruckner settled in America in 1936. Unlike many of his fellow exiles, he returned to Germany after the war.

MIKHAIL BULGAKOV (1891-1940)

Russian playwright and novelist. The son of a professor at the Kiev Theological Academy, Mikhail Afanasyevich gave up the practice of medicine to become a writer. From the beginning he showed a dangerous disregard for official sensitivities. *The Day of the Turbins* (1926), a partly autobiographical play about the Kiev Rebellion of 1918–19, portrayed White soldiers in too sympathetic a light. Stalin allowed it to be staged for only a few performances, and denounced Bulgakov's subsequent offering, *The Red Island*, as "trash".

Of more than thirty plays Bulgakov wrote, most were harassed from the stage (if they ever got there) before they could do the Russian public any lasting harm. *Bliss, The Cabal of Holy Hypocrites* (1936) about MOLIÈRE, *Don Quixote* (1940) and *The Last Days* (of PUSHKIN) (1943) were all scrutinized for subversion, and censored. Understandably, the spectre of imprisonment was to haunt Bulgakov for the rest of his life. Stalin refused him

The joyous energy that made **Fanny Brice** a great mimic lasted throughout her career. In middle age she created one of her most famous characters, the inimitably bouncy Baby Snooks

permission to emigrate, but as a gesture allowed him a living by appointing him Theatrical Editor at the Moscow Art Theatre.

He devoted his last ten years to *The Master and Margarita*, a novel in which the devil, with a retinue of two demons, a naked girl, and a cigar-smoking, Mauser-toting cat, get up to some very un-Stalinist antics. Bulgakov died blind and alone; his novel was published thirty years later.

AGATHA CHRISTIE (c 1891-1976)

English novelist and playwright. Theatregoers have proved just as eager as the reading public to match wits with Mrs Christie. The first of her many stage whodunnits was *Alibi* (1928), a dramatization of her classic novel *The Murder of Roger Ackroyd*, with Charles LAUGHTON as the supremely unflappable Hercule Poirot. Adaptations, original plays and revivals kept the Christie name in lights for the next fifty years. In 1953–54 she had three productions – *The Mousetrap* (1952), *Witness for the Prosecution* (1953) and *Spider's Web* (1954) – all running in London's West End at once. After twenty-eight years *The Mousetrap* is still playing to packed houses (1980) and making theatrical history.

Agatha Christie's own life had one episode which might have been drawn from her own devious imagination when, in December 1926, she mysteriously vanished. Missing for ten days, she turned up at a health resort suffering from "amnesia" and registered under the name of her husband's mistress. Her disappearance was never satisfactorily explained.

ERICH ENGEL (1891-1966)

German director. Engel ended his career in the theatre as he had begun, directing the plays of Bertolt BRECHT, yet there was a period of over twenty years when the two could not collaborate at all. This was because Engel chose to remain in Germany under Nazism, concentrating on prestigious productions of SHAKESPEARE and lightweight comedy films.

In 1922 Engel was a little-known director at the Staatstheater in Munich. His meeting there with Brecht was to have an enormous influence on both their careers. Engel's production of Brecht's *Im Dickicht der Städte* was transferred to Berlin, and they worked together on all Brecht's early plays up to the spectacularly successful *Dreigroschenoper* of 1928. But after this, it was not until 1950, when Engel went to join the Berliner Ensemble, directing *Herr Puntila und sein Knecht Matti*, that they were able to renew their old partnership.

YVAN GOLL (1891-1950)

Franco-German poet and playwright. In his own words Goll was "Jewish by destiny, French-born by chance, designated a German by a piece of stamped paper". Two world wars served to exaggerate his rootlessness, the first driving him to Switzerland, the second to the United States. The resulting alienation is evident in plays such as *Methusalem, oder Der erwige Bürger* (1922), in which he employed films and masked actors to satirize bourgeois society. *Die Chaplinade* and the two *Überdramen* (1920) similarly exploit avant-garde techniques and the imagery of surrealism, a concept still unknown to most of his contemporaries.

SIDNEY HOWARD (1891-1939)

American playwright. Howard's vivid descriptions of American life enriched the stage with plays that were at

The writer of "Anything Goes" and "I've Got You under my Skin" came late to show business. **Cole Porter** (*left*) went from Harvard to the French Foreign Legion, and thence to high society, where his music entertained friends such as the Prince of Wales and Noel Coward

Four playwrights (*right*) whose satirical plays brought social conscience to the fore in the American theatre: from left to right, **S. N. Behrman**, **Maxwell Anderson**, **Robert Sherwood**, and **Elmer Rice**. These men formed the "Playwrights' Company" to put on their plays

Two great comic actresses (*far right*) of opposite style: **Margaret Rutherford**, awkward and resolute, receives a cup of tea from the forever elegant **Marie Tempest**. The former is just beginning her stage career and the latter is an astonishing seventy-one. Both of these women came to acting only in their thirties; and both in time were made Dames of the British Empire

once popular and thoughtful. A compassionate attitude to infidelity in *They Knew What They Wanted* (1924) won a Pulitzer Prize and established the author as a major dramatist. With *The Silver Cord* (1926), Howard attacked the heart of the nation itself, lashing out at the possessive American "Mom" as a "self-centred, self-pitying, son-devouring tigress". Other successful plays included *Ned McCobb's Daughter* (1926), *The Late Christopher Bean* (1932) and *Yellow Jack* (1934).

Howard was killed in a tractor accident on his farm in Massachusetts, at the age of forty-eight.

PÄR LAGERKVIST (1891-1974)

Swedish novelist, playwright and poet. Lagerkvist shocked Scandinavians in 1918 with his revolutionary essay, *Modern Theatre*. Comparing the revered plays of IBSEN to a "silent treading on carpets through five long acts with words, words, words", he declared that realism was "out"; STRINDBERG and expressionism were "in". The next year his trilogy of one-act plays, *The Difficult Hour*, was produced in Düsseldorf, where an infuriated public assaulted the director after the performance.

Not all of Lagerkvist's plays provoked such a strong reaction, but the best, which include *He Who Lived His Life Over Again* (1928) and *The Philosopher's Stone* (1947), are violent and stylized depictions of mankind's brutal nature. *The Hangman* (1934) is possibly Lagerkvist's most powerful work for the stage. "Since the beginning of time I have looked to my task," says the symbolic title character in his pessimistic conclusion, "and it seems I shall not have finished with it yet awhile."

As a novelist Lagerkvist is best known abroad for *Barabbas* and for *The Dwarf*.

UGO BETTI (1892-1953)

Italian playwright and poet. Betti believed that "the facts of life are basically uninteresting" compared to the "human condition"; but the central facts of Betti's own life bear directly on his work. Born into a middle-class family, he was raised in Parma, where his early passions were literature and soccer. He was good enough at the first to publish a translation from Catullus when he was eighteen, and at the second to play with two top-ranking local clubs. After university studies in law, he fought in the First World War, emerging from an Austrian prisoner-of-war camp a committed pacifist.

After the war, Betti embarked on his life-long career as police magistrate and judge, serving in the provinces before his appointment to the Roman bench in 1930. His literary reputation had begun with the prize-winning play *La Padrona* (1927), but *Frana allo scalo Nord* (1936) established him as a major and distinctive voice. It depicts a courtroom inquiry's attempt to fix the blame for a disaster; the investigation becomes more philosophical than legal, ultimately arraigning both society and human existence itself. Betti's assertion that his drama owes "nothing in particular, everything in general" to his judicial experience is borne out not just by his fondness for legal settings, but in this preoccupation with guilt and responsibility. Essentially religious, he saw the world's violence, passion and ambition proceeding simply from the flaws of human nature. Men yearn for a peace and stability that can only come from outside themselves. In the great plays of his last years, among them *Corruzione al Palazzo di giustizia* (1949) and *La Regina e gli insorti* (1951), he expounds this philosophy.

Not everyone responds to such mystical and allegorical exercises. Americans in particular (masters of a very different sort of courtroom drama) have baulked at his "vague Christian goodness", but Betti is respected in England and regarded in Italy as the true successor to Luigi PIRANDELLO.

EDDIE CANTOR (1892-1964)

American singer. A five-dollar first prize in a 1906 talent contest filled Cantor's huge, round "banjo eyes" with visions of success. After some years in vaudeville, where he began the blacking-up that was so much a part of his appeal, he was offered a one-night trial in 1916 in the New York show *Midnight Frolic*, held upstairs above the *Ziegfeld Follies*. His exuberant act ran for twenty-seven weeks and, with songs like "That's the Kind of Baby for Me", he was soon one of the stars of the *Follies* below. He lost all his money in the Wall Street Crash, but continued his career on radio and television and returned to Broadway in *Banjo Eyes* in 1941.

FRITZ KORTNER (1892-1970)

Austrian actor and director. The leading actor of German expressionist theatre and cinema, Kortner was at his finest as Richard III, his eyeballs rolling and teeth agnash. After making his name in Vienna in HEBBEL's

Herodes und Mariamne, he moved to Berlin, where as Gessler in SCHILLER's *Wilhelm Tell* he began a long association with Leopold JESSNER.

Leaving Germany after a performance interrupted by pro-Nazi demonstrations, Kortner had a lean time in the United States, despite an attempt to re-create his celebrated Herod in English with Katharine CORNELL playing Mariamne.

After the war Kortner turned to directing, rehearsing his casts implacably until they assumed the very essence of their characters. He worked mainly with the classics, but also produced and acted in the plays of Samuel BECKETT, his grotesque, craggy features making a memorable Krapp in *Krapp's Last Tape*.

ARCHIBALD MACLEISH (1892...)

American poet and playwright. During the 1930s and 1940s MacLeish was known to a literate few as a distinguished poet. To many more he was familiar as an eloquent and controversial spokesman for Roosevelt's New Deal. By the time he retired from public life in 1949 he had held several government appointments, from Librarian of Congress to Assistant Secretary of State.

Although he had proven his abilities as a dramatist with a number of successful radio verse plays, including *The Fall of the City* (1937), it was not until 1958 that MacLeish became a familiar name to theatregoers. *J.B.* was a Broadway hit which ran for 364 performances, an astonishing record for a play that was both religious and poetic. It also won MacLeish a Pulitzer Prize. *J.B.* recounts a modernized version of the *Book of Job*, performed as a play within a play in a circus tent. J.B.'s three comforters are a priest, a psychiatrist and a social historian. Like their biblical counterparts, they bring no comfort, but J.B. prevails over his sufferings (which include an atomic attack) and survives with renewed faith.

COLE PORTER (1892-1964)

American composer and lyricist. For several years after the First World War Porter lived in Europe where, thanks to his wealthy wife, he amused a fashionable circle of friends. Not until 1928 did five songs from *Paris*, including "Let's Do It", catch on in New York. There followed a series of successful musicals: *The Gay Divorce* (with "Night and Day", 1932), *Anything Goes* (1934), *Kiss Me Kate* (1948) and *Can-Can* ("I Love Paris", 1953). Porter's knowing lyrics and lush harmonies won him a slightly decadent reputation as the rich man's Irving BERLIN.

ELMER RICE (1892-1967)

American playwright, director and novelist. Rice's first play, *On Trial* (1914), made its author famous (and $100,000 richer) at the age of twenty-two. His prolific, varied and uneven output is occasionally sentimental or melodramatic, but at best reveals great skill in handling large casts, adventurous effects and complex plots. Attracted by the bold ideas of the expressionist movement, Rice was always concerned with the theatre's power to influence, and in his celebrated *The Adding Machine* (1923) he savagely attacked the dehumanizing effects of automation. Among his targets in other works were Nazism, racism, snobbery, materialism and the legal profession; not surprisingly he was often in conflict with censors and bureaucrats.

An arresting combination of reality and symbol, Rice's evocation of everyday city life, *Street Scene* (1929, later rewritten as a musical play with Kurt WEILL) moved one critic to write: "You can almost feel the mysterious grit that sifts all over Manhattan."

MARGARET RUTHERFORD (1892-1972)

English actress. In her autobiography, Margaret Rutherford remarks stoically: "If you have a face like mine the thing is to learn to live with it and come to terms with it." But her determined mouth and dreadnought chin did not immediately commend her as a young ingénue seeking work in the West End. For years she lived as a teacher of elocution and piano; her stage debut did not come until she was in her early thirties. She eventually became famous for her portrayals of *grandes dames* of both the kindly and the embattled variety, from Miss Prism in *The Importance of being Earnest* to Agatha CHRISTIE's Miss Marple. Perseverance brought success; even her husband waited fifteen years before asking for her hand.

SAMUEL NATHANIEL BEHRMAN (1893-1973)

American playwright and essayist. S. N. Behrman's comedies of manners provided irresistible vehicles for stars such as Noel COWARD, Laurence OLIVIER and Alfred

LUNT. His typical male hero is a world-weary lounge lizard trying entertainingly to resolve the twin vices of hedonism and conscience within himself. *The Second Man* (1927) and *End of Summer* (1936) were notable in a string of formulated successes. *Jacobowski and the Colonel* (1944) was a successful adaptation of WERFEL's novel.

As the Second World War approached, Behrman tried to encapsulate his misgivings about the role of slick Broadway comedy in *No Time for Comedy* (1939). The title proved prophetic: critics disparaged his attempts to insert a serious message beneath the surface gloss, and Behrman increasingly abandoned original writing in favour of adaptations. In the earlier *Amphitryon 38* (1937) he had pruned Jean GIRAUDOUX's play of most of its philosophic ramblings (and much of its meaning).

NORMAN BEL GEDDES (1893-1958)

American designer and architect. For Max REINHARDT's *The Miracle* (1924) Bel Geddes transformed a whole theatre into a cathedral. A disciple of Adolphe APPIA, he aimed at maximum use of three-dimensional space. Large movable ramps, plinths and steps combined with bold lighting to project an abstract, ever-changing tableau. Many of his more grandiose and visionary projects remained too ambitious and costly ever to be realized.

JIMMY DURANTE (1893-1980)

American comedian. The comedy team of Durante, Lou Clayton and Eddie Jackson was one of the hottest acts in New York in the 1920s. The focal point of their wild clowning was Durante's enormous nose – hence his nickname "Schnozzola" and his perennial joke "I'm the only man in America who can smoke a cigar in the shower." They appeared in nightclubs at first, then the big vaudeville theatres and finally Broadway musicals. The team broke up when Durante began to work in films. He returned to Broadway in shows that included *Strike Me Pink* (1933) and *Keep Off the Grass* (1940), but in 1943 took his noisy humour and ungovernable Brooklyn accent back to the nightclubs where he was most at home.

HEINRICH GEORGE (1893-1946)

German actor and director. Whether or not he was sincere, George embraced National Socialism with the same fervour that he had previously demonstrated as a Communist. Guests at his house claimed they had been forced to kneel in front of an altar to the Führer, which may be true, for the massive, Falstaffian George was capable of anything when drunk.

In the twenties his enormous vitality combined with quiet, subtle humour had made him a true popular hero of the German stage. He worked with all the leading figures in left-wing theatre, appearing frequently for Erwin PISCATOR at the Volksbühne. In later years his gentleness receded, his temper waxed and he came to favour tougher, more martial roles, his great favourite being in GOETHE's *Götz von Berlichingen*. Interned by Soviet troops at the end of the War, George died the following year in what had formerly been a Nazi concentration camp.

LILLIAN LEITZEL (1893-1931)

Bohemian aerialist. Queen of the combined Barnum and Bailey and Ringling Brothers circuses, Leitzel was curiously graceless on the ground: she was less than five feet tall, with the arms and shoulders of a heavyweight boxer. Her courage and endurance thrilled audiences, who counted aloud the seemingly endless spirals she performed above them. Spurning a net, she fell to her death in Copenhagen on the ominous date (circus people are notoriously superstitious) 13 February, 1931. The tragedy did not end there, however. The news of her fall convinced a rival performer that his days too were numbered. Such is the power of auto-suggestion that he was killed the very same evening.

Lillian had been married to Alfredo Codona, the man who perfected the terrifying triple somersault: three complete turns in mid-air, from one trapeze to another. After her death he married another aerialist, Vera Bruce. Although they were both spared from death in the ring, their union was equally short-lived. After a serious fall, Codona took to the bottle. Eventually they found themselves in a law-office discussing divorce. While the lawyer was out of the room, Codona resolved their differences by shooting first his wife, then himself – a final, terrifying "double".

ALFRED LUNT (1893-1977)

American actor and director. Lunt's name is inseparable from that of his wife and co-star, Lynn FONTANNE. For forty years they were at the hub of glittering New York society, making their names in the crisp comedies of Noel COWARD, S. N. BEHRMAN and Robert SHERWOOD. But Lunt's popularity was not just the creation of Broadway razzmatazz; it owed much to his hypnotically expressive command of gesture, timing and vocal inflection.

His stage persona and his marriage (hailed as "the most outrageously perfect love story of the twentieth century") were inextricably linked in his and the public's imagination. Audiences and critics flocked just to observe the Lunts and their sometimes erotic mutual understanding and joy in one another. Even in the weightier comedies of SHAKESPEARE, SHAW, GIRAUDOUX and DÜRRENMATT, Lunt tended to impose his own character on those he portrayed. In the same way he has been accused of making more of trifling roles than they deserved.

VLADIMIR MAYAKOVSKY (1893-1930)

Russian poet and playwright. As a boy of fourteen, Vladimir Vladimirovich joined the clandestine Bolshevik Party. After a year in prison, he placed his futurist muse at the service of the revolution, and his brilliant declamatory political poetry became its voice. Maxim GORKY originally encouraged him to write for the theatre. His first play, in 1913, was a *succès-de-scandale*. Called *Vladimir Mayakovsky*, it naturally starred himself. MEYERHOLD, with the painter Malevich, staged *Mystery-Bouffe* in 1918; *The Bedbug* appeared in Moscow in 1929.

This eclectic poet who could master tender love lyrics as well as coarse, original metaphor, also contributed to the experiments of the cubists and constructivists; costumes, sets and graphics were all within his range.

To celebrate the twenty-fifth anniversary of the 1905 revolution, Mayakovsky wrote *Moscow is Burning*, a circus spectacle. Later that year he committed suicide.

IVOR NOVELLO (1893-1951)

Welsh-born playwright, composer and actor-manager. Novello was one of the most versatile personalities in theatrical history, having an almost complete understanding of the requirements of pure entertainment.

His song "Keep the Home Fires Burning" (1915) was so beloved of British soldiers in Flanders that their allies often mistook it for the national anthem. He later wrote and sometimes starred in films, thrillers and serious plays, including a memorable *Henry V*. But Novello is best remembered as composer, author and star of a stream of lavish and frothy musical romances presented at the Drury Lane Theatre, notably *The Dancing Years* (1939). With their redeeming element of self-parody, they invoke what *The Times* called a "highly agreeable nostalgia for time past, or time perhaps that never was".

ERWIN PISCATOR (1893-1966)

German director. Bertolt BRECHT may have had the greater influence on twentieth-century drama, but it was Piscator who first put the twentieth century on the stage. He used film, slides, animated comic strips, placards and loudspeakers, all the essential hardware of Brechtian political theatre.

Although not a playwright himself, Piscator cut and altered the works he produced so drastically that the classics became unrecognizable, and living authors often had recourse to the law. He first shook the Berliner Volksbühne with *Fahnen*, a documentary account of the struggle by Chicago unions to win an eight-hour day, but it was his 1926 production of SCHILLER's *Die Räuber*, set in the trenches of the First World War (complete with incidental saxophone music), that provoked the greatest controversy. Many did not agree with the view of the radical actress Tilla DURIEUX that it "swept away the

Erwin Piscator, seen here (*below*, seated left, examining a set) introduced many modern effects, but he sought "a play without decor, without costumes . . . even without clothes . . . to discover finally where the truth lies"

The lissom **Ivor Novello** (*right*) who was born Davies, wrote and starred in some twenty West End plays and musicals

"It's not the man in my life, but the life in my man": **Mae West** (*above*) is the great embodiment of a satisfied and languorous sexuality

The British playwright and novelist, **J. B. Priestley** (*below*) sets off in the boat-train in 1931 to conquer America

stale air, the pomposity, all that missed the essence".

It was Durieux who put up much of the money to install Piscator at the Theater am Nollendorfplatz in 1927. The Piscator-Bühne, as the theatre soon came to be known, had its greatest triumph with *Die Abenteuer des braven Soldaten Schweik* (1928), based on the great Czech novel by Jaroslav Hašek. Its success owed much to the talents of Brecht, who collaborated on the script, George Grosz, the savage cartoonist, who designed the sets and marionettes, and Max PALLENBERG, who played the title role.

The rise of the Nazis forced Piscator into American exile. At the Dramatic Workshop of the New School for Social Research in New York his students included TENNESSEE WILLIAMS and ARTHUR MILLER. His influence has been greater in Europe, however, Joan LITTLEWOOD and Roger PLANCHON being particularly important exponents of his style of multi-media production.

When the Un-American Activities Committee took an unfriendly interest in him, Piscator turned to work in West Germany. For some years he had to struggle as a freelance producer before eventually becoming director of the new Freie Volksbühne in Berlin. One of the first plays he accepted for the theatre was Rolf HOCHHUTH's *Der Stellvertreter*. In the young man's work Piscator declared he had at last found the documentary style that all his life he had sought to create: "Total Theatre."

ERNST TOLLER (1893-1939)

German playwright. Most of Toller's early works were performed during the five years he spent in prison after the abortive Bavarian revolution of 1919. There are both visions of hope and cries of despair in *Die Wandlung* (1919) and *Der deutsche Hinkemann* (1923), powerful variations on the commonplace theme of the soldier returning home from the war. In *Masse-Mensch* (1922) the heroine, Sonja (the only character in the piece with a name), fails to prevent a revolution from turning into a bloodbath. This play and *Die Maschinenstürmer* (1922), based on the history of the Luddites, are dominated by the writer's anger at the stupidity of the masses.

Hoppla, wir leben (1927) was produced with a spectacular multiple set by Erwin PISCATOR. *Feuer aus den Kesseln* (1930), his last major work, has been frequently revived since the war. In 1933 Toller left Germany but could not adjust to life in exile, and committed suicide in New York after the German invasion of Czechoslovakia.

MAE WEST (1893...)

American actress and playwright. W. C. FIELDS's "little brood mare" is much better known for films than for theatrical work. But Mae West shaped that unique character of bejewelled, platinum-blonde earth mother, exuding and satirizing sexuality in a stage career of over thirty years. Some time after an innocent debut at the age of seven in *Little Nell and the Marchioness*, she discovered she possessed, in her own words, "the force of an extraordinary sex personality", and made potent use of it both as actress and authoress. In 1926 her first play, disarmingly called *Sex* ("a catchy title and the basis of all life"), established her as a wholly original combination of seductress and comedienne, though it also resulted in a ten-day gaol sentence and a $500 fine for immorality. Subsequent plays confirmed her talent for finding tantalizing and hilarious double meanings everywhere, and in 1932 she left the New York stage for the screen, where in films like *She Done Him Wrong* and *My Little Chickadee* she could appear appropriately larger than life. For the next few years, this proved true, though her innuendo was gradually tamed by the censors.

FRED ALLEN (1894-1956)

American comedian. An early act as "Freddie St James, The World's Worst Juggler" took Allen into vaudeville. Changing his name to Fred Allen (his real name was John F. Sullivan) he continued on the vaudeville circuit for a number of years with a crazy act in which he would often sit down on the stage in mid-routine and read his press cuttings to the band leader. His first big spot on Broadway was in the revue *The Passing Show of 1922*. Of the shows that followed, *The Little Show* (1929) and *Three's A Crowd* (1930) had great successes. Allen became immensely popular for his dry humour, gloomy face and a rasping voice that was "like a man with false teeth chewing on slate pencils". He later starred in *Allen's Alley*, one of the most successful radio shows of its time.

IZAAK BABEL (1894-c 1941)

Soviet writer and dramatist. A protégé of Maxim GORKY, Babel served in a Revolutionary Cossack regiment during the Russo-Polish Campaign of 1920. The experiences of that year were to be the basis of his vivid and violent short stories: *Red Cavalry*. The sweetness of the sun of Odessa set against the bitterness of growing up a Jew in the last years of Tsarist Russia is the background of the rest of his slim output. A writer of genius, he wrote only two plays: *Sunset* and *Mariya*, which has been performed in London and in Germany, but never professionally in Russia.

In the late 1930s, Babel was denounced. It was said he was arrested for having an affair with the sister of Yagoda, the purged chief of political police. The official charge was Trotskyism, and he was sent to a concentration camp, where he died.

GIZI BAJOR (1894-1951)

Hungarian actress. Gizi Bajor won fame not only for herself but also for the National Theatre of Budapest, of which she was made a life member in 1928. Excelling in classic roles, notably SHAKESPEARE's heroines, Bajor also encouraged interest in modern Hungarian drama.

Her sensitive portrayals of the more complex female parts in plays such as IBSEN's *A Doll's House* were much admired. In 1950 she was named "People's artist of the Republic of Hungary", for her work in the theatre.

JACK BENNY (1894-1974)

American comedian. Although he never reached the age of forty, Benjamin Kubelsky had a very long and successful career in comedy. His Jewish Orthodox parents envisioned him as a classical musician, but by fifteen Benny was playing violin at the local vaudeville theatre. Soon he was on the road with a musical act and during the 1920s toured America with his show *A few minutes with Jack Benny*, which finally reached New York. By now a star, Benny went on to play in revues and variety shows.

In 1932 he left the stage for a weekly radio programme that was to exploit his talent for self-parody. He returned to Broadway in 1963 with a show called *One hour and sixty minutes with Jack Benny*. On stage, radio and television (frequently with his wife, Mary) Benny created a character of excessive meanness and ridiculous vanity. Until his death at "thirty-nine", he was a consummate master of the long pause and the raised eyebrow.

PAUL GREEN (1894...)

American playwright, novelist and scriptwriter. Green's boyhood on a North Carolina farm gave him a deep understanding of the Southern poor, both black and white. In plays such as *In Abraham's Bosom* (1926) and *The House of Connelly* (1931) he exposes their hopeless struggle to improve their condition. Later "symphonic dramas", among them *The Common Glory* (1947), were patriotic musical pageants for open-air settings. Green, a professor at North Carolina University, was not primarily interested in popular recognition and often wrote for independent theatre groups, which attracted him much more.

BEN HECHT (1894-1964)

American journalist, playwright and novelist. Hecht was, among other things, an acrobat before he joined a Chicago newspaper in 1910. There he became well known for his articles on the seamier side of city life, later published as *One Thousand and One Afternoons in Chicago*.

At first Hecht's plays had mixed receptions, but *The Front Page* (1928), a fast, funny and vulgar play about journalism (written with Charles MacArthur), was an outstanding success on Broadway. When one critic spoke badly of it, Hecht, who loved a joke, sabotaged his theatre seat. Of the other plays that he wrote with MacArthur, the best received was *Twentieth Century* (1932), a comic satire on show business. They also wrote many Hollywood screenplays. Hecht's own more serious play, *To Quito and Back* (1937), was praised by the critics, but did not have the commercial success of his collaborations.

HANS HENNY JAHNN (1894-1959)

German playwright and novelist. Jahnn's plays both fascinated and horrified audiences with their brutal eroticism and obsession with perversion. Some saw such violence as senseless; others saw it as an expression of man's need to give meaning to life. His plays include *Pastor Ephraim Magnus* (1921), *Die Krönung Richards III* (1921), *Medea* (1926) (in which Medea is a bloated, old Negress whose life is ruled by lust) and *Thomas Chatterton* (1956). In contrast to his plays, Jahnn was a pacifist and an expert on organ-making; he farmed, bred horses and did genealogical research.

CHARLES MORGAN (1894-1958)

English novelist, playwright and critic. For most of his career Morgan was a leading London drama critic. Although better known for his rather pretentious analytical novels, he also wrote three plays: *The Flashing Stream* (1938), *The River Line* (1952) and *The Burning Glass* (1954), dealing, in his own words, with "the conflict between the spirit and the flesh". Morgan had a great following in France, where he was honoured with election to the Académie Française.

JOHN BOYNTON PRIESTLEY (1894...)

English playwright and novelist. Foremost among Britain's experimental playwrights in the 1930s, J. B. Priestley began his career as a novelist, but in 1932 wrote *Dangerous Corner* in one week to prove that he could write for the stage. This was the first of a number of "time plays". In *Time and the Conways* (1937), the family gathers in Act I to celebrate Kay Conway's twenty-first birthday. Act II takes place twenty years later; the ambitions of Kay and her siblings have come to nothing. When, in Act III, the action returns to the present, Kay still has vague "memories" of what the future holds.

Priestley also wrote popular middle-class comedies. One of the best is *Laburnum Grove* (1933), a sharp dig at the middle classes' ambivalence about money. Among his moral tales for the stage, the best known is *An Inspector Calls* (1945). The respectable Birling family is visited by a police inspector, who questions them about a young girl's suicide and exposes their moral implication in the tragedy. They are alarmed by his visit, but soon discover that police officials have never heard of the inspector. Sinking back into complacency, they receive a phone call to say that the girl has committed suicide and an inspector will be coming to call.

BUSBY BERKELEY (1895-1976)

American choreographer. "A new dance director has been born on Broadway," wrote a New York critic in 1927, reviewing Rodgers and HART's *A Connecticut Yankee.* Just over three years later, Busby Berkeley (the neonate in question) settled in Hollywood to put the American Dream definitively on film, but in that short time he had directed, choreographed or acted in twenty Broadway shows. The complex rhythms and precise geometry that were to typify his dance routines in the movies were the glossy fruit of stage productions such as *Present Arms* (1928) and *The Earl Carroll Vanities of 1928.*

ARNOLT BRONNEN (1895-1959)

Austrian playwright. In the 1920s Bronnen rivalled Bertolt BRECHT as the most performed playwright in Germany. *Vatermord* (1922), his tale of parricide and incest, caused an uproar in Berlin, and subsequent works showed a move to an even more brutal, erotic realism. They included *Geburt der Jugend* (1922), a violent play about rebellious schoolchildren, *Die Exzesse* (1923) and *Anarchie in Sillian* (1924). *Rheinische Rebellen* (1925) revealed Bronnen's growing Nazi sympathies, but in 1945 he became a Communist.

OSCAR HAMMERSTEIN II (1895-1960)

American lyricist and librettist. When young Oscar Hammerstein asked his employers at the law office for a rise, they turned him down. "If they'd given me another twenty dollars a week I'd have stayed on and probably become a lawyer," he confessed. Instead he started work for his uncle Arthur, a Broadway producer.

After the failure of a four-act tragedy, Hammerstein established that his greatest talents lay in putting words to music. By 1924 the success of *Rose-Marie*, with music by Rudolph Friml, had introduced these talents to most of North America. *Showboat* (1927) was an even greater achievement and the best of several collaborations with Jerome Kern. But Hammerstein was to experience a number of relative failures before teaming up with Richard Rodgers for *Oklahoma!* (1943). What made that show revolutionary, as well as an unparalleled box-office success, was that the two collaborators had harnessed their talents to produce a musical in which songs were an integral part of the action. It was, like Gershwin's *Porgy and Bess*, a genuine American opera. The best Rodgers and Hammerstein shows that followed now read like an outline of American musical history: *Carousel* (1945), *South Pacific* (1949), *The King and I* (1951) and, a year before Hammerstein's death, *The Sound of Music* (1959), one of the biggest hits of all time.

Hammerstein's lyrics are often cloyingly sentimental. At their best, however, they are both simple and surprisingly moving, qualities that defy explanation except in the author's own words (from "Some Enchanted Evening"):
Who can explain it? Who can tell you why?
Fools give you reasons, wise men never try.

LORENZ HART (1895-1943)

American lyricist and librettist. The collaboration between Richard Rodgers and Lorenz Hart is a Broadway legend. They worked together exclusively from the time of their first meeting (in 1918) until the year of Hart's death. Among their twenty-seven musicals are *The Connecticut Yankee* (1927), *Babes in Arms* (1937), *The Boys From Syracuse* (1938) and *Pal Joey* (1940), while more than one thousand songs include "The Lady Is A Tramp" and "Falling in Love With Love".

Hart was a sophisticated lyricist, wittier than his great successor Oscar HAMMERSTEIN II, and with a seemingly endless store of improbable rhymes. His lyric writing was occasionally over-hasty—a practice which sometimes led to imprecision. His personal life was plagued with anxiety over his homosexuality and his height (he was just over five feet tall). Increasingly afflicted by alcoholism, he left the theatre during the New York première of *A Connecticut Yankee* (1943) and died after a two-day spree.

BERT LAHR (1895-1967)

American comedian. Bert Lahr's "dog face" is now best remembered peering from behind the mane of the Cowardly Lion in the 1939 film of *The Wizard of Oz*, but he was always more at home on the stage. His immense energy, loud humour, grotesque expressions, shouts, howls and his famous catch-phrase "Gnong! Gnong! Gnong!" made audiences roar with laughter: laughter that he could not live without.

Born Irving Lahrheim, Lahr was on stage in a "kids' act" by fifteen. After some difficult years he became a leading burlesque comedian, probably the last great American comic to come out of this tradition. He formed his own vaudeville act in 1921 with his first wife, Mercedes Delpino. Lahr's talent and determination took the show to Broadway but the strain was too much for Mercedes.

In 1928 Lahr played a prize-fighter in *Hold Everything*, the first of many musicals that were to confirm him as a star for more than forty years. Later shows included *Life Begins at 8:40* (1934) and the last big musical revue, *Two on the Aisle* (1951). After the war Lahr ventured into serious drama and was acclaimed as Estragon in Samuel BECKETT's *Waiting for Godot* and as Bottom in *A Midsummer Night's Dream.* Even these "straight" roles often allowed him to indulge the hilarious comic style he had developed on the musical and burlesque stage.

MAX MILLER (1895-1963)

English music-hall star. Miller, the Cheeky Chappie of music-hall, wore clothes of quite immaculate bad taste: flashy shoes, kipper ties, opalescent jackets and gargantuan plus-fours. His genius lay in a confiding – almost conspiratorial – manner that persuaded audiences to overlook the awfulness of his material.

Miller's tales (of Jack and Mary in the Dairy, and other lengthy amorous adventures) had an air of moral innocence that enthralled the public. Like an Elizabethan jester, he pleased his audience by conniving playfully with them to nurture, express and condone their own moral frailty. "It's people like you that get me a bad name", he explained with a feigned helplessness. Only the magistrate who fined him for his cheekiest jokes remained stubbornly unamused.

FLORENCE MILLS (c 1895-1927)

American singer and dancer. Florence Mills, a Harlem girl, rose to fame in *Shuffle Along* (1921), one of the first

Bert Lahr and **Ethel Merman** starred in the Cole Porter musical, *Du Barry Was a Lady*, in 1939. Both began as vaudeville performers. Merman developed her clear, brassy voice in cabaret, and Lahr was "the last and most marvellous of the American clowns cradled in burlesque"

all-Negro shows to become popular in the 1920s. Florence was small and dynamic, with an enthralling, bird-like voice; the public loved her and her song "I'm Just Wild About Harry". She also took the show *Blackbirds* to Paris and London, where the Prince of Wales became one of her greatest fans. But New Yorkers were never to see her on stage again; she died of appendicitis shortly after her return to the United States.

PAUL MUNI (1895-1967)

Polish-born American actor. "To Paul Muni," said ARTHUR MILLER, "acting was not just a career, but an obsession." Muni's obsession began as a twelve-year-old when he successfully played an old man at a Yiddish theatre in Cleveland. Not until he was thirty-one did he make his English-language debut. During the 1930s and 1940s he starred in films such as *Scarface* and *The Story of Louis Pasteur*, but he frequently returned to the stage, where his greatest roles were Willy Loman in *Death of a Salesman* and Henry Drummond in *Inherit the Wind*. So great was his compulsion to "become" the role he was currently playing that he attended the London opening night party for Miller's play slumped and dejected, still the world-weary salesman.

MARCEL PAGNOL (1895-1974)

French playwright, film director and novelist. Pagnol's ancestors had lived in the South of France ever since fleeing Spain to escape the Inquisition, and his love of Provence is the inspiration for much of his writing. His first successful play was *Jazz* (1926), but it was *Topaze* (1928), a comic satire on money's power to corrupt, that brought him international fame. He went on to write his poetic trilogy *Marius* (1929), *Fanny* (1931) and *César* (which was produced first as a film in 1933). These popular, sentimental comedies about people of the Marseilles waterfront – Fanny a fishmonger, Marius her errant lover, and his father César, a barman – were welcomed for their wise humour and evocative southern atmosphere and dialect. In 1954 *Fanny* reappeared as a hit Broadway musical. Pagnol ceased to write for the theatre in 1933, turning his attention to the cinema.

JIMMIE SAVO (1895-1960)

American comedian. Like Charlie Chaplin, Savo was a mixture of down-at-heel, pathetic innocence and capricious cunning. He did comic sketches and worked in pantomime and Broadway revue. One of the most popular comedians in the business, he later appeared in such shows as *The Boys from Syracuse* (1938), (a take-off of SHAKE-SPEARE's *The Comedy of Errors*) and *What's Up* (1943).

FREDERICK VALK (1895-1956)

Czechoslovakian actor. A large, thick-set man with a powerful voice, expressive face and noble gestures, Valk became famous as a tragedian in London when anti-semitism had forced him from the German-speaking stage. Kenneth Tynan described Valk's Othello as "a great stunned animal strapped to the rack" and remarked that few actors could, at his age, "deliver those great sledge-hammer blows to the solar plexus".

ANTONIN ARTAUD (1896-1948)

French actor, director, playwright and poet. Artaud completed only one full-length drama, but his most dramatic theories have spawned a host of plays by writers such as Jean GENET and Arthur ADAMOV and been an influence on such directors as BLIN and BARRAULT. Originally an actor, in 1930 he started the Théâtre Alfred Jarry with Roger VITRAC. They produced four plays, including Artaud's sketch *Le Jet de Sang*, in which a prostitute eats a young man's eyes.

In 1931 a performance by a troupe of Balinese dancers revolutionized Artaud's ideas, inspiring him to write a number of essays on what he called the "Theatre of Cruelty". Collected in *Le Théâtre et son double* (1938), these writings have been vital to the development of modern drama. Theatre, he asserted, must break away from its purely literary connections and become an exorcism in which the audience is frightened, bewitched and spiritually overwhelmed. He put his ideas into practice in 1935 in his play *Les Cenci*. The chaotic first production, with its jarring light and sound effects and its revolving scenery, was only fully appreciated in the decades that followed.

Artaud had many periods of mental instability and in 1937 entered an asylum, to be released only two years before his death.

A monkish cowl is oddly appropriate to **Antonin Artaud**, the demonic visionary of modern theatre. He wanted drama to cast a spell like primitive ritual, tapping the forces of the unconscious

PHILIP BARRY (1896-1949)

American playwright. Whether social comedies or psychological dramas, the plays of Philip Barry were heavy with meaning. Not surprisingly, his best works were those which tempered their moralizing with sparkling comedy. While *Hotel Universe* (1930) and *Here Come the Clowns* (1938) were at times pretentiously symbolic, comedies such as *Paris Bound* (1927) and particularly *The Philadelphia Story* (1939) charmed audiences and critics with good-humoured sentiment. The latter was a popular vehicle for Katharine HEPBURN, both on stage and screen.

PIERRE BLANCHARD (1896-1963)

French actor. A sensitive actor with a strangely disturbing face, Blanchard was particularly esteemed for playing mysterious characters, neurotics and eccentrics. He arrived on the Paris stage in 1919, and from 1921 also acted in films, in which he later fascinated audiences with his breathless speech and staring eyes, in fact a result of being gassed in the war.

Blanchard's long list of performances includes leading roles in the first productions of Marcel PAGNOL's *Jazz*, Armand SALACROU's *L'Inconnue d'Arras* and Henry de MONTHERLANT's *Malatesta*. In 1939 he joined the Comédie-Française, and excelled in interpretations of Julius Caesar and Oedipus.

GEORGE BURNS (1896...)

American comedian. At the age of thirteen, Burns, then Nathan Birnbaum, started in show business with his Peewee Quartet, a child group that sang for handouts outside New York bars. In 1923, after a number of difficult years in vaudeville, he met Gracie Allen (1906–64) and together (albeit single at the time) they started their famous husband and wife act. With Gracie as the impossibly scatty wife and George the bemused and exasperated husband, they were to delight audiences for more than thirty years. They married offstage in 1926, the same year as their show *Lamb Chops* went to New York. Signed up by a big theatre group, Burns and Allen toured America and Europe and in 1932 began their long career in radio and TV. Burns returned to the stage in the 1960s with his own one-man show, featuring the inevitable cigar and the inimitable timing.

IRA GERSHWIN (1896...)

American lyricist. So great was Ira's admiration for his younger brother that until 1924 he wrote under the name of Arthur Francis, in order not to dim the rising star of George Gershwin. In that year he reassumed the family name and collaborated with his brother for the first time on the popular *Lady, Be Good!* Until George's death in 1937 the Gershwins produced a series of innovative musicals, including *Oh, Kay!* (1926), *Funny Face* (1927), *Of Thee I Sing* (1931) and *Porgy and Bess* (1935). In songs such as "'S Wonderful", "Strike Up the Band" and "It Ain't Necessarily So" Ira neatly matched the sophisticated colours and fascinating rhythms of George's scores.

RUTH GORDON (1896...)

American actress, playwright and script-writer. Ruth Gordon was advised to leave drama school after her first year, but did not let this interfere with her ambition to act. Her early performances, although popular with the public, did not please the critics. One remarked, "Anyone who looks like that and acts like that must get off the stage." Undeterred, she gradually won recognition as a fine actress for her humour and great individuality. Roles she played with distinction include Mrs Pinchwife in William WYCHERLEY's *The Country Wife*, Nora in IBSEN's *A Doll's House*, and Dolly Levi in *The Matchmaker* by Thornton WILDER.

Ruth Gordon wrote three plays, of which *Over Twenty-one* (1944) and *Years Ago* (1946) were very successful in New York. Also well known as a film actress, she won an Oscar in 1969 for a frightening performance in *Rosemary's Baby*, and with her husband, Garson KANIN, wrote many screenplays such as *Adam's Rib* and *Pat and Mike*.

OTTO GRIEBLING (1896-1972)

German-born clown. When Griebling moved to America in his teens he knew no English. It was thus of necessity that he learned the art of mime, of which he was half a century later to become a supreme exponent.

He worked first as a bareback rider, but in 1930 broke both legs in a fall. While convalescing he taught himself juggling and read widely about miming and clowning. He then spent twenty years working up his act to become a star of the Ringling Brothers and Barnum and Bailey Circus in New York.

A "tramp" or "hobo" clown, Griebling wore clothes of unbelievable dilapidation. His most famous routine consisted of a hilariously prolonged attempt to deliver a block of rapidly melting ice to an imaginary Mrs Schultz. His genius lay in his ability to manipulate an audience's mood by unpredictably changing his own. Unrivalled in the art of "body-language", Griebling never spoke. Ironically, this virtue once again became a necessity when his larynx was surgically removed in 1970.

WALTER MEHRING (1896...)

German cabaret artist. Mehring was the most important cabaret artist to emerge from the anarchic Dada movement in Berlin after the First World War. With the satirical artist George Grosz he performed such pieces as *Race Between the Sewing Machine and the Typewriter*, and *Private Conversation of Two Senile Men Behind a Fire-screen*. Mehring went on to use cabaret as an organ of dissent, becoming immensely popular with his quick repartee, vulgar Berlin dialect and racy, satirical songs.

Mehring worked in Berlin until 1924, also writing sketches for Max REINHARDT's left-wing cabaret *Schall und Rauch*. After four years in France he returned for a production of *Der Kaufmann von Berlin*, his satirical version of *The Merchant of Venice*, which exposed the link between capital and the arms market. He now used his cabaret act to attack the Nazis, but had to flee to France in 1933. Mehring spent the war in America, and worked briefly in Hollywood before finally deciding to make Switzerland his home.

HENRY DE MONTHERLANT (1896-1972)

French playwright, novelist and essayist. For many years Montherlant showed little interest in the theatre, but he later emerged as one of France's greatest post-war dramatists. Expelled from school on account of a fervent friendship with another boy, he enlisted as a private in the First World War and was seriously wounded. During the next twenty years he wrote highly successful novels on the courage of bullfighters, sportsmen and soldiers.

Montherlant's first play, the tragedy *La Reine morte*, appeared in 1942. He went on to write a number of important stage works, including *Malatesta* (1950), and his "Catholic trilogy": *Le Maître de Santiago* (1948), *La Ville dont le Prince est un enfant* (1953) and *Port-Royal* (1954), psychological dramas dealing with spiritual problems. For plays of great seriousness and intensity, Montherlant's stage works enjoy surprising popularity.

Obsessed, in his writing, with the subject of suicide, he finally fell victim to it himself, as he became progressively terrified of going blind in his old age.

ROBERT CEDRIC SHERRIFF (1896-1975)

English playwright and novelist. R. C. Sherriff disappointed and baffled his admirers by writing one grandly successful play and then withdrawing to a modest life of cricket, rowing, archaeology and literary competence. *Journey's End* (1928) was a stunning hit, the first English play to deal unsentimentally with the trench warfare of the previous decade. It tells the story of nerve-shattered Captain Stanhope (played in the first performance by Laurence OLIVIER) and his doomed soldiers on the Western

Front. Albert Einstein urged its production in Germany; the manuscript fetched £1500 when sold by the League of Nations. But gentle Sherriff wrote nothing more like it. *Badger's Green* (1930), a comedy about cricket, and the screenplay of *Goodbye Mr Chips* are characteristic of his other dramatic works.

ROBERT SHERWOOD (1896-1955)

American playwright. Sherwood's moral commitments led him from pacifism to a militant hatred of fascism, beliefs which are mirrored in his plays. *The Road to Rome* (1927), his first Broadway hit, was a gentle comedy offering a pacifist's explanation as to why Hannibal failed to capture Rome, but with *The Petrified Forest* (1934) (in which the then unknown Humphrey Bogart starred as the killer, Duke Mantee) and *Idiot's Delight* (1936), a black comedy which eerily predicted the Second World War, Sherwood came to believe that tyranny must be opposed. *Abe Lincoln in Illinois* (1938) and *There Shall Be No Night* (1940) were further dramatic arguments in favour of the vigilant protection of democracy.

CARL ZUCKMAYER (1896-1977)

German playwright and novelist. For over fifty years Zuckmayer wrote consistently well-made, thought-provoking pieces on topical issues. The controversy aroused by *Pankraz erwacht, oder Die Hinterwälder* (1925), a harrowing saga of rustic incest, died down when the author produced *Der fröhliche Weinberg* (1925), a jovial comedy set in his native Rhineland. The latter work showed great sympathy and understanding for the ordinary man. This is also evident in Zuckmayer's comic master-piece, *Der Hauptmann von Köpenick* (1931), a brilliant satire on officialdom based on the true story of an ex-convict who successfully deceives a whole town by wearing the uniform of an army captain.

The Second World War, during which he sheltered in Switzerland and the USA, provided fresh inspiration for Zuckmayer. *Des Teufels General* (1946) analyses the guilt and responsibility of those who collaborated with Nazidom, the Luftwaffe general of the title being modelled on a real-life character. *Das kalte Licht* (1955) also tackled a topical and emotive subject, in this case the unquiet conscience of an atomic physicist (who bears a strong resemblance to Klaus Fuchs).

ROBERT ALTON (1897-1957)

American choreographer and director. Alton danced in the 1924 *Greenwich Village Follies* staged by John Murray Anderson before transforming Broadway shows with his own innovative choreography. His adroit routines broke away from mass-kicking chorus lines and perfectly complemented the sophisticated musicals of the

Carl Zuckmayer's plays depict a wide range of characters and situations with unfailing insight. His most famous work, *Der Hauptmann von Köpenick* (*above*) exposes the stuffy pretensions of authority in a delightful manner

This ominous night scene (*right*) illustrates the kind of mood that **Caspar Neher's** designs wove for the plays of Bertolt Brecht. But he was also renowned for his sensitive staging of Mozart's operas

thirties and forties. From 1933 to 1944 Alton was directing at least one show a year on Broadway, many of them smash hits, such as *Anything Goes* (1934), *Du Barry Was a Lady* (1939) and *Pal Joey* (1940).

PIERRE FRESNAY (1897–1975)

French actor. In his early twenties, Fresnay was the leading player in the Comédie-Française, excelling in the classical roles of RACINE as well as in the Romantic comedies of Alfred DE MUSSET. But in an extraordinary gesture of independence, he rejected the future his career there offered him and broke his contract with the company.

The ensuing litigation won his freedom – at a price of 200,000 francs. Thereafter he became renowned for the "scrupulous, almost ruthless integrity" of his performances in plays by such as Marcel PAGNOL and Jean ANOUILH, as well as in many films. The intelligence and subtlety of Fresnay's work is rare for the period. It certainly unnerved his colleagues from time to time, one of whom remarked: "He's a marvellous actor, but he always makes you feel you are using the wrong spoon."

FREDRIC MARCH (1897–1975)

American actor. Though born auspiciously in Racine, Wisconsin, Fred Bickel was at first intent on becoming a banker. To this end he went to New York in 1920, but boredom, a landlady's theatrical reminiscences and a taste for amateur acting drew him inexorably to the stage. Several plays later he was Fredric March, with a reputation for "earnest" and "unaffected" performances that could also be "heroic and masterful". Over a long career in theatre and films he bore out his promise as a disciplined actor of considerable versatility whose successes ranged from Mr Antrobus in Thornton WILDER's *The Skin of Our Teeth* to Willy Loman in a film version of ARTHUR MILLER's *Death of a Salesman*. March's powers were shown to best advantage in his award-winning role as the father in O'NEILL's *Long Day's Journey into Night*, combining pettiness and magnificence in a "character portrait of grandeur".

CASPAR NEHER (1897–1962)

German stage designer. Neher is particularly famous for his work with Bertolt BRECHT, with whom he collaborated on a number of plays, including *Der Hofmeister* (1949) and *Herr Puntila und sein Knecht Matti* (1950). He was one of the first German stage designers to experiment with all-round theatre, an attempt to reduce the gulf between the audience and the stage. Evocative rather than realistic, his sets tended to be stark, with sombre background colours and brilliant lighting. Brecht praised his designs for their exceptional ability to inspire the actors. Neher worked with many directors and was in demand through-

Eternally feminine, **Arletty** (*above*) was once accused of collaboration by a French court because a German officer had been her lover during the Occupation. She responded simply, "But I am a woman", and the court bowed to the timeless logic of her defence

Bertolt Brecht at work (*right*). The spare furnishings of the room reveal not just the playwright's ideological dislike of ostentation, but the firm discipline that enabled him to turn out masterpieces even while living in exile

As a director, **Hans Jacob Nilsen** raised critical hackles with his uncompromisingly modern productions. But as an actor (*below*) he would still don romantic costumes

out Europe. He also created new and exciting designs for opera productions, as well as writing librettos.

HANS JACOB NILSEN (1897-1957)

Norwegian director and actor. Nilsen was initially known for his acting, but it was as a director that he made his greatest contribution to Norwegian theatre. Though strongly influenced by German and Russian drama, his treatment of both modern and classic plays was fresh and intense. In 1948 Nilsen provoked hostile reaction with a particularly famous, "anti-romantic" production of *Peer Gynt*. This was a complete rejection of the traditional Norwegian approach to IBSEN, but his new, realistic theatre was soon accepted and admired.

THORNTON WILDER (1897-1975)

American playwright and novelist. Thornton Wilder's substantial contribution to the theatre reflected his contempt for traditional drama: "The trouble began in the nineteenth century and was connected with the rise of the middle classes – they wanted their theatre soothing," he explained. According to Wilder, the unique power of the theatre was its combination of particular actions and universal truths, but the fixed location of place in conventional drama restricted its ability to relate the particular to the universal.

In his early one-act plays (published in 1931) Wilder defied theatrical conventions of time and place, attempting "to capture not verisimilitude but reality". In *The Happy Journey to Trenton and Camden*, four chairs represent a car in which a family travels seventy miles in twenty minutes; and ninety years of Christmases pass during *The Long Christmas Dinner*. Wilder's main dramatic works develop further his concept of theatre. *Our Town* (1938), one of the landmarks of American drama, discovers in the everyday life of Grover's Corners, New Hampshire, a metaphor for human existence. Distanced by an informative and omniscient Stage Manager, the audience sees the past, the future, life and death inextricably interwoven in this most moving of Wilder's plays. Wilder said that the work was "an attempt to find a value above all price for the smallest events in our daily life . . . but I have set the village against the largest dimensions of time and place". The Antrobus family in *The Skin of Our Teeth* (1942) live both in prehistoric times and a modern suburb. For Wilder life is cyclical but inevitable, however banal it might be. The Stage Manager in *Our Town* describes life as "the cottage, the go-cart, the Sunday afternoon drives in the Ford, the first rheumatism, the grandchildren, the second rheumatism, the death bed, the reading of the will. Once in a thousand times it's interesting."

Wilder admitted his debt to such authors as James Joyce, and though he regretted that he himself was "not one of the new dramatists we are looking for", he hoped he had prepared the way for them with his drama. It is ironic that *Hello, Dolly!* (1964), the musical version of Wilder's play *The Matchmaker* (1954), has been such an enormous success at charming and soothing middle-class theatre audiences.

JUDITH ANDERSON (1898...)

Australian-born American actress. Judith Anderson made her debut in Sydney in 1915, but her successful stage career has been mainly in the United States, where she has consistently excelled in powerful, tragic roles, particularly in SHAKESPEARE. Her Medea in Sir John GIELGUD's 1947 production of EURIPIDES' play was a triumph. Dame Judith has played Lady Macbeth twice with great distinction, opposite Laurence OLIVIER in 1937 and Maurice Evans in 1941. In 1936 she played the Queen to Gielgud's Hamlet, and in 1970 she herself played Hamlet. She has also had a distinguished film career.

ARLETTY (1898...)

French actress. Arletty (Arlette-Léonie Bathia) is best known as a distinguished film actress, whose most famous stage role was Blanche in Jean COCTEAU's adaptation of TENNESSEE WILLIAMS's *A Streetcar Named Desire*. Her early career in music-hall and operetta began when she walked into a theatre by chance and auditioned for a review by singing "It's a Long Way to Tipperary". She later claimed that had she been passing the high-minded Théâtre Odéon that morning, she might just as easily have become a classical actress.

BERTOLT BRECHT (1898-1956)

German playwright and poet. Although nobody would dispute Brecht's radical influence on the theatre, he cannot be said to have changed it (as he intended) from a place of escapist entertainment to a centre for political education. Even in his most polemic pieces, his poetry, humour and humanity have made his revolutionary messages palatable to the well-heeled middle-classes of the West, who rarely leave the theatre intent on destroying the capitalist system.

Contrasting the traditional "dramatic theatre" with his new style of "epic theatre", Brecht claimed that the danger of the former was in identifying too strongly with the characters on stage. Conventional audiences reacted with the actors. "I weep when they weep, I laugh when they laugh", they said, and concluded that human nature was immutable. The audiences of the ideal Epic Theatre, on the other hand, should be detached observers who say to themselves, "I laugh when they weep, I weep when they laugh", and conclude therefore that human nature can be changed for the better. Hence Brecht's famous *Verfremdungseffekt* (alienation effect). Audiences must always be reminded that they are watching an unreal spectacle. There should be no illusion of continuity between the scenes, nor should the actors be consistently naturalistic in their roles. The only props should be those essential to the action, and the lights should glare down stark and white upon the stage.

Already a leading figure in German theatre before his definitive confirmation as a Marxist, Brecht in his early twenties lived a life of nihilistic anarchy, fuelled by sex and alcohol in the style of his great hero, the medieval French poet François Villon. This antisocial period is reflected in his first two plays, *Baal* (1922) and *Trommeln in der Nacht* (1922), the hero of which retires to bed rather than fight in the revolution.

About the time of *Mann ist Mann* (1926), his first use of the parable-form, Brecht began to study Marx in earnest, making capitalist greed the prime target for his works. At the same time he formed his brilliant partnership with the composer Kurt Weill, with whom he produced *Aufstieg und Fall der Stadt Mahagonny* (1927) and *Die Dreigroschenoper* (1928). The latter, his version of John GAY's *The Beggar's Opera*, has remained the most popular of all Brecht's works, though more for its stirring music and moving lyrics than for its portrayal of the bourgeoisie as a band of robbers.

In 1933 all Brecht's writings were banned, and thus began his astonishingly fruitful years of exile. While he and his considerable entourage were accommodated by a series of wealthy Scandinavian patronesses, he worked on the plays that form the essential nucleus of his work. They received their first performances in Zurich during the war and included *Mutter Courage und ihre Kinder* in 1941, *Der gute Mensch von Sezuan* and *Leben des Galileo Galilei* in 1943. No amount of alienation can prevent one from sympathizing with the tragic but irrepressible Mother Courage, or with the idealistic, all-too-human Galileo. *Der gute Mensch*, which also demonstrates the uselessness of being "good" in an evil society, is in the form of a Chinese fable. This highly poetic style was used again by Brecht in *Der Kaukasische Kreidekreis* (*The Caucasian Chalk Circle*).

Brecht settled in California in 1941, remaining until 1948, when he made his momentous decision to accept the invitation of the East German government to form a state theatre company, the legendary Berliner Ensemble. Producing and rewriting SOPHOCLES, MOLIÈRE, SHAKESPEARE and FARQUHAR left him limited time for original work in his final years. The great controversy of this period was his failure to make any statement on the Berlin workers' revolt of 1953, during which his company continued to rehearse his adaptation of *Coriolanus*. These events were the subject of ironic speculation by Günter GRASS in his "German tragedy" *Die Plebejer proben den Aufstand*. It is sad that the century's most influential dramatist should have become a pawn in the Cold War, both sides claiming him as their own.

Expressionism

Audiences in 1917 were amazed to see a snow-covered tree transformed into a skeleton in Georg KAISER's *Von Morgens bis Mitternachts* and were terrified to hear the prolonged scream that opened Reinhard GOERING's *Seeschlacht*. Today such effects are commonplace, for in the fields of design and direction Expressionism has had an enormous influence throughout the theatre.

The label expressionist is now applied to almost any non-realistic production, especially if it uses extraordinary lighting effects. But it originally referred to a short-lived experiment in German theatre that reached its height at the end of the First World War. Many of the experimenters were not primarily dramatists: Oskar KOKOSCHKA was a painter, Ernst Barlach a sculptor and Fritz von Unruh and Franz WERFEL were poets. Their common cause was a rebellion against rigid social structures in an increasingly mechanized world. Kokoschka believed that the artist should listen to his "inner voice" and "release control". Then "all laws are left behind. One's soul is a reverberation of the universe."

Already STRINDBERG's later plays, particularly *The Road to Damascus* (1900) and *A Dream Play* (1901), had attempted to project a subjective vision of the world on the stage, while Frank WEDEKIND's tragedies of suppressed sexuality foreshadowed another major preoccupation of the movement. A typical combination of these two influences was Walter HASENCLEVER's incitement to parricidal rebellion, *Der Sohn*.

Like Filippo Marinetti and the Italian futurists, expressionist playwrights and poets often wrote without articles or qualifiers, stripping language to its essential, most powerful elements: nouns and verbs. Such violent language was well suited to the cataclysmic dramas of Kaiser and Ernst TOLLER, the two major playwrights of the period. Their works are often likened to *Everyman*, for the heroes tend to be nameless young men, isolated from society as history around them goes mad.

The end of the First World War brought the homecoming soldier to the expressionist stage, notably in Toller's *Der deutsche Hinkemann*. The horror of war had been so overwhelming that in opposition to it expressionists like Kokoschka had merely invoked a vague cosmic unity of spirit. Now writers began to ask once more what should or could be done to change society. Characteristic of this early political genre was *Trommeln in der Nacht*, a play by the young Bertolt BRECHT.

Meanwhile a new generation of directors had begun to politicize the theatre in accordance with the troubled times. Although their declared intention was to express the writers' ideas as powerfully as possible, the guiding principle of a production by Leopold JESSNER or Jürgen FEHLING was the director's own conception of the play. There was a general revolt, both against the constrictions of naturalism as an end in itself and against the artistic lyricism of Max REINHARDT. The means available to the director now included sound recordings, back projection and sequences of film. The most revolutionary of the new directors, Erwin PISCATOR, seized on such paraphernalia to create a form of dramatic poetry appropriate to the twentieth century. The most significant of the new dramatists, Brecht, wrought from the varied techniques of Expressionism a theatre of genius.

An expressionist classic, **Bertolt Brecht**'s *Mutter Courage und ihre Kinder* indicted war and war-mongering. The indomitable title character is a camp follower whose profiteering costs her her whole family. Brecht's wife **Helene Weigel** (*second from left*) stars in his own staging of the play

KATHARINE CORNELL (1898-1974)

American actress and producer. Cornell and her husband, the producer and director Guthrie McClintic, formed one of the most celebrated theatrical partnerships of the twentieth century, playing on Broadway, throughout the United States and to enthralled Allied soldiers in Europe. Contemporary writers praised her "integrity and devotion", her "pulsatile and electric presence", her "ability to reveal the inner life of a character and to clarify what the text itself did not make explicit", and her impassioned voice, which could "lick at the dialogue like a flame". These gifts produced performances of great power in her Juliet, her Cleopatra, and in SHAW heroines.

ÉTIENNE DECROUX (1898…)

French mime, actor and author. Decroux is considered the father of modern mime. Rejecting the traditions of Romantic pantomime, he developed a codification of bodily movements that excluded the expressive use of the face and hands in order to tell a story with elegant and unhurried precision.

Decroux trained as a speaking actor at Jacques COPEAU's Vieux-Colombier, a centre of avant-garde art and theatrical reform. From the late 1920s through the 1940s he performed on the Paris stage and in films and radio. During the same period he developed his theories of mime. *La Vie primitive*, the culmination of his research, was performed in 1931 without text, scenery, costumes or music. The Théâtre de l'Atelier, which he ran with Charles DULLIN, became a platform for presenting new works, often performed by his students. His son Maximilian continues his work as teacher and mime.

Decroux was not thought a great actor and was a severe instructor but, as the spiritual heir of the mime DEBURAU, he inspired the loyalty of many students, including MARCEL MARCEAU and Jean-Louis BARRAULT. In Carné's film *Les Enfants du Paradis* (1945) he played the father of Deburau, a role immortalized by his student Barrault.

GRACIE FIELDS (1898-1979)

English singer and comedienne. Gracie Fields was born above a fish-and-chip shop in Rochdale, Lancashire, and built her act largely on the very poverty of her origins. Clad in a humble headscarf and an old mackintosh, "Our Gracie" would belt out comic monologues and songs such as "The Biggest Aspidistra in the World", then switch to the mawkish "Sally" in a sentimental *fortissimo*.

During the Second World War, Gracie Fields became something of a national monument, and raised over one million pounds for the war effort. She also amassed a tidy fortune for herself, retiring with her third husband to the Isle of Capri (about which she sang another song and where she opened a restaurant).

FEDERICO GARCÍA LORCA (1898-1936)

Spanish poet and playwright. On a summer night in 1936, without either trial or apparent motivation, fascist sympathizers shot García Lorca and killed at once Spain's greatest modern poet and a playwright of genius and international standing.

As a student in Granada, Lorca was gifted at both music and writing. After briefly studying law, he returned to these interests and at the University of Madrid became known as an able pianist and a brilliant poet. Although he had experimented with drama in his youth, it was not until 1927 that he had his first stage success with *Mariana*

Katharine Cornell (*above*) was renowned as a distinguished and dedicated exponent of serious theatre. But she also illuminated lighter roles. Here she plays the mistress of Casanova

An image of pure mime from one of the great masters and theoreticians of the art. **Étienne Decroux** (*below*) inspired a generation of performers to express emotion through the body

Pineda, about the legendary Spanish patriot. His friend Salvador Dali, an eccentric young surrealist artist, designed the production. Lorca subsequently wrote several interesting and highly stylized poetic dramas, but his real theatrical education began in 1932, when he led La Barraca, his own company, in tours throughout Spain.

The three great tragedies for which Lorca is universally acclaimed date from the four last years of his life. All have rural settings and deal with the most essential human passions: lust, maternity, hatred, envy and love. *Bodas de sangre* (*Blood Wedding*, 1933) is the first and most frequently performed of the trilogy. It describes the inevitable tragedy that results from a conflict between love and loveless honour. The heroine of *Yerma* (1934) longs fruitlessly for a child and finally strangles her husband. In *La Casa de Bernarda Alba* (a prose work written in 1936) the newly widowed Bernarda attempts to cloister her five grown-up daughters. As in the earlier two plays, such an arbitrary suppression of life and lust leads only to death. Lorca's own end was a senseless affirmation of this dramatic obsession.

MICHEL DE GHELDERODE
(1898-1962)

Belgian playwright. Michel de Ghelderode wrote over fifty plays, some in Flemish, but most in French. It was only when *Hop! Signor, Escurial* and *Mademoiselle Jaïre*
were performed in Paris after the war that his work became well known outside Belgium. An invalid, Ghelderode lived a secluded, scholarly life in a house full of masks and puppets. His drama, a poetic and imaginative blend of the macabre, the grotesque, folklore and the Bible, is reminiscent of the Theatres of Cruelty and the Absurd. But Ghelderode was a devout Catholic and declared in an interview, "I believe in Man and I think that one can sense this in my work."

THERESE GIEHSE (1898-1975)

German actress. Therese Giehse was one of the most distinguished of modern German actresses. She began her career at the age of four in provincial theatres, but it was not until the première of Bertolt BRECHT's *Mutter Courage und ihre Kinder* in 1941 that she discovered her greatest role.

Among her many other major roles were Vassa Zheleznova in the 1949 Berliner Ensemble production of Maxim GORKY's play of that name, and Claire Zachanassian in the 1956 Zurich production of Friedrich DÜRRENMATT's *Der Besuch der alten Dame*. Like many of her colleagues, Therese Giehse contributed to the satirical cabaret culture between the wars.

Six years later, in the first production of Dürrenmatt's bizarre tragicomedy, *Die Physiker* (*The Physicists*, 1962), she created the challenging role of Mathilde von Zahnd.

You, the audience IV

A classic image of stage glamour: fans besiege a matinée idol outside the West End theatre where he is starring, while a gleaming Rolls-Royce awaits. The time is the glamorous thirties when as Noel COWARD proudly recalled, the people on stage were even better dressed than their elegant audiences. But the moment is timeless. Though sometimes more an occupational hazard than a blessing, public exposure has always been part of a star's life. When a celebrated beauty like MAXINE ELLIOTT simply drove down Broadway, the event became a royal progress, attracting the envious gaze of gawping crowds. In fact, like many another actress before her, Miss Elliott numbered royalty among her admirers, being a personal friend of Edward VII. Yet a monarch's favour might not necessarily please the larger public. Londoners loved Nell GWYNN, mistress of Charles II, but objected to the king's current French Catholic paramour. Challenged by a suspicious crowd one night, bright Nell delighted them by identifying herself as "His Majesty's *Protestant* whore".

Worlds away from capitals and courts, audiences were no less responsive. In the nineteenth-century American West, grizzled miners applauded the songs and dances of little Lotta CRABTREE by tossing gold nuggets at her feet. But frontier manners could also be dangerously rough and ready: on a Texas tour, Maurice BARRYMORE, father of John, Lionel and Ethel, admonished a local tough for filthy language. Unimpressed by the aura of the stage, the rowdy pulled a gun, shot Barrymore in the arm and killed another actor before bystanders (including JOHN DREW) disarmed him.

Earlier in the nineteenth century, rival supporters of the actors Edwin FORREST and William MACREADY had sparked violence on a much more grievous scale. Forrest was the champion of American theatre and democracy; Macready supposedly stood for England and class distinction. Macready's 1848 tour of America was continually sabotaged by audience hostility. "One ruffian", he reported in disbelief, "threw into the middle of the stage the half carcass of a sheep!" The tragic climax came on 10 May, 1849, at New York's Astor Place Opera House. Furious demonstrators in the theatre brought Macready's performance to a halt, while outside mobs attracted by inflammatory posters, rioted. Troops and police opened fire, with many casualties.

Though its consequences are rarely fatal, audience approval can be crushingly emphatic. Authors are no more immune than actors. In a famous episode, Henry James was lured to the footlights only to be stunned by a volley of boos. With such precedents, the wise entertainer learns never to rely on fickle adulation. No matter how ecstatic its response to one play or one performance, the audience is always, as John Barrymore said, "a great hulking monster with four thousand eyes and forty thousand teeth . . . that . . . makes or breaks men like me".

EDGAR Y HARBURG (1898...)

American lyricist and librettist. Although not as familiar a name as HAMMERSTEIN or LORENZ HART, E. Y. "Yip" Harburg wrote some of the most familiar and witty words ever heard on an American stage. As a teenager he worked on the high school paper with his good friend Ira GERSHWIN, but after college he went into business. Not until he was in his thirties did he give up "this dreamy abstract thing called business" in favour of songwriting, "the business of dreams". "Brother, Can You Spare a Dime?" from *New Americana* (1932) was a hit during the depressed 1930s while the 1940s adopted the Academy Award winning "Over the Rainbow" from the film *The Wizard of Oz* as its escapist anthem. Two of Harburg's best musicals date from 1944 and 1947 respectively: *Bloomer Girl* (with his longtime collaborator Harold Arlen) and *Finian's Rainbow*. A later successful collaboration with Arlen, *Jamaica* (1957), gave Lena HORNE her greatest role.

Harburg's political and social concerns are evident in several of his best songs. "The Eagle and Me" from *Bloomer Girl* has been called "a hymn to human dignity", but many, like "April in Paris", are merely great expressions of an American dream.

EMMETT KELLY (1898...)

American clown. Emmett Kelly was known to two generations of Americans as the tramp-clown Weary Willie.

Always in character, "Weary Willie" sorrowfully shows a young autograph-hunter his battered, elongated shoe. **Emmett Kelly** made the clown's woes a source of delight to millions of circus-goers

Kelly, who had wanted to be an artist, first created Willie as a cartoon character. But when he brought him to life as a clown in 1924, the shabby, unshaven Willie was considered too dirty to be entertaining. It was not until 1933, after the Depression had made the tramp a part of American life, that the sad clown who never talked or smiled replaced the conventional white-face character that Kelly had previously assumed. Willie, according to Kelly, is "the hobo who found out the hard way that the deck is stacked, the dice 'frozen', the race fixed and the wheel crooked, but there is always present that one, tiny, forlorn spark of hope still glimmering in his soul which makes him keep trying". Kelly was so attached to Willie that he refused to use him when he played the part of a clown murderer in a film, and he was distraught when his son adopted the character of Willie in his act.

GERTRUDE LAWRENCE (1898-1952)

English actress. "In adolescence she was barely pretty. Now, without apparent effort, she gives the impression of sheer loveliness," said Noel COWARD, amazed at the transformation of Gertrude Lawrence Klasen, whom he had known as a stage-struck girl of fourteen. After early successes in revue and musical comedy, she starred with Coward in the première of his *Private Lives* (1930) and revealed that her dramatic abilities were also reaching an unforeseen maturity. Her grace, wit and perfect timing were perfectly suited to Coward's work.

In the 1940s Lawrence starred in MOSS HART and Kurt Weill's *Lady in the Dark*, SHAW's *Pygmalion* and Coward's *Blithe Spirit*. Totally dedicated to the theatre and adored by the public, she collapsed while appearing in *The King and I*, and shortly afterwards died.

BEATRICE LILLIE (1898…)

Canadian-born comic actress. Lillie's autobiography is called *Every Other Inch a Lady*, a title that neatly characterizes her alluring mixture of aristocratic hauteur and raffish charm. This image was publically reinforced by her marriage to an English baronet and by her intimacy

Fred and **Adele Astaire** disport themselves as tots in one of the show-stopping numbers from *The Band Wagon*. His sister's retirement led to Fred's sparkling alliance with Hollywood and with Ginger Rogers

with such brilliant personalities as Ivor NOVELLO and Noel COWARD.

Her most celebrated revue-sketch was an act, reminiscent of a Fragonard painting, in which she dangled over the audience on a swing and removed her garters. But much of her comedy was more subtly satirical than this. Critics praised her "fluttering urbanity" and "pixyish, antic personality". It was these qualities that Coward saw in Lillie when he wrote "Mad Dogs and Englishmen" for her, and which made her one-woman shows, such as *An Evening with Beatrice Lillie* (1952), such a success.

MARILYN MILLER (1898-1936)

American musical comedy star. Miller made her debut at the age of five, performing in a vaudeville trio with her parents. A decade later, Lee Shubert engaged her for his revue *The Passing Show of 1914*. Besides singing and dancing with memorable grace, she gave brilliant impressions of leading actresses and even of a female impersonator.

Miller's bewitching radiance did not escape the attention of the ever-watchful Flo ZIEGFELD. She appeared for him in *The Ziegfeld Follies of 1918* and in the Jerome Kern musicals *Sally* (1920) and *Sunny* (1925). She later appeared with Fred and Adele ASTAIRE and performed material by George and Ira GERSHWIN, P. G. WODEHOUSE, MOSS HART and Irving BERLIN. At the height of her fame she was earning $5000 a week.

Admiring critics strained for sufficiently flattering epithets: the "Titania of the jazz-age", one called her; the "very essence of feminine allure", the "twinkle-toed, dainty darling of a gaudy, poignant era", gasped two others. Whatever her title, she undoubtedly projected an innocence and freshness lacking in her rivals.

Marilyn's first husband was killed in a car-crash; thereafter, possibly as a result of her liaison with the rapacious Ziegfeld, her personal life went awry. She left the musical *As Thousands Cheer* (1933) in mid-run and never returned to the stage, dying three years later of complications following a trifling infection.

KAJ MUNK (1898-1944)

Danish playwright. As a young Lutheran minister, Munk attacked moral pettiness from both stage and pulpit. By contrast he celebrated the noble spirit of man and expressed sympathy with the youthful fascist movement. *Herod the King* (1928) and *Cant* (1931) show great characters locked in passionate conflict. In *Ordet* (1932), his best play, God himself intervenes to undo the tragic effects of narrow piety. But in the late 1930s Munk began to concentrate on the gross impiety of Adolf Hitler. When the Nazis occupied Denmark they banned such works as *He Sits at the Melting-Pot* (1938) and *Niels Ebbesen* (written in 1942), which explicitly advocated resistance to the Germans. Despite their threats Munk continued to speak out against the invaders, until he was murdered by the Gestapo.

PAUL ROBESON (1898-1976)

American actor and singer. A star student and the first black all-America college football player, Robeson nevertheless abandoned a career in law to become an actor. His power and dignity on stage, particularly in Eugene O'NEILL's *The Emperor Jones*, combined with his deep and resonant voice to assure international popularity. As Joe in *Showboat*, singing "Ol' Man River", he astonished both Broadway and the West End, but his greatest role was Othello, for which a London audience insisted on twenty curtain calls one night in 1930. He spent many years in Europe, enjoying the relative freedom and respect that Negroes could achieve there. It was not until 1943 that America was ready to see a black man kiss a white woman on stage, but when *Othello* did reach Broadway, it broke all records for a Shakespearean production there.

Robeson's outspoken socialism and involvement with civil rights made him a natural target in the McCarthy era. His passport was withdrawn in 1950; fear and ill-feeling subsequently made it difficult for him to find work. In 1958, at liberty to travel once again, Robeson resumed his international recitals, but after an illness in 1963 he withdrew from public life.

TOTÒ (1898-1967)

Italian comedian. The frenetic parodies and physical contortions of Totò first reached a wide audience in the smart cafes of Rome, Turin and Milan. He then returned to his native Naples, where he had been born with the unmanageable title of Antonio de Curtis, Prince of Bisanzio. There, as part of a variety company, he convulsed audiences with grotesque animal imitations as Tarzan, and his hilarious satire on militarism as D'Artagnan (he wore a chicken feather in his Chaplinesque bowler and was armed with a coat-hanger). Throughout the war, he appeared in revue in Rome (often with the support of Anna Magnani) and continued to use patently anti-fascist and anti-German material in his sketches.

Totò's immensely successful series of post-war films made him a national institution, but often the poor scripts caused those who could remember them to hanker for his earlier days in variety and revue.

MARCEL ACHARD (1899-1974)

French playwright and actor. Achard started writing as a boy on his parents' farm in the Rhône valley. Although his first mature play was roundly booed (or rather whistled, according to Gallic custom), he early established himself as France's leading "boulevard dramatist". He retained that position for nearly half a century.

Many of his plays are infused with the traditions of pantomime and the Commedia dell' Arte, notably *Voulez-vous jouer avec moâ* (1923). The hero of this burlesque is a clown, a character then in vogue among the literati, who delighted in discovering grief beneath the antic exterior of Achard's pierrots. In his most celebrated work, *Jean de la Lune* (1929), the hero Jef blindly reassures the heroine Marceline that she loves him, despite her protestation of preferring affairs with other men. The point of the piece is that Jef's naïve insistence succeeds. Achard's heroes, in fact, are remarkably consistent in their similarity. They inhabit an unreal and indolent world, from which they emerge only to blunder.

FRED ASTAIRE (1899...)

American dancer, actor and singer. Though one of the great all-round entertainers, Astaire has always insisted that he was "just a hoofer". His remarkable talent revealed itself while he was still little Fred Austerlitz of Omaha, Nebraska. His mother took him and his sister Adele to New York, and by 1906 the children were tap-dancing in vaudeville. In 1917 they acquired a new name and a starry Broadway reputation. Their popularity grew throughout the 1920s in such shows as *For Goodness Sake*, *Lady, Be Good* and *Funny Face*. For their London debut in 1923 *For Goodness Sake* changed its name to *Stop Flirting* and ran for 418 performances. "Adele is a genius," said *The People*, "Her partner is also a clever dancer." This show featured one of the Astaires' most popular and inexplicably funny routines, a comic race in which the two simply ran round in circles side by side. The "oompah trot", as it became known in England, was to reappear years later in the film *A Damsel in Distress*, but by then Gracie Allen was Fred's partner.

After *The Band Wagon* in 1931, Adele retired to marry Lord Charles Cavendish, and the next year Fred made his first appearance with another partner in Cole PORTER's *The Gay Divorce*. Critics raved about him, but it proved to be his last stage show. A great Hollywood career made the hoofer, as the novelist John O'Hara said, "the living symbol of all that is best in show business".

JACQUES AUDIBERTI (1899-1965)

French playwright, novelist and poet. Audiberti did not become known as a journalist and poet until he was nearly forty, and he had to wait even longer for the first productions of his plays. His joy in language and breadth of vision have been attributed by some to a strain of southern exuberance in his blood (he was born on the Riviera); but they tend to mask his deeper concern with the problem of combating evil.

This difficulty is well illustrated by his masterpiece, *Le Mal Court* (1947), in which the theme of the corruption of innocence is concealed within a bizarre fantasy set in the eighteenth century, which also shows the influence surrealism had upon him.

His production is very varied, ranging from the satirical *Quoat-Quoat* (1946) to the historical comedy *Pucelle* (1950), a re-creation of the story of Joan of Arc. Critics have found his sometimes grotesque intermingling of farce, tragedy, facility and profundity hard to digest, and have tended to pigeon-hole him as a typical *enfant-terrible* of the Theatre of the Absurd. His *Times* obituarist, perhaps in a moment of desperation, praised Audiberti for his "meaningful ambiguity".

JAMES CAGNEY (1899...)

American actor. Hollywood's sneering, snarling "public enemy" started his professional life as a Broadway dancer. After solo turns in vaudeville and revues, he had his first dramatic break in 1925 with a successful drama called *Outside Looking In*. Briefly he was forced to return to song and dance, but in 1929–30 two box-office flops paradoxically set him on the way to Hollywood. The first was GEORGE KELLY's *Maggie the Magnificent*, which Al JOLSON, in the opening-night audience, thought the best play he had ever seen. He persuaded Darryl Zanuck to send a scout to see *Penny Arcade* in which Cagney played just the sort of vicious, fast-talking cherub that he was to monopolize on film. Warner Brothers bought the rights and, with *Sinner's Holiday*, made Cagney a star.

A postscript to Cagney's stage career is *Yankee Doodle Dandy*, a film biography of George M. COHAN. Cagney's masterly song and dance routines revealed how great had been Broadway's loss.

NOEL COWARD (1899-1973)

English playwright, composer, actor, dancer and singer. To the Las Vegas audiences who patronized his cabaret act in the 1950s, Coward was an hilarious reincarnation of the twenties English toff. But behind the button-hole, the perfectly-tailored suit and the cigarette holder poised exquisitely between two fingers was far more than a clever child of his times. As the actor Micheál MacLIAMMÓIR has pointed out, Coward "did not merely echo the age he lived in . . ., but helped to create it".

He was born into a middle-class family who lived in an unexciting London suburb. His unerring professionalism and polish developed early; he made his acting debut before he had reached his teens, and had his first comedy produced in 1920. He acted in it, too, a habit he was rarely to break.

One of the early works in which he starred was *The Vortex* (1924), a drama which now seems uncharacteristically serious. Coward's frank treatment of sex and drugs horrified the conservative public, who accused the work of decadence and immorality. Despite this excursion into the "problem play", Coward is far better known for the witty comedies that reveal him as a master of mockery. The ironic muscial *Bitter Sweet* (1929), the wry *Private Lives* (1930, which he claimed to have written in a mere four days while recovering from flu in Shanghai) and the fantastical comedy *Blithe Spirit* (1941) attracted the very best actors of the day. They reveal more than a mere "talent to amuse" (Coward's own deprecating self-description), for they quietly attack the shallowness and hypocrisy of the English upper-crust.

Coward was also a prolific author of revues and songs. "Don't put your daughter on the stage, Mrs Worthington" and "Mad dogs and Englishmen" have become classics, while in "The stately homes of England" he coined a lasting phrase.

Coward revelled in the debonair role which the public assigned to him, but he was a serious craftsman, who made his art out of superficiality. Although much of what he wrote is destined for obscurity, the products of his prime – masterpieces of high comedy – are permanently established in the repertoire.

GUSTAF GRÜNDGENS (1899-1963)

German actor, director and administrator. Gründgens is one of the most respected actors and directors of modern times. He studied drama in Düsseldorf before serving briefly on the Western Front. After the war he joined Max REINHARDT's Deutsches Theater, working simultaneously in the Prussian State Theatre and Opera as well as in films.

Remaining in Germany under the Third Reich, Gründgens resisted Nazi pressure to put on crude pageant-plays. It was probably for this non-co-operation that he was released unharmed by the occupying Russians. When peace came he returned to direct and act in Berlin, Düsseldorf and Hamburg.

Innovative though never modishly avant-garde, Gründgens's interpretations of SHAKESPEARE, FRIEDRICH SCHILLER and BRECHT were admired both for their originality and for their fidelity to the playwrights' intentions. But his heroically evil Mephistopheles in GOETHE's *Faust*, a role he first assumed in 1932 and later brought triumphantly to film, is for many audiences his greatest accomplishment.

IDA KAMINSKA (1899-1980)

Russian-born actress and director. The nomadic career of Ida Kaminska has taken her from Russia to Poland, to Russia again (during the Second World War), back to Poland and finally to the United States. She has directed the Warsaw Jewish Art Theatre and, from 1949 to 1968, the Jewish State Theatre of Poland. Leading her own companies, the indomitable Kaminska has toured Europe and the United States, winning especial praise for Yiddish productions of such classic plays as *A Doll's House*, BRECHT's *Mutter Courage* and *Fuenteovejuna* by LOPE DE VEGA. She has also enjoyed a prominent career in films and television.

Noel Coward and Gertrude Lawrence
compare classic profiles in his debonair
comedy *Private Lives*. Starring in the
original production as the divorced couple
blithely reunited in adultery, they perfectly
embodied Coward's ideals of wit, suavity and
romance. The play retained its charm in a hit
1980 revival

THE PLAY

PICTORIAL

" PRIVATE LIVES "

No.
344

VOL.
LVII

NOËL COWARD

GERTRUDE LAWRENCE

1 S.
NET

MONTHLY

212

Eva Le Gallienne (1899…)

American actress, director and writer. The daughter of an English poet and a Danish authoress, Eva Le Gallienne studied at London's Royal Academy of Dramatic Art before moving to New York. There she established herself in a long career as a leading actress in the plays of Ibsen and Hauptmann.

At the remarkably early age of twenty-seven she founded the Civic Repertory Theatre (1926–33) in a decrepit shack-theatre in Greenwich Village. This pioneering off-Broadway venture did not always attract the most discerning of patrons; the critic Alexander Woollcott pilloried the theatre's opening-night audience for "laughing mutinously at the wrong places" in Chekhov's *Three Sisters*. But the project survived, doing vital service to Le Gallienne's goal of educating the American theatre-going public. She wrote two autobiographies: *At 33* and *With a Quiet Heart*.

Micheál MacLiammóir (1899-1978)

Irish actor. The greatest Irish actor of his generation, MacLiammóir was co-founder of the Gate Theatre in 1928, with his lifelong companion Hilton Edwards. The Gate gave Dublin audiences an alternative theatre to the Abbey, which, by the 1930s, had fallen into a rustic, nationalist style. MacLiammóir broadened and internationalized the repertory, producing 350 plays at the Gate (nine of them written by himself). The most popular was Eugene O'Neill's *Mourning Becomes Electra*, which he described as Ireland's *Charley's Aunt*.

MacLiammóir was born in Cork, but his parents moved to London, where he became a child actor, playing in Herbert Beerbohm Tree's company under the name of Alfred Williams at the age of eleven (alongside another new boy called Noel Coward). After studying art at the Slade School, he settled in Ireland, learning its language fluently, and only rarely returning to London. His mannered style did not endear him to the critics there until late in his career, when he performed one-man shows, the best being about Wilde: *The Importance of Being Oscar* (1960). After his *Hamlet* failed in London, he expressed his grievance in a characteristically extravagant style: "London is like a big blonde woman with a high-pitched voice who said all she had to say years ago." In the same florid prose MacLiammóir produced one of the finest theatrical biographies, *All for Hecuba*, which he eventually translated himself from Irish into English.

Armand Salacrou (1899…)

French playwright. Despite the support of men such as Charles Dullin, Salacrou's early plays were little performed, and dismal failures when they were. At one time he worked as an advertising copywriter, promoting the anti-louse liquid invented by his father. He also spent periods as a law-student, a medical student and as a journalist on the left-wing paper *L'Humanité*. Success came, however, with the comedy *Une Femme libre* (1934).

Salacrou's masterpiece is *L'Archipel Lenoir* (1947), which critics have viewed variously as a macabre farce, a satirical burlesque and an existential statement about

Fifteen years of rootlessness came to an end for Bertolt Brecht when the Russian authorities invited him to settle in East Berlin. He founded the Berliner Ensemble as a brilliant showcase for his dramatic beliefs, and it has continued to flourish since his death

the hopelessness of life. His output as a whole is an almost anarchical mixture of different themes and styles. Absurdity, left-wing comment, realism, fantasy and psychological anguish are often combined within a single work. The novelist Colette described this recipe as "le sel et le sucre".

Salacrou's success as a dramatist (and the astuteness he showed in buying up cubist paintings when they were cheap) brought him the wealth he had longed for from his early boyhood in Le Havre. His other ambition, of equalling the achievements of SHAKESPEARE, proved more elusive. His life has been characterized by a desperate restlessness which is easily discernible in his plays; contentment seems to have escaped him.

ROGER VITRAC (1899-1952)

French playwright and poet. A pioneer in the anarchic Dada movement, Vitrac was a precursor of the Theatres of the Absurd and Cruelty. His vicious satire, *Victor ou les enfants au pouvoir* (1928), exerted a lasting influence on his friends Jean ANOUILH and Eugène IONESCO. The monstrous Victor of the title is a nine-year-old child with the mental and physical faculties of a grown-up, whose attempts to cope with the illogic of the adult world culminate in his death. *Les mystères de l'amour* (1927), which exposes the erotic and sadistic fantasies of two lovers, is similarly macabre.

MARIE BELL (1900...)

French actress. Before and after the Second World War, Marie Bell played leading roles at the Comédie-Française, excelling especially in the plays of the seventeenth-century French classicists. Her portrayals of Esther, Agrippine, Phèdre and Bérénice are still considered by many to be definitive. She was quite as at ease in her own ignoble century, becoming a convincing Madame in Jean GENET's *Le Balcon*; indeed the parts of prostitutes were later to become something of a speciality for her. Bell is also a noted comedienne, both on the stage and in several otherwise undistinguished films.

ELISABETH BERGNER (1900...)

Austrian actress. In Berlin in the twenties, each new play starring Elisabeth Bergner was eagerly awaited. The appeal of her slight, boyish figure and enormous eyes made up for occasional miscasting, in a series of leading roles ranging from SHAKESPEARE to Eugene O'NEILL. Her attractions were accentuated in any part with a hint of sexual ambiguity, and it was inevitable that her greatest successes should come as Rosalind in *As You Like It* and as BERNARD SHAW's Saint Joan.

After a triumphal tour of Europe, Elisabeth Bergner settled in England, where James BARRIE was inspired to take up his pen for the last time, and write for her a thoroughly characteristic role in *The Boy David*.

PAOLA BORBONI (1900...)

Italian actress. From scantily-clad appearances in the 1920s to her recent marriage (to a man forty years her junior) Paola Borboni has kept Italian gossip columns supplied with an unceasing flow of copy. Early successes in light comedy owed more to her striking looks than to her eccentric acting, but after appearing in *Come prima, meglio di prima* in 1935, she became a passionate devotee of the plays of PIRANDELLO, an enthusiasm that inspired her to work seriously on technique. Borboni's new-found maturity as an actress was seen to great effect in the title

The intriguing **Paola Borboni** (*above*)

Marie Bell (*above*) excelled in French tragedy

Eva Le Gallienne (*below*) as Lewis Carroll's White Queen

Kids always love clowns, but the great **Coco** (*left*) seemed almost to enchant his young audiences wherever he went

role of GEORGE BERNARD SHAW's immortal comedy *The Millionairess*.

ELLIOTT MARTIN BROWNE (1900...)

English director. E. Martin Browne shared T. S. ELIOT's dual commitment to verse drama and religion, and was Eliot's personal choice to direct all his plays. He established a religious acting company, the Pilgrim Players, and in 1945 produced a London season of modern works in verse. In 1951 Browne presented the York cycle of mystery plays in their native city for the first time in almost four hundred years.

ERNST BUSCH (1900-80)

German actor. Busch's authentic working-class credentials and strong personality made him a prominent figure in the left-wing theatre of pre-Nazi Germany. After playing the lead in Ernst TOLLER's *Hoppla, wir leben* at the Piscator-Bühne, he began his long association with Bertolt BRECHT, which was to be renewed after the war in the Berliner Ensemble. His greatest Brechtian interpretation was the Cook in *Mutter Courage und ihre Kinder*, a role of coarse humour and vicious sarcasm, qualities which are also the chief ingredients of the many political ballads Busch has composed.

PAUL VINCENT CARROLL (1900-68)

Irish playwright. As the nationalist trauma of the 1920s subsided, Carroll, a teacher by profession, was able to concentrate on the conflicts in Ireland. His best known play was *Shadow and Substance* (1937), but his theme is best described by an elderly Canon in *The White Steed* (1939), who says: "We rule this nation with laws that no one writes, but everyone instinctively accepts." Such a mood of tolerance and resignation prevailed in Ireland until the political eruption in Ulster in 1968.

COCO (1900-74)

Anglo-Russian clown. Nicolai Poliakoff's life demonstrates why, as he said, "a clown learns to be something of a

philosopher". During his early years in Russia he was beaten and imprisoned by the police, and almost killed in the Revolution. Later a serious accident hospitalized him and closed the little circus in which he had done almost everything except fire-eating and contortionism. In 1930 his association with the Bertram Mills Circus in England brought him popularity and some security, but the show disbanded during the Second World War. Again Coco was in financial difficulties in the 1950s and again he was severely injured in an accident. But none of his misfortunes kept him from becoming and remaining one of the great circus performers. His ginger wig, bulbous nose, baggy check suit and huge shoes were beloved trademarks for two generations. At length the philosophical old clown died happy, in the midst of yet another successful comeback.

EDUARDO DE FILIPPO (1900...)

Italian playwright and actor. Against all the odds, for much is inevitably lost when the picturesque Neapolitan of his plays is translated, de Filippo has begun to receive international recognition as a master of modern comedy. To capture the imagination of the rest of Italy with plays written in dialect was a considerable feat in itself, yet as early as 1931 Eduardo, his sister Titina (1898–1963) and brother Peppino (1903–80) had become popular stars while touring with their Teatro Umoristico I de Filippo.

Peppino, the most conspicuously comic actor of the three, was also at first the most prolific writer, producing variations on stock comic themes in the time-honoured manner of the Commedia dell' Arte. Eduardo, however, especially after his meeting and brief collaboration with PIRANDELLO, aspired to something higher than this stereotyped buffoonery. The two brothers eventually fell out and each formed his own company. Their hatred became so intense that for years they never spoke, avoiding each other on all occasions.

Titina remained with Eduardo and in 1946 had her greatest individual triumph as the single-minded heroine of *Filumena Marturano*. The title character is a middle-aged prostitute, who feigns terminal illness to persuade a former steady customer to marry her. She wishes to legitimize her three sons, one of whom (she says) is his.

Now honoured as a great lady of the theatre, **Helen Hayes** (*left*) delighted audiences in the 1920s as a vital, glowing young star

One of **Tyrone Guthrie**'s early successes was this version of Shakespeare's *The Tempest* (*left*) staged at London's Sadler's Wells Theatre in 1934. Charles Laughton is a saturnine Prospero in a far-fetched wizard's hat. His nubile daughter is played by Elsa Lanchester – Mrs Laughton in real life

Deceived into marriage, the man burns to know which is his son, but Filumena steadfastly refuses to tell him, knowing he will unfairly favour whichever she names. In this and other of Eduardo's ironic comedies, traditional, moral standards do not apply to the complexity of human (and particularly family) relationships.

Even in his vision of poverty-stricken Naples, *Napoli milionaria* (1945), Eduardo wrote much pure farce. *Questi Fantasmi* (1946) is set in a supposedly haunted house, where the husband mistakes his wife's lover for the ghost, while *Le voci di dentro* (1948) contains a character who rejects normal methods of communication, preferring to use fireworks. Later plays, including *Mia famiglia* (1955) and *Il sindaco del Rione Sanità* (1960), had enormous success in Italy, but it was *Sabato, domenica e lunedì* (1959) which finally brought Eduardo to the attention of English audiences. Laurence OLIVIER and Joan PLOWRIGHT had a totally unexpected hit with the English version (*Saturday, Sunday, Monday*) in 1973. *Filumena Marturano* (previously better known as a film distressingly titled *Marriage Italian Style*) has also taken its place as a favourite at the National Theatre.

MILDRED DUNNOCK (1900...)

American actress. Mildred Dunnock gave one of her finest performances as Linda in the first production of *Death of a Salesman* in 1949. Especially suited to the plays of TENNESSEE WILLIAMS, she created the role of Big Mama in the 1955 première of *Cat on a Hot Tin Roof*, and more recently portrayed the deluded Amanda Wingfield in *The Glass Menagerie*. Her career of over forty years has also included such Williams films as *Baby Doll* and *Sweet Bird of Youth*, and much work for television.

TYRONE GUTHRIE (1900-71)

English director. At six feet and five inches tall, Guthrie felt he was too conspicuous to be a successful actor; his true stature as a director appeared soon enough. After work in the provinces he joined London's Westminster Theatre in 1931. His production of J. B. PRIESTLEY's *Dangerous Corner* so impressed Lilian BAYLIS of the Old Vic that she made him the company's youngest director,

in 1933. Over a long association with the Vic (of which, together with the Sadler's Wells Theatre, he was Administrator from 1939–45) Guthrie became famous for endlessly innovative staging, particularly in his ensemble effects. When these succeeded, as in his epic production of MARLOWE's *Tamburlaine* in 1951 with Sir Donald WOLFIT, critics hailed him as a "master of spectacle and movement". When they didn't he was accused of directing "as though he were staging a circus". But whether presenting *Hamlet* in modern dress or *All's Well That Ends Well* in Edwardian costume, Guthrie was never dull. He was one of the first directors to become an international star, and his contributions included the founding of repertory theatres in Stratford, Ontario, and in Minneapolis.

HELEN HAYES (1900...)

American actress. A true doyenne of the American stage, Miss Hayes made her debut at the age of five in Washington, D.C. She capped the juvenile phase of her career in 1918 with James BARRIE's *Dear Brutus*. *To the Ladies* (1922) by George S. KAUFMAN and Marc CONNELLY was her first great adult success. Other coups of the 1920s included starring roles in SHAW's *Caesar and Cleopatra* and Barrie's *What Every Woman Knows*. In 1927 she opened a long run, playing the hussy in George ABBOTT's *Coquette*. The show was still at peak popularity in 1928 when she married the playwright Charles MacArthur (1895–1956). It closed only when she left the cast in 1929 to have a baby.

In the 1930s she discovered the centre of her career: the title part in Laurence Housman's *Victoria Regina*. The play covers the whole course of the Queen's sixty-year reign. Miss Hayes's performance was a *tour de force*, evoking, in the words of MAXWELL ANDERSON, both "such moving young grace and such heartbreak." She played the role 969 times from 1935 to 1939. Her triumphs in the forties included the London production of TENNESSEE WILLIAMS's *The Glass Menagerie*, but the decade ended tragically with her actress-daughter's death from polio. She retired in 1968, but returned to star in a revival of her husband's classic comedy *The Front Page*. The role she played, Mrs Grant, had been written by MacArthur about her own mother.

KATINA PAXINOU (1900-73)

Greek actress. Paxinou and her husband Alexis Minotis were the vital force behind the Greek National Theatre, which they joined at its inception in 1932. Under her husband's direction, she was celebrated for such classic roles as Clytemnestra in AESCHYLUS' *Agamemnon*, but she also starred in modern works, including those of Eugene O'NEILL, for which she provided translations.

In 1940 she played Mrs Alving in IBSEN's *Ghosts* in London and, after a war-time voyage in which her ship was torpedoed, his *Hedda Gabler* in New York. A by-product of that success (and of her "Spanish" complexion) was her leading role in the film of *For Whom the Bell Tolls*, which made her famous in middle-America but no less keen to return to Greece.

NIKOLAI POGODIN (1900-62)

Russian dramatist. Nikolai Pogodin was the pen-name of Stukalov, a journalist turned playwright. With AFINOGENOV, he was an associate of RAPP, a society of working-class writers, and his plays based on reportage and Party slogans followed the patterns set by The Bureau of Agitation and Propaganda. He is credited with one innovation in Soviet drama: for the first time, Lenin and Stalin appeared on stage as living characters, albeit gilded and heavy as patriotic icons. In that most popular drama, *The Man with the Gun* (1937), the actor portraying Stalin went mute with fright when confronted with the live Stalin in the audience. Nikolai Feodorovich's other plays are documentaries of the Revolution. *Poem About An Axe* (1931) deals with difficulties in the steel industry; Lenin appears in *Kremlin Chimes* (1942); *Missouri Waltz* ridicules President Truman. When Khrushchev appealed for young men and women to make the Asiatic Russian steppes bloom, Nikolai Pogodin came up with the delightfully appropriate *Three to the Virgin Lands*.

SPENCER TRACY (1900-67)

American actor. Tracy made a mute Broadway debut playing a robot in Karel ČAPEK's *R.U.R*. A long apprenticeship in stock companies followed before a fill-in part prompted George M. COHAN to call him "the best actor I have ever seen". Cohan later became something of a father-figure to Tracy, giving him a star part in *The Baby Cyclone*, his own weak play, and helping him with such simple but apparently effective advice as "Take your hands out of your pockets and listen to the other actors". A flop called *Conflict* was followed in 1930 by *The Last Mile*, in which Tracy as the condemned Killer Meers revealed talents far greater than any of his previous comic performances had suggested.

Tracy's subsequent career, except for one brief return to Broadway in Robert SHERWOOD's *The Rugged Path* (1945), was entirely in films, so memorably in partnership with Katharine HEPBURN.

ETHEL WATERS (1900...)

American actress and singer. According to her autobiography, Waters was conceived in rape when her mother was only twelve years old. In this light it is encouraging that her personality should have later projected such a life-enhancing quality; her laugh has been described as "a trumpet of pure joy".

She has appeared in vaudeville and revues such as the all-Negro *Africana* (1927), and in more serious plays, notably *Mamba's Daughters* (1939) and *The Member of the Wedding* (1950). In the latter work the producer Harold Clurman praised her expressiveness and range, but found her prone to terrifying lapses of memory. He speculated that her nervousness might arise from the burden she felt at representing the black race in a white cast.

Ethel Waters is also respected for her moving interpretations of songs such as "Dinah" and "Stormy Weather" and – in later life – for her equally convincing performances in Billy Graham's Youth for Christ rallies.

HELENE WEIGEL (1900-71)

Austrian actress. Helene Weigel's career was inextricable from that of Bertolt BRECHT, whom she married in 1928. Her two greatest roles were in her husband's plays: the long-suffering mothers in *Die Mutter*, which she played in Germany before she and Brecht were forced into exile, and in *Mutter Courage und ihre Kinder*, one of the first pieces put on in 1949 by the Berliner Ensemble, the great company of which she was director until her death. Brecht considered her to embody his ideal of the actress, worker, wife and mother, and wrote many moving poems in her praise.

KJELD ABELL (1901-61)

Danish playwright, designer and director. Abell's blend of social satire and poetic fantasy, as in *Eva aftjener sin*

Her great friend Ernest Hemingway ungallantly referred to **Marlene Dietrich** (*left*) as "the Kraut". But she captivated him as surely as she did all other men

Katina Paxinou (*right*) made her stage debut as an opera singer and later composed music for productions of the classical Greek dramas in which she starred so powerfully

A typical set by **Jo Mielziner** (*far right*), at once simple, functional and striking. Trained as an actor himself, Mielziner always produced designs that caught a play's distinctive character

Barnepligt (1936) and *Vetsera blomstrer ikke for enhver* (1951), often left audiences impressed but perplexed. The threat of Nazism inspired the more straightforward *Anna Sophie Hedvig* (1939) and *Judith* (1940), both of which show the reactions of the individual to tyranny and violence, problems Abell himself had to face during the German occupation of Denmark. In 1944, on hearing of the assassination of his fellow playwright Kaj MUNK, he stopped the performance in his theatre to express his horror and disgust, a gesture which obliged him to spend the rest of the war in hiding.

GINO CERVI (1901-74)

Italian actor. Even as a young man, Cervi radiated such bonhomie that it was difficult to suspend disbelief when he played a passionate tragic role. While his Othello and Romeo were unconvincing, those who saw his magnificent portrayal of Falstaff could thereafter imagine no other actor in the part.

During a long career in the theatre, the cinema and television, Cervi made many other characters his own, including the Mayor in the Don Camillo films and, on stage, the title role in ROSTAND's *Cyrano de Bergerac*.

MARLENE DIETRICH (1901...)

German actress and singer. With the exception of a minor role in Frank WEDEKIND's *Frühlings Erwachen*, Marlene Dietrich's early stage appearances under Max REINHARDT in Berlin gave little indication of the legend she was to become. After her overnight rise to stardom as the ice-cool enchantress in the film *The Blue Angel*, she gave up the theatre and set off for Hollywood to have her new persona thoroughly exploited by Paramount.

Her film career over, Dietrich toured the world in a series of one-woman concerts. An extensive wardrobe did not always compensate for her limited repertoire, consisting of "Where have all the flowers gone" plus old favourites from her films. In 1975 a fall in Australia (caused by an ill-mended broken leg) at last allowed "The Boys in the Backroom" to rest their elbows after forty years of solid drinking.

MARIELUISE FLEISSER (1901-74)

German short-story writer and playwright. One of the few talented writers to remain in Nazi Germany, Marieluise Fleisser chose marriage and anonymity in her home town of Ingolstadt rather than exile in Hollywood. Events in this small Bavarian town had been the subject of her two successful plays, produced with the help of Bertolt BRECHT in 1929. *Fegefeuer in Ingolstadt* was a provincial tragedy, while *Die Pioniere von Ingolstadt* took an ironic look at hypocrisy and sexual taboos. Only at the end of the war did she start to publish once more, with *Der starke Stamm* (1946), a folk-play.

OSCAR HOMOLKA (1901-38)

Austrian actor. Homolka's striking slavonic features were a casting director's dream, and secured for him a long succession of sinister supporting roles in American and British movies. On stage too he had begun as a character actor, but after scoring a big hit in Berlin in Eugene O'NEILL's *The Emperor Jones*, he attempted further leading roles in the early plays of BRECHT. *Edward II* he almost ruined with his unintelligible delivery, but he regained some of his lost reputation in *Baal*.

ÖDÖN VON HORVÁTH (1901-38)

Austrian playwright and novelist. The ironic title of Horváth's *Geschichten aus dem Wiener Wald* (*Tales from the Vienna Woods*, 1931) concealed a harshly realistic portrait of the true Vienna, far removed from the sentimental world of operetta and cream cakes. It was this play that won him his reputation as one of the most promising writers working in pre-Nazi Germany. That same year he had written *Italienische Nacht*, a dark prophecy of the looming threat of fascism. Two years later he was duly driven into exile.

Many of Horváth's eighteen plays deal with the responsibility and guilt of the individual. In *Der jüngste Tag* a frightened railway official tries to cover up his part in a disastrous accident. Horváth himself must take the blame for his own untimely death. While strolling along the Champs Elysées, he unwisely sheltered under a tree during a thunderstorm, with predictable results.

JO MIELZINER (1901-76)

American designer. "His work has the balance and beauty and sanity of fine prose, but it never flies to the heights nor falls to the depths of poetry," wrote one of Mielziner's contemporaries. This balance was neatly exemplified in his design for ARTHUR MILLER's *Death of a Salesman*, where the family house was painted on to a translucent

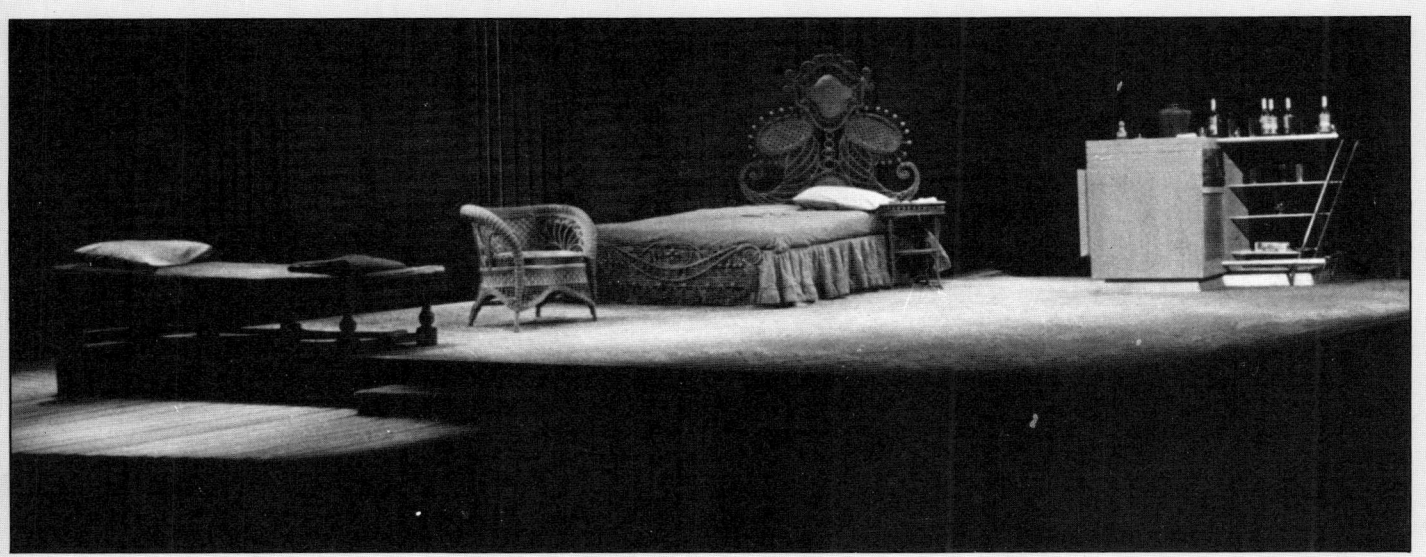

Greasepaint enables **Ralph Richardson** (*above*) to create a character's physical appearance. But the mental labour of interpreting and absorbing a role goes on through months of effort

Inga Tidblad (*above*) was every inch Strindberg's Queen Kristina

Donald Wolfit's imposing Shylock (*below*) was one of his wartime successes

back-cloth. Back-lighting cast a wintry glow on it, while front projection could instantly impart a spring-like aura. Mielziner's work is thus imaginative and ingenious, but also – unlike that of his more avant-garde rivals – immediately comprehensible. He contributed greatly to the early success of such playwrights as Miller, Elmer RICE and TENNESSEE WILLIAMS.

In all he designed some 300 productions, ranging in genre from *Hamlet* to *Guys and Dolls*. His genius lay in his ability to make sets look both stylish and lived-in, giving them what one admirer described as a "rich patina of occupancy". Mielziner is also the author of two outstanding books on theatre design.

LEE STRASBERG (1901...)

American director, teacher and writer. Strasberg is America's leading exponent of the Method, an acting system based on the teachings of Konstantin STANISLAVSKY. With Harold Clurman he was successively a member of the Theatre Guild and of the Group Theatre; but Strasberg has exerted his greatest influence as director of the Actors' Studio, an institution whose alumni include Marlon BRANDO, Paul Newman and JULIE HARRIS.

The Method's method is to encourage an actor to experience the reality of the role he is playing; he should, in a sense, relive his own emotion and in doing so forget that he is acting. Although the Method's more fanatical adherents sometimes forget to act and become what one critic called mere "mumbling back-scratchers", Strasberg's most famous protégés are the backbone of the American theatre.

INGA TIDBLAD (1901-75)

Swedish actress. Inga Tidblad was one of Sweden's finest interpreters of SHAKESPEARE and STRINDBERG. A refreshingly gay and stylish performance as Ariel in *The Tempest* brought her immediate success in her 1921 debut. Tidblad joined the Royal Dramatic Theatre in Stockholm in 1932 and soon became one of its leading actresses. She had a musical voice, and combined fragile femininity with immense energy. Her famous parts included Shakespeare's Juliet, Rosalind in *As You Like It*, and the title-role in Strindberg's *Miss Julie*.

JOHN VAN DRUTEN (1901-57)

Anglo-American playwright and director. Van Druten trained as a lawyer and lectured briefly on this subject at the University of Wales before finding notoriety with his drama *Young Woodley*. This charming but frank study of adolescence was banned by a timid Lord Chamberlain in 1925, though it was produced the same year in New York without interference. The United States also proved more receptive to Van Druten's wry romantic comedy *The Voice of the Turtle* (1943); its appeal was lost on audiences in war-torn London, and Van Druten became an American citizen the following year.

Several of his plays have been well received, notably *I am a Camera* (1951), adapted from Christopher Isherwood, and *Bell, Book and Candle* (1950). But many critics have found his work craftsmanlike rather than original, and sentimental rather than profound.

PER AABEL (1902...)

Norwegian actor. Aabel's acting was natural, intuitive and full of gaiety; he excelled in comedy and farce. In 1926 he began directing at the Nye Theatre in Oslo, but his talent as an actor did not emerge until 1931. Aabel went on to act and direct at a number of Oslo theatres, and later toured Scandinavia and the rest of Europe. MOLIÈRE's Tartuffe and BEAUMARCHAIS' Figaro were two of his greatest parts, and he gave other memorable performances in the plays of the expatriate Norwegian Ludvig HOL-BERG. His public readings of the works of Hans Christian Andersen and others have made Aabel a firm favourite throughout Scandinavia.

MARCEL AYMÉ (1902-67)

French novelist and playwright. Aymé was a timid and retiring man, indeed he was known as the most silent man in all Paris. But his uninhibited imagination and macabre sense of humour had their outlet in his writing; his novels, plays and stories are minutely observed, yet full of surreal fantasy. The first of his novels to arouse great interest was *Brûlebois* (1926). Its success enabled him to abandon a series of jobs ranging from bank clerk to builder and to devote himself to writing.

Aymé wrote his first play, *Lucienne et le boucher*, in 1932. This chilling tragicomedy had an enthusiastic reception at its first performance sixteen years later. The grotesque satire *Clérambard* (1950) brought international fame. Clérambard is an obsessive and impoverished aristocrat who mistreats cats and dogs and keeps his family slaving over looms to pay the debts. When Saint Francis appears, preaching charity, Clérambard swings to the other extreme; he even insists that his son marry a local prostitute. The saint strongly advises moderation, but the whole family sets out in a cart to spread the Word. Other notable plays by Aymé include *La Tête des autres* (1952), a bitter middle-class satire, and *Les Quatre Vérités* (1954).

CHRISTIAN BÉRARD (1902-49)

French artist and designer. It took Bérard a remarkably short time to be acclaimed as a genius. From the outset of his career he was a favourite of Louis JOUVET, then the dominant figure in French theatre, and he soon became the pampered darling of high-society ladies. His very first stage design was for a Diaghilev ballet; consequently, working with the great held no terrors for him. His earliest triumphs in the theatre were for *La Voix humaine* and *La Machine infernale* by Jean COCTEAU, an accomplished artist himself, and another of Bérard's admirers.

Bérard's greatness lay not in one readily recognizable style but in his immediate grasp of the demands of the play, be it a MOLIÈRE classic or an avant-garde work by Jean GENET. It was while checking the set and lighting for a production of Molière's *Les Fourberies de Scapin* that he collapsed and died.

LANGSTON HUGHES (1902-67)

American poet, short-story writer, playwright and librettist. The "Harlem Renaissance" of the late twenties, when black writers and artists were the toast of white intellectuals, produced many nine-day wonders. With *The Weary Blues*, however, Hughes produced a volume of poetry that inspired a lifetime's work as writer, lecturer and journalist. He toiled ceaselessly to help establish a literary and historical identity for his people.

Hughes's serious dramas such as *Mulatto* (1935) and *The Sun Do Move* (1942) never reached such wide audiences as his musicals and musical adaptations (he wrote the fine libretto for Kurt Weill's music in a version of Elmer RICE's *Street Scene*). His most popular fictional creation was Jesse B. Semple, known as "Simple", who first appeared in Hughes's column in the *Chicago Defender*. In 1957 the

"Simple" short stories were turned into a musical, *Simply Heaven*. It was predictable (but a little depressing after all Hughes's efforts to extend black culture) that his greatest stage successes, *Black Nativity* (1961) and *The Prodigal Son* (1964), should have been in the Gospel tradition.

RALPH RICHARDSON (1902...)

English actor and director. Ralph Richardson first impressed London critics with his Cockney performance in a 1928 modern-dress *The Taming of the Shrew*. Through the thirties he played SHAKESPEARE at the Old Vic while securing a West End reputation in works by Somerset MAUGHAM and J. B. PRIESTLEY. After service in the Royal Air Force he returned to the Vic, and the post-war years brought full recognition of his powers. The role of Peer Gynt perfectly suited his subtle, resourceful interpretation, earning him general praise–and a medal from the king of Norway. Jubilant critics agreed too that he made Falstaff "a credible creature at last, with some dignity in obesity". Later triumphs included ANOUILH's *The Waltz of the Toreadors*, Robert BOLT's *Flowering Cherry*, David STOREY's *Home* and Harold PINTER's *No Man's Land*, the last two with his friend Sir John GIELGUD. Sir Ralph's consistent achievement has been to reveal a depth of character in even the most hackneyed roles. He himself has always remained quietly complex, the hard-working actor unimpressed by himself and riding a motorcycle to rehearsals; the English gentleman whose profound sensibilities reveal themselves only (but unfailingly) on stage.

FLORA ROBSON (1902...)

English actress. Unhappy in *ingénue* roles, Flora Robson retired from the stage in 1925 to become a social worker in a cereal factory. On her return in 1929 she immediately found an ideal role as the murder victim in James BRIDIE's *The Anatomist* and continued her success in plays by Eugene O'NEILL and J. B. PRIESTLEY. At the Old Vic she was a chilling Lady Macbeth. A critic noted her skill at expressing "quivering strain", and she became almost typecast playing sinister roles on stage and screen. Yet Dame Flora remained equally adept at portraying a very un-neurotic Prism in *The Importance of Being Earnest*.

DONALD WOLFIT (1902-68)

English actor-manager. Wolfit's repertory experience taught him to love the life of the strolling player. He had starred in the West End, Stratford and the Old Vic when, in 1937, he formed his own company and took it on tour. They were a hit in the provinces, but perhaps their finest hour came in London during the Second World War. The blitz had closed all theatres, but the hardy Wolfit troupe, working on a shoestring budget, kept drama alive with lunchtime scenes from SHAKESPEARE. Sir Donald's expressive range and heroic energy were the company's main assets. Although he often played comic roles, including Malvolio and Sir Peter Teazle, he was at his best as Oedipus, MARLOWE's ranting Tamburlaine, or as a King Lear of a stature that may never be equalled.

LUTHER ADLER (1903...)

American actor and director. Adler got his early training with the Yiddish Theatre, in which his actor-parents were deeply involved. After an adult debut at eighteen, he had a busy career in New York and on tour overseas. In 1931 he and his sister Stella joined the Group Theatre in its attempt to provide a serious alternative to standard Broadway fare.

Most of the women in this relaxed scene are probably men. Exhausted by war and bludgeoned by inflation, Germany in the twenties needed its places of fantasy. Cabaret offered a potent mixture of satire, jazz, and sexual titillation—this transvestite club provided one variation

Cabaret II: Berlin

After the First World War, Berlin became a haven for international refugees. It was thronged with Russians fleeing the revolution, Balkan conspirators, Poles, Hungarians, and Ukrainians. Cabaret developed in two directions: one catered simply for the erotic entertainment of pleasure-seekers; the other took on itself the serious need to attack an increasingly right-wing government.

In its more decadent incarnation, Berlin was far from dull. Private boxes at the cabaret were known sometimes to have floors which could be lowered at the touch of a button; after a particularly inflammatory act, an aspiring seducer could pneumatically lower his own private floor and mount his champagne-sodden beloved of the evening. So cynical did the whole scene become, that chopping-boards complete with onions were here and there available to help the patrons cry. It is not surprising that German satire failed to acquire the playfulness of its Parisian model.

The movement began early in the century, at such intimate venues as Der Hungrige Pegasus, where young artists would perform and discuss their work. Max REINHARDT, then a young actor, conducted literary parodies based on the work of establishment writers such as MAETERLINCK and SCHILLER. But, in front of all this, there were telephones on the tables of the more expensive clubs so that a customer might telephone and send across a bottle of *Sekt* to a neighbouring blonde (heterosexual patrons were rarely deceived by the size of a blonde's bust: transsexuals with wax-filled breasts were common property in such places).

More importantly, the great satirist Kurt TUCHOLSKY (who committed suicide when the Nazis rose to power) attacked the growing militarism of the state. BRECHT, who was on the Nazi black-list as early as 1923, brilliantly de-romanticized the life of the soldier in a series of poems and songs, and attacked the industrialists who profited from the astronomical inflation of the time. But the satirists who mocked the sacred cows of absolute rule became the prime targets in their turn of the humourless Third Reich. When Hitler seized power, satire was first to be exterminated.

Yet its influence continued. It was there that Brecht learned of the informal but vital link between a player and his audience. His plays, written in small, pointed scenes, are now the most vivid legacy of that extraordinary era.

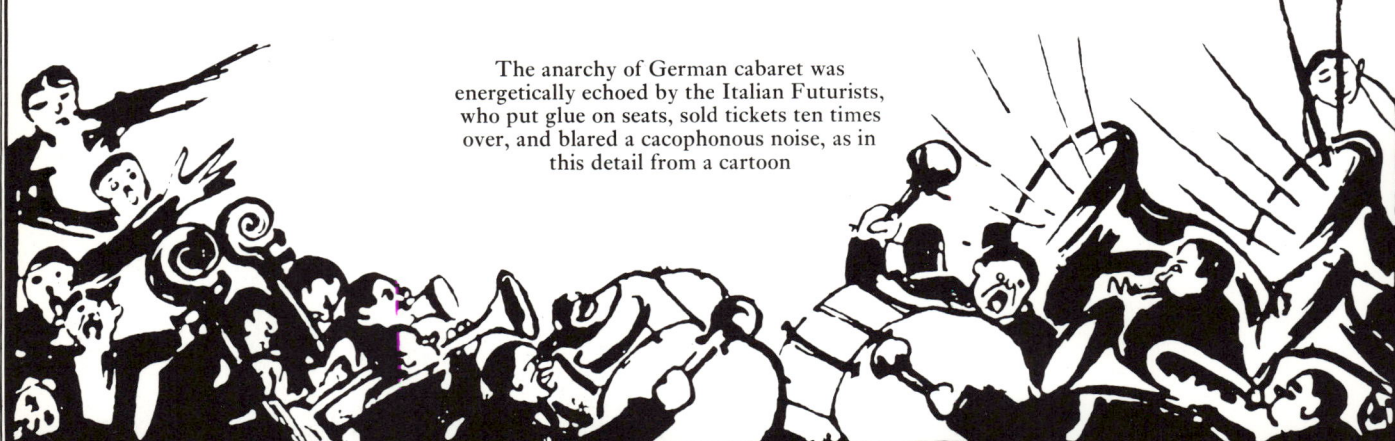

The anarchy of German cabaret was energetically echoed by the Italian Futurists, who put glue on seats, sold tickets ten times over, and blared a cacophonous noise, as in this detail from a cartoon

TALLULAH BANKHEAD (1903-68)

American actress. London fell in love with Tallulah
Bankhead's irrepressible good humour and throaty,
unoiled voice when she first appeared with a play called
The Dancers in the twenties. Back home many suspected
that her outrageous *joie de vivre* was a sham, designed to
mask a basic lack of talent. Only with her chilling performance as Regina Giddens in Lillian HELLMAN's *The
Little Foxes* did Broadway audiences realize that behind
all the exaggerated theatrical behaviour there lurked a
great actress. Serious pieces like *The Little Foxes* and
Thornton WILDER's *The Skin of Our Teeth*, in which she
was the original Sabina, brought out her finest work, while
in comedy she tended to indulge herself shamelessly.
Questioned about her playing of Amanda in a revival of
Noel COWARD's *Private Lives*, she admitted blithely, "I'm
Tallulah in this play, and I'm not a bit ashamed of it."

CLYDE RAYMOND BEATTY (1903-65)

American animal-trainer. When someone suggested that
Beatty "tamed" his lions and tigers, he replied indignantly,
"If they are tamed, there is no act." In any case, he insisted
that big cats never develop any affection for their trainer.
Armed with a reinforced chair, a revolver and a whip, he
gave them little chance of becoming friendly; danger was
always the principal ingredient of his act. The featured
performer of his own Clyde Beatty Circus, he was the first
to appear with lions and tigers of both sexes together, and
on occasions his menagerie was expanded by the addition
of leopards, pumas and hyenas. His animals demonstrated
their lack of affection by dispatching him to hospital more
than sixty times, a lion called Nero once had him unconscious for twelve days.

EDGAR BERGEN (1903-78)

American ventriloquist. Admired for his brilliant dialogue
by no less a master of repartee than Noel COWARD, Bergen
was the unchallenged leader of his profession throughout
a career that spanned the years of vaudeville, radio and
television. The shy Bergen was merely a foil for the jibes
of the impertinent, top-hatted Charlie McCarthy. For
twenty years Charlie was his only dummy; the act was
then expanded to include the grinning yokel, Mortimer
Snerd and Miss Effie Klinker, an old maid with a "spry
libido". There were never any trade secrets behind
Bergen's superiority over his rivals; he revealed all his
techniques in his comprehensive entry on ventriloquism
for the *Encyclopaedia Britannica*.

ALEJANDRO CASONA (1903-65)

Spanish playwright. Casona's first major play, *La sirena
varada* (1933), was performed while he was touring with
La Barraca, a university theatre group directed by Federico
GARCÍA LORCA. Forced by the Civil War to leave Spain, he
took refuge in Argentina, where his lyrical fantasies lost
some of their contemporary relevance. Of his later plays,
La dama del alba (1944), which drew on legends of
Casona's homeland, the Asturias, and *Los arboles mueren
de pié* (1949), a comedy in the manner of PIRANDELLO,
enjoyed the greatest success. When in 1962 he was allowed
to return to Spain, he settled quietly in the Asturias, the
region he had evoked so often throughout his long exile.

MADELEINE RENAUD (1903...)

French actress. Against all precedents, Madeleine Renaud
went from dignified traditional roles in her youth to

The outrageous, husky-
voiced **Tallulah Bankhead**
(*above*) was the toast of
England's younger generation
in the roaring twenties.
Recognition came more
slowly in her native America

A harrassed lifetime spent in
the company of his short,
sharp-witted friend, Charlie
McCarthy (holding forth
below) taught the American
entertainer **Edgar Bergen**
how to keep his mouth shut

Worlds away from his classic Shakespearean roles, **John Gielgud**'s performance as the "piss-pot poet" of Harold Pinter's *No Man's Land* (*left*) was another triumph

Graham Greene (*below*, at left) rehearsing his first play, *The Living Room*. A late starter in the theatre, he still became an important and distinctive dramatic voice

avant-garde extravagances in her old age. Before she was thirty, she had mastered MOLIÈRE, MARIVAUX and DE MUSSET; aged over seventy, she was appearing buried up to her neck as Winnie in Samuel BECKETT's *Oh! Les Beaux Jours* (*Happy Days*). The principal reason for this unusual sequence of events was her marriage to the great actor Jean-Louis BARRAULT. Together they decided to leave the Comédie-Française, where Madeline Renaud had reigned supreme for twenty-five years, and set up their own, more progressive company.

In the course of her two careers, Madeleine Renaud has created many of the great tragic roles of Paul CLAUDEL, Jean GIRAUDOUX and Henry de MONTHERLANT, but she has always been best-loved for the sparkle and intelligence she brings to comedy (and not only comedy of high intellectual content, witness her perennial success in Georges FEYDEAU's farce, *Occupe-toi d'Amélie*).

JEAN TARDIEU (1903...)

French playwright and poet. When the poet Tardieu was made director of French radio and television's experimental workshop in 1947, he became so excited by its possibilities that he began to write sketches, parodies and "poems for acting". He experimented with "sound drama", using music and rhythms of speech as means of dramatic expression, rather than traditional sentence construction. His sketches include *Les Amants du métro* (1952), "a comic ballet without music or dance" that might be described as a ballet of speech, and *L'ABC de notre vie*, which consists of rhythmically murmured excerpts from the dictionary.

ALEXANDER AFINOGENOV (1904-41)

Russian playwright. In the 1920s, RAPP, an organization of proletarian writers (and writers who considered themselves proletarian) came to the defence of the Soviet working class. Part of its literary guard duty was to rebuke dissenting free-thinkers and Marxist heretics in the theatre. In these activities Alexander Nikolaevich was an obedient participant until he himself fell victim to official displeasure for a time.

His many plays, as Marxist apologia and social criticism, were well constructed, thoughtful and, despite official reservations about *The Eccentric* (1929), well received. *Distant Point* was the hit of 1935; *Mashenka* a success in 1941. His best political drama, however, was *Fear* (1931), an early work which suggests that Afinogenov himself was not so confident in the state as his correct solutions would indicate. The play tells of old Professor Borodin, who feels the Soviet Union is governed by fear. "Fear compels the repudiation of mothers, the falsifying of social origins and the wriggling into high positions," he says. In Act IV the professor finally realizes that he has been misled by anti-Soviet colleagues. "I can still be useful," he insists, and promises to work for a true socialist state.

CECIL BEATON (1904-80)

English designer, photographer and writer. For the past fifty years Beaton has been one of the most colourful and visible men in the worlds of theatre, photography and fashion. As a child he had a passion for photography, and as a belated aesthetic at Cambridge University designed (and took female leads in) many productions. From 1927 he began professionally to design sets and extravagantly stylish costumes for the theatre, ballet and opera. His designs for WILDE's *Lady Windermere's Fan* (1946) were, in his own words, "an orgy of Edwardian luxury". Beaton is probably best known for the extraordinary fantasy of his costumes for the stage and screen versions of *My Fair Lady*.

RAY BOLGER (1904...)

American entertainer and actor. Loose-limbed and rubber-faced, Ray Bolger excelled both as dancer and comedian for forty years. *George White's Scandals* of 1931 gave him his first featured part, and *On Your Toes* made him a star in 1936. His greatest success, *Where's Charley?* (1948), ran for over two years. He played, of course, the inimitable transvestite, Charley Wykeham, who dresses up as his own rich aunt Donna Lucia D'Alvadorez. A familiar and delightful figure on television as well as the stage, Bolger may be best known as the Scarecrow in Victor Fleming's film *The Wizard of Oz*.

Theatre begins and ends backstage, and even deserted, a dressing room transmits an air of expectancy. The trappings of performance are gathered here, ready to complete the long process of a play's evolution from idea to dramatic experience

HARRY BUCKWITZ (1904...)

German director and manager. To put on the plays of Bertolt BRECHT in the German Federal Republic during the 1950s was to risk one's livelihood and even one's life, for public feeling against the "defector" to the East ran high. Buckwitz had to contend with demonstrations and pickets outside his theatre in Frankfurt, which from his 1952 production of *Der gute Mensch von Sezuan*, was the Brechtian capital of the West. When Brecht, who had been so vigorously boycotted, was later canonized by German playgoers, Buckwitz, who had always tried to bring out the contemporary political relevance of Brecht's works, was naturally suspicious. Not wishing to produce "classics", he turned instead to up-to-the-minute works like the *Viet Nam Diskurs* of Peter WEISS.

JOHN GIELGUD (1904...)

English actor and director. As a student, Gielgud could make himself weep by listening to his own voice. The Old Vic was not so easily impressed. In his first appearance with the company in 1921 he delivered his single line so clumsily that his next three roles were silent. But it soon became clear that Ellen TERRY's grand-nephew had both an extraordinarily beautiful voice and the intelligence to use it with subtlety and grace. His Romeo was a masterpiece of tenderness and energy (though a critic complained that he possessed "the most meaningless legs imaginable"). Already in 1929 his Hamlet was deemed "the high-water mark of English Shakespearean acting in our time". Branching out, he staged a *Merchant of Venice* which Tyrone GUTHRIE called "elegant and witty, light as a feather". As director and actor again in 1932 he won both critical esteem and popular enthusiasm for *Richard of Bordeaux* by Gordon Daviot (better known to mystery readers as Josephine Tey). The next year he directed and starred in an even more triumphant *Hamlet*, a play which, with *The Importance of Being Earnest*, he has had a long association.

Gielgud's career seemed never to peak; well into his seventies, he still comes up with dazzling performances. He produced and acted in a classic season of plays at the Queen's Theatre in 1937–38 and another at the Haymarket Theatre in 1944–45. His Lear at Stratford in 1951 gave belated notice that "his genius had come of age". During the 1960s he idled somewhat, touring widely with a solo Shakespearean recital *The Ages of Man*. But in 1975 he sallied bravely forth into Harold PINTER's *No Man's Land* with another old campaigner, Sir RALPH RICHARDSON. His co-star, summing up Sir John's dazzling and varied career, described him as "a Catherine wheel of ideas".

WITOLD GOMBROWICZ (1904-69)

Polish novelist and playwright. Gombrowicz's plays anticipate the Theatre of the Absurd in their concern with the illusory nature of reality, and man's hopeless attempts to escape from an environment that is constantly trying to mould him. He emerged as an important avant-garde writer on publication of his novel *Ferdydurke* in 1937.

His first play, *Princess Ivona* (written in 1935), was a farcical tragedy in a weird fairy-tale setting. His next (and most famous) play was *The Marriage*, a parody of Shakespearean tragedy, written in 1946. A soldier dreams that he has returned home to his fiancée, family and friends. The dream becomes a nightmare as they cease to be themselves and assume roles such as king, princess and policeman, showing that reality can only exist in the distorted images that others form.

Operetka (1967) was performed almost as a musical comedy. Its fragmented dialogue and action demonstrate Gombrowicz's belief that a play could have no value as a text, only as a score that comes to life on the stage. Gombrowicz has had a great influence on young Polish writers, despite the fact that he lived in Argentina and France for most of his life.

GRAHAM GREENE (1904...)

English novelist, essayist and playwright. Like his sombre novels, Greene's plays depict the cruel tedium of modern life, which only religious faith can ease. *The Living Room* (1953) asserts "we can't *not* suffer". *The Potting Shed* (1957) combines family alienation, lost belief and a miraculous resurrection. The mood of *The Complaisant*

Lover (1959) is summed up by the betrayed husband: "The trouble about marriage is, it's a damned boring condition even with a lover." Greene's perspective derives from the crises of his own life. He has progressed from suicide attempts and games of Russian roulette to religious orthodoxy, and finally to precarious stability as an "agnostic Catholic".

PATRICK HAMILTON (1904-62)

English playwright and novelist. Hamilton's popular reputation rests on three spine-chilling melodramas: *Rope* (1929), *The Governess* (1945) and *Gaslight* (1938). The latter, set in the eerie fog of Victorian London, depicts a fortune-seeker's attempts to drive his wife mad, with a view to inheriting her riches. The inspiration for numerous stage and film thrillers, *Gaslight* is a classic of pregnant tension and macabre atmosphere. Hamilton's own experience as an actor taught him much about what actually *works* in the theatre. His output is remarkable for its unfailing "stageability".

MOSS HART (1904-61)

American playwright and director. Hart and his collaborator George S. KAUFMAN earned a reputation as the BEAUMONT & FLETCHER of the twentieth century, especially for their frivolous but penetrating comedies *You Can't Take It With You* (1936) and *The Man Who Came to Dinner* (1939). These joyfully celebrate chaos and confusion; the pratfall is seen as the governing principle of the universe. The latter play involves such farcical contrivances as the imprisonment of an actress in a mummy-case, though a more serious message may underly the sardonic portrayal of the overweening critic Sheridan Whiteside.

A professional of great versatility, Hart also wrote the books for shows by Irving BERLIN and Cole PORTER, and directed stunning productions of *My Fair Lady* (1956) and *Camelot* (1960). He found playwriting a strain, complaining, "Your last play always shows up on your next electrocardiogram." But medical considerations did not deter him from finding interesting ways to spend all of the five million dollars he earned from his work: "I have none of the money left," he remarked, "and I have no regrets." Fate spared him from the sobering experience of old age.

PIERRE BRASSEUR (1905-72)

French actor and playwright. Brasseur was one of France's most outstanding actors. Natural and uninhibited on stage, he made his Paris debut in 1925 and became known at first for gigolo roles in plays like Edouard Bourdet's *Le Sexe faible*, but it was with the company of Jean-Louis BARRAULT and Madeleine RENAUD that his talents matured. In 1948 he appeared in *L'État de siège* by Albert CAMUS and Paul CLAUDEL's *Partage de Midi*, giving his finest performances as Goetz in SARTRE's *Le Diable et le Bon Dieu* (1951) and as Edmund KEAN in Sartre's adaptation of DUMAS *père*'s *Kean*.

Brasseur also acted in films; he will always be remembered as the Actor in *Les Enfants du paradis* (1945), one of the masterpieces of French cinema. He also appeared in a number of his own plays, including *L'Ancre noire* (1927) and *Un Ange passe* (1943).

ELISABETH FLICKENSCHILDT (1905...)

German actress. Never a great beauty, Elisabeth Flickenschildt did not receive due recognition until her late thirties, when she worked for Gustaf GRÜNDGENS at the Staatstheater in Berlin. From then on she was acknowledged as Germany's foremost classical actress, although she did not necessarily play the role of the tragic heroine. In GOETHE's *Faust*, for instance, she was always Marthe rather than Gretchen, and in SCHILLER's *Maria Stuart*, Queen Elizabeth rather than Mary, Queen of Scots. Similarly in SHAKESPEARE, her greatest triumphs came in her unloveliest roles, notably as Gertrude in *Hamlet*, and as Lady Macbeth. In 1941, the part of Mistress Quickly in *The Merry Wives of Windsor* exploited her comic talents.

HENRY FONDA (1905...)

American actor. Fonda, an aspiring young writer, was first coaxed on to the stage in Omaha, Nebraska, by the mother of Marlon BRANDO. Despite his shyness he took to the theatrical atmosphere immediately, and in 1929 was ready to try his fortunes in New York. His breakthrough there came with the lead in *The Farmer Takes a Wife* (1934), in which critics praised his "manly modest performance in a style of captivating simplicity". Those have remained his distinctive qualities ever since, just as the theatre has remained his first love, whatever his cinematic reputation. He gave up years of Hollywood rewards to play 1700 performances of *Mister Roberts*, probably his most famous role, and "never got tired of it". Still publicly identified with such archetypal, decent Americans, he is known in the profession for a deep and thoughtful dedication to his craft. For Fonda himself acting retains its original appeal: "If it ever stops being fun, I'll go back to my garden and my bees and my painting."

LILLIAN HELLMAN (1905...)

American playwright. "I cannot and will not cut my conscience to fit this year's fashions." With this stirring defence Hellman defied Senator McCarthy's infamous House Un-American Activities Committee. Unnerved by such an all-American response, her inquisitors feared to gaol her for refusing to testify against her friends. But the defendant had visited post-revolutionary Russia and war-torn Spain; she had even met Marshal Tito of Yugoslavia. Inevitably, therefore, she appeared on the Hollywood blacklist.

Ironically, Hellman had already described the consequences of malicious accusation in her very first play, *The Children's Hour* (1934), which depicts the hounding of two schoolmistresses falsely suspected of lesbianism. Later works – *The Little Foxes* (1939), *Another Part of the Forest* (1946) and *Toys in the Attic* (1960) – intimately investigate the neurotic passions of her native South. But these are not merely self-indulgent studies of spiritual pathology; Hellman's primary target is society itself. This moral commitment, coupled with her meticulous craftsmanship, gives her work a wholeness which transcends the occasional morbidity of its subject matter. Though unattractively self-seeking, her characters are observed with an accuracy and conviction reminiscent of IBSEN.

McCarthy's imprecations spelt an abrupt end to the fame and wealth which Hellman's early work had brought her. Her literary mentor and lover of thirteen years, Dashiell Hammett, was imprisoned despite his age and infirmity; Hellman's own scriptwriting assignments vanished, and she was forced to sell the farm on which she and Hammett had lived.

With *Toys in the Attic* and the autobiographical film *Julia* (1976), Lillian Hellman has regained some of her earlier public eminence. But feeling that the avarice and false idolatry she has continually attacked are as manifest as ever, she has increasingly retreated into a disenchanted retirement.

ALEXANDER KORNIYCHUK (1905-72)

Russian dramatist. It was this Ukrainian party official's play *Wings* which, in 1955, finally exorcized the worst terror of the secret police. Khrushchev's tumultuous applause of a caricature of Stalin's secret-police chief, Beria, was to change the state's attitude towards the arts. It was the beginning of "The Cultural Thaw".

Though Alexander Yevdokimovich's play *The Banker* was carefully buried by the censors, most others were performed with great success: *Platon Krechet* (1934) is a paean to Soviet medicine; *Destruction Of A Squadron* (1934), set in the Civil War, concerns the destruction and scuttling of a sailor's rebellion before it falls into the hands of the Whites.

SAMUEL LEVENE (1905...)

American actor. Sam Levene's gloomy, furrowed, face has been amusing American audiences for over fifty years—and delighting producers, who find Levene not only willing to take any part offered but able to make entertainment out of the most mediocre play and add his own inimitable sparkle.

He does not always get bad roles. In George S. KAUFMAN and Edna Ferber's *Dinner at Eight* (1932) Sam found a vehicle to match his comic talent, and in *Guys and Dolls* he was the incurable gambler, Nathan Detroit. Another role that verged on the serious was Horace Vandergelder in Thornton WILDER's *The Matchmaker* (which later was made into the hit musical comedy, *Hello, Dolly!*). But mostly Levene is content to let things happen: "They say, 'You want to do it?'" he shrugs, "So I do it."

OLIVER MESSEL (1905-78)

English designer and artist. Messel was one of the most original British theatre designers of the century. His rococo sets, unusual colour schemes, floating, transparent costumes and fantastic masks created exquisite visual effects which were always handled with humour and imagination. He often experimented with materials: hair, for example, could be made of painted metal and paper.

From 1926 to 1931 Messel worked mainly for the impresario C. B. COCHRAN. Later productions which he distinguished with his designs include *The Lady's Not for Burning* (1949) and *The Dark is Light Enough* (1954), both by Christopher FRY, and Jean ANOUILH's *Ring Round the Moon* (1950); fresh also in the minds of audiences are numerous designs for opera, ballet and films.

JEAN-PAUL SARTRE (1905-80)

French philospher, novelist and playwright. Now the "grand old man" of the French intellectual left, Sartre emerged as a leading philosopher and exponent of existentialism with the publication of his treatise *L'Être et le néant* in 1943. His first play, *Les Mouches*, was produced in the same year; although set in ancient Greece, it was clearly a call for resistance to the German occupation of France and the attitudes of the Vichy government. Fortunately the Germans failed to recognize this. Orestes

A typical piece of gorgeous whimsy from **Oliver Messel**, this set graced C. B. Cochran's *Helen*, directed by Max Reinhardt

arrives in Argos to find the city obsessed with guilt (symbolized by swarms of flies) for the murder of their king Agamemnon by his wife Clytemnestra and Aegisthus, her lover Orestes refuses any part in this guilt, and kills the lovers. In choosing this action he is responsible only to himself; he is imposing a meaning upon an existence that is otherwise pointless.

Sartre continued to explore such existentialist themes in plays that avoided the trend towards the Theatre of the Absurd, yet were successful dramatic expressions of his own philosophy. In *Les Mains sales* (1948), his most popular play, a young revolutionary chooses to die for a political murder expressly in order to give to his act and to his victim a significance they would otherwise be denied. *Kean* (1954) analyses the deceptions and illusions of existence with brilliant wit. The feelings of the hero (the actor Edmund KEAN) as a misfit or impostor, constitute his "original sin". Sartre's other plays include *Huis Clos* (1944), *Morts sans sépulture* (1946) and *Le Diable et le Bon Dieu* (1951).

CARL WALLENDA (1905-78)

German-born tight-rope artist. In 1928 Carl Wallenda, his brothers Herman and Joe and sister Helen premièred the terrifying high-wire act that made them famous. At its climax two brothers walked the wire a hundred feet up with a chair balanced on a pole between them, on which the third brother stood with Helen standing on his shoulders. Over the years, the size of the act increased, and so did its risks. A series of disastrous falls killed four members of the troupe and crippled Carl's son. Fifty years after the debut of his family act, the elderly Carl set out on a wire high above a street in San Juan, Puerto Rico. Half-way to safety he was caught by a gust of wind and, in front of a helpless and terrified crowd, fell to his death.

GEORGE EMLYN WILLIAMS (1905...)

Welsh actor and playwright. Williams is one of the fraternity of great all-rounders who have dominated the London stage in this century. Born humbly—his parents were shopkeepers—he won a scholarship to Oxford and read languages, a training that was instrumental in getting him minor parts requiring fluent French. After he had proven he could also act in English, he gave notable interpretations of Shylock, Iago and Richard III. He reached wider audiences on international tours with his taxing solo performances as Dickens (a recitation of 15,000 words) and Dylan Thomas.

Williams's most celebrated play is the psychological thriller *Night Must Fall* (1935), notorious for the severed head which lies invisibly in a hat-box on stage for the whole length of the play. A lifelong preoccupation with his own background is popularly and lyrically expressed in another successful play, the semi-autobiographical *The Corn is Green* (1938).

JOSEPHINE BAKER (1906-75)

American-born entertainer. A phenomenon of the twenties, Josephine Baker danced her way from the black ghetto to Broadway chorus lines and then to star billing at the Folies-Bergère. Her legs and her smile attracted attention in such New York shows as *Shuffle Along* (1923), but it was in Paris, with *La Revue Nègre* (1925), that she first caused a sensation. The sensation became a furore when the Folies-Bergère lured her away from revue and presented her as "Dark Star", dancing on a mirror and wearing only a G-string of bananas.

Josephine was liberated by Europe. She settled in Paris, walked a leopard down the Champs-Elysées and eventually owned her own nightclub. In the 1930s she added songs to her act and became a glamorous *chanteuse* with sophisticated patter and fabulous gowns. For work with the resistance during the war she was awarded the Légion d'Honneur. Long after her official retirement in 1956 she was in the public eye, though as much for humanitarian activities as for entertainment.

The **Wallandas** (*facing page*). The net made things easier for the audience

Originally a Harlem chorus girl, **Josephine Baker** (*above*) blossomed in Paris

SAMUEL BECKETT (1906...)

Irish playwright. In the 1950s and the 1960s Beckett was the most famous playwright in the English language, a position confirmed by the award of the Nobel Prize for Literature in 1969. Beckett, always an intensely private person, characteristically refused to collect the prize himself. The London *Times* in an editorial on that occasion, wrote: "Beckett's greatest gift to our age, already exploited by others whose outlook is remote from his, is his creation of a dramatic form which needs no intervening fable to give shape and direction to experience." The first line, spoken by Estragon in the most famous of his plays is: "Nothing to be done." Soon after, Estragon says to his companion, Vladimir, on a lonely country road: "Don't let's do anything, it's safer."
Vladimir: "Let's wait and see what he says."
Estragon: "Who?"
Vladimir: "Godot"
Estragon: "Good idea."
After the first performance of *En attendant Godot* in

Samuel Beckett (*above*) made nihilism popular. His unblinking, ironic vision of the world brought him fame and the Nobel Prize

The elegant high spirits of **Cab Calloway** and **Pearl Bailey** (*below*) injected a new life into the long-running musical *Hello, Dolly!*

Paris in 1953 (its first English performance was three years later) the audience anxiously searched for the meaning of the play. It took some time for them to discover that there was no meaning, only pain, incomprehension and a number of good laughs. Since that is what enough people in the audience felt about their lives, Beckett became very popular. Others sought a more traditional explanation for the play's success. Beckett's most enthusiastic critic in London, Harold Hobson, wrote after the first night: "It was immediately clear that *Waiting for Godot* had the immutable essence of great drama: it had a plot, a climax, several star parts, rousing rhetoric, and a dilemma; it had pity and deep understanding."

Beckett was born in the Dublin suburbs and, as a young man, his ambition was to play cricket for Ireland. This he failed to achieve, though he did play one first-class match in England, thus being the only Nobel Prize winner to earn a mention in *Wisden*, the cricketer's bible. He was an accomplished scholar and linguist at Trinity College, Dublin, though soon after he graduated he fled Ireland (or, perhaps, an over-possessive mother) and lived in Paris, where he did odd literary jobs for the most famous Irish exile, James Joyce. He wrote novels of such pessimistic obscurity that his readership remained very narrow—which is how it very nearly remained, because in Paris in 1938 he was stabbed by a pimp named Prudent to within an inch of his life. (Beckett later visited Prudent in jail to inquire why he had done it, and received an answer which might have come from one of his plays: "I do not know," said the pimp.) During the German occupation he joined the French Resistance, eventually escaping to the south of France after an arduous, depressing journey on foot which some critics suggest gave him the idea for *Waiting for Godot*. The later plays—*Endgame* (1957), *All that Fall* (1957), *Krapp's Last Tape* (1958) and *Happy Days* (1961)—were reverentially received, though none had the impact of the first play. Beckett's most recent work, called *Breath* (1969), was an exercise in self-parody which had no dialogue, no actors, and lasted for thirty seconds. Perhaps it was intended to give Beckett the last laugh.

DINO BUZZATI (1906-72)

Italian novelist, playwright and journalist. Buzzati, who wrote for the newspaper *Corriere della Sera*, first made his name as a novelist. His novels, in particular *Il Deserto dei Tartari* (1940), use allegory and fable tempered with satire, and deal with the anguish of modern man in a world that turns its back upon the spiritual. This is the problem dealt with in his most famous play, *Un Caso clinico* (1953). An incurably ill man gradually loses touch with reality as he progresses upwards through the seven floors of a clinic towards death. Buzzati's other plays include *Piccola passeggiata* (1942), *Il Mantello* (1960) and *L'uomo che andrà in America* (1962).

SIDNEY KINGSLEY (1906...)

American playwright. While a teenager in New York City, Kingsley began writing the kind of earnest, socially concerned plays at which he was still labouring thirty years later. The first of these to be performed was *Men in White*, a realistic view of the medical profession, complete with a vivid operating scene. Its 1933 production by the Group Theatre earned him a Pulitzer Prize. *Dead End* (1935) was equally successful, again making effective theatre out of a social theme, this time the plight of children trapped in tenement slums.

Kingsley's didacticism palled in his later plays. Audiences were less responsive, and critics decided his works showed "far more of a theatre sense than either a

mind or imagination". But *The Patriots* (1943) won at least qualified praise, and *Detective Story* (1949) was a hit on stage and screen.

CLIFFORD ODETS (1906-63)

American playwright and actor. In 1935 Odets went from complete anonymity to tumultuous success with three controversial plays on Broadway in little over a month. He was a charter member of the Group Theatre, whose production of his second play, *Waiting for Lefty*, was a surprise hit on Broadway. Passionate and overtly political, *Lefty* depicted the human causes and effects of a taxi drivers' strike, building to a tremendous climax. In short order the Group Theatre produced *Awake and Sing*, a play they had previously rejected, and *Till the Day I Die*, an anti-Nazi polemic. Some critics admired Odets' verbal intensity and angry compassion; others dismissed him as strident and pretentious. His next plays for the Group hammered the same social-economic themes, but with less success. Typical of them is *Golden Boy* (1937), whose deprived hero must abandon his musical talent to become a boxer. Of his last plays, *The Country Girl* (1950) won praise for its sensitivity, but by then its author was well beyond living up to his own claim of being "the most talented young playwright in the business".

SALVO RANDONE (1906...)

Italian actor. Randone, a severe, hollow-cheeked Sicilian, has done most of his acting in Rome and Milan. An uncompromising actor, continually testing his art with the most demanding parts, he has consistently given powerful and sensitive performances in many of the great traditional and modern roles. These include Luigi PIRANDELLO's Enrico IV, Becket in T. S. ELIOT's *Murder in the Cathedral*, and Malvolio in *Twelfth Night*. He has also helped to promote the work of such modern Italian playwrights as Ugo BETTI.

LUCHINO VISCONTI (1906-76)

Italian director and designer. Although world famous as a master of Italian neo-realist films, Conte Luchino Visconti di Modrone was also extremely active in the theatre. In 1936 he went to France and became involved in left-wing intellectual life, working on Jean Renoir's film *Une Partie de campagne*. His own first film, *Ossessione* (1942), opened up a career both in cinema and the theatre. He directed modern European and American drama, often putting on plays which had a social or political message, such as Jean ANOUILH's *Antigone* and *The Fifth Column* by Ernest Hemingway, and shocking a rather conservative Italian public with works by COCTEAU and Jean-Paul SARTRE.

Visconti's strength as a director lay in the powerful creation of atmosphere. He had a strong sympathy with the plays of TENNESSEE WILLIAMS and ARTHUR MILLER. The latter were particularly suited to his own feeling for social realism. But he also enjoyed extravagance and fantasy in the theatre, as was seen in 1948 in *Rosalinda*, his balletic version of *As You Like It* designed by Salvador Dali. His own designs, in Testori's *L'Arialda*, for example, were atmospheric masterpieces.

Visconti's productions of Carlo GOLDONI and CHEKHOV

were much admired, as was his treatment of nineteenth-century opera, one of his great loves. He has had a lasting influence on Italian theatre, helping to end its isolation from the rest of the theatrical world, while managing at the same time to preserve his country's own dramatic and operatic traditions.

PEGGY ASHCROFT (1907...)

English actress. Peggy Ashcroft is one of the greatest Shakespearean actresses of this century. Her Juliet (in GIELGUD's famous production) had a ravishing simplicity of spirit that quite overcame audiences; while Kenneth Tynan described her Portia as a "jewel" and the actress herself as a "cool zephyr". She has also displayed great comic skill in SHAKESPEARE's comedies, and her interpretations of modern roles such as Hedda Gabler, and Nina (in CHEKHOV's *The Seagull*) are thought by many critics to be definitive. Even in Norway, IBSEN's own territory, her Hedda was spectacularly successful.

Peggy Ashcroft was made a Dame in 1956 and in later life has become an actress of distinctive power and majesty, the grandest dame of the English theatre.

WYSTAN HUGH AUDEN (1907-73)

English poet, essayist and playwright. W. H. Auden's choirboy training in enunciation inspired the "profound respect for words" that marked both his lyric and dramatic poetry. *The Dog Beneath the Skin* (1935), *The Ascent of F6* (1936) and *On the Frontier* (1938), all co-authored with Christopher Isherwood, are his major dramatic works. These plays show Auden's mastery of speech rhythms, gift for satire and his awareness of the social and political tensions that were to ignite the Second World War.

For the Time Being (1944), an oratorio, and *The Age of Anxiety* (1947), a modern morality play, were also written in dramatic form. Auden's poetic versatility has made him an ideal opera librettist, whether creating *Paul Bunyan* for the English composer Benjamin Britten (who was always a great admirer of the poet's work) or *The Rake's Progress* for Igor Stravinsky.

ROGER BLIN (1907...)

French director. From his earliest productions, Blin has been associated with the sensational and the experimental. A disciple of Antonin ARTAUD, in 1935 he helped produce Artaud's *Les Cenci*, in which his master's Theatre of Cruelty came to brief life. After the Second World War, Blin's name became linked with the emerging Theatre of the Absurd. Four years spent trying to persuade theatres to take Samuel BECKETT's *En attendant Godot* ended in 1953 with his direction of the first production, in which he himself was Pozzo. The play was an immediate success, and remains one of the most significant productions in post-war drama. Blin was also known for his work with the plays of Jean GENET, directing *Les Nègres* in 1959 with his own black company.

CAB CALLOWAY (1907...)

American singer and bandleader. Calloway was famous for his flashy personality, hi-de-ho scat-singing and extravagant taste in clothes. He led one of the best swing bands of the 1930s and 1940s after making his first impact singing "Ain't Misbehavin'" in the musical *Connie's Hot Chocolates*. When the big bands faded he returned to musicals, playing the slick, ebullient Sportin' Life in *Porgy and Bess* and co-starring with PEARL BAILEY in the all-black version of *Hello, Dolly!*

ANGNA ENTERS (1907...)

American mime and dancer. Miss Enters's unique solo dramatizations of moods and themes evolved from her research as a painter. To learn to analyse physical movement, she studied with a Japanese dancer. His expressive gestures led her to create her first *Compositions in Dance Form*. Performed in a 1923 revue, *Moyen Age* sought to evoke in mime the spirit of a Gothic statue. Since then, Angna Enters has constantly expanded her repertoire, incorporating contemporary satire and motifs from her travels, particularly in Spain and Greece. Ranging from the tender to the macabre, her sketches can convey the impatience of young love or the spectral mystery of death.

EDWIGE FEUILLÈRE (1907...)

French actress, Feuillère, who had previously appeared in light comedy and films, joined the Comédie-Française in 1931, playing Suzanne in BEAUMARCHAIS' *Le Mariage de Figaro*. But she became dissatisfied with her work within the company, and in 1933 returned to films. There, she gained confidence in her own seductive beauty and was first recognized as a great actress. Her moment of triumph on the stage (which she had never entirely deserted) came in 1937 in DUMAS *fils' La Dame aux camélias*. Her beauty, energy and deep, sensuous voice gave her a magnetic stage presence. Among her finest performances were the Queen in Jean COCTEAU's *L'Aigle à deux têtes* in 1946 and Ysé in *Le Partage de midi* by Paul CLAUDEL in 1948.

CHRISTOPHER FRY (1907...)

English playwright and poet. *The Lady's Not For Burning* (1948), Christopher Fry's most successful play, describes the effect on a small community of a world-weary young man who demands to be hanged and a pretty young woman condemned to death for witchcraft. An anonymous *Times* reviewer struck a surprisingly prophetic note in reviewing the first London production: "The only notable effect of these two [characters] is to drive everyone to interminable talk." Fry's pyrotechnic verbal conceits and paradoxes cannot convince many recent critics that he has anything to say (though all admit he says it brilliantly).

Yet in that first post-war decade Fry was–with T. S. ELIOT–the herald of a new age of poetic drama. His verse-plays *A Phoenix Too Frequent* (1946) and *Venus Observed* (1950) were thought to portend a return to an Elizabethan delight in the enchantment of language; and the joyfully promiscuous extravagance of his writing was a refreshing antidote to the sterility of post-war England. Fry's daring juxtaposition of modern slang and flowery archaisms lent an air of contemporaneity to his work, and attracted such stars as Laurence OLIVIER and John GIELGUD.

The change in his fortunes came with *The Dark Is Light Enough* (1954): "As static as a candle-lit tableau or darkling waxworks," complained Kenneth Tynan. Dismayed by accusations of dramatic stagnation, and perceiving a vogue for the more acerbic talents of John OSBORNE and Arnold WESKER, Fry increasingly relinquished original stage works in favour of translations and–somewhat incongruously–scriptwriting for such films as *Ben Hur* (1959), with Charlton Heston.

CANADA LEE (1907-52)

American actor. Leonard Lionel Canegata took his "stage-name" as a young professional boxer, long before he had ever appeared on stage. When an eye injury forced him out of the ring, he made a living in New York playing the violin and eventually leading his own orchestra at the Lafayette Theatre. After such an unlikely early career, he surprised no one by joining the Harlem Players and becoming one of the greatest black actors of the century.

Lee was an actor of immense range whose roles encompassed the villainous Bosola in WEBSTER's *The Duchess of Malfi* (a part he played in white make-up opposite Elisabeth BERGNER) and a black Banquo in Orson WELLES's West Indian *Macbeth*. His greatest success, however, was as the bitter American black, Bigger Thomas, in Richard Wright and PAUL GREEN's *Native Son*.

One of the saddest victims of Senator McCarthy's campaign against Communism, Lee was blacklisted for "left-wing activities" and died in poverty soon after.

After spells as prizefighter and musician, **Canada Lee** became an actor of rare physical presence, intelligence and grace. But a dubious charge of political subversion blighted his career

LAURENCE OLIVIER (1907...)

English actor and director. At drama school Laurence Olivier learned that his hairline was too low, his eyebrows too close together and his bearing too bumptious. What his critical teacher surprisingly failed to notice was the youth's extraordinary physical presence. His athletic physique, brooding handsomeness and commanding voice combined to make him a natural romantic lead in plays ranging from COWARD's *Private Lives* (1930) to the famous 1935 *Romeo and Juliet*, in which Olivier and his friend John GIELGUD played alternately the roles of Romeo and Mercutio. He was an inevitable choice too for Heathcliff in the film of *Wuthering Heights* (1939).

In fact it is on film that some of his best known stage roles are most familiar. The series of Shakespearean films he directed himself are by no means perfect conceptions: *Henry V* (1945) smacks too much of war-time chauvinism, while his *Richard III* (1955) and *Othello* (1965) were too histrionic to transfer comfortably to the intimacy of film. A similar tendency to excess has marred, for some, his stage and screen performances of *Hamlet* (filmed 1948). Yet even in two dimensions Olivier has the power to bully the most begrudging of audiences into a fearful admiration. Indeed his extreme emotional range and expressive power are at once his strength and his weakness. Olivier is the most virile and princely actor of modern times, quite incapable of portraying ordinariness or of letting the lines do the work for him. Thus in a light role such as Mr Puff in SHERIDAN's *The Critic* (1945) he was accused of overacting and mangling the words.

Olivier is above all a showman, taking a clownish

delight in the simple task of physical impersonation. Significantly, his greatest non-classical role was, for many, the vaudeville star Archie Rice in John OSBORNE's *The Entertainer* (1957). It is very much in keeping with his flamboyant style that he should have enjoyed so many accolades: besides his decade from 1963–73 as first director of the National Theatre, he was the youngest ever actor-knight in 1947 and the first ever actor-lord in 1970.

But beneath the bravura is a subtlety that makes his brashest interpretations startlingly complex. By using to the full his commanding vocal, facial and physical resources, he can suggest a quite terrifying–almost mystic–emotional depth. His friend RALPH RICHARDSON envied "Larry's splendid fury"; and Peter O'Toole praised that "grey-eyed myopic stare that can turn you into stone". But Olivier simultaneously imparts a sense of womanish vulnerability; it is this bewitching paradox that reverberates in his portrayals of Coriolanus, Hamlet, Othello and Richard III, while as James Tyrone, in O'NEILL's *Long Day's Journey Into Night*, he perfectly caught the wasted power of the embittered old actor.

As much the subject of gossip columns as of theatre reviews, Olivier has fought and won a long battle with ill-health, which at one time included cancer. His second marriage to the stunningly beautiful Vivien LEIGH was the romantic match of the century; but with his third wife, the actress Joan PLOWRIGHT, he has created one of the happiest artistic partnerships of the English stage.

ARTHUR ADAMOV (1908-70)

Russian-born French playwright. The incomprehensible and Godless world that obsessed Adamov in his youth is the landscape for his early, absurdist plays. In *La Parodie* (1950) a faceless clock hangs on the wall while two nameless characters carry on the futile pursuit of a girl; one ends up in prison, the other dead in a dustbin.

When he began to see Marxism as a possible solution to social evil, Adamov gradually emerged from what he called the "no-man's-land of poetry" to write more socially committed drama. *Le Professeur Taranne* (1953, a nightmarish story of persecution based, in fact, on a nightmare) and *Le Ping-Pong* (1955) mark this transition. *Paolo Paoli* (1957) shows capitalists who trade in butterflies and ostrich feathers as the cause of war in 1914. In plays such as *La Politique des restes* (1962) Adamov continued to make political statements, but these later works never totally discarded the neuroses of his youth.

MILTON BERLE (1908…)

American comedian. Child film star and vaudeville comic, Berle was encouraged by a "Mom" who, for her premature and piercing shrieks of laughter from the audience, became almost as famous as he. In 1932 their mutual determination got him to Broadway in *Earl Carroll's Vanities*, and he went on to star in two of the *Ziegfeld Follies*. With his energetic delivery and vast repertoire of jokes (estimated in 1949 to number 50,000) Berle was a top night club entertainer in the 1940s, and in 1948 became America's leading television star, earning the nickname "Mr Television". He was even the subject of the Broadway show *Top Banana*. More recently he played himself (alias Jerry Biffle) in its 1963 revival.

ALAIN CUNY (1908…)

French actor. Originally a stage and set designer for the cinema, Cuny began to train as an actor in 1938 under Charles DULLIN. Undeterred by the cancellation of his debut (due to the outbreak of war), he went on to appear

Authentically Elizabethan, the young **Olivier** (*above*) stars as Katharina in *The Taming of the Shrew*

Angna Enters (*below*) makes a dashing but poignant man-about-town in one of her inimitable solo routines

in such plays as ANOUILH's *Eurydice*, SARTRE's *Les Morts sans sépultures*, and *Mourning Becomes Electra* by Eugene O'NEILL. In 1955 he joined the Théâtre National Populaire. A later performance as Romeo Daddi in Luigi PIRANDELLO's *Non si sa come* has been a particular highlight of his career. Cuny has also appeared in films directed by Fellini, Buñuel and Antonioni.

PIERRE DUX (1908...)

French director and actor. Early in his career with the Comédie-Française Dux established his versatility by distinguishing himself both as BEAUMARCHAIS' lively Figaro and the morose Alceste in MOLIÈRE's *Le Misanthrope*. He acted with the company from 1929 to 1946, during which years he also directed such plays as HUGO's *Ruy Blas* and Henry de MONTHERLANT's *La Reine Morte*. In 1948 he became codirector of the Théâtre de Paris, where Roger VITRAC's *Le Sabre de mon père* was among his productions. Dux's work was careful and traditional, although in 1962 he did venture to do *Le Misanthrope* in modern dress. He returned to the Comédie-Française in 1970 as Administrator.

REX HARRISON (1908...)

English actor. A deliciously urbane and casual comic actor, Harrison found overnight fame in the 1936 production of Terence RATTIGAN's *French Without Tears*, which enjoyed a long run in the West End. His natural style has also attracted critical acclaim in plays by CHEKHOV, VAN DRUTEN, ELIOT and COWARD.

But Harrison's international renown derives from his performance in the popular musical (and later film) *My Fair Lady* (1956), based on SHAW's *Pygmalion*. Playing Professor Higgins, the linguist who teaches savoir-faire to Eliza Doolittle (Julie Andrews), Harrison mesmerized audiences with his eccentric but kindly charm and convinced everyone that he could sing by speaking (more or less) at pitch.

MARTIN HELD (1908...)

German actor. Dazzled reviewers of Held's performances have often been forced into facile paradox. Thus his Wehrhahn in Gerhart HAUPTMANN's *Der Biberpelz*, the part that established him as a leading actor, was praised for its superbly intelligent portrayal of stupidity, and his interpretation of the talentless comic Archie Rice in John OSBORNE's *The Entertainer*, was a striking exhibition of his talents. At his best as ageing, disillusioned heroes, Held has used his fine sense of irony to illuminate works ranging from MOLIÈRE's *Dom Juan* to Samuel BECKETT's *Krapp's Last Tape*, in which he received the rare honour of being directed by the author.

JOSHUA LOGAN (1908...)

American director, writer and actor. Logan is best known as co-author and director of such spectacular Broadway hits as *Mister Roberts* (1948), *South Pacific* (1949) and *The Flower Drum Song* (1958). He studied in Moscow with STANISLAVSKY before settling in New York. Logan's work is effective without calling attention to itself: "When people come up and tell me the direction is wonderful, then I know I have failed."

RINA MORELLI (1908-76)

Italian actress. Although she had appeared on stage from childhood, Rina Morelli was thirty before the public came fully to appreciate her abilities. After the war she was a notable success in Luchino VISCONTI's production of Jean COCTEAU's *Les Parents Terribles*, and in 1946 she and Paolo Stoppa formed the Morelli-Stoppa company with Visconti as director. An extremely versatile actress, Morelli was at home in many genres, from SHAKESPEARE and CHEKHOV to ARTHUR MILLER, TENNESSEE WILLIAMS and Noel COWARD. Her understanding of modern drama and unerring grasp of character made her one of Italy's finest actresses.

ROBERT MORLEY (1908...)

English actor, playwright and wit. Destined for the diplomatic service, Morley spent a period as a beer salesman before achieving his ambition to "loaf about on the stage". He is best at eccentric extroverts: as Oscar WILDE in 1936 (an untypically serious role) or the egocentric Sheridan Whiteside in *The Man Who Came to Dinner* (1941).

His shaggy eyebrows permanently arched in feigned horror, Morley is the victim of his easy ability to make people laugh. Though he has had some success as a playwright (most notably with *Edward My Son*, 1947) in recent years his talents both on stage and screen have been increasingly directed to agreeable self-parody.

MILDRED NATWICK (1908...)

American actress. Mildred Natwick has appeared in everything from Noel COWARD comedies to Hollywood westerns and teenage movies. She has excelled at eccentrics such as Mme Arcati in Coward's *Blithe Spirit* and was ideal as the mother in Neil SIMON's *Barefoot in the Park*. A London critic praised her 1965 performance in this role as the "benevolent suburbanite with a crucified smile who . . . when put to the test can outdo anyone on the stage in craziness".

MICHAEL REDGRAVE (1908...)

English actor, director and playwright. "One of the greatest pieces of acting I have ever seen"; the English critic Michael Billington's assessment echoed the sentiments of many who saw Redgrave's 1958 Hamlet. For the same critic, his Uncle Vanya (in CHEKHOV's play) was "a brilliantly controlled acceleration of emotion".

Besides his Hamlet, Redgrave's interpretations of Shylock, Lear and Antony have been widely acclaimed. He excels especially at roles requiring the subtle suggestion of internal conflict. In recent years, illness has curtailed his stage appearances.

WILLIAM SAROYAN (1908...)

American storywriter and playwright. In Saroyan's plays as in his fiction, the innocent and humble triumph over cruelty and misery. Famous for his short story collection, *The Daring Young Man on the Flying Trapeze*, he became a playwright in 1939 with *My Heart's in the Highlands*, the sentimental tale of a poor Armenian-American family who keep smiling despite losing their home. The same year he produced the Pulitzer Prize-winning *The Time of Your Life*. Set in a San Francisco bar, it depicts a group of down-and-outs given a miraculous second chance by a rich benefactor. Human sympathy and buoyant energy are Saroyan's great qualities, "be alive" his constant motto. His later plays, including *The Beautiful People* (1941) and *Hello Out There* (1942), all have appealing moments but suffer from a lack of structure.

JACQUES TATI (1908...)

French film director, actor and comedian. Today Tati, whose full name is Tatischeff, is known as the gentle and silent M Hulot from such films as *Mon Oncle* and *Trafic*; but his career began in music hall. A keen sportsman, he discovered a talent for comedy when entertaining his rugby club, and by 1931 was appearing in Paris with his mimed parodies of men at play. The novelist Colette wrote with enthusiasm that he was able to be "the player, the ball and the racquet . . . the boxer and his opponent, the bicycle and the cyclist". An extremely popular performer, Tati was already involved with films in the 1930s. His fame became international when, in 1946, he gave up the stage to devote himself to the cinema.

MAX WALL (1908...)

English comedian. Wall spent many years as an "acrobatic dancer" before emerging after the Second World War as one of Britain's most popular music hall comics. His grotesque contortions added to the macabre humour of his act, especially when he became the bandy-legged Professor Wallofsky who, in black tights and oversize shoes, tried to play the piano with the help of a map and a spirit level.

Although he made a second career as a radio comic, the decline of music hall and the advent of television left Wall forgotten in the late fifties. In the last ten years, however, he has been rediscovered. Mostly as principal actor at the newly-founded Greenwich Theatre, he has played roles that have taken him far from pure comedy: Archie Rice, Malvolio, the tramp in PINTER's *The Caretaker*. In one-man shows he has included an outstanding performance of *Krapp's Last Tape* by Samuel BECKETT.

On stage Wall is an almost tragic figure, yet when he shouts "Don't laugh, it's cruel!" it is hard to know who is laughing at whom.

AGNES DE MILLE (1909...)

American choreographer. "When we did *Brigadoon*," said Agnes de Mille, "everyone involved learned classic Scottish dancing, and then I kind of exploded it." Such explosions of traditional dance forms have been a de Mille speciality throughout her ballet and Broadway careers. With *Oklahoma!* (1943) she revolutionized the American musical, putting serious dance and trained dancers on stage. This gave country dancing such a face-lift that straw hats and gingham skirts were suddenly the rage and briefly became known as the "ballet look". Later shows have included *Carousel* (1945), *Allegro* (1947), *Gentlemen Prefer Blondes* (1949) and *Paint Your Wagon* (1951). In each she has insisted on movement being as inseparable from the development of a story as the words and music themselves. For the remarkable effect her folk choreography has had, de Mille has a disarming explanation: "There is nothing so absolutely startling as the truth."

ROBERT HELPMANN (1909...)

Australian dancer, actor, choreographer and director. Robert Helpmann had already appeared as actor and dancer in his native Australia when he arrived in England in 1932. His debut the next year with the Vic-Wells Ballet revealed both technical skill and dramatic flair. In 1937 he gave an impressive display of his purely theatrical gifts at the Old Vic as Oberon in *A Midsummer Night's Dream*, and until 1950 he moved effortlessly from one art to the other, dancing principal roles with the Wells company while also starring in Elizabethan plays. His physical grace was a natural asset in such parts as Hamlet, but critics also praised his "rare quality of verbal passion". In the late 1940s he began to create his own dance compositions, uniquely incorporating elements of mime. Helpmann also had considerable success as a director before assuming leadership of the Australian Ballet.

KATHARINE HEPBURN (1909...)

American actress. On stage and screen, Katharine Hepburn is the high-strung thoroughbred: dominating but vulnerable, self-possessed but loving. She first came to Broadway's notice in *The Warrior's Husband* (1932), a pseudo-Greek comedy in which she played a fetchingly formidable Amazon. The role won her a Hollywood contract, and the next few years established her as a star of great ability and considerable independence. She returned to Broadway triumphantly in 1939 in *The Philadelphia Story*. PHILIP BARRY wrote the leading part of Tracy Lord, the wilful aristocrat who finally succumbs to love, with Hepburn specifically in mind.

Except for another Broadway appearance in 1942, Hepburn spent the next decade in Hollywood, beginning her classic partnership with Spencer TRACY. In 1950 her career took a new tack with a well-received performance of Rosalind in SHAKESPEARE's *As You Like It*. Through the 1950s her reputation was enhanced by success in several other Shakespearean parts, most notably that of Portia in *The Merchant of Venice*, which she played with the Old Vic on tour in Australia. Such heroines demand the qualities – strength of purpose, wit and femininity – that still characterize Katharine Hepburn, privately as well as professionally. Wryly, she calls herself "a battle-axe with a heart of gold".

Robert Helpmann as Oberon in *A Midsummer Night's Dream*

ELIA KAZAN (1909...)

American director. As an apprentice actor at the left-wing Group Theatre Kazan was considered untalented and asked to leave, but he stayed on doing odd jobs. His obstinacy was rewarded, first by acting and then by directorial assignments, mostly for socialist-realist plays.

Kazan's subsequent career is a roll-call of triumphant premières: Thornton WILDER's *The Skin of our Teeth* (1942), ARTHUR MILLER's *Death of a Salesman* (1949), TENNESSEE WILLIAMS's *A Streetcar Named Desire* (1947), *Cat on a Hot Tin Roof* (1955) and *Sweet Bird of Youth* (1959). During this period Kazan was, with Lee STRASBERG, a powerful voice in the Actors' Studio and the mentor of Marlon BRANDO and James Dean. His style is, at its best, abrasive, simple and direct, owing more to melodrama than to realism. This is especially apparent in his best films: *On the Waterfront* (1954), *East of Eden* (1955) and *Splendor in the Grass* (1961).

Though he resisted Communist attempts to dominate the Group Theatre, Kazan was himself a party-member in the 1930s. By the 1950s, however, he had alienated many of his liberal and socialist colleagues by co-operating with the witch-hunting Senator McCarthy. Shortly afterwards he signed a lucrative Hollywood contract. Denying suggestions of careerist expediency, he has pointed to the allegedly anti-union *On the Waterfront* as evidence of a genuine change of allegiance.

An aggressive exponent of the "Method" school of acting, Kazan views directing as the "transformation of psychology into behaviour". Cynics have wondered whether his political metamorphosis might be an example of the Method in reverse, or of the "transformation of behaviour into psychology".

BURGESS MEREDITH (1909...)

American actor and director. Meredith discovered his vocation as an actor when the boredom of a sea voyage drove him to declaim poetry. As a member of Eva LE GALLIENNE's repertory company, he had his first Broadway success in 1933. Critics hailed him (rather confusingly) as "the Hamlet of 1940" for his title performance in Ferenc MOLNÁR's *Liliom*. He later appeared

Burgess Meredith with **Tallulah Bankhead**
at a rehearsal of *Crazy October* in 1958

in works by PIRANDELLO, SYNGE and SHAW, and directed a number of plays, including James BALDWIN's *Blues for Mister Charlie*. On television, he was a memorable Penguin in the *Batman* series.

ETHEL MERMAN (1909...)

American musical comedy star. Apprenticed in vaudeville and cabaret, Merman found overnight fame in *Girl Crazy* (1930) for her explosive rendition of George Gershwin's "I got rhythm". Subsequent show-stoppers have included "Life is just a bowl of cherries" in George White's *Scandals* (1932), "You're the tops" in Cole PORTER's *Anything Goes* (1934) and "Anything you can do" in Irving BERLIN's *Annie Get Your Gun* (1946), in which she was an especially confident cow-girl. These and other composers wrote with her trumpet-toned voice specifically in mind.

Described by the American critic Brooks Atkinson as "a female juggernaut", Merman preserved her vitality well into a robust middle-age. Four decades (and husbands) after *Girl Crazy*, she triumphantly assumed the lead in the musical *Hello, Dolly!* (1970).

JEAN ANOUILH (1910...)

French playwright and director. Anouilh was inspired to write by Jean GIRAUDOUX's play *Siegfried*; as secretary to its director, Jean JOUVET, he was even able to furnish his flat with sets from the play. Encouraged by the reception of his first work, *L'Hermine* (1932), he devoted himself to writing, and achieved popular success in 1937 with *Le Voyageur sans bagage*.

Anouilh described his earlier plays as *pièces roses* or *pièces noires*; they share the same themes of purity, lost innocence and the rejection of a corrupt society, but the *pièces noires* are darker and more passionate. In *La Sauvage* (1938) Thérèse refuses to compromise and lose her integrity by accepting a comfortable bourgeois existence. *Eurydice* (1942), Anouilh's first adaptation of a classical myth, has a modern setting. Orphée is a street musician, Eurydice an actress and Death a travelling salesman. *Antigone* (1944), based on SOPHOCLES' tragedy, was produced during the war and creates a surprisingly subtle analogy between Greek myth and the German occupation. Antigone defies the ruler, Creon, by burying her brother. She acts according to her principles and refuses to compromise, as Creon has, for the sake of public order.

The *pièces roses* are lighthearted, although the comedy often disguises pathos. *Le Bal des voleurs*, one of Anouilh's most successful plays, written in 1932, is a farce about thieves, lovers, disguise and mistaken identity. In the same style is the "charade with music" (or *pièce brillante*) *L'Invitation au château* (1947), known in English as *Ring Round the Moon*. *Ardèle* (1948) and *La Valse des toréadors* (1952) are frenzied and bitter comedies which the author described as *pièces grinçantes* (grating pieces).

Later Anouilh took political and historical subjects for such plays as *L'Alouette* (1953) about Joan of Arc, *Pauvre Bitos, ou le diner des têtes* (1956) and *Becket, ou l'honneur de Dieu* (1959). His most recent plays have tended to be comedies, including *Cher Antoine* (1969).

Although he has been criticized for returning to the same themes and characters, Anouilh is a skilled dramatist whose frequent levity masks a serious and often despairing response to an unhappy world.

JEAN-LOUIS BARRAULT (1910...)

French actor and director. According to the novelist André GIDE, Barrault had "an admirable face, breathing enthusiasm, passion and genius". These qualities have made him one of the most courageous and inspiring men in the modern French theatre.

While training as an actor with Charles DULLIN from 1931 to 1935, Barrault met Étienne DECROUX, from whom he learned the mime that was to be so important in his theatre. He also assisted Antonin ARTAUD, who had been impressed by the power of his early work as a director. Over the next five years Barrault continued to experiment with the idea of a "total theatre" that would get away from purely spoken literature to a fuller exploration of drama.

During the war Barrault worked as actor and director with the Comédie-Française, where his most memorable production was *Le Soulier de satin* by Paul CLAUDEL. During these years he also created one of his most remarkable film roles: the mime DEBURAU in *Les Enfants du Paradis*. In 1946 he and his wife, Madelaine RENAUD, left the conservative Comédie-Française to form a company of their own. The Compagnie Renaud-Barrault, with Barrault as director and leading actor, became one of the great forces in post-war French theatre. They produced many new plays, including *Les Nuits de colère* by Armand SALACROU, *L'État de siège* by Albert CAMUS, *Rhinocéros* by IONESCO and Henry de MONTHERLANT's *Malatesta*, while with *Partage de midi* Barrault again proved himself a sympathetic interpreter of Claudel.

As director of the state-owned Théâtre de l'Odéon from 1959, Barrault staged revivals and continued to champion contemporary plays, including Jean GENET's controversial *Les Paravents*. In May 1968 his obvious sympathy with rebellious students lost him his job. Not easily defeated, he and Renaud opened the Théâtre de l'Orsay, where they continue their innovative work.

ABE BURROWS (1910...)

American librettist and director. During the 1940s Burrows became a minor cult figure for radio comedy and for such satirical songs as "I Looked Under a Rock and I Found You". His first attempt at a musical (with Jo Swerling) was one of Broadway's biggest hits; Frank LOESSER's jazzy score and the earthy dialogue of Damon Runyon were perfect material for Burrows's New York humour, and *Guys and Dolls* (1950) ran for 1200 performances. Later shows, most written in collaboration, include *Can-Can* (1953), *How to Succeed in Business Without Really Trying* (1961) and *Cactus Flower* (1965), though none is likely to survive as well as his maiden, and still more popular, effort. Like many comic writers, Burrows is earnest about his craft. "Everything I do is serious," he wrote. "It just turns out funny."

JOHN CLEMENTS (1910...)

English director and actor. Sir John's long career has been both distinguished and unspectacular. As a young man he founded the aptly-named Intimate Theatre in a suburb of London. There he directed forty-two performances and played thirty-six roles in 1936 alone. The next year lost some of its intimacy when his Hamlet brought crowds to quiet Palmers Green. Since the war Clements has played a vast range of roles, from Petruchio in *The Taming of the Shrew* to Mr Zuss in Archibald MACLEISH's *J.B.* As a director he is best known for his years (from 1965–73) at the Chichester Festival Theatre.

JEAN GENET (1910...)

French playwright, novelist and poet. Abandoned by his mother when he was an infant, Genet was sent to a reformatory at the age of ten for stealing. Frequent subsequent imprisonments confirmed his criminality and homosexuality; they also provided him with time and material for two of his most famous novels: *Notre Dame des Fleurs* (1944) and *Miracle de la Rose* (1946). So great was his literary reputation that when he was facing a life sentence in 1948, Jean COCTEAU, Jean-Paul SARTRE and other writers intervened to secure him a Presidential amnesty.

Genet's sympathies lie with those whom society has outlawed. His plays portray a lonely world of evil, eroticism and perversion. They reveal the influences of both the Theatres of Cruelty and the Absurd, but are by no means derivative, reflecting as they do an extremely personal view of life. Audiences have frequently rebelled at his work; in *Les Paravents* (1961), for instance, his depiction of the French army in the Algerian war caused riots and provoked bitter attacks.

Genet's two earliest plays were *Les Bonnes* (1947) and *Haute Surveillance* (1949). *Le Balcon* (1957), perhaps his best known work, is set in a brothel, a world of illusion where men indulge their perverse fantasies while acting out roles from the "respectable" world: judge, general and bishop. In this work, as in *Les Nègres* (1959), illusion and reality, good and evil, become hopelessly confused for actors and audience alike. Genet does not allow complacency; he is an evangelist of nihilism. At the end of *Le Balcon* Irma, the madam of the brothel, sends the audience back to their world, where everything "will be even falser than here".

JOYCE GRENFELL (1910-79)

English comedienne. Whether a schoolmistress, housewife or shopgirl, Joyce Grenfell was the quintessential Englishwoman, resolutely cheerful in the face of hilarious adversity. She made her first appearance on radio, but an impromptu performance at a dinner party led to a spot in *The Little Review* of 1939. Other revues followed, as well as films, but she came into her own with a solo recital, *Joyce Grenfell Requests the Pleasure*, in 1954. A collection of comic one-sided conversations, the show ran for a year in London, played successfully in New York and became a model for subsequent one-woman entertainments entitled simply, *Joyce Grenfell*.

FRANK LOESSER (1910-69)

American composer and lyricist. After winning the Second World War with hit-songs like "Praise the Lord and Pass the Ammunition", Loesser, already King of Tin Pan Alley, set out to conquer Broadway. This he did with both music and lyrics for *Where's Charley?* (1948) and *Guys and Dolls* (1950). He went on to write book, lyrics and music for *The Most Happy Fella* (1956), an ambitious and popular show which Loesser himself called an "extended musical comedy" but which is almost operatic in form. *How to Succeed in Business Without Really Trying* (1961), though not in the same league, was his most successful musical, running for 1417 performances on Broadway and winning a Pulitzer Prize.

GEORGES SCHÉHADÉ (1910...)

French poet and playwright. Born in Egypt of Lebanese parents, Schéhadé has managed in his plays to combine the mystery and charm of classical Arab fable with the nihilistic pessimism of contemporary Western civilization. He was already highly regarded in France as a poet when he wrote his first play, *Monsieur Bob'le* (1951), the life and death of a humble Everyman. Its success led to

Terence **Rattigan**'s comedy *French Without Tears* (in a 1949 revival, *right*) ran for over 1000 performances. His drama remained popular until the plays of the "angry young men" elbowed it offstage. He came out of the wilderness at the end of his life, when audiences realised that the new and the traditional drama could both be enjoyed

his being taken up by the RENAUD-BARRAULT company, whose productions of bizarre pieces such as *La Soirée des proverbes* (1954) and *Le Voyage* (1961) brought out all the magical poetry of Schéhadé's extremely individual drama.

LEE J COBB (1911-76)

American actor. After his success in Clifford ODETS' *Golden Boy* for the Group Theatre, Cobb was lured away to a career in films. But of his eighty-odd character parts in Hollywood, he declared that only two had given him any satisfaction (one being the gangster in *On the Waterfront*). His deep, gravelly voice and meaty physique doomed him to movie roles of violence or villainy, and the stage remained his first love. In 1949, ARTHUR MILLER's *Death of a Salesman* finally provided him with the role he felt (and audiences and critics agreed) he was born to play: "When I read the script, I knew there was no living unless I played Willy Loman's part." It was Loman's buoyant frailty that gave Cobb a chance to exercise talents so rarely exploited on film.

DIEGO FABBRI (1911...)

Italian playwright. Fabbri's devout Catholicism is matched by a certainty that man will never discover a solution to earthly evils. Despite such an uncommercial philosophy ("tragic Christianity" as it has been called), his craft and conviction place him among the most important Italian playwrights since PIRANDELLO.

He regards his plays as trials (*processi*) evaluating men's guilt or innocence, hence such titles as *Inquisizione* (1950) and *Processo di famiglia* (1953). His famous *Processo a Gesù* (1955) reconstructs the trial of Jesus in a play-within-a-play. *Veglia d'armi* (1956) re-examines the meaning of modern Catholicism. Fabbri's plays are not entirely pessimistic; he encourages man to accept his position and to find strength in fraternity. Nor are they all serious. *La Bugiarda* (1956), about a lying and adulterous woman, is a much lighter work. It was a great success at the 1965 World Theatre Season in London.

MAX FRISCH (1911...)

Swiss playwright and novelist. In his macabre political parable, *Biedermann und die Brandstifter* (1958), known in England as *The Fire Raisers*, Frisch uses "alienation effects" (including a comical chorus of firemen) in the manner of his mentor, Bertolt BRECHT. But it is a different kind of alienation that is the prime concern of Frisch's work: the individual's loss of identity through extreme social pressure. An absurd example of this is found in *Don Juan oder die Liebe zur Geometrie* (1953). Don Juan, who wishes merely to retire to a monastery and study geometry, cannot escape from his false reputation as a great lover. On a more serious level, *Andorra* (1961) shows how a man, wrongly suspected of being a Jew, comes to accept that he is Jewish and perishes when his country is conquered and overrun by an (imaginary) anti-Semitic power.

It had, in fact, been his reaction to the horror of the Second World War that first inspired Frisch to write for the stage. *Die chinesische Mauer* (1946), a panoramic survey of the history of the world up to the atomic bomb, ends with the cheerful message, "The rest is silence – radioactive silence."

FRITZ HOCHWÄLDER (1911...)

Austrian playwright. The attempt by the Jesuits to found a religious state in Paraguay was an improbable subject for a play by an Austrian refugee in Switzerland at the height of the Second World War. Yet *Das heilige Experiment* (1943) won Hochwälder a world-wide reputation as a dramatist, playing in London and New York under the title *The Strong are Lonely*. He never repeated this initial success, but he is continually experimenting with new dramatic forms, refusing to publish works with which he is dissatisfied. Hochwälder remains his own severest critic. The mysterious *1003*, produced in 1964, contains just two characters, the author and his imagination, suggesting to some critics that the former has rather lost control of the latter.

Tennessee Williams (*far left*, smoking a cigarette) with Elia Kazan, Mildred Dunnock and Barbara Bel Geddes at a rehearsal of *Cat on a Hot Tin Roof*, 1955. The great American dramatist spares no effort to remind his audience in this play of the wretchedness and the complexities of merely being alive

The Italian Catholic **Diego Fabbri** (*left*) is one of the few playwrights who have successfully transferred their faith to the stage

TERENCE RATTIGAN (1911-79)

English playwright. Noel COWARD once said that there were only two real dramatists writing for the English stage: himself and Terence Rattigan. The reason for Rattigan's inclusion in this wild claim was his adherence to the traditional virtues of a well-constructed plot and natural dialogue. His long career as the mainstay of middle-class theatre began with *French Without Tears* (1936), a piece of comic bravura in the manner of Coward, which enjoyed the then longest-ever West End run. He subsequently bettered his own record with *While the Sun Shines* (1943). A second wartime success was *Flare Path* (1942), which drew on his own experience in the RAF.

In *The Winslow Boy* (1946), Rattigan broke new ground with a dramatic Edwardian scandal. His meticulous research and sure sense of period made him much in demand as a film script-writer. This earned him a reputation as a hack, as did his declaration that he wrote for the typical London theatregoer, whom he saw as "a nice, respectable, middle-class, middle-aged, maiden lady with time on her hands and money to help her pass it".

Although his plays remained conventional in form, they were, for commercial successes, surprisingly serious and uncondescending. The curtain rises on *The Deep Blue Sea* (1952) to reveal a woman lying before the gas fire, having just failed to commit suicide. *Separate Tables* (1955) deals with humiliation and despair, while *Ross* (1960) tackles the awkward subject of Lawrence of Arabia's homosexuality. The success of Rattigan's last play, *Cause Célèbre* (1977), a courtroom piece on another historical scandal, proved that there were still plenty of Aunt Ednas (as he called his maiden ladies in the audience), even though many of them were by now imported from abroad.

ANDRÉ ROUSSIN (1911...)

French playwright, actor and director. If judged solely by commercial success, Roussin challenges strongly for the title of leading French playwright of this century. His years as an actor in popular theatre in and around Marseilles gave him an unerring sense of what makes an audience laugh, and after the unexpected triumph of a piece of surreal lunacy called *Am-Stram-Gram*, he devoted more and more of his time to writing. In *Une grande fille toute simple* (1942) he ambitiously attempted serious, reflective comedy, but thereafter preferred to comment on the human condition in a lighter vein, as in his best-known plays, *Nina* (1949) and *La Petite Hutte* (1947), in which the traditional triangle of wife, husband and lover find themselves a trifle overexposed when stranded on a desert island. Having revived the spirit of Georges FEYDEAU with his impeccable plotting, he showed himself no less gifted as a satirist of bourgeois manners and morals in *Les Oeufs de l'autriche* and *Bobosse*. In 1973 Roussin's unpretentious brand of comedy was given the ultimate seal of intellectual approval with his elevation to the Académie Française.

PHIL SILVERS (1911...)

American comedian. Now known to millions as television's Sergeant Bilko, Silvers began his career at thirteen in vaudeville musical comedy. Joining the Minsky Burlesque Troupe in 1934, he rapidly rose to become "top banana" (top comic) for his enthusiastic custard pie clowning. To heighten the comic effect he brightened up his "sort of blank face" with the black-framed spectacles, which over the years have become a permanent prop. Success in the Broadway shows *High Button Shoes* (1947) and *Top Banana* (1951) took Silvers into television, but he has often returned to Broadway.

TENNESSEE WILLIAMS (1911...)

American playwright, novelist and poet. In the late 1930s Tom Williams became "Tennessee" because, he said, his father's family had fought Indians in that state and he knew that "the life of a young writer was going to be something similar to the defense of a stockade against

Theatre of the absurd

The theatre being a conservative institution, it took audiences time to accept that Eugène IONESCO's characters turning into rhinoceroses could come to be seen as meaningful entertainment. The absurdity of life was an important theme of European theatre long before Eugène Ionesco changed his characters into rhinoceroses or Samuel BECKETT dumped his into dustbins, "How weary, stale, flat, and unprofitable seem to me all the uses of this world" complained Hamlet 350 years earlier. The dramatists of the absurd shared this view, but they turned words into action. In the twentieth century, metaphor, always acceptable in poetry, became a basic tool of the theatre.

At first absurdity was a handy notion invoked by all budding existentialists in post-war Paris. Albert CAMUS, it is true, made it the basis of a coherent philosophy, but his idea of stoic struggle against an intransigent world was not sufficiently novel to capture the public's imagination. The word achieved world-wide currency instead through the grotesque comedies of Ionesco.

When, after laborious preparations, the Orator in Ionesco's *Les Chaises* arrives to give a meaningless speech to a hall full of empty chairs, it is not difficult to recognize the frustrating logic of the dream. This kind of absurdity is the direct descendant of Surrealism. The Smiths' living room in *La Cantatrice chauve* or the Professor's room in *La Leçon* are extremely "realistic". One slight shift from normality is enough to make the conventional world absurd, as when the Smiths start to speak in complete non-sequiturs or when the Professor browbeats his student to death. PETER HALL, staging the first English production of *La Leçon*, thought forty a rather high number of young ladies for the professor to have killed, but there is no point in attacking the logic of Ionesco's world, it is as arbitrary as that which prevails in life.

A mere chaotic dream world is that of Arthur ADAMOV, whose characters are alienated from themselves by a terrifying unreality. In *Le Ping-Pong* this alienation is given a Marxist interpretation; the world is absurd because of capitalist exploitation, seen in terms of a monstrous pin-table racket. Adamov's violent, disorganized pieces seem quite conventional, however, when compared with Fernando ARRABAL's "Theatre of Panic". Here all human hypocrisy is supposedly stripped away in erotic and cloacal rites, which include displays of nudity and trapeze artistry. Both Adamov and Arrabal contain echoes of the "Grandfather of the Absurd", Alfred JARRY, whose monstrous Père Ubu had bewildered audiences sixty years before. They paved the way for "The Living Theatre" and other manifestations of theatrical anarchy in the 1960s.

Meanwhile a more sedate, almost motionless, absurdity was to be found in the theatre of Beckett. His characters do not inhabit sexually perverted tyrannies, or even rhinoceros-infested suburbia; they live mainly inside their own heads. Theirs is a world grown old, where all desire is dead; there remain just habit and a few residual flickerings of human spirit.

The most striking thing these playwrights of the absurd have in common is the fact that though not one of them is French, they all chose to write in the language of their common land of exile. This unusual situation may have heightened their sense of man's precarious hold on reality, but the intellectual climate in France was already moving towards such a vision of life. Jean TARDIEU, for one, was producing work very similar to Ionesco's before the latter tried to learn English and became instead the leading playwright of the absurd.

That life is absurd few will deny, even if there is continuous debate as to where that absurdity lies. So too with the writers of the Theatre of the Absurd who, through their creation of alternative worlds, are thrown together for the sake of convenience into one motley movement.

---

a band of savages".

Williams's youth was a series of shocks and violations. The "tenement wilderness" of St Louis replaced his idyllic Mississippi birthplace. His father and schoolmates mocked his bookish delicacy, while his mother and sister lived in nostalgia and fantasy. He won literary prizes at college, but his father withdrew him for failing Officer Training. The pressure of continuing to write while enduring the "indescribable torment" of his job as a shipping clerk brought on a nervous breakdown. After recuperating and finishing his degree, he travelled and worked around the country. He also wrote tirelessly, his apprentice plays winning attention and awards. At last *The Glass Menagerie*, a Broadway hit in 1945, established him as a major dramatist.

This lyrical evocation of his St Louis years embodied what Williams has called his Dominating Premise: "The need for understanding and tenderness and fortitude among individuals trapped by circumstances". In *Menagerie* the "circumstances" are external, the drab hopelessness that Amanda and Laura Wingfield can only relieve by illusion. But later plays show that they can be internal as well. Blanche DuBois, of *A Streetcar Named Desire* (1947), is a victim of sexual repression and ill-starred sensitivity.

Opposing pressures typify Williams's work. He believes in freely acted desire but loathes "unkindness and violence". He maintains that people must "make voyages", while aware that death can make any endeavour seem meaningless. These conflicts account for the intensity of his plays, in which extreme situations represent the very extremes of reality.

Williams's most successful works – *Cat on a Hot Tin Roof* (1955) and *The Night of the Iguana* (1961), in addition to *Menagerie* and *Streetcar* – convert these tensions into brilliant drama. Other plays appear merely

Ionesco's short play *Motor Show* (*left*) in a lunchtime production at the open-air theatre in London's Regent's Park, 1974

In **Samuel Beckett**'s *Endgame* (*below left*) Nell and Nagg have no legs and are accordingly well equipped to live in dustbins; they are obsessed with a need for food

The great English comedian **Max Wall** found a classic vehicle for himself as the preposterous hero of Jarry's *Ubu Roi* (*below*). Designs for this London production were by David Hockney

extravagant, macabre and hysterical. Their turmoil serves to point up the contradictory strains within the personality of the playwright. "Truly", Williams says, "I have two sides to my nature," referring to more than just his publicly professed homosexuality. Critics might object that the theatrical anguish of his own life only occasionally shapes itself into good drama. But despite two decades of ill-health, professional failure and personal ordeal, he continues to write, committed in his own words "to experience and to witness" and show, if he can "how to live beyond despair and still live".

WILLIAM DOUGLAS HOME (1912...)

English playwright. Home's craftsmanlike comedies of everyday, upper-class life have packed theatres in London and New York for over thirty years. *Now Barabbas* (1947), a grim prison drama, was a distinguished excep-

tion to the string of popular successes that include such commercial classics as *The Chiltern Hundreds* (1947) and *The Reluctant Debutante* (1955). *Lloyd George Knew My Father* (1972) and *The Secretary Bird* (1968) do include some food for thought, but remain highly digestible.

The son of an earl and brother of Sir Alec Douglas Home (a former Prime Minister), Home writes with authority about the English aristocracy.

EUGÈNE IONESCO (1912...)

Romanian-born French playwright. Questioned about his first play, *La Cantatrice chauve* (*The Bald Prima Donna*, 1950), the founding father of so-called "anti-theatre" replied, "I had not the slightest intention of becoming a playwright. I just wanted to learn English." The platitudes and *non sequiturs* drawn straight from a well-known English course (with stage-directions like

"The clock strikes twenty-nine times") were taken by some as an assault on traditional theatre by others as an assault on the bourgecis mentality, but by most as an insult to their intelligence. Even the irrelevant title was the result of an unlikely slip of the tongue during rehearsals. Instead of saying "l'institutrice blonde" (the blonde governess) an actor came out with "la cantatrice chauve", which so appealed to author and cast that it was retained.

With *La Leçon* (1951), which shows the effectiveness of language as a means of violence, and *Les Chaises* (1952), which shows its complete inadequacy as a means of communication, Ionesco's intentions became clearer (at least to some). The French theatrical establishment started to take notice. Unexpected enthusiasm came from dramatists as established as Jean ANOUILH, who announced that he preferred *Les Chaises* to both MOLIÈRE and STRINDBERG.

As yet Ionesco had only written one-act plays. His first full-length venture into the absurd was *Amédée ou comment s'en débarrasser* (1954), the tale of a corpse which gradually expands to fill a whole flat. This macabre image has been taken to symbolize the guilt and remorse in a marriage that has failed, but the play also makes relatively traditional use of dialogue. Ionesco, who had hitherto maintained that language was useless, had begun to use it to communicate.

All Ionesco's later works are in the form of allegories, his constant theme being man faced with death, as in *Tueur sans gages* (1958), *Le Roi se meurt* (1962) and *Jeux de massacre* (1970). The play which secured his worldwide reputation was *Rhinocéros* (1959), produced in France by Jean-Louis BARRAULT and in England by Orson WELLES. The inhabitants of a city are mysteriously turning into rhinoceroses. Even Berenger, the well-intentioned little man who is the hero of several of Ionesco's plays, finally succumbs to the epidemic of pachydermia. The play is usually taken as a demonstration of how suggestible men are to totalitarian doctrines.

Thus the playwright who began by mocking literary endeavour in the theatre has become essential reading for high-school literature students. Ionesco himself enjoys this absurd state of affairs, willingly contributing to debates on his own work, although he sometimes claims that he does not know what his plays are about either.

WENDY HILLER (1912...)

English actress. As if destined for the theatre from baptism, Wendy Hiller was named after the young heroine in James BARRIE's *Peter Pan*. She went straight from school to three years' repertory in Manchester, and her first London success came in *Love on the Dole* in 1935. That performance prompted GEORGE BERNARD SHAW to choose her to play Saint Joan the following year. Thereafter she was one of Shaw's favourite actresses, playing the heroines of *Pygmalion* and *Major Barbara* both on stage and screen. A consummate professional, Hiller has been as effective in SHAKESPEARE as in Eugene O'NEILL, though Americans may not have been pleased to hear her very professional response when she won an Oscar for the film of Terence RATTIGAN's *Separate Tables*: "Cold, hard cash. That's what it means to me."

GARSON KANIN (1912...)

American writer, director and actor. Early in his career Garson Kanin had the good fortune to be associated with the eminent writer-director George ABBOTT. The young actor helped to stage such Abbott hits as *Three Men on a Horse* and *Boy Meets Girl* as well as performing in them,

and his mentor later gave him directing assignments of his own. The practical experience of making plays work bore spectacular fruit in 1946 when *Born Yesterday*, a comedy written, directed and produced by Kanin, began a run of 1642 performances. A Broadway masterpiece, the play combined energy, wit and sentiment in its tale of a war-time profiteer exposed by his dumb-blonde girl friend and an idealistic reporter. Similar ingredients were less successful in *The Smile of the World* (1949), *The Rat Race* (1949) and *The Live Wire* (1950). As director alone, Kanin has been responsible for such diverse projects as *The Diary of Anne Frank* and the hit musical *Funny Girl*. His many film credits include the early TRACY/HEPBURN movies, co-written with his wife, the actress Ruth GORDON.

GENE KELLY (1912...)

American dancer, actor, choreographer and director. Gene Kelly describes his own dancing as "strong, wide-open, bravura", a graceful and athletic style that has inspired such film classics as *An American in Paris* and *Singin' in the Rain*. After some unhappy boyhood lessons, he resumed dancing in college, although only as one of his many interests in the theatre. In 1940, however, he became the heir-apparent to Fred ASTAIRE, when two contrasting Broadway roles made him a star: the good-hearted dancer in William SAROYAN's *The Time of Your Life* and the cynical title character of Rodgers and HART's *Pal Joey*. His later career has been mainly cinematic, though he has appeared in summer stock with all the old energy.

JEAN VILAR (1912-71)

French director, actor and manager. In Vilar's opinion, "An auditorium where you can embrace your neighbour, eat and drink and piss on the floor is better for our drama than theatres for the privileged." Throughout his life he strove to end the middle-class monopoly of the theatre by making it popular and approachable.

After training as an actor with Charles DULLIN and touring the provinces for two years, Vilar returned to Paris in 1943 and directed STRINDBERG's *The Dance of Death*. Two years later he won the Prix du Théâtre with ELIOT's *Murder in the Cathedral*. During the summer of 1947 Vilar created his first Avignon Festival, which was to become an annual centre for theatrical experiment. Distinguished productions at Avignon have included *Richard II*, Georg BÜCHNER's *Dantons Tod*, in which Vilar was a magnificent Robespierre, KLEIST's *Prinz Friedrich von Homburg*, and *L'Avare* by MOLIÈRE.

In 1951 Vilar took over the Théâtre National Populaire in Paris. Continuing to encourage a popular audience, he offered seats at low prices and staged original productions of plays chosen mainly from the classical repertoire. The sets were simple, the style heroic, with impressive use made of space, costume and lighting. CORNEILLE's *Le Cid*, BRECHT's *Mutter Courage und ihre Kinder* and *Ubu Roi* by Alfred JARRY were among the many successes during his twelve years at the theatre. Vilar continued to run the Avignon Festival until his death.

LILLA BRIGNONE (1913...)

Italian actress. Brignone made her debut in 1934, but it was not until she joined the newly formed Piccolo Teatro di Milano as leading actress in 1947, that she proved herself one of Italy's most delightful and versatile actresses. During her long career she has played an enormous variety of parts ranging from Elektra in the verse tragedy by SOPHOCLES to Elizabeth in ARTHUR MILLER's *The Crucible*. Closer to home, she has been outstanding as

Mommina in *Questa sera si recita a soggetto* by Luigi PIRANDELLO and as Smeraldina in Carlo GOZZI's masked comedy *Il Corvo*. She is also well known as the coquettish Clothilde in Henry BECQUE's *La Parisienne*, a part she monopolized for years on stage, radio and television.

ALBERT CAMUS (1913-60)

Algerian-born novelist, philosopher, journalist and playwright. The earliest interest of the great novelist Camus was the theatre. In 1935, while still in his early twenties, he helped to form the Théâtre du Travail, a Communist theatre company for which, with his colleagues, he collaborated on his first play. *La Révolte dans les Asturies* (1936) was the beginning of a brief but intense association with the company (later called the Théâtre de l'Équipe) as writer, producer and even as actor.

Camus was obsessed with the intrinsic absurdity of existence, which he saw as neither the fault of Man himself nor of the Universe, but of their perpetual, unfortunate juxtaposition. Two plays written during the war years, *Le Malentendu* (1944) and *Caligula* (1944), have "heroes" that use their freedom wrongly and cause their own destruction. Caligula finds no happiness in his orgy of cruelty, only a great emptiness. A post-war play, *L'État de siège* (1948), is an allegorical account of totalitarianism and resistance to it. Plague (with his secretary Death) takes over a city. Drunken Nada reacts by leading a rule of death and horror, while Diego gives his own life to save the girl he loves (and incidentally saves the city).

The plays of Camus are the most passionate expressions of his ideals; if sometimes they fail as drama, it is because the allegory is too deliberate. His characters lose their

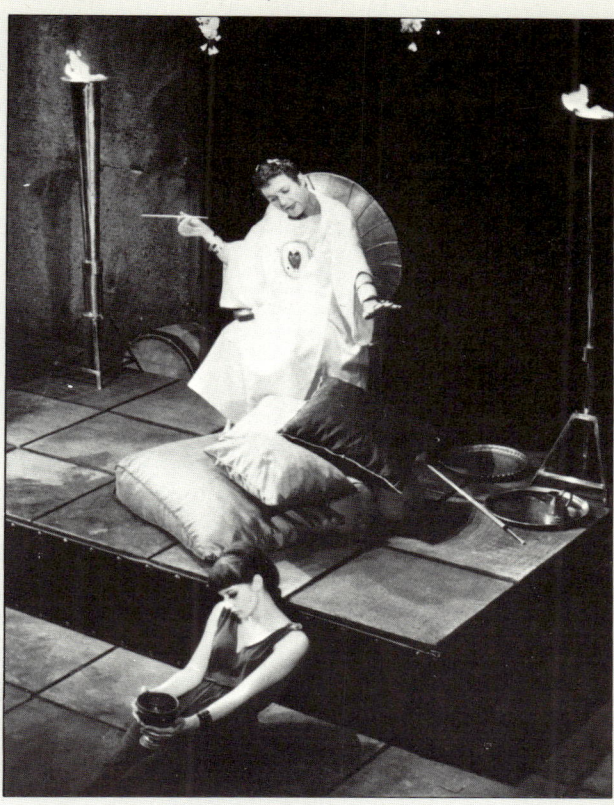

Caligula (*above*) by **Camus** is a terrifying moral tale about the downfall of the megalomanic young emperor

ENSA (Entertainments National Service Association) brought Gielgud, Vera Lynn, and other stars to fighting men

human individuality under an involved construction of symbol and formalized idea. More successful (if by definition less original) are his stage adaptations, such as *Requiem pour une nonne* (1956, after William Faulkner's novel) and *Les Possédés* (1959, after DOSTOYEVSKY). In 1960 Camus was killed in a motor accident, a senseless death for one so conscious of life's absurdity.

WILLIAM INGE (1913-73)

American playwright. Enthralled by the theatre at an early age, Inge dreamed of becoming an actor, and performed in tent shows in his native Kansas. But the Depression forced him to teach instead of seeking his fortune on Broadway. Then a wartime stint as drama critic brought him into new contact with the theatre, and an interview he did with TENNESSEE WILLIAMS inspired him to compose a play of his own. In 1947 a Dallas theatre group produced *Farther Off From Heaven* on Williams's recommendation. Inge continued to write, and in 1950 *Come Back Little Sheba* brought him to Broadway at last. Some critics found the play's realistic description of alcoholism "depressing", but Inge confirmed his promise with the highly charged *Picnic* (1953) and *Bus Stop* (1955). *The Dark at the Top of the Stairs* (1957), another psychological drama, gave him his fourth consecutive hit, but three later plays were less successful.

VIVIEN LEIGH (1913-67)

English actress. Leigh is the bewitching Scarlett O'Hara in the film *Gone with the Wind* (1939). It was her seraphic and then unfamiliar beauty that led David O. Selznick to sign her for the part after a two-and-a-half-year search.

On the stage she was a superb Lavinia in a 1955 Stratford production of *Titus Andronicus*, though she is best remembered in roles such as Ophelia and later as Blanche in *A Streetcar Named Desire*, where her attractiveness was all the more beguiling because it contained a suggestion of fragility. Indeed this was borne out in her personal life; respiratory and depressive illness, combined with obsessive overwork, provoked a series of nervous breakdowns that eventually destroyed her marriage to Laurence OLIVIER and led to her early death.

JEAN MARAIS (1913...)

French actor and director. Built like a Greek god, with chiselled features and deep eyes, Marais is best known internationally as Orphée in the film by Jean COCTEAU. The two worked closely for many years, an association which began in 1937 when Marais (then training with Charles DULLIN), auditioned for Cocteau's play *La Machine infernale*. When he was cast as Oedipus, the other actors were so angry that Cocteau had to relegate him to the part of Chorus, for which he spent the play balanced, statue-like, upon a pedestal.

In 1938 Marais played the son, Michel, in Cocteau's *Les Parents terribles*. It was a great success, and made his name as an actor. He has since appeared in the play a number of times, most recently in 1977. Marais directed and performed in an outstanding production of RACINE's *Britannicus* in 1941. In 1946 he had another triumph as Stanislas in Cocteau's *L'Aigle à deux têtes* with Edwige FEUILLÈRE. A more recent success was his production of SHAW's *The Devil's Disciple* in 1968.

FÉLICIEN MARCEAU (1913...)

Belgian-born playwright and novelist. Both *L'Oeuf* (1956) and *La Bonne soupe* (1958), Marceau's best known plays, reveal unexpected events from the past lives of the main characters (respectively, a criminal and an adventuress). Marceau himself kept secret for many years the fact that he had once been condemned to fifteen years' hard labour by a Belgian court. This was on account of his work on Belgian radio under the Nazi occupation. Most of the war, however, he spent working in the Vatican Library.

Now an eminent man of letters in France, Marceau has also been a mainstay of traditional theatre. In his skilful blends of the comic and the dramatic, he has pursued a preoccupation with confessions, notably in *La Preuve par quatre* (1964), the story of an industrialist who tries to maintain three women to satisfy his need for three different kinds of love.

ANTHONY QUAYLE (1913...)

English actor and director. Having made his reputation as a "glowingly evil" Iago, Quayle was from 1948 to 1956 director of the Shakespeare Memorial Theatre in Stratford-upon-Avon, where he had under his wing such glittering celebrities as EDITH EVANS, John GIELGUD, RALPH RICHARDSON, Laurence OLIVIER and Paul SCOFIELD. In 1949–50, he took the company on a highly successful tour of the Antipodes.

He still found the opportunity to cast himself as a plumply lovable Falstaff and (despite a rather weak voice) a powerful Othello. Since those days Quayle has established himself as an actor of considerable versatility (witness his brilliant Galileo in New York in 1967), though he has thoughtfully rejected stardom.

IRWIN SHAW (1913...)

American playwright and novelist. Shaw's finest dramatic achievement is *Bury the Dead* (1936), in which six slain soldiers refuse to stay dead, to the horror of their relatives and superiors. Misinterpreted as pacifist, it is in reality a bitter prophecy of "the war that is to begin tomorrow". Indeed Shaw's other major success, *The Gentle People* (1939), is a plea for action; fascism is personified by a gangster who is finally murdered by his victims.

MARGUERITE DURAS (1914...)

French novelist and playwright. Duras was born in Indo-China, but there is nothing exotic or colourful about her works, even the early novels set in the East. Best known outside France for the film-script of *Hiroshima, mon amour*, she consistently creates a world of emptiness and death. Since the success of her first play, *Le Square*, adapted from one of her own novels, she has concentrated more and more on the theatre, even though any communication between her (not numerous) characters is an exceedingly rare occurrence.

Duras's protagonists are usually lonely women; two of her greatest successes have been the result of inspired solo-playing by Madeleine RENAUD. In *Des Journées entières dans les arbres* (1965) there is no action at all, while in *L'Amante anglaise* (1967), based on the true case of a woman, who, for no apparent reason, killed her cousin and cut her into pieces, the murder is only the prelude to a long interrogation of the murderess.

ALEC GUINNESS (1914...)

English actor. In private life Guinness is a silent, retiring man. At work he retains some of these same qualities, investing his performances with a subtlety that is often more striking on film than in the theatre.

Seemingly destined to be the definitive Hamlet, Guinness tried the part twice. In Tyrone GUTHRIE's modern-dress production of 1938, he was accused of attempting "neither play of feature nor gesture", while in 1951 he produced the play himself, again leaving audiences puzzled rather than convinced. But he has generally excelled in the roles of tortured, isolated men. As Garcin in SARTRE's *Vicious Circle* (*Huis Clos*), T. E. Lawrence in Terence RATTIGAN's *Ross* and the title role in Boland's *The Prisoner*, he hinted at unimaginable horrors in the human soul. Indeed his unique ability to portray the visionary quality of his characters has been successfully exploited by Hollywood, in *Star Wars*. His voice, even at its quietest, has a haunting resonance that can rivet an audience to attention. A chilling performance as Fagin in *Oliver Twist* is further testament to this.

In comic parts Sir Alec is no less compelling, with an ironic twinkle in his eye that never fails to charm. An obvious role that combined these two extremes of his enormous range was the Fool in *King Lear*.

GYPSY ROSE LEE (1914-70)

American striptease artist and actress. The hit musical comedy *Gypsy* celebrates Mrs John Olav Hovick, the mother who pushed Gypsy Rose Lee and her sister (later the actress June Havoc) to vaudeville stardom. Mom Hovick manipulated every aspect of her darlings' careers, including arranging the unfortunate accidents that occasionally befell competing kiddie acts. The girls became headliners, but Gypsy found her true calling in Toledo, Ohio, on filling in for an "exotic dancer" who had been arrested. By the 1930s she was the most renowned figure in burlesque, admired equally for her wit as for her dancing. There had been other comedienne-strippers, as Gypsy said, but she was "the only one of them who ever talked". She could write too, turning out thrillers, (*The G-string Murders*), memoirs and a Broadway comedy that even George S. KAUFMAN was moved to produce. She continued dancing into the fifties, but later, as host of her own TV talk show, amused her audiences fully clothed.

When people are asked to name a famous strip-tease artist, only two ladies spring readily to mind: Salome, and **Gypsy Rose Lee** (*right*). Other great practitioners of the art have enjoyed extremely ephemeral fame. Their specialities, involving novel pieces of equipment or previously unattempted contortions of the body, were soon assimilated into the acts of other strippers. Gypsy Rose Lee, however, was blessed with a show-business personality as well as the far from unique ability to take off her clothes to music. The bumping, grinding gyrations employed by the majority of conventional strippers have their beginnings in the hootchie-kootchie dance of the early 1900s.

The first public performance of this frank imitation of the sexual act is usually axcribed to the legendary Little Egypt (who, in fact, wore a great deal more than a button and a bow) at the St Louis Exhibition of 1904, but the more explicit Burlesque artists had been performing similar motions for years before then. The great Millie De Leon was said to be capable of "a purely muscular side to side movement, generally deemed the peculiar gift of horses". The effect that displays of feminine nudity have had on other forms of entertainment has rarely, if ever, been beneficial. The decline of the Music Hall in Britain and France, and of Vaudeville in America, can be directly attributed to the spread of strip-clubs and nude revues. Although stand-up comics continued to fill in while the young ladies "changed", how could they hope to satisfy an audience still panting for its pound's-worth of flesh

Vivien Leigh (*above*) was brilliant in roles combining passion with fragility

Circus now

Some veteran circus-goers lament that the big top is not what it was. They recall the fever of excitement that would overwhelm a town as soon as the circus arrived, and the cry of "hold your 'osses, here come the elephants", that would send a glorious parade of wagons, artistes, animals and music winding down Main Street like a medieval pageant. But today, shows travel only by train and truck. Often

they perform in stadiums rather than tents. Rising costs and the competition of movies and television have forced even such mighty spectacles as the Bertram Mills show to close.

And yet the circus still touches the public's imagination with its unique and ageless appeal. "The Big One", Ringling Brothers and Barnum and Bailey, may not play under canvas, but it still tours all over the United States. The circus is as popular as ever on the continent of Europe, and

Big top's coming to town! An attraction in themselves, circus posters convey all the gaudy excitement of the show. Here are the thrills that the ring will bring to life – the animals, the artists, the death-defying feats, that are all part of the show

Adrian Wettach became **Grock** (*above*) because his first comedy partner was called Brick. But it was his solo performances in theatres as well as circuses that made him the greatest clown of his time

The circus would not be the circus without its animals, and they receive the treatment stars deserve. A princely pachyderm (*below*) is given a foot-shine by two properly deferential attendants

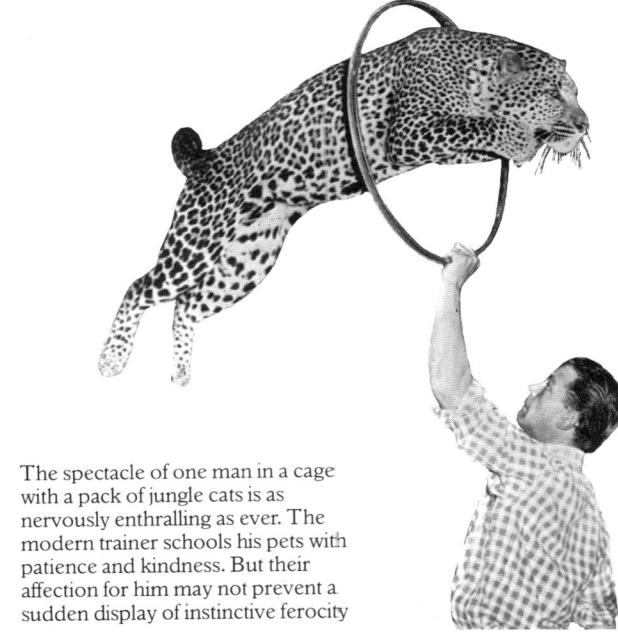

The spectacle of one man in a cage with a pack of jungle cats is as nervously enthralling as ever. The modern trainer schools his pets with patience and kindness. But their affection for him may not prevent a sudden display of instinctive ferocity

village greens in England provide tent sites for the considerable number of shows that are still active. In Russia alone there are one hundred circuses, and the art is given state support on a level with music or ballet. In 1974 Prince Rainier of Monaco initiated his Festival International du Cirque, bringing together top performers from all over the world. For the circus remains a unique amalgam of danger and laughter where the larger-than-life comes to life and the incredible becomes fact.

Early troupes of rope-walkers performed on their own, but for generations no circus has been complete without them. And lovely ladies have always been part of the big-top's glamour

Jaunty in stripes, checks and patches, a uni-cyclist shows off his comic and acrobatic ability. Even the circus acts that aim for laughs can wow their audiences with their skill as well as their fun

The big top is no place for amateurs. The show is thrilling only because the risks are real, and triumph is only a hair's breadth away from disaster

People flock to the circus to see the marvellous. Here everything is bigger, brighter, funnier, more spine-tingling than anywhere else, and ordinary men and women perform extraordinary feats. This young star's speciality is balancing chairs on his mouth. Beginning with two, he works up to twenty-two, with a total weight of almost 200 pounds to carry

Horses and their riders were the first stars of the circus, from the bare-back acrobatics of the Romans to the equestrian dramas of Philip Astley. The standard size of the riding ring and the dazzling virtuosity it presents have remained the same for 200 years. Crowds still respond with excitement and anticipation to the old cry of "bring on the 'osses!"

JOAN LITTLEWOOD (1914...)

English director. Despite the fact that the Theatre Workshop was a collective venture, it would never have succeeded without Joan Littlewood's inspirational capacity for hard work. The idea was born in Manchester, where Littlewood and her then husband (the folk-singer and playwright Ewan McColl) had worked in radio and fringe theatre since before the war. In 1953 the Theatre Workshop moved to East London, making its home at the Theatre Royal, Stratford. Keeping "alternative" theatre alive in a working-class area was no easy task; the censors kept close watch on a company which shared the radical ideals of Bertolt BRECHT (Littlewood herself played Mother Courage in her 1955 production of Brecht's play). The brilliance of their productions and the advent of talented new writers to the theatre (Brendan BEHAN's *The Quare Fellow* and *The Hostage*, and Shelagh DELANEY's *A Taste of Honey* all received their first performance there) rapidly lured sophisticated audiences from the West End to the East End.

Ironically, success spoiled the Theatre Workshop for Littlewood. Since the early 1960s she has returned only occasionally to direct, but her latter productions have included the entertainment for which she is best known. *Oh What a Lovely War!* (1963) is an ironic collage of short scenes and First World War songs in which comic-opera generals play idiotic war-games, while thousands die in the Flanders mud. For all the jollity, war has rarely appeared so unattractive on stage.

WILL QUADFLIEG (1914...)

German actor. Germany's leading classical actor of the last forty years, Quadflieg has played all the major tragic heroes of SHAKESPEARE, GOETHE and SCHILLER. As a young man, his most famous role was as Schiller's Don Carlos, but in 1957 he had an even greater success as Faust, when both parts of Goethe's vast work were put on in Hamburg by Gustaf GRÜNDGENS. Quadflieg had played Faust before, but this time he brought out the detached,

studious side of the character. His Mephistopheles in the same play at the Salzburg Festival of 1961 was even more detached, giving the impression that there were many things the diabolic emissary would rather be doing than chasing after Faust's immortal soul.

In the sixties Quadflieg turned to direction, and with Maria BECKER formed the travelling company Schauspieltruppe. The greatest successes of their original repertoire were their revivals of lesser-known works of August STRINDBERG.

ARTHUR MILLER (1915...)

American playwright and novelist. Miller's *Death of a Salesman* (1949) comes closer than any other play to restating the values of classical tragedy in terms of the common man and the industrialized West. The hero, Willy Loman, finds his powers as a salesman failing and is sacked. Unable to reject the false commercial values by which he has lived, he dreams wistfully of what might have been, and finally confuses fantasy and reality. His self-esteem as a family man is also mercilessly demolished when his own sons refute his pretensions to nobility. In a final attempt to salvage some personal usefulness and honour he commits suicide to provide insurance money for his family. The play is a moving social document, but Loman is also a true tragic hero in the Grecian and Shakespearean mould; his doom is brought about both by the world's ill-will and by his own hubristic need to be "well liked".

Miller's feeling for the harsh realities of the modern world is firmly based upon experience. His own father was a small-time manufacturer and Miller himself undertook various manual jobs, observing at first hand the destruction of men's self-respect by a system he considered to be exploitive.

Given the thematic material of his work, it is no surprise that Miller was indicted in 1955 by the Un-American Activities Committee for refusing to incriminate his friends. His political stance, and his own short-lived marriage to Marilyn Monroe, are the subject of *After the*

Peter Weiss and the elderly director **Erwin Piscator** (*left*) discuss the production of *Die Ermittlung*, Weiss's play about the trials of Auschwitz guards. Both men had to flee from Nazi Germany in the 1930s

Zero Mostel is seen (*right*) in his most famous role as Tevye, the traditional Jewish father in *Fiddler on the Roof*. In the midst of recurring disaster he finds strength and simple wisdom by talking matters over with God

Fall (1964). His only other universally acclaimed drama is *The Crucible* (1953), which – being set in the days of the Salem witch-hunts – deals more symbolically with the problem of persecution.

Later successful works such as *A View from the Bridge* (1955), *Incident at Vichy* (1964), *The Price* (1968) and *The Creation of the World and Other Business* essentially re-examine the same moral dilemmas as *Death of a Salesman* and *The Crucible*, though they lack perhaps the impact of his earlier work.

ZERO MOSTEL (1915-77)

American actor. At school Samuel Mostel was the class clown, his shaky academic record earning him the nickname "Zero". He later used his comic skills to support himself while studying art, and an appearance at a private party led to a successful Broadway debut in the 1942 revue *Keep 'Em Laughing*. Thereafter his mobile face and rotund though graceful body figured in a series of films and stage productions, including *Beggar's Holiday*, the Broadway adaptation of John GAY's *The Beggar's Opera*. Mostel achieved superstardom in the 1950s and 1960s in remarkably varied roles. He excelled in such dramatically demanding plays as Bertolt BRECHT's *The Good Woman of Setzuan* and *Ulysses in Nighttown* (after James Joyce), then upstaged his way triumphantly through two great musical comedy hits, *A Funny Thing Happened on the Way to the Forum* and *Fiddler on the Roof*.

ORSON WELLES (1915...)

American actor and director. By his mid-twenties, Welles had received every possible accolade as an actor, and in *Citizen Kane* had made one of the most influential films in the history of the cinema. Inevitably his later career has been an anti-climax.

The emergence of Welles's prodigious talent has become the subject of legend in his own lifetime, especially his brazen presentation of himself in *Jew Süss* at the Gate Theatre, Dublin, as a lad of sixteen on holiday in Ireland.

Back in the United States, after touring with Katharine CORNELL, he organized a festival at Woodstock, Illinois, and was hailed as a director of genius.

Welles proceeded to take outrageous liberties with SHAKESPEARE and other classics, the most extreme examples being his West Indian version of *Macbeth* with an all-black cast, and his *Julius Caesar* at the Mercury Theatre in 1937. This was staged as the assassination of a modern-day fascist dictator at a Nuremberg-style rally.

Welles also produced and appeared in a number of distinguished radio productions, notably *The War of the Worlds* (1938). Since the war, however, his work has never had the same impact. The avant-garde overtook him, and although he has continued to experiment on stage and screen and has given some great performances (his 1951 Othello stands out in particular), his vast frame, unmistakable growl and meteoric history have made it difficult for him to be anything other than Orson Welles.

WOLFGANG HILDESHEIMER (1916...)

German playwright, novelist and short story writer. Contributions by Germans to the Theatre of the Absurd in the fifties were as rare as their contributions to the British war effort in 1939–45; the unconventional Hildesheimer contributed handsomely to both causes. After serving as a British Information Officer in Palestine, then as a simultaneous translator at the Nuremberg war-trials, he resettled in Germany. Forsaking painting and design for writing, he had his first play *Der Drachenthron* put on by Gustaf GRÜNDGENS in 1955. A satirical version of the Turandot story, it was more readily appreciable than his later weird pieces in the manner of IONESCO. *Die Uhren* (1959) ends with a couple living in a darkened room full of clocks. They each get inside a clock and go tick-tock themselves.

PETER WEISS (1916...)

German playwright, novelist, painter and journalist. When rioting lunatics simulated copulation in the bath-

The Swedish director **Ingmar Bergman** (*above*) brings the same intensity to his stage productions as to his celebrated films

The powerful **Irene Worth** is the actress behind the make-up in the title role of Edward Albee's unnerving play, *Tiny Alice* (*below*)

room of their asylum in Weiss's *The Persecution and Assassination of Jean-Paul Marat, as performed by the Inmates of the Asylum at Charenton, under the Direction of the Marquis de Sade* (1964, a literal translation of the German title) even the most sophisticated theatregoers were shocked. A complex investigation of revolution and revolutionary theatre, *Marat/Sade* was acclaimed as the most exciting (or at least violent) new play of the 1960s. In Britain Peter BROOK's production had enormous influence on the development of avant-garde theatre.

Before this success, Weiss had only dabbled in the theatre; his reputation was based chiefly on novels written in Swedish (his family had settled in Sweden when they fled from Nazi Germany). Overnight he became the leading modern German playwright. He was unofficially appointed investigator of Germany's post-war conscience, attending the Frankfurt trials of Auschwitz war criminals in order to write a documentary play based on the hearings. When *Die Ermittlung* (*The Investigation*) appeared in 1965, it was put on simultaneously at seventeen theatres in West and East Germany.

Since then Weiss's importance has declined. *Gesang vom Lusitanischen Popanz* (1967) and the *Viet Nam Diskurs* (1968), condemnations of Portuguese colonialism in Angola and American involvement in Vietnam, were remarkable for their form, but anti-imperialism was no longer a theatrical novelty. In *Trotzki im Exil* (1970), Weiss returned to conventional plot and dialogue, but without the excitement of his earlier calls to arms.

IRENE WORTH (1916...)

American-born actress. "I really must stop seeing Miss Worth. She leads to disappointment with practically everyone else," complained the *New York Times* critic in 1967. But he was lucky to have seen her at all; a quarter-century earlier, despairing of finding a serious outlet for her talents in America, Worth had left for England, where she was ultimately recognized as a distinguished tragedienne. Besides playing Desdemona, Portia and Goneril with refinement and majesty, Worth has brought her intelligence and passionate commitment to the service of such demanding modern writers as T. S. ELIOT, Lillian HELLMAN and TENNESSEE WILLIAMS.

ROBERT ANDERSON (1917...)

American playwright. Though acclaimed as a "brilliant new dramatist" for his 1953 hit *Tea and Sympathy*, Robert Anderson was already a practised professional. He had written and directed plays at Harvard, won a wartime drama contest and adapted dozens of productions for radio and television. *Tea and Sympathy* was a polished piece of theatre, depicting a sensitive prep-school boy tormented by his classmates but ultimately consoled by the wife of his headmaster. Anderson's later successes included *You Know I Can't Hear You When the Water's Running* (1967), a group of one-act comedies, and *I Never Sang for My Father* (1968), a study of family conflicts.

OSSIE DAVIS (1917...)

American actor and playwright. An advocate of both racial pride and inter-racial laughter, Ossie Davis has appeared in such disparate black productions as Marc CONNELLY's *The Green Pastures* and Lorraine HANSBERRY's *A Raisin in the Sun*. His own comedy success *Purlie Victorious* (1961) shaped memories of his Southern boyhood with modern dramatic technique into a blend of folk humour, satire, realism and fantasy. He starred in the play with his wife Ruby Dee, and in 1964 they toured with a programme of readings from Negro literature. Davis's efforts to entertain and communicate took yet another form when he turned his hit play into *Purlie*, a hit musical.

LENA HORNE (1917...)

American singer. Lena Horne made her debut in an all-black revue at Harlem's Cotton Club, where bouncers at the door ensured that the clientele remained all-white. Her triumph here led to a succession of films in which she wrapped her inimitably sexy voice provocatively round such numbers as "Just One of Those Things", and draped her voluptuous frame against pillars and palm trees. MGM insisted she wear thick chocolate make-up to render her more convincingly negroid, one of several indignities which made her increasingly outspoken about racist attitudes in Hollywood. Her opposition to the cattle-market approach of casting-directors encountered inevitable hostility among black bit-part actors, who were happy to endure it so long as it brought in work.

Horne has appeared with Basie and Ellington and in a host of night clubs. Her greatest Broadway triumph was *Jamaica* (1957), of which *Life* magazine wrote: "She shines like a tigress in the night, purring and preening and pouncing into the spotlight."

JOHN WHITING (1917-63)

English playwright. Though now overshadowed by Ken Russell's clamorous film, Whiting's *The Devils* (after Aldous Huxley's novel) was hailed as breaking new ground for the British theatre in 1961. The story of a priest who seeks salvation in seduction and sedition and induces mass hysteria in a community of nuns, the play combined poetic power with an almost chaotic dramatic boldness. It was the result of an open-ended commission by director PETER HALL, whose courage must be judged in the light of the fact that Whiting had by that time almost given up writing for the stage, as most of his early work had been critically derided. *The Times* had pilloried his *Saints Day* (1951) as having "a badness that must be thought indescribable"; but *The Devils*, together with *Penny for a Song* (1951) and *Marching Song* (1954), represent a substantial and enduring contribution to the English stage.

PEARL BAILEY (1918...)

American singer and actress. Dead-pan, sceptical, worldly-wise, "Pearlie Mae" first delighted Broadway in *St Louis Woman* (1946), holding off an ardent suitor to the song "Legalize My Name". Primarily a night-club performer, she is beloved for her lazy, insinuating vocal style and droll asides. Pearl Bailey starred in the 1954 musical *House of Flowers*, but her greatest stage triumph came in 1967, heading the cast of the all-black *Hello, Dolly!*

INGMAR BERGMAN (1918...)

Swedish film-maker and stage director. Long before his stark cinematic studies of the human condition made him world famous, Bergman was one of Sweden's most controversial stage directors. At university, one of his contemporaries recalled: "He was considered to be very gifted but utterly crazy," referring perhaps to a production of STRINDBERG's *The Pelican*, which he rehearsed with a hammer in his hand, occasionally throwing it at the actors. Intense and scornfully Bohemian, Bergman also possessed, as a lady friend said, "an unconcerned charm which was so forceful that after a few hours' conversation I had to drink three cups of coffee ... to get back to normal."

By 1944 he had won his first full-time directing post.

Bergman's fascination with drama began as a child, with the gift of a puppet theatre and magic lantern. In 1935 a production of Strindberg's *A Dream Play* overwhelmed him and confirmed his vocation. Since then, he has shown his special affinity for Strindberg's tense and tormented world in his remarkable staging of such plays as *The Ghost Sonata*. But his theatrical work has also been notable for its variety, embracing not just CHEKHOV and IBSEN, but MOLIÈRE and even Mozart's *The Magic Flute*. Formerly principal director of the municipal companies at Göteborg and Malmö and, with particular distinction, of the Royal Dramatic Theatre in Stockholm, since 1966 Bergman has concentrated on cinema. But he is still active in the theatre, describing it as "a faithful wife" while film remains "the costly, exacting mistress".

ARTHUR LAURENTS (1918...)

American playwright. In *West Side Story* (1957) Laurents had the advantage of lyrics by Stephen SONDHEIM, music by Leonard Bernstein, choreography by Jerome ROBBINS and a plot by William SHAKESPEARE.

He deported Romeo and Juliet from Renaissance Italy to the twentieth-century New York slums. The warring Capulets and Montagues became the feuding Sharks and Jets; the airy balcony became a humble fire-escape; and Shakespeare's stylish and exciting psychological romance became a stylish and exciting sociological cartoon. Laurent's next hit-musical, *Gypsy* (1959), revealed similar invention, though one eminent reviewer complained that the evening tapered off "from perfection to mere brilliance".

ALAN JAY LERNER (1918...)

American librettist. Written in collaboration with the composer Frederick Loewe, *My Fair Lady* (1956) alone places Lerner in the front rank of Broadway librettists. Son of a wealthy clothing manufacturer, he decided early on a song-writing career and produced his first shows while a student at Harvard.

His partnership with Loewe began in 1942; in addition to *My Fair Lady*, they achieved respectable hits with *Brigadoon* (1947), *Paint Your Wagon* (1951) and *Camelot* (1960). Lerner's later work with other composers has been less successful, though he won a Tony Award for his–and Loewe's–*Gigi* in 1973.

RENÉ DE OBALDIA (1918...)

French playwright and novelist. Obaldia's mother was French, his father a Panamanian diplomat; he himself was raised in Hong Kong by a Chinese nurse. His first dramatic works were sketches for private performance, and his plays still resemble zany, if sometimes scandalous, improvisations. *Génousie* (1960) lightheartedly evokes a mythical country, passionate love and murder; *Le Satyre de la Villette* (1963) spares a kind word for middle-aged men hungering after little girls, and *Du Vent dans les branches de sassafras* (1965) parodies American westerns in ribald Gallic style.

JEROME ROBBINS (1918...)

American choreographer, director and dancer. Among a dozen other Broadway triumphs, the phenomenal *West Side Story* (1957) best epitomizes Robbins's gifts. He conceived the idea, created the galvanic dances and, as director, filled the whole production with violent and sensual action. Energy and ingenuity have been the hallmarks of his work since he choreographed his first ballet, *Fancy Free*, in 1943, later turning it into a hit Broadway musical, *On the Town*. Ever since, Robbins has alternated between the two mediums, creating distinctive modern dance pieces while directing and choreographing Broadway shows. Musicals that have benefited from his ability to impart motion and excitement include *The King and I*, *The Pajama Game*, *Gypsy* and *Fiddler on the Roof*.

OLIVER SMITH (1918...)

American stage designer and producer. Whether representing an enchanted forest or a Manhattan tenement, Oliver Smith's designs combine abstract beauty with a strong sense of place. He joined the Ballets Russes in 1941, but three years later Jerome ROBBINS and Leonard Bernstein's *On The Town* (which he also co-produced) began his long Broadway career. Since then he has devised sets for the most spectacular hits, including *My Fair Lady*, *West Side Story*, *The Sound of Music* and *Hello, Dolly!*, as well as contributing designs for numerous ballets and plays. Despite his commercial success, as co-producer Smith has often presented such cerebral classics as Jean-Paul SARTRE's *Huis Clos* (*No Exit*) and Samuel BECKETT's *Endgame*, simply out of a "love for ideas".

UTA HAGEN (1919...)

American actress. The daughter of a German art lecturer and musicologist, Hagen arrived in America at the age of five. On her debut in 1937 she played Ophelia, towering over a Hamlet incongruously portrayed by the actress Eva LE GALLIENNE. While still a teenager she played Nina in a Broadway production of CHEKHOV's *The Seagull*, managing, it was said, to upstage the famous LUNTS. About this time she met her first husband, José Ferrer, whom she got to know more informally after accidentally knocking him out on stage.

In the mid-1940s Hagen toured as Desdemona to Paul ROBESON's Othello, giving a "glorious and heart-gripping performance". Her friendship with this black socialist actor displeased Washington, and Hagen appeared on Hollywood and television blacklists, though she was never indicted nor even questioned. Her success on stage was unimpaired, however, and she has since played an astonishing variety of roles in works by GOETHE, SHAW, IBSEN, CHEKHOV, BRECHT and TENNESSEE WILLIAMS. Audiences on both sides of the Atlantic will probably best remember Hagen's definitive performance as Martha in Edward ALBEE's *Who's Afraid of Virginia Woolf?* as the high spot of her great career.

DONALD PLEASENCE (1919...)

English actor. Unable to pay his tuition to drama school, Pleasence worked for the railways and rose to become a station-master. In the RAF during the Second World War, he was shot down and spent two years in a POW camp run by a "psychotic German killer". This experience may have provided him with the authority to become a chilling Arthur Goldman (a role inspired by Adolf Eichmann) in Robert Shaw's *The Man in the Glass Booth* (1967).

Pleasence has had a versatile stage and film career, but his most memorable roles are those which quiver with suppressed violence (the pitiful and frustrated Dr Crippen being a classic example). He was outstanding as the tormented Bitos in ANOUILH's *Poor Bitos*, and has struck just the right tone of veiled menace in three plays by Harold PINTER: *The Caretaker* and *Tea Party*. His technique is a curious variant of the Method; he prefers to identify with animals rather than people, choosing for instance an alley-cat to characterize Davies, the tramp in *The Caretaker*.

MARIA BECKER (1920...)

German actress. Becker's precocious but restless youth took her to playhouses in Switzerland, Austria and Germany. In 1960 she made a virtue of her wanderlust and helped to found the adventurous and distinguished Schauspieltruppe, a touring company which she has since managed. A dignified, graceful and thoughtful actress, Becker has given moving interpretations of SHAKESPEARE, SOPHOCLES and SCHILLER, besides bringing her considerable authority to bear on Jean GENET's *Le Balcon* and Edward ALBEE's *Who's Afraid of Virginia Woolf?*

JACQUES CHARON (1920-75)

French actor and director. Defeated by the vagaries of the language, Charon gave up the attempt to sell French haberdashery to the English and, after serving in the French army, joined the Comédie-Française. The Germans occupying Paris were generous and strangely liberal patrons of the theatre, which they hoped would divert the populace from political activity; hence they succeeded in enticing all but a handful to continue working under the Nazi régime.

It was during this artificial Golden Age that Charon first established himself as a "wonderfully effusive" comic actor. He later expressed frank nostalgia for those days, being dismayed by the austerity he encountered on a tour of post-war England.

The powerful cabal which Charon eventually ruled at the Comédie did much, according to their detractors, to distort the original aims of the company. In one six-month period they gave 113 performances of farces by LABICHE, but could manage only a paltry six tragedies by RACINE. The alarmed intervention of the Minister for Culture, André Malraux, did much to redress the balance, but the irrepressible Charon continued to delight audiences with MOLIÈRE and FEYDEAU.

EILEEN HERLIE (1920...)

British actress. Eileen Herlie's queenly bearing has suited her to such regal roles as Hamlet's mother, O'NEILL's Anna Christie and EURIPIDES' Medea. An established star in England, she went to the United States in 1955 with Thornton WILDER's comedy *The Matchmaker* and has remained ever since. According to Walter Kerr, her performance in Karel ČAPEK's *The Makropulos Secret* "seemed to have been spirited right out of the heart of the warm-blooded nineteenth century". But she is just as capable of dominating a musical like *Take Me Along* with twentieth-century energy.

JOSEF SVOBODA (1920...)

Czech designer. Svoboda's ingenious and prolific use of every kind of mechanical, electrical and optical device resembles the technique of cinema – except that he manages, by using all three dimensions, to transcend the spatial limitations of film. When a device is not available, he invents it, such as his Polyecran system of simultaneous projection.

Svoboda's genius for "heightened realism" is classically illustrated in his design for a Salzburg production of *En attendant Godot*: he extended the auditorium walls, with their ornate boxes, on to the stage; he further enhanced the illusion by placing, at the back of the set, a huge mirror in which actors and audience were reflected.

The Czech designer, **Josef Svoboda,** is the creator of brilliant effects of illusion. This set for Chekhov's *Three Sisters* (*left*) is made of string

The American **Oliver Smith** brings a fine eye for detail to the spectacular designs he has made for a long succession of musicals on Broadway. In the opening scene of *My Fair Lady*, the poor flower girl, Eliza Doolittle, stands outside the imposing Covent Garden Opera House (*below*)

Possibly the most useful item in stage design is the old-fashioned painted canvas–the "flat" (*above*). A deft artist can use its surface to suggest anything from Miss Havisham's cluttered sitting-room to a sunlit coast of Bohemia. Until about a century ago it was customary to act some scenes in front of flats which could slide open to reveal a more elaborate set behind. This led to smoother transitions than the modern style, where whole scenes (including flats) are often changed at the drop of the curtain. Some modern sets, of course, discard realism: a generalized locality or mood can be created by fairly abstract settings, while instant transitions of scene are effected by lighting

Top right of the page: Brecht's play, *Galileo*, was the subject of one of **Giorgio Strehler**'s most inspired productions with the Piccolo Teatro di Milano.
Right: four faces of **Peter Ustinov**; or, alternatively, four disguises of the wicked Carabosse, who is out to bewilder the princess in Ustinov's own remarkable fantasy play, *The Love of Four Colonels*

BORIS VIAN (1920-59)

French poet, novelist, playwright, songwriter, singer, actor, translator, jazz-trumpeter and engineer. Vian inflicted upon himself a staggering profusion of activity, in defiance of the heart-complaint which he knew was killing him. Unpersuaded by engineering, he became a leading light both of the absurdist JARRY's Collège de Pataphysique, and of the "St Germain set", where he could exchange ideas with such influences as Édith Piaf and Jean COCTEAU. Some of his work was banned for immorality, but much survives, notably the moving novel *L'Écume des jours*. His most celebrated play is *Les Bâtisseurs d'empire*, performed after his death in 1959. This terrifying satire portrays a family who try to escape from an eerie noise probably emanating from a lumpish semi-animate object called a Schmürz, a creature whose exact symbolism died with its author.

GIORGIO DE LULLO (1921...)

Italian actor and director. Post-war Italian theatre was given a new lease of life by the Compagnia dei Giovani, a young and vigorous theatrical group established in 1954. Its founder and leading light was Giorgio de Lullo, who played the lead in their first production: Alfred de MUSSET's *Lorenzaccio*. It was an outstanding success, as was his debut as director, with *Gigi*, later that year. Subsequent productions included *The Diary of Anne Frank* and William INGE's guilt-ridden *The Dark at the Top of the Stairs*. In 1965 de Lullo brought the troupe to London for the World Theatre Season, and scored a hit with Diego FABBRI's *La Bugiarda* (also starring Rossella FALK). He has also directed opera at La Scala in Milan.

FRIEDRICH DÜRRENMATT (1921...)

Swiss playwright. *Der Besuch der alten Dame* (1956), Dürrenmatt's best known play, has been called a tragifarce, a satiric parable, a black morality and a grisly fable. It tells of a grim widow who uses the corrupting power of her wealth to incite a village to murder. Dürrenmatt's boldness, ambiguity and brutal irony resembles that of Bertolt BRECHT, but he sternly dismisses attempts to find a usefully Brechtian message in his work. The world for him is an "enigma of calamity that has to be accepted". This pessimistic stoicism also colours *Die Physiker* (1962), a macabre farce about nuclear scientists feigning insanity, one of whom is trying to prevent his deadly secret from destroying the world.

Dürrenmatt's early artistic training may explain his strong visual imagination; his plays are extremely effective on stage and have attracted a surprisingly wide audience. *Der Besuch* (as *The Visit*) was chosen by Alfred LUNT and Lynn FONTANNE for the first production at the Lunt-Fontanne Theatre in 1958.

RAY LAWLER (1921...)

Australian playwright. Lawler's father, a labouring man, considered the theatre an unsuitable career for any of his eight offspring. Young Ray left school at thirteen. Only after ten years spent in factories did he finally – first as an actor – reach the stage.

His tragic masterpiece, *Summer of the Seventeenth Doll* (1955), is a milestone in the history of Australian drama, which had until then resorted to embarrassed mockery of Australian "types". Lawler paints the common man as he is, without caricaturing, politicizing or romanticizing him; an achievement which has invited favourable comparison with ARTHUR MILLER and

TENNESSEE WILLIAMS. Later plays, including *Piccadilly Bushman*, have been less successful abroad.

JOSEPH PAPP (1921...)

American producer and director. Papp believes that "theatre is important to people's lives" and should therefore be available free. In 1954 his New York Shakespeare Festival began presenting Elizabethan plays without charge, first in a church basement, later outdoors in Central Park. Critics hailed the production as "unadulterated SHAKESPEARE", and Papp's persistent appeals for funds finally secured the Festival a permanent home. In 1967 he obtained municipal support for The Public Theatre, a drama complex dedicated mainly to the presentation of new American plays. Papp's two landmark productions have both, however, been musicals: *Hair* and, more recently, *A Chorus Line*. Fund-raising for his ventures has superseded Papp's own directing activities. Nowadays, he says only half-humourously, "I spend money, that's what I do. I spend a fortune."

KIM STANLEY (1921...)

American actress. After hearing Miss Stanley's attempts at SHAKESPEARE, the producer at her first New York audition advised her to go back to Texas. But the Actors' Studio was more encouraging, and she made her debut in W. H. AUDEN's *The Dog Beneath the Skin*. Two award-winning performances in plays by William INGE, *Picnic* (1953) and *Bus Stop* (1955), gave her a Broadway reputation for freshness and vitality. Much of Miss Stanley's later work has been in television, which she is quoted as preferring, because "I never think anybody's watching." But her intense performance in CHEKHOV's *Three Sisters* (1964–5) attracted admiring attention in both London and New York, and affirmed her position as arguably the most accomplished American actress of her generation.

GIORGIO STREHLER (1921...)

Italian director and manager. Strehler's work has helped change the face of Italian theatre. After the Second World War he became involved with a movement intent upon reviving the theatre as a means of combating fascism; since then socialism has remained a strong inspiration. In 1947, with Paolo Grassi, he formed the Piccolo Teatro di Milano. This was the first and most important of many permanent theatre troupes, a new departure in a country where companies were traditionally itinerant.

At the Piccolo Teatro Strehler directed plays by SHAKESPEARE, CHEKHOV and PIRANDELLO; GOLDONI's *Arlecchino servitore di due padroni*, with the acrobatic stunts of Marcello Moretti, became a world-famous production. In 1956 BRECHT, one of the playwrights who most interests Strehler, visited the Teatro and was impressed by their imaginative work with his *Die Dreigroschenoper*. In 1963 Strehler also directed a magnificent production of Brecht's *Galileo*.

Frustrated with the Milanese bureaucracy, and unable to get a larger theatre, Strehler left the Piccolo Teatro in 1968. He continued to direct opera, for which he is well known, and theatre, but returned to Milan in 1972. With Strehler once more at the helm, the Piccolo Teatro celebrated its thirtieth anniversary in 1977.

PETER USTINOV (1921...)

English actor and playwright. Ustinov's early impersonation of Madame Liselotte Beethoven-Finck (his own creation) began a lifetime of mimicry. He has brought this

The intensity of post-war drama found its expression through a new generation of passionate actors. **Maria Casarès** (*right*) starred in plays by Sartre and Camus. **Maureen Stapleton, Irene Worth** and **Jason Robards** (acting together, *far right*) found their métier in the work of such playwrights as Eugene O'Neill and Tennessee Williams

talent to many of his own satirical comedies, including *The Love of Four Colonels* (1951) and *Romanoff and Juliet* (1956). Among his successful later plays are *Photo Finish* (1962) and *The Unknown Soldier and his Wife* (1968). Whimsical and humane, they still reveal a promising rather than a mature author. Even his friend Robert MORLEY has remarked of Ustinov, "He's never done as much as he should."

Today Ustinov is best known to television chat-show audiences as a rotund, erudite and consistently entertaining "personality". This is a role he loathes. Partly to dispel the taint of buffoonery, he played Lear at the 1979 Stratford festival in Canada, though before the production his attitude was characteristically flippant: "I've got three daughters, which is a more thorough rehearsal for the part than anything STANISLAVSKY ever suggested."

GEORGES WILSON (1921…)

French actor and director. Wilson seemed destined for provincial obscurity until, at the age of thirty, he came under the wing of Jean VILAR at the Théâtre National Populaire in Paris. There he rapidly prospered, specializing in such prodigious roles as Georg BÜCHNER's Danton, Alfred JARRY's Ubu and Bertolt BRECHT's Galileo. Since succeeding Vilar as director in 1963, Wilson has provoked both adulation and fury in his staging of such modern foreign dramatists as OSBORNE, DÜRRENMATT and Brecht.

BENNO BESSON (1922…)

Swiss director. The leading figure in the presentation of BRECHT's work at the Berliner Ensemble, after the author's death, Besson was responsible for reverently detailed productions of such plays as *Mann ist Mann* and *Die heilige Johanna der Schlachthöfe*. An excellent linguist, he has also translated many of Brecht's works into French and adapted French classics. It was with his version of MOLIÈRE's *Dom Juan* that he made his debut as a director in Rostock in 1952.

In the sixties, as director of the Deutsches Theater, Besson became associated with the work of Peter HACKS, the foremost of East Germany's young generation of playwrights. When East-West relations began to thaw, his company toured East Germany with Hacks's adaptation

of ARISTOPHANES' *Peace*. They received standing ovations, lasting as long as three-quarters of an hour. In 1969 Besson became director of the Berliner Volksbühne.

TINO BUAZZELLI (1922…)

Italian actor. "An actor born to play Falstaff," said *The Times* of Buazzelli's performance in *Henry IV, Part 1*, an assessment prompted by his power and spontaneity (and, no doubt, by his Falstaffian dimensions). Buazzelli, one of Italy's most interesting post-war actors, made his debut in 1947 as the Father in ARTHUR MILLER's *All My Sons*. Since 1952 he has worked extensively with the Piccolo Teatro di Milano. In the early sixties, under its director Giorgio STREHLER, he gave superb performances as Schweik in *Schweyk im zweiten Weltkrieg* and as another of BRECHT's protagonists, Galileo. Buazzelli has since formed his own Compagnia di Prosa, which he took to London in 1975, playing Dr Stockmann in IBSEN's *An Enemy of the People*.

MARIA CASARÈS (1922…)

Spanish-born French actress. After a testing and intense apprenticeship in the existential dramas of Albert CAMUS and Jean-Paul SARTRE, Casarès built a formidable reputation for herself at the Comédie-Française and the Théâtre National Populaire, and with Jean-Louis BARRAULT's Théâtre de France. The warmth of her speaking-voice and the power of her "force nerveuse" have made her an electrifying Lady Macbeth and an awe-inspiring Phèdre. In less highly charged roles, however, her emotional palpitations – unkindly described as a "taste for paroxysms" – have occasionally seemed inappropriate.

SID CAESAR (1922…)

American comedian. It was in his father's New York restaurant, filled with the chatter of immigrant workers, that Caesar's talents for comic impersonation and the imitation of dialects no doubt developed. After appearing in the US Coast Guard's musical *Tars and Spars* (1945), he spent a couple of years as a nightclub entertainer, before being offered a part in *Make Mine Manhattan* (1948). An instant success, the revue moved to Broadway and Caesar stole

Vittorio Gassman (playing Hamlet, *far left*) and Tino Buazzelli (*left*) are two of Italy's most versatile actors. Buazzelli plays serious and comic character roles with equal flair. The fluent, athletic Gassman can compass practically anything, but he has dominated post-war Italian theatre especially in his dazzling repertoire in tragedy

the show. Since 1949 he has been an outstandingly successful television comedian, but he returned to Broadway in *Little Me* (1962) by Neil SIMON in which he played the men in the life of film star "Belle Poitrine".

VITTORIO GASSMAN (1922...)

Italian actor and director. Gassman has achieved a reputation unique among modern Italian actors, comparable to TALMA or KEAN. His 1943 debut revealed talents extraordinarily mature and his fame was quick to spread. Remarkably, he not only excelled in realistic modern drama such as ARTHUR MILLER's *All My Sons*, but inherited the grand Romantic style of the previous century; he was outstanding in Vittorio ALFIERI's *Oreste*, and *Antony* by ALEXANDRE DUMAS *père*.

Gassman was to become equally well known as a director. At the Teatro d'Arte Italiano, which he joined in 1952, SENECA's tragedy *Thyestes* was among his outstanding productions. With his own company, in 1956–57, he alternated the parts of Othello and Iago with Salvo RANDONE, while Federico Zardi's play *I Tromboni* provided twenty characters for his virtuoso talents. Keen to popularize the theatre, in 1960 Gassman formed the Teatro Popolare Italiano, touring the provinces with lavish productions of the *Oresteia* by AESCHYLUS and Alessandro Manzoni's *Adelchi*. In 1977 a lengthy one-man "happening" reached its climax in a week-long auction at which Gassman tried (unsuccessfully) to sell himself. He has also worked extensively for television and for the cinema.

JUDY HOLLIDAY (1922-65)

American musical star. Changing her name from Tuvim to its (misspelt) gentile equivalent, Holliday found overnight fame by the classic route when asked to stand in for an established actress in the Broadway comedy *Born Yesterday* (1946). This proved a perfect vehicle for her comic talents and initiated a successful film career. Surviving official accusations of Communist leanings, she went on to one further stage triumph, *Bells are Ringing* (1956), written for her by Betty Comden and Adolph Green, who had been her friends and colleagues eighteen years earlier in a struggling night-club act.

MARGARET LEIGHTON (1922-76)

English actress. Leighton's private life was almost as varied as her stage *personae*. The wife (in turn) of Max REINHARDT, Laurence Harvey and Michael Wilding started out in provincial repertory theatre when she was only sixteen. By 1944 she had reached the Old Vic company and, though initially her parts were small, in 1950 she played a definitive Celia (at the New Theatre) in the London première of T. S. ELIOT's *The Cocktail Party*.

Her acting revealed the strength and directness of the person beneath. She excelled in the demanding role of playing two complex and different women in RATTIGAN's double bill *Separate Tables* (1954), and in 1961 her portrayal of the virgin Hannah in TENNESSEE WILLIAMS's *The Night of the Iguana* won her New York's coveted Tony Award. She also appeared in many films, though the theatre remained uppermost in her affections. Her untimely death (from cancer) robbed audiences of one of the stage's great stars.

GÉRARD PHILIPE (1922-59)

French actor. At the Avignon Festival in 1951, Philipe swept away centuries of cobwebs from CORNEILLE's *Le Cid*, in which, as the great Spanish hero, he seemed the very incarnation of heroic idealism. Yet at the height of his fame he declined lucrative offers of starring roles in order to stage at his own expense a play by an unsuccessful writer whom he admired. This selfless dedication to his art also enabled him to assume roles far removed from his own socialist ideals. Heinrich von KLEIST's aristocratic Prince of Homburg, for instance, was one of his greatest triumphs. Philipe died in his prime while preparing an eagerly anticipated *Hamlet*. He was buried in the costume of Le Cid.

JASON ROBARDS JR (1922...)

American actor. After a 1947 New York debut as the back half of a cow in *Jack and the Beanstalk*, Robards joined José QUINTERO's Circle in the Square company. In 1956 he played the lead in Eugene O'NEILL's *The Iceman Cometh* with "chilling authority", then won a critics' award for his turbulent performance as the alco-

CONTINUED ON PAGE 258

The puppet show

Puppets are one of the most ancient and widespread forms of theatre. Their mysterious or comic effects have been employed in every kind of show from rituals to fun-fairs. Hand puppets like Punch and Judy represent the art at its most basic, and their rough-and-tumble antics have delighted audiences for three hundred years. But puppetry is also capable of great sophistication, from the charming intricacies of marionettes to the compelling stylization of Indian and Javanese stick figures. Modern puppet theatres exploit all of the medium's possibilities. Made from a variety of materials, their inanimate actors can be funny, bizarre or touching: a source of delight to young and old alike.

At its most basic, puppetry is a parlour game. In the middle ages (*above*) two simple figures and some string created a battlefield

Besides acting out traditional stories, the puppets of India are expressive objects in themselves. Carving and decorating them is a special craft in every part of the sub-continent, and the products of each area are unique. None are more colourful and evocative than the rod-and-string puppets of Rajasthan (*left*), resplendent in their full-length gowns

The puppet-maker's workshop (*right*) is a gallery of odd characters – likeable, laughable or sinister. If the leading actor in a show cracks open his skull, the producer always has a perfect understudy to hand

The versatility of puppets is limitless. How better could the ritual nature of Greek tragedy be evoked than by the gaunt, masked figures (*below*)? They were designed for a performance of *Oedipus Rex*, the stark opera-oratorio by Stravinsky, with a libretto by Jean Cocteau after the tragedy of Sophocles.

As every child knows, striking puppets can be created without painstaking and messy work with glue and papier mâché. Here (*below right*) a few household objects – including a mop and a watering can – are transformed into a Hollywood harridan of unparalleled horror

No more dramatic display of puppet magic exists than the shadow plays of Indonesia (*left*). The action takes place in silhouette behind a screen and represents the heroic deeds of mythic figures. The puppets are connected to rods, and the puppet master can move their limbs with a flick of his finger. Performances can last throughout the night, accompanied by the hypnotic tintinnabulations of a gamelan gong-orchestra

Puppet theatres have long been popular in Central and Eastern Europe. In Czechoslovakia, itinerant puppeteers helped to keep national culture alive while the country was under Austrian rule, with performances of native legends and folk tales. Puppetry still flourishes everywhere in the region. Bulgaria maintains eight permanent puppet theatres and its Institute of Theatre Art (*above*) includes a full-fledged Puppet Faculty

The world-famous Salzburg Marionettes (*below*) set puppetry to music with small-scale performances of grand opera. Their lyrical gaiety makes them ideal interpreters of Mozart

holic Jamie in O'Neill's *Long Day's Journey into Night*. His rugged integrity and world-weary countenance have since made him a popular Broadway star, though his loud and casual way with blank verse has hampered his few attempts at SHAKESPEARE. Robards has received two Oscars as a film actor, but dismisses his movie work, calling the stage "my anchor to reality".

FREDERICK SCHNECKENBURGER (1922-67)

Swiss puppeteer. Among his four-foot-high rod-puppets Schneckenburger frequently included the figure of Kaspar, the German equivalent of Mr Punch, but there was nothing traditional about his grotesque, surreal shows. His Kaspar was reduced to little more than a monstrous nose on a wire frame, while other figures were purely symbolic, the secret police being represented by a head full of eyes with sprouting guns for fingers. Schneckenburger's provocative scripts (some written in German, some in French) were considered sadistic and shocking by many adults, yet he used the same frightening puppets (including a soldier with half his face shot away) in his shows for children.

PAUL SCOFIELD (1922...)

English actor. Few actors are so well loved and widely admired, or so deeply committed to their art as Paul Scofield. He was discovered in the 1940s at the Birmingham Repertory Theatre by director BARRY JACKSON, who brought him to Stratford. There, at the Shakespeare Memorial Theatre, he was enormously successful as Mercutio and Hamlet, while with such performances as the rebellious Pierre in Thomas OTWAY's *Venice Preserved* and twin brothers in ANOUILH's *Ring Round the Moon* he became an established London star. His often mannered acting style has been shown off to perfection in such mannered comedies as *The Way of the World*.

Scofield first played Sir Thomas More in Robert BOLT's *A Man For All Seasons* in 1960; later, his performance in the film brought him international fame, though it has branded him forever with a spiritual nobility that is at times inconvenient. Appearances abroad have included *Hamlet* (Moscow, 1955) and a world tour as King Lear in 1964, both directed by Peter BROOK. He is concerned too in bringing foreign drama to Britain, and has appeared in English versions of PIRANDELLO's *The Rules of the Game* and ZUCKMAYER's *The Captain of Kopenick*. In 1979-80 Scofield played the guilt-ridden Salieri in Peter SHAFFER's *Amadeus*.

GIORGIO ALBERTAZZI (1923...)

Italian actor and director. While still in his twenties Albertazzi co-founded Italy's leading theatrical group of the post-war period, from 1956 known as the Compagnia Proclemer-Albertazzi. For a decade it was unrivalled, largely due to the intelligence and virtuosity of Albertazzi himself. Classical and modern plays, comedies and tragedies, all were handled with an insight and imagination that were unmatched. His performance as Oswald in Henrik IBSEN's *Ghosts* was particularly outstanding, as was his debut as director (in 1959) with Jean-Paul SARTRE's tortured drama *Les Séquestrés d'Altona* – in which he also played the lead.

One other role which must be mentioned was his magnificent portrayal of Hamlet in ZEFFIRELLI's renowned 1963 production. He has also appeared in a number of films, and in 1959 adapted DOSTOYEVSKY's *The Idiot* for television, playing the part of Prince Myshkin.

LINDSAY ANDERSON (1923...)

English director. In the 1950s Anderson was in the forefront of "free cinema", the British documentary film movement, and with films such as *This Sporting Life* (1963), *If...* (1969) and *O Lucky Man!* (1973) he has won an international reputation. But his anger at the mercenary attitudes of the British film industry has prompted him to pursue a simultaneous career in the theatre. In 1959 he accepted an offer to direct WILLIS HALL's *The Long and the Short and the Tall* at the Royal Court Theatre in London. *Progress to the Park* by Alun OWEN and *Serjeant Musgrave's Dance* by John ARDEN followed the same year. While continuing to make films, he has since directed a number of plays, including David STOREY's *The Changing Room* (1971) and, in 1975, a sensitive and extremely funny production of Joe ORTON's *What the Butler Saw*.

BRENDAN BEHAN (1923-64)

Irish playwright. Behan was a legendary figure in Dublin, London and New York as much because of his capacity for good whiskey and uproarious conversation, as for his plays. As a boy he joined the Irish Republican Army, though he was never a particularly capable terrorist. He was arrested in Liverpool at the age of sixteen and sent to Borstal, which furnished the material for a prose work, *Borstal Boy*. Another jail term in Ireland in 1942 gave him the subject for his first play, *The Quare Fellow* (1956). On that second conviction he was sentenced to fourteen years. When he was released by a political amnesty in 1946, he took up the traditional occupation of IRA men of his generation: painting (houses, not pictures).

Behan did not begin to write until the mid-1950s and then his output was irregular, but he was fortunate to find a theatre, at Stratford in the East End of London, and a director, Joan LITTLEWOOD, who could draw a delightful combination of drama and fun out of the original script. *The Hostage* emerged from this collaboration in 1958, and it was produced regularly in Paris and New York after its London opening. Behan celebrated his success unwisely and too well, telling stories to his companions rather than writing them down, and much of his later work was dictated into a tape recorder. He was, perhaps, an ephemeral figure in the theatre, but anyone who heard him talk, or saw the talk translated on to the stage by Joan Littlewood, will never forget him.

ROLAND DUBILLARD (1923...)

French playwright, poet and actor. Dubillard's early experience in cabaret gives his acting an improvisatory air; it may also help to explain the near plotless absurdity of his plays. The hero of *Naives hirondelles* (1961) lives with a friend and an aunt. A girl arrives. One of the men probably leaves with her. The other possibly sleeps with the aunt. In *Le Jardin aux betteraves* (1969) four musicians, rehearsing for a concert, die in a violin-shaped *maison de culture* situated in a beetroot-field. But it must be added that the "absurdité tragique" of these uneventful works has impressed both Jean ANOUILH and Eugène IONESCO.

SIOBHAN McKENNA (1923...)

Irish actress. When she played SHAW's Saint Joan in a Galway accent in 1954 Siobhan (pronounced Shivawn) became England's favourite Irish actress. She justified this partiality by performing the finest Pegeen Mike (in SYNGE's *The Playboy of the Western World*) London had ever seen. She was born in Belfast but brought up in Galway, the dutiful daughter of a mathematics professor.

CONTINUED ON PAGE 262

Paul Scofield, (*above* as the alcoholic priest in *The Power and the Glory*), is a virtuoso performer with a strongly personal style. His superbly controlled voice can travel easily between the texture of gravel and a honeyed smoothness

Brendan Behan (*below*) in characteristic circumstances – and an uncharacteristic listening posture. The burly Irishman spent much of his life in drinking, quarrelling, and talk – his genius for words was directed too rarely into books and plays

The art of mime

Mime – the art of using the body to express feeling – has its most popular modern champion in Marcel MARCEAU. Without words, and on a bare stage, the extraordinary Marceau conjures a world of imaginary butterflies, lions, ladders and chairs. Because the objects are invisible he is compelled to refine his gestures so that each action may be totally understandable. The audience, forced to concentrate solely on movement, discovers in the human body a rich, inner world of feeling.

Mime as a Western solo form of entertainment has a distinguished pedigree, but its modern renaissance derives from Marceau's teacher, Étienne DECROUX, whose study and practice in the 1930s expanded the repertoire of the art enormously. Another great pupil of Decroux, Jean-Louis BARRAULT, has developed a form of "total theatre" where mime is incorporated with the text.

Mime has often emerged in the popular, non-literary theatre, which is generally prepared to use any kind of physical expression to hold an audience. In France the sad, silent Pierrot figure (ancestor to Marceau's Bip) reaches back more than a century to the immortal DEBURAU. Traditionally, Pierrot was part of a show which also includes acrobatics, dance and song. John Rich was playing a silent harlequin in similar circumstances in eighteenth-century England. (Deburau and Rich were forbidden to speak: their governments, afraid of the seditious power of words, allowed speech in only a few selected theatres.) As Pedrolino and Arlecchino, both these mute characters can be traced back to noisy origins in the professional street-theatre of Renaissance Italy, the Commedia dell' Arte, where the actors mimed and talked.

In fact "mime" was originally the name for the talkative, indecent market-place farces which began in ancient Greece and were for centuries the most popular form of theatre in the Roman empire. Speech and the body were equally eloquent in this very physical drama, and miming was an expedient aid to performance when the strolling players and their audience spoke different languages.

The body is such a vulnerable piece of physical apparatus that it is not surprising mime artists tend to have a fine sense of farce. Marceau was influenced by the vulnerable little tramp of Charles Chaplin (the silent cinema is of course a storehouse of mime). Some contemporary mime artists, including the American Bob Berky and Nola Rae, dress as clowns. Indeed POPOV and GROCK were excellent mimes.

Overleaf: The Russian mime, Boris Amarantov (*left*) flourishes umbrella and portmanteau. The French mime duo, "Théâtre du Mouvement" (*top left*) use dance, acrobatics, and exotic masks and costumes for a more impersonal effect. They comprise Yves Marc and Claire Heggen, who are former students of the austere Étienne Decroux. *Top centre,* a performance from the Decroux Workshop: from left, Éliane Guyon, Maximilien Decroux, and Étienne himself. Nola Rae (*top right*) takes on some seventy characters in her delicate and comic "Some Great Fools from History". *Bottom row, right:* **Marcel Marceau** as "Bip"

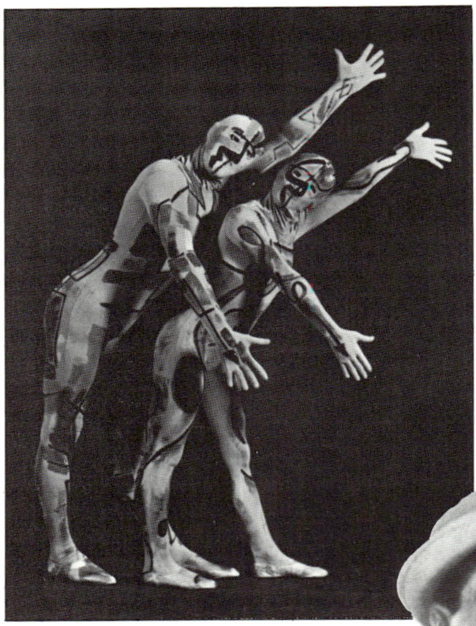

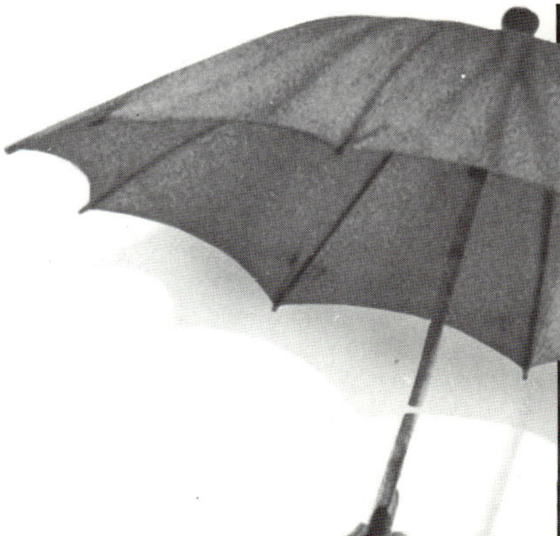

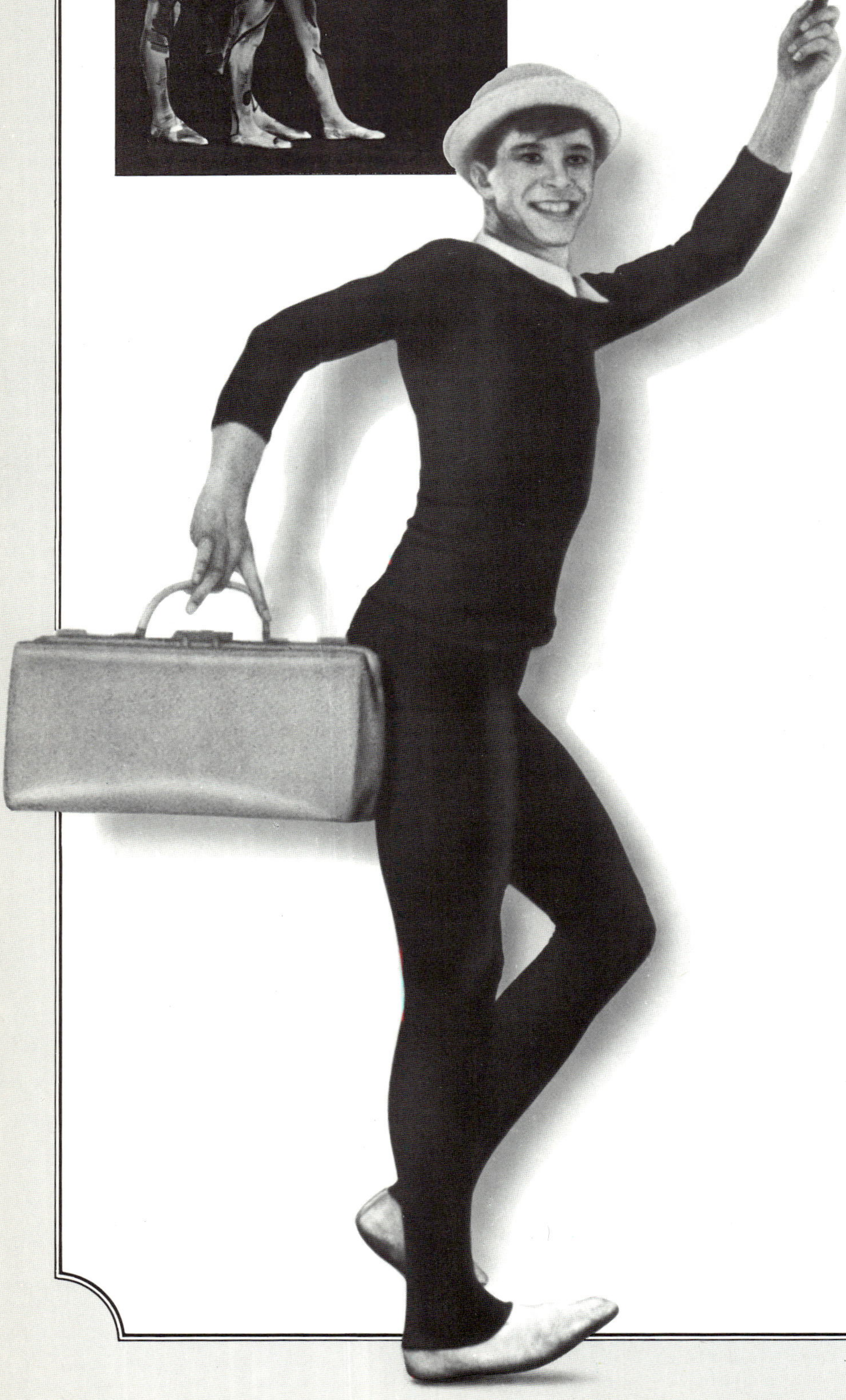

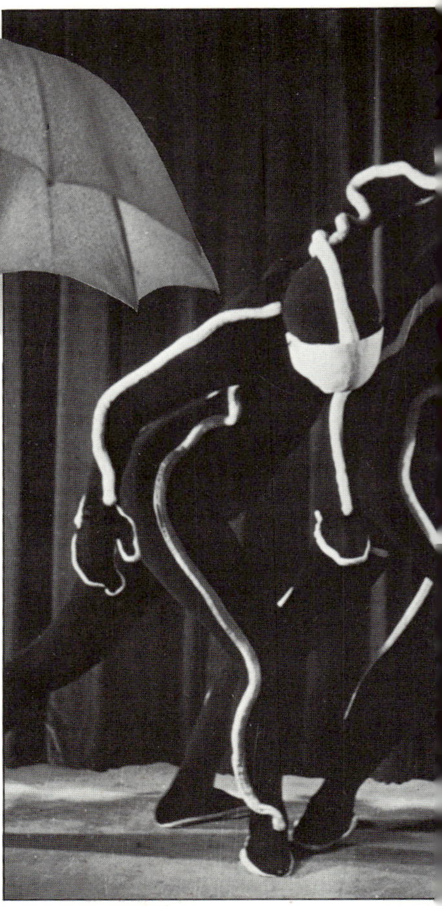

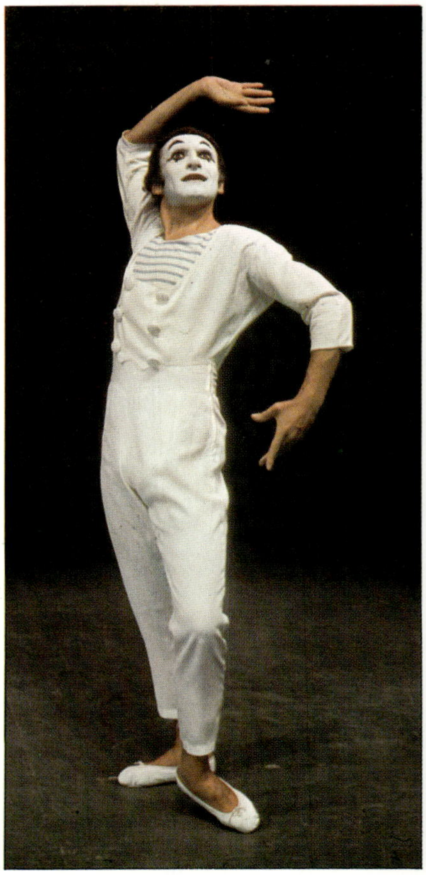

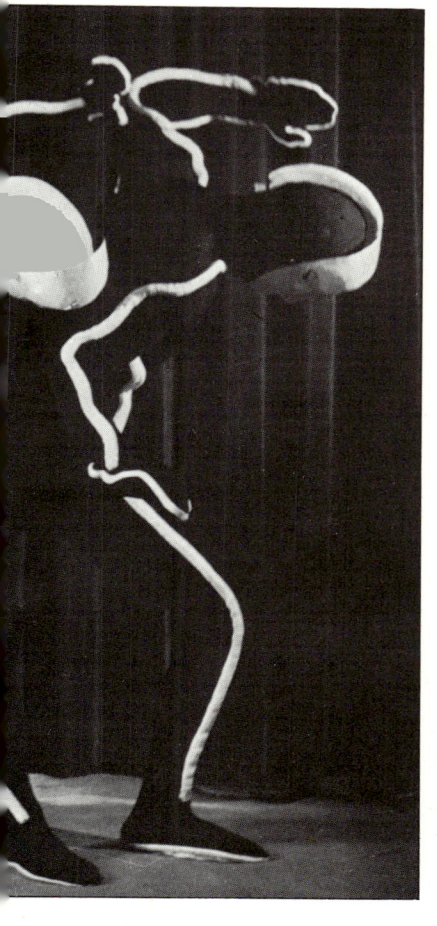

James Baldwin (*above*) was one of the first black American authors to gain a wide audience. His novels and plays have had a disturbing effect, not only by their angry dissection of racism, but also by their openly bisexual attitudes

Geraldine Page acted with the young Paul Newman in Tennessee Williams's play, *Sweet Bird of Youth*, in 1959 (*below*). Her performance as an ageing film star established her reputation and earned her an award as Best Actress of the Year

Aged eighteen she played Lady Macbeth – in Irish – and joined the Abbey Theatre company in the 1940s, when she was described as being "as quiet as a squirrel and as shy as a badger". Success revealed in her the more flamboyant Irish-actress qualities, but her reputation suffered little from her fashionably Republican outbursts in the late 1950s. On stage she was disciplined, refusing to play Sean O'CASEY's *Juno* until she was forty. In her fifties McKenna concentrated on one-woman shows, about Irish women and about Sarah BERNHARDT.

MARCEL MARCEAU (1923…)

French mime. Marceau was born in Strasbourg, the son of a Jewish butcher named Mangel (who was later killed by the Nazis). His skill at mimicry was apparent even at the age of five, when a Charlie Chaplin film inspired his first silent imitations. He studied with the great mimes DULLIN and Étienne DECROUX and in 1946 briefly worked with yet another master of the art, Jean-Louis BARRAULT. The following year he appeared for the first time as Bip, whose white Pierrot face, short jacket and trousers, striped jersey and crumpled top hat would become his world-famous trademarks.

Marceau's unprecedented popularity is due not just to technical mastery but to his naïve faith in humanity. For him mime is "the art of touching people . . . the drama of silence that speaks direct to mind and emotion", and the Bip sketches express the range of feelings aroused by even the simplest event. Bip's well-known encounter with a butterfly begins in eagerness and delight and ends in pathos. The joy in his broad clown's grin turns gradually to panic as he discovers that his face is stuck in that expression. Marceau's virtuosity is incomparable. In one sketch he plays ten different characters; in *David and Goliath*, using a screen, he seems to play two at once. But as he says, his skill is based above all on the "thought and observation" necessary to achieve a "human radiance". "Bip feels. . . . And everyone knows how he feels. This then is my art."

JOHN MORTIMER (1923…)

English playwright and novelist. Mortimer's comedies are affectionate attempts to portray "the lonely, the neglected, the unsuccessful", whose typical response to life is wishful self-delusion. However absurd his characters may seem, he invests them with a kind of redeeming gusto, like the lawyer in his first play, *The Dock Brief*, who secures an acquittal not by the fantastic defence he dreams of delivering, but because the court finally rules him incompetent (the author is himself a leading London barrister). Mortimer is at his best in such sympathetic and ingenious one-acters, a recent example of which has been the religious double-bill, *Heaven and Hell* (1976). He has also produced successful full-length works, including *Two Stars for Comfort* (1962) and *A Voyage Round My Father* (1970).

DONALD SINDEN (1923…)

English actor. By alternating between unpretentious television comedy and prestigious productions of SHAKE-SPEARE, Sinden has made it difficult to assess his own standing in the profession. His voice is equally elusive, making him by turns a caricature of the plummy Englishman and a sonorous declaimer of verse. Since his early days in the Shakespeare Memorial Company at Stratford, he has travelled much in the realms of trivia, but has returned regularly to give such outstanding performances as Sir William Harcourt Courtly in BOUCICAULT's

London Assurance, Richard Plantagenet in *The Wars of the Roses*, and Lord Foppington in VANBRUGH's *The Relapse*.

FRANCO ZEFFIRELLI (1923...)

Italian director and designer. Though known to the largest public as a film director, Zeffirelli has worked mainly in the theatre (and the opera-house). He first came to notice in the post-war years as designer for VISCONTI's productions of *A Streetcar Named Desire*, *Troilus and Cressida* and *Three Sisters*. It was not until 1953 that he turned to directing, initially opera. In the late 1950s he was a familiar name to English audiences for his frequent productions at Covent Garden.

While in London Zeffirelli returned to the theatre with a moving and original production of *Romeo and Juliet* at the Old Vic in 1960. The following year he went on to bring a powerful version of *Othello* to Stratford-upon-Avon. More recently in London he has directed and designed plays by Eduardo DE FILIPPO: *Saturday, Sunday, Monday* in 1973 and *Filumena* (1978). These productions, with their meticulous re-creations of Neapolitan family life, are typical of Zeffirelli's insistence on precise detail.

JAMES BALDWIN (1924...)

American novelist, essayist and playwright. Like all his writings, James Baldwin's plays express his most passionate concerns: the roots of black identity, racial prejudice, and the abuse of love and sexuality. As a teenager in Harlem, he became a celebrated preacher in order to compete with the Holy Roller stepfather who had rejected him: his play *The Amen Corner* (1955) examines without rancour the true and false values of ghetto religion. *Blues for Mister Charlie* (1964) is infinitely angrier, written while Baldwin was in the South campaigning for civil rights. Based on the true story of a black Mississippi youth who lost his life for looking at a white woman, the play attacks racism as a white disease arising from frustrated love and self-loathing. Without denying the work's raw power, some critics felt it was evidence that the preacher in Baldwin was winning his battle with the artist.

ROBERT BOLT (1924...)

English playwright. While working as a schoolmaster, Bolt had several plays broadcast by the BBC (including the now famous *A Man For All Seasons*). His first West End play was *Flowering Cherry* (1957). The title, characters and atmosphere all deliberately recalled CHEKHOV, and, with RALPH RICHARDSON in the lead, it was a popular success.

When *A Man For All Seasons* was finally produced in 1960, with Paul SCOFIELD giving a magnificent performance as Sir Thomas More, Bolt's "epic" style of historical drama was compared both to BRECHT and to the Elizabethans. Although he did not have a comparable stage success until he returned to the sixteenth century with *Vivat! Vivat Regina!* (1970), the scripts for *Dr Zhivago* and *Lawrence of Arabia* maintained Bolt's reputation as one of England's most successful dramatic writers.

MARLON BRANDO (1924...)

American actor. Tallulah BANKHEAD described the young Brando as "terribly talented" but "rather strange". Moody and self-conscious, he had come to New York in 1943, where his teachers, Erwin PISCATOR and Stella Adler, immediately perceived a natural "inner rhythm". He attracted attention in such unlikely roles as Marchbanks in SHAW's *Candida*, but it was his visceral performance as Stanley Kowalski in TENNESSEE WILLIAMS's *A Streetcar Named Desire* that proclaimed a revolutionary acting style. Hailed as a "once in a lifetime" experience, it was also Brando's last major stage role. Restless as ever, he moved on to Hollywood to become *The Wild One* and *The Godfather*.

ARMAND GATTI (1924...)

French playwright and director. Gatti's plays deal with oppression and rebellion. Frequently they use a sequence of short, linked scenes, a technique probably accounted for by his experiences as a journalist. *Le Crapaud-buffle* (1959), his first work to be performed, is a satire on dictatorship, while his experiences in a concentration camp inspired *L'Enfant-rat* (published in 1960) and *La Deuxième existence du camp de Tatenberg* (1962).

A bewildering mixture of past and present, real and imaginary comprise Gatti's plays. This is well exemplified in *La Vie imaginaire de l'éboueur Auguste Geai* (1962), where the dreams and actual experiences of the street-cleaner Geai are enacted simultaneously on no less than seven different sections of the stage.

In 1961 Gatti made a prizewinning film, *L'Enclos*. More recent plays include *V comme Viêt-nam* (1967), *La Naissance* (1968) and *Les 13 soleils de la rue Saint-Blaise*.

GERALDINE PAGE (1924...)

American actress. Geraldine Page worked in summer stock outside Chicago "while wintering and starving in New York" until 1952 when José QUINTERO cast her in the lead of TENNESSEE WILLIAMS's *Summer and Smoke*. The off-Broadway production gave emphatic notice that a new star had arrived, and her performance the following year in an otherwise saccharine play confirmed her status. But in 1959, the part of the spent and desperate movie star in Williams's *Sweet Bird of Youth* revealed completely new capacities. What Walter Kerr called her old "finger-at-the-forehead shyness" was replaced by an authority that "reverberated like an anvil". Miss Page has continued to surprise and delight, whether playing O'NEILL, CHEKHOV or AYCKBOURN, justifying the confidence she felt even in her early days: "I always knew I was good." She is married to the actor and director, Rip Torn.

JOSÉ QUINTERO (1924...)

American director. In 1950 Quintero and several friends rented a vacant bar in Greenwich Village, arranged seats around the dance floor and opened the Circle in the Square theatre. This classic off-Broadway enterprise had its first big hit in 1952 with TENNESSEE WILLIAMS's *Summer and Smoke*, staged by Quintero and starring Geraldine PAGE. In 1956 his atmospheric production of Eugene O'NEILL's *The Iceman Cometh* inspired the playwright's widow to put him in charge of the American première of *Long Day's Journey into Night*. Despite other successes, Quintero has been regarded as an O'Neill specialist ever since, winning a Tony award for *A Moon for the Misbegotten* in 1973. He has many television credits, including an outstanding production of Thornton WILDER's *Our Town* (1959), and has also directed opera at the Met in New York.

BRIAN RIX (1924...)

English actor-manager. A typical dénouement of any Brian Rix farce is the point at which the wife discovers her crestfallen north country husband (Rix) with the au pair, trouserless but innocent. So popular were such harmless romps as *Dry Rot* and *Simple Spymen* that Rix's Whitehall Theatre eventually broke the record for continuous presentation of bedroom farce, previously held by the Aldwych and Ben TRAVERS. After twenty-eight years the joke wore thin on Rix himself, who remarked, "I've fallen into the terrible trap of being a cliché in my own time."

JULIAN BECK (1925...)

American director and actor. Together with his wife Judith Malina, Beck founded The Living Theatre in New York in 1947. They were radicals then, they are radicals now; and their theatrical search has always taken them to the extremes of art and life. Between 1951 and 1963 they served the literary avant-garde, doing works by Gertrude Stein, William Carlos Williams, W. H. AUDEN and Jean COCTEAU as well as plays by BRECHT, STRINDBERG and RACINE. They also provided the "new wave" of American theatre in the early sixties with two of its most audacious plays: Jack Gelber's *The Connection* and Kenneth Brown's *The Brig*.

The Living Theatre exiled themselves in Europe in the mid-sixties, returning with a radical message and radicalized epic happenings like *Paradise Now*, *Frankenstein* and *Mysteries* – evenings which created tumult and scandal in their call for sexual and political liberation. In 1971 the troupe was imprisoned in Brazil. Since then, the Becks have continued to take their theatre to the people. Their events, always based on wide-reading and bold scenic devices, are a call to change. As Beck wrote in *The Life of the Theatre*, "We are going so far out that they will never be able to catch us."

PETER BROOK (1925...)

English director and theorist. Brook made his directing debut as a teenager, and while still in his twenties was working with John GIELGUD in SHAKESPEARE and collaborating, while resident director at the Royal Opera House, with Salvador Dali. His fame spread in 1962 with a bleak and controversial version of *King Lear*, in which Paul SCOFIELD played Lear as a crotchety dotard. While many saw the sense of this interpretation, some critics felt that Brook, by divesting the king of his nobility, had also demolished his tragic stature. Controversy has also greeted his advocacy of such demanding writers as Jean-Paul SARTRE, Friedrich DÜRRENMATT and Peter WEISS. In the latter's *Marat/Sade* (1963), the alienating effect of "actors acting actors" revealed a clear debt to Bertolt BRECHT, while the play's disturbing cruelty recalled Antonin ARTAUD. These influences also permeated the semi-improvisatory *US* (1966), an attack on American imperialism in Vietnam combining burlesque and shock-tactics. Not all Brook's productions have been violent or political. One of the greatest triumphs of the Royal Shakespeare Company has been his gay 1970 staging of *A Midsummer Night's Dream*.

Since 1971 Brook has worked mainly in Paris, declaring that "the English resent naked truth". There he has orchestrated such extraordinary ventures as a trip to Persia with a company that acted only in "Orghast" (a language invented for the occasion) and a tour of central Africa by a mime-troupe. Opposed to the "deadly theatre" of tradition (and specifically to conventional auditorium interiors), he is still striving to realize his ideal of uniting actors and audience in a holy and orgiastic rite.

LENNY BRUCE (1925-66)

American comedian. Lenny Bruce died taking heroin, but a friend observed bitterly that the real cause of death was "an overdose of police". For years he was harassed for his lacerating, sometimes surreal, comic monologues on forbidden subjects, delivered in forbidden language. Son of a burlesque dancer, Bruce believed that "people should be taught what is, not what should be". Typical routines taunted moral and religious conventions, imagining Moses and Jesus entering a cathedral during Mass, for instance, or speculating on the rise of Hitler as a public-relations stunt that got out of hand. He attracted a considerable underground following, but a dubious 1964 conviction for obscenity effectively silenced him. Dying a bankrupt addict, he was resurrected as a cult hero in the 1970s when obscenity became chic. As profitable eulogies poured out, another friend observed, "Alive Lenny was a problem. Dead he's a property."

RICHARD BURTON (1925...)

Welsh actor. "Make up your mind, dear heart, do you want to be a household word or a great actor?" admonished Laurence OLIVIER early in Burton's career. "Both," was the reply.

Burton is the son of a miner and the youngest of thirteen children. After Oxford and the RAF he appeared in the plays of Christopher FRY, whose poetic dialogue he enriched with a sonorous Celtic delivery. There followed a powerful Henry V (moving a fellow-actor to remark: "He brings his cathedral on with him"), an heroic Hamlet and a quietly majestic Othello; but these interpretations were noted more for their promise than for their authority. A New York run of *Hamlet* in 1964, directed by John GIELGUD, broke attendance records, though Burton's attractively extrovert approach dismayed the older actor.

By now Burton's film career was taking over, along with the notoriety attending his expensive skirmishings with Elizabeth Taylor. He has yet to refute Olivier's doubts, though such a feat may still be in his power.

SAMMY DAVIS JR (1925...)

American cabaret star. When Frank Sinatra heard that he was the butt of a popular impersonation by a skinny little black man, he went to have a look for himself and came away impressed. As singer, dancer, trumpeter, drummer and comedian, Davis's mastery of timing has continued to be arrogantly casual, and brings an unforgettable zest to such numbers as Cole PORTER's "Night and Day" or Gershwin's "It Ain't Necessarily So". A broken nose and an artificial eye strangely enhance his rakish charm.

But he was not always so popular. The racial bigotry he lightly mocks in his act attended both his army service and his early marriage to a Swedish actress, while a London visit was greeted by the racist slogan: "Sammy go back to the trees." His adoption of the Jewish faith was a dramatic gesture of solidarity with other minorities, though an outspoken endorsement of President Nixon alienated many of Davis's liberal admirers.

JOHN DEXTER (1925...)

English director. War service rescued Dexter from a plumbing-equipment factory and introduced him to touring theatricals, but an attack of polio shattered his dream of training as an actor, and for years he scraped a living as a factory hand and theatrical odd-job man. For some time he was heard in *The Archers* (a rustic radio soap-opera) before he finally found his way – via the Royal Court Theatre and the plays of Arnold WESKER – to the Old Vic, where he directed OLIVIER in a celebrated *Othello* (1964). Later that year his almost choreographic methods found striking expression in Peter SHAFFER's spectacular

The Royal Hunt of the Sun, for which Dexter employed the mime Claude Chagrin as an advisor. In 1967 incredulity greeted his plans for an all-male rock version of *As You Like It* – the result was brilliant.

Dexter then diversified into opera and cinema; his subsequent return to the stage was triumphantly celebrated by a beautifully stylized production of Shaffer's *Equus* (1973), with animal-mimes again devised by Chagrin. Dexter has since returned to opera, at the New York "Met", where his acerbic methods and profoundly original visual imagination have continued to inspire both horror and delight.

TANKRED DORST (1925...)

German playwright. Dorst made his debut working for a puppet theatre. His early plays reveal a number of influences ranging from Jean GIRAUDOUX to Eugène IONESCO, but recently a more obvious political awareness has informed his work. First performed in the supercharged atmosphere of 1968, his famous play *Toller* documents playwright Ernst TOLLER's role in the 1919 Munich rebellion. A kaleidoscopic variety of technique encompasses puppets, cabaret acts, songs and readings from Toller, much of which takes place simultaneously. The character of the playwright himself is none the less developed with sensitivity and authority.

JULIE HARRIS (1925...)

American actress. A harsh voice and angular features have not stood in the way of Julie Harris. After rejecting the debutante's life her parents urged on her, she studied at the Actors' Studio and made her debut on Broadway in 1945. Ten subsequent plays brought her an admiring critical following, and Carson McCullers's 1950 hit *The Member of the Wedding* gave her the public exposure she deserved. Her wistful performance as Frankie, the lonely twelve-year-old tomboy, led to a string of remarkably diverse roles, including Sally Bowles in John VAN DRUTEN's *I am a Camera* and Joan of Arc in Jean ANOUILH's *The Lark*. She has been just as convincing in SHAKESPEARE and Restoration comedy and as Emily Dickinson in her 1976 solo show *The Belle of Amherst*.

JULES IRVING (1925...)

American producer, director and actor. In 1952 Irving and Herbert Blau founded the San Francisco Actors' Workshop "to provide the circumstances in which actors can practise their art". Over the next thirteen years their company became a critic's byword for "selfless allegiance to the repertory ideal", presenting unadorned and intelligent productions of such playwrights as BECKETT, BRECHT and PINTER. As a result, in 1965 Irving and Blau were invited to New York to head the recently established Lincoln Center Repertory Theater. There, in spite of a frequently cool press, Irving (and – initially – Blau, who resigned in 1967) continued the work until 1973, with more productions of such as Pinter and Beckett together with plays by HAVEL and Ed BULLINS. One of the peaks of Irving's career (before his resignation in 1972) must be his foresight and discernment in being the first to give a proper professional production to a play by Sam SHEPARD (*Operation Sidewinder*, 1970).

ALEC MCCOWEN (1925...)

English actor. McCowen dropped out of drama school and spent years in obscurity before a remarkable performance as Mercutio in *Romeo and Juliet* (1960) brought him recog-

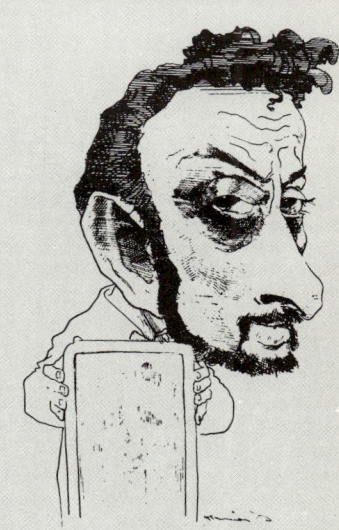

Julie Harris (*above*) makes a speciality of playing unusual women. The lonely life of the poet Emily Dickinson provided the occasion for some brilliant solo acting in *The Belle of Amherst*

Lenny Bruce (*right*) battled with the censors. His sardonic utterance of forbidden words and ideas proved to be a great influence in dispelling the taboos against obscenity

Alec McCowen (*below*, as Henry Higgins in Shaw's *Pygmalion*) has gained a reputation as a self-effacing player in major roles. He brings this quality even to the remarkable solo performance in which he reads the Gospel of St Mark

The success of *Accidental Death of an Anarchist* in London in 1980 established **Dario Fo** (*above*) as an international figure

Lovely, intense and vulnerable, **Rossella Falk**, (*below*) played the doomed Marguerite in this production of *La Dame aux camélias*

nition. Since then this "actor's actor" has repeatedly proven that energy and intelligence are far more useful assets than instant charisma. He has won acclaim in roles ranging from the Fool in *King Lear* (1962) to Martin Dysart in *Equus* and has made something of a speciality of deluded heroes: his portrayal of the would-be Pope in *Hadrian the Seventh* (1968) was hailed by critic Ronald Bryden as "one of the major performances of the decade".

JAMES SAUNDERS (1925…)

English playwright. The heroine of *A Scent of Flowers* (1964) is already dead, and argues with her family about the reasons for her suicide. In *Next Time I'll Sing to You* (1962), the leading actor himself portrays an actor playing a hermit, while other "actors" dispute with him in an attempt to explain his rejection of the world. Indeed, in Saunders's more dialectical works, the cast even argues with the audience. Yet these experimental methods do not obscure his commitment to truth and compassion. *Bodies* (1978), a successful West End production, protracted the moral debate.

MAUREEN STAPLETON (1925…)

American actress. When Anna Magnani's English wasn't good enough for her to play the tempestuous Italian widow in TENNESSEE WILLIAMS's *The Rose Tattoo* in 1951 Maureen Stapleton took the role and scored an indisputable triumph. Subsequent performances in the playwright's *27 Wagons Full of Cotton* and *Orpheus Descending*, as well as a 1965 revival of *The Glass Menagerie*, made her something of a Williams specialist, though such contrasting roles as the motherly matchmaker of S. N. BEHRMAN's *The Cold Wind and the Warm* proved her versatility. Later, her success in *Plaza Suite* and *The Gingerbread Lady* identified her with the nervous, witty world of Neil SIMON. But Miss Stapleton's real specialities have always been commitment and adaptability. Attracted to drama first by Hollywood fantasies, she soon discovered the craft was "a lot harder than I thought". Method acting with the Actors' Studio trained her to immerse herself completely in whatever role she was playing, and being "true and real and alive and fresh" remains her ideal – but she adds, "You show up at 8.30 and whether you feel true or not, Charlie, *go*."

HELMUT BAIERL (1926…)

German playwright. The political bias of Baierl's plays ensures that they remain unknown in the West. *Die Feststellung* (1958), the tale of a peasant who misguidedly flees to the West, so delighted the East German authorities that the writer was rewarded with the position of dramaturge to the Berliner Ensemble.

Baierl's best known play is *Frau Flinz* (1961), a present-day postscript to BRECHT's *Mutter Courage*. Helene WEIGEL herself played the title role, looking very much as she had done as Mother Courage. Frau Flinz is a dissatisfied factory-worker who conducts a spirited campaign against a zealous party official. Eventually, realizing where her interests lie, she comes round to the Party line.

COLLEEN DEWHURST (1926…)

American actress. Colleen Dewhurst loves Eugene O'NEILL's female characters because "they move from the groin rather than the brain. To play O'Neill you have to be big." Her own robust acting has often been too big for Broadway. In the 1950s and 1960s she won awards and critical praise in SHAKESPEARE with Joseph PAPP and in other off-Broadway productions such as Jean COCTEAU's *The Eagle Has Two Heads*. But her Broadway parts, though invariably acclaimed by professionals, received scant attention from the public. Recent successes, such as O'Neill's *A Moon for the Misbegotten* in 1973, have awakened a growing audience to her formidable talent.

ROSSELLA FALK (1926...)

Italian actress. After Falk left drama school her angular beauty and emphatic delivery won her a stage debut as the stepdaughter in a 1948 production of PIRANDELLO's epoch-making *Sei personaggi in cerca d'autore*. It remains one of her finest roles. In 1954 she joined Giorgio DE LULLO and other young actors to form the Compagnia dei Giovani. During many years with this troupe, which was for a long time one of the mainstays of Italian theatre, Falk starred in several outstanding productions: as Isabella in FABBRI's delightful *La Bugiarda* (which she also played in London in the 1965 World Theatre season), as Masha in CHEKHOV's *Three Sisters* and in a host of other roles. Some critics have seen the zenith of her career as a stunning Hedda Gabler in a 1968 production of IBSEN's drama.

DARIO FO (1926...)

Italian actor, playwright, director and manager. Fo is a highly controversial figure, who has been imprisoned for his outspoken political theatre. With his wife, Franca Rame, he formed his first company in 1950. For nine years they worked within the established theatre, producing and performing Fo's highly popular plays, vehicles for thinly masked political and social comment. These included *Isabella, tre caravelle e un cacciaballe* (1963) and *Gli arcangeli non giocano a flipper* (1959). In the 1950s, together with the playwright Franco Parenti, he also wrote two entertainments: *Il Dito nell' occhio* and *I Sani da legare*.

In 1968 Fo and Rame became outlaws of the conventional theatre, first forming the Associazione Nuova Scena, a troupe supported by the Communist Party, and, two years later, La Comune, an independent and radical company. One of their earliest productions was *Morte accidentale di un anarchico* (1970). In this highly charged but humorous political drama Fo gives his version of the story of Giuseppe Pinelli, a young anarchist who fell to his death from the window of a police station in 1969.

In 1974 La Comune occupied and restored the crumbling Palazzina Liberty in the centre of Milan, running the theatre as a club in order that they might refuse admittance to the police. With works like *Il Fanfani Rapito* (1975), a wild fantasy about a Christian Democratic Party plot to kidnap one of its own leaders, Fo's political and cultural evangelism continues unabated.

ALUN OWEN (1926...)

Welsh-born playwright. "Liverpool and Wales: they're the two things I really know, and yet I'm not completely at home in either." The clash between cultures has been a theme for Owen's best stage works: Protestant against Catholic in *Progress to the Park* (1959), and Christian against revolutionary in *The Rough and Ready Lot* (1959). In dialogue that captures reality without anger, and lyricism without falsehood, Owen has been one of the most effective dramatists to emerge from the British working class. He served a useful apprenticeship as an actor in the 1940s and 1950s but has since turned to writing full-time, mostly for radio and television. In 1964 he put Liverpool on the map for millions with his best known film script, The Beatles' *A Hard Day's Night*.

MURRAY SCHISGAL (1926...)

American playwright. In 1959 Schisgal's thirteen-year failure as a writer of fiction prompted him to switch to drama and, a year later, to leave the United States. In London two of his one-act plays, *The Typists* and *The Postman* (1960), impressed critics and audiences with their bleak, absurdist view of contemporary life, and in 1963 the same double bill (with *The Postman* retitled *The Tiger*) was also successful in New York. His biggest hit, the full-length *Luv*, followed in 1963, its neurotic antics demonstrating Schisgal's belief that "love . . . has lost its meaning for us". Later plays have failed to attract (or hold) the attention of his earlier work.

PETER SHAFFER (1926...)

English playwright. Shaffer understands the demands of theatre; his plays are carefully structured and intensely dramatic, but they are impossible to categorize, for each is a new venture. His first stage play, *Five Finger Exercise* (1958), is a subtle and closely observed middle-class drama, while *The Royal Hunt of the Sun* (1964) is a bold experiment in "total" theatre using music, masks and mime. In *Equus* (1973) a middle-aged psychiatrist is confronted with the fantasy and passion of a teenage boy who has brutally blinded the horses that he worshipped. *Amadeus* (1979), his most recent play, is based on the theory that Mozart may have been poisoned by a rival composer, Salieri. Shaffer's twin brother Anthony is also a playwright; *Sleuth* (1970), a psychological thriller, had a long run in the West End.

FRITZ WEAVER (1926...)

American actor. Weaver studied physics at university but spent almost as much time on stage as in the laboratory. He made a 1954 New York debut in CONGREVE's *The Way of the World* and established himself as a leading man in the heroic mould. Working most often in repertory, he has concentrated on the classic parts in SHAKESPEARE, IBSEN and O'NEILL. But he has also starred as Sherlock Holmes in the musical *Baker Street*, and successfully adapted his grand style to contemporary roles.

FRANÇOIS BILLETDOUX (1927...)

French playwright, actor and novelist. With *Tchin-Tchin* (1959), Billetdoux was fêted in avant-garde circles throughout France. Variously interpreted as a grinding farce and as a celebration of redemption through self-destruction, it portrays a man and a woman who descend together into drunken degradation after their respective spouses have decamped together. The deliberate obscurity of works such as this and *Va donc chez Törpe* (1961) is viewed by hostile commentators as an attempt to disguise their own vacuity; but Billetdoux's theatre relies to a degree upon non-communication and alienation, especially in his treatment of the "clown triste", a pathetic figure which has continually fascinated French intellectuals.

GÜNTER GRASS (1927...)

German novelist, playwright and poet. The great literary spokesman of the not-too-extreme Left in West Germany, Grass came to prominence when his picaresque masterpiece, *The Tin Drum*, proved that a novel still had power to amaze. Many of the hero's experiences were autobiographical. The young Grass had, like the dwarf Oscar, worked as a stonemason before he took himself off to paint and sculpt in Paris. His early plays, however, did not cause the same sensation as his novels. They were short, absurdist pieces, like *Hochwasser* (1957) and *Die bösen Köche* (1961).

Grass's one major play has been *Die Plebejer proben den Aufstand* (1966, *The Plebeians Rehearse the Uprising*), a pointed fantasy about Bertolt BRECHT's part in the East German workers' rebellion of 1953. It shows the great man rehearsing the scene in *Coriolanus* in which the Romans rise up against their leader. Berlin workers rush in to ask him to give his blessing to the revolt. Brecht will neither support them nor, when the Government also seeks his support, will he denounce them. To the end he remains in the play a lonely, guilt-ridden figure. Perhaps to avoid such isolation himself, Grass has always been the first to speak out on major political issues.

PETER NICHOLS (1927…)

English playwright. Experiences as the father of a spastic child inspired Nichols, who had written plays for television, to write his first stage-play, *A Day in the Death of Joe Egg* (1967). His poignant yet humorous observations of how people cope with suffering brought equal success to *The National Health* (1969), in which patients' grim experiences are contrasted with satirical interludes of television hospital melodrama, and *Forget-Me-Not Lane* (1971), which follows the life of Frank Bisley, first trying to escape his parents' bickering marriage and, twenty years later, trapped by his own. *The Freeway* (1974), a pessimistic look into the future set in an enormous traffic jam, was badly received; it was with relief that the critics welcomed *Privates on Parade* (1977), full of lively sequences of song and dance. *Born in the Gardens* (1980) returns to that desolate trap, the English family; again it is Nichols's humour that lightens the gloom.

TOM O'HORGAN (1927…)

American director and composer. O'Horgan's search for more expressive stage imagery, his experiments with movement and a theatre language beyond speech, were the spearhead of the brief off-Broadway renaissance in the mid-1960s. As the director of the influential La Mama Troupe, O'Horgan mounted successful and often sensa-

tional productions that included Paul Foster's *Tom Paine* and Rochelle Owens's *Futz*. After off-Broadway became chic, O'Horgan took his avant-garde experiments with masks and movement and made them pay on Broadway. He scored a tremendous success with *Hair*; and also directed *Lenny* and *Jesus Christ Superstar*, which he conceived for the stage.

ESTELLE PARSONS (1927…)

American actress. Famous for her Oscar-winning portrayal of an hysterical fellow-traveller in the film *Bonnie and Clyde*, Estelle Parsons is herself something of a maverick. In a college show she played a striptease artist so enthusiastically that "the dean of women cut my scene". She made her 1956 debut in a Broadway musical, but became known off Broadway and in repertory. Her stage career still flourishes, with such successes as the 1974 *Mert and Phil*, despite her belief that "the theatre is full of dopes".

CHRISTOPHER PLUMMER (1927…)

Canadian actor. Plummer gained formidable acting experience with the Canadian Repertory Theatre, playing nearly one hundred roles from 1950 to 1952. In 1955, a year after his New York debut, he played Count Zichy in Christopher FRY's *The Dark is Light Enough* with Katharine CORNELL and Tyrone Power, and in 1961 he was a memorable Richard III at Stratford-upon-Avon. That same year he won the London Evening Standard Award as King Henry in Jean ANOUILH's *Becket*, but he had more trouble getting to grips with the parts of Jupiter and Amphitryon in Jean GIRAUDOUX's *Amphitryon 38* while with the National Theatre from 1971 to 1972. Plummer has acted in many films including the seemingly everlasting *Sound of Music*. In a recent movie, *Murder by Decree*, he portrays a saturnine Sherlock Holmes in pursuit of Jack the Ripper through foggy, gas-lit London.

MORT SAHL (1927…)

American comedian. American comedians have found their country stony ground for political cabaret. But a few cities provide havens of cynicism where men like Mort

Left: A scene from *Seascape* (1975) by **Albee**, who is the only playwright of stature to deal with America in terms of tragic farce. His absurdist style is opposite to the elegant, naturalist comedy of Simon

Right: two acute observers of American affluence. *Barefoot in the Park* (1963) was an early success for playwright **Neil Simon** (*left*) and satirist turned director **Mike Nichols** (*right*). Robert Redford's name is a reminder that many film stars began on Broadway

Far right: the hand-puppet show *Punch and Judy* has a horrific plot which has delighted children for two centuries. Punch kills the baby when it cries and beats his wife to death when she objects: also a doctor, a policeman, and sundry others. He tricks the hangman into putting the noose round his own neck, and thrashes the devil too

Sahl can make a living. He began at San Francisco's "hungry i" in 1953, attacking militarism, McCarthyism and Eisenhower ("We need a man on a white horse. Well we got the horse, but there's nobody on him"). At first branded as a "sicknik", he had become positively respectable by the early 1960s, and at clubs in Las Vegas and Miami Beach was receiving a reported $7,500 a week for satirizing his audiences. At his peak, Sahl was so popular (and so establishment) that John F. Kennedy was asking him to supply campaign jokes, and sending jet-planes for their safe delivery. By then a real sicknik had taken his place, and Lenny BRUCE had become the villain of the popular press.

GEORGE C SCOTT (1927...)

American actor. Scott's nose took its aggressively flattened shape during his early days as a hard-drinking bit-part actor and ex-Marine. This prominent feature may well have contributed to making him "the meanest Richard III ever seen by human eyes" on his starring debut in New York. But soon after, his performance as Jaques in *As You Like It* confirmed him as an actor of subtlety and distinction. Scott then used his earnings to found a theatre. It failed, but he chose to buy it out of insolvency, a gesture of unselfishness which contrasted ironically with his next major role, Shylock. In this part he won praise for his characteristic refusal to render the role superficially attractive. Such indeed is the authenticity of Scott's style, that even in the controversial Actors' Studio version of CHEKHOV's *Three Sisters* (given in London in 1965), he was spared the critics' disapproval.

Scott's outspoken sincerity was manifested in 1970, when he publicized his repugnance for Hollywood ethics by refusing an Oscar for his performance in the film *Patton*.

NEIL SIMON (1927...)

American playwright. Re-reading the thirteen plays he had written in sixteen years since he made his debut on Broadway in 1961, Neil Simon said, "When I was good, I was very, very good . . . and when I was bad, we folded." Not many of Simon's plays folded, and the ones that remained open became some of the most popular and the biggest money-makers of the century. Having started out as a television gag writer, Simon now owns his own Broadway theatre (The Eugene O'Neill) and estimates that from his royalties he earns about £15,000 a day.

Simon's plays are about the audience who pay to see them. He has a wry understanding of middle-class Jewish life, and he puts these problems on stage with a modicum of humour that they lack in life. His two best plays, *The Odd Couple* (1965), about two separated husbands setting up house together, and *The Sunshine Boys* (1972), a tale of the comeback of two crotchety vaude-villains, go beyond the run of the Broadway treadmill with fine characterizations.

In all Simon's plays, a recurring theme is urban man's losing battle against the city, loneliness and death. "I'm terribly conscious of the powerlessness of the people in the plays," Simon has said. "In *The Odd Couple*, Oscar says to Felix: 'You mean you have no idea of changing.' And Felix says: 'I am what I am.' When I look around in life, most people who are in trouble know what the problems are. This becomes sadder to people over forty because they feel their characters are determined . . . they're trapped. The trap is themselves, not necessarily life."

Among Simon's other hit plays which give a boulevard gloss to the problems of urban living are: *Barefoot in the Park* (1963), *Plaza Suite* (1968), *The Last of the Red Hot Lovers* (1969) and *The Prisoner of Second Avenue* (1971).

EDWARD ALBEE (1928...)

American playwright. *Who's Afraid of Virginia Woolf?* (1962) was greeted by one New York critic as a "calculated exercise in depraved obscenity". It portrays the "exorcism", during a night of drunken and painful self-examination, of a fantasy-child invented by George and Martha, a disintegrating academic couple. The catalyst for their painful awakening is a younger couple, the only other characters in the play. Impotence, infertility and infidelity predictably shocked and enthralled Broadway audiences who flocked to see it, but the play survived the sensationalism of its première and has remained one of the most important American dramas of the decade.

The themes of failure and disenchantment pervading

CONTINUED ON PAGE 272

The director

The art of directing is largely the art of prophecy. An established director receives dozens of scripts from managements, agents, playwrights and even actors themselves. He must judge in cold blood what will work in the theatre and what will not. Having committed himself to a script – which may advance or ruin his career – he then has to choose which actors will be right for the parts. And, more importantly, what combination of actors will produce theatrical excitement. At the same time he has to select the correct designer for the show and work with him in meticulous detail to create a setting that will exploit the drama to the full.

In the eighteenth century there is the story of SHERIDAN writing the last act of a comedy while the actors were performing the first. They weren't very pleased, but they got through the evening because there were accepted conventions about how a piece should be performed. Now there are no such conventions; it is up to the director to invent them. The job is impossibly difficult, and actors are not noted for their charity to those that have led them. As a consequence the director has to be a mixture of showman, psychoanalyst, lover, thug and friend.

The profession is full of frauds and fools. Some managements welcome this, and would much prefer to employ a pleasant idiot who didn't get in the way of the stars to a man of independence and vision. But in the end the job of director depends on the company he is working for, and the prestige he has acquired within the profession. He can be an innovator and a trail-blazer of fashion and thought. It is the dream of most directors to start a company where they can rely as much on the invention of the actors as on their own interpretation, and where the loneliness of command can be made more tolerable by the respect and trust of those working around them on a production.

The needs of the 1950s and 1960s, however, raised the position of the director to guru level. And many directors (PETER HALL and PETER BROOK, for example) have suffered the inevitable backlash. People who were hailed as masters are savagely attacked and (unlike film directors) they cannot point to a tangible body of work to justify themselves. BOUCICAULT, the great nineteenth-century playwright (and one of the first, true, unofficial directors) described the public as "a monster who forgets".

Though the job of director may eventually become redundant – and there are many who think it will – the position will always survive in some form. Indeed the theatre has never been without directors; but in the past it has simply been the leader of the pack, whether actor, playwright, manager or call-boy. The question is whether the leader of the future will simply be dominant because he can supply money for the shows, and whether this money will involve intolerable bureaucratic restraints. Direction – and consequently theatre – may still be crushed by misdirection from without.

A great director needs to be something of a perfectionist, and the typical richness and freshness of a production by the Italian **Franco Zeffirelli** (*above*) is in fact the result of meticulous attention to detail and of exhaustive research. He often goes to the length of being the designer for his own productions

Peter Hall (*below*) directs Peggy Ashcroft in Beckett's *Happy Days*. His talent is for seizing on the essential shape of a play – for letting it speak for itself in a lucid, spare production. He has put great energy into developing Britain's major companies, and was also an early backer of the work of Beckett and Pinter

Lindsay Anderson (*right, on the floor*) is a fine director of farce whether the wild dissent of Joe Orton and John Arden, or the urbane anarchy of Ben Travers. Here he confers with John Moffat, Joan Plowright, and the nonagenarian Travers on a production

The British director **Tyrone Guthrie** (*top*) was an exponent of speedy dialogue and spectacular choreographic effects in his productions of Shakespeare. He was always ready to experiment – his version of *Hamlet* in modern (1938) dress, starring Alec Guinness, caused a sensation. **Harold Prince** (*above*) has directed many Broadway musicals. Here facing the camera, he rehearses Lotte Lenya, Bert Convy, and Jack Gilford for *Cabaret*

On stage as in film, the strength of the Italian director **Luchino Visconti** (*right*) lay in creating psychological intensity. To this end he was often also the designer for his own productions of plays and opera. His interest in social issues led him to enrich the Italian theatre with the work of foreign playwrights

Who's Afraid of Virginia Woolf? are not foreign to Albee. He himself was dismissed from college and spent years in a distressing variety of odd jobs. Employment as a telegram delivery boy enhanced his fascination for the vast range of types he met, to the point where he finally decided to write. *Zoo Story* (1959) is an absurdist encounter between a bourgeois and a Bohemian. The dialogue ends with suicide, seemingly the ultimate means of communication. A similar pessimism seems to inform *The Death of Bessie Smith* (1960), inspired by the tragic death of the black blues singer. Oddly, Smith herself does not appear, for Albee is more concerned to analyse the psychological problems which impel her exclusion from a "whites-only" hospital. The social problems raised here figure more prominently in *The American Dream* (1961), a gruesome satire on the clichés of American society.

Later works, ranging from *Tiny Alice* (1964) to *The Lady from Dubuque* (1980), reveal Albee as a writer never seemingly at ease in any well-proven vein; his most overtly experimental venture has been *Box/Mao/Box* (1968), which alternates monologues on fundamental issues with quotations from Mao Tse-Tung.

All Over (1971) depicts a family quarrelling round a dying man. John Gielgud's American production presented it as an abstract and stylized ritual, and possibly Albee's gravest work to date. In view of his unremitting preoccupation with being serious, it is not surprising that he still encounters immense difficulties in getting new plays performed.

PETER HACKS (1928...)

German playwright. As one of the very few writers to migrate from West to East (he made the move at the height of the Cold War in 1955) Hacks has experienced censorship on both sides of the border. The pieces he produced as dramaturge to the Deutsches Theater in East Berlin met with official approval until he began to deal with contemporary East German problems. *Die Sorgen und die Macht* (1960), which demonstrates how both sexual impotence and falling production in a briquette factory can be cured by joining the Communist Party, had to be substantially revised before it could be presented.

Most of Hacks's major works are historical. *Die Schlacht bei Lobositz* and *Der Müller von Sanssouci*, written while he contemplated his change of flag, received their first performance in the East in 1956 and 1958 respectively. The theme of both plays is the role of the common man in history, and his realization that he is being exploited.

Der Frieden (1962), an adaptation of Aristophanes' *Peace*, revived West German interest in Hacks's work. In *Amphitryon* (1967) he forgot the world of warring classes and nations to concentrate on the politics of sex. The enthusiastic reception of the play on both sides of the Iron Curtain was a high point of cultural détente.

DAVID MERCER (1928...)

English playwright. Mercer is a political playwright whose belief in the value of individualism has made him reject his early Marxism. Some of his characters, such as Peter in *Ride a Cock Horse* (1965), are sadly warped by society; others such as Morgan, in the television play (later a film) *A Suitable Case for Treatment* (1962), or the lecherous old vicar of the comic melodrama *Flint* (1970), exuberantly ignore normality and authority. But Mercer has continued to be concerned by the need for political activity in a healthy society. In *After Haggerty* (1970) he contrasts Bernard Link, intellectually aware but politically ineffectual, with Haggerty, who can handle a gun: and the two Russian dissidents of *Cousin Vladimir* (1978) are horrified at the way their new English friends live, totally isolated from their society.

HAROLD PRINCE (1928...)

American director and producer. Hal Prince made his first mark on Broadway as the producer of such highly successful and entertaining musicals as *The Pajama Game* (1954), *Damn Yankees* (1955), *West Side Story* (1957) and *A Funny Thing Happened on the Way to the Forum* (1962). But as a director and co-producer of Stephen Sondheim's musicals, he has come to dominate musical theatre over the last decade. In his slick, sardonic and somewhat pretentious attempts to push the musical into deeper water, he has given Broadway such award-winning shows as *Company* (1970), *Follies* (1971), *A Little Night Music* (1973), *Pacific Overtures* (1976) and *Sweeney Todd* (1979).

TONY RICHARDSON (1928...)

English director. In 1956 Richardson directed a play that was to revolutionize British drama: John Osborne's *Look Back in Anger*. The next year he scored an equal success with Osborne's *The Entertainer*, which, like the first, he took to Broadway. A master of evoking British shabby gentility on stage, Richardson has also proved himself a sympathetic director of absurdist drama with such productions as Ionesco's *Les Chaises*. He directed his then wife, Vanessa Redgrave, in Chekhov's *The Seagull* in 1964; Shakespeare's *Hamlet* and *Antony and Cleopatra* have been among subsequent admired productions. Richardson's balance of realism and wit has made him a particularly successful director of such films as *A Taste of Honey* and *Tom Jones*.

JULES FEIFFER (1929...)

American satirist and playwright. Feiffer came into prominence in the early 1960s as the sardonic cartoonist of *The Village Voice*. In his syndicated strip, his characters talked out the absurdities of American politics and the bourgeois psyche. A prolific writer (he is the author of two novels and eleven collections of his cartoons), Feiffer wrote his first play, *Crawling Arnold*, in 1961. "Plays which have meant something to me have disturbed me. That is something I'm trying to reproduce." He succeeded with *Little Murders* (1967), one of the decade's outstanding satires. "Satire," Feiffer says, "has to be antagonistic to the system within which it's operating. I don't think of Noel Coward, for instance, as satire. They're pastiche, parodies. Satire is much more subversive." *Little Murders* "took the Andy Hardy family, the situation comedy, and set them loose in a country that's been living for a long period with a Cold War morality, the America of Vietnam." Feiffer tackled governmental hypocrisy in *The White House Murder Case* (1970), and *Knock, Knock* (1976). He has also written the screenplays for *Little Murders*, *Carnal Knowledge* and *Popeye*.

WILLIS HALL (1929...)

English playwright. Hall is a versatile and prolific playwright, who has written successfully for stage, radio, television and cinema. His first and best known play, *The Long and the Short and the Tall* (1958), was about a group of soldiers trapped and eventually killed in a jungle war. *Billy Liar* (1960) was the first in a series of successful collaborations with Keith Waterhouse (the author of the original novel). They followed this mordant comedy with such plays as *Celebration* (1961) and the clever farce *Say Who You Are* (1965).

HENRY LIVINGS (1929...)

English playwright and actor. Livings, an actor at Joan LITTLEWOOD's Theatre Workshop, sought to make theatre more fun. In 1961 he succeeded with *Stop It, Whoever You Are*, a comic fantasy about the adventures of a lavatory attendant. Livings has continued both to act and to write. His plays, such as *Eh?* (1964) and the two collections of comic *Pongo Plays* (1971 and 1975), are often about the little man and his minor victories over authority. More serious are *Kelly's Eye* (1963) and *The Little Mrs Foster Show* (1966). The latter, reminiscent of Littlewood's *Oh, What a Lovely War!*, presents the atrocities of war in music-hall style.

JOHN OSBORNE (1929...)

English playwright and actor. Osborne claims he was born into a "brawling, laughing, drinking, moaning" family of failed innkeepers. University was out of the question, and he spent his disenchanted youth working on trade journals, before employment as an actor stimulated him to write seriously.

The hero of *Look Back in Anger* (1956) is Jimmy Porter, an irate working-class intellectual whose unfortunate middle-class wife serves as a surrogate target for his venom against a vaguely defined Establishment. Porter's spleen now seems too generalized for a political message to emerge, but in the 1950s he provided a convenient focus for the manifold frustrations of post-war Britain, and his creator was popularly hailed as leader of the "Angry Young Men".

Osborne's next venture, *The Entertainer* (1957), also depicts a crumbling society, symbolized by the very institution of the theatre itself. The "entertainer" is Archie Rice, a failed comedian brought face to face with his own inconsequence. In his own act, Rice unwittingly provides an allegory of his and society's decadence, a feature of structural complexity inspired by Osborne's discovery of Bertolt BRECHT in the same year. The play provided a magnificent vehicle for Laurence OLIVIER, though Osborne

John Osborne (*left*) is as angry at left-wing establishments as at the right. Looking back, his Jimmy Porter is a violent study in alienation, but not the symbol for a programme of political change

himself thought the actor distorted the point of the play. Indeed, when the real-life comedian Max WALL starred in a more naturalistic revival, many critics detected structural weaknesses which Olivier's sheer power had previously obscured.

Osborne's subsequent plays have rarely lived up to critical expectations. He has been accused of "self-satisfied shrillness", and "bilious ventriloquism". *Luther* (1961), *A Patriot For Me* (1965) and *West of Suez* (1971) have had considerable success, but the best of the later plays has probably been *Inadmissible Evidence* (1964). Here the solicitor hero rages in impotent solitude, a pathetic and morally bereft figure who has twice been brilliantly brought to life by Nicol WILLIAMSON. Indeed many world-class actors have relished Osborne's ability to create great characters, if not always great plays.

For TONY RICHARDSON, who directed his early successes at the Royal Court Theatre, Osborne wrote the joyful film script of *Tom Jones*.

JOAN PLOWRIGHT (1929...)

English actress. In the late 1950s Plowright's graceful simplicity did much to sweeten the splenetic output of Arnold WESKER, John OSBORNE and Eugène IONESCO. In 1961 she married Laurence OLIVIER, since when she has considerably broadened her range. One critic has found her attempts at loftiness merely "glassy-eyed", but her stylish sincerity and warmth have made her an admired exponent of CHEKHOV and IBSEN, while the recent discovery in England of the comedies of Eduardo DE FILIPPO has provided her with two glorious Neapolitan roles.

PAOLO POLI (1929...)

Italian actor, director, playwright, librettist and designer. Despite his popularity as a television entertainer in the early sixties, especially for his *controfavole* (upside-down fairy-tales), Poli has preferred to work in the theatre. Early in his career he acted at the Borsa di Arlecchino, an avant-garde theatre in Genoa, and in 1961 returned to the stage with *Il Novellino*, his own lively medley of prose, music and dance. Its successor, *Il Diavolo* (1962), revived and extended in 1965, was even more popular. Both were also designed by Poli. Appropriately he also directed Arthur ADAMOV's *Paolo Paoli* in 1963. More recently, Poli's two plays *Arcadia* and *Milizia Forestale*, reflecting current alarm about pollution of the environment, were performed in Florence. He is also renowned as Italy's first successful "drag" performer.

JOHN ARDEN (1930...)

English playwright. Arden's war on the conventional theatre began with no obvious provocation. From private school in the north of England to Cambridge University he experienced the advantages of a privileged middle-class education. Only after training as an architect did he begin to write the plays which established him as a daring and anarchic (but hardly unprecedented) dramatist. *Live Like Pigs* (1958), *Serjeant Musgrave's Dance* (1959), *The Workhouse Donkey* (1963) and *Armstrong's Last Goodnight* (1964) all bespoke a debt to the plays of BRECHT, a love of song and verse and a robust pessimism.

In the early 1960s, Arden realized that life was much simpler than he had realized. "I have become a participant," he wrote, describing his commitment to popular socialist theatre. *The Non-Stop Connolly Show* (1975), one of the many entertainments he has written with his wife Margaretta D'Arcy, took theatre to the people of Dublin. For twenty-six and a half hours a cast of professionals and amateurs rambled through the life of the Irish patriot. "The cheapest doss in Dublin," sneered a critic. But Arden, the *eminence rose* of English letters, could now ignore such clapperclawing.

LIONEL BART (1930...)

English composer and librettist. Bart is one of the few Englishmen to have taken America on at its own game and won a resounding victory. Broadway critics in 1963 loathed the Dickensian sentiment ("witless amiability," said *Newsweek*) of *Oliver!*, but the public flocked to see it.

In London, Bart's acceptability was never in question. That same year three of his musicals – *Lock Up Your Daughters!* (1959), *Oliver!* (1960) and *Blitz* (1962) – were running simultaneously. Bart, who learned his trade with Joan LITTLEWOOD's company, lost his commercial touch with *Twang!* (1965), an enormously costly setting of the Robin Hood fable which proved a mighty "flop!"

PETER HALL (1930...)

English director. Sir Peter Hall admits to being a "workaholic". "Throughout my life I have been running to pass examinations . . . to get on," he says. In 1960, from the Shakespeare Memorial Theatre in Stratford he created the Royal Shakespeare Company, with its year-round home at the Aldwych in London. He has also directed the Royal Opera Company, Glyndebourne Opera, and, in 1973, took on one of Britain's most massive cultural institutions, succeeding Laurence OLIVIER as director of the National Theatre.

Hall is the grandson of a rat-catcher and son of a station-master. From an early age he was intent on directing, and soon after leaving Cambridge had his first break. As director of the Arts Theatre in 1955 he recognized BECKETT's *Waiting for Godot* as a masterpiece. His production, the first in English, proved what he called "an extraordinary door-opener". Another early achievement was his consecutive staging of all the Shakespearean history plays at Stratford, while a particularly fruitful collaboration with Harold PINTER has resulted in premières of *The Homecoming* (1965), *Old Times* (1971), *No Man's Land* (1975) and *Betrayal* (1978).

Hall's reign at the National Theatre has been beset with labour disputes and public criticism, but few would so ably assume a role that he defines as "play director . . . cum-object that people throw rotten eggs at".

LORRAINE HANSBERRY (1930-65)

American playwright. In 1959 New York drama critics considered plays by O'NEILL, MACLEISH and TENNESSEE WILLIAMS, but they gave their prestigious award to *A Raisin in the Sun* by a young black woman none of them had heard of a year before. Lorraine Hansberry's first work was a drama of urban black Chicago, with an appealing cast headed by Sidney Poitier and a rousing let's-battle-on theme that (the author said) described "the unbelievable courage of the Negro people". A second play, *The Sign in Sidney Brustein's Window* (1964), was relatively unsuccessful. Its brief Broadway run ended with Hansberry's death from cancer.

HAROLD PINTER (1930...)

English playwright, director, actor and poet. Pinter describes his first full-length play, *The Birthday Party* (1958), as "a mammoth flop, a flop *d'estime*". Critics were either scandalized or mystified by its mixture of absurdist comedy and inexplicable terror. The comfortably aimless existence of the play's protagonist is shattered by the arrival of two strangers who berate and threaten him, accuse him of an array of crimes from heresy to murder, subject him to a mock celebration of his birthday, then lead him off to some nameless punishment. It was only two years later, with the production of Pinter's second long work, *The Caretaker*, and his earlier one-acters, *The Room* and *The Dumb Waiter*, that these menacing effects were generally appreciated.

Cultivated by his long experience as poet and actor, Pinter's special gifts are a peerless knack for capturing the illogical, haphazard patterns of everyday speech and an infallible sense of timing and juxtaposition that turns them into gripping theatre. Influenced both by Samuel BECKETT and by American gangster movies, he says his characters feel "a world bearing upon them which is frightening". But this threatening universe is also the result of their personal failure, of "the poverty within us". The fragmented exchanges and eloquent silences that make Pinter's work both funny and fearful stem from deliberate attempts to conceal that emptiness. His plays typically take place in anonymous interiors, where characters try to insulate themselves from discovery but are exposed by some sinister intrusion.

Although recent works, among them *The Homecoming* (1965), *Old Times* (1971), *No Man's Land* (1975) and *Betrayal* (1978), are increasingly specific regarding time and place, they continue to expand the mood of *The Birthday Party*, where the victim's true crime is his nonentity. As his tormentors sneer, "You can't live, you can't think, you can't love. You're dead . . . You're nothing but an odour."

OLEG POPOV (1930...)

Russian clown. Popov, "the sunny clown", sees himself as "a simple fellow in love with life" and rejects the outlandish garb and make-up of traditional joeys. He charms his audience by his skills as a mime, perhaps imitating a musician unable to decide whether to play his flute or eat a carrot, or as a pompous, gesticulating orator who rebukes his listeners when they laugh. His view that the circus must serve the high dignity of man does not diminish the pure pleasure he gives as "the greatest clown in the world".

STEPHEN SONDHEIM (1930...)

American composer and lyricist. In collaboration with his director/producer Hal PRINCE, Sondheim has given a sense of occasion back to the musical and moved it away from the Shubert Alley formula of "no girls, no gags, no chance". He has set himself the task of reforming the musical, while young enough to have absorbed the professional expertise from the master craftsmen with whom he has worked: his mentors Oscar HAMMERSTEIN, Leonard Bernstein, Jerome ROBBINS, Richard Rodgers and Jule Styne. Lyricist and composer of *A Funny Thing Happened on the Way to the Forum*, *Anyone Can Whistle*, *Company*, *Follies*, *A Little Night Music*, *Pacific Overtures* and *Sweeney Todd*, and grudging wordsmith to such great shows as *Gypsy* and *West Side Story*, Sondheim is undisputed king of what remains of the American musical.

His ambition to write musicals was fired by the friendship and tutelage of Oscar Hammerstein, who lived nearby in Pennsylvania. After graduating in music from Williams College, he won a two-year scholarship to study with the composer Milton Babbitt. Sondheim's superb early lyrics were written to other people's tunes. His first show was *West Side Story*, and he followed it with another hit, *Gypsy*. Songs like "Something's Coming" and "Everything's Coming Up Roses" gave eloquent expression to the vein of hope and attainment that musical comedy traditionally sings about. Sondheim himself has said, "I believe *Gypsy* is one of the two or three best musicals ever written. The last good one in the Rodgers and Hammerstein tradition."

"Anybody can rhyme 'excelsior' and 'Chelsea or'," Sondheim has said. "I'd rather have an ear-catching thought than an eye-catching rhyme." Since *Company* (1970), he has tried to bring the musical up to date with the disenchanted times. His deepest lyric impulse is not love but anger, and his most memorable songs celebrate

CONTINUED ON PAGE 278

Once a reluctant student at the Royal Academy of Dramatic Art, **Harold Pinter** (*above*) later transformed English theatre

Stephen Sondheim (*above*) accompanies Leonard Bernstein, rehearsing the chorus for the original *West Side Story*

Oleg Popov's clowning (*below*) is enhanced by his partner Oleg Jr., who disrupts his master's attempts at magic and juggling

On painting the face

Under first-class modern theatre lights, an actor may need no make-up. Under the primitive gas or wax lighting of times now gone, he needed a great deal – though most of it was, by present standards, crude. (The word "ham" – used to describe an actor thought to be exceeding his histrionic brief – harks back to an overuse of ham fat and brick dust, the basic make-up which once was used.) Grease-paint is the traditional make-up, though modern products are often water-soluble.

The job overleaf was to transform a young male face into that of the villainous Fagin from Lionel BART's *Oliver!* As in every kind of make-up, a foundation or "base" is the first requisite. Here it is not the usual healthy flesh-tint, but a sallow olive overlaid with a tired grey. Lines and shadows to age the face and neck are added with pencil, brush and fingertips, forming and exaggerating shadows in the incipient hollows of the young actor's face. The bony and protruding parts of his face are likewise highlighted with a white paint. Note particularly the effect at the bridge of the nose, and upon the neck sinews.

The next stage shows the addition of a basic "Fagin" nose. While applying the earlier base and lining, the actor will already have begun to "think himself" into the part, making the grimaces and facial gestures that his character will portray, and shading and highlighting appropriately. Now a suitable nose is built up with nose putty, a traditional method that has been largely superseded by the more speedy premodelled plastic features. The putty is difficult to apply – patience and spoon-handles are both necessary. The extra effort is worth it for both the finished result, and the confidence it gives (a putty nose is less likely to fall off if knocked against the scenery).

In the third stage illustrated, the nose has been skilfully blended in with its surroundings. The beard is also under construction. As with the nose, some players use premade features; the work of mocking-up whiskers is becoming obsolete, though it remains the best. Teased-out hanks of wool are built up from the back upon a layer of tacky spirit gum. The finished beard and moustache in the next picture enhance the effect. The personality of the character he is to play is also in the actor's mind; thus the eyelids too are treated, for he wants them heavy and hawk-like.

By the last stage the wig has been added. It is made of real hair (the best comes from the convents of northern Italy). When the wig is mounted, some of the side-pieces are stuck to the side of the actor's face, to keep it in place.

The underlip is further exaggerated to reveal the character, and the eyelids highlighted to hood as evilly as possible. Red lining within them and upon the lips is done last; these are things – like blacked-out teeth – that come off all too readily. The whole make-up takes about two hours to apply; traditionally (and properly) it is done by the actor himself.

this rage: "I'm Still Here", "The Ladies Who Lunch", and "Could I Leave You". With the exception of "Send in the Clowns" from *A Little Night Music*, Sondheim's love songs are surprisingly ordinary. His memorable love lyrics are written in collaboration with other composers who have a melodic grace that Sondheim's music lacks such as Bernstein ("Maria", "Somewhere"), Styne ("Small World," "You'll Never Get Away From Me") and Rodgers ("Do I Hear A Waltz?").

Sondheim's musicals continue to challenge the shape and content of the form. "You must go on breaking down old musical forms and creating new ones, otherwise there's nothing but repetition."

DOROTHY TUTIN (1930…)

English actress. Depressed by her performance in a 1952 production of *Much Ado About Nothing*, Tutin was on the verge of giving up acting when the role of Rose in GRAHAM GREENE's *The Living Room* tempted her to continue. By the end of the run she was a star, ready to tackle such diverse women as Sally Bowles in *I Am A Camera* and Joan of Arc in ANOUILH's *The Lark*. She has performed memorably with the Royal Shakespeare Company as Juliet, Portia and the hunchbacked Sister Jeanne in John WHITING's *The Devils*.

As leading lady of the National Theatre, Tutin still admits to a lack of confidence, a weakness that was not apparent in her icily majestic Lady Macbeth of 1978.

DOUGLAS TURNER WARD (1930…)

American playwright, director and actor. In 1966 Douglas Turner Ward warned of the sterility of "theatre for whites only", and in 1967 he became artistic director of the newly formed Negro Ensemble Company. His one-act satires *Happy Ending* and *Day of Absence* (1965) were well known; for the company he wrote such plays as *Brotherhood* (1970). But his contributions as director and actor have been just as important, injecting new life into American theatre with such sensitive productions as Joseph A. Walker's *The River Niger* and his own *The Reckoning* (1969).

ANNE BANCROFT (1931…)

American actress. As a baby in New York, Anne Bancroft was an incorrigible sidewalk entertainer, but she only appeared on a Broadway stage after seven years in Hollywood. In 1958, weary of hack movies, she won the lead in William Gibson's *Two for the Seesaw*. Her performance as a carefree Greenwich Village Bohemian enchanted the critics, and the next year she confirmed her star status in a very different play, Gibson's *The Miracle Worker*, portraying Annie Sullivan, teacher of the blind, deaf-mute Helen Keller. She has since divided her time between New York and Hollywood (where her husband Mel Brooks involved her in his chaotic *Silent Movie*).

ROLF HOCHHUTH (1931…)

German playwright. Critics may now belittle Hochhuth's virtues as a dramatist, but the controversy aroused by his re-examination of recent history continues to this day. *Der Stellvertreter* (1963, known in English either as *The Deputy* or *The Representative*) took as its target Pope Pius XII's failure to condemn Nazi atrocities against the Jews. Erwin PISCATOR, the grand old man of German documentary theatre, who produced the play, saw it as "one of the few really significant attempts to come to terms with the past".

The subject of *Soldaten* (1967), Hochhuth's second denunciation of a world leader, was Winston Churchill. The play centres around Churchill's assent to the saturation bombing of German cities and his supposed connivance in the air crash that killed the Polish Prime Minister.

Both these "documentary" works contained invented episodes and characters. Hochhuth's next piece entered the world of fantasy. *Guerillas* (1970) concerns a plot by a US senator to take over the country and introduce socialist reforms.

JAMES EARL JONES (1931…)

American actor. As a schoolboy, Jones cured a paralysing stammer by forcing himself to participate in debate and public speaking. In college he compensated for feeling "big, ugly and shy" by acting in plays. Through such self-therapy he found his profession, making his New York stage debut in 1957. His balletic performance in Jean GENET's *The Blacks* brought him critical recognition, but his 1967 portrayal of boxer Jack Johnson in *The Great White Hope* made him a box-office star. Despite lucrative success in films, Jones has remained true to the stage, winning particular acclaim in SHAKESPEARE, and in 1977 playing an unpaid workshop season as Oedipus.

MIKE NICHOLS (1931…)

American director and actor. When he met Elaine MAY in Chicago, Mike Nichols thought her "extremely rude, a very dark Bohemian girl in a trench coat". By contrast, he was polished and blond, but their common talent for witty improvisations on contemporary society made them ideal comic partners. In nightclubs and theatres they became famous for their sketches on all aspects of American life from adultery to motherhood. Their most remarkable feat was concocting skits on the spot from opening and closing lines supplied by the audience. The partnership ended in 1962, primarily because Nichols wanted to concentrate on directing. His spectacular success with Neil SIMON's *Barefoot in the Park* was the first of a long series of stage hits and awards, and such slick film triumphs as *The Graduate*. But Nichols and May fans will continue to recall the great days, and especially such Nichols characters as "Alabama Gross", the Southern writer curiously reminiscent of TENNESSEE WILLIAMS, whose latest ravaged heroine has fallen victim to "drink, prostitution and puttin' on airs".

ROGER PLANCHON (1931…)

French playwright, actor, director and manager. Planchon's work at Villeurbanne, a working-class industrial suburb of Lyon, has earned him an international reputation. He became director of the theatre there in 1957 and, with his company of friends, went out in search of an audience, talking to the local residents until they came to regard the theatre as their own. Productions have included MARLOWE's *Edward II*, ALEXANDRE DUMAS *père*'s *Les Trois Mousquetaires*, a perennial favourite, MOLIÈRE's *Tartuffe* (one of Planchon's finest parts) and modern works like Arthur ADAMOV's *Paolo Paoli*.

La Remise (1962) was Planchon's first play. He has gradually devoted more of his time to writing. *L'Infame* (1969), in which a priest murders a girl he has impregnated and then cuts her open to baptise the child, shows a strange preoccupation with belief, as does *Le Cochon noir* (1974). Planchon has directed all his plays, including *Gilles de Rais* (1976). In 1972 the Théâtre National Populaire was moved from Paris to Villeurbanne and he was made its director.

Cabaret III: America

For Americans at least, one man's cabaret is another man's poison. The tourist in Las Vegas expects glamour and girls, a "name" singer (a real pro like Sammy Davis Jr. if he's lucky) and an atmosphere of superficial informality. He would be repelled to find instead a dim and crowded room, where through the dubious smoke a bearded little man is telling him scatological but pointed jokes about the human condition: such was the work of Lenny BRUCE.

Both these entertainments are called cabaret in America, but while the first is slick showbiz trying to let its hair down, only the second is close in spirit to the cynical cabaret of Montmartre in the 1880s or the fierce political cabaret of Berlin in the 1920s. Frank Sinatra and Tom Jones may become "cabaret artists" when they weave noisily among the tables of hotel banqueting rooms, but the setting is irrelevant.

Cabaret as social protest first emerged in America in the early 1950s, a time when "the silent majority" was trying its best to ensure that the minority remained silent too. In reaction to President Eisenhower's reign of smug conformity, and the repressive crusade of Senator McCarthy, young people took to outraging their parents by going arty, hairy and dirty. Beatniks never exactly penetrated the heart of middle America, but they

did create an alternative entertainment, of which the first undisputed leader was a comic called Mort SAHL. Although Sahl had become quite acceptable (if still irreverent) by the 1960s, in the early days he joked about America in a way that turned the apple pie to ashes in Mom's mouth.

Sex, religion, politics and race, formerly taboo subjects for successful comedians, became the obvious targets for the entertainers of the new counter-culture. MIKE NICHOLS and Elaine MAY lampooned adultery and attacked racism. Lord Buckley introduced nervous audiences to "The Naz" in a lyrical and strangely devout monologue about Jesus of Nazareth. Dick Gregory described how the police brought black men to justice – by firing a warning shot in the leg.

But the man who shocked even the most partisan audiences was Lenny Bruce. Dragging his own insecurities out into the open, he imposed an unbearable burden of self-analysis on the public. It was only after his early death in 1966 that people could fully cope with the violence of his material:

"Now there's a curtain line for great Jewish theatre ... The old Jewish couple, there they are, they open up the *Muzuzah*, and the old guy goes:
'*Gevult*, they stashed a joint.'
Boom! Curtain."

Cabaret at "Caesar's Palace", Las Vegas, means an expensive dinner with the show. The mellow atmosphere makes up for the lack of intimacy

Short, tall, chubby or thin, with frizzy wigs or funny hats, Clowns come in all shapes and sizes and in more colours than you can imagine. This merry crew (*left*) is American, but the clown's jolly diversity is an international trademark

In the RAF, **Arnold Wesker** felt "politically a marked man". His Jewish, Communist, working-class background exposed him to constant prejudice. In *Chips with Everything* (*right*) his bitter experiences became potent, compassionate drama

Delphine Seyrig's warmth and intelligence make even unlikely dramatic situations unbelievable. In Georges Schéhadé's *Histoire de Vasco* (*far right*) she responds sympathetically to a quizzical shaggy dog

FERNANDO ARRABAL (1932…)

French playwright. Arrabal left his native Spain for France when his father was imprisoned by the fascist régime. His plays, written in a French that is violent and aggressive, combine elements of extreme brutality, comedy and the absurd. *Pique-nique en campagne* (1959) is a satire condemining militarism. In *Le Cimetière des voitures*, Emanov, a Christ-figure, tries to spread kindness in his shanty town of car skeletons, but is crucified on a bicycle and put to death. Childlike, he is typical of many Arrabal characters who are unable to cope with the modern world.

Arrabal's later *Théâtre Panique* is strongly surrealistic. In the short sketch *La Communiante* (1966) a girl is being dressed for her first communion while a necrophiliac pursues a coffin on and off the stage, finally jumping in to rape the cadaver; the young girl returns and plunges a knife into the coffin. Two men are stranded on an island in *L'Architecte et l'empereur d'Assyrie* (1967). They act out roles until one kills and eats the other, only for their identities to be reversed and the action to resume. Arrabal's most recent collection, *Théâtre Bouffe*, contains such plays as the satirical comedy *Vole-moi un petit milliard*. His stimulating, surprising and often shocking work is pervaded throughout by a keen intelligence and a perverse wit. It is these qualities, together with some fine *coups de théâtre*, that keep Arrabal's work in demand in many countries and on both sides of the Atlantic.

ATHOL FUGARD (1932…)

South African playwright, director and actor. Fugard's first play, *No-Good Friday* (1956), was inspired by his experience as clerk in a South African court, where "we sent an African to jail once every two minutes". But he regards racial hatred as just one kind of human alienation, a particularly compelling example of the general need for sympathy. One of the half-brothers in *The Blood Knot* (1960) is coloured, the other white. The play demonstrates not just the iniquities of apartheid but the brothers' obligation to accept each other. *Boesman and Lena* (1969) are coloured wanderers, but their rootlessness, though thrust on them by government action, is a metaphor for everyman's basic state. More recently, Fugard's work with a native theatre group, the Serpent Players, has produced two one-act plays, *Sizwe Bansi is Dead* and *The Island* (1972). Devised in collaboration with two black actors, John Kani and Winston Ntshona, they too illustrate Fugard's central thesis: "If you tell the human story, the propaganda will take care of itself."

SEAN KENNY (1932-73)

Irish stage designer. The architectural quality of Kenny's sets delighted London producers and audiences in the 1960s. The explanation for this was simple: Sean Kenny was an architect. He studied in Dublin, and then under Frank Lloyd Wright in America. The most memorable of thirty-two West End productions he designed were for expensive musicals such as *Oliver!* (the most successful of them). Yet Kenny was a restless person, fond of innovation, perhaps for its own sake. He said of traditional theatre design: "The only thing to do is to go down to the basement and, with a bloody great bomb, blow the lot sky high, COWARD, RATTIGAN and all."

ELAINE MAY (1932…)

American actress, director and playwright. In a typically mordant MIKE NICHOLS/Elaine May sketch, Miss May played a wheedling, suffocating mom trying to coerce her adult son into needing her. Under the pressure of her misery he moans, "I feel awful," and she fervently replies, "Honey, if I could believe that I'd be the happiest mother in the world." Ridiculing such American types made Nichols and May the brightest comedy team of the late 1950s. The daughter of an itinerant Yiddish actor, Miss May met her partner in an improvisatory theatre group in Chicago. Their success lasted from 1957 until 1962, when they disbanded to pursue individual careers. Miss May turned her acute comic talents to writing and directing plays like the one-act *Adaptation* (1969).

DELPHINE SEYRIG (1932…)

French actress. A graceful and persuasive exponent of such varied authors as CHEKHOV, PIRANDELLO and PINTER,

Seyrig owes much of her versatility to her cosmopolitan background. She was born in Beirut and studied with French and Russian teachers before joining Lee STRASBERG's Actors' Studio in New York. Like many graduates of this Method academy, she excels at conveying a meaning in the smallest gesture, inventing a whole life-history for a character before she feels ready to perform even the briefest scene. She is popularly known for her pensive film roles, but her stage career reveals an impressive range of style and mood. This variety was triumphantly displayed in Fernando ARRABAL's *Le Jardin des délices*, a tour-de-force which required her to remain on stage for the duration of the play.

ARNOLD WESKER (1932...)

English playwright. Wesker's socialism has been a continual inspiration both for his writing and for wider activities in the theatre. A job as a pastrycook provided the material for his first naturalistic play, *The Kitchen*, written in 1957. Autobiography also played a large part in the "Wesker trilogy", *Chicken Soup with Barley* (1958), *Roots* (1959) and *I'm Talking About Jerusalem* (1960) that marked him as one of England's most original dramatic voices. These three plays follow the Kahn family and its political thinking over twenty years.

Chips with Everything (1962), his only success in the commercial theatre, explored class consciousness in the RAF, drawn from the author's personal experience.

Wesker was arrested at a nuclear disarmament rally and imprisoned for a month in 1961, the same year that he formed the trade-union-backed Centre 42, an organization dedicated to popularizing the theatre. Its success, however, was limited, and in 1971 it was dissolved. *Their Very Own and Golden City* (1965) can be seen as an expression of Wesker's disillusionment with trade union commitment to socialist ideals. Recent plays have included *The Friends* (1970), *The Old Ones* (1972) and *The Wedding Feast* (1974).

MICHAEL FRAYN (1933...)

English playwright, novelist and journalist. Frayn is one of the most versatile of English satirists. As a columnist for *The Guardian* and later *The Observer* from 1959 to 1968, he became the voice of the self-conscious liberal, and his plays are on their way to becoming required viewing for the same audience. Since 1970 he has written six stage works, including the successful comedies *Alphabetical Order* (1975), *Donkey's Years* (1975), *Clouds* (1976) and *Liberty Hall* (1980). A student of Russian, for the National Theatre he has translated *The Cherry Orchard* and LEO TOLSTOY's *The Fruits of Enlightenment*.

JERZY GROTOWSKI (1933...)

Polish director. In the provincial city of Opole in 1959, Grotowski established his Laboratory Theatre, one of the most radical theatrical experiments of all time. Stripping his actors of costumes and make-up, his stage of scenery and his audiences of all the reassuring illusions of traditional productions, he strove to create a mystical experience between the "holy actor" and the public – what he (confusingly) called a "poor theatre". When his troupe toured Europe and America in 1969 they dazzled critics and directors with their discipline and athleticism. "No one since STANISLAVSKY has investigated the nature of acting . . . as deeply and completely as Grotowski," said Peter BROOK. Audiences (generally kept to less than fifty) were surprised to discover themselves part of the production. In an adaptation of MARLOWE's *Dr Faustus* they joined the actors at long wooden tables, reminiscent of the Last Supper; in *The Constant Prince* (after CALDERÓN) they peered into a wooden pit; in *Kordian*, a Polish play, they sat on hospital beds – patients in a mental hospital.

In his own country Grotowski's theatre does not attract the same adulation. "It is naive, childish, inconsistent, amateurish," said the director of the National Theatre of Poland.

JOE ORTON (1933-67)

English playwright. Orton was the first modern playwright to translate the clown's rambunctious instincts from the stage to the page. A natural anarch, he was born in Leicester and did badly at school. He won an acting scholarship to RADA, however, and while there met his lifetime friend and mentor Kenneth Halliwell, who was seven years older. Failing as actors, they decided to write. For a decade they wrote novels together until, caught defacing public library books, both were sentenced to six months in prison. When Orton emerged in 1962, his writing and his personality had changed. "I tried writing before I went into the nick but it was no good. Being in the nick brought detachment to my writing. I wasn't involved any more and suddenly it worked." Between 1963 and 1967, when he was bludgeoned to death by Halliwell, who then took his own life, Orton became a playwright of international reputation. His *oeuvre* was small but his impact large. By 1967, the term "Ortonesque" had worked its way into the English vocabulary, a shorthand adjective for macabre outrageousness. He wrote three first-class full-length plays: *Entertaining Mr Sloane* (1964), *Loot* (1966) and his posthumously produced farcical master-piece *What the Butler Saw* (1969). He also wrote four one-act plays: *The Ruffian on the Stair, A Good and Faithful Servant, The Erpingham Camp* and *Funeral Games*, which was never produced. Two films were made of his plays, and *Loot* was voted the *Evening Standard*'s Best Play of 1966.

Orton's plays often scandalized audiences, but his wit made the outrage scintillating. Orton brought the epigram back to the contemporary stage to illuminate a violent world. "It's life that defeats the Christian Church, she's always been well equipped to deal with death" (*The Erpingham Camp*). "All classes are criminal today. We live in an age of equality" (*Funeral Games*). Orton's laughter created a panic both figuratively and literally. His stage gargoyles tried to frighten their audience into new life. "One must shake the audience out of its expectations," Orton said. "They need not so much shocking, as *surprising* out of their rut." He accomplished this by reinventing boulevard farce, making it face serious issues. And by writing, line for line, the funniest dialogue on the English stage since Oscar WILDE.

DAVID STOREY (1933...)

English playwright and novelist. Storey loathed the Yorkshire mining society of his boyhood and the punishing life of a professional rugby player. But his best work is nourished by the adversities of his youth. *This Sporting Life*, his first novel, is a bitter reaction to the early days. *The Restoration of Arnold Middleton* (1966) and *In Celebration* (1969), his first two plays, present unhappy and alienated characters desperately trying to keep their heads above water. *Home* (1970) withdraws to a mental institution, where four old people strive to gather about them the illusions of sanity. *The Contractor* (1969) and *The Changing Room* (1971) consider group survival, the latter returning to professional rugby for its central image. Storey sees life as hard; he describes the survival of his characters as "a flower growing in a bed of concrete".

ALAN ARKIN (1934...)

American actor. Arkin saw his first movie at five and immediately became a "film junkie", craving the Hollywood stardom he later achieved in such pictures as *Catch 22*. But he gained initial public notice on Broadway with a 1961 revue by the Second City improvisatory theatre group, and by a show-stealing part in the farce *Enter Laughing*. Then in 1964 critics and audiences cheered his inspired performance as Harry Berlin, the woebegone neurotic of Murray SCHISGAL's *Luv*. Director MIKE NICHOLS called him "the best actor in America", and Hollywood was within easy reach. His first film, *The Russians are Coming, The Russians are Coming*, was in 1966.

ALAN BATES (1934...)

English actor. Bates has attracted unusually mixed notices. He was allegedly a lifeless Richard III and, as Petruchio, made heavy weather of taming SHAKESPEARE's Shrew; but he was complimented on his surly understanding of Harold PINTER, while his Hamlet seemed surprisingly likely to "drink hot blood". Bates's emotional subtlety has been especially effective in the plays, including *Butley* and *Otherwise Engaged*, written for him by his friend Simon GRAY. He has quietly become a star for his work in such films as *Women in Love* and *The Go-Between*.

ALAN BENNETT (1934...)

English playwright and actor. Bennett co-wrote and performed in the hugely successful satirical revue *Beyond the Fringe*, appearing most memorably as a benign parson, who preaches a sermon on the text "My brother Esau is a hairy man".

His first play, *Forty Years On* (1968), was a humorous look at England's culture and traditions set in a public school, full of verbal games and sometimes successful parodies: "All women dress like their mothers, that is their tragedy. No man ever does. That is his." *The Old Country* (1977) also comments on the English; this time their incurable irony. *Getting On* (1971) is a painful comedy of approaching middle age and *Habeas Corpus* (1973) a farce on the coming of the permissive society to the staid seaside town of Hove. Bennett has written a number of more realistic television plays.

BARRY HUMPHRIES (1934...)

Australian comedian. Dame Edna Everage is a middle-class Australian housewife, who has become a superstar without losing any of her naive charm or embarrassing bad taste. She is also Barry Humphries, author, actor and elegant satirist, mocking his audience with a caricature that is both grotesque and perfectly truthful. Dame Edna, in a permed wig and loud two-piece dress, chats confidingly about her daughter Valmai (with the alcohol problem) or son Kenny (an *art deco* buff who has opened an antique shop called "Dead People's Gear"). Suddenly she will pounce: "Got a little discharge, have you?" to a woman weeping with laughter.

Success puzzles Dame Edna. "My show is designed to appeal to expatriate Australian housewives *only*," she protests. This is a crafty definition that few of her sophisticated English admirers would care to accept.

LEROI JONES (1934...)

American playwright. Jones is one of the most important figures in American Black literature. Essayist (*Home*), historian (*Blues People*), poet and novelist, Jones became an angry and articulate playwright in *The Toilet* (1964). He followed it that same year with *The Slave* and *Dutchman* (later made into a film). Jones's increasing militancy compelled him to give up his slave name and take the name Imamu Amiri Baraka. Under it, he wrote *Slaveship* (1969), a raging history lesson which was nothing less than a call for blacks to rise up against whites. Separating himself from white society and commercial theatre, Baraka continued to write plays to slidify the political goals for blacks. "This is a theatre of assault . . ." he has written. "The play that will split the heavens for us will be called *The Destruction of America*. The heroes will be Crazy Horse, Denmark Vesey, Patrice Lumumba . . . and their enemies most of you who are reading this." In 1980, he reassumed the name LeRoi Jones.

JONATHAN MILLER (1934...)

English director, writer and doctor. Miller earned extra money entertaining at debutantes' balls while studying to qualify as a doctor. In 1960, with Peter Cook, Dudley Moore and Alan BENNETT, he created the immensely popular satitical revue *Beyond the Fringe*, which enjoyed over a year's run in London and eighteen months in New York. He has since combined medical research with directing, becoming known for his stimulating (if not invariably successful) production of plays and operas. In 1968 he set *The Rivals* by SHERIDAN in an uncharacteristically squalid eighteenth century, and his 1970 production of *The Tempest* was a comment on colonialism. Miller's work for television includes a Freudian *Alice in Wonderland*, a slightly macabre series on the human body, and some chilling ghost stories.

MAGGIE SMITH (1934...)

English actress. Maggie Smith is one of the funniest serious actresses on the stage today. She first came to London with a small revue group and was spotted by Leonard Sillman, an American producer, who used her in his New York revue *New Faces of 1956*. Returning to London, she starred in Bamber Gascoigne's revue *Share My Lettuce* (1957), and in 1959 spent a year with the Old Vic Company. Proving that she could make a weak play good and the dullest line funny, in 1963 she won a Variety Club Award for her performance in Jean Kerr's *Mary, Mary*. In fact she tells that Edith EVANS once advised her, "My dear, if you don't understand it, just make it sound filthy." This she can do as well as any actress in the business, her husky voice inviting a cornucopia of interpretations.

She spent seven years with the National Theatre Company from 1963, playing Desdemona to Laurence OLIVIER's Othello, and repeating the role on film. As Amanda in a revival of Noel COWARD's *Private Lives* in 1972–3, she was an enormous success. Since 1976 Maggie Smith has acted in Canada at the Stratford Ontario Shakespeare Festival in such roles as Rosalind in *As You Like It* and Lady Macbeth, while in Tom STOPPARD's *Night and Day* in the West End she found a role ideally suited to her. She has also made several films, including the Oscar-winning *The Prime of Miss Jean Brodie*.

WOLE SOYINKA (1934...)

Nigerian playwright. Soyinka is both an honours graduate of the University of Leeds and a Yoruba; a European man of letters and a tribal African, imbued with the rhythms and myths of his people. His plays, which include *The Lion and the Jewel* (1959), *The Trials of Brother Jero* (1961), *The Strong Breed* (1964) and *Madmen and Specialists* (1971), unite song, dance and a lyrical English that owes as much to the Irish playwright J. M. SYNGE as to West Africa. His themes, understandably, are the agonized transition of Africa and the misuse of history by false prophets. For his efforts to negotiate a peace during the Nigerian Civil War, he was imprisoned in 1967 for two years. Since his release he has returned to academic life and the theatre in Nigeria, resuming his role as one of Black Africa's most eloquent spokesmen.

BIBI ANDERSSON (1935...)

Swedish actress. Bibi Andersson was long a symbol of blonde purity and freshness, an image that was only dispelled in the English-speaking world by her complex role as the nurse in BERGMAN's *Persona*. For theatre audiences in Uppsala, Malmö and Stockholm, however, she escaped such stereotyping. She has been a whore in GENET's *Le Balcon*, Irina in *Three Sisters*, the vomiting Honey in *Who's Afraid of Virginia Woolf?* and Maggie (Marilyn Monroe) in ARTHUR MILLER's *After the Fall*. In 1973 she first appeared on stage in America. *Full Circle* was a flop on Broadway, but Andersson persuaded Clive Barnes that she was "a superlative actress". Since then, in both films and the theatre, her career has become increasingly international.

EDWARD BOND (1935...)

English playwright. In *Saved* (1965), Bond's second play, a group of young toughs stone a baby to death in its pram. Five babies are murdered in the oriental fable *Narrow Road to the Deep North* (1968). Some saw the violence as cathartic; many saw it as gratuitous and disgusting; the Lord Chamberlain wanted no one to see it at all and banned both works, plus the historical fantasy *Early Morning* (1968), thereby gaining the playwright a host of allies. "Experience is depressing," argued Bond and reworked SHAKESPEARE to create a *Lear* (1971) in which his transformed and villainous Cordelia abuses power more shamefully than her father ever had. In *Bingo* (1971) he attacked Shakespeare himself, retired and miserable in Stratford. Recent plays such as *The Woman*, produced by the National Theatre in 1978, indicate that Bond is increasingly acceptable but still unrepentant.

ED BULLINS (1935...)

American playwright. Raised in the Philadelphia backstreets among hoodlums and bootleggers, Bullins began to write plays in California in the early sixties (producing them himself when no one else would). From 1967 to 1973 he was associate director of the New Lafayette Theatre, Harlem, where most of his plays have been staged. Committed to community theatre, he writes for blacks about blacks. Their urban ghetto existence, their relationships, their hopes and frustrations are portrayed with sympathetic realism, evincing power without sentimentality, and using music, song and dance. His ambitious Twentieth-Century cycle is to consist of twenty plays. Five have already appeared, among them *In the Wine Time* (1968), *The Duplex* (1970) and *Home Boy* (1976). According to Bullins, "In the area of playwriting, Ed Bullins, at this moment in time, is almost without peer in America – black, white or imported." Many would agree.

JOSEPH CHAIKIN (1935...)

American director and actor. In *The Serpent*, five writhing actors interpreted the title role; for *Terminal*, members of the cast studied embalming, and even went to a criminal court to see "a real judgement situation". Developing a new theatre language of sounds and gestures, Chaikin's Open Theatre (founded 1963) was one of America's most exciting experimental groups. Improvising from scenarios suggested by such writers as Sam SHEPARD and Jean-Claude VAN ITALLIE (but relying as much upon mime and abstract sound as words) Chaikin and company disbanded in 1973, alarmed that success might lead to complacency. But he has not been inactive since then, continuing to direct and act in the United States. A particularly outstanding performance was the lead in BÜCHNER's *Woyzeck* in 1976.

JOHN MCGRATH (1935...)

English playwright and director. McGrath's discovery by critic Kenneth Tynan while still at Oxford led to a

CONTINUED ON PAGE 286

Inside the modern theatre

There are two schools of thought in modern theatre design: that of preserving older forms but improving them with new technology – and that of breaking with convention altogether. This diagram of the Yvonne Arnaud Theatre in Guildford, England (opened in 1965) shows the former. There is some compromise with modern ideas: with the cover over the orchestra pit, the design attempts to make the theatre flexible enough for the thrust-stage style of production as well as conventional shows, musicals and operas.

Otherwise there is little difference between this and a Victorian theatre – save in the technical innovation. On the right-hand side of the picture (known as the prompt side or *stage left*) is the prompt desk. From here the stage manager cues the electricians seated in a lighting box at the back of the theatre. This is done by means of a series of light cues (red for stand-by, green for go, etc.) and is accompanied by spoken instructions over a microphone system. Nowadays the whole lighting plan can be pre-recorded on to a memory tape, and the electrician's job is simply to push buttons all night. But such machines can break down; and "Sparks" (as the electrician hates to be called) then switches to manual override and works the show himself. Such occasions are not uncommon.

The stage manager also gives the actors their calls from the prompt desk. Dressing rooms are fixed with a Tannoy system that can relay the dialogue spoken on stage; the stage manager cuts into this to call members of the cast required to go to the wings.

Two revolving stages are also illustrated.

Revolves are often used in musicals where quick-changing spectacle can be the essence of the show, but more and more modern plays (influenced by the cut-away techniques of film and television) now require these noisy and cumbersome devices. Silent revolves *are* possible, but they require such expensive electrical equipment that most theatres are compelled to use the hand-winched devices shown in the diagram.

Fixed scenery, such as the double doors at the back of the set (4), is moved manually by stage hands. Flown scenery (5) is operated by hemp sets or by counterweights. Hemp sets can drop a piece of scenery anywhere, but they need at least two stage hands on every line, and such labour is costly. (Stage hands may sometimes earn much more than the actors.) Counterweights can be operated by one man on each line, but are limited by being fixed to a particular place. Cues to stage hands, in the days before electricity, were whistled by the stage manager: it is hence considered unlucky for anyone to whistle inside a theatre.

Many modern designers express dissatisfaction with conventional theatre structure. To them the stalls, circle and gallery represent the hierarchy of an obsolete society, and they feel the structure should represent contemporary forms of social organization. The trouble with this philosophy is that an adequate substitute has not yet been invented to replace it. Conventional techniques are not simple to make obsolete, for they embrace the sum total of knowledge about how to build theatres.

1 Orchestra pit
2 Prompt desk
3 Revolving stages
4 Fixed scenery
5 Flown scenery
6 Hemp sets
7 Counterweight sets
8 Safety curtain

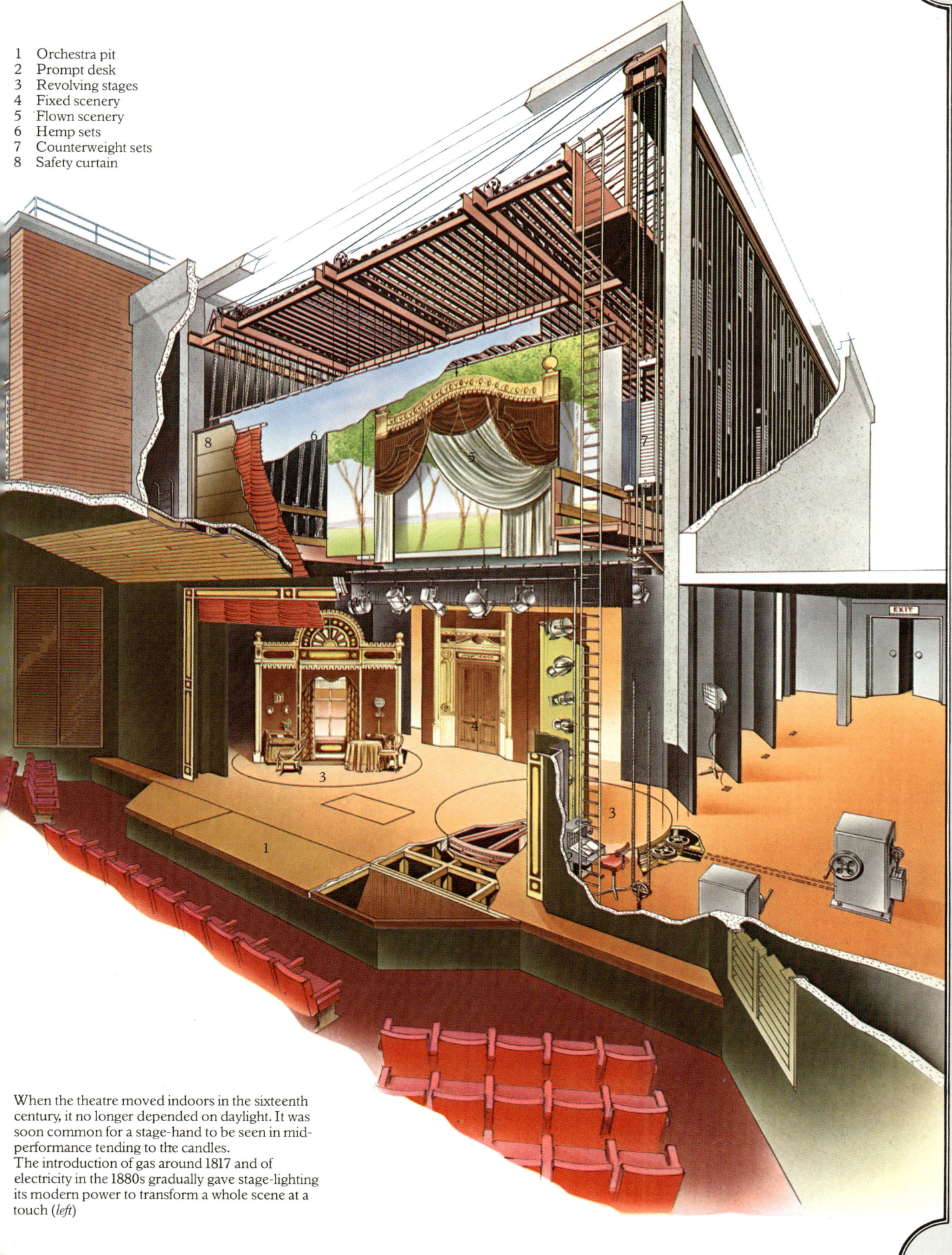

When the theatre moved indoors in the sixteenth century, it no longer depended on daylight. It was soon common for a stage-hand to be seen in mid-performance tending to the candles.
The introduction of gas around 1817 and of electricity in the 1880s gradually gave stage-lighting its modern power to transform a whole scene at a touch (*left*)

London production of *Why the Chicken* (1959), but attempts to render the work "acceptable" for West End audiences badly mangled the show. Despairing of the "pressure and evil that surrounds the whole business", McGrath retreated into film and television work.

He returned to the stage with *Events while guarding the Bofors Gun* (1966), and in 1971 he used his earnings to found the 7:84 Theatre Company (named after the claim that 7 per cent of the population possesses 84 per cent of its wealth.

ALBERT FINNEY (1936...)

English actor. Finney, the son of a Lancashire bookmaker, has been unfairly categorized as the "prototype of the prole next door". He began his career in repertory, coming to the notice of Charles Laughton for a "bloody terrible" Macbeth. Graduating to Stratford-upon-Avon, Finney took over the role of Coriolanus from Laurence OLIVIER and proved that he could rage just as well as the older actor. In 1960 he won popular fame in the exhausting comic role of Billy Liar and the following year confirmed his range with a monumental interpretation of John OSBORNE's *Luther*. Since then, this powerful and aggressive performer has confirmed his eminence in naturalistic performances ranging from Samuel BECKETT to Christopher MARLOWE. In 1975, he won both fame and notoriety for an "engaging, sexy, mischievous, witty and merciless" Hamlet at London's National Theatre.

SIMON GRAY (1936...)

English playwright. *Wise Child* (1967), a comedy typifying Gray's output, illustrates the tyranny of role-playing over reality. Alec GUINNESS, its original star, has irreverently likened it to *Charley's Aunt*: the hero is a fleeing criminal dressed as a respectable lady, in which guise he induces a shapely maid to disrobe. Gray is also a lecturer, an activity plainly reflected in later works – notably *Butley* (1971) and *Otherwise Engaged* (1975) – which tend to portray disaffected intellectuals. His verbal and psychological finesse creates characters of unusual complexity, whose problems are attractively illuminated by their heterosexual and homosexual appetites. Gray's manner, both risqué and erudite, has thus proven ideal for the commercial West End, at the cost of alienating some former critical supporters.

VÁCLAV HAVEL (1936...)

Czech playwright. Havel's satires *The Garden Party* (1963) and *The Memorandum* (1965) depict the grotesque and dehumanizing results of conformity in faceless bureaucracy. *The Increased Difficulty of Concentration* (1968) portrays a man who seeks in sexual experience the fulfilment he otherwise lacks, only to find mere ejaculation no substitute for orgasm, and that every new liaison boringly replicates the details of his marriage.

Havel's participation in the short-lived "Prague Spring" led in 1968 to the banning of his work. In a macabre confirmation of the absurdity which he himself had satirized, the authorities built an observation-post at the bottom of his garden, censored his mail and cut off his telephone, while he had to seek official permission to walk his dog. He has since incurred even further displeasure, and was imprisoned in 1979.

GLENDA JACKSON (1936...)

English actress. "I knew there had to be something better than the bloody chemist's shop." Jackson's explanation of her change of vocation also illustrates a streak of toughness which has memorably coloured such roles as IBSEN's Hedda Gabler and John WEBSTER's Vittoria (in *The White Devil*).

She first attracted attention in an experimental venture run by Peter BROOK, with a nude impersonation of the call-girl Christine Keeler. There followed a starring role as Charlotte Corday, the demented assassin WEISS's *Marat/Sade*, while in *Hamlet* she gave a performance sufficiently virile to merit the proposal that the play be renamed *Ophelia*. Jackson's earthiness also made her, for many reviewers, more effective in CHEKHOV's *Three Sisters* than the refined Joan PLOWRIGHT, who played the same role in the same month. Increasingly active in the cinema, Jackson's stern sensuality has been caught to great advantage in films which include *Women in Love* and *Sunday, Bloody Sunday*.

JEAN-CLAUDE VAN ITALLIE (1936...)

American playwright. With mime, music, improvisation and archetypal symbolism, van Itallie savagely parodies American religion, politics, commerce, medicine and art. From 1963 to 1968 he was playwright-in-residence at Joseph CHAIKIN's Open Theatre in New York. For this company he created his two best known works: *America Hurrah!* (1966) and *The Serpent* (1968). The first contains three short plays (*Interview, TV, Motel*) which bitterly tear into the faceless violence of modern America. "Blah, blah, blah, blah – hostile. Blah, blah, blah, blah – penis," is van Itallie's *précis* of cocktail party conversation. *The Serpent* is the result of a collaboration between author and actors. Starting with the assassinations of John F. Kennedy and Martin Luther King, it seeks to discover the roots of violence (originally exemplified by the title character). Death and sin are defeated in the optimistic finale, when the cast advance singing into the audience.

Van Itallie resents the description of his plays as "nightmarish" or "unreal". "I am simply trying to be clear," he explains.

TOM COURTENAY (1937...)

English actor. Courtenay's north country accent–preserved in defiance of his drama school training–helped to establish him as a leader of the new naturalistic style of acting, along with Albert FINNEY, from whom he triumphantly inherited the title role of *Billy Liar* in 1961. Subsequent appearances have included the lecherous hero of Alan AYCKBOURN's *The Norman Conquests* (1974) and the rustic poet John Clare in Edward BOND's *The Fool* (1975). The latter role in particular confirmed Courtenay's alluring mix of romantic introspection and earthy vigour.

DUSTIN HOFFMAN (1937...)

American actor. Before his leap to movie fame in 1967, Dustin Hoffman was a connoisseur's secret on the New York stage. His Los Angeles boyhood had included junior high school stardom as Tiny Tim, an abortive attempt to become a concert pianist and acting classes at the Pasadena Playhouse. In 1958 he left California to seek his fortune in Manhattan, figuring "it would be easier to fail at that distance". A modest debut at a college theatre in 1960, a role in a Broadway flop in 1961, summer stock and repertory experience were the rewards of the first seven years in the east. Offstage, life was a cold-water apartment and menial odd jobs.

In 1965, although he was considering trying his luck

as a director, Hoffman auditioned for the Off-Broadway *Harry, Noon and Night* by Ronald Ribman, and won the leading role. His sensitive portrayal of a crippled German homosexual proclaimed his skill at playing "outsiders". He won Off-Broadway awards for similar roles in *The Journey of the Fifth Horse* and Henry LIVINGS's *Eh?*

On the strength of his stage reputation he graduated to Hollywood with MIKE NICHOLS's film *The Graduate*; the theatre has seen little of him since.

ARTHUR KOPIT (1937...)

American playwright. When Kopit was twenty-one and a senior at Harvard University, his end-of-term play, a spoof on the Theatre of the Absurd called *Oh Dad, Poor Dad, Mama's Hung You in the Closet and I'm Feelin' So Sad* (1960), was snapped up by a Broadway producer and subsequently became one of the decade's smash hits. Kopit's plays are distinguished by their strong but complicated construction and their bold approach to serious problems. He dramatized his sophisticated under-standing of the pattern of deceit in America in *Indians* (1968), a superb play which uses Buffalo Bill and a Wild West show to illustrate the contradictions between exploitation and obfuscation in American history. In *Wings* (1978), Kopit again found a brilliant metaphor for the experience of aphasia. Although he works slowly, his output is distinguished by its scope and depth. He has also written a series of short plays published under the title *The Day the Whores Came Out to Play Tennis*.

HARTMUT LANGE (1937...)

German playwright. Even as dramaturge to the Deutsches Theater, Lange had difficulty in having his work per-formed in the East. Yet after a dramatic escape to the West via Yugoslavia, he expressed remarkably little criticism of the East German authorities, continuing to pursue the same Marxist line as before. His anger was reserved for his personal bugbear, Stalin, the unlovely subject of two one-act plays performed in 1968. *Der Hundesprozess* and *Herakles*. The former is an horrific picture of a Stalinist show-trial, in which the friends of the accused are beheaded one by one and given the heads of dogs.

Lange's hatred of brutal inhumanity was then directed against the rigid Prussian sense of morality in *Die Gräfin von Rathenow* (1969), an adaptation of Heinrich von

KLEIST's famous short story "Die Marquise von O", treating the subject of passion with great sympathy.

VANESSA REDGRAVE (1937...)

English actress. Vanessa is the daughter of MICHAEL REDGRAVE and Rachel Kempson, and her acting forebears extend back a further two generations. Her 1958 West End debut (with her father) heralded a series of stage and screen triumphs ranging from a stormy Katharina in *The Taming of the Shrew* to a reinterpretation of Noel COWARD's Gilda in *Design for Living*. A statuesque and beautiful woman, she excels in "difficult" roles: Cleopatra, Nina in *The Seagull* and Ellida in *The Lady from the Sea*.

The major obstacle to a fuller stage career has been Redgrave's involvement (with her brother Corin) in revolutionary politics, which began in 1960 with the anti-nuclear campaign. This commitment has frequently attracted the interest of the press, most notably in 1975, when police raided a country house that was bought as a training centre for like-minded actors.

TOM STOPPARD (1937...)

English playwright. After kicking his heels for years as a provincial journalist, Stoppard astonished the British stage in 1966 with *Rosencrantz and Guildenstern are Dead*. This trenchant verbal fizgig concerns the two hapless courtiers in *Hamlet*, appearing in the scenes SHAKESPEARE *didn't* write for them. Refusing to flesh them out with a life they lack in the original play, Stoppard allows them to retain their anonymity and irrelevance. Indeed the problem of human inconsequence in an uncaring universe is a major theme of this comedy. Knowing they are being sent to their doom, the courtiers decide to complete their mission in the hope that death will bring a significance previously denied them. Both here and in such later works as *Jumpers* (1972), *Travesties* (1974) and *Dirty Linen* (1976), Stoppard's verbal bravura and brilliant theatricality have a life strangely independent of his apparent pessimism. Critics hostile to his popular success have accused him of concealing his moral uncertainties behind an amusing façade of linguistic sparkle, telling "one-liners" and spectacular *coups-de-théâtre*; certainly his point is more often enlivened than really illuminated by his instinctive and inimitable dramatic flair.

Spurred on perhaps by his own Czech origins, Stoppard

The title role in *Rose* (1980) by Andrew Davies gave **Glenda Jackson** (*above*) the opportunity to show a softer side to her talent

Tom Stoppard's *Jumpers* (*right*) is a murder mystery which manages to spend its energies delightfully exploring the implications of philosophy and gymnastics

Alan Ayckbourn excels at discovering the comic possibilities in everyday situations. In *Time and Time Again* (*above*) a bikini-clad girl chats with **Tom Courtenay**, unconcernedly holding one of his shoes

Janet Suzman (*below*) cradles her baby Orestes (who later will kill her) in Euripides' *Iphigenia in Aulis*. She also played Helen in this day-long English version of ten classical plays on the Trojan War, *The Greeks*

has lately become a champion of human rights in the Communist bloc; works such as *Night and Day* (1979) and *EGBDF*, though no less witty and abstruse than their precursors, suggest that freedom, in all its dimensions, is becoming a growing preoccupation, and that Stoppard is searching for an unambiguous moral stance worthy of his astonishing technique.

NURIA ESPERT (1938…)

Spanish actress and director. Spain's greatest actress, the dark and beautiful Nuria Espert, started in the theatre at the age of eleven. Her own company, formed in 1959, put on Spanish plays at first, but soon broadened their interests. It was BRECHT's *Der Gute Mensch von Sezuan* that first attracted workers and students to this popular experimental group. Espert gave one of her finest performances in GENET's *Les Bonnes* in 1969 and has also played Hamlet, as well as the lead in Garcia LORCA's *Yerma* (on a trampoline). She is now a director of the National Theatre in Madrid, where her recent production of GORKY's *Summer Folk* was an outstanding success.

JOHN GUARE (1938…)

American playwright. Guare is one of the most playful and inventive playwrights to come out of off-Broadway in the mid-sixties. His work is full of parody, songs, and farcical reversals. High spirits, outrageous images and fine comic writing set his plays apart from those of most of his contemporaries, both in their ability to please and in their satirical investigations of social problems. Among his best plays are *Muzeeka* (1967), *Cop-Out* (1968), *The House of Blue Leaves* (1970) and *Bosoms and Neglect* (1979). Guare had an international success with a rock adaptation of *The Two Gentlemen of Verona*, for which he also wrote the ear-catching songs.

DEREK JACOBI (1938…)

English actor. Struck by the young man's abilities, Laurence OLIVIER invited Jacobi to take part in the 1963 Chichester Festival. This led to an engagement with the National Theatre Company in London, where he remained until 1971, adding to his repertoire such widely differing roles as Gurion Bliss in Noel COWARD's *Hay Fever*, Touchstone in *As You Like It* and Prince Myshkin in an adaptation of DOSTOYEVSKY's *The Idiot*. In recent years Jacobi has frequently appeared with the Prospect company: in 1974 playing Rakitin in TURGENEV's *A Month in the Country*. On television he has been particularly effective as the stammering emperor in *I Claudius*, and in the dramatization of *The Pallisers*.

NICOL WILLIAMSON (1938…)

English actor. Williamson was showered with critical bouquets for his agonized solo performance as the disintegrating lawyer, Bill Maitland, in John OSBORNE's *Inadmissible Evidence* (1964). Among a bewildering variety of subsequent roles, he revealed a gift for comedy as Vladimir in *Waiting for Godot* (1964), while in 1969 he was a controversial Hamlet who "scoffs and snarls and wields the soliloquies like a switchblade". The moody energy that he generates in the theatre sometimes erupts into his private life too, and directors have learned to fear his temper. He reviles uncritical audiences and actors alike, and at curtain-time has on occasion borrowed the stage as a platform from which to air his disenchantment. These high principles did not prevent him starring in a disastrous film of GREENE's *The Human Factor*.

ALAN AYCKBOURN (1939...)

English playwright and director. From his provincial base in Scarborough, where he is artistic director of the local theatre, Ayckbourn unfailingly answers the prayers of London's commercial impresarios. He once had five plays on in the West End at the same time. His creative method, however, can cause a few nervous breakdowns. Each year he announces a new piece, but omits to write it until the very last moment. This happened even with *Bedroom Farce*, a work commissioned by the National Theatre for 1977.

Ayckbourn's extraordinary series of hits began in 1967 with *Relatively Speaking*. As in all his plays, the characters are unmemorable except as wickedly accurate types in English society. Everything is in the timing and the precision of the plot. This precision has become increasingly mathematical. *How the Other Half Loves* (1970) employs a double set with two dinner parties taking place at once, while in *The Norman Conquests* (1974) he contrives to construct three contemporaneous plays out of one series of events, each play being set in a different part of the house.

Ayckbourn is naturally compared to Neil SIMON for his unfailing commercial success. And as with his American counterpart, his works do not always travel well, faring best before the very people he so deftly mocks.

SHELAGH DELANEY (1939...)

English playwright. Bored by a Terence RATTIGAN play and sure that she could do better, Delaney wrote *A Taste of Honey* when she was only seventeen. First produced by Joan LITTLEWOOD in 1958, this sad drama told of an adolescent girl, her irresponsible mother, the black sailor by whom she becomes pregnant, and the homosexual friend who helps her. It was an extraordinary success, with long runs in London and New York and a splendid film version directed by TONY RICHARDSON. On the eve of the sixties Delaney seemed to represent yet a younger generation of young British playwrights. But *The Lion in Love* (1960) was less successful; it has proved to be her only subsequent work for the stage.

JANET SUZMAN (1939...)

South African-born actress. In 1962, the very year of her theatrical debut, Suzman was invited to join the Royal Shakespeare Company. Since then she has grown in stature and popularity with almost every major role she has assumed. Her handsome and commanding presence made her a natural choice for SHAKESPEARE's forceful heroines, particularly Rosalind, Portia, and Katharina in *The Taming of the Shrew*. Even these triumphs were eclipsed by her magnificent Cleopatra of 1972. More recently she has played Masha in CHEKHOV's *Three Sisters* and (less successfully) Hedda Gabler. One rare departure from the classical stage was to play Hester in fellow-South African Athol FUGARD's *Hello and Goodbye*.

FRANK LANGELLA (1940...)

American actor. Langella's first two Broadway roles were as a lizard and a vampire. He had previously established his ability to play human beings in André GIDE's *The Immoralist*, Gibson's *A Cry of Players* and VANBRUGH's *The Relapse*. Then in his Broadway debut in 1975 he won a Tony Award as Leslie in Edward ALBEE's *Seascape*, and recreated it again later that year in Los Angeles.

His menacing and sensual Count Dracula (1978), a role he has subsequently played on film, has established Langella as a box-office star, no less in Europe than in the United States.

TREVOR NUNN (1940...)

English director. After directing Cambridge undergraduate productions, Nunn began working professionally at the Belgrade Theatre, Coventry. In spite of a shaky start at the Royal Shakespeare Company, he soon came to prominence with a triumphant production of the then little known Jacobean play *The Revenger's Tragedy* by Cyril TOURNEUR. At home with the RSC he has directed most of SHAKESPEARE's plays – some more than once. A number of these have toured as far afield as Australia and Japan. In 1968 he was appointed the RSC Artistic Director and Administrator. Nunn pursues his ideal that "there must be serious purpose in each artistic endeavour."

AL PACINO (1940...)

American actor. After a lonely Bronx childhood and years of drifting, Pacino studied acting at the Berghof Studio, New York, and became an actor, director and comedy writer in the avant-garde Café La Mama and Living Theatre companies. Training at the Actors' Studio, he was awarded an Obie as the best actor in 1967–68 for his performance in *The Indian Wants the Bronx*.

He made his Broadway debut playing a psychotic junkie, and was subsequently typecast in his first film and again in 1971 in *The Panic in Needle Park*. It was the latter that won him the part of Michael Corleone in *The Godfather* and made him a movie star. Pacino continues to work in the theatre believing that "there are no rewards except in what you are doing".

DAVID RABE (1940...)

American playwright. Rabe was a soldier in Vietnam, an experience he has used to great effect in his dramatic criticisms of American society. In *The Basic Training of Pavlo Hummell* (1971) a young man accepts the mindless discipline of army training and dies an absurd death. The war-blinded hero of *Sticks and Bones* (1971) returns home to his complacent and morally corrupt all-American family, themselves too blind to see his disability. *Streamers* (1976) is the third play in this trilogy; between them they have collected almost every major critical award.

WOLFGANG BAUER (1941...)

Austrian playwright. In the atmosphere of permissiveness and student unrest of 1968, almost every major German city presented Bauer's *Magic Afternoon*. The effect this had was to confirm many an honest burgher's suspicion that the young were a lot of good-for-nothing, pot-smoking layabouts. The play's one act aims at total realism; much of the inarticulate dialogue could be from tape-recordings of four stoned people sitting in a room. The dramatic events, however (vicious sexual horseplay that leads to a death by stabbing), are artfully contrived.

Change (1969), about a fraud in the art world, did not represent a substantial change in mood. The same mixture of dope, sex and violence rooted it firmly to the 1960s, but Bauer's improving craftsmanship made it a more successful piece of theatre than its predecessor.

TERRY HANDS (1941...)

English director. After university and RADA, Hands co-founded the Liverpool Everyman Theatre. Here his productions attracted the attention of the Royal Shakespeare Company, who in 1966 appointed him director of their touring company, Theatre-Go-Round. In coping with limited or improvised sets, he won a reputation for directness and ingenuity, and his later work for the parent company has revealed similar strengths: fidelity to the test, and a simple – almost balletic – formalism. In 1978 his integrated version of *Henry V* and all three parts of *Henry VI* won him several awards and made the latter play seem a neglected masterpiece.

PETER HANDKE (1942...)

Austrian-born playwright. Handke's early works, like *Publikumsbeschimpfung* (1966), in which four "speakers" first flatter, then violently abuse the audience, made valid points as practical jokes, but hardly made him a playwright. Since *Kaspar* (1968), however, he has been considered the most original talent writing for the German stage. Based on the true nineteenth-century case of a sixteen-year-old boy who was found wandering the street, unable to speak, it shows how language determines what people are. For Kaspar, who already is somebody, the language he is taught proves a totally unsuitable means of expression. The results are both comic and tragic; his last words are, "I am I only by chance."

Although always concerned with the inadequacy of language, Handke has attempted something different in each new play. *Das Mündel will Vormund sein* (1969) is entirely in mime, while *Der Ritt über den Bodensee* (1971) has a cast of well-known silent film stars such as Emil Jannings. In a strange dream sequence they consistently misinterpret one another's words and gestures.

SAM SHEPARD (1943...)

American playwright. Rancher, drummer and film star (*Days of Heaven*), Sam Shepard is one of the most elusive figures of modern American drama. He has consistently shied away from the limelight, and has left New York to live variously in Nova Scotia, London and now California. His range of experience gave his plays an unusual variety. No writer evokes with more power and precision the sense of rural America better than Shepard. He loves the land and lives on it. The slang, archetypal characters and music of America consistently find their way into his work.

In the early 1960s Shepard came to New York from California and fell in with Greenwich Village musicians and actors. His word-play often has the improvisational

fantasy of jazz, and he acknowledges the connection between music and his dialogue. With a strong sense of visual and verbal surprise, Shepard's surreal one-acters became the bijou pieces of the avant-garde. Shepard writes fast, and a great many of his short pieces are surprisingly inept – run-ups to the bold ideas he works out in his major works. His best full-length plays include *Operation Sidewinder* (1970), *The Tooth of Crime* (1972) and *Buried Child* (1978), for which he won a Pulitzer Prize. He remains the avant-garde's finest playwright.

TIM RICE (1944...)

English librettist. Rice and his composer-partner Andrew Lloyd Webber were quite unknown when a school commissioned their mini-oratorio *Joseph and the Amazing Technicolor Dreamcoat* in 1968. This rock version of the biblical story of Joseph and his brothers was such a hit that it was performed in St Paul's Cathedral. Recognizing that Holy Writ could be box-office, Rice and Lloyd Webber set to work on a "rock opera" based on the last days of Jesus. *Jesus Christ Superstar* was a stunning success, first as an album, then as a musical that conquered New York in 1971 and the rest of the world shortly thereafter. Switching from redeemers to dictators, the partners based their next project on the charismatic wife of Argentinian strongman Juan Perón. Already familiar on disc, *Evita* opened in London to enthusiastic crowds in 1978 with every expectation of tyrannizing the city for years to come.

MARTIN SPERR (1944...)

German playwright. With murder, suicide, homosexuality and rape on stage, Sperr's first play *Jagdszenen aus Niederbayern* (1966) could hardly have passed unnoticed. Brutal realism or, as he put it, "the honesty to shit for real" was his means of revealing the hypocrisy of small-town Bavaria. After the horrific persecution of a homosexual, who is driven to murder the girl he has made pregnant, there is an ironic happy ending. This successful device Sperr used again in a second rural saga, *Landshuter Erzählungen* (1967).

Sperr was on less sure ground when he tackled the wider subject of the student unrest of 1968 in *Münchner Freiheit* (1971). This, like all his previous work, was primarily a warning against the ever-present threat of fascism in southern Germany.

Helen Mirren played the raunchy, chaotic lead singer of a third-rate band (and revealed an unexpected musical ability) in David Hare's *Teeth 'n' Smiles* (*left*). These are two of the most talented of a generation in Britain who have often taken a radical and independent stand in theatrical matters

The nightmare of city life lies at the heart of the plays of **Stephen Poliakoff** (*right*). Yet the denizens of his sordid world are presented with sympathy

RAINER WERNER FASSBINDER (1946...)

German director, actor and writer. Fassbinder, who has led the revival of West German cinema with his low-budget films, began his career directing no-budget theatre in Munich bars and disused cinemas. Many of his well-known films, like *Die bitteren Tränen der Petra von Kant* (1972), began as stage-plays for the motley, communal company of those early days.

In 1974 Fassbinder, by now a national figure, worked for a time at the Theater am Turm in Frankfurt, directing such classics as CHEKHOV's *Uncle Vanya* and STRINDBERG's *Miss Julie*. He ultimately ran into trouble because the villain of one of his own plays, a Frankfurt property speculator, happened to be Jewish. Hysterical accusations of anti-Semitism obliged him to leave; since then he has concentrated on films and television.

HELEN MIRREN (1946...)

English actress. Helen Mirren broke out of her convent background with the National Youth Theatre, graduating as Cleopatra in 1965. After a stint in Manchester, she joined the Royal Shakespeare Company at Stratford playing Cressida, Lady Anne in *Richard III* and Ophelia. She went on to play Tatyana in GORKY's *Enemies* and the title role in *Miss Julie*. She toured Africa and the US with Peter BROOK's extraordinary Centre Internationale de Recherches Théâtrales and returned to the RSC to play Lady Macbeth. Publicly critical of RSC expenditure, she left to play the pop singer in *Teeth 'n' Smiles* and continues to assert her independence. She has appeared frequently on television, notably as Rosalind in the BBC production of *As You Like It*.

DAVID HARE (1947...)

English playwright and director. Educated at Cambridge University, Hare co-founded Portable Theatre, an experimental group that toured where theatre was not normally seen. Between 1969 and 1971 he was literary manager and resident dramatist of the Royal Court Theatre. Before founding the Joint Stock Theatre Group, Hare wrote such plays as *Slag, The Great Exhibition* and *Knuckle*. He has also directed radical new plays and collectively written others such as *Brassneck* (with Howard Brenton) and *Fanshen*. He has also written television plays, including *Licking Hitler*. His work diagnoses the English social condition and draws inspiration from myriad sources: from Mickey Spillane to Bertolt BRECHT.

DAVID MAMET (1947...)

American playwright. Born in the Jewish district of Chicago, Mamet started in theatre by working backstage. Declining to follow his father into law, he studied literature and theatre at the experimental Goddard College in Vermont, and acting in New York. Via a great variety of jobs, he returned to his alma mater, writing short plays for acting exercises. In Chicago, his play *Duck Variations* (and others) were staged, and in 1974 *Sexual Perversity in Chicago* won a local award. After opening on Broadway, *American Buffalo* was named the best play of 1977, and Mamet was no longer just a regional playwright.

Mamet has found poetry in rough everyday speech. As he says, "If it's not poetic on the stage, forget it."

MERYL STREEP (1950...)

American actress. Fresh out of drama school, Meryl Streep auditioned for a small part for Joseph PAPP. He was impressed: "She took terrible risks . . . She's not afraid to fall on her face," and that year, 1975–76, at his Public Theatre, she played Katherine in *Henry V*, Isabella in *Measure for Measure*, and Dunyasha in CHEKHOV's *The Cherry Orchard*. Streep has since won a wide audience in films that include *The Deer Hunter*, but has expressed the intention of returning to the theatre.

STEPHEN POLIAKOFF (1952...)

English playwright. By any standards Poliakoff's success is astonishingly precocious. While still in his early twenties he graduated from the circuit of club productions to see his work performed in the West End. *Clever Soldiers* (1974) was a rather insular attempt to exorcise his public school and Cambridge background; but later works such as *City Sugar* (1975) *Strawberry Fields* (1977) and *Shout Across the River* (1978) are firmly rooted in reality. Poliakoff's vision is a Hogarthian fantasy of urban living: his locales are launderettes, Wimpy Bars, discos and radio stations. The hero of *City Sugar*, a sharp, exploitive disc jockey, is a classic survivor of the swinging sixties. Indeed, much of Poliakoff's work seems to concern itself with the spiritual pollution of the sixties dream.

You, the audience V

The present-day audience can be required to do more than sit in indolent comfort and refrain from crackling their sweet-wrappers. Avant-garde theatre originally blurred the line between spectator and actor, but today even well-heeled patrons of Broadway and the West End can find themselves part of the action. BRECHT and PIRANDELLO initiated the trend with assaults on a complacent public detached from the issues presented on stage: more recent playwrights have made audience involvement a basic theatrical principle. And when nudity is also involved, the revels may return to the wild Dionysian rites that were their distant origins.

ORIENTAL THEATRE

In 1603, a handful of Europeans in a Shinto shrine in Kyoto, Japan, watched Okuni and her troupe of prostitutes perform the ecstatic Buddhist dances, the *nembutsu odori*. Some of the Japanese in the audience wore Portuguese doublets and ruffs. Okuni herself wore a crucifix in one of the little dramatic scenes that she added to her performance. For a brief moment the West looked on a new Asian dramatic form in the making, and even provided a few props.

Kabuki theatre, whose origins are found in Okuni's dances, was a late addition to the wealth of Asian drama, but it shows many of the qualities which distinguish Oriental theatre from that of the West. Its fusion of dance, drama, instrumental music, mime and singing is characteristic of nearly all Asian theatre. "The song and playing of musical instruments being well executed, the performance of drama does not encounter any risk," declares an ancient Sanskrit work on Indian dramatic art. It was only under the influence of nineteenth-century Western theatre that Asia produced any purely spoken drama. Instead, the East has developed a complex theatre of gesture, speech and singing. Its rich, unspoken dramatic language allows a simple gesture, like the gentlest movement of a sleeve in Japanese Nō drama, to convey the deepest of emotions. A fan in Peking Opera can be used as a sign of frivolity. A massive treatise on Sanskrit drama, the *Natyashastra*, concerns itself with the significance of every technical detail including the permissible movements of neck and eyeballs. Time and place are subject to a similar theatrical language. Many years can pass in an instant and many thousands of miles can be travelled in a step on the Eastern stage. This emphasis on tradition has meant that, at times, Asian theatre has been more concerned with repeating the old than creating the new. Languages and dialects often survived in drama long after they could be easily understood by the audiences. Consequently, it is impossible to understand much of the actors' speech in Nō theatre without some textual knowledge of the play: lines like "I am suffering unbearable agony" and "The cherry trees are in blossom" can sound very similar to the inexperienced ear.

Masks and puppets are naturally important to such a stylized theatre. While in Western drama the individual expression of the voice and face of the actor is the main focus of attention, in the East the mask (by tradition an object of worship and incarnation of divinity) can be used to prevent the individual personality of the actor imposing itself on the rituals of his art. In Japan it was said that "the distant being, perceptible only far off, flows into our presence through the mask." The puppeteer, along with the storyteller, has for centuries been a link between the literate and illiterate in Asia. Theatrical magic and religious rite merge in the movements of his puppets. In the West the puppet is made to imitate the free movements of a human individual. In the East both the actor and the puppet conform to rigid disciplines that tradition has imposed upon them.

None of these traditions appeared fully formed overnight; the unchanging East does change. Indeed, the writing down of conventions in works like the *Natyashastra* are as likely to be a sign of their decay after many years of unwritten practice as to be proof that their prescriptions were obeyed to the letter. Kabuki went through a number of changes before it was an established dramatic form. It became so successful with the growing urban population of Japan because Nō, which originally was a popular theatre, had become the preserve of the aristocratic warrior class. Myth and magic, the spiritual and the erotic have all played their parts in Western theatre, but they have never fused together as harmoniously as in Asia. It was not exceptional that Okuni's troupe sold their charms in addition to performing ancient, religious dances. In India, the temple dancing girls (*devadasi*) were wedded to a deity but bedded with mortal men. Both male and female prostitutes performed the classical Chinese Yuan plays. It was not uncommon then for an actress to later become a nun or a Taoist priestess.

Licentiousness was not, however, the predominant feature of traditional Asian theatre. Authorities often tried with varying hypocrisy to curb the more unseemly side of the theatre. Kabuki became reputable only after troupes of prostitutes were banned from performing it. The use of drama to create a communal, spiritual mood is essential to much of Oriental theatre. But the more earthbound side of human experience has been just as much a part of the Asian theatrical world as the search for spiritual fulfilment.

Although theatrical performances often last much longer in the East, audiences are not always expected to sit in reverential silence concentrating on everything that happens on the stage. A Kabuki play can last up to twelve hours, but the audience can come and go and chat during the performance. The training of performers can also take a very long time and be very rigorous. It is said to take nineteen years for the narrator in the Japanese puppet theatre to master the different kinds of weeping.

The West's perception of Eastern theatre has been limited. Interest has often been greater than understanding. GOETHE greatly admired the Sanskrit playwright Kalidasa. VOLTAIRE wrote a play called *l'Orphélin de la Chine* (1755) based on an incomplete translation from the Chinese, but the work did not depart in any way from French neoclassical conventions. The poet W. B. YEATS drew inspiration from Japanese Nō plays to write works which are distinguished poems–but no plays. Antonin ARTAUD borrowed from the East for his theories of the theatre. Some successful dramatists have only adopted specific Eastern techniques to suit a particular dramatic purpose. Thornton WILDER used four chairs to represent a motor car in one of his plays, just as a man straddling a stick can represent a rider in Chinese drama. He also made effective use of sudden changes in time as in Nō plays. Perhaps the most accomplished play to be influenced by the theatre of the East has been Bertolt BRECHT's *The Caucasian Chalk Circle*, inspired by an adaptation of *The Chalk Circle*, a Chinese play. On the whole, however, the West's interest in Asian theatre has been most usefully employed in the encouragement by Western scholars of the revival of ancient traditions that were threatened with extinction. Some Westerners, at least, wish the East to remain inscrutable.

INDIA

Indian drama and dance have had a widespread influence on the rest of Asia. Buddhist missionaries and pilgrims, Hindu merchants and conquering armies introduced Indian culture to other Asian societies. Lion dances in China and Japan and dance-dramas throughout Southeast Asia based on stories from the two great Indian epic poems, the Ramayana and the Mahabharata, are examples of this cultural debt. In some cases, such as with Balinese dance, Indian forms have survived elsewhere long after they have disappeared from India itself.

The way in which a formal written Indian drama developed from temple dances and folk rituals is unclear. The first surviving written plays date from *c.* AD 100 and the rest of the millennium saw the flourishing and decline of classical Sanskrit drama which was primarily for the entertainment of an educated, courtly society. Of the six outstanding Sanskrit playwrights three were kings, Sudraka, Harsa and Visakhadatta and the others, Bhasa, Kalidasa and Bhavabhuti, close friends of kings. Sudraka was also a distinguished mathematician and an expert in the "art of courtesans and the science of elephants".

Kalidasa is considered to have produced the greatest of Sanskrit drama. An ancient saying goes: "In literature, the drama is best and in drama *Sakuntala*." This celebrated drama by Kalidasa tells the story of Sakuntala, who leaves her father to join her husband, King Dusanta. A curse makes Dusanta fail to recognize Sakuntala when they meet again. It is only after a fisherman discovers Sankuntala's lost wedding ring inside a fish that Dusanta remembers his wife, who by this time has given birth to their son.

Tragedy in the Western sense was unknown: poetry, music and dance combined to create a whole range of delicate dramatic moods. The *Natyashastra*, the great treatise on Sanskrit drama (dating from before the third century AD) discusses at length the aesthetic principles which were thought to determine each particular dramatic mood and sentiment.

Sanskrit had ceased to be a common spoken language by the time these plays were written, and the playwright's increasingly ornate and overelaborate use of poetic embellishment contributed to the decline of the drama. Not all the characters in the play spoke in Sanskrit: according to the *Natyashastra*, women (excepting courtesans), servants, doorkeepers, soldiers, persons of low birth, lunatics and phallus-worshippers should speak in

Prakrit, the everyday language of the time. A character in *The Little Clay Cart*, a play of uncertain authorship which GOETHE so greatly admired, declares: "When a woman talks Sanskrit, she is like a cow with a rope through her nose: All you hear is 'soo, soo, soo'."

A comedian was often used to explain the story of the play to those of the audience who could not follow Sanskrit, and the performers, who used very few props, were able to express themselves through a whole language of physical movement and gesture. A single hand gesture, such as the Pataka with all the fingers extended close together and the thumb bent, could have, when combined with different body positions, many meanings: heat, rain, wind, a crowd of men, to cut, night, forest, self, horse, or a flight of birds. The make-up of an actor and the tone of his voice also followed particular conventions. Kings were painted lotus pink, Gods and heavenly nymphs in orange. The comic or the erotic was conveyed by middle or bass voice registers, while a higher pitch was adopted for the heroic.

Ritual in Sanskrit drama started even before the play began, there being as many as twenty pre-play ceremonies to perform. The Sutradhara, who was the director, leading actor and stage manager of the company, would offer homage to the stage and introduce the play, often with help of his actress wife. Plays were usually performed in temporary theatres erected in temples or palaces. The time of the performance depended on which of the many types of play was being acted. A play based on a story of virtue would be performed before noon, while a play with erotic sentiments would have to wait until dark.

Actors and actresses had their own place in the elaborate Indian caste system. They were normally members of wandering troupes and had a much more humble status than the more distinguished of the Sanskrit playwrights. Like other mummers throughout the history of theatre, they often attached and endeared themselves to the rich and the powerful.

The Mohammedan invasions from the twelfth to the fifteenth centuries contributed to the decline of more formal Indian drama, Islam being opposed to representational arts. Popular and folk drama, which did not depend on the patronage of courts, was better equipped to survive under the new rulers. Popular variety theatre, farce and dramatic monologues were to be found in this medieval period. Plays based on the legends of Rama and Krishna (who was the focus of the Vaishnava cult) grew into the great public religious pageants that are celebrated to this day.

India developed a very rich and varied folk theatre. Jatra and Bhavai are but two of the many different forms which are still popular today. Jatra is an operatic Bengali theatre dramatizing mythological and historical themes.

Life for most rural folk actors was harsh. Bhavai players adopted ingenious methods of financing themselves, such as sending the player of an impoverished queen into the audience with a begging bowl. The engrossed spectators then felt obliged to aid the royal suppliant.

Native audiences have not been the only ones persuaded to suspend their disbelief by Indian folk drama. So powerful is the art of the Kathakali dancers (who use over 500 gestures and wear violently expressive make-up) that when one performer mimed the throwing of a stone at an Englishman's dog, the animal went lame. The Englishman took the dancer to court.

JAPAN

Japanese culture has an unequalled ability to absorb, evolve and preserve different dramatic forms; dance and drama have had a continuous history in Japan of well over a thousand years.

Nō, the great classical Japanese theatre, dates from the fourteenth century, when an actor called Kan-ami introduced a chanted dance into the largely musical entertainments of the time, thus facilitating the telling of a dramatic story. His son, Zeami (1363–1443), developed and refined this new style of drama, which became known as Nō. Nō began as a popular theatre performed in temples or shrines, but the military ruler of Japan, struck by Zeami's beauty, took the boy into his patronage. Faced with an educated court as his audience, Zeami improved the literary quality of Nō, introducing old and distinguished passages of poetry and prose into the drama. Aesthetic excellence was more important to Zeami than dramatic action. *Komachi at Sekidera*, for instance, has very little plot. A young disciple and some priests listen to an old woman revealing

the secrets of poetry only to realize that, in fact, she is a famous poet. The success of such a play is determined by the quality of the poetry and its presentation.

Dance, mime, song, costumes and masks are vital to Nō theatre. A chorus sings and discusses events in the play with the *shite*, principal actor, and the *waki*, supporting actor. Both the *waki* and the *shite* sing, but only the latter is permitted to mime and dance. Many plays are in two scenes: the *shite* who appears in the first scene as a boatman or a peasant is revealed to be a god or the ghost of a distinguished person in whose form he appears in the second scene. In the interval between scenes, another player helps explain the play in a simpler language than is used in the poetical passages. As interludes between the pieces there was often a short farce or Kyogen. These plays, usually in colloquial dialogue, rarely have more than three characters. The humour is simple. In *The Ink-Smeared Lady* the trickery of a mistress who uses a basin of water to feign tears over her departing lord is revealed when the basin is replaced by an ink-well.

Nō became the theatre of the samurai, the aristocratic warrior class. Actors were even granted minor samurai status. Ordinary people were barred from studying Nō and could only watch a performance on special occasions. By the beginning of the seventeenth century, Nō was the official court ceremonial music. New plays have been written, but in antiquated styles.

The townspeople and the merchant classes in the Edo period (1603–1867) turned to other forms of theatre for their entertainment – Kabuki, and Bunraku puppet plays. Puppet plays have had a long history in both India and China, but it was in Japan that they achieved their greatest importance in formal drama. As early as the fifteenth century puppets were performing Nō and Kyogen plays, but puppet theatre came to life when given its own written texts and music to the accompaniment of the three-stringed samisen in Bunraku plays. The plots were not at all dramatic, being based on medieval stories and consisting of long literary descriptions without dialogue. Kabuki originated with a female dancing troupe in the seventeenth century, and at first consisted mainly of songs and unwritten dialogue. The history of these two forms of drama, the puppet and the human, came to be closely related. Their development was due largely to the work of Chikamatsu Monzaemon (1653–1725), Japan's greatest playwright. Chikamatsu first achieved fame with his Bunraku play, *The Soga Heir*, which contained such devices as a staged beheading (of a puppet). The best of his Kabuki plays was *Courtesans and the Great Recitation of the Name of Buddha at the Mibu Temple*. It gave actors a wonderful opportunity to exhibit their powers, especially in the long, mimed monologue on the glories of prostitution. At the end of the seventeenth century contemporary scandals became popular subjects for Kabuki plays. Chikamatsu, who concentrated on Bunraku plays, introduced such a subject into the more conservative puppet theatre. *The Love Suicides* is based on the true story of a suicide pact between a shop assistant and a prostitute. The topicality of this play, which was performed by the great Bunraku narrator Takemoto Gidayu (1650–1714), made it an enormous success among the merchant classes.

For half a century after Chikamatsu's death, Bunraku, helped by technical improvements in the capabilities of the puppets (including the introduction of a puppet operated by three men) flourished at the expense of Kabuki. Chikamatsu's work was continued by the disciples. The most famous Bunraku play was *Chushingura: the Treasury of Loyal Retainers*, which takes eleven hours to perform in its entirety. *Chushingura* was the highpoint of this great period of puppet theatre. Its enormous success was marred when the theatre company split because of a quarrel between the puppeteer and the chanter over the recitation of a passage. This great era of Bunraku ended when Osaka ceased to be Japan's cultural capital; after 1800 there were few new puppet plays written.

Though Kabuki influenced Bunraku, which increasingly used dialogue and more dramatic situations, it could not compete with the puppet theatre at the height of its popularity. In the eighteenth century Kabuki actors were more important than the playwrights, but in the next century in the city of Edo (now Tokyo), Kabuki achieved a literary status unequalled since the days of Chikamatsu with the plays of Tsuruya Namboku IV (1755–1829) and Kawatake Mokuami (1816–93).

The abolition of feudalism in 1867 delivered a near fatal blow to Nō theatre which no longer had a samurai class to support it. Before the middle classes began to take an interest, there was a time when there were no performances of Nō plays. The puppet theatre continued to decline despite a brief revival in the 1870s and even Kabuki, like Nō and Bunraku, became by the early twentieth century a repository of tradition rather than a contemporary theatre.

CHINA

Well before the birth of Christ, there was a form of theatre in China, probably originating from religious ceremonies in honour of harvest gods. Religion, however, did not play such an important role in the development of theatre in China as in India. Confucianism is concerned with human morality rather than with mysticism, and Chinese drama reflected the whims of its earthly rulers.

The Emperor Ming Huan (AD 712–754) was a great early patron of Chinese theatre, founding the famous Pear Garden academy for performing artists at Ch'ang-an. By the time of the Northern Sung dynasty (960–1126) there was a spectacular form of variety play in North China, and during the ensuing Southern Sung dynasty a speciality southern drama evolved, combining music and verse.

The ensuing Mongol (or Yuan) dynasty oppressed the Chinese in the middle ages, but were more interested in watching entertainments than in controlling the ideas of degraded scholars, and these new playwrights found that they had much more intellectual freedom to express themselves than when the government was dominated by conservative Confucianism. There were many forms of Yuan plays which were based on old stories, legends and dramas. Vengeance against unjust oppression, as in *The Orphan of Chao* (late thirteenth century) by Chi Chun hsiang, was a common theme in Yuan drama. Love between man and woman, which was not regarded by Confucianism as a proper concern of literature, was also the subject of such Yuan drama as *The Romance of the Western Chamber*.

Only the main character in Yuan plays sang the poetical lyrics; others were restricted to spoken dialogue. Northern and southern China continued to develop different styles of drama. The northern school used colloquial expressions and vigorous songs to string accompaniment, while the southern school favoured literary expressions and the mellow music of the flute.

Women had a prominent place in Yuan theatre, and were noted for their artistic as well as physical accomplishments. Actors and actresses took both male and female roles. Men vied with each other for actresses' favours. A scholar killed his magnificent horse when one of them, Any Time Beauty, developed a yearning for equine tripes. Not all actresses were famed for their looks. Pingyang Slave, who was tattooed all over and blind in one eye, excelled in brigand roles. One actress was described as having "a voice as perfect as a xylophone, a body like a xylophone-hammer".

The traditional Chinese drama, *The Sun and the Moon* (*top*). In India, the intricate choreography of the Kathakali dramatic dances (*top right*) is still strictly maintained. The mask for a Japanese Nō play (*above*); and a performance (*right*). The swordsmanship in Chinese Opera can reach a terrifying precision (*far right*)

The Yuan period was not without its bans on certain entertainments, but when the Mongols were replaced by native Chinese Ming rulers (1368–1644) much drama was, for a time, forbidden altogether. Although Ming emperors often took a keen personal interest in the theatre, drama became increasingly the preserve of the scholarly few.

Southern drama survived better in this period than the northern style and, at the beginning of the sixteenth century, there evolved from southern theatrical forms a new style of drama, k'un ch'u, which was to be dominant in Chinese theatre for the next 300 years. K'un ch'u was the product of a collaboration between Liang Ch'en-yu, an eminent poet, and Wei Liang-fu, a musician who had spent years developing the new k'un ch'u music from which the drama took its name. Soochow, the home of k'un ch'u, was a cultural centre of China, and the new opera form became popular with both the high and low in society. The Emperors K'ang Hsi (1661–1722) and Ch'ien Lung (1735–96) were particular devotees of k'un ch'u. However, attempts by the secular authorities to restrict dramatic entertainments of which they disapproved, continued. K'un ch'u became increasingly the theatre of a dilettante elite. Imperial edicts at the end of the eighteenth century tried in vain to preserve the form by curbing other styles of music and drama. Even the scholars began to turn from k'un ch'u, and when Soochow was captured in 1853, the drama went into decline.

Peking opera came to replace k'un ch'u as the dominant Chinese theatrical form. Though the authorities never completely gave up imposing restrictions on theatre-going, Peking opera flourished under the patronage of Tz'u-hsi (1835–1908), the Empress Dowager, who even performed in plays herself. In the middle of the Boxer troubles of 1900 she sat for four days watching plays.

Peking Opera fused a number of elements into one of the most complex and stylized theatres in the world. The plays are of less literary value than in k'un ch'u drama, being mostly devised by actors from popular romances and historical novels. Peking Opera had its origins in northern-style drama. Musically, it had a more limited range than k'un ch'u and used loud clappers, cymbals and strings rather than the softer sounds of the southern-style drama.

The popularity of k'un ch'u was partly due to the famous courtesans who performed it so well, but Peking opera was predominantly a theatre of actors. Male theatrical troupes were throughout Chinese history a part of a homosexual culture. An actor had a rigorous training from an early age and specialized in playing one particular type of character, which might be male or female. Ch'eng Chang-keng of Anhui was the first great actor of Peking opera, having the unique honour of being awarded an official rank by the Emperor although actors were barred from government service. The greatest actor of the Peking Opera in modern times has been Mei Lan-fang, who raised the art of female impersonation to new heights of artistic excellence.

The name "Opera" derives from the Italian "*Opera in musica*", or "a dramatic work with music". The Italians themselves now speak of "*la lirica*", short for "*opera lirica*".

Opera exists in many forms, but common to all is that words in a musical play are partly or entirely sung rather than spoken. Opera is regarded by opera lovers as the highest form of musical expression (and at the same time as the highest form of dramatic expression). There is a basic objection to opera, frequently advanced: is there not something inherently ridiculous in a drama that is sung?—it is not a normal means of communication in real life. Quite apart from the fact that opera *is* real life to the confirmed addict, the question has been answered once and for all by *Grove's Dictionary of Music and Musicians* (fifth edition): "In opera verses are sung instead of spoken, in order that they may be invested with a deeper pathos than the most careful form of ordinary declamation can reach."

The idea of heightening the effect of poetic declamation was in the minds of a group of educated Florentines who set out at the end of the sixteenth century to try and revive the ancient Greek drama, and who instead succeeded (accidentally) in creating opera. It is not easy to visualize the discussion, study, experiment and rehearsal that attended the birth of the first opera, because these men (and women) were imbued with the classical spirit of the Renaissance and strove to re-create the arts of ancient Greece and Rome.

The first opera was *Dafne*, privately performed in Florence in 1597. The words were by Ottavio Rinuccini, the music—unhappily lost—by Jacopo Peri. It seems likely that others of this group of friends, meeting regularly for years, had had a hand in both words and music, for when Peri published his second opera *Euridice* (first performed in 1600, and the earliest opera to survive) he revealed in the preface that parts of the music were by Caccini, who also published his own setting of this text (again by Rinuccini) in 1600, although it was not performed until two years later.

These distinguished Florentines (the Camerata) had no doubts at all that the music was to be the servant of the word. They longed for drama, and their rebellion against polyphony was not because they disliked the music of such as Palestrina, but because they wanted to hear the words. An attempt had earlier been made to produce musical plays consisting of madrigals, but these were unconvincing. The place for madrigals was in the home, for private music making, and the great choral works could go on being performed in the church, where they belonged. What was wanted for the theatre was something that would set the words free and accentuate their power to move the hearers. They "invented" recitative, a method of singing words in free declamation to a musical accompaniment that is not too rigidly fixed, so that the instruments could follow the singer as he moved from period to period. The Florentines had only to look to the music of the people to find this method—the art of the *cantastorie*, to be found in Italy to this day—but the achievement of Peri, Caccini and Marco da Gagliano was to take this seemingly improvised declamation, free it from all the vulgarity and monotony of folk music, and sing it so expressively that the *stile rappresentativo*, as the new style of musical play was called, was an instant hit. Everyone was moved by the new declamation in recitative, and felt that what they were hearing was what they had always been waiting for—in fact, they thought that at last they had rediscovered Greek drama.

The first operatic performances were all given by *dilettanti*—Peri, Caccini and da Gagliano were singing composers—when the term "dilettante" implied no kind of inferiority to professional standards. Nobly-born instrumentalists, discreetly placed behind the scenes, accompanied the singing. It was not to be expected that they would be able to maintain this aristocratic style of performance for ever, nor that the subservience of music to the word would long survive the advent of a really great composer. The death-knell of the poet's supremacy was sounded in 1607, when the audience at the first performance of Monteverdi's *Arianna* at Mantua sighed and sobbed as Arianna sang her great lament, "*lasciatemi morire*". Monteverdi's music, like his predecessor's, was described as being in the *stile rappresentativo* (in the theatrical manner) and was based, like

theirs, on the recitative; but his melodic gifts and showman's instincts enabled him to introduce songs and duets. He was the first major composer who did not sing in his own operas, and he had no objection to writing difficult airs that would give his singers opportunities to dazzle the audience. This development, however, was inherent in the genre. Peri himself had introduced the occasional song: "*Gioite al canto mio*" from his *Euridice* is the earliest operatic aria that figures regularly in modern singers' repertoires.

Monteverdi was also a skilled madrigal composer, and therefore did not hesitate to show off his skill in vocal counterpoint whenever the dramatic situation seemed to call for it; so polyphonic music, considered by the Florentine theorists as the arch enemy of the word, took its place in opera (albeit a subordinate place, to begin with).

Comic scenes, often in local dialect, were first introduced into opera in Rome and Naples; the first out-and-out comic opera was *Che Soffre, Speri*, a joint work of the friendly rival composers Mazzocchi and Marazzoli (Rome, 1639). The comic and dialect scenes were not written merely to please the gallery; even today the remains of the nobility of Rome and Naples retain a delight in the hearty and healthy vulgarity of their native dialects. This enthusiasm for comic works led to the invention of "Intermezzi" or slight musical comedies, one scene of which would be given at the end of each act of the evening's serious opera—a typically Italian compromise.

The final death blow to the cause of the ancient Greek drama was the opening in 1637 of the first public theatre for operas—the Teatro di San Cassiano in Venice—with Manelli's *Andromeda*. Until then operas had been princely entertainments at which the majority of men in the audience would have had at least a nodding acquaintance with the classics; now, for the first time, there would be people present who could afford a ticket but who had never heard of Andromeda except as a character in that night's show. Marco da Gagliano himself was responsible for the first opera on a non-Greek subject, *Medoro* (1619), the story taken from ARIOSTO. The first woman to write an opera, Francesca Caccini, followed suit in 1625 with her *La Liberazione di Ruggiero dall' Isola d' Alcina*.

The Italian operas that were produced all over Europe in the seventeenth century by princely courts with lots of money to spend, were fabulous spectacles. Opera was supposed to be a blend of poetry, music and architecture; and as if the splendid scenery, beautiful and elaborate beyond anything imaginable today, were not enough, elements of the circus and the disaster movie were introduced: pageants, equestrian and naval battles, live animals, floods and fires. It is not surprising to read that the architect BERNINI, in that day of the all-round educated gentleman, wrote the music and words of an opera as well as designing the costumes and scenery (which is believed still to exist in a Roman palazzo). As the finale of one of his Roman carnival productions, the whole back wall of the stage of the Teatro Tor di Nona melted away so that the audience could see straight across the river to the Castel Sant'Angelo, where a firework exhibition closed the evening's entertainment.

There was something for everyone in these operas, and so they proved readily exportable. Anyone who was fond of the theatre found in the Italian operas the maximum of what theatre had to offer; the same is true today. With exportation, however, came the problem of whether or not it was important to understand the words—a debate that has likewise continued. "... for there is no question but our great-grandchildren will be very curious to know the reason why their forefathers used to sit together like an audience of foreigners in their own country, and to hear whole plays acted before them in a tongue which they did not understand." (*The Spectator*, 1710.)

The first opera to be heard outside Italy was *Andromeda* (1610) by Girolamo Giacobbi, produced in Salzburg in 1618. The first opera by a German composer was, however, *Dafne* by Schütz (Torgau, 1627), sung in Italian to Rinuccini's text and, like Peri's, lost. The cradle of true German opera was Hamburg, where Johann Theile produced the first *Singspiel*, *Adam und Eva* in 1678. The *Singspiel* had spoken dialogue alternating with sung musical numbers, and this form of musical play held absolute sway in Germany until Wagner banished the spoken word from German opera and the *Singspiel* degenerated into operetta. The *Singspiel*, alternating between the comic and the sentimental, was aimed at a middle-class audience; the Court Operas of Berlin, Vienna, Dresden etc., for long maintained a preference for the Italian models, and for many years the greatest Italian singers were to be heard in those cities, whose princes dabbled in the art of composition enough to be able to write arias for their favourites.

Italian operas found a willing public in England from the beginning of the eighteenth century–political disturbances had prevented any earlier acclimatization. From the first performance of Handel's *Rinaldo* in London in 1711 Italian opera was unassailable artistically, if financially very weak on its legs. Handel not only knew how to write music to show off the voices of the greatest singers to the best advantage. It is a question whether this naturalized Englishman, born and taught in Germany, was not the greatest of all Italian composers. Native English opera had no chance, and it has never amounted to more than a mere handful of idiosyncratic works (the finest of which, Purcell's *Dido and Aeneas*, was written for a girls' school and so is, at least, easy to perform). The greatest English opera of the eighteenth century, Arne's *Artaxerxes*, an imitation Italian opera in the style of Bononcini (and others–the score also includes English popular ballads) is unperformable today because of the extreme difficulty of the songs and arias.

The Spectator, in the number quoted above, inadvertently gives the reason for the failure of the English to shine in opera composition: "If the Italians have a genius for music above the English, the English have a genius for other performances of a much higher nature, and capable of giving the mind a much nobler entertainment . . . I must confess I would allow it [music] no better quarter than Plato has done, who banishes it out of his common-wealth." Italian opera had to wait until the nineteenth century to be able to include Paris in its Empire; the first importations in the seventeenth century were an instant success, but they met with the most deadly kind of opposition: a local, purely French attempt to revive the Greek drama. The "ballet dramatique", in which sung poems alternated with dances, led to the development of "comédie-ballet" in which sung recitative based on the authoritative model of the declamation of the Comédie-Française alternated with spectacular ballets, choruses and songs. Lully, an Italian from Florence, collaborated with MOLIÈRE in the establishment of this genre, in which Louis XIV himself would occasionally dance at court performances. By the end of the eighteenth century, the more popular form of opéra-comique had grown up alongside the formal, spectacular operas. Here spoken dialogue took the place of sung recitative, as in the German *Singspiel* and the English Ballad Opera (GAY's *The Beggar's Opera* for instance).

By the beginning of the eighteenth century, opera had become a rather different kind of entertainment from that provided by Monteverdi. The opera house had become the focal point of Italian social life, to an extent that all but suffocated the "stright theatre". The Italians had produced the *Commedia dell' Arte*, and it is reasonable to suppose that a healthy theatrical life could have gone on developing with such an inventive people, but the overwhelming popularity of opera left the *teatro di prosa* (spoken theatre) in the position of a Cinderella. High society lived in the opera house; if it is surprising to us at first to learn that people had gaming and dining tables in their private boxes, and made liberal use of them during the performances, we should remember that opera was no longer an occasional entertainment for royal weddings; each season would offer only two, three or four operas, with many performances of each. Furthermore, it was felt that the highly successful libretti by Zeno and, particularly, METASTASIO–the Italian SHAKESPEARE, or so it was thought–were good enough for anyone. Rather than search out new librettists, composers went on setting Metastasio's texts again and again. "The plays were beautiful, the public knew them by heart; so much the better, it enjoyed them here and there, and gave its main attention to the music . . ." (Vernon Lee, *Studies of the Eighteenth Century in Italy*, 1887). So the first performance of any new setting of a well-loved libretto would be listened to with all attention, to see how it compared with other favourite settings; after the second or third performance, everyone would know which bits were worth listening to, and talk happily through the rest. This may shock us today, but music-making in those days was supposed to be primarily entertain-ment, and was utterly devoid of the pseudo-religious atmosphere that has surrounded concert- and opera-going in the twentieth century.

From today's point of view, the operas of the eighteenth century are disappointing because they lack the variety of arias, duets, trios and other concerted numbers found in the works of Cavalli and Monteverdi, not to mention the interesting harmonic experiments of stage and chamber music of that early period. The strict limitation of operas to a string of arias with just one duet in the evening and perhaps (as in many of Handel's operas) a brief ensemble of all the singers to close the opera–including even those characters who have died during the development of the story–was perfectly natural to the eighteenth century. The action was carried on in recitative, and the endless string of arias told of the emotions of the character at that particular moment of the plot. Feeling was best expressed by the solo voice; it was confusing if too many people were gabbling all at once. Unwittingly, opera had in part returned to the precepts of the *stile rappresentativo*.

Although the conventional rigidity of the accepted forms of serious opera makes the eighteenth-century masterpieces seem like odd prehistoric monsters today, the greatest composers experimented as much as they dared within those limitations. Handel has many well-known examples of breaking off a phrase when the audience is expecting a conventional repeat, and also of introducing passages–a brilliant extemporization on the harpsichord, for example–in the ritornellos. At the same time, in Italy, the forgotten genius Rinaldo da Capua (whose son sold all the scores of his father's operas to the dustman) was writing some music of extraordinary dramatic effect, with daring innovations; in the once famous scene of Berenice from the last act of *Vologeso*, recitative singing of great dramatic force is alternated with short orchestral passages which set off the great aria "*Ombra che pallida*" to the maximum advantage. The art of expressing emotion in song has really made no advance since those days; more modern operas have simply bombarded us with ever more luxurious sensuality.

The art of singing had reached its apogee by Handel's day. There is no mystery why singers were so much better two or three hundred years ago than they are today. If a boy proved to have a beautiful voice, he was set to study. Before his voice could change, he or his family would be lured by the prospect of great wealth to consent to a "small operation", performed as painlessly as possible, that would preserve the boy's soprano or alto voice. These *castrati* then continued studying in the great Conservatorios of Italy until they were ready to make a debut. All told, they might have ten years of preparation before singing in public. Their art had a generally beneficial influence, for naturally the women singers would imitate them and try to emulate their skill and success, which very few succeeded in doing. The secret of the singing of these great artists was quite simple; the art of managing the breath was mastered so that the voice was free of any muscular restraint or effort. The voice could then, by dint of years of practice, execute florid passages of great difficulty, and express by purely vocal colour every shade of human emotion that it was thought fitting to express on stage. A composer wrote his opera for a certain group of singers, and it was understood that when another artist had to sing what had been written for Farinelli or Pacchierotti, the composer (or, more likely, the singer himself) would rewrite the music to suit his own range and style. There was nothing shocking in this, for the castrato received a musical education quite equal to that of the best composers.

We can distantly glimpse the castrati through the records made in 1902 by Moreschi, of the Cappella Sistina choir. He is a poor singer with a debased *verismo* style, but the voice itself is brilliant and powerful–there need be no surprise that such a voice was thought suitable to impersonate the heroes of ancient Greece and Rome on the operatic stage. To understand something of the vocal style of these days, there remains an echo of it in the records made in 1905–6 by Adelina Patti, then an old lady. When in 1902 she unwisely ventured an isolated concert in Rome, her opening bars of Arditi's "*Il bacio*", in which the singer appeals for a kiss on the lips, were greeted by coarse voices from the gallery calling out: "Too late!"–but when, as an unsolicited encore, she added Mozart's "*Voi che sapete*", the Romans realized that they were listening to something they had

298

thought long vanished: the art of freely floating a beautiful voice on the breath, with no tiresome technical tricks, and a wide range of expression achieved by purely musical means.

In a wonderful record (1907) by the baritone Mattia Battistini of "Alfin siam liberati" from *Don Giovanni*, we have one of the very few examples of true recitative singing; colour, charm, variety and expression are all achieved, together with great rapidity and clarity of enunciation, in tone that is truly sung and not whispered or in any way faked. This art is now utterly lost – but not, it is to be hoped, beyond recall.

Mozart's *Don Giovanni* seemed at the time a revolutionary work, for throughout the eighteenth century the *opera seria* and the *opera buffa* had been kept rigidly apart. Comic opera contained all kinds of ensembles and elaborately worked out finales that were not found in the serious works, where the hidebound Metastasian forms held sway. This is one reason why the comic operas are easier to revive today, for they fit in more with current ideas of what an opera should be, but there is also another reason: the best singers sang only in the serious works, and the composers wrote their best music for them. The best music is also the most difficult to sing, even leaving out of account the fact that the singers improvised a great deal of the music, especially in repeats (many printed and manuscript examples survive).

Don Giovanni mixes together elements of serious and comic opera in what Mozart termed *dramma giocoso*, a combination usually referred to as "opera semi-seria" (Rossini's *La Gazza Ladra* is a later example). For Lord Mount Edgecumbe, a great critic of the late eighteenth and early nineteenth century, Mozart – whose genius he fully appreciated – was ill advised to have done this, and to have (so inexplicably!) written the title role for a bass voice, hitherto confined to gross comic parts.

Of operatic reform in general, he goes on to say: "The dialogue, which used to be carried on in recitative, and which in Metastasio's operas is often so beautiful and interesting, is now cut up (and rendered unintelligible if it were worth listening to) into *pezzi concertati*, or long singing conversations, which present a tedious succession of unconnected, ever-changing motives, having nothing to do with each other: and if a satisfactory air is for a moment introduced, which the ear would like to dwell upon, to hear modulated, varied, and again returned to, it is broken off before it is well understood or sufficiently heard, by a sudden transition into a totally different melody, time and key, and recurs no more. . . . Single songs are almost exploded, for which one good reason may be given, that there are few singers capable of singing them" (*Musical Reminiscences of an old amateur*, 1827 edition).

By 1827, the French Revolution had swept away the castrati together with much else of the old order; opera was developing with rapid strides into an art form capable of great variety. The new operas were noisy to the ear of the "old amateur", but a public that had wept over the *Sorrows of Werther* and shuddered over a generation of horror stories was not to be contented for ever with the operas of Sarti, Cimarosa and Sacchini, however beautiful and varied they seemed when fresh and new.

The operas which are regularly played in theatres all over the world today as part of an international repertoire nearly all date from after the French Revolution. Different national schools began to develop sufficiently to be able to challenge the Italian operas. The reign of Paer and later Rossini as director of the Italian theatres in Paris influenced French singers and composers to a marvellous extent. At the end of the eighteenth century Carlo GOLDONI had remarked of French grand opera: "Tis a paradise for the eyes, but a hell for the ears." In the nineteenth century, however, operas by Auber, Boieldieu, Halévy, Hérold, Gounod and Massenet, among many others, were unmistakably French and yet exportable to Germany, England and even Italy.

Operas continued to be composed in Germany, but there is no real German repertoire. Beethoven's one attempt, *Fidelio*, which owes not a little, it now appears, to Paer's *Leonora* which he deliberately went to see before setting his own version of the same story, contains such fine music, and even one or two striking dramatic effects, that it has kept the stage; he was not, however, an operatic composer. Weber's *Der Freischütz* holds the stage for the same reasons, but his other operas are very inferior, although *Euryanthe* was an interesting attempt to free German opera from the curse of spoken dialogue. The Italian Spontini (like Cherubini whom he greatly resembles) was able to produce music of profound scholarship and no little dramatic fire without any real genius. He was the true founder of German opera; his *Agnes von Hohenstaufen* (Berlin, 1821) anticipated Wagner in almost every move, and directly inspired the latter's *Lohengrin*. It is surely the first opera ever composed in which each act is one long, through-composed entity without breaks at the end of numbers.

The operas of Wagner, which he himself did not regard as "operas" in a conventional sense but as complete art-works of a unique type, are quite separate. They tore musical Europe apart; no one could foresee at the time that they were at once supremely great and yet eccentric, in that they founded no school and established no precedent. There they remain, the works of Wagner, with their place in the repertoire and nothing really like them before or since. Many small fry were lost in the attempt to imitate the success of Wagner, but the only truly great operatic composer to emerge in Germany after him was Richard Strauss.

The Hungarian school of opera got off to an early start with Ferenc Erkel's *Hunyadi László* in 1844, a delightful blend of Liszt and Donizetti. The Russian school's first masterpiece was Glinka's *A Life for the Tsar* of 1836. The Russian operatic masterpieces, a small but rich collection, enjoyed the inestimable advantage of the great bass Chaliapin, who performed many of them in the greatest theatres of Europe and America. Smetana's

Richard Wagner was an exact contemporary of Verdi. *Das Rheingold* (1869) is the first of the four operas that make up the mighty *Ring* cycle. These works are ideally suited to a stylized Romantic staging, like the one shown here

The Bartered Bride of 1866 started the Bohemian school, and Polish opera sprang into life with the beautiful operas of Moniuszko. None of these schools of opera, however, had an international ambassador of the status of Chaliapin; but they offer no great roles such as Boris or Ivan the Terrible, in which he was able to scare two entire generations of opera-goers.

Opera meant Italian opera. All through the nineteenth century success after success was scored at home and abroad not only by Rossini, Donizetti, Bellini and Verdi but also by Vaccai, Persiani, Mercadante, Pacini and a host of others. The public wanted novelty, and the repertoire of the great theatres was made up of recently composed works. Those of Verdi had a political significance, but even works by lesser firebrands who presented no worries to the censor were eagerly awaited by a public agog for anything new. The success of Mascagni's *Cavalleria Rusticana* initiated the flood of *verismo* operas. This success was world-wide because it seemed genuinely new.

Things are very different today; only a pathetically small number of operas written in the twentieth century have entered the regular repertoire of opera houses, or made any lasting appeal to the public. More than one writer has pointed out that opera composers no longer cater for the audience that go night after night for entertainment to Covent Garden, La Scala or the Metropolitan. The American musical has been indicated as the true successor to nineteenth-century Italian opera, but those music lovers who stop short of that may enjoy a round of revivals of old works, written to entertain their great-great-grandfathers, in the opera house—once the centre of cultural life, but now a museum.

Many governments are now of the opinion once expressed by GEORGE BERNARD SHAW, that an opera house had a beneficial effect on any community that possessed one; accordingly millions are spent to keep the doors open where private subscriptions are not forthcoming. The opera house now presents a repertory of works ranging over three centuries and more, a very happy arrangement in comparison with the limited choice available to past generations. Unfortunately opera (and music generally) differs from other museums of the arts in one essential respect; whereas one may simply look at the treasures of Tutankhamun, or read SHAKESPEARE and Dante, music relies upon performance. It is not to be supposed the singers and orchestral players who, during one season, have to perform works by Gluck, Handel, Mozart, Monteverdi, Rossini, Bellini, Verdi, Wagner, Strauss and Berg, will perform all of them in a manner which would be pleasing to all those composers, were they able to be present. The older the opera, the more of a distortion the performance is likely to be. There are now musicologists all over the world who dedicate themselves to studying from contemporary sources how the written-down notes of Handel, Mozart or Rossini should be sung or played, but few conductors are really interested in knowing about it, and even fewer singers. Who today could be said to sing in a genuinely Mozartian manner?

Audiences too are different in their needs from those of two hundred years ago. The change was noted by Melba, when she sang in the first performance at Covent Garden after the First World War (1919 season): "It was that night at Covent Garden which made me realize the full extent to which London had changed. . . . But though there was as much, if not more enthusiasm, than before, there was so little of the old brilliance. Can you imagine in the old days, men walking into Covent Garden on a Melba night, or on any other night, and sitting in the stalls in shabby tweed coats? . . . I could not help feeling a sensation almost of resentment that men who could afford to pay for stalls could not also afford to wear the proper clothes." (*Melodies and Memories*, 1926.)

For Melba, the performance of an opera was a social rite somehow incomplete without a glamour and glitter in the aristocratic audience rivalling that of the singer's own (real) jewels and personal costumes on stage. Although it is now customary to scoff at such an audience, the sad fact is that in the days of aristocratic leisure the art of singing (like piano-playing) was widely cultivated in the home, and regular opera-goers had far more knowledge of singing technique and style than they have today. Singers themselves naturally tend to imitate the current stars, so that during a hundred years of increasingly loud orchestras and more authoritarian conductors, each generation has tended to be a louder but inferior copy of the preceding hierarchy of stars.

The future of opera is largely bound up with financial considerations, and may have priced itself out of the market. As a museum, it is exceptionally alive; theatres everywhere are full, and there is a large audience for televised and filmed opera. The founders of the *stile rappresentativo* would not have been delighted to learn that INGMAR BERGMAN's delightful film *Die Zauberflöte*, a German opera after all, is sung in Swedish and shown all over the world to audiences who applaud but do not understand the words, and have to content themselves with a vague paraphrase in the sub-titles. The success of this film lies partly in its visual charm, but also in the fact that although none of the singers is a great international star, each has a fresh and pleasant voice, so the music is well served.

Opera lives by music and not by virtue of the words. But opera librettos are subject to the vagaries of changing taste even more than the music; Cammarano's libretto for *Il Trovatore*, long derided, is now seen for the poetic gem that it is, whereas Boito's *Otello* and *Falstaff*, once regarded as holy writ, are now seen as more modest creations. Nothing can now touch the music of those three Verdi operas; they are enthroned for ever as masterpieces. No opera has remained in the repertoire just because it had a good libretto. The music is lord over all, and fortunately singers such as Melba, Caruso, Battistini, Chaliapin and Callas have been able to leave all the best part of their art for posterity to admire on the gramophone.

Verdi's *Falstaff* (1893) was his last opera. In this work, and in the passionate tragedy *Otello* (1887), which preceded it, Shakespeare inspired the composer to produce his two greatest dramatic works

Some people date musical comedy from *Show Boat*, *The Maid of the Mountains* or *Véronique*, which is naïve; some from *H.M.S. Pinafore* or *The Black Crook*, which is at least historical; some from *The Magic Flute*, which shows flair. But musical comedy–farcical and sentimental entertainment with music in the popular idiom–dates back at least to the middle ages. The classic citation, Adam de la Halle's *Le Jeu de Robin et de Marion* (*The Play of Robin and Marion*, circa 1283), bears in its rustic simplicity little resemblance to modern musical comedy, but its modest score and use of spoken dialogue between numbers suggest the essential identifying difference between musical comedy and opera.

By the eighteenth century, when establishment opera (except in France) was Italian in style and language, heroic in subject and static in dramatics, musical comedy was nationalistic, naturalistic and lively, with funny or charming rather than noble characters, scores derived from traditional tunes and original lyrics, and a generally satiric viewpoint. The English form, ballad opera, found its paragon in John GAY's *The Beggar's Opera* (1728), widely regarded as the reply to Handelian opera in its self-spoofing thieves and tarts, its casual score collected hither and yon (including a slice of Handel's *Rinaldo*) and its biting contemporaneity. "It made Gay rich and RICH (Gay's producer) gay," ran a joke of the time. Even then, this showbiz side of musical comedy distinguished it from the grander types of music theatre. Musical comedy must please the simplest public; opera plays to a more educated audience–sometimes it need only please itself.

The division between pop and "art" music that we observe today was not so clear-cut in the eighteenth and nineteenth centuries, and some of the most distinguished musicians were attracted to musical comedy because its theatrical exuberance promised more effective communication than opera. German musical comedy, *Singspiel*, was derived from ballad opera, but it soon developed a stronger musical affiliation than the English genre. Whereas in England Gay's contemporaries were too busy imitating the operas of Handel or Bononcini to take notice of the home-grown product on their doorstep, in Europe, Mozart, Beethoven and Weber all produced *Singspiele*. The French, too, upgraded the musical component of their *opéra comique*, and by the mid-1800s both *Singspiel* and *opéra comique* functioned as kinds of diluted opera. Ballad opera had totally vanished.

It was Jacques Offenbach who revived musical comedy's satiric energy in his *opéra bouffe* in the latter half of the nineteenth century. His contemporaries W. S. GILBERT and Arthur Sullivan likewise enlivened the English theatre with their Savoy operas. Gilbert was wittier than Offenbach's collaborators and Sullivan a more devastating parodist of musical styles. But Gilbert and Sullivan were patriotic and essentially respectful of status quo for all their lampoons; Offenbach was disreputable. Gilbert's librettos for *H.M.S. Pinafore* (1878) and *The Gondoliers* (1889), for instance, mock the social hierarchy, but don't really challenge it, and *Iolanthe* (1882), his most promising satire, seems set to pillory the English class system (a chorus of pompous Lords being an especially tempting target) only to back off into gentle caricature before it had gone too far. In France, a land of cultural self-importance, Offenbach was thought really dangerous. Pedants fumed about the classical burlesques *Orphée aux Enfers* (*Orpheus in the Underworld*, 1858) and *La Belle Hélène* (1864), in which the composer ridiculed not only Hellenic mythology and history but the very dignity of art, quoting the revered tune from Gluck's *Orfeo* with something less than dignity. Offenbach dubbed his style *le genre et gai*, emphasizing what would now prove to be musical comedy's most basic asset: lowdown farce.

But post-Offenbach musical comedy in France and Germany tended to the exotic, the glamorous or the sedately romantic. Johann Strauss's *Die Fledermaus* (1874) and *Der Zigeunerbaron* (*The Gypsy Baron*, 1885) cut their respective urbanity and fantasy with obtrusive comic characters, a drunken gaoler in the first and a pushy pig farmer in the second. But generally the Viennese school favoured the fantasy, and Strauss's successor Franz Lehár relegated comedy to tertiary status. Lehár seemed most comfortable when the atmosphere was at its headiest.

Japan, Russia and various Ruritanias furnished the colour for his pastiche numbers, while hussars and *Dirndlmädchen* fielded his choruses. Though early *opéra comique* was nothing like *Singspiel*, by the late 1800s French musical comedy had come to resemble the Viennese. André Messager's *Véronique* (1898) typifies early urban musical comedy, with its utility choruses, speciality bits, "Swing Duet" and its spirited heroine, an heiress disguised as a shopgirl. Masquerade at all costs was indispensable to this romantic sort of musical–what we call operetta nowadays. In Messager's *Monsieur Beaucaire* (1919), from Booth Tarkington's novel, a nobleman passes himself off as a barber. This was an international project–French composer, English libretto, London première (Maggie Teyte as the inevitable haughty lady). The commercial success of shows such as this delivered a final blow to the cultural borders that had once defined ballad opera, *Singspiel*, and *opéra comique*. From Gilbert's shrewdness, Offenbach's risqué verve, light Viennese love plots, the English chorus lines, and earthy, anarchic American comedy, the twentieth-century musical comedy began to take shape. There is no question that American artists brought this new international crossbreed to its highest stages of development.

One outgrowth of the American domination was the emphasis on stage personalities at the expense of the material. A comic's grab-bag of *shtick*, a prima donna's coloratura perquisites, a dancer's irrelevant gambols, or a ukelele player's ten o'clock spot (guaranteed by contract) were the sort of ingredients that did not promise an evening of taut and coherent entertainment. Plotted shows were often little better than revues, the story serving as a makeweight between set pieces. But the better composers sought to weave a score out of character and action. Victor Herbert, the kingpin melodist of the early 1900s, found a solution in *The Red Mill* (1906), essentially a vehicle for the star comic duo David Montgomery and Fred Stone. These buffoons concentrated on the dialogue scenes, giving Herbert his head on love songs, choruses, and a suitably creepy "Legend of the Mill". Then Herbert fitted in the comics' numbers, a ridiculous pseudo-Italian mock-up, "Good-a-bye, John," and a lilting Bowery waltz, "In Old New York".

The worldwide success of Lehár's *Die lustige Witwe* (*The Merry Widow*, 1905) helped the all-important love plot in the musical to mature. Lehár's sophistication appealed to American audiences, though his Widow, Hanna Glawari, had to be renamed Sonya in English translation or risk sounding like a goosegirl. Even more important was the emergence of American naturalism in the work of George M. COHAN. Producer, playwright, composer, librettist and stage director, Cohan abandoned the dreamy romantic musical (Ivan Caryll's *The Pink Lady*, 1911, with its violin-playing beauty Hazel Dawn, for instance) for the more lively comic musical. As of Cohan's *Little Johnny Jones* (1904) and *Forty-Five Minutes from Broadway* (1906), the musical broke up into operetta and musical comedy, and in such numbers as "The Yankee Doodle Boy", "I'm Mighty Glad I'm Living and That's All" and "Mary's a Grand Old Name," Cohan invested the latter form with what one might call apolitical populist art, an aesthetic for middle America (though on the other hand Cohan consistently derided the "rubens" who inhabited it). The romantic musical's aesthetic rooted itself in fabulous visions and pretended to a certain fairyland universality. Victor Herbert's characters seldom sang anything as aggressive as "The Yankee Doodle Boy" or bothered to express so humdrum a notion as to be glad they were living. And a grand name was something on the order of Princess Sylvia of Zilania, as in Herbert's *Sweethearts* (1913). True, she was stolen at birth and grew up as the daughter of a laundress. But it was inevitable that she be revealed in her true beauty (i.e. social rank) in time to marry Prince Franz.

Cohan would have thought nothing of making a laundress his heroine; nor did he believe in princesses. And his successors, Jerome KERN, Guy BOLTON, and P. G. WODEHOUSE, introduced a new refinement in their "Princess Shows" (named for the tiny theatre in which they launched the series). Cohan, for all his democratic openness, was loud, abrupt and smug. The Princess dandies doodled less abrasively, blending the plot plan of farce with easy-going love and no sentimental overkill. In a typical Princess show, *Very Good Eddie* (1915) by Kern, Bolton and Schuyler Greene, two honeymooning couples are separated on a

Hudson River cruise; when the four catch up with each other, they decide they were mismatched in the first place and elect to honour the new alignments. Such clear and simple plotting made more of character than Cohan, yet avoided the monotonous grandeur of romance; Kern offered in his music a beautifully genuine American sound abstracted out of ballad and ragtime. Where Cohan unfurled the flag and strutted screaming, Kern unveiled the banjo and strummed.

The development of an American sound utterly revolutionized musical comedy. As with early *opéra comique* and *Singspiel*, the form would now be speaking to its audience in a transcendently indigenous language, taking from to give back to its public. Kern's tunes were so pure, the harmony seemed to flow out of them like honey; meanwhile, Irving BERLIN, who was said to play the most incompetent piano in all Tin Pan Alley, worked a wizardry in rhythm, and as lyricist radiated an effortless proletarian humanism. Some lyricists exploit cliché; Berlin coined cliché: "A Pretty Girl Is Like a Melody", "Soft Lights and Sweet Music", "Harlem on My Mind", "There's No Business Like Show Business". Cohan first, then Kern and Berlin, broke the middle-European monopoly on music in English-language musical comedy. Shortly after them, Cole PORTER, George and Ira GERSHWIN, and Richard Rodgers and LORENZ HART completed the rout. Porter's adult subject matter and advanced chromatics, Gershwin's vital blues accent and Hart's naïve worldliness made it possible for musical comedy to tackle more varied subjects and to deal with ampler characters. Porter's *Fifty Million Frenchmen* (1929) treated love, for once, as sex; the Gershwins' *Oh, Kay!* (1926) reconciled the warring components of comedy and romance in its score, allowing for an emotional gradation in the love songs ("Do, Do, Do" is pert, "Maybe" expansively serene, "Someone to Watch Over Me" a little troubled). Rodgers and Hart wrote plot songs—the stuff between the Big Tunes, and the very essence of music theatre—like nobody's business. Yet many hung back from the modern style, putting their all into operetta. Noel COWARD and Ivor NOVELLO in England, and Sigmund Romberg and Rudolf Friml in America, kept Lehár's spirit glowing—as did Lehár, who peaked in *Giuditta* (1934), premièred at the Vienna State Opera, no less. Coward eventually grew into brash musical comedy in *Sail Away* (1961), but Romberg and Friml had got out of musical comedy into operetta and had no intention of getting back. "A full-blooded libretto with luscious melody, rousing choruses, and romantic passions"—that was Friml's personal genre. His *The Vagabond King* (1925) and *The Three Musketeers* (1928) and Romberg's *The Student Prince* (1924) and *The Desert Song* (1926) fought naturalistic musical comedy with period decor, cloak-and-dagger plots and delirious self-belief. Yet because both men worked with Oscar HAMMERSTEIN II, a librettist of meticulous rationality in storytelling, they too helped point the way to a more penetratingly unified form.

Kern and Hammerstein's *Show Boat* (1927) marks the breakthrough for the modern musical. While the authors did not entirely do away with conventional trappings—the "curtain-going-up" choruses, the comic secondary couple, the inconsequential dance turns—they still managed to include a serious theme, contrasting the transformation of earthly vanities with the changeless truths of human destiny. Edna Ferber's novel, *Show Boat*'s source, uses the Mississippi River as a symbol of the anarchic energies of industrial age man; to Kern and Hammerstein, the Mississippi is epic, ageless, and true, and man is a sometime thing. Kern used pastiche to suggest the passage of time, moving from cakewalk and the old story ballad to the Charleston. Hammerstein's lyrics to *Show Boat*'s theme song, "Ol' Man River", combined with the elemental sweep of Kern's tune, brings their theme home as the song grows in scope at each reprise.

Show Boat had few imitators. It wasn't even that successful at first. Broadway had doted on blends of frolic, sentiment, and uplift before, but conceptual sweep was something new. The original *Show Boat* was a hit, but not a sensation. Only at the time of the 1946 Broadway revival did everyone realize it was a classic, possibly The Classic. In London in 1971, *Show Boat* again reaffirmed itself; it is hopelessly dated and strangely hybrid, but absolutely tremendous.

Show Boat marks the culmination of operetta; the 1930s emphasized earthier musical comedy. It was also a golden age

of the suave revue—Noel Coward, Beatrice LILLIE, Bert LAHR, MARILYN MILLER, Ethel WATERS, Clifton Webb and Fred and Adele ASTAIRE all combined their own dazzling accomplishments with superb material. Coward wrote his own; Lahr improvised a mixture of tough-guy and debonair put-on; Astaire reshaped American romanticism with his unpretentious elegance. Arthur Schwartz and Howard Dietz supplied exemplary scores for *The Little Show* (1929), *Three's a Crowd* (1930), *The Band Wagon* (1931), and *Flying Colors* (1932), the songs of which offer a lively pastiche: German beer hall ("I Love Louisa"), American rustic ("Louisiana Hayride"), wry sleazo ("Smokin' Reefers") and sultry ballads ("Moanin' Low", "Dancing in the Dark"). Between the stars' specialities, the revues tried social spoof, encouraging the rise of the political musical. Innocence still reigned: the Gershwins' *Girl Crazy* (1930), Porter's *Anything Goes* (1934), Rodgers and Hart's ballet-rich *On Your Toes* (1936), hey-kids-let's-put-on-a-show *Babes in Arms* (1937), and the Shakespearean burlesque of *The Boys from Syracuse* (1938). But three other Gershwin shows, all with books co-authored by George S. Kaufman, challenged the state of things: *Strike up the Band* (1930) ridiculed militarism, *Of Thee I Sing* (1931) party politics and *Let 'Em Eat Cake* (1933) radical conspiracy. Other works, some less friendly than these, helped re-establish musical comedy's satiric component. Kurt Weill, in the process of his emigré's assimilation, smoothed over what remained of his Brechtian edge in PAUL GREEN's anti-war fantasy *Johnny Johnson* (1936) and actually sounded almost congenial in MAXWELL ANDERSON's celebration of the American anti-totalitarian temperament, *Knickerbocker Holiday* (1938). These were not products of the musical show shop, but plays liberated, so to speak, in music. *Johnny Johnson*, staged by the idealistic Group Theatre, didn't even boast a single "Broadway voice" in its cast. By far the most politicized entry was Marc Blitzstein's *The Cradle Will Rock* (1937), a savage anti-capitalist spoof. The federal government, Blitzstein's sponsor under one of Roosevelt's relief programmes, thought this too hard a show in such hard times and padlocked the theatre on opening night, but cast and crew discovered an empty (and open) theatre nearby. Taking the audience with them, they staged one of the most remarkable premières in theatrical history: Blitzstein alone at a wrecked upright piano, one grouchy spotlight, and a cast forbidden by its union to perform.

By the 1940s, American musical comedy had advanced way past what other cultures produced in the same line, through a combination of formidable production polish and the experimental audacity of its artists: composers, trained and amateur, poets and hacks alike. The ancient elements survived—the star comic (Bobby CLARK, Phil SILVERS), the glamorous celebrity turn (Gertrude LAWRENCE in *Lady in the Dark*, 1941), nags at contemporary problems, endorsements of timeless escapist sententia, dance and the exotic. But now creators were blending these elements organically. Harold Arlen's naturalistic fantasy *Cabin in the Sky* (1940) and period-flavoured *St Louis Woman* drew on black performing talent (Ethel WATERS, Todd Duncan, Katherine Dunham, PEARL BAILEY) to celebrate a subcultural life. Leonard Bernstein's *On the Town* (1944) derived a large part of its twenty-four-hour adventure of sailors on leave in New York out of the momentum of Jerome ROBBINS's choreography. *Finian's Rainbow* (1947) dealt frankly with capitalism, consumerism and race relations. Rodgers and Hammerstein's *Oklahoma!* (1943) and *Carousel* (1945) extrapolated the ethnic feeling of the west and New England respectively. Their *Allegro* (1947), a cult classic whose propaganda is repeatedly humiliated by Hammerstein's sluggish book, daringly told its tale of an idealistic young doctor through Agnes DE MILLE's free-form, set-less staging, an extension of her psychological and folk ballets in *Oklahoma!* and *Carousel*. By comparison, Emmerich Kálmán's last work, *Arizona Lady*, just a few years later, seemed hopelessly aimless with its czardas-crazed cowboys and empty libretto.

Perhaps most important was the strengthened musical base. Working on the same theory that inspired Gershwin to write the opera *Porgy and Bess* (1935), "legit" musicians mated Broadway's theatrical sophistication with scores of substance, dismantling the academic distinction between opera and musical comedy: Weill's *Street Scene* (1947) and *Lost in the Stars* (1949), Jerome Moross's *The Golden Apple* (1954) (to John Latouche's witty updating of Homer) and Bernstein's "comic operetta" *Candide* (1956), bedevilled by a problem of tone. Bernstein and his partners caught VOLTAIRE's bitter wit but also their sentimental hearts; a garish revision corrected the tone at the cost of the wit and a substantial fraction of the score.

In Europe, the 1950s saw the phenomenal imperialism of the American musical, led by Berlin's *Annie Get Your Gun* (1946) and Porter's *Kiss Me, Kate* (1948) in countless productions of varying authenticity. (Dolores Gray's Annie offered London a persuasive alternative to Broadway's Ethel MERMAN and the American touring company's Mary Martin, but the Wagnerian tenor Max Lorenz must have made a bizarre mouthful of Frank Butler in a Vienna staging, not least in "Alles was du Kannst, das Kann ich Viel Besser".) The French responded with Robert Dhéry's quasi-pantomimed revue *La Plume de Ma Tante* (1954) and Marguerite Monnot's *Irma-La-Douce* (1956), the light-hearted tale of a *poule* and her penniless lover, though the work became best known through Peter BROOK's drolly austere London staging with Elizabeth Seal. Sandy Wilson helped inaugurate a heyday for the British musical with a thin but charming spoof of the 1920s, *The Boy Friend* (1953); aficionados claim that the Broadway edition, with the seventeen-year-old Julie Andrews and a hot period jazz band, outdid the London original, which featured the great Anne Rogers but suffered from its inadequate piano accompaniment. Julian Slade's *Salad Days* (1954) furthered Wilson's "little-show" foolishness with an absurd vaudeville loosely centred on a subversive piano that makes people dance against their will. But Wilson himself lost his innocence in his wickedly faithful adaptation of Ronald Firbank, *Valmouth* (1958), with Cleo Laine as a sinister masseuse, Doris Hare as a mouldy religious fanatic, and Fenella Fielding as lascivious Lady Parvula de Panzoust. The critics were scandalized; one headline screamed, "HAS THE CENSOR QUIT?"

Performers, too, could act as censors. "Call me Miss Birdseye", Ethel Merman told Irving Berlin when he tried to replace a lyric just before the opening of *Call Me Madam* (1950), "This show is frozen!" She was righter than she knew. A period of stasis followed the really quite radical developments of the 1930s and 1940s through topical, technical and musical experiments; the whole art was frozen. Often, the biggest hits seemed to be more or less conventional adaptations of old properties—Frederick Loewe and Alan Jay LERNER's *My Fair Lady* (1956) and *Camelot* (1960), Rodgers and Hammerstein's *The King and I* (1951). The Boy Meets Girl syndrome, the chain of ballads, comic spots, plot numbers, the dancers' cues, the proscenium-bound decor, the star's "eleven o'clock song"–everything from overture to curtain calls sank into ruts, though Broadway polish and sheer gutsy elation kept the form alive. And there were still standout events, such as Frank Loesser's advanced use of

recitative, ensemble and free song form in the pleasantly low-down *Guys and Dolls* (1950), Meredith Willson's midwestern nostalgia in *The Music Man* (1957) and the precise collaboration of Bernstein's music and Robbins's choreography in *West Side Story* (1957). Another surprise was Jule Styne, Stephen SONDHEIM, and Arthur LAURENTS' *Gypsy* (1959), which threw out the traditional love plot for a look at the compulsions of a stage mother–GYPSY ROSE LEE's, in fact, done to the nth by Ethel Merman and, in revival, Angela LANSBURY.

The rise of the super-director helped defeat convention, introducing the "staging-concept" show, in which all elements grow out of a fundamental look and motion. Such thinking was old on Broadway; Rouben Mamoulian's productions of *Oklahoma!*, *Carousel* and *Lost in the Stars* and Agnes de Mille's of *Allegro* insisted on unity as a first principle of the art. But in those days the material was written first, then staged, and (usually) lightly polished in tryouts. In the 1960s, directors collaborated with the writers and sometimes overhauled works *in toto* on an extended pre-Broadway tour. (This, too, was not entirely new: *No, No, Nanette*, in 1925, spent so much time on the road that "Tea for Two" and "I Want to be Happy" had become standards before the piece reached New York.) Anthony Newley and Leslie Bricusse's parable-like *Stop the World–I Want to Get Off* (1961) drew its interest from its circus-ring set, Newley's clown-like protagonist Littlechap, Anna Quayle's rendering of the women in his life, and an all-purpose girls' chorus; these diverse quantities merged in a single-minded atmosphere. Similarly, Jerry Bock and Sheldon Harnick's *Fiddler on the Roof* (1964) was strengthened by the framework of Jerome Robbins's Russian–Jewish village style and Boris Aronson's Chagall-like designs. Even Zero MOSTEL, an occasionally undisciplined performer who would let an indulgent public encourage his spontaneity in the obsolete style of the old burlesque-trained comics, transcended type as Tevye, the poor milkman with five daughters to marry off. Perhaps Topol, who played the role in London and on film, is the superior artist. But Mostel's manic buffoonery ultimately enriched the part and made the pathos all the more telling. Topol's was the truer Tevye, but Mostel's was the classic.

Jerry Herman's *Hello, Dolly!* (1964) is simply a first-rate pop package: star spotlight, a sound farcical source (Thornton Wilder's *The Matchmaker*) and title-tune showstopper all neatly placed. But John Kander and Fred Ebb's *Cabaret* (1966) shows the result of artistic forethought, all conventions either integrated into the whole or omitted. This is no star vehicle. The source is unusual, even "unsuitable" (Christopher Isherwood's tales of interwar Berlin). The title tune offers no production number, but an ironic reflection of the work's concept: escapism ("Life is a cabaret, old chum") promotes catastrophe. Harold PRINCE staged *Cabaret* to use the nightclub set pieces as com-

One of the most original musicals of recent years, *Cabaret* (*left*) abandoned the healthy, high-stepping chorus line for the suspendered squalor of the night-club

The already considerable fame of George Bernard Shaw's *Pygmalion* was totally eclipsed by the phenomenal success of its musical version, *My Fair Lady* (*right*). Here Rex Harrison is intrigued by Julie Andrews's improbable vowel-sounds

The material on which great musical comedies are based has often undergone countless metamorphoses, before assuming its final form. *Hello Dolly!* (*far right*) had as its distant ancestor a Viennese comedy, written over a century before by Nestroy

mentary on the story, dispensing with pop's obsequious respect of its audience, even denying them the traditional rise of the curtain and formal bows that symbolize the ancient reassurance that "it's only a play".

The old guard continued to pursue romance (i.e. operetta) in such works as Broadway's *Man of La Mancha* (1965) and London's *Robert and Elizabeth* (1964), an adaptation of *The Barretts of Wimpole Street*. Both shows proved the power of all-out vocalism. *La Mancha* reduced CERVANTES' tragicomedy to "The Impossible Dream" and Ron Grainer's *Robert* score pulled his Elizabeth (June Bronhill) up to a stunning high D in the turbulent "Woman and Man". Show-shop impresarios tried vainly to follow *Hair* (1967) with a canon of rock musicals – vainly, for rock is eclectic and doesn't always behave according to expectations. It is notable that Andrew Lloyd Webber and TIM RICE's "rock opera" *Jesus Christ Superstar* (1971) has more blues and ragtime than rock, and their *Evita* (1978) has no rock at all. Indeed, both these works, arguably operas, demonstrate standard musical comedy "parts" that the rock shows, including the money-grubbing *Hair*, never got down: extensive musical pastiche, commentative "alienation" from a character who participates in the action and addresses the audience, and high production values. (Tom O'HORGAN's staging of the Broadway – as opposed to the original off-Broadway – *Hair* was competent, but an often sloppy or absentee cast made a mess of the production in short order.)

Rock briefly encouraged the hopes of those who wanted to hear something contemporary in the musical, and it is certainly true that while theatre music dominated the pop music scene from the 1920s through the 1950s, the revelation of rock's experimental possibilities (mainly in the work of the Beatles), combined with the superior economics of rock recordings and concerts, elbowed theatre music aside. Yet no alternative to Broadway traditionalism presented itself. Rock couldn't adapt, and such modern pop excursions as Burt Bacharach and Hal David's score for *Promises, Promises* (1968) constituted a momentary stunt. Even John Barry, as instrumental as Bacharach in colouring the contemporary pop sound in his film soundtrack scores, turned conservative in *Billy* (1974), an adaptation of *Billy Liar*. Barry deftly manipulated parodies of hymn, music hall, and fifties rock and roll while tracking Billy's impetuous dream worlds. This most adult of British musicals, more threatening than *Cabaret* in its working-class relevance, remains a neglected masterpiece despite Michael Crawford's high-powered performance in the title part. One British musical to cause a sensation wherever it went, was Richard O'Brien's gaily anarchic *Rocky Horror Show*.

It was Stephen Sondheim who patterned the new sound in a series of innovative musicals staged by Harold Prince: *Company* (1970), *Follies* (1971), *A Little Night Music* (1973), *Pacific*

Overtures (1976) and *Sweeney Todd* (1979). As with his *Cabaret* and *Evita* productions, Prince created a non-realistic fluidity, confronting characters with ghosts of their former selves in *Follies* and combining musical comedy conventions with those of the Kabuki theatre in *Pacific Overtures*. Sondheim's subjects ignore the cardinal rule of pop theatre: flatter the customers. *Company* evoked an unnervingly eloquent ambivalence about marriage; *Follies* shattered old myths through the use of parodies of old theatre styles and antique performers; *Sweeney Todd* gave a Marxist reading of the exploits of a mass murderer in Victorian London. Sondheim's verbal point and musical gifts are unsurpassed. *Company*'s driving currency, *Follies*' panorama of stage types, *Night Music*'s sumptuous waltzes, *Pacific Overtures*' conceptual organization and *Sweeney Todd*'s penetrating characterization are the wonders of the decade.

Yet this sophistication notwithstanding, musical comedy has retained the formative elements – musical parody, socio-political burlesque and contraposition of the ideal and the natural – that can be traced far back in its history, through Offenbach to *The Magic Flute* and beyond. Two shows of 1975 demonstrate the modern versions of romance and satire: *A Chorus Line* and *Chicago*. The former's auditioning dancers involve the spectators on an emotional level, beseeching sympathy and belief; the latter's almost Brechtian detachment laughs at its jazz-age criminals, hustlers and stooges. Marvin Hamlisch and Edward Kleban's whimsical and fervent *Chorus Line* score suspends one's cynicism; Kander and Ebb's *Chicago* arouses it with Kern "cheer up" ditties, Bert Wheeler's self-pity, Rudy Vallee's megaphone, Eddie CANTOR, and the "my man" torch song all get mercilessly lampooned. There is another difference between the two, basic to show-biz technology. *A Chorus Line*'s cast were all unknowns, except one character, a former principal down on her luck, who, in this musical-verité, would naturally be played by a real-life counterpart, Donna McKechnie (though her New York replacement, Ann Reinking, was on the rise rather than the skids). *Chicago*, because it exploded the glamorous lies of communications, needed stars, and got them: Gwen Verdon, Chita Rivera and Jerry Ohrbach, Verdon being succeeded as Roxie Hart by Liza Minnelli and Reinking again (by far the best and meanest of the three Roxies).

Both *A Chorus Line* and *Chicago* are products of the age of the super-director. Michael Bennett steered *A Chorus Line* through months of rewrites, and Bob Fosse (credited as co-author of the book) created *Chicago* out of his trademark splayed-elbow, finger-snapping, ghoul-tango style. No two works could have felt more mid-seventies than these, yet both together comprise the two ageless sides of musical comedy, *A Chorus Line* supplying the operetta and *Chicago* supplying the satire. The farce, sentiment and idiom of ancient days are, for all their constant reinvention, nimbly permanent.

Alienation Technique

Also known as the "A effect", it was invented by Bertolt BRECHT in a reaction against the meticulous naturalism of STANISLAVSKY's theatre. It is a theory of presentation which never allows the audience to forget they are in a theatre. Certain techniques of writing, acting and directing are used to elicit a more critical response to the action from the audience, and to discourage their emotional identification with the characters. Often a story teller or singer "distances" the spectator from the plot, focussing his attention on the reasons behind a character's behaviour. Brecht perfected this technique with the **Berliner Ensemble** in plays like *Mutter Courage* and *Galileo*.

Alternative Theatre

A term encompassing all theatre work which rejects the conventional West End and Broadway establishments. Alternative companies are usually community orientated and often politically committed, preferring to play to a non-theatregoing audience in unconventional venues. See **Happening**, also **Fringe**.

Ballad Opera

A form invented (and unsurpassed) by John GAY in *The Beggar's Opera* of 1728. It is a popular play with many songs set to well-known tunes of the time. As a genre it was short-lived, although popular tunes were used in the English theatre for many years afterwards.

Barnstormers

Term applied to nineteenth-century strolling players who would set up their stage in a large barn. Their performances were distinguished by much shouting, raving and violent gestures, hence the name.

Berliner Ensemble

Company founded by Bertolt BRECHT in 1949 to perform his own plays and explore his theories of theatre. See **Alienation Technique**.

Boulevard Theatre

Term applied after 1850 to any popular French drama from **Farce** to domestic plays. It especially refers to the Boulevard Voltaire, built on an old fairground site, now the home of many popular commercial theatres.

Broadway

The main theatre street in New York, equivalent to London's West End. Since the inception of theatre in America, all the principal New York theatres have been found on Broadway or its side streets.

Burlesque

Originally an eighteenth-century form referring to a play parodying a current success. In late nineteenth-century America it came to mean a type of show aimed at exclusively male audiences with a bias towards comedy and sex. Moral outcry banned burlesque from New York in 1942.

Cabaret

An intimate entertainment of Parisian origin, built around a single performer who establishes a close relationship with his or her audience in clubs or theatres. In the case of particularly well-known entertainers, cabaret is now often packaged as a spectacular revue. In pre-Nazi Germany, political cabaret clubs were especially popular, influencing the young BRECHT.

Clown

A comic performer. There are two distinct types of clown, the court jester or all-seeing "fool" to be found in SHAKESPEARE, and the circus buffoon of the **Commedia dell' Arte**. The lovable innocent and the quipping cynic combine to make the clown as we know him today: an extremely funny, but somehow pathetic figure now rarely seen outside the circus. Each clown creates his own "character" and patents the make-up that expresses it.

Commedia dell' Arte

A popular form of Italian comedy during the sixteenth and seventeenth centuries. Actors of the Commedia would each specialize in their own masked stock character. Plays were improvised around comic situations and included jokes, acrobatics and much stage business. Enjoyed equally by the upper and lower classes, the various Commedia companies toured Europe, extensively influencing writers like MOLIÈRE and GOLDONI. The emphasis was totally on the actors' craft and their ability to invent spontaneously together on stage. See also page 38.

Curtain Raiser

A one-act play, usually farcical, designed to whet the audience's appetite for the more meaty drama to follow. Now rarely seen.

Dada

Shorthand for the eccentric life and work of Tristan Tzara and his followers around 1920. Tzara turned all artistic and social conventions on their heads and founded the Dada movement. The name Dada is apparently arbitrary, part of life's nonsense. Dada's famous visual descendants include the iconoclastic Dali and Duchamp, while the **Theatre of The Absurd** developed Dada's dramatic potential.

Dramaturge

A kind of literary manager attached to a theatre company, whose function is to select scripts for production, often working closely with the author on revisions. Unfortunately English theatres have not imported this German idea.

Epic Theatre

Bertolt BRECHT's term for the kind of theatre he was creating with the **Berliner Ensemble**. See **Alienation Technique**.

Equity

Compulsory trade union for British, American and Australian actors, founded in America in 1912, and in Britain in 1929.

Expressionism

An artistic movement which burgeoned in Germany around 1910. The expressionists in art and theatre reacted against nineteenth-century **Naturalism** in an attempt to portray a larger, more spiritual vision of life and its dark underside. Their style was urgent and bold, often resulting in works of grotesque fantasy. Principal dramatists of this movement were KAISER and TOLLER. See also page 204.

Farce

A fast-moving light comedy in which a series of stereotyped characters manoeuvre through intricate situations and improbable coincidences. It is difficult to draw a precise distinction between comedy and farce, but if the plot involves complicated amorous exploits and hasty exits through a number of well coordinated doors, it is probably farce.

Fringe

Small-scale theatre companies specialising in **Alternative Theatre**. Some of the best shows in London can be found "on the fringe", as these companies often experiment with new writers and innovatory styles that commercial managements are afraid to touch.

Happenings

An experimental form of **Alternative Theatre** with origins in **Dada**, where an artist creates an event in which the audience feel free to participate as they choose. Examples of happenings are the affixing of dollar bills to bare January branches (Alan Kaprow), Jim Dine's audio-visual psychodrama, "The Car Crash", or a man diving into a vat of banana custard (Ken Campbell). Many of these events have an environmental bias, closely allied to performance art as explored by John Cage in experiments with musicians, painters and dancers at Black Mountain College, North Carolina, in 1952. Making a snowman is a happening—especially if you stay around to watch it melt.

Harlequin

From *Arlecchino*, the most popular character of the **Commedia dell' Arte**. Harlequin is an enigmatic character. Childlike but also an inveterate lecher, he feigns stupidity but is very cunning; his mask has pert, chubby features but often looks downcast. In the eighteenth century Harlequin donned a costume patterned with coloured diamond shapes to become the romantic lover of Columbine in the English mime spectacle, the Harlequinade.

Improvisation

Acting without a set script. This technique was at the heart of **Commedia dell' Arte** performances, in which actors would invent dialogue to develop their characters inside a given story line. As an exercise (particularly for **Method** actors) improvisation is often used to help an actor explore his role by exposing him "in character" to situations not encountered in the script. Basically, improvisation is a sophisticated game of make-believe, now gaining popularity especially in **Alternative Theatre**.

Ingénue

General term for the roles of innocent young girls in the theatre.

Interlude

A short dramatic piece inserted into a longer play. It can also mean a theatrical entertainment at a social function. The play of *Pyramus and Thisbe* in SHAKESPEARE's *A Midsummer Night's Dream* is an interlude.

Libretto

The text of an opera or other lengthy musical composition.

Melodrama

Of eighteenth-century French origin, meaning a play with musical accompaniment. At moments of great pathos or sentimentality, a small orchestra would underscore the dramatic mood. Later the term came to refer to any particularly sensational drama, and now is only used derogatorily to describe exaggerated wallowing in emotion. Popular melodramas were *East Lynne*, *The Bells* and *The Ticket-of-Leave Man*.

Method

The Method is a theory of training actors evolved by Lee STRASBERG at the Actors' Studio, New York, on the principles of STANISLAVSKY. Method actors concentrate on the inner life of the role, using improvisation and other exercises to encourage complete identification with the character they are playing. This technique leads to extreme **Naturalism**, and has been criticised for neglecting diction and style, but it has nonetheless reared some of America's greatest actors.

Middle Comedy

The transitional stage between **Old Comedy** and **New Comedy**, of which mainly fragments have survived.

Miracle Play
Synonymous with **Mystery Play**, now a term rarely used.

Monologue
A lengthy speech delivered by one person. Now also used to refer to any dramatic composition for a single actor.

Morality Play
A late medieval allegorical drama in which personified virtues and vices struggle to win man's soul. The anonymous play *Everyman* is the most famous to survive.

Music Hall
Introduced to England in the mid-nineteenth century, it remained the most popular working-class entertainment for nearly a hundred years. Originally attached to public houses, music halls like the Surrey and the Canterbury were rapidly purpose-built to meet the demand. Performers would present their acts when announced by the chairman, a voluble figure who engaged the audience in banter between items. Many music hall songs were salacious or laced with social satire. Other acts included diverse forms of dance (like the popular "Sanddance"), monologues, magic acts, tableaux and character comics. Music hall reached its peak with a Royal Command Performance in 1911. After the war it degenerated and was finally snuffed out by the cinema, radio and television. See also page 144/5.

Musical Comedy
A play punctuated by songs and dance which evolved from the light operas of the late nineteenth century. During the 1920s, romantic operettas were superseded by the more sophisticated fast-moving musical shows of George Gershwin, Cole PORTER and Irving BERLIN. Musical comedy has a tendency towards trite subject matter, but serious experimenters have explored the integration of singing, dancing and text to produce something exciting and substantial, e.g. *West Side Story* (1957) and *Sweeney Todd* (1979).

Mystery Play
Sometimes called **Miracle Plays**. Short medieval pieces dramatizing scenes from the Bible often with gory detail and rough jokes. In England, members of trade guilds would perform a cycle of these plays on feast days. Only four cycles survive, those of York, Coventry, Wakefield and Chester.

Naturalism
A nineteenth-century movement which rejected theatrical artifice and fancy spectacle in favour of stark realism. Emile ZOLA's dramatisation of his own low-life novel, *Thérèse Raquin*, captured just the blend of psychological insight and uncompromising social realism that the naturalists sought. Both IBSEN and STRINDBERG strayed from the movement after an inspired flirtation. Naturalism was especially successful in Russia with GORKY's dramas, and was championed in England by GEORGE BERNARD SHAW.

New Comedy
A late form of Greek Comedy, exemplified by MENANDER. These urbane comedies of manners involve plots of disguise and mistaken identity, with the chorus relegated to a minor role. The Roman PLAUTUS (and later SHAKESPEARE in *The Comedy of Errors*) imitated this form.

Off-Broadway
New York sister to **Fringe**. Off-Broadway can be said to lead the world in experimental **Alternative Theatre** with exciting ventures by companies like the Living Theatre, and the La Mama troupe.

Old Comedy
The earliest form of Greek Comedy, using a chorus and strict processional forms based on religious rituals but also connected with more spontaneous fertility rites and revels. ARISTOPHANES' topical satires fall into this category.

Pantomime
Originally synonymous with Mime, now referring to a peculiarly English form of Christmas entertainment with songs and dances. In these plays the hero is traditionally played by a girl (the "Principal Boy") and the comic mother (the "Dame") by a man. Various tales e.g. *Cinderella* or *Jack and The Beanstalk* are used as apologies for a story line.

Pierrot
A childlike clown character, who began as Pedrolino in the **Commedia dell' Arte** but who became a naturalized Frenchman, distinguished by his floppy white costume and a dunce's cap. Pierrot rarely speaks, and celebrated mimes like DEBURAU and MARCEL MARCEAU have based much of their work on this innocent, sentimental figure.

Pit
The ground floor of a theatre, where seats used to be cheap.

Prompter
A person who sits in the wings to "feed" actors when they forget their lines.

Proscenium
The picture-frame effect on the front of the stage. Proscenium-arch theatres were introduced in the seventeenth century. The stage was divided into two areas with most of the action taking place on the forestage, while the scenic background remained behind the arch. By the nineteenth century the whole stage was framed by the proscenium arch, giving the traditional theatres still used everywhere today.

Punch
Mr Punch originated as Pulcinella, a character of the **Commedia dell' Arte**. He is now a hook-nosed and hump-backed glove puppet. Cruel, selfish and pretentious, he murders nearly everyone who appears on stage with him, including the hangman. Mr Punch can be found in English seaside puppet booths along with his wife Judy and dog Toby.

RADA
Royal Academy of Dramatic Art. London's most prestigious acting school, now in Gower Street, was founded by BEERBOHM TREE in 1904.

Repertoire
The term for the total selection of plays that a company has ready for performance in the same season. Up to this century most English and American theatres had an extensive repertoire of plays, but the practice has become prohibitively expensive for all but the wealthiest companies. Repertoire and repertory were originally synonymous, but the latter term now generally refers to a company that has several plays "in repertoire".

Repertory
See **Repertoire**.

Revue
A selection of comic sketches, songs and dances following on in quick succession, often with a topical or satirical slant.

Soliloquy
A reflective monologue spoken by a character alone on stage, in which he reveals his hidden hopes and fears.

Soubrette
Actress specializing in comic roles of pert, saucy young girls–often French maids.

Stock
A form of American **Repertory** company who perform during the Summer in out-of-town theatres.

Sturm und Drang
German, literally "Storm and Stress". A generic term applied to a group of late eighteenth- and early nineteenth-century German dramatists who took Shakespearean tragedy as their model. These Romantic poets treated extreme emotions on a large scale, usually celebrating the triumph of violent passion over high-minded principle. GOETHE's *Faust* and the historical dramas of FRIEDRICH SCHILLER best illustrate this movement. See also page 104.

Theatre in the Round
A form of presenting a play with the audience seated in radiating circles around the acting area. The idea dates from the middle ages, but has only recently returned to vogue. When used effectively it can result in a vibrant and involving theatre for both actors and audience.

Theatre of Cruelty
A theory advanced by Antonin ARTAUD in his book, *The Theatre and Its Double*. Artaud believed that the theatre should be a place of ritual and magic, releasing subconscious, elemental forces in the audience. To achieve this, narrative and naturalistic dialogue have to be replaced by violently obsessive characters, images, incantations and stylized gesture, giving direct expression to the emotions. Jean-Louis BARRAULT and Peter BROOK both espoused Artaud's theory in their work.

Theatre of the Absurd
Term for the plays of a group of dramatists working in the 1950s who transferred the irrational to the stage. Strongly influenced by Albert CAMUS's analysis of the absurdity of the human condition, they mirrored this in the form as well as the content of their plays. Although very funny, they are marked by a vein of desperation as characters behave illogically, and impossible, fantastic events occur on stage. The best absurd plays are one-act pieces, notably by ARRABAL, IONESCO, BECKETT and PINTER. See also page 238.

Tony
A prize awarded annually by the League of New York Theatres and Producers for best actor, best actress, best play etc. Established in 1947 to encourage excellence in the theatre, Tonys are named after the actress and director Antoinette Perry, and consist of a revolving medal mounted on a plastic base.

Total Theatre
A concept of theatre as primarily the director's medium. Design, sound, lights and images have equal status with actors in order to create a "total" theatrical effect.

Vaudeville
The term originally applied to light satirical French plays with songs, but in the nineteenth century it became an American form of **Music Hall**. Tony Pastor pioneered Vaudeville in New York, and it was later refined by impresarios into a slick and punchy family entertainment.

West End
The traditional heart of London's theatreland, centred around Shaftesbury Avenue. It is run by commercial managements, the emphasis being on well-known names and long-running tourist attractions.

306

INDEX
COMPILED BY FREDERICK SMYTH, MEMBER OF THE SOCIETY OF INDEXERS

Page numbers in **bold type (25)** indicate biographical sections and other headed articles and important references. *Italic* page numbers *(25)* direct the reader to illustrations or their captions. All other page references are in normal roman type (25). "q." stands for "quoted".

The titles of stage works and films only are alphabetically indexed and, unless otherwise qualified, are those of plays. Under the names of authors, composers, etc., are listed only those of their works to which reference in text or captions is made *other than* in the headed sections relating to the persons concerned. The duplication of multiple entries relating to individual stage works has been avoided, for the works of Corneille, Ibsen, Molière, Racine and Shakespeare, by cross-referencing

ACKNOWLEDGEMENTS

The editors and publishers would like to express their grateful thanks for the valuable assistance given by the following: Victor Stevenson for the original concept of the book, Betty Beesley of the Garrick Club in London, Ethel Hurwicz, Raymonde Largaud, John P. O'Neill of The Metropolitan Museum of Art in New York, Amber Newell, Kenneth Rea, Martin Rogerson, Richard Small, and the Librarian and staff of the Westminster Central Reference Library in London

GENERAL CREDITS

Make-up feature on page 276/7: Photographed by Duncan McNicol, make-up by Douglas Young and wig by Wig Specialities Ltd., London
Jacket and Prelims: Photographs of John Beresford Slinger commissioned by Sue Casebourne and taken by Kim Sayer

ARTISTS' CREDITS

Studio Briggs: 51, 61B, 134
Hugh Dixon/Spectron Artists: 285
Howard Levitt/Young Artists: 156/7
Dan Pearce/Beint & Beint: 42/3, 68/9, 77
Helena Zakrzewska-Rucinska: 141
Retouching: Michael Mann Studios

PICTURE CREDITS

B: Bottom C: Centre L: Left
R: Right T: Top

8: Ronald Sheridan 8/9(B): Photo Resources 9: Brian and Sally Shuel 10/11: Michael Holford/British Museum 12(TL): Ronald Sheridan 12(CL): Ronald Sheridan 12(R): Wagner Museum, Wurzburg 13(L): Michael Holford/British Museum 13(R): Ronald Sheridan 14: Michael Holford 15(TL): Rheinisches Landmuseum, Trier 15(TR): Michael Holford/British Museum 15(C): Rapho 15(BL): Ronald Sheridan 15(BR): Scala/Roma, Musei Capitolini 16(L): Archiv fur Kunst und Geschichte 16(R): Archiv fur Kunst und Geschichte 17: Hirmer Fotoarchiv 20(T): Scala/Roma Museo delle Terme 20(B): John Hillelson Agency/Erich Lessing 23(T): Bibliothèque Nationale 23(B): J. C. D. Smith 24/25: Musée de Cluny/Cliché Musées Nationaux, Paris 25(L): J. C. D. Smith 25(R): Bodleian Library, Oxford 26(T): Bibliothèque Nationale 27(T): Galleria Sabauda, Torino/Chomon-Perino 26/27(B): Crown Copyright/Victoria and Albert Museum 28/29: Mary Evans Picture Library 30: BBC Hulton Picture Library 31: BBC Hulton Picture Library 32(L): Uffizi Gallery, Florence 32(R): Mary Evans Picture Library 33: Victoria and Albert Museum/Elly Beintema 35: Mary Evans Picture Library 36(T): BBC Hulton Picture Library 36(B): BBC Hulton Picture Library 37: Mary Evans Picture Library 38/TL): The British Museum 38(TC): Victoria and Albert Museum/Elly Beintema 38(TR): The British Museum 38(B): BBC Hulton Picture Library 39: Mary Evans Picture Library 41(TL): BBC Hulton Picture Library 41(TR): Mary Evans Picture Library 41(B): Robert Harding Associates 44(TL): Dominic Photography 44(TC): Mander and Mitchenson Theatre Collection 44(TR): Mander and Mitchenson Theatre Collection 44(CL): Ullstein Bilderdienst 44(CR): Octavian Books/Victoria and Albert Museum 44(BL): Mander and Mitchenson Theatre Collection 44(BR): Mander and Mitchenson Theatre Collection 45(TL): Dominic Photography 45(TR): René Dazy 45(BL): BBC Hulton Picture Library 45(C): Mander and Mitchenson Theatre Collection 45(BC): Mander and Mitchenson Theatre Collection 45(BR): Osterreichische Nationalbibliothek 46(L): National Portrait Gallery, London 46(R): Mary Evans Picture Library 47(L): Mary Evans Picture Library 47(R): Dulwich College Gallery 49: Mary Evans Picture Library 50: Farabola Foto 51(T): BBC Hulton Picture Library 52/53: BBC Hulton Picture Library 55(T): BBC Hulton Picture Library 55(B): Time Life–Library of Art–*The World of Bernini*/Photograph by Dmitri Kessel, © 1970 Time Inc. 57: BBC Hulton Picture Library 58: Metropolitan Museum of Art 59: BBC Hulton Picture Library 60(T): Victoria and Albert Museum/Elly Beintema 60(C): Victoria and Albert Museum/Elly Beintema 60(B): National Museum, Stockholm 61(T): Victoria and Albert Museum/Elly Beintema 61(CB): Victoria and Albert Museum/Elly Beintema 61(B): Victoria and Albert Museum/Elly Beintema 62(T): BBC Hulton Picture Library 62(C): Robert Harding Associates 62(B): BBC Hulton Picture Library 65(T): National Gallery, London 65(B): National Gallery, London 66/67: Mansell Collection 68: Comédie Française 69(L): Mander and Mitchenson Theatre Collection 69(R): Osterreichische Nationalbibliothek 71(T): Biblioteca Marciana/Foto Tosa 71(CL): Callwey/Helga Schmidt-Glassner 71(CR): Callwey/Helga Schmidt-Glassner 71(B): Callwey/Helga Schmidt-Glassner 72: Mary Evans Picture Library 73: BBC Hulton Picture Library 74: BBC Hulton Picture Library 75(L): Mary Evans Picture Library 75(R): George Rainbird Ltd/courtesy Lord Brooke 77: "Nell Gwynn and the infant Duke of St. Albans" by Sir Peter Lely from The Denys Eyre Bower Collection, Chiddingstone Castle, Kent 79(T): Mary Evans Picture Library 79(C): Mary Evans Picture Library 79(B): National Portrait Gallery, London 80(T): BBC Hulton Picture Library 80(BL): Mansell Collection 80(BR): Garrick Club 82(T): BBC Hulton Picture Library 82(B): Mary Evans Picture Library 85(L): BBC Hulton Picture Library 85(TC): Garrick Club 85(TR): Mary Evans Picture Library 85(B): BBC Hulton Picture Library 86: BBC Hulton Picture Library 87(L): René Dazy 87(R): Archiv fur Kunst und Geschichte 89(TL): BBC Hulton Picture Library 89(TR): Mary Evans Picture Library 89(C): Institut fur Theater Wissenshacht, Universität Köln 89(B): Garrick Club 90(T): BBC Hulton Picture Library 90(B): BBC Hulton Picture Library 92(L): National Portrait Gallery, London 92(R): Italian Institute, London 93: Garrick Club 95: BBC Hulton Picture Library 96: Archiv fur Kunst und Geschichte 98: BBC Hulton Picture Library 98/99: Moro/Roma 101: BBC Hulton Picture Library 102: Osterreichische Nationalbibliothek 103: National Portrait Gallery, London 105(L): Kunsthalle, Hamburg 105(R): BBC Hulton Picture Library 107: BBC Hulton Picture Library 108(TL): BBC Hulton Picture Library 108(TR): Victoria and Albert Museum/Elly Beintema 108(B): BBC Hulton Picture Library 110(L): BBC Hulton Picture Library 110(R): Osterreichische Nationalbibliothek 111: René Dazy 112(T): BBC Hulton Picture Library 112(C): Mary Evans Picture Library 112(B): Giraudon 114(L): BBC Hulton Picture Library 114(R): BBC Hulton Picture Library 115(L): BBC Hulton Picture Library 115(R): Mander and Mitchenson Theatre Collection 117(T): BBC Hulton Picture Library 117(B): BBC Hulton Picture Library 119: Mary Evans Picture Library 123: Victoria and Albert Museum/Elly Beintema 124(TL): Kevin MacDonnell 124(TR): BBC Hulton Picture Library 124(BL): Publi Foto 124(BR): BBC Hulton Picture Library 126: BBC Hulton Picture Library 129(T): BBC Hulton Picture Library 129(B): BBC Hulton Picture Library 131(T): Cassell and Co. 131(CL): BBC Hulton Picture Library 131(BL): John Frost 131(R): Garrick Club 132: Archiv fur Kunst und Geschichte 133(L): Mander and Mitchenson Theatre Collection 133(C): Milbourne Christopher 133(R): Mander and Mitchenson Theatre Collection 134: Bettmann Archive 135: Mander and Mitchenson Theatre Collection 136(T): National Portrait Gallery, London 136(B): Giraudon/BN/S.P.A.D.E.M. 138: Klaus Budzinski Archiv 141: BBC Hulton Picture Library 142: BBC Hulton Picture Library 144(TL): Mander and Mitchenson Theatre Collection 144(BL): Victoria and Albert Museum/Elly Beintema 144(C): Mander and Mitchenson Theatre Collection 144(BC): Mander and Mitchenson Theatre Collection 144(BR): Mander and Mitchenson Theatre Collection 145(T): Daily Telegraph Colour Library 145(BL): Mander and Mitchenson Theatre Collection 145(BC): Mander and Mitchenson Theatre Collection 145(BR): BBC Hulton Picture Library 150(TL): BBC Hulton Picture Library 150(TR): Society for Cultural Relations with USSR 151: BBC Hulton Picture Library 153(T): Archiv fur Kunst und Geschichte 153(B): Mander and Mitchenson Theatre Collection 155: Farabola 156: New York Public Library, Lincoln Center 156/157: New York Public Library, Lincoln Center 160(T): Mander and Mitchenson Theatre Collection 160(BL): BBC Hulton Picture Library 160(BR): Novosti 163: Lords Gallery 165(T): Culver Pictures 165(B): Culver Pictures 167: Culver Pictures 168(T): Photopress, Switzerland 168(B): BBC Hulton Picture Library 170: BBC Hulton Picture Library 171(L): BBC Hulton Picture Library 171(R): BBC Hulton Picture Library 172: BBC Hulton Picture Library 174: Victoria and Albert Museum/Elly Beintema 175(T): BBC Hulton Picture Library 175(C): New York Public Library, Lincoln Center 175(B): BBC Hulton Picture Library 178(T): BBC Hulton Picture Library 178(C): Kobal Collection 178(B): BBC Hulton Picture Library 181: New York Public Library, Lincoln Center 182(TL): BBC Hulton Picture Library 182(TR): BBC Hulton Picture Library 182(B): BBC Hulton Picture Library 184(L): BBC Hulton Picture Library 184(C): New York Public Library, Lincoln Center 184(B): Ullstein Bilderdienst 185(L): René Dazy 185(R): BBC Hulton Picture Library 189: New York Public Library, Lincoln Center 190: Camera Press 191(L): New York Public Library, Lincoln Center 191(R): BBC Hulton Picture Library 193(T): Mander and Mitchenson Theatre Collection 193(B): Ullstein Bilderdienst 194(T): New York Public Library, Lincoln Center 194(B): BBC Hulton Picture Library 197: New York Public Library, Lincoln Center 198: René Dazy 200: Archiv fur Kunst und Geschichte 201: Archiv fur Kunst und Geschichte 202(TL): René Dazy 202(TR): Ullstein Bilderdienst 202(B): Norsk Telegrombyra Billedarkivet 204: ADN/Zentrabild 205(T): New York Public Library, Lincoln Center 205(B): Étienne Bertrand Weill 206: BBC Hulton Picture Library 207: New York Public Library, Lincoln Center 208: New York Public Library, Lincoln Center 211: John Frost 212: ADN/Zentrabild 213(T): Farabola 213(C): René Dazy 213(B): New York Public Library, Lincoln Center 214(L): BBC Hulton Picture Library 214(R): BBC Hulton Picture Library 215: BBC Hulton Picture Library 216(L): Ullstein Bilderdienst 216(R): BBC Photograph Library 217: Joseph Abeles Collection 218(T): BBC Hulton Picture Library 218(C): Swedish Institute/Beata Bergstrom 218(B): BBC Hulton Picture Library 220(T): Bildarchiv Preussischer Kulturbesitz 221(T): Joseph Abeles Collection 221(B): Culver Pictures 222(L): Donald Cooper 222(R): BBC Hulton Picture Library 223: BBC Hulton Picture Library 225: BBC Hulton Picture Library 226: BBC Hulton Picture Library 227: Bettmann Archive 228(T): Dominic Photography 228(B): Joseph Abeles Collection 229: John Frost 230: Culver Pictures 231(T): BBC Hulton Picture Library 231(B): Culver Pictures 233: Mander and Mitchenson Theatre Collection 234: Joseph Abeles Collection 236: BBC Hulton Picture Library 237(L): Joseph Abeles Collection 237(R): Farabola 239(T): John Timbers 239(L): John Timbers 239(R): Dominic Photography 241(T): Dominic Photography 241(B): BBC Hulton Picture Library 243(T): BBC Hulton Picture Library 243(B): Popperfoto 244(TL): BBC Hulton Picture Library 244(TR): Photopress, Switzerland 244(BL): Mander and Mitchenson Theatre Collection 244(BR): BBC Hulton Picture Library 245(T): BBC Hulton Picture Library 245(C): BBC Hulton Picture Library 245(CR): Mander and Mitchenson Theatre Collection 245(BL): BBC Hulton Picture Library 245(BR): Mark Rusher 246: Deutscher Press Agentur 247: Joseph Abeles Collection 248(T): Svensk Pressfoto 248(B): Dominic Photography 251(T): Dominic Photography 251(B): Joseph Abeles Collection 252(TL): BBC Hulton Picture Library 252(TR): Italian Institute, London 252(CL): BBC Hulton Picture Library 252(CR): BBC Hulton Picture Library 252(BL): BBC Hulton Picture Library 252(BR): BBC Hulton Picture Library 254(L): René Dazy 254(R): Joseph Abeles Collection 255(L): Mander and Mitchenson Theatre Collection 255(R): Farabola 256(T): Bibliothèque Nationale 256(CL): Cassell and Co. 256(CR): Society for Cultural Relations with USSR 256(BL): Detroit Institute of Arts/Cassell and Co. 256(BR): Popperfoto 257(TL): Claus Hansmann 257(TR): Daily Telegraph Colour Library/Ted F. Barker 257(B): Daily Telegraph Colour Library 259(T): BBC Hulton Picture Library 259(B): BBC Hulton Picture Library 260(TL): Joseph Seelig/Cockpit Theatre 260(L): Novosti 260(BR): Étienne Bertrand Weill 260/261(T): Étienne Bertrand Weill 261(TR): Joseph Seelig/Cockpit Theatre 261(BL): Étienne Bertrand Weill 261(BC): Étienne Bertrand Weill 261(BR): Étienne Bertrand Weill 262(T): Popperfoto 262(B): Joseph Abeles Collection 265(T): Dominic Photography 265(C): New York Review 265(B): Dominic Photography 266(T): Farabola 266(B): Farabola 268: Joseph Abeles Collection 269(L): Joseph Abeles Collection 269(R): Popperfoto 270(T): Popperfoto 270(B): Dominic Photography 271(TL): BBC Hulton Picture Library 271(TR): Dominic Photography 271(CL): Joseph Abeles Collection 271(BR): Farabola 273: Donald Cooper 275(T): Donald Cooper 275(C): Joseph Abeles Collection 275(B): Popperfoto 279: Western Americana 280: Daily Telegraph Colour Library 281(L): Dominic Photography 281(R): Etienne Bertrand Weill 284(TL): Donald Cooper 284(TR): Donald Cooper 284(BL): Donald Cooper 284(BR): Donald Cooper 287(L): Donald Cooper 287(R): Dominic Photography 288(T): Dominic Photography 288(B): Donald Cooper 290(L): Donald Cooper 290(R): Mark Rusher 291: DPA Bild/Press Association 294(TL): Mansell Collection 294(TR): Reg Wilson 294(BL): Japanese Information Centre 294(BR): Japanese Information Centre 295: Donald Cooper 298: Royal Opera House, Covent Garden/Donald Southern 299: Royal Opera House, Covent Garden/Donald Southern 302: Joseph Abeles Collection 303(L): Joseph Abeles Collection 303(R): Culver Pictures
Rights and Permissions: Celia Dearing